Praise for *Asia-Pacific Transfer Pricing Handbook*

"Feinschreiber and Kent offer an especially useful guidebook—*Asia-Pacific Transfer Pricing Handbook.* The comprehensive information is seasoned with refreshing insights and practice tips essential for multinational businesses."

Eduardo Goldszal
Director of Tax, NCR Corp.

"This book will be a valuable and handy resource for all stakeholders—professionals, revenue authorities, and multinational enterprises. It is extremely timely considering the next decade(s) of growth from Asia and consequent increased flow of goods, services, funds, and intangibles. The transfer pricing regime is also evolving in many Asian countries with focused examination of cross-border transactions by revenue authorities and this book will assist in navigating the same."

Samir Gandhi
Partner, Deloitte Haskins & Sells,
Mumbai, India

"This book brings a timely and fresh look at the rapidly changing transfer pricing landscape in the region. Whether you are you implementing a new business model in Asia, documenting your intercompany transactions, or are in the middle of defending your historical filing positions, *Asia-Pacific Transfer Pricing Handbook* will help you understand local rules and procedures and provide you with valuable and practical insights."

Horacio Peña
Partner & Senior Economist,
U.S. & Americas Transfer Pricing Practice Leader,
PricewaterhouseCoopers, LLP

"Once again Mr. Feinschreiber has provided us with a go-to guide for transfer pricing. This time it's a guide to the Asia-Pacific region with an abundance of useful and practical information for the transfer pricing practitioner."

Stuart Simons
Partner, International Tax,
Deloitte Touche Tohmatsu,
Bangkok, Thailand

"Robert Feinschreiber and Margaret Kent continue to provide comprehensive and up-to-date guidance in the complex and dynamic transfer pricing field. In this book, they focus in a very concrete and useful way on what is certainly the most economically explosive region of the world—Asia."

Michael Kliegman
PricewaterhouseCoopers, LLP

"This book provides practical solutions and guidance to assist multinational corporations (MNC) to effectively mitigate transfer pricing tax exposure. It provides practical solutions with examples that demonstrate the use of "allocation keys" under the Transactional Profit Split method that can provide equitable and consistent results in connection with allocating MNC global profits to affiliates in different tax jurisdictions. I believe the information provided by Feinschreiber and Kent's book will be valuable to business executives, tax professionals, and tax administrative officers."

Alexander Pan, PhD, MBA, MBT, CPA
Partner (retired),
PricewaterhouseCoopers, LLP;
University of California, Irvine

Asia-Pacific Transfer Pricing Handbook

ROBERT FEINSCHREIBER
MARGARET KENT

WILEY
John Wiley & Sons Singapore Pte. Ltd.

Published by John Wiley & Sons Singapore Pte. Ltd.
1 Fusionopolis Walk, #07-01, Solaris South Tower, Singapore 138628

Other Wiley Editorial Offices

John Wiley & Sons, 111 River Street, Hoboken, NJ 07030, USA
John Wiley & Sons, The Atrium, Southern Gate, Chichester, West Sussex, P019 8SQ, United Kingdom
John Wiley & Sons (Canada) Ltd., 5353 Dundas Street West, Suite 400, Toronto, Ontario, M9B 6HB, Canada
John Wiley & Sons Australia Ltd., 42 McDougall Street, Milton, Queensland 4064, Australia
Wiley-VCH, Boschstrasse 12, D-69469 Weinheim, Germany

ISBN 978-1-118-35937-2 (Hardcover)
ISBN 978-1-118-35939-6 (ePDF)
ISBN 978-1-118-35938-9 (Mobi)
ISBN 978-1-118-35940-2 (ePub)

Typeset in 10/13 pt Photina Regular by MPS Ltd., Chennai, India
Printed in Singapore by Markono Print Media

10 9 8 7 6 5 4 3 2 1

To Steven Feinschreiber and Kathryn Feinschreiber Hagedorn, and to our grandchildren, Alexander, Elizabeth, and Henry, in the hope that they will follow our footsteps.

Contents

Preface

WELCOME TO THE *Asia-Pacific Transfer Pricing Handbook*. This book is the sixth volume of the Transfer Pricing Handbook series, a series that we began 20 years ago with John Wiley & Sons. The first two transfer pricing volumes have a U.S. perspective; the third volume focuses on the rest of the world. The fourth volume looks specifically to transfer pricing methods. The fifth volume examines the 2010 OECD Regulations, *OECD Transfer Pricing Guidelines for Multinational Enterprises and Tax Administrations*. The sixth volume looks to transfer pricing developments in the Asia-Pacific region, encompassing countries from India and Sri Lanka to Australia and New Zealand, from Japan and South Korea to Singapore and Indonesia. While each country relies heavily upon the OECD transfer pricing provisions, each country stands on its own when it comes to transfer pricing.

Once again, we are pleased to be selected by John Wiley & Sons to be the authors of this comprehensive book on transfer pricing, whether this selection is based on our practical transfer pricing experiences as practitioners during the past 40 years or otherwise. We are grateful to Sheck Cho at John Wiley & Sons for developing and nurturing the transfer pricing project and to Tim Burgard and Stacey Rivera at John Wiley & Sons. We are thankful to Nick Melchior at John Wiley & Sons, Australia, for making this volume a reality. In addition, we owe a debt of gratitude to Natu Patel, then the principal tax official at John Wiley & Sons, for continuing to encourage us to undertake this project despite our extensive international schedule.

Readers are welcome to contact us to suggest additional topics or suggestions, or to inform us about transfer pricing planning or audit and litigation techniques: e-mail us at multijur@aol.com. Our Web site is TransferPricingConsortium.com.

Robert Feinschreiber
Margaret Kent
Key Biscayne, Florida
August 2012

PART ONE

Country-by-Country Analysis

CHAPTER ONE

Introduction

TRANSFER PRICING is a central ingredient to trade and commerce, to financing and accounting, and to law and economics. We have selected 15 countries in Asia and the Pacific where these transfer pricing components have grown in importance.

We have divided the *Asia-Pacific Transfer Pricing Handbook* into two parts: Part One: Country-by-Country Analysis and Part Two: Advanced Applications—complex transfer pricing issues.

PART ONE: COUNTRY-BY-COUNTRY ANALYSIS

For the convenience of the reader, we provide alphabetical country-by-country analysis. We examine these countries in the Asia-Pacific region:

Australia
China

Hong Kong
India
Indonesia
Japan
Korea
Malaysia
New Zealand
Philippines
Singapore
Sri Lanka
Taiwan
Thailand
Vietnam

PART TWO: ADVANCED APPLICATIONS

The *Asia-Pacific Transfer Pricing Handbook* then examines transfer pricing issues that take place across borders:

- Hong Kong and Singapore
- India and Hong Kong
- Australia, Canada, Japan, and the United States
- Singapore and the United States
- Japan and South Korea
- China and Taiwan
- Malaysia and Singapore
- Hong Kong and India

Multinational institutions play a major role in the transfer pricing context. These organizations include the Organisation for Economic Co-operation and Development (OECD) and the Association of Southeast Asian Nations (ASEAN), including ASEAN + three. At this time, the OECD has 34 members, only 4 of which are in the Asia-Pacific region: Australia, Japan, New Zealand, and South Korea. Nevertheless, the broader Asia-Pacific group of 15 countries, which are the subject of this analysis, follow OECD principles. Most of the nonmember countries are already on track to become OECD members.

Today the ASEAN pact, including ASEAN + three, have moved slowly in addressing transfer pricing issues. In part, the ASEAN pact and ASEAN + three are reticent because some members do not have their own transfer pricing regimes.

Each country stands on its own, despite the impact of the OECD. In particular, these six developments are notable:

1. Japan took the lead in profit split techniques, and the OECD follows these techniques.
2. China and Vietnam address control issues, which the OECD fails to address.

3. Singapore is applying important techniques for the treatment of services in the transfer pricing context.
4. Hong Kong has developed anti–tax haven techniques and put these rules with its transfer pricing guidelines.
5. India is far ahead in case law developments, leaving the United States behind.
6. Australia is far ahead in developing pre-audit techniques for midsize businesses.

CHAPTER TWO

2

Australia's Risk Assessment Transfer Pricing Approach

THE AUSTRALIAN GOVERNMENT, through its Australian Tax Office (ATO), issued in March 2005 an international transfer pricing document entitled "A Simplified Approach to Documentation and Risk Assessment for Small to Medium Businesses." As tax practitioners working in the field of international transfer pricing, it is our position that the ATO's document is neither simplified nor designed for small and medium businesses. The ATO, in response to this comment, increased the small business threshold. Nevertheless, despite these shortcomings, this document provides multinational taxpayers with a worthwhile risk assessment approach toward transfer pricing issues.

The U.S. taxpayer is cautioned that the ATO transfer pricing review and audit process involves two essentially separate procedures:

1. The ATO pervasively applies the transfer pricing review process, evaluating the business and its transfer pricing activities as an intermediate audit-related step. Many companies can find themselves as being on the ATO's watch list, but few companies face transfer pricing audits.
2. The ATO rarely audits business for transfer pricing issues, which suggests that a company facing a transfer pricing audit likely can be subject to transfer pricing adjustments and penalties.

INTRODUCTORY ISSUES

The ATO's transfer pricing simplified approach applies to businesses with an annual turnover of less than A$100 million, which the ATO defines as small to medium businesses. The threshold is based on total transactions, not just on international transactions. Thus, a business having domestic Australian sales of A$5 million and international sales of A$90 million would be within the confines of the small- to medium-businesses parameters. In contrast, a business having domestic sales of A$100 million and international sales of A$5 million would be outside the confines of those parameters. Earlier we suggested that the ATO would be well advised to base the small- to medium-businesses parameter on international transactions standing alone. However, the ATO increased the parameters in 2009, thus alleviating some of the objections that we previously had made.

The ATO overrides the A$100 limitation for small to medium businesses in two respects:

1. The enterprise is part of a multinational group that is listed on any stock exchange. The term "any stock exchange" might possibly include stock exchanges outside Australia.
2. The enterprise is part of a private group with any international subsidiary or other offshore related party that "has the resources" to deal with global transfer pricing issues. The ATO provides no guidance to access the parameters that would constitute "having the resources."

The small- to medium-businesses guide seeks to explain:

- The transfer pricing review process
- The ATO's methodology in selecting businesses for review
- The "simplified" transfer pricing documentation that the ATO suggests businesses maintain
- A four-step process for setting up related party pricing and reviewing the transfer pricing outcome
- The mechanism under which the ATO scores the business reality of the business's profit and the quality of the company's transfer pricing records to determine the ATO's further response
- The outcomes of the transfer pricing review or audit

TRANSFER PRICING REVIEWS

The ATO views the prices in the transfer pricing mechanism as reflecting a fair return for activities carried out by or for an Australian business based on:

- What is done
- What assets are used
- Who bears the risk in carrying out the activities

Australian transfer pricing addresses related party international dealings. These dealings cover the sale, purchase, finance, or asset transactions to or from an Australian taxpayer and an overseas company or other overseas business entity or non-Australian resident person who is related to the taxpayer by common ownership or by family ties. These transfer pricing provisions do not pertain to all-Australian transactions. The dealings cover goods, services, services, and intangibles.

The small to medium business in Australia must complete and lodge a Schedule 25A with the annual income tax return if the total value of related cross-border transactions is more than A$1 million. Thus, the taxpayer having transactions less than A$1 million has nothing to report; the taxpayer having transactions between A$1 million and A$100 million might be able to come within the so-called simplified approach to small to medium businesses.

The ATO looks to two specific facets of the business's tax return to determine its response, if any:

1. The bottom-line profitability of the business
2. How the taxpayer answers Schedule 25A

The business may face from the ATO:

- A transfer pricing review
- A transfer pricing tax audit and subsequent adjustment and penalties if the business scored a high risk as a result of the review

The ATO field audit teams conduct a risk review process covering all areas of tax risk. Transfer pricing issues are a part of this wider review process. If the ATO judges transfer pricing as an area of concern for a business, it will conduct a transfer pricing review as a prelude to an audit action. The process is mandatory in Australia regardless of the size of the business.

The ATO, in selecting businesses for a transfer pricing review, considers factors such as:

- The number and value of related party cross-border transactions
- The performance of the business over time (i.e., whether the business makes commercial profits or incurs consistent losses or low profits)

These categories of businesses in Australia are at the greatest risk of a review and a possible follow-up audit:

- Businesses with significant cross-border transactions
- Businesses having year-on-year Australian losses
- Businesses having consistent low profits
- Businesses having noncommercial profits

The transfer pricing review involves the ATO's review of transfer pricing documentation, coupled with interviews of a business through desk and fieldwork. The

ATO's aim is to assess the quality of the processes and documentation on hand and with the commercial realism of the outcomes of the business's dealing with related parties. In this regard, the ATO uses economists and data from public databases that the business and its tax advisor can access. Small to medium businesses do not have to create documents beyond the minimum necessary to arrive at an arm's length outcome in the context of their business.

The ATO applies a scoring process to the business, evaluating:

- The quality of the business's processes
- The quality of the business's records
- Commercial outcome arising from related party cross-border transactions

After the ATO undertakes the scoring process, it evaluates whether a transfer pricing review shows that there is a risk to the revenue associated with a business's related cross-border transactions. The business may face an ATO audit if the risk occurs.

DOCUMENTATION REQUIREMENTS

The ATO expects significantly less transfer pricing documentation for a small to medium business than for a large business. The extent of the documentation the ATO requires increases as the significance and complexity of the transactions increase. For example, the ATO would expect a business having A$48 million in related party cross-border transactions to have more extensive documentation than a business having A$8 million in related party cross-border transactions.

Small businesses having relatively low levels of cross-border transactions need not create documents beyond the minimum necessary to arrive at arm's length outcomes in the context of their business. A less detailed functional analysis, coupled with an assessment of any external data available about price and/or performance, provides a greater degree of certainty and a reduced risk of tax adjustments.

Business managers might want to consider the next issues regarding the documentation that would satisfy the requirement that the taxpayer has applied the arm's length principle:

- Is the cross-border transaction that deals with a related party significant in terms of dollar value compared with the turnover of the business?
- Is the cross-border dealing unusual, and not part of similar activities, enabling a group to be priced and tested to show that the taxpayer has generally taken these factors into account?
- Should the ATO question the basis of the taxpayer's pricing against the profitability of the business?

The ATO suggests that if the taxpayer were to respond affirmatively to one or more of the preceding inquiries, the taxpayer should take some action that is "reasonably balanced" against the cost of complying. The "reasonable balance" criterion is far from universal, but Singapore also uses such a reasonable balance approach.

PREPARATION OF THE DOCUMENTATION FILE

The ATO uses the term "transfer pricing documentation" in a broad manner. Thus, transfer pricing documentation includes more than transaction data and requires the taxpayer to undertake much of the transfer pricing analysis a priori, even before seeking to undertake a transfer pricing analysis per se.

Transfer pricing documentation is more than recording and filing invoices. Transfer pricing documentation involves creating records outside the everyday business record keeping that shows how the business deals with cross-border transactions. Transfer pricing documentation requires:

- Writing down and describing how the business operates—in other words, functional analysis.
- Writing down and describing how the business sets its prices in cross-border transactions with related parties. The business should name the transfer pricing methods it uses and explain why it selected that method. Justifying its transfer pricing approach using global lists of related parties might not be sufficient for the business merely to justify its transfer pricing approach.
- Justifying that the transfer price used was an arm's length price, a price that independent parties would find appropriate. The taxpayer should undertake one of two approaches to determine comparability:
  - Compare the price charged to the related party with the price charged to unrelated parties (the comparable uncontrolled price method), or
  - Compare its profit outcome based on gross profit or on net profit before interest and tax with other companies in its industry. This comparison might be as simple as comparing the profit outcome to public data on the ATO's Web site or undertaking a more complex review if the business's profitability is not similar.
- The taxpayer should prepare a documentation file that would include the functional analysis and include evidence of how the taxpayer determines cross-border pricing. The ATO expects the taxpayer to undertake at least a basic benchmarking study to show broadly that the outcome of the business reflects arm's length pricing.
- The taxpayer can take advantage of its knowledge of its market and pricing, and can take budgets and management tools into account.
- The taxpayer can take advantage of making both independent and affiliated party sales.

The ATO recognizes that the taxpayer might find it difficult to gather external information on prices or margins to support the business's actions. This difficulty can occur because of the following:

- The business might differ from other companies in its industry, or
- The business might have a unique business operating in Australia

The ATO also recognizes that it might be difficult for the taxpayer to obtain publicly available data as to bottom-line profits for similar companies that are not controlled by related parties to compare net profit outcome. The ATO warns, though, that the presence of these adverse situations is not an excuse for doing nothing.

At its option, the taxpayer can obtain data from commercial databases and tailor these data to the company's documentation report. The taxpayer should weigh the cost of obtaining these data internally or using an external service provider against the likelihood of a transfer pricing review and subsequent tax audit adjustments.

The ATO encourages businesses to keep the most valuable transfer pricing documentation, which the ATO refers to as contemporaneous documentation. The ATO, then, does not specifically require the taxpayer to undertake contemporaneous documentation. It defines "contemporaneous documentation" as the documentation that existed at or before the time of preparing the business's tax return for the given year. The taxpayer is to use contemporaneous documentation to set or review the outcome of the company's related party cross-border transaction pricing. The ATO expects the taxpayer to prepare some documentation specifically created to show the business applied the arm's length principle.

According to the ATO, contemporaneous documentation is a self-contained report with evidence attachments that describe:

- The business itself.
- The environment in which the business operates.
- The method the business uses to set or review related party pricing, including a discussion of why the businesses rejected acceptable methods for each type of transaction.
- A comparability study that uses publicly available accounting data to indicate a range of prices or profit that demonstrates or proves that the business was at arm's length in its dealing with unrelated parties. This comparability study should include the analysis of comparables (i.e., independent company data) that were accepted or rejected in the study and specify why the selected data are comparable and reflect arm's length results when applied to the business.

The ATO will select certain cases for a transfer pricing review. In all such cases that it selects, the ATO will undertake its own benchmark review to gauge what outcome it thinks the business should reflect in its taxable income relative to the industry it is engaged in. If the taxpayer is subject to the simplified transfer pricing approach, during the transfer pricing review, the ATO may discuss the use of benchmarking with the business and its advisors to let them know what to expect in testing the arm's length outcome of the prices the business uses in its cross-border transactions.

The ATO provides an example of the pre-review process. Thus, in this example, the ATO might discuss how the business's low profit outcome, based on gross profit or net profit before interest and tax, compares with higher comparably broad Australian Bureau of Statistics data profit outcomes. The ATO might also ask the business to explain how its related party dealings have influenced this comparison and/or how market and other environmental issues are relevant. Such factors include business cycles, market competition, and foreign exchange risks. This pre-review process is designed to help businesses understand what action they need to take in future years.

APPLYING THE ARM'S LENGTH PRINCIPLE

The first step in applying the arm's length principle is to select an arm's length method and test it. The ATO recommends that small to medium businesses use a four-step process to demonstrate compliance with the arm's length principle. This four-step process is not appropriate for businesses that are part of large multinational groups that can avail themselves of more resources.

Some businesses might have relatively simple cross-border transactions with related parties. Other businesses might have low-value cross-border transactions with related parties. In these two situations, the ATO states that the extent of the data collection and analysis and the contents of the documentation might be minimal.

The ATO asks small to medium businesses to put a name to the transfer pricing method it uses, although the ATO acknowledges that some businesses of this size may find doing so or testing the price burdensome. The instructions to Schedule 25A describe transfer pricing methods that might or might not be considered arm's length.

SIMPLIFIED APPROACH TO DOING A BENCHMARKING STUDY

The ATO recognizes that the cost of doing the benchmarking analysis and placing it in the documentation file before lodging the company's annual tax return may be a material cost burden for small to medium businesses. As a result of incurring this burden, the management of the small to medium business incurs the risk of any subsequent Tax Office adjustment as being low, and proceeds to rely on the company's internal procedures and records only. A profitable business is unlikely to be prejudiced by this approach, but loss businesses run higher risks if no action is taken.

The ATO expects that businesses having related cross-border transactions that are using documented business plans to, in fact, have documented these business plans. The ATO expects businesses to have the resources to undertake a basic benchmarking study, doing so by using Tax Office publicly available information. The small to medium business might not prepare a benchmarking study or might not place the study in the documentation file. In that event, the ATO expects that the business and the ATO would work together, much like this transfer pricing system in Singapore. Under this working-together process, the ATO presents the business with a benchmarking study using publicly available data and asks the business to explain why its profit outcome is below the benchmarking information.

The profit outcome benchmark is a risk indicator the ATO uses to assess whether the pricing of related party transactions results in a low tax position in Australia. There can be other explanations of a low tax position, such as:

- Bad product sales
- Management issues
- Foreign exchange exposure
- Other business cycle pressures on the business

The benchmarking study that the ATO hands to the business under this simplified approach might not be the only benchmark pointing to the pricing that the business should accept to demonstrate that it has applied the arm's length principle to related party cross-border transactions. The ATO might not be satisfied with other explanations. In the event that the business does not provide a sufficient explanation to the ATO, the business might need to undertake a more detailed benchmarking study or seek additional time from the ATO to comply within the spirit of the simplified approach.

FOUR STEPS FOR TESTING INTERNATIONAL TRANSFER PRICES

Step 1. The business accurately characterizes international dealings between the associated enterprises in the context of its business and documents that characterization.

The small to medium business should know this information, and record them in the documentation file:

- The nature of the business activities being carried on
- An explanation as to how cross-border transactions with related parties fit into its ordinary business
- An explanation as to how industry and/or economic conditions affect the business

The business is to identify any major business strategy that it is conducting, such as a market penetration strategy. Usually this information is to be presented in a functional analysis report.

Step 2. The business selects the most appropriate transfer pricing methodology or methodologies and documents its choice. The business should add to the documentation file this information, which reflects the manner in which the business sets and records prices:

- Price lists
- Budgets
- Correspondence
- Working papers
- Agreements with related parties

According to the ATO, what the business actually calls the pricing method it uses is not important. Nevertheless, the business must have some basis to show how it sets prices. The business should reflect the price it uses and that the price reflects arm's length prices used, for example, by its competitors. The business is to identity whether its competitors are part of a controlled group, as their prices may be influenced by their transfer pricing policy; in such cases, prices might not provide a reliable comparison. Note that this consideration impacts antitrust considerations and that the U.S. tax authorities typically avoid this comparison issue.

The business might know, for example, that cost plus markup is normal in its industry, and it might be able to use this industry "plus" percentage to set its prices and test its position. The business needs to make sure that the industry "plus" is based on arm's length dealings and not on controlled party dealings. The business might have charged a related party the same or similar price as it charged a third party for same or similar goods or services. The ATO calls this method the comparable uncontrolled price method. The United States calls this method the comparable uncontrolled price method using an in-house comparable.

The business might have set its related party prices based on a business plan that used sale prices from or to related parties that result in a planned gross profit that is sufficient to cover administration and selling costs, returning to the business a fair net profit. Such a business should prepare its documentation file to explain how it calculated that profit. The business needs to test whether the "fair net profit" reflects an arm's length result.

Step 3. The business applies the most appropriate transfer pricing method, determines the arm's length outcome, and documents the process. The business should add to the documentation file the actions it has taken to test that the price it has set and recorded reflects an arm's length outcome. For example, the business should reflect in its documentation file whether it undertook a benchmarking study. This study might be a general comparison of the business's profit result with the Tax Office for the type of business the company carries on. The business should reflect in its documentation file a more detailed study conducted by an outside advisor using profit level indicators that are acceptable arm's length methods.

Step 4. The business implements support processes and review processes to ensure adjustment for material changes and to document these processes. The business should review the transaction pricing and the benchmarking study if there are any changes to:

- The nature of the transaction
- The parties to the transaction
- Economic conditions

The business should record the outcome of these changes in its documentation file.

DECISION TREE

The beginning point for the decision tree is to ascertain whether the business has internal or external data to compare prices or profits from related party transactions. The ATO views internal data and external data in the same manner. If the response to the inquiry is negative, the ATO would have the business consider other approaches that give comfort to the profit outcome the business obtained or the business can seek an amendment to its income tax returns to reflect an arm's length result.

If the business does have internal data or external data to compare prices or profits from related party transactions, the next question is whether it has evidence of a comparable uncontrolled price. If the response to the comparable uncontrolled price inquiry is affirmative, the final step is to ascertain whether the comparison shows that the business's pricing and profits are acceptable.

A separate method applies if the business does have internal data or external data to compare prices or profits from related party transactions but no evidence of a comparable uncontrolled price. When the business has no evidence of a comparable uncontrolled price, the next question becomes whether it has evidence of gross margins. If the business does have evidence of gross margins, it is to use the resale price method or the cost method using comparables using similar products traded by independent companies having similar functions, asset bases, and risk profiles. If the business does not have evidence of gross margins, it is to apply the transactional net margin method at the net margin level, using comparables for similar companies with similar products or services, similar levels of assets used in their businesses, and similar risk profiles in the industry.

Internal evidence might support the arm's length nature of the pricing the business uses with related parties. Nevertheless, profit comparisons might either strengthen or weaken the case if the profit outcome of the business falls outside the comparable profit range. The ATO points out that the reasons for this situation may not relate only to transfer pricing.

HOW THE ATO SCORES RISK

The ATO originally introduced five risk levels for scoring the quality of the transfer pricing processes and for documentation of cross-border transactions with related parties. Three of these five risk levels survive for small to medium businesses. The ATO recognizes that many small to medium businesses do not have the in-house resources or cannot afford to engage external advisors to prepare the medium- to high-quality documentation expected of large businesses. The ATO nonetheless encourages small to medium businesses to aspire to a medium to high quality of documentation. At the same time, the ATO recognizes that in most cases, the business would not be required to provide the same amount of documentation as would be required of large businesses. Accordingly, in developing a transfer pricing review, the quality of the processes and documentation applied to related party cross-border transactions generally falls into one of these three levels:

- **Low score, score 1.** This score increases the likelihood of an audit. However, the business and its advisor can cooperate by using the simplified approach if the business works with the ATO to provide an acceptable level of documentation and explain the level of profitability.
- **Medium score, score 3.** This approach also allows the business and its advisors to work with the ATO to provide an acceptable level of documentation and explain the level of profitability.
- **Medium to high score, score 4.** The ATO generally accepts this approach. It requires little interaction with the ATO and provides a decreasing level of audit. This score recognizes the limitations of obtaining comparables in the Australian market. The high-quality level, level 5, is rarely obtained in practice.

SCORING THE THREE LEVELS

The ATO uses a scoring system to evaluate the taxpayer's activities. The ATO then uses this analysis to ascertain its response to the taxpayer.

Score 1 Low Quality

- The business provides no analysis to describe the functions, assets, and risks of the business, the markets in which it operates, and the business strategies that business management uses to gain a commercial return.
- The business provides no documentation or insufficient documentation or processes to enable a check on the selection of its pricing method.
- The business does not provide comparables.
- The business provides no documentation to allow a check on the application of the pricing methods the business uses.

Score 3 Medium Quality

- The business provides inadequate analysis to describe the functions, assets, and risks of the business; the markets in which the business operates; and the business strategies that business management uses to gain a commercial return.
- The business provides a selection of the transfer pricing method it uses, supported by some contemporaneous documentation.
- The business uses broad inexact comparables or comparables based on data from external related comparables. For example, the business uses data used by an overseas related party to justify the pricing.

- The business provides an application of the pricing method, supported by some contemporaneous documentation.

Score 4 Medium to High Quality

- The business provides sound analysis to describe the functions, assets, and risks of the business; the markets in which it operates; and the business strategies that business management uses to gain a commercial return.
- The business provides a selection of the transfer pricing method it uses, supported by some contemporaneous documentation.
- The business uses comparables that are based on, and limited to, adequate data from independent dealings. This reliability is taken into account in the choice of comparables.
- The business provides an application of the pricing method, fully supported by contemporaneous documentation.

SCORE GRAPH

The ATO provides a score graph to measure the risk of a transfer pricing audit. The ATO scores the risk of a transfer pricing audit as being very high, high, medium to high, medium, low to medium, or low. Then the ATO categorizes the profit outcome of the business as being within one of three categories:

- A. A commercially realistic result
- B. A less than commercially realistic result
- C. Consistently provides losses

The ATO then seeks to categorize both the quality of the documentation and the audit risk in this manner:

1. Regarding profit outcome A, the ATO categorizes scores in this manner:
   - The commercially realistic result as applicable to the medium-risk score of 1, low quality
   - The commercially realistic result as applicable to the low- to medium-risk score of 3, medium quality
   - The commercially realistic result as applicable to the low-risk score of 4, medium to high quality
2. Regarding profit outcome B, the ATO categorizes scores in this manner:
   - The less than commercially realistic result as applicable to the high-risk score of 1, low quality
   - The less than commercially realistic result as applicable to the medium- to high-risk score of 3, medium quality
   - The less than commercially realistic result as applicable to the medium-risk score of 4, medium to high quality

3. Regarding profit outcome C, the ATO categorizes scores in this manner:

   - The losses consistently returned result as applicable to the very-high-risk score of 1, low quality
   - The losses consistently returned result as applicable to the high-risk score of 3, medium quantity
   - The losses consistently returned result as applicable to the medium- to high-risk score of 4, medium to high quality

   The ATO provides examples of its scoring system:

- A score of C1 shows the business had a high risk, indicating that a Tax Office audit is possible. To avert an audit, the ATO would encourage the business to prepare and maintain a documentation file to at least the 3 quality level. The ATO would also encourage the business to examine its profit position relative to available statistical data for benchmarking purposes. The ATO would offer the business an opportunity to enter into an advance pricing agreement if the ATO commences an audit.
- A score of B3 would indicate that the taxpayer has medium to high risk of an audit. The ATO would provide the business with statistical data benchmarking information if the business has related party cross-border transactions that present medium to high risk in the ATO risk review process. The ATO might undertake "a cooperative discussion" with the business. The ATO might place the business on a watch list to review the business's progress in demonstrating compliance with the arm's length principle. The audit may result if the business makes little progress in future years.
- A score of A4 would suggest that the business has made a big effort to manage its related party cross-border transactions on an arm's length basis. The results would indicate to the ATO that it would require no audit action as to its transfer pricing issues.

OUTCOME OF TRANSFER PRICING REVIEW OR AUDIT

The ATO might decide to audit a business after a transfer pricing review. If the ATO decides to undertake such an audit, the business is likely to face tax adjustments and penalties. Any such adjustment is subject to normal Tax Office review and legal review and appeal processes. The adjustments might also be subject to discussions with another revenue administration involved in the mutual agreement procedure of the relevant double tax agreement. The ATO, as part of the audit process, normally will issue a position paper and give the business an opportunity to comment before the ATO assesses any adjustments and enforces any resulting tax and penalties.

The ATO has issued a flow chart that shows how it conducts transfer pricing reviews and transfer pricing audits and how it undertakes other follow-up action specifically for small to medium businesses. The ATO will work with a business and its tax advisor to help the business understand the minimum steps it must take to comply with the arm's length principle. The ATO might provide benchmarking information applicable to the business that indicates the outcome expected as to a business that is trading at arm's length with all parties in which the business deals.

The ATO's aim is to improve the documentation held by the business and to encourage commercially realistic outcomes from related party dealings. As a result, the ATO might give the business the time before the business finishes the review to explain why the business has performed below industry standards. The business is to explain how the business must address the issue, both commercially and in documenting the arm's length nature of the dealings with related parties.

AUDITS TAKING PLACE IN LOW-RISK SITUATIONS

The transfer pricing review process focuses on cross-border transactions. The transfer pricing review process, then, focuses only on the manner in which the parties deal with each other. The purpose of the transfer pricing review process is to demonstrate whether these activities taken on behalf of the parties demonstrate arm's length outcomes. Although the risk of a transfer pricing audit may be low, the ATO still might audit a business if a broader review indicates that other tax-related issues demonstrate a risk to the revenue.

The ATO recognizes that low profit performance by a business is not necessarily the result of transfer pricing action. Nevertheless, the ATO states that the presence of the next factors might precipitate an audit:

- The business uses tax havens, for example, where the business is part of a re-invoicing arrangement.
- The business uses back-to-back transactions to mask the true consideration involved in a transaction.
- The business uses a triangular or a circular structure to shield related party dealings.

TRANSFER PRICING REVIEW PROCESS

The ATO interviews the business and its agents as part of the transfer pricing review process. The ATO's objective is to verify the facts presented by the business and its agents and to examine the business's documentation file. The ATO, as part of this transfer pricing review process, reviews internal comparable uncontrolled prices or comparables the business uses to set or to justify the arm's length outcome. The ATO asks the business these questions:

- Has the business prepared any documentation to describe the functions, assets, and risks that are associated with related party transactions?

- Has the business put in place any process to set the pricing of related party transactions using arm's length pricing methods?
- Has the business put in place any process for checking that the application of the pricing method results in an arm's length outcome?

CATEGORIZING THE RESULTS OF THE TRANSFER PRICING REVIEW

As a result of undertaking the transfer pricing review process, the ATO will score the review to grade:

- The commercial reality of the business's profit outcome, as discussed earlier in this analysis, as having a grade of A, B, or C
- The quality of the business's documentation, as discussed earlier in this analysis, as being a grade of 1, 3, or 4

Combining the letter and number results provides the ATO with an outcome. The ATO has three potential outcomes:

- **Outcome 1.** This outcome applies to A3 and A4 businesses. These businesses provide a commercially realistic result in A and a low to medium or low audit risk having a grade of 3 or 4. The ATO will take no further action on the transfer pricing dealings under review.
- **Outcome 2.** This outcome applies to A1, B1, B3, B4, C3, and C4 businesses. The ATO works with a business and its agent in these categories and places them on a watch list. The ATO might look for a positive response on a follow-up interview. If the follow-up result is positive, the ATO will take no further action concerning the business. If the follow-up result is negative, the ATO will undertake a transfer pricing audit. Outcome 2 applies to these six business categories:
  - **A1.** The business provides a commercially realistic result, but the risk of a transfer pricing audit is at the medium level.
  - **B1.** The business provides a less than commercially realistic result, with low or variable profit, but the risk of a transfer pricing audit is at high level.
  - **B3.** The business provides a less than commercially realistic result, with low or variable profit, but the risk of a transfer pricing audit is at medium to high level.
  - **B4.** The business provides a less than commercially realistic result, with low or variable profit, but the risk of a transfer pricing audit is at medium level.
  - **C3.** The business provides consistent losses, but the risk of transfer pricing audit is at the high level.
  - **C4.** The business provides consistent losses but the risk of transfer pricing audit is at the medium to high level.
- **Outcome 3.** This outcome applies to C1 businesses, which are businesses that have consistent losses, and the risk of the transfer pricing audit is extremely high. The ATO undertakes a transfer pricing audit of C1 businesses.

HOW THE AUSTRALIAN TRANSFER PRICING AUDIT PROCEDURE WORKS

The ATO reviews all of the business's related party transactions during a transfer pricing audit. Then, using internal economists, the ATO forms a view of the business's arm's length outcome. The ATO then questions whether the outcome of the transfer pricing audit is materially different from that of the business.

If the transfer pricing results are not materially different from that of the business itself, the ATO then works with the business and its agents to put the company on a watch list. If the transfer pricing results are different from that of the business itself, the ATO prepares a position paper and invites the business to respond to reevaluate the ATO's position if the difference is material. The ATO can reevaluate its position, working with the business and its agents, and putting them on a watch list or exonerating the business. If the ATO determines that it should make an adjustment, the Commissioner can rely on a double tax agreement, if applicable, and the ATO can take assessment and penalty action.

AUSTRALIA'S FOUR-STEP PROCESS FOR BUSINESSES

Australia applies a four-step process for businesses:

1. Accurately characterize business dealings between associated enterprises in the context of the taxpayer's business, and document that characterization.
2. Select the most appropriate transfer pricing methodology or methodologies, and document that choice.
3. Apply the most appropriate transfer pricing method, determine the arm's length outcome, and document that process.
4. Implement support processes, including the installation of the review process to ensure adjustment for material changes, and document these processes.

Step 1 involves the determination of the next points, which would accurately characterize the business dealings:

- The business is to identify the scope, type, value, and timing of its international transactions with associated enterprises in the context of the taxpayer's business. This identification may require an understanding of the context of the business's dealings, including:
  - Organization, decision processes and systems, and incentive structures
  - The conditions affecting the industry, the nature of competition the business experienced, and economic and regulatory factors
  - Business objectives, strategies the business adopts, and financial performance
  - Intellectual assets the business uses, their contribution, ownership, and reward

  - The economically important activities undertaken by each of the associated enterprises, the recourses the business uses, and the risks that the business assumed in each case
- The business is to identify the specific elements of the international dealings that it is to consider.
- The business is to prepare a preliminary functional analysis.
- The business is to explain the conditions affecting the industry and the business strategies available to the taxpayer as these conditions affect functional analysis.
- A critical part of this functional analysis is to ascertain which of these functions are the most economically important functions, assets, and risks, and how these functions, assets, and risks might be reflected by a comparable price, margin, or profit on the dealings.
- The business is to determine if it appropriately rewards intangibles in light of contribution and ownership.
- The business is to document the process it adopts.

Step 2 involves the determination of these points, which should accurately select the most appropriate transfer pricing methodology or methodologies:

- The business would identify the available data that might establish an arm's length consideration for each of its dealings and for the dealings taken into account in their entirety.
- The business would determine the most appropriate methodology or methodologies, based on the facts and circumstances of the particular case.
- The business is to document its choice of methodologies.

Step 3 involves the determination of the next points, which would accurately apply the most appropriate transfer pricing methodology or methodologies:

- The business should refine, examine, and organize data pertaining to comparable dealings, or comparable enterprises, for each of the business's dealings for the purpose of enabling the business to properly assess comparability. To improve comparability, it is necessary for the business to:
  - Adjust the data to account for material differences in comparability
  - Group or aggregate data
  - Extend its analysis over a number of years
- The business should develop data points and ascertain whether a range of results appears.
- It might be necessary to broaden and refine the business's functional analysis.
- The business should undertake a comparability analysis.
- The business should establish a level of reliability that it can place on the answers that it derives from the application of selected methods and its consequences.
- The business may need to apply several transfer pricing methods.
- The business is to decide on the arm's length outcome.

- The business is to document practical transfer pricing considerations, such as:
  - Assumptions and judgments the business makes
  - The interpretation of data points or ranges
  - How the business uses results from different methods

Step 4 involves the determination of these points, which would accurately implement support processes:

- The business should monitor international dealings and their economic content to identify any material changes as they occur.
- The business should collect data relevant to evaluating the impact of these changes based on an arm's length consideration.
- The business should review the process and the choice of methodology if the data that the business uses establish the outcome of the change.
- The business should put a system in place to support the ongoing application of the chosen method in future years.
- The business should establish a review mechanism to ensure that, if material changes occur, the comparability analysis or its methodology is adjusted as appropriate.

CHAPTER THREE

Profit Attribution for a Dependent Agent's Permanent Establishment in Australia

THE AUSTRALIAN Tax Office (ATO) issued a guide in September 2005 that explains how Australia's permanent establishment (PE) attribution rules apply to a PE activity that arises through the activities of a third party (i.e., through a dependent agency PE). As a general matter, dependency agency status has come to the fore in transfer pricing issues as India and other countries seek to take a more stringent approach in applying PE status. Much of the ATO's guidance titled "Attributing Profits to a Dependent Agent Permanent Establishment" is relevant inside and outside Australia.

Other countries in the region, including New Zealand and Thailand in particular, tend to rely on Australia transfer pricing developments. The ATO published this guidance in September 2005. We analyze these provisions here because the Organisation for Economic Co-operation and Development (OECD) addressed the same dependent agency PE profit attribution issues, and these OECD issues impacted the PE approach in 2010.

PERMANENT ESTABLISHMENT CONCEPTS IN AUSTRALIA

Australia generally provides PE rules in sections 136AE(4) through (7) of Division 13 of Part III of the Income Tax Assessment Act of 1936 (ITAA). The Business Profits Article in Australia's double tax agreements determines PE status. Both the ITAA and the double tax agreements determine dependent agency PE status. Consider these two examples:

1. Australia treats an agency that has the power to contract on behalf of the principal as a PE in certain circumstances.[1]
2. Australia treats a party that possesses goods on behalf of another as a PE.[2]

Australia's guide to a dependent agency PE arises from a taxpayer enterprise that takes place through the activities of associated enterprises. The guide applies when both parties are members of the same multinational enterprise.[3] Australia's guide, for the most part, presupposes that a foreign party has an Australian activity that might or might not be a PE.

PROFIT ATTRIBUTION CONCEPTS IN AUSTRALIA

The ATO applies a two-step process in determining profit attribution to a PE, with both facets applying transfer pricing principles:

1. **Undertake a functional analysis.** This functional analysis attributes to the PE the functions performed within the PE, the assets used in the PE, and the risks that take place within the PE. The taxpayer is to determine its functions, assets, and risks as to the business that the taxpayer carries on through its PE.
2. **Undertake a comparability analysis.** Under this comparability analysis, the taxpayer is to determine an arm's length return for its functions, assets, and risks.

Australia, then, requires the taxpayer in a PE situation to undertake a full-blown transfer pricing analysis, including its functions, assets, and risks, and then undertake a comparability study. This two-step process applies to all PEs in Australia, including all dependent agent PEs.

THE ATO'S OPERATIONAL APPROACH

The Australian approach delineates two types of taxpayer enterprises, as these enterprises have different functions, assets, and risks, and the inevitable ensuing taxable profits:

1. The taxpayer's nonresident enterprise, or ForCo. ForCo earns taxable profits through its dependent agency PE.

2. An associated enterprise that is a resident of the host jurisdiction and whose activities give rise to dependent agent PE of ForCo as SubCo. SubCo earns taxable profits through its agency activities.

The ATO explains the ForCo(HO), ForCo(PE), and SubCo categorizations, regrettably without providing examples that would better explain these terms.

The ATO takes the view that the functions, assets, and risks of the dependent PE are the functions, assets, and risks of ForCo, not the functions, assets, and risks of SubCo as to the agency activity. The dependent agency PE is the attributed profit of ForCo, not the attributed profit of SubCo arising from the agency activity. Thus, the ATO takes the position that the profit attributable to ForCo's dependent agency PE is not merely an arm's length profit for the agent entity. Rather, the ForCo's dependent agency PE is an arm's length profit for the functions, assets, and risks of ForCo as to its agency activity performed by SubCo on behalf of ForCo.

According to the ATO, the taxable profit of the dependent agent PE is calculated by taking some part of ForCo's income from the activity performed by the agent. ForCo is to deduct the expenses that it incurs in deriving that income, including the service fee paid to SubCo. An arm's length service fee paid for ForCo to SubCo may be an arm's length reward for the agent's functions, assets, and risks. Nevertheless, it does not follow that the reward for the agent's functions, assets, and risks also constitutes the arm's length reward for the dependent agent PE functions, assets, and risks.

DETERMINING FUNCTIONAL ANALYSIS FOR A PERMANENT ESTABLISHMENT

The first step in the ATO process is to determine the functional analysis for dependent agent PE. This functional analysis takes into account:

- Any functions performed by the agent on behalf of the enterprise
- Any assets used by the enterprise through the agent
- Any risks assumed by the enterprise through the agent

The functional analysis seeks to determine the extent to which ForCo carries on its business, directly or indirectly, through its dependent agency PE. The taxpayer is to undertake this analysis by examining the functions, assets, and risks of ForCo, as to this business are attributable to the PE. Consider a sales example and a manufacturing example.

Sales Example

SubCo acts as a sales agent of behalf of ForCo. The functional analysis in this instance looks to the functions, assets, and risks that ForCo applies in its business of selling goods and how much of its selling profit are attributable to its dependent agent PE.

Manufacturing Example

SubCo acts as contract manufacturer (described as a toll manufacturer) on behalf of ForCo. The functional analysis in this instance determines the extent to which ForCo's functions, assets, and risks apply to its business of manufacturing goods and to the magnitude of its manufacturing profits that are attributable to its dependent agent PE.

The ATO provisions delineate the nature of the functions that are attributable to dependent agent PE. The functions so attributable are those performed by SubCo on behalf of ForCo. These amounts include those activities compensated by the service fee that SubCo receives from ForCo. These functions might give rise to assumption of risks by ForCo as principal. If ForCo does in fact assume these risks, the risks are attributable to the dependent agent PE of ForCo.

SubCo, while acting on behalf of ForCo, might employ third parties to perform specified functions. In that event, these functions are attributable to the dependent agent PE just as if the agent itself had performed the functions. These functions might give rise to assumption of risks by ForCo as principal. In that event, the risks that ForCo assumes are attributable to the dependent agent PE.

The ATO provides guidance in determining the assets attributable to the dependent agent PE. The ForCo assets that are attributable to the dependent agent PE are assets used in the functions performed by SubCo on behalf of ForCo. Consider the next sales agency example.

SubCo is performing sales agency activity on behalf of ForCo. SubCo is responsible for warehousing and managing a stock of product inventory owned by ForCo, doing so for the purpose of filling customer orders. Such inventory is attributable to the dependent agent PE. According to the ATO, only the assets of ForCo, not the assets of SubCo, can be attributed to ForCo's dependent agent PE.

The ATO provides that the taxpayer can attribute the asset to a PE that is using the asset. The attribution of an asset to a PE that is using the asset does not, in and of itself, result in the PE attributing all of the profit derived from the use of the asset.

ForCo's dependent agent PE can use ForCo's assets. When that situation happens, it is necessary that ForCo attribute profits to the PE. ForCo is to attribute profits to the dependent agency PE based on functions performed and risks assumed by ForCo in creating, acquiring, or maintaining that asset. Step 2 in this analysis provides the basis for which the taxpayer is to award functions and risks to the PE in attributing profits. The taxpayer might, depending on its particular circumstances, attribute profits to the PE or to another ForCo activity. Consider this manufacturing activity example.

SubCo performs contract manufacture (tolling) activities on behalf of ForCo. The functions and risks involved in research and design create ForCo's product intangibles. ForCo uses these product intangibles in the contract manufacture activity. Those product intangibles are outside of the dependent agent activity. ForCo is to reward that portion attributable to these functions and risks in attributing profit to the PE.

According to the ATO, functional analysis assesses the relative economic significance of various functions (i.e., the assets are risks that are relevant to the business activity involving the dependent agent PE). The ATO recognizes that it is particularly important for the taxpayer to determine the functions that involve assuming and managing the significant risks of that business. The extent to which the dependent agent PE performs these functions is equivalent to the extent to which SubCo undertakes these functions on behalf of ForCo. The extent of the above-mentioned activities determines the amount of profit as a reward for functions, assets, and risks attributable to the PE.

COMPARATIVE ANALYSIS FOR THE PERMANENT ESTABLISHMENT

According to the ATO, the taxpayer is to determine a PE for its functions, assets, and risks by following the guidelines for arm's length pricing in associated enterprise cases.[4]

- The taxpayer, in applying the ATO's approach, is to use an economic model of the PE to select the most appropriate "separate enterprise characterization," such as that of a distributor, agent, or service provider.
- The taxpayer is then to apply the "most appropriate" arm's length pricing method (i.e., comparable uncontrolled price, cost plus, resale price, profit split, or transactional net margin method [TNMM]) to determine the arm's length compensation for the PE based on that characterization.
- This process requires the taxpayer to apply a comparability analysis, using the most reliable available data as to arm's length comparables.

The ATO recognizes that it is important for the taxpayer to recognize the differences in functions, assets, and risks, and hence profits, between the PE and SubCo in using an arm's length pricing method to attribute profit to a dependent agent PE.

SubCo: The ATO presupposes that SubCo is rewarded for its functions, assets, and risks as being a service provider.

ForCo: The PE is rewarded for its functions, assets, and risks of ForCo as being an entrepreneur or principal in regard to SubCo agency activity.

Data that concern uncontrolled comparables as to market rates of commission for sales agents are relevant to determining an arm's length commission for SubCo. However, data concerning uncontrolled comparables as to market rates of commission for sales agents are not directly relevant to determining an arm's length attribution of profit to a dependent agent PE.

The ATO recognizes that it is essential for the taxpayer to use an arm's length compensation for SubCo in applying certain arm's length pricing methods to determine the arm's length profit for ForCo's dependent agent PE. The ATO views the arm's length compensation as a service fee. ForCo's service fee to SubCo is ForCo's expense that is attributable to its dependent agent PE.

The ATO recognizes that the cost plus method or the TNMM might be a reliable method to determine an arm's length profit for the PE. Such a taxpayer is to benchmark a gross markup on costs or a net markup on costs. In that event, the amount of these costs, including the service fee to SubCo, must demonstrably be arm's length.

The ATO believes that the transfer pricing method that most likely will give the taxpayer the best estimate of an arm's length profit for the dependent agent PE in a particular case will depend on these inputs:

- The outcome of the functional analysis
- The comparables available
- Taxpayer data available for the comparability analysis

The ATO reasons that an arm's length profit for the dependent agent PE provides the best estimate for transfer pricing purposes for three reasons:

1. In many cases, the taxpayer might find it difficult to obtain uncontrolled data that enable the taxpayer to directly benchmark an arm's length return for the functions, assets, and risks of the dependent agent PE.
2. Each dependent agent PE is unique. The function and risk profile of the dependent agent PE commonly is not similar to the function and risk profile of any available uncontrolled comparables. This example illustrates the uniqueness of the dependent agent PE: The sales agency arrangement creates a dependent agent PE. In this situation, the dependent agent PE typically will not have functions, assets, or risks that are comparable to either a full-risk buy-sell distributor or to a selling agent.
3. It might also be difficult for the taxpayer to make reasonably accurate comparability adjustments that would have permitted the taxpayer to use potential comparables to reliably estimate an arm's length compensation for the dependent agent PE.

Having determined that an arm's length profit for the dependent agent PE typically provides the best estimate for transfer pricing purposes, the ATO suggests that the comparable uncontrolled price (CUP), resale price, cost plus method, or TNMM is not the most appropriate method. In that situation, it is necessary for the taxpayer to resort to an indirect transfer pricing method, such as a profit split method, to estimate the arm's length result for the PE. Nevertheless, the ATO suggests that the taxpayer consider the application of a traditional transfer pricing method (CUP, resale, or cost plus) before resorting to the use of a transactional profit method.

APPLICATION OF THE RESALE PRICE METHOD

The ATO suggests that one possible approach in determining the profit of a dependent agent PE in the sales agency arrangement process is to characterize the dependent agency PE as reseller of the goods. The taxpayer would then apply a resale price method to the transaction. This allocation process would allocate the profit as if:

- ForCo sold the goods to a dependent agent PE.
- The dependent agent PE resold the goods to the customer.

The ATO explains the three-step profit attribution process:

1. Ascertain the price to ultimate customer.
2. Determine the arm's length transfer price between ForCo and the PE.
3. The difference between the amounts specified in step 1 and step 2 is gross profit attributable to the PE.

The taxpayer would then benchmark an arm's length gross sales margin using comparables having functions, assets, and risks that are similar to those of the dependent agent PE. The resulting transfer price would therefore exclude, from the amount attributed to the dependent agent PE, any costs and profit attributable to the ForCo activities related to the costs of goods sold, other than costs attributable to the PE. Such excluded costs include purchasing, manufacturing, and/or selling activities undertaken by other parts of ForCo—ForCo(HO).

APPLICATION OF THE COST PLUS METHOD

The taxpayer might be able to use a cost plus method to determine the profit that is attributable to dependent agent PE. The ATO's approach is to benchmark a markup on the cost of the agent's services. The extent of the markup, then, would depend on the taxpayer's particular circumstances.

Under the application of the cost plus method, the level of profit that is attributable to the dependent agent PE is the level of profit that ForCo, as an independent party, would expect to make. Such amount is over and above its costs related to the activity that SubCo performs on behalf of ForCo. Such amounts, then, include service fee payments to the agent.

USING A TRANSACTIONAL NET MARGIN METHOD

In some cases, it might be more appropriate for the taxpayer to use the TNMM in attributing profits to a dependent agent PE. The taxpayer, then, uses the TNMM by benchmarking a net margin based on resale price; alternatively, the taxpayer can use the TNMM by benchmarking a net margin based on cost. The selection of the TNMM would depend on the availability of comparables data. The taxpayer's concern should be the lack of data regarding comparables needed to reliably apply the resale price method or the cost plus method.

USING A PROFIT SPLIT METHOD

In some cases, it might be more appropriate for the taxpayer to use a profit split method in attributing profits to a dependent agent PE. The taxpayer can apply a profit split method by:

- Determining ForCo's profit from its business operations involving the agency activity
- Splitting ForCo's profit between the dependent agent PE and ForCo(HO)

The taxpayer, in undertaking the profit split method, would split the profit based on the relative value of the contributions of dependent agency PE, on one hand, and the contributions of ForCo(HO), on the other hand. The taxpayer would take into account these profit contributions for this profit split purpose as determined by the functional analysis, step 1 in attributing profits to a dependent agent PE.

The ATO then significantly adds to the complexity of the profit split process, mandating that the taxpayer value these contributions using external market data to the extent possible. In reality, the taxpayer is likely to find that the external data do not exist, or, if the external data do exist, the taxpayer will have to make an extraordinary level of external data assumptions to assess profitability. Notwithstanding its external data profit split requirement, the ATO recognizes that the taxpayer may have difficulty in reliably determining ForCo's actual profit from its business operations involving the same activity. This profit analysis is likely to require the taxpayer to apportion revenues and expenses between those operations and from ForCo's other operations. For example, ForCo might have profits from both manufacturing and the sale of products, but the agency activity relates only to the sales activities.

The ATO specifies that ForCo's relevant profit must reflect an arm's length amount. This arm's length standard means that when ForCo includes transactions with its associates, such as with SubCo, ForCo must establish that its profit outcome with these transactions is an arm's length amount.

The ATO recognizes that it may difficult for the taxpayer to reliably value contributions when it is not possible for the taxpayer to obtain external market data to benchmark such as through the contributions of the functions, assets, and risks of the dependent agent PE or the contributions of the functions, assets, and risks of ForCo(HO).

Because of the paucity of applicable data in this instance, the taxpayer might find it necessary to use some sort of allocation key or to substantially judge the relative value of the contributions. The allocation key might pertain to, for example, risks, assets, or headcount. Alternatively, the taxpayer can substantially judge the relative value of the contributions in generating the profit earned from the activity performed by SubCo on behalf of ForCo.

The ATO encourages the taxpayer to consider possible alternative profit split approaches when it has difficulty in applying a reliable application of a profit split method in the usual way. Such alternative profit split methods ideally should use available comparable data to the fullest extent possible. The goal here is to use these data to achieve the most reliable estimate of an arm's length profit for the dependent agent PE.

In this alternative profit split approach, the taxpayer should apply the available comparable data so as to enable the benchmarking of a combined result for ForCo and SubCo taken together. The ATO mandates that the taxpayer should apply the combined results for ForCo and SubCo in respect of their contributions in generating profit of the business that involves the agency activity. Then the taxpayer can split the activity to produce a reliable estimate of the arm's length profit for ForCo's dependent agency PE.

The ATO provides two examples that illustrate the different profits split approaches in applying the profit split method:

1. The taxpayer might be use available comparables data to benchmark an arm's length combined result for SubCo and the dependent agent PE taken together. Such a taxpayer could then deduct a benchmarked arm's length return for the dependent agency PE.
2. The taxpayer can split the benchmarked combined result between SubCo and the PE by using an appropriate allocation key (e.g., return on assets or return on costs).

The ATO follows up these two examples with a more detailed example using the sales agency arrangement. Here, in another situation, a sales agency arrangement causes a dependent agent PE to arise. The fact pattern specifies that the PE and SubCo, acting together, have functions, assets, and risks that are comparable to a full-risk buy-sell distributor.

In that sales agency situation, the taxpayer may obtain data as to controlled distributors to benchmark an arm's length combined result for SubCo and the dependent agent PE. The taxpayer would then seek to deduct an arm's length compensation for SubCo and would benchmark sales agent comparables to determine this compensation amount. This deduction approach might produce a reliable estimate of the arm's length compensation for the dependent agent PE.

TOLL MANUFACTURERS

The ATO addresses profit split method analysis in the context of toll manufacturing (contract manufacturing). One approach might be for the taxpayer undertaking the profit split to attribute profits to a dependent agent PE using a two-step process:

1. The taxpayer uses full-risk manufacturing comparables to benchmark a combined result for SubCo and the dependent agent PE.
2. Having benchmarked a combined result for SubCo and the dependent agent PE, the taxpayer then deducts a benchmarked result for SubCo, using toll manufacturer comparables, to get an arm's length result for the dependent agent PE.

The ATO then elucidates an alternative profit split approach in the contract manufacturer situation. Under this alternative approach, the taxpayer can determine a combined result for SubCo and the PE by benchmarking using contract manufacturer comparables rather than full-risk manufacturer comparables. The taxpayer can apply the contract manufacturer comparables if SubCo and the PE are together considered to have functions, assets, and risk comparable to those of a contract manufacturer.

However, the ATO limits the use of the comparable contract manufacturer approach. The ATO points out that a contract manufacturer commonly holds inventory and that the inventory-owning relationship largely explains the difference between the return of the contract manufacturer and the toll manufacturer. The ATO concludes that the alternative contract manufacturer is unlikely to be used if the inventory and risk are not attributable to the PE. The ATO similarly concludes that functions, assets, and risks other than related to inventory are likely to account for significant profit attributable to the PE.

According to the ATO, the taxpayer can use the comparable contract manufacturer approach as a reliable measure only if SubCo and the dependent agent PE were together considered to have similar functions, assets, and risks to selected comparables. The taxpayer is unable to use the comparable contract manufacturer approach without adjustment or modification where significant functions, assets, and risks are attributable to ForCo(HO).

The ATO suggests two ways in which the taxpayer can modify or adjust the contract manufacturer analysis:

1. The taxpayer can adjust the results of the comparables to account for a return for the functions, assets, and risks attributable to ForCo(HO) and the adjusted results that the taxpayer used to benchmark a return for SubCo and the dependent agent PE.
2. The taxpayer can use unadjusted results of the comparables to benchmark the combined result for SubCo and the dependent agent PE and ForCo(HO). The data under review are more than SubCo and the independent agent PE.

The ATO provides an example under which the taxpayer applies and modifies the contract manufacture situation to benchmark the combined result for SubCo and the dependent agent PE and ForCo(HO). The taxpayer would apply the next four steps, assuming it were to adopt the combined approach as to toll manufacturing arrangement:

1. The taxpayer would benchmark an arm's length combined result for ForCo(HO) plus dependent agent PE plus SubCo. The taxpayer, in arriving at this benchmark, would use either full-risk manufacturer comparables or contract manufacturer comparables, as appropriate.
2. The taxpayer would benchmark an arm's length result for SubCo standing alone. The taxpayer, in making this analysis for SubCo, would use toll manufacturer comparables.
3. The taxpayer would deduct the results from step 2 from the results in step 1. The purpose of this subtraction is to arrive at an arm's length result for ForCo (both the HO segment and the dependent agent PE segment).
4. The taxpayer would use the "most reliable basis" to split the results of step 3. The goal of this profit split is to give an arm's length result for the dependent agent PE standing alone.

The ATO further explains the purpose of ascertaining the arm's length return for the combined functions, assets, and risks of ForCo(HO) and the dependent agent PE, the results of step 3: The taxpayer uses the arm's length return for the combined functions, assets, and risks of ForCo(HO) and the dependent agent PE as a proxy for ForCo's actual profit from its manufacturing operations involving the agency activity. Thus, the taxpayer overcomes any practical problems in this determination.

In essence, the taxpayer applies a residual profit analysis. The taxpayer must split this residual profit in some way between ForCo(HO) and the dependent agent PE. This residual profit analysis requires the taxpayer to value relative contributions and presents the same difficulties a traditional profit split approach.

FOUR EXAMPLES

The ATO provides four examples under which the taxpayer undertakes (1) a function analysis and then (2) a comparability analysis in the process of attributing profits to a dependent agent PE. Examples 1 and 2 illustrate the ATO's approach to attributing profit to a dependent agent PE arising from a sales agency arrangement. Examples 3 and 4 illustrate the ATO's approach in a toll manufacturing situation.

The ATO examples are, by design, intentionally limited to highly simplified fact patterns and analysis so that the reader can more readily understand the approach taken. The ATO recognizes that most situations may be significantly more complex and difficult to deal with in practice. This complexity should not alter the principles that underlie the attribution process.

Example 1: Sales Agency Arrangement, Step 1 Functional Analysis

The underlying facts are these: ForCo sells computer products to independent ultimate customers Country A. ForCo has no direct relationship with these customers. Instead, ForCo sells its computer products through its selling agent, SubCo.

SubCo has a sales force. SubCo's sales force performs all activity related to selling ForCo's computer products in Country A. ForCo has no presence in Country A and no connection with Country A other than through SubCo.

There is an agency agreement between ForCo and SubCo. The agency agreement provides that SubCo acts for account and risk of ForCo. SubCo performs the marketing, sales, and distribution activities in Country A for ForCo's computer products. In return, the agency agreement provides that ForCo pays SubCo a commission for its agency services. This commission is calculated as a percentage of sales revenue.

The ATO applies a three-step functional analysis in attributing the functions, assets, and risks to the PE between the parts of ForCo other than the PE, SubCo, and ForCo's dependent agent PE. The taxpayer or the ATO would reflect the functional analysis in two stages:

Table 1 reflects the allocation between the principal entity and the agency entity (i.e., ForCo and SubCo). The taxpayer or the ATO ignores the dependent agent PE at this step of the analysis.

Table 2 takes the Table 1 allocations a step further by adding the dependent agency PE of ForCo. The taxpayer or the ATO excludes the functions, assets, and risks that are attributable to ForCo as product manufacturer because the agency arrangement relates only to product distribution and marketing.

Table 3 reflects the manner in which the ATO would attribute the various selling cost functions, quantifying the costs associated with the activities.

Example 1: Functions, Assets, and Risks

Table 1 addresses the functions, assets, and risks attributable to Situation 1:

- **Functions.** In Situation 1, all of the relevant functions are attributable to SubCo, with no relevant functions attributable to ForCo. These functions are: product ordering, marketing; sales force, marketing; advertising strategy, warehousing; inventory management, delivery; shipping, debt management, and collections; and after-sales support.
- **Assets.** In Situation 1, the assets are divided between ForCo and SubCo. The inventory and receivables are attributable to ForCo. The property, plant, and equipment pertaining to distribution are attributable to SubCo.
- **Risks.** In Situation 1, the risks are attributable entirely to ForCo, with none of the risks attributable to SubCo. Such risks are inventory risk, credit risk, and foreign exchange risk.

Adding to this analysis, the dependent agent PE of ForCo causes the dependent agent PE of ForCo to assume functions that in part were ascribed to SubCo in Table 2. These functions are: product ordering, marketing; sales force, marketing; advertising strategy, warehousing; inventory management, delivery; shipping, debt management, and collections; and after-sales support. The categorization of assets and risks remains the same, notwithstanding the fact that the data then reflect the dependent agent of ForCo.

Table 3 allocates the functions between SubCo and ForCo PE. ForCo PE is charged with the costs of the commission, advertising, bad debts, and stock losses. SubCo is charged with sales and marketing, delivery, after-market support, and debt collection and management.

After the taxpayer and/or the ATO analyze the functions, assets, and risks, the taxpayer and/or the ATO is to undertake a comparability analysis as step 2 of the process of attributing profits to a dependent agent PE.

Example 1: Sales Agency Arrangement, Step 2 Comparability Analysis

The ATO requires the taxpayer to undertake a comparability analysis:

1. Seek internal (in-house) comparables. In Example 1, there are no internal comparables because SubCo acts exclusively as an agent for ForCo.
2. Seek external comparables, to directly benchmark an arm's length compensation or margin for the dependent agent PE for its particular functions, assets, and risks. Here such external comparable as a whole does not exist.
3. Seek a comparable for SubCo's dependent agency services standing alone. This comparable is said to exist in Example 1. Under the hypothetical, independent selling agents in Country A establish that the $15 million commission amount is an arm's length amount for SubCo's independent agency services.

Now we turn to the risk analysis impacting the full-risk marketers and distributors of computer products in Country A, determined on a combined basis. The hypothetical data as to these comparables reflects companies with similar functions, assets, and risks compared with SubCo and the dependent agent PE, determined on a combined basis. The data reflects a 3 percent return on sales ($100,000,000) at the earnings before interest and taxes (EBIT) level, or return on sales of $3 million. Later we need to divide the division of income between SubCo and the dependent agent PE.

The first step in the process is to ascertain whether the taxpayer has a direct benchmark to determine the compensation of the dependent agent PE. Based on the data that the taxpayer obtains—data that are typical in attributing profits to a dependent agent PE—and given the outcome of the functional analysis and the available comparable data, it is unlikely that the taxpayer can use an arm's length pricing method as a direct benchmark regarding compensation of the dependent agent PE.

After the taxpayer determines that it has no direct benchmark regarding compensation of the dependent agent PE, the ATO suggests that the taxpayer apply the profit split method.

The ATO would have the taxpayer apply an arm's length pricing method if the taxpayer could reliably use this method to directly benchmark the compensation of the dependent agent PE. However, the ATO also recognizes that the taxpayer is unlikely to apply such an arm's length pricing method to benchmark the compensation of the dependent agent PE, given the outcome of the functional analysis and the available comparables data. The ATO suggests, then, that given the lack of a taxpayer's ability to apply such an arm's length pricing method to benchmark the compensation of the dependent agent PE, the taxpayer should then resort to a profit split transfer pricing method.

ForCo might be able to determine its operating margin on a reliable basis for its sales operations that involve SubCo. In the event that ForCo in fact can do so, the functional analysis would then indicate that the whole of that profit is properly attributable to the dependent agent PE. In the event that ForCo can determine its operating margin on a reliable basis for its sales operations that involve SubCo, the functional analysis would then indicate that there is no contribution for ForCo(HO) for such profit. The taxpayer is likely to find that it may be difficult to apply this profit under the profit split method.

The ATO suggests that, after the taxpayer cannot successfully apply the profit split method, it might not be possible for the taxpayer to select another transfer pricing method. In the event that the taxpayer cannot select another transfer pricing method, the ATO suggests that the taxpayer apply a formulary approach to the EBIT amount. Returning to the basic Example 1 situation, the data for independent full-risk marketers of computer products in Country A having similar functions, assets, and risks of SubCo and the dependent agent PE, on a combined basis of 3 percent return on sales at the EBIT level, ForCo derives \$100 million in sales income.

The combined arm's length EBIT amount as to dependent agent PE and SubCo is 3 percent of \$100 million, or \$3 million. SubCo has an arm's length commission of \$15 million and incurs operating expenses of \$13 million (sales and marketing of \$6 million; warehousing and inventory management of \$2 million; delivery of \$2 million; after-sales support of \$2 million; and data collection and management of \$1 million), leaving SubCo with a net profit of \$2 million of the \$100 million. The final step to determine the EBIT of the dependent agent PE is to subtract the arm's length EBIT of SubCo (\$2 million) from the combined arm's length EBIT of the dependent agent PE and SubCo (\$3 million), which leaves \$1 million for the arm's length EBIT of the dependent agent PE.

The situation could have involved a conversion of SubCo from a full-risk marketer or distributor into a selling agent. This conversion could take place as part of a supply chain restructuring, for example. Such a restructuring would not have caused any change in the overall profit on which the multinational enterprise is subject to tax in Country A. The conversion of SubCo from a full-risk marketer or distributor into a selling agent would reduce the taxable profit of SubCo. However, the conversion of SubCo from a full-risk marketer or distributor into a selling agent would create a taxable profit in the PE of ForCo corresponding to that reduction as to SubCo. The ATO suggests that the taxpayer could justify the conversion of the profit from SubCo to the profit of the PE of ForCo because the lack of functions, assets, and risks attributable to ForCo(HO) would indicate that SubCo's conversion was not accompanied by any changes on the ground in Country A.

Example 2: Sales Agency Arrangement

Example 2 shows the effect that different contractual arrangements between ForCo and SubCo would have on the profit of the dependent agent PE. The underlying facts in Example 2 are the same as in Example 1. The taxpayer receives and expends these amounts in connection with the products in Country A:

ForCo derives sales income of $100 million in sales income and manufactures the products at a cost of $60 million.

ForCo incurs costs of $28.5 million related to sale of products, including these specific expenditures:

- Commission of $6.5 million paid to SubCo
- Advertising costs of $12 million paid to SubCo
- Bad debt losses of $2 million for ForCo's handling of all debt management and collections from a central location
- Inventory stock losses of $1 million in damages caused by the warehousing of the goods by SubCo
- Payments of $4 million made to a third-party freight forwarder that ForCo employs for inventory management and delivery
- Payment of $2 million paid to a third-party contractor that ForCo employs for technical services of products
- Debt collection and receivables management of $1 million

In addition to the preceding revenues, costs, and expenses for ForCo, SubCo incurs operating expenses of $6 million. These agency activities are for sales and marketing, including the costs of SubCo's sales force.

Step 1 is to undertake a functional analysis in attributing the functions, assets, and risks to the PE. Based on the preceding set of facts, the ATO would attribute the significant functions, assets, and risks to ForCo(HO), to SubCo, and to ForCo's dependent agent PE. The ATO would employ two steps to attribute the significant functions, assets, and risks to ForCo(HO), to SubCo, and to ForCo's dependent agent PE. The first step in the attribution process would be to allocate the functions, assets, and risks between ForCo and SubCo, ignoring the dependent agent PE at this step in the analysis. The second step in the attribution process would be to allocate the functions, assets, and risks between ForCo and SubCo by adding ForCo's dependent agent PE.

The first step in the analytical process reveals that, as to functions, the product ordering function and the marketing sales force function are attributable to SubCo while the marketing advertising strategy, the warehouse inventory management function, the delivery shipping function, the debt management and collection function, and the after-sales support services function are attributable to ForCo. All of the assets are attributed to ForCo: inventory; property, plant, and equipment for distribution; and receivables. All of the risks are attributed to ForCo: inventory risk, credit risk, and foreign exchange risk.

The second step in the analytical process causes a partial shifting of the product ordering function and the shifting of the marketing sales force function from SubCo to ForCo PE. The remaining functions, assets, and risks that were attributable to ForCo in the first instance are now attributable to ForCo(HO).

The third step in the analytical process is to quantify the cost items among ForCo(HO), SubCo, and ForCo PE. Based on the set of facts, the $6.5 million intercompany commission from ForCo(PE) to SubCo is attributable to ForCo(HO); SubCo's $6 million for sales and marketing is attributable to SubCo. The other costs of $22 million are attributable to ForCo(HO): advertising of $12 million, bad debts of $2 million, inventory stock losses of $1 million, warehousing inventory management delivery services of $4 million, technical support services of $2 million, and debt collection and management services of $1 million.

Example 2: Comparability Analysis

The next step in Example 2 is to undertake a comparability analysis. The facts as to the comparability analysis in this instance pertain to the availability of uncontrolled comparables, which are generally the same as in Example 1. However, in this instance the combined functions, assets, and risks of SubCo and the dependent agent PE are not similar to those of independent full-risk managers or distributors.

Under the facts and circumstances of Example 2, the transfer pricing method most likely to provide the best estimate of the arm's length profit of the dependent agent PE may be a form of the cost plus method, given the outcome of the functional analysis and the available comparable data. The ATO points out that the functional and risk profile of the independent agent PE is little different from that of the agent, SubCo. Accordingly, and under those circumstances, the most reliable method is to mark up ForCo's costs of the agency activities.

Example 1 used the profit split method, based on EBIT activity. Example 2 is a situation in which the profit split method would not be the most appropriate transfer pricing method. The dependent agent PE and agent together do not have the functional profile that is comparable to a full buy-sell distributor. The ATO concluded that it does not seem possible for the taxpayer to make sufficiently accurate adjustments to reliably use the profit split method. The ATO reached this conclusion given the number and size of the comparability adjustments that the taxpayer would have to make to obtain an appropriate result for the dependent agent PE, beginning with distributor results.

The ATO acknowledges that it might be possible for the taxpayer to estimate an appropriate markup on cost for the dependent agent PE. The taxpayer could achieve this result by using the same comparables data that determined an arm's length commission for the agent. The taxpayer could apply this comparable result if the taxpayer used a TNMM to benchmark the commission.

The ATO provides an example of the "comparable result" technique. Assume, in this instance, the taxpayer benchmarked the $6.5 million commission fee by applying a TNMM for limited-risk service providers. Then assume that the rate of return on cost was 8 percent. Under this method and data, the arm's length profit for the dependent agent PE would be 8 percent. The arm's length profit for the dependent agent PE would be 8 percent of $6.5 million, or approximately $500,000.

Example 3: Toll Manufacturing Arrangement

Toll manufacturer SubCo manufactures computer products in Country A for ForCo. ForCo then sells the computer products in Country A. SubCo performs all the activity related to manufacturing the products in Country A. There is a contract or toll agreement between ForCo and SubCo. The agreement between ForCo and SubCo provides that SubCo acts of behalf of ForCo in performing the manufacturing activities of these products in Country A. In return for SubCo acting on behalf of ForCo in performing the manufacturing activities in Country A, ForCo pays SubCo a processing fee, which the ATO describes as SubCo's agency services.

Example 3: Facts

The ATO visualizes that the production process itself contains more than 15 separate production functions. This delineation is important, as the ATO process necessitates a more extensive involvement than do the tax authorities in other taxing jurisdictions. The next step, then, in attributing profits to a dependent agent PE is to examine the following significant functions and risks pertaining to the toll manufacturing agreement, based on these facts:

- ForCo has master agreements with materials suppliers. These master agreements specify the terms of the material supplier agreements, including quantities and pricing.
- ForCo negotiates these materials supplier contracts.
- ForCo pays for material that materials suppliers supplied under the agreements.
- SubCo requisitions the materials supplied under these materials supplier contracts, ordering these materials when needed to meet its production schedules.
- ForCo provides SubCo with a demand plan regarding product scheduling. This demand plan details ForCo's requirements as to the quantities and timing of the products to be delivered to SubCo.
- SubCo uses its demand plan to determine its daily production schedule.
- SubCo performs the manufacturing processing function on behalf of ForCo.
- ForCo is responsible for providing SubCo with the intangibles, designs, and specifications needed to manufacture the product.

- ForCo determines quality control standards on a national basis.
- SubCo undertakes the plant activities.
- ForCo requires that SubCo's production conform to its quality control standards.
- ForCo has the right to dictate the production process to SubCo.
- ForCo makes plant inspections of SubCo's plant.
- SubCo undertakes quality assurance testing to make sure that its products conform to ForCo's standards.
- SubCo hold the finished goods in its warehousing operations.

The risks and assets as to SubCo and ForCo are:

- ForCo has the entire risk and ownership as to the production process. SubCo has no ownership interest in the production process but does have risk as to the raw materials, work-in-process, or finished goods inventories.
- ForCo owns all of the intangible rights of the intangibles, including all intangible property rights for the products being manufactured. Such intangible property rights include patented designs, processes, know-how, brand names, trademarks, and logos.
- Research and development (R&D) performed by ForCo outside Country A create the intangibles.
- SubCo owns or leases all of the property, plant, or equipment it uses in manufacturing ForCo's products.
- ForCo has sole liability for product defects and for customer warranty claims.
- ForCo agrees to indemnify SubCo for any losses and damages.
- ForCo bears any foreign exchange risk it incurs in respect of amounts payable for raw materials.

ForCo and SubCo expend and receive these amounts in connection with the manufactured products received and expended in country A:

- ForCo derives $100 million in sales income from the manufactured products, incurs costs of $59 million related to the manufacture of the products, and incurs costs of $30 million for distributing and marketing the products.

  The $59 million in costs that ForCo incurs comprise:
  - $14 million processing fee ForCo pays to SubCo
  - $10 million R&D costs for developing product intangibles
  - $30 million raw material purchase costs
  - $3 million product liability and warranty claim costs
  - $1 million operating raw material purchasing and production scheduling department costs
  - $1 million in inventory stock losses caused by damage to the warehousing of components and finished products by SubCo
- SubCo incurs operating expenses of $13 million for its toll manufacturing activities.

Example 3: Functions

The next step in the analysis is to ascertain the functions, assets, and risks to ForCo(HO), SubCo, and ForCo's dependent agent PE. The taxpayer (and the ATO) apply this analysis in two steps:

1. The taxpayer (and the ATO) ignore the presence of the dependent agent PE and allocate amounts between the principal and agent entities, ForCo and SubCo.
2. The taxpayer (and the ATO) add to the allocations the dependent agent PE of ForCo.

This analysis excludes the analysis of the functions, assets, and risks relating to product distribution and marketing because the toll manufacturing arrangement relates only to product manufacture.

We look at ForCo and SubCo standing alone as to functions, assets, and risks. ForCo undertook the functions pertaining to raw materials purchasing, R&D, production scheduling, and quality control. SubCo undertook the manufacturing and warehousing functions. As to the assets, ForCo had the inventory and the intangibles. SubCo had the property, plant, and equipment pertaining to manufacturing. As to the risks, ForCo had all risks, including inventory risks, product liability and warranty risks, and foreign exchange risks.

ForCo originally had all risks, including inventory risks, product liability and warranty risks, and foreign exchange risks. After the division of the risks between ForCo(HO) and ForCo(PE), ForCo(HO) has the foreign exchange risk; ForCo(PE) has the inventory risk and the product liability and warranty risks.

After dividing up ForCo's assets between ForCo(HO) and ForCo(PE), ForCo(PE) has the inventory and the intangibles. SubCo has the property, plant, and equipment for manufacturing.

Dividing up ForCo's functions between ForCo(HO) and ForCo(PE), SubCo has the manufacturing functions and the warehousing functions, but ForCo also has the same functions. ForCo(HO) has these functions: raw material purchasing, R&D, production scheduling, and quality control.

The ATO attributed the cost items in this way:

- To ForCo(PE): the $14 million processing fee paid to SubCo; the ATO attributed none of this processing amount to ForCo(HO).
- To ForCo(HO): the $10 million R&D expense; the ATO attributed none of the R&D expense to ForCo(PE).
- To ForCo(PE): the $30 million raw material expenditure; the ATO attributed none of the raw material expenditure to ForCo(HO).
- To ForCo(PE): the $3 million product liability and warranty claims costs; the ATO attributed no product and liability and warranty costs to ForCo(HO).
- To ForCo(HO): $1 million in purchasing and production scheduling department costs; the ATO attributed no purchasing and production scheduling

department costs to ForCo(PE). The ATO's own schedule (Table 8) erroneously reflects the purchasing and production scheduling department costs as being part of the product liability and warranty claims cost.

- To ForCo(PE): $1 million inventory stock loss cost; the ATO attributed none of the inventory stock loss cost to ForCo(HO).
- To SubCo: the entire $13 million manufacturing cost

Step 2 in Example 3 provides for a comparability analysis as to ForCo and SubCo. Here there are no internal comparables as SubCo acts exclusively on behalf of ForCo. There are no external comparables that would benchmark an arm's length compensation or margin regarding the functions, assets, and risks of the dependent agent PE. There is, however, an external comparable, independent toll manufacturers in Country A, to establish the $14 million arm's length fee for SubCo's processing services. There are sufficient data for independent contract manufacturers of computer products in Country A. These data establish that SubCo and the dependent agent PE combined, as to functions, assets, and risks, have a 10 percent net return on costs. However, it is not possible to reliably determine ForCo's operating profit for the manufacturing operations involving SubCo.

The ATO concludes that it is possible to reliably use an arm's length pricing method to directly benchmark the compensation to the dependent agent PE, given the outcome of the functional analysis and the available data for the comparability analysis. This result suggests a need on the part of the taxpayer and the ATO to resort to a profit split transfer pricing method. However, it is not possible for the taxpayer and the ATO to apply the profit split method using ForCo's actual operating profit results. The ATO suggests that the taxpayer apply a transfer pricing profit split alternative.

Under the ATO alternative transfer pricing method, the taxpayer would determine the combined arm's length return of costs, taking into account ForCo's dependent agent PE and SubCo. This amount is approximately $5 million, 10 percent of $48 million in consolidated costs. Then the taxpayer would subtract the arm's length profit for SubCo, the processing fee of $14 million less the operating expenses of $13 million, a net amount of $1 million. The net amount and arm's length profit of ForCo's dependent agent PE is $4 million—the $5 million for ForCo's dependent agent PE and SubCo on a combined basis less the $1 million amount for SubCo.

Example 4: Toll Manufacturing Arrangement

Example 4 illustrates that different contractual arrangements between ForCo and SubCo impact the profit of the dependent agent PE. The facts in Example 4 are the same as in Example 3 except:

- While ForCo had complete control of the raw material purchasing function in Example 3, in Example 4, SubCo has agreements with materials suppliers. These agreements specify terms, including quantities and pricing. SubCo negotiates these raw material purchasing functions and pays for all material supplied under these contracts. However, ForCo reimburses SubCo for these raw material purchasing costs.

- While ForCo had provided SubCo with a demand plan for production scheduling in Example 3, in Example 4, SubCo uses the international enterprise's intranet systems to ascertain the required quantities and product to be delivered and to determine its production schedule.
- The manufacturing functions are identical in Example 3 and Example 4. SubCo performs the processing function on behalf of ForCo.
- Example 3 had provided that the multinational enterprise set quality control standards on a global basis, with ForCo requiring that SubCo's production conform to these global basis quality standards. In contrast, Example 4 provides that, although the multinational enterprise sets global quality control standards, SubCo has the responsibility to ensure that its production conforms to these standards.
- The warehousing functions are identical in Example 3 and Example 4. SubCo holds the finished goods awaiting ForCo's delivery and shipment.
- In both Example 3 and Example 4, when it comes to inventory ownership and risk, SubCo has no ownership or risk in raw materials, in work-in-process, or in finished goods inventories.
- Example 3 and Example 4 provide that ForCo owns all intangible property rights for the products being manufactured. Such rights include patented designs, processes, know-how, brand names, trademarks, and logos. Example 3 provides that ForCo create trade intangibles internally through R& D outside of Country A. In contrast, in Example 4, ForCo licenses the product intangibles for SubCo's use.
- For both Example 3 and Example 4, SubCo owns or leases all property, plant, and equipment that it uses for manufacturing ForCo's products.
- For both Example 3 and Example 4, as to product liability and warranty risk, ForCo has sole liability for product defects and customer warranty claims. ForCo agrees to indemnify SubCo for any losses or damages.
- For both Example 3 and Example 4, ForCo bears any foreign exchange risk regarding amounts payable for raw materials.
- For both Example 3 and Example 4, ForCo derives $100 million in sales income and incurs total distribution and marketing costs of $30 million.
- For both Example 3 and Example 4, ForCo incurs costs of $59 million related to the manufacture of the products, but the components of this $59 million amount differ from each other. ForCo paid SubCo a $14 million processing fee in Example 3 and $15 million in Example 4.
- In Example 3, ForCo had a $10 million R&D allocation for developing product intangibles; in Example 4, ForCo incurred $10 million in royalties for licensing intangibles.
- In Example 3, ForCo paid $30 million in intangibles for raw materials; in Example 4, ForCo paid $30 million to reimburse SubCo for raw material costs.
- For both Example 3 and Example 4, ForCo incurred $3 million in product liability and warranty costs and incurred $1 million in inventory stock losses caused by SubCo's damage to components and finished products during warehousing.

Example 3 reflected a $1 million expenditure to operate the raw material purchasing and production scheduling department. Example 4 had no comparable expenditure.

- In Example 3, SubCo incurred operating expenses of $13 million for its toll manufacturing operations. In Example 4, SubCo incurred operating expenses of $14 million for its toll manufacturing activities, other than costs reimbursed by ForCo as above. These amounts include the $1 million for purchasing and production scheduling departments.

Example 4: Functional Analysis

The ATO attributes functions, assets, and risks to ForCo(HO), SubCo, and ForCo's dependent agent PE by first allocating functions, assets, and risks to the principal and agent activities, ForCo and SubCo, ignoring the functions, assets, and risks pertaining to the independent agent PE. Then the ATO attributes functions, assets, and risks to the independent agent PE.

Viewing functions, assets, and risks to ForCo and to SubCo, SubCo incurs all of the functions: raw material purchasing, manufacturing, production scheduling, quality control, and warehousing. As to assets, the inventory and intangibles belong to ForCo while the property, plant, and equipment for manufacturing belong to SubCo. All of the risks belong to ForCo: inventory risk, product liability and warranty risk, and foreign exchange risk.

Different results apply when we take into account the dependent agent PE. All functions are split between SubCo and ForCo: raw material purchasing, manufacturing, production scheduling, quality control, and warehousing. Regarding assets, the inventory and intangibles belong to ForCo(PE); the property, plant, and equipment for manufacturing belong to SubCo. All of the risks belong to ForCo(PE): inventory risk, product liability and warranty risk, and foreign exchange risk.

The ATO would attribute these cost items based on the facts specified in Example 4:

- $15 million processing fee—ForCo(PE)
- $10 million royalties—ForCo(PE)
- $30 million raw materials—ForCo(PE)
- $3 million product liability and warranty—SubCo
- $1 million purchasing and promotion scheduling departments—ForCo(HO)
- $1 million inventory stock losses—ForCo(PE)
- $13 million manufacturing—SubCo

Example 4: Comparability Analysis

The ATO ascertained the next facts regarding ForCo, SubCo, and uncontrolled comparables. There are no internal comparables in this situation, as SubCo acted exclusively on behalf of ForCo and its other affiliates. There are no external comparables to benchmark an arm's length compensation or margin for particular combination of functions, assets, and risks of the dependent agent PE. Independent toll manufacturers in Country A provide external comparables that establish that $15 million as an arm's length fee for SubCo's processing services.

The ATO then seeks to apply return on assets computations. Independent full-risk manufacturers of computer manufacturers in Country A with similar functions, assets, and risks have data as to SubCo and the dependent agent PE combined that reflect a 10 percent return on assets. The ATO determines the relevant assets of SubCo as being $20 million for SubCo and $50 million for ForCo. All of these amounts are attributable to the dependent agent PE.

The ATO suggests that the transfer pricing method most likely to give the taxpayer the best estimate of the arm's length profit for the dependent agent PE may be a similar type of profit split as that used in Example 3, given the outcome of the functional analysis and the available data for the comparability analysis. Using this approach:

1. Ascertain the combined arm's length return on assets taking into account the dependent agent PE and SubCo. The combined assets are $20 million for SubCo plus $50 million for ForCo, or $70 million in total. At the 10 percent rate, the combined return is $7 million.
2. Deduct SubCo's arm's length profit. The arm's length processing fee is $15 million and the operating expenses are $14 million, resulting in an arm's length profit of $1 million.
3. To determine the residual amount, subtract $1 million from the initial $7 million amount, for a total of $6 million.

The ATO comments that, given this outcome under the profit split method, this analysis might reflect SubCo's conversion from a full-risk manufacturer to a toll manufacturer. Such conversion would not cause any change in the overall profit on which the multinational enterprise is subject to tax in Country A. SubCo's conversion from a full-risk manufacturer to a toll manufacturer would reduce the taxable profit of SubCo but would have created a taxable profit of the PE of ForCo corresponding to that reduction.

This shift in the location of profits appears to be justified. The lack of the functions, assets, and risks attributable to ForCo(HO) indicates that conversion from a full-risk manufacturer to a toll manufacturer has not been accompanied by any changes on the ground in Country A.

NOTES

1. ITAA 1936 Section 6(1)(a); for example, Vietnamese-Australian Double Tax Agreement, Article 5, paragraph 5(a).
2. ITAA 1936 Section 6(1)(d); for example, Vietnamese-Australian Double Tax Agreement, Article 5, paragraph 5(c).
3. See Tax Ruling TR 2001/11, paragraphs 5.37 to paragraphs 5.42, as to dependent agency PEs.
4. TR 2001/11, paragraphs 4.40 to 4.42.

CHAPTER FOUR

Australia's Advance Pricing Arrangement Program

AUSTRALIA CONTINUES to apply its advance pricing arrangement (APA) program. According to the November 2008 APA Program report, Australia increased the issuance of its APAs in 2007–2008 compared with that of prior years. The Australian Tax Office (ATO) completed 48 APAs during the 2008 financial year, comprising these activity categories:

- 30 APAs are renewals that result from existing APAs
- 7 APAs are new APAs that arise as result of the ATO's compliance activity and the ATO's involvement in the transfer pricing review and audit process
- 11 APAs are new APAs, unprompted by the ATO

Taxpayers at all size levels can request APAs. These taxpayers include large businesses and small to medium enterprise markets. Large businesses with revenues of more than A$250 million more readily use APAs than do smaller businesses. The ATO completed two-thirds of its APAs with large business taxpayers in 2007–2008 year. The ATO completed the remaining one-third of the APAs with small to medium businesses.

The completed APAs cover a wide range of related party inbound dealings and cover a wide range of related party outbound dealings. These APAs include purchases and sales of these business activities:

- Consumer products
- Medical products
- Business products
- Information technology software and hardware
- Business and management services
- Metals and minerals

The businesses that apply for an APA include these activities:

- Agency permanent establishments
- Distributors
- Service providers
- Toll manufacturers
- Full manufacturers

PRE-FORMAL APA DISCUSSIONS

The ATO encourages potential APA participants to take advantage of discussions with the ATO before the taxpayer files a formal APA application. The taxpayer and the ATO can undertake pre-formal APA discussions to address:

- Whether the case is suitable for an APA
- Preliminary views as to the transfer pricing method
- The information the taxpayer will need to give the ATO so that the ATO can properly look at the APA request before the taxpayer files an APA application

The ATO cautions that many APA proposals are complex or are unique.

Applicants to the APA process must provide these materials to the ATO long before the taxpayer–ATO conference occurs:

- Background material
- Outline of the proposal

The goals of the taxpayer–ATO conference are to achieve these objectives:

- Use the time well.
- Offer considered views.
- Make sure that the most appropriate staff attends.

APA PROCESSING TIMES

The ATO moves rapidly compared with most other tax offices in formulating APAs. Thus, the ATO expects to complete an APA within 12 months after the taxpayer files the application. The ATO expects the taxpayer to cooperate with the ATO and to provide the ATO with timely, detailed, and accurate information. The completion of the APA process within 12 months depends on:

- Availability of information
- Amount of cooperation among the ATO, the taxpayer, and the foreign tax authority, assuming the APA is a bilateral APA
- The APA's available resources to undertake the APA process

Australian APAs completed in 2007–2008 took, on average, 11 months to process, determined from the inception or filing of the APA to the finalization of the APA. The processing time during the prior year, 2006–2007, was 13 months. The average time to complete the APA depends on whether the APA was unilateral or bilateral:

	Unilateral	Bilateral
2006–2007	8 months	17 months
2007–2008	8 months	16 months

The processing time to complete the APA in Australia is much less than the processing time in the United States. The disparity in processing times between countries applies to both unilateral APAs and bilateral APAs. The median processing times in Australia were similar to the average processing times.

In 2007–2008, on average, the taxpayer's renewal APA application took the same time to process as would a new APA application. In contrast, in 2006–2007, a renewal APA application took 30% less time than a new application took.

An APA application in 2007–2008 involving a small and midsize taxpayer took about 60% less time than a large taxpayer APA application took. In contrast, an APA application in 2006–2007 for a small and midsize taxpayer took about 45% less time than for a large taxpayer application.

The ATO permits a small to midsize taxpayer to enter into an APA application process when the ATO undertakes transfer pricing review and/or transfer pricing audit. Small and midsize APA applications were often prompted by the compliance activity on the part of the ATO. These small and midsize APA applications were usually unilateral. The ATO's knowledge of the business helped to improve processing times for these cases.

APA processing time for bilateral applications increased over the six years beginning in 2002–2003 from 13 to 23 months in 2004–2005 and then decreased to 16 months in 2007–2008. The processing time for unilateral applications ranged from 8 to 12 months. Australia had one multilateral APA application.

According to the ATO, unilateral APA applications are more common. It attributes this high percentage to:

- A unique joint venture arrangement in which bilateral APAs were not appropriate
- Small to midsize businesses, which could not justify the costs of submitting a bilateral APA application

UNILATERAL AND BILATERAL APAS

Australia completed bilateral APA applications with four countries in 2007–2008: Canada, Japan, New Zealand, and the United States. As tax practitioners conversant with developments in the area, we anticipate that Australia will soon be developing bilateral APA applications with Singapore.

The number of total APAs in Australia increased from 20 or fewer APAs per year in the pre-2000, 2000, and 2001 period to 38 in 2005, 27 in 2006, 31 in 2007, and 48 in 2008. Bilateral and multilateral APAs have never reached 20 of Australia's total APAs. In fact, there were just 4 bilateral and multilateral APAs in 2000. These data reflect program life, including renewals.

THE ATO'S APA WORK IN PROCESS

The ATO divides in APA work in process into these categories:

	At June 30, 2007	At June 30, 2008
Discussion stage	18	29
Pre-filing stage	3	20
Filed and in process	41	23
Includes bilateral APAs	18	23

APA ISSUES AND METHODS

The ATO categorizes APAs by type of activity during the 2007–2008 year:

Type of Dealing	Primary Activities	All Activities
Tangible Property	36	36
Intangible Property	3	5
Services	9	18
Total completed	48	

Several APAs cover more than one type of activity. For example, an APA might cover the selling of tangible property and the receiving of management services. The

ATO lists the primary activity first and totals all covered activities in the right-hand column. The broad categories encompass these activities:

- Sales and purchases of goods, made by marketers, distributors, and manufacturers
- Sales of commodities and sales of semicompleted goods
- Licensing of intellectual property
- Services, including financial services and research and development
- Management services and other support services

The APA process in Australia involves the selection of primary transfer pricing methods. As in previous years, taxpayers and the ATO primarily use the transactional net margin method (TNMM). Taxpayers in Australia have ready access to independent comparable data in Australia and elsewhere to show that their related party dealings achieve an arm's length outcome. The tested party might be in Australia or elsewhere, depending on the facts of the case. The taxpayer can also use the TNMM to establish routine returns in a residual profit split:

Primary Methods	
TNMM—Return on Assets	8
TNMM—Sales	24
TNMM—Costs/Berry	4
Method	
Profit Split	3
Comparable uncontrolled price	7
Cost Plus	2
Total	48

The taxpayer should note that Australia's primary methods do not include the resale method.

CHAPTER FIVE

5

China Implements Transfer Pricing Procedures

THE CHINESE tax authorities have implemented transfer pricing regulations. These transfer pricing provisions came into force in January 1, 2008, but the tax authorities postponed the contemporaneous documentation requirements until December 31, 2009.

OVERVIEW

The tax practitioner should be aware of three specific facets of the Chinese transfer pricing regulations in particular:

1. The Chinese tax authorities cast "associated enterprises" in a broad net. As a result, the tax authorities in other countries might not view these associated parties, and relationships among these parties, as constituting control. Nevertheless, the Chinese tax authorities would treat these associated parties as constituting associated enterprises and therefore as constituting control. The reader should examine Article 9 in particular.

2. The Chinese tax authorities have emphasized the transfer pricing enforcement process. This enforcement process emphasizes the collection of contemporaneous documents and on the tax authority's remedies when the enterprise fails to submit these documents.
3. The Chinese transfer pricing regulations are comprehensive in scope. As such, the Chinese transfer pricing regulations address advance pricing arrangements, cost sharing agreements, controlled foreign corporations, thin capitalization, and anti-avoidance provisions.

REGULATIONS

The Chinese transfer pricing regulations comprise 13 chapters:

Chapter	Topic Articles
1	General Principles—Articles 1–8
2	Reporting and Filing Related Party Transactions—Articles 9–12
3	Administration of Contemporaneous Documents—Articles 13–20
4	Transfer Pricing Methods—Articles 21–27
5	Transfer Pricing Audit and Adjustment—Articles 28–45
6	Administrative Guidance Concerning Advance Pricing Arrangements—Articles 46–63
7	Administrative Guidance Concerning Cost Sharing Agreements—Articles 64–75
8	Administrative Guidance Concerning Controlled Foreign Corporations—Articles 76–84
9	Administrative Guidance Concerning Thin Capitalization—Articles 85–91
10	Administrative Guidance Concerning General Anti-Avoidance—Articles 92–97
11	Corresponding Adjustments and International Negotiation—Articles 98–104
12	Legal Responsibility—Articles 105–109
13	Supplementary Provisions—Articles 110–118

The Chinese tax authorities issued transfer pricing regulations for the purpose of standardizing the administration of special adjustments.

CHAPTER 1: GENERAL PRINCIPLES

The Chinese regulations are comprehensive in scope. Many taxpayers are facing problems in implementing these regulations because of the all-Chinese requirement, the strict timing requirements in the regulations, and the lack of forgiveness of the part of the tax authorities. As transfer pricing practitioners, we suggest that multinational enterprises pay more attention to Chapter 10, anti-avoidance techniques.

Relevant Documents

The Chinese tax authorities formulated Article 1 in accordance with the documents that comprise three categories:

1. **Enterprise Income Tax Law.** The People's Republic of China (PRC) Enterprise Income Tax Law, which the Chinese transfer pricing regulation refers to as the EIT Law, together with its implementation rules, which the Chinese transfer pricing regulation refers to as the EIT Implementation Rules.
2. **Tax Collection Law.** The PRC Tax Collection and Administration Law, which the Chinese transfer pricing regulation refers to as the Tax Collection Law, together with its implementation rules, which the Chinese transfer pricing regulation refers to as the Tax Collection Implementation Rules.
3. **Tax treaties and arrangements.** The relevant provisions that pertain to tax treaties or arrangements that the taxpayer undertook to avoid double taxation that otherwise would have taken place between the Chinese government, on one hand, and governments of other countries or regions, on the other hand. The Chinese transfer pricing regulation refers to the tax treaties or arrangements as tax treaties.

Applicable Relationships

Article 2 provides that this transfer pricing regulation applies to these relationships:

- The administration of special adjustments that tax authorities can take for transfer pricing purposes
- Advance pricing arrangements (APAs)
- Cost sharing agreements (CSAs)
- Controlled foreign corporations (CFCs)
- General anti–tax avoidance rules and so forth

Transfer Pricing Administration

Article 3 provides that EIT Law Chapter 6 and the Tax Collection Law Article 36 define the term "transfer pricing administration" to mean the "the tax authorities' administrative work" in relation to:

- Verification
- Evaluation
- Investigation
- Making adjustments

These investigative powers that the Chinese tax authorities assert pertain to transactions between an enterprise and its associated parties, which the Chinese transfer pricing regulation refers to as related party transactions. The underlying objective for the Chinese tax authorities is to determine whether the taxpayer carries out these transactions in accordance with the arm's length principle.

APA Tax Administration

Article 4 provides that EIT Law Article 42 and the Tax Collection Law Article 53 define the term "APA tax administration" to mean:

- The tax authorities' administrative work in relation to the verification of documents
- The tax authorities' administrative work in relation to the evaluation of pricing principles and calculation methods for related party transactions that the enterprise will raise in future years
- The tax authorities' administrative work in relation to negotiating with the enterprise to reach the APA

Cost Sharing Agreement

Article 5 provides that the cost sharing agreement (CSA) tax administration refers to the tax authorities' administrative work, based on EIT Law Article 41, Paragraph 2. Such CSA work includes:

- Verification of the CSA
- Evaluation of the CSA
- Investigation of the CSA
- Adjustment of the CSA

The CSA tax administration seeks to examine whether an agreement entered into by an enterprise and its associated enterprise is in accordance with arm's length principle and related concerns.

Controlled Foreign Corporations

Article 6 provides that the CFC's administration refers to the tax authorities' administrative work, based on EIT Law Article 45. Such CFC work includes:

- Verification of the CFC
- Evaluation of the CFC
- Investigation of the reasonableness of the CFC's no profit distribution, investigation of the reasonableness of the CFC's reduced profit distribution, and/or making adjustments as to the taxable income of the Chinese tax resident enterprise from the CFC

Thin Capitalization

Article 7 provides that thin capitalization tax administration refers to the tax authorities' administrative work, based on EIT Law Article 46. Such thin capitalization work includes:

- Verification as to the thin capitalization
- Evaluation as to the thin capitalization

- Investigation and adjustment of the ratio of an enterprise's debt investment from its associated parties and equity investment as to whether the taxpayer carries out the underlying transactions in accordance with the promulgated ratios or the arm's length principle

Anti–Tax Avoidance

Article 8 provides that general anti–tax avoidance tax administration refers to the tax authorities' administrative work, based on EIT Law Article 47. Such general anti–tax avoidance work includes:

- Verification as to the tax avoidance activities
- Evaluation as to the tax avoidance activities
- Investigation and adjustment of the enterprise's business arrangement that results in a reduction of its taxable revenue or income without reasonable business purpose

CHAPTER 2: REPORTING AND FILING OF RELATED PARTY TRANSACTIONS

China takes a strong position in ferreting out related party interests. As a parallel, the reader should contrast the position taken by Vietnam in ascertaining related party interests.

Associated Enterprises

Article 9 makes reference to the term "associated enterprises" as mentioned in EIT Implementation Rules Article 109 and Tax Collection Law Implementation Rules Article 51. Article 9 defines "associated enterprises" to include one of the next eight relationships between an enterprise and another enterprise, business, or individual:

1. **Share ownership creates related party status.** One party holds—directly or indirectly—a total of 25% of another's shares. Alternatively, a third party holds—directly or indirectly—25% or more of the shares of both parties. One party might hold the shares of another party through an intermediary. In such an intermediary situation, the party that holds 25% or more of the shares of intermediary is treated as the party's shareholder percentage to the same extent.[1]
2. **Debt relationship creates related party status.** One party might owe debt to another party where that debt exceeds 50% of the party's actual received capital. Alternatively, the party might owe debt to another party that exceeds 10% or more of the total debts the party owes, and which debt another party guarantees. This analysis does not take into account the debt to an independent financial institution.

3. **Appointment of senior management personnel creates related party status.** One party might appoint its senior management personnel over the operations of another party. The term "senior management personnel" includes members of the board of directors and managers. Such an appointment creates related party status in two situations:
    1. **More than half.** One party appoints more than half of its senior management personnel, or the party appoints at least one senior member of the board of directors, where that party is able to exert control over the board of directors of the opposite party.
    2. **Two parties.** The same third party appoints two parties with more than half of its senior management personnel, or the same third party appoints more than one senior member of the board of directors who is able to exert control over the board of directors of the opposite party.
4. **Concurrent management creates related party status.** One party might incur its senior management operations over another party. The term "senior management personnel" includes members of the board of directors and managers. Such an appointment creates related party status in two situations:
    1. **More than half.** More than half of one party's senior management personnel concurrently include senior management positions of another party.
    2. **One senior member.** At least one senior member of the board of directors, who is able to exert control over the board of directors, concurrently holds the position of senior member of the board of directors of another party.
5. **Dependency on intangibles creates related party status.** One party's normal production and operational activities depend on intangibles that the party licensed from another party. Such intangibles include industrial property rights or know-how.
6. **Control of purchase or sales creates related party status.** The purchases that one party controls over another create related party status if that one party primarily controls the other's purchases. The sales that one party controls over another create related party status if the one party primarily controls the other's sales.
7. **Providing controlled services creates related party status.** One party's providing of services or its receipt of services creates related party status if one party controls the providing of services or receipt of services to the other party.
8. **Substantial control creates related party status.** One party might have substantial control over another party's production, operations, and transactions so as to create related party status. Alternatively, the party might have other relationships or interests so as to create related party status, such as where one party shares basically the same interests with major shareholders of another party. This situation can arise even though the parties would not satisfy the shareholding percentage requirements of (1) above. Family relationships can determine substantial control.

Principal Categories

Article 10 describes the four principal categories of related party transactions:

1. **Transfers of tangible assets.** Transfer pricing applies to the purchase, sale, and use of tangible assets. Such transfers include the purchase, sale, transfer, or lease of houses and buildings, vehicles, machinery and equipment, tools, commodities, and products.
2. **Transfers of intangible assets.** Transfer pricing applies to the transfer and use of intangible assets. Such transfers include the transfer of ownership, the provision of land rights, copyrights (authorship), patents, trademarks, customer lists, distribution channels, brands, technical know-how, and intellectual property rights, such as exterior designs or practical and new designs.
3. **Transfers of capital.** Transfer pricing applies to capital financing. Such capital financing includes all kinds of long-term borrowing and short-term borrowing, lending and guarantees, and all kinds of interest-bearing advance payments and deferred payments.
4. **Transfers of services.** Transfer pricing applies to the providing of services. Such services include market surveys, marketing, management, administration, technical services, maintenance, design, consulting, agency, scientific research, legal and accounting services, and so forth.

Tax Returns

Article 11 addresses the resident enterprise tax returns. The enterprise is to file its tax returns on the basis of an actual profit basis, and nonresident enterprises with establishments in China are to be taxed on an actual profits basis. The enterprise is to prepare and submit the "PRC Annual Related Party Transactions Reporting Form," which is to include these documents:

- Associated Parties Form
- Related Party Transaction Form
- Purchase and Sales Form
- Services Form
- Intangible Assets Form
- Fixed Asset Form
- Financing Form
- Outbound Investment Form
- Outbound Payments Form

Extension

Article 12 specifies that enterprises might have difficulties in submitting documents, such as documents specified in Article 11. Such an enterprise might apply for an extension, doing so in accordance with the relevant provisions of the Tax Collection Law and its Implementation Rules.

CHAPTER 3: ADMINISTRATION OF CONTEMPORANEOUS DOCUMENTATION

China follows the strict contemporaneous documentation approach that the United States initiated. The reader should consider various contemporaneous documentation approaches in the Pacific Administrators Tax Administration (PATA) Guidelines.

Contemporaneous Documentation Requirement

Article 13 specifies that, according to EIT Implementation Rule Article 114, the enterprises should prepare and maintain relevant contemporaneous documentation regarding each related party transaction and for each taxable year. The enterprises must submit these documents to the tax authorities upon the tax authorities' request.

Contemporaneous Documents

Article 14 specifies the contents of the contemporaneous documents are to principally include:

1. **Organizational Structure**
   a. **Organizational and shareholding structure.** The enterprise is to prepare a relevant organizational structure of the group with which the enterprise is affiliated, together with the enterprise's shareholding structure.
   b. **Development and changes.** The enterprise is to prepare records concerning the development of relationships and its associated parties, and change in relationships between enterprises and its associated parties.
   c. **Primary information.** The enterprise is to prepare information as to the associated parties with which the enterprise conducted its related party transactions. This information request is to include the following as to the associated enterprises:
      i. Name
      ii. Legal representatives
      iii. Senior management personnel, such as directors and managers
      iv. Registered address and the place where the enterprise conducts its business
      v. Name of the associated person
      vi. Nationality
      vii. Residency
      viii. Family members
      ix. Additional relevant information regarding the association

d. **Parties exerting direct influence.** The enterprise is to indicate the parties exerting direct influence over the pricing of the related party transactions.
e. **Tax rates and tax incentives.** The enterprise is to indicate, for each associated party, the tax rates and eligible tax incentives, indicating those taxes having an income tax–type nature.

2. **Overview of Business Operations**
   a. **Economic issues.** The enterprise is to include its business operation summary, including information as to its major economic issues affecting the enterprise and the industry, such as the enterprise development summary, industry development summary, business strategy, industry policy or industry restrictions, group supply chain arrangement, and position that the enterprise has in the chain.
   b. **Main business.** The enterprise is to indicate the composition of its main business. Further, the enterprise is to indicate the percentage of the business that the enterprise incurs in proportion to its main business. The enterprise is to include the revenue and profit of the main business together with its percentage to this total revenue and profit, respectively.
   c. **Industry position.** The enterprise is to provide an analysis of its position within the industry and an analysis of the relevant market environment from a competition standpoint.
   d. **Internal organization.** The enterprise is to provide its internal organizational structure. This internal structure includes information regarding the functions that it performs, the risks that it assumes, and the assets it employs as to the enterprise and as to its associated parties in the related transactions. The enterprise is to fill out the "Functional and Risk Analysis for Enterprises" form accordingly.
   e. **Group consolidated report.** The enterprise is to prepare a group consolidated report, which it can prepare according to financial year of the group. The enterprise must prepare and include the group consolidated report no later than December 31 of the year following the year in which the related party transactions took place.
3. **Information Regarding Related Party Transactions**
   a. **Basic information.** The enterprise is to indicate the following information as to its related party transactions: types, participants, timing, amount, currency denominated or settled, and commercial terms of the related party transactions.
   b. **Transactional model.** The enterprise is to describe the transactional model and the terms that apply to related party transactions, together with relevant changes and justifications.
   c. **Operational flows.** The enterprise is to indicate operational flows, including product flow, cash flow of the related party transactions, and a flow comparison between related party transactions and unrelated party transactions.
   d. **Intangible assets.** The enterprise is to specify the intangible assets that are involved in the related party transactions. The enterprise is to indicate the influence of these intangible assets on the pricing of these transactions.

e. **Copies or agreements.** The enterprise is to provide copies or agreements related to the related party transactions. The enterprise is to provide an explanation as to their executed status.
f. **Economic and legal factors.** The enterprise is to analyze the main economic factors and legal factors that impact the pricing of the related party transactions.
g. **Allocations.** The enterprise is to allocate revenues, costs, expenses, and profits between related party transactions and nonrelated party transactions. The Chinese tax authorities expect the enterprise to provide directly segmented financial data. If the enterprise cannot directly segment these financial data, the enterprise is to allocate these data using reasonable methods supporting explanations supporting the allocation rationale. The enterprise is to fill out the "Annual Financial Analysis on Related Party Transactions for Enterprises" Form accordingly.

4. **Comparability Analysis**
   a. **Factors.** The enterprise is to indicate the factors it considered in performing a comparability analysis. These factors include the characteristics of the transacted goods or services, the functions and risks the transaction parties assume, together with the transaction parties' contractual terms, economic environments, business strategies, and so forth.
   b. **Functions.** The enterprise is to provide information as to the functions it performs, the risks it assumes, and the assets it employs compared with that of comparable enterprises.
   c. **Comparable transactions.** The enterprise is to describe comparable transactions. Such comparable transactions are the physical characteristics, quality, and efficacy of the goods; interest rates, amount of financing, currency, duration, guarantees, credit ratings, terms of repayment, methods of interest computation, and so forth for financial activities; the nature and extent of the services; the types and transaction forms of the intangible assets, the right to use intangible assets, and the benefits from using the intangibles.
   d. **Comparable information.** The enterprise is to provide the source, the selection criteria, and the rationale for the comparable information.
   e. **Comparable data adjustments.** The enterprise is to provide the rationale for making the comparable data adjustments.
5. **Selection and Application of Transfer Pricing Methodologies**
   a. **Method selection.** The enterprise is to select its transfer pricing methodologies and provide a rationale for such selection. The enterprise can select a profit-based selection method. However, if the enterprise does select a profit method, the enterprise must explain its contribution to the group overall profit, or the enterprise must explain its contribution to the residual profit.
   b. **Data applications.** The enterprise is to explain how the comparable data can support the application of the transfer pricing methods the enterprise has selected.
   c. **Assumptions and judgments.** The enterprise is to provide information as to the assumptions and judgments it made when determining the comparable uncontrolled prices or determining the comparable uncontrolled profits.

d. **Reasonability and judgment.** The enterprise is to apply reasonable transfer pricing methods. The enterprise is to apply comparability analysis results to determine comparable uncontrolled prices or profits, and the enterprise is to provide justifications of the arm's length prices or profits.
e. **Other documents.** The enterprise is to provide other documents that can justify the selection of transfer pricing methods.

Exemptions

Article 15 exempts enterprises that meet one of these three standards from the requirement that the enterprise prepare contemporaneous documents:

1. **Size criteria.** The Chinese tax regulations exempt enterprises in which the amount of related party purchases or sales is lower than RMB200 million. For toll manufacturing operations, the enterprise is to determine the exempt amount based on the import/customs declared prices. The exemption that the Chinese tax regulations provide for small businesses applies only if the annual amount of other related party transactions is lower than RMB40 million. In determining the applicability of the size criteria as to related party financing, the enterprise is to calculate the amount based on the interest that it received or is paid. The enterprise should exclude from this determination the above-mentioned related party purchases of related party sales or other transactions where the enterprise already included these amounts in a CSA or in an APA that is effective for that year.
2. **APA transactions.** The Chinese tax regulations exempt enterprises in which an APA that is in effect covers these related party transactions.
3. **Domestic associated parties.** The Chinese tax regulations exempt enterprises in which the foreign shareholder percentage is less than 50 percent, but the exception applies only if the related party transactions occur among domestic associated parties.

Timing Requirements for Submission

Article 16 provides that the enterprise is to prepare contemporaneous documents for the current year before May 31 of the following year. The enterprise is to submit these contemporaneous documents within 20 days after the tax authorities issue this request. Chapter 7 of this regulation might stipulate otherwise. An enterprise that is unable to submit the documents for reasons beyond its control should submit the documents to the tax authorities within 20 days of obtaining these rights over the documents.

Submitting Formal Documents

Article 17 provides that when the enterprise submits documents under the tax authority's request, the enterprise must submit these documents under the company's legal seal and with the legal signature of the legal representative or the legal signature of the delegate whom the legal representative designates.

Merger and Division

Article 18 provides the situation in which an enterprise might conduct its tax deregistration due to a merger or division. In the event that an enterprise conducts its deregistration in the event of its merger or division, the surviving enterprise after the merger or division must maintain its relevant contemporaneous documents.

Chinese Language Only

Article 19 provides that the enterprise must submit contemporaneous documents in Chinese. The original documents can be in a foreign language, but the enterprise must submit copies in Chinese.

Ten-Year Maintenance

Article 20 specifies that the enterprise is to maintain contemporaneous documents for 10 years, beginning with June 1 of the year following the year in which the related party transactions took place.

CHAPTER 4: TRANSFER PRICING METHODS

The Chinese government issued these rules before the Organisation for Economic Co-operation and Development (OECD) updated its method selection process. China has signified its desire to comply with OECD transfer pricing rules but nevertheless has not specified whether it will apply the old OECD Guidelines or the 2010 OECD Guidelines. As a result, taxpayers might find the Chinese method selection more limiting.

Arm's Length Principle

Article 21 provides that enterprises should follow the arm's length principle and select and apply reasonable transfer pricing methods where these enterprises have related party transactions and the tax authorities can verify and evaluate these related party transactions. Article 21 then makes reference to EIT Implementation Rules Article 111, which provides that the transfer pricing methods include:

- Comparable uncontrolled price method
- Resale price method
- Cost plus method
- Transactional net margin method
- Profit split method
- Any other methods that comply with the arm's length principle

Comparable Analysis

Article 22 provides that a comparable analysis should consider the next five aspects when selecting a reasonable transfer pricing method:

1. **Characteristics.** Characteristics of the transacted assets or services, which primarily include: the physical characteristics, quality, and the tangible properties; the nature and scope of the services; the types, the transaction forms, the duration, and the scope of asset or service being transferred; and the expected returns of the intangible properties.
2. **Functions.** The functions that all parties to the transactions perform and the risks that all parties to the transactions assume. Such functions principally include: research and development (R&D), design, purchasing, processing, assembling, manufacturing, inventory management, distribution, after-sale services, advertising, transportation, storage, financing, finance, accounting, legal, human resource management, and so forth. When the enterprise compares functions in undertaking comparable analysis, it should pay close attention to the similarity of the assets the enterprise employs to perform these functions. Risks principally include: R&D risks, purchase risks, production risks, distribution risks, marketing risks, management and financial risks, and so forth. The risk provisions do not address liability risks, such as labor dispute risks, slip and fall risks, or the like.
3. **Contract terms.** Contract terms principally include: the subject of the transaction, the quantity and prices of the transactions, the forms and type of payment, the terms of delivery, the scope and terms of the after-sale services, the agreement to provide additional services, the rights related to modifying and amending the content of the contract, the valid duration of the contract, the termination rights of the contract, and the extension rights of the contract.
4. **Economic environment.** The economic environment principally includes: industry overview, geographic region, market scale, market level, degree of market competition, consumer purchasing power, suitability of the goods and services, prices of production factors, cost of transportation, governmental regulation, and so forth.
5. **Business strategy.** Business strategy principally includes innovation and R&D strategies, business diversification strategies, risk avoidance strategies, market penetration strategies, and so forth.

Comparable Uncontrolled Price Method

Article 23 provides that the enterprise is to base the comparable uncontrolled price method for related party transactions on the arm's length price for the prices of the same or similar transactions between unrelated parties. In applying the comparable uncontrolled price method, the enterprise, in undertaking the comparability analysis, should examine the differences in the characteristics of the transacted properties and services that impact contractual terms and economic environment between related party transactions and unrelated party transactions. The enterprise should consider differences regarding different types of transactions, including:

1. **Tangible properties.** The purchase or sale pertaining to transfer of tangible properties
   a. **Purchasing.** The process of purchasing, selling, or transferring tangible properties, which principally includes the time and venue of the transaction; the

terms of delivery, delivery procedures, payment terms, the quantity of the transaction, the time and venue of after-sale services, and so forth.

   b. **Manufacture.** The stage of purchase, sale, or transfer, which principally includes the stages of manufacturing, wholesale, retail, export, and so forth.
   c. **Previously purchased products.** The products purchased, sold, or transferred, including the name, brand, specifications, models, performance, structure, appearance, packaging, and so forth.
   d. **General environment.** The environment as to the purchase, sale, or transfer of tangible properties. These issues principally include local customs, consumer preferences, degree of political stability, fiscal policies, taxation policies, foreign policies, and so forth.
2. **Employing assets.** The employment of tangible assets:
   a. **Physical assets.** The tangible assets, physical constraints (i.e., the assets' performance, specifications, models, configuration, types, and asset depreciation).
   b. **Usage rights.** The usage right provisions (i.e., time, duration, and use).
   c. **Costs.** Cost issues (i.e., the owner's investment expenditures and maintenance costs as to these assets).
3. **Transfer and use.** The transfer and use of intangible assets:
   a. **Types.** The types, usage, applicable industries, and expected returns as to the intangible assets.
   b. **Costs.** Other costs, such as: development costs, terms of the transfer, exclusivity, the degree and duration of the protection to the extent that relevant laws and regulations protect the intangible assets, the cost and expenses of the transfer, the functions and risks, the suitability of the intangible assets, and so forth.
4. **Financing.** The amount, currency, duration, financing guarantee, credit rating of the borrower, terms of repayment, method of interest calculation, and so forth.
5. **The providing of services.** The nature of the services, their technical requirements, professional proficiencies, the responsibilities the enterprise assumes, the terms of payment, direct and indirect costs, and so forth. Significant differences can arise in the above-mentioned factors between the related party transactions and unrelated party transactions. If the preceding significant differences do arise, the enterprise should perform a reasonable adjustment to reflect the impact of these differences on transaction price. Such an adjustment might not be possible. However, in the event such adjustment is not possible, the enterprise should select other reasonable transfer pricing methods according to the provisions in this chapter. The comparable uncontrolled price method is applicable to all types of related party transactions.

Resale Price Method

Article 24 examines the resale price method procedure. Under the resale price method, the enterprise determines the arm's length price for goods purchased from an associated party by deducting the gross profit of a comparable uncontrolled party transaction from the resale price to unrelated parties for goods purchased. This purchase formula is: The arm's length purchase price is the unrelated party's resale price multiplied by 1 minus the comparable unrelated party transaction gross margin. The comparable unrelated party transaction gross margin is the gross profit of the comparable unrelated party transaction divided by the net sales of the comparable unrelated party transaction times 100%.

Focus on Differences

The enterprise, when conducting a comparability analysis, should pay special attention to investigating the differences between related party transactions and unrelated party transactions in regard to: functional profile, risk profile, contract terms, and other factors that might impact the gross margin. Such differences might include any of the following: sales, marketing and service functions, inventory risk, value and useful life of the machinery and equipment, the use and value of the intangible property, retail or sales channels, business experiences, accounting treatments, management efficiency, and so forth.

Making Reasonable Adjustments

Significant differences might exist between the related party transaction and the unrelated party transaction. If these differences do occur, it is essential for the enterprise to make reasonable adjustments on gross margin influences caused by the differences. However, it might not be feasible for the enterprise to make such a reasonable adjustment. In such a situation, where the present method does not enable the enterprise to make such reasonable adjustments, the enterprise should select other reasonable transfer pricing methods in accordance with the provisions of this chapter.

Material Processing

The enterprise normally applies the resale price method to situations in which resellers do not provide material processing. The term "material processing" includes changing the shape, performance, structure, and trademark of the property. An enterprise applying the resale method might conduct processing activities, or conduct the pure resale of goods.

Cost Plus Method

Article 25 examines the facets of the cost plus method. Under the cost plus method, the enterprise's arm's length price for a related party transaction is the reasonable cost of the related party transaction plus the gross profit of a comparable unrelated party transaction. The cost plus formula is the reasonable cost of the related party transaction times 1 plus the cost margin of the comparable unrelated transaction. The cost margin of the comparable unrelated transaction is equal to the gross profit of the comparable unrelated party transaction divided by the cost of goods sold of the comparable unrelated party transaction times 100 percent.

Investigating Differences

When the enterprise conducts a comparability analysis as to the cost plus method, the enterprise should pay special attention to investigating the differences between related party transactions and unrelated party transactions. The enterprise should examine differences such as: the function and risk profile, contractual terms, and other factors that might impact the cost plus margin. Factors that might impact the cost plus margin are: manufacturing, processing, installation and testing functions, market risk and exchange risk, the value and useful life of the machinery and equipment, the use and value of intangible property, business experiences, accounting treatments, management efficiency, and so forth.

Making Reasonable Adjustments

Significant differences can exist between related party transactions and unrelated party transactions. If such differences do exist, it is essential for the enterprise to examine reasonable adjustments that these differences cause on the influence of cost plus margin. It might not be feasible for the enterprise to make reasonable adjustments. In such a situation, the enterprise should consider selecting other reasonable transfer pricing methods according to the provisions of this chapter. The enterprise normally applies the cost plus method to related party purchase transactions, sales transactions, transfer transactions, the use of tangible properties, providing related party services, and related party financing.

Transactional Net Margin Method

Article 26 describes the transactional net margin method. The term "transactional net margin method" refers to the methodology under which the enterprise uses profit-level indicators of comparable unrelated party transactions to determine the net operating margin of related party transactions. The profit level indicators include: return on assets, return on sales, net cost margin, the Berry ratio, and so forth.

Investigating Differences

When an enterprise conducts a comparability analysis, it should pay special attention to investigating the differences between related party transactions and unrelated party transactions. These differences impact the functional profile, the risk profile, economic environment, and other factors that might affect the operating profit. Such differences could include: functions performed, risks assumed, assets employed, the industry and market situation, business scale, economic cycle, and product life cycle. These differences also can include the allocation of cost, expenses, earnings, and assets among transactions; accounting treatments; management efficiency; and so forth.

Making Reasonable Adjustments

Significant differences might exist between a related party transaction and an unrelated party transaction. If such significant differences do exist, it is essential for the enterprise to undertake reasonable adjustments as to the impact of these differences on the influence on operating profit. The enterprise might determine that it is unfeasible to make such adjustment. In the event that the enterprise finds making such adjustment infeasible, the enterprise should select other transfer pricing methods according to this chapter. The enterprise usually is to apply the transactional net margin method to related party sales, related party transfers, the use of tangible properties, providing related party services, and the related party transfer of intangible assets.

Profit Split Method

Article 27 examines the profit split method. The term "profit split method" refers to the methodology in which the enterprise allocates a portion of the consolidated profit to each associated party according to the respective contribution of each associated party. The Chinese transfer pricing regulations provide two types of profit split methods: (1) the general profit split method and (2) the residual profit split method. The general profit split method splits profits according to the functions the enterprise performs, the risks the enterprise assumes, and the assets that each entity of the enterprise performs in a related party transaction.

Two Steps

The residual profit split method has two steps: The enterprise first identifies the residual profit. The enterprise then makes this residual profit determination by beginning with the total consolidated profit and then deducting routine profit for each associated party.

Investigation

When an enterprise seeks to apply the profit split method, it should pay special attention to investigating the functions that each associated party performs, the risk that each associated party assumes, and the assets that each associated party employs. The enterprise is to examine the allocation of cost, expense, earnings, and assets between associated parties involved in the transaction, together with accounting treatments and the information and assumptions the enterprise uses to evaluate the contribution that each associated party makes to the residual profit. The enterprise normally applies the profit split method in cases where the related party transaction is highly integrated and it is difficult for the enterprise to evaluate the operating results in isolation.

CHAPTER 5: TRANSFER PRICING AUDITS AND ADJUSTMENTS

The Chinese tax authorities focus heavily on state powers rather than on taxpayer's rights. The tax authorities are loath to give taxpayers extensions of time, and the authorities are sometimes ignorant of the complexities taxpayers face, especially where taxpayers have a location that is outside of the commercial mainstream.

Tax Authorities' Powers

Article 28 provides that the tax authorities have the right to select target enterprises for transfer pricing audit and adjustment. The tax authorities rely on the relevant provisions of the Tax Collection Law and its implementation rules as to a tax audit. Article 28 provides that the audited enterprise must report its related party transactions truthfully and provide relevant documents without concealment.

Key Audit Targets

Article 29 provides that tax authorities will select seven key targets for transfer pricing audit:

1. **Large amount.** Enterprises that have a large amount of related party transactions, or enterprises that have multiple types of related party transactions
2. **Losses.** Enterprises with a long-term loss, marginal profit, or fluctuating profit
3. **Small profits.** Enterprises whose profit level is lower than the industry level
4. **Mismatch.** Enterprises whose profit levels obviously do not match with the functions the enterprise performs or the risks the enterprise assumes
5. **Tax havens.** Enterprises that have transactions with associated parties where the parties register in a tax haven
6. **Failure to declare.** Enterprises that fail to declare their related party transactions or enterprises that fail to prepare contemporaneous documentation based on the regulations
7. **Non-arm's length.** Other enterprises that obviously disobey the arm's length principle

Exempted Parties

Article 30 exempts domestic Chinese enterprises from transfer pricing review. Thus, the Chinese tax authorities exempt transactions between domestic related parties that have the same actual tax rate. The tax authorities require no transfer pricing audit or adjustment in principle so long as the transaction does not directly or indirectly result in the reduction of tax revenues as a whole.

Desktop Audit Process

Article 31 addresses the desktop audit process. The article, however, appears to treat desktop audits as a preliminary pre-audit procedure, taking place after the tax authorities preselect the audit targets. The tax authorities are to collect desktop verification and analysis to select enterprises for audit during their daily tax collection duties and while pursuing their administrative duties. The tax authorities should apply desktop verification and analysis to make an overall evaluation of an enterprise's production and operational status and related party transactions. The tax authorities are to apply the desktop audit process principally based on the enterprise's historical tax returns, the enterprise's related party transaction reporting forms, and on other related documents. An enterprise may provide the tax authorities with contemporaneous documents during the tax authority's desktop verification and analysis.

Field Office Transfer Pricing Audit

Article 32 explains the transfer pricing field audit process. The tax authorities expect to conduct field audits on its selected audit targets, relying on these authorities: EIT Law Chapter 6 and the EIT Implementation Rules, Tax Collection Law Chapter 4, and Tax Collection Implementation Rules Chapter 6. Article 32 would apply these eight transfer pricing field audit process.

1. **More than two.** The field office team must comprise more than two officials.
2. **Inspection certificate.** The field office team is to provide the enterprise with a "Tax Inspection Certificate," and is to issue a "Notice on Tax Audit" when the field office team conducts a field audit.
3. **Audit process.** The field audit might include: inquiry, review of the accounting books, and on-site investigation, undertaken in accordance with legal procedures.
4. **Personnel.** The field office can inquire as to the relevant personnel. The field office team will appoint a person to prepare the "Inquiry (Investigation) Record." The field office team inspectors will inform the enterprise's personnel of the relevant legal liabilities related to providing untruthful information. Relevant personnel must check and confirm the "Inquiry (Investigation) Record."
5. **Documents.** The field office team inspectors can request accounting books and relevant documents from the enterprise. When the inspectors request such documents, the directors are to follow Tax Collection Law Implementation Rules Article 86 by preparing a "Notice on Obtaining the Accounting Book" and the "List of Obtained Accounting Books." The inspectors are to follow legal procedures to take away documents and main documents such as accounting books, vouchers, and so forth. The inspectors are to return the accounting books and relevant documents within the duration of the audit in accordance with the regulation.
6. **Issues and problems.** The inspectors might discover issues or problems during the field office audit. If the inspectors discover these issues or problems, the inspectors are to prepare an "Enquiry (Audit) Record." Two or more inspectors are to sign the record. The audited enterprise is to check on or confirm the "Enquiry (Audit) Record" as necessary, but the enterprise might refuse to confirm or to sign it. If the enterprise refuses to confirm and sign the "Enquiry (Audit) Record," more than two inspectors may sign the record.
7. **Note taking.** The inspectors might choose to take notes, record audio or video, make photographs, or photocopy the documents or materials related to the case during the field office inspection. However, the inspectors must indicate the source of the original documents and specify how the inspectors are to maintain these documents. Furthermore, the suppliers of the documents or those who maintain the documents should sign these photographs, paintings, and duplications with the words "consistent with the Original."

8. **Witnesses.** The tax inspectors might need witnesses. If the inspectors do need witnesses, the inspectors are to inform the witnesses of the legal liabilities they have that pertain to providing untruthful information. The tax authorities can require the witnesses to sign off as to the record of testimony.

Documentation

Article 33 describes the documentation process under a Chinese government tax audit. EIT Law Article 43 Paragraph 43 and EIT Implementation Rules Article 114 are the authorities under which the Chinese tax authorities can request the enterprise to provide documents. When the tax authorities conduct transfer pricing audits, the tax authorities have the right to require that the enterprise provide relevant documents, parties associated with the enterprise provide relevant documents, and other enterprises related to the related party transaction audit provide relevant documents. Article 33 calls enterprises related to the related party transaction comparable enterprises. In making that documentation request, the tax authorities are to issue a written "Tax Matter Notice." Note the next two documentation process issues:

1. **Deadline and extension.** The tax authorities can set a "Tax Matter Notice" deadline. The tax authorities expect the enterprise to submit these documents within that deadline. However, the enterprise might not able to submit these required documents by the deadline because of special circumstances. An enterprise facing delay should file an application for the extension with the tax authorities. An enterprise that receives approval from the tax authorities can submit these documents later, but within 30 days from the original deadline. The tax authorities are to provide a response to the enterprise within 15 days of receiving an application for its extension. If the tax authority does not respond to the enterprise regarding the extension request, the tax authority is treated as accepting the application.
2. **Providing information within the deadline.** The associated parties and the comparable enterprises are to provide relevant information to the tax authorities within the deadline. The associated parties and associated enterprises should have agreed as to the deadline with the tax authorities. The submission deadline should normally not exceed 60 days. Rule 33 provides that the enterprise, the associated parties, and the comparable enterprises should provide true and complete information, in accordance with the requirements of the tax authorities.

Checking and Confirmation

Article 34 provides that the tax authorities will check and confirm the information the enterprise's declaration provides, according to the provisions in Chapter 2 of this regulation. The tax authorities will request the enterprise fill in the "Enterprise Factor Analysis Form." The tax authorities are to fill in the "Associated Parties Relationship Conformation Form," the "Related Party Transaction Confirmation Form," and the "Enterprise Comparability Factor Analysis Form," based on the information that the enterprise declares and the documents the audited enterprise provides. The audited enterprise is to verify and confirm the preceding documents.

"Notice of Tax Audit"

Article 35 addresses a transfer pricing audit that involves the investigation and the collection of evidence from associated parties and comparable enterprises. The tax authorities will issue a "Notice of Tax Audit" in such an investigation and collection situation to collect the evidence.

Verification Process

Article 36 provides that the tax authorities are to verify and analyze the information the enterprise, the associated parties, and the comparability enterprises provide. The tax authorities are to verify and analyze this information by applying approaches such as field investigation, sending assistance request letters to other tax authorities, searching information from public sources, and so forth. The tax authorities might need additional information. In such an event, the tax authorities may initiate the information procedure specified in the relevant tax treaties; alternatively, the tax authorities can investigate and collect relevant information through China's overseas resident governmental organizations. The information the tax authorities request might relate to overseas independent parties. When the tax authorities request such information, they may require the enterprise to notarize the documents.

Compliance with the Arm's Length Principle

Article 37 provides that the tax authorities are to analyze and evaluate whether an enterprise's related party transactions comply with the arm's length principle. The tax authorities, in making that arm's length determination, are to select transfer pricing methods as Chapter 4 of this regulation prescribed. The tax authorities can use either public information or nonpublic information for making this analysis and evaluation.

Adjustment Process

Article 38 defers the adjustment process, shifting the adjustment process from the tax auditors to the State Administration of Taxation (SAT). The tax authorities are to analyze and evaluate an enterprise's related party transactions as part of the audit process, and then analyze and evaluate the enterprise's related party transactions. Article 38 cautions that the tax authorities should not adjust for differences in operating profit caused by operating asset differences between the enterprise and the comparable enterprise. While the tax authorities might determine that it is necessary for the tax authority to adjust for such differences, the tax authority is to report these findings to the SAT and seek SAT approval.

Risks and Losses

Article 39 addresses the issues of risks and losses in a functional analysis context. Article 39 itself addresses the treatment of enterprises that engage in process manufacturing under an associated party's orders, where that enterprise does not perform functions such as operational decision making or product R&D. Such sales should not bear the risks and losses that the enterprise would associate with wrong decisions, low capacity utilization, or sluggish sales. Such an enterprise should normally maintain a certain level of profit. The tax authorities are to select appropriate comparable prices or comparable enterprises for these loss-making enterprises to determine a profit level based on economic analysis.

Offsets

Article 40 provides that payments can offset between an enterprise and its associated parties. In the event that such offsets do occur, the tax authorities in principle are to restore and evaluate the related party transactions separately when conducting a comparability analysis and make adjustments.

Interquartile Results

Article 41 provides that tax authorities can analyze and evaluate the enterprise's profitability using the quartile method, but the tax authorities must make an adjustment if the profit level of the enterprise is lower than the median of the comparable enterprises' profitability range. In principle, the tax authority should adjust the tested enterprise's profit up to a level that is not lower than the median of the range the comparable enterprises establish.

Notice of Special Tax Audit Conclusion

Article 42 addresses the conclusion process after the tax audit. The tax authorities might conclude after audit that the enterprise's related party transactions are in line with the arm's length principle. In such an event, the tax authorities will reach a transfer pricing audit conclusion and issue the enterprise a "Notice on Special Tax Audit Conclusion."

Presence of Non–Arm's Length Results

Article 43 addresses the tax authority's procedure when the enterprise does not prove that its related party transactions are in line with the arm's length principle, and these results cause China to receive reduced taxable revenue or taxable income after audit. The tax authorities can apply a transfer pricing adjustment, based on these five procedures:

1. **Preliminary special adjustment plan.** The tax authorities are to prepare a preliminary special adjustment plan. The tax authorities, in preparing such a preliminary special adjustment plan, are to base the plan on calculation, on verification, and on comparability analysis.
2. **Negotiation.** The tax authorities, in preparing such a preliminary adjustment plan, are to consult with and negotiate with the enterprise. The parties are to negotiate

the special adjustment plan in the following manner: The two parties will both appoint chief negotiators. The inspectors will prepare the "Negotiation Notes." The chief negotiators of both parties are to sign and confirm the preliminary adjustment plan. However, the enterprise might refuse to sign the preliminary adjustment plan. If the enterprise refuses to sign this plan, more than two inspectors can sign the preliminary adjustment plan.

3. **Disagreement.** The enterprise can disagree as to the preliminary adjustment plan. The tax authorities are to provide the enterprise with a time period to respond. The enterprise is to provide the tax authorities with further relevant information during this time period. The tax authorities are to verify the information it receives and make timely, deliberate decisions after receiving the information.
4. **"Preliminary Special Adjustment Notice."** The tax authorities are to review their decision and issue the enterprise a "Preliminary Special Adjustment Notice." If the enterprise disagrees with the preliminary adjustment notice, the enterprise is to inform the tax authorities in writing within seven days after the enterprise receives this notice. The tax authorities and the enterprise are to negotiate and deliberate again after the tax authorities receive the enterprise's submission. The tax authorities may regard the enterprise as agreeing with the tax authorities as to the preliminary adjustment notice if the enterprise does not raise any disagreements with the tax authorities during that time period.
5. **Final adjustment.** The tax authorities are to determine the final adjustment to the enterprise and issue a "Special Tax Audit Notice" to the enterprise.

Payment Period

Article 44 provides that enterprises are to pay their tax and interest due within the specified period after the enterprise receives the "Special Tax Audit Adjustment Notice."

Follow-Up Supervision

Article 45 provides that the tax authorities are to implement a five-year follow-up supervision period after a transfer pricing adjustment comes into effect from the year following the last year assessed. The enterprise is to provide contemporaneous documents for a supervision year, providing these documents before June 20 of the following year during the follow-up supervision period. The tax authorities are to analyze and evaluate four key contents based on contemporaneous documents and tax filing information:

1. **Investment.** The enterprise's investment, its operating status, and its changes
2. **Filing amount.** Changes to the enterprise's tax filing amount
3. **Operating result.** Changes in the enterprise's operating result
4. **Related party transactions.** Changes in the enterprise's related party transactions, and so forth

Follow-Up Supervision Period

The tax authorities might conclude during the follow-up supervision period that enterprise's transfer pricing is abnormal. If the tax authorities do determine that the enterprise's transfer pricing is abnormal, the tax authorities are to communicate with the enterprise, informing the enterprise as to these abnormalities. The tax authorities are to require the enterprise to make self-adjustments. Alternatively, the tax authorities can conduct transfer pricing adjustments in accordance with the relevant provisions of this chapter.

CHAPTER 6: ADMINISTRATIVE GUIDANCE CONCERNING ADVANCE PRICING ARRANGEMENTS

The Chinese tax authorities authorize the taxpayer to engage in advance pricing arrangements, but, in practice, such APAs remain uncommon. We expect that the APA process will become more important in future years.

APA Authorization

Article 46 provides that an enterprise can enter into an APA with the tax authorities pursuant to EIT Law Article 42, EIT Implementation Rules Article 113, and Tax Collection Law Implementation Rules Article 53. This APA can address pricing principles and calculation methods for related party transactions in the future period. An APA generally includes six phases: (1) pre-filing meeting, (2) formal application, (3) review and evaluation, (4) negotiations, (5) signing of the agreement, and (6) monitoring and execution. The enterprise can conclude an APA unilaterally, bilaterally, or multilaterally.

APA Internal Procedure

Article 47 provides that the enterprise should initiate the APA process with municipal level tax authorities, including districts.

Basic APA Conditions

Article 48 provides that APA generally applies to enterprises that meet all of these three conditions:

1. **Amount.** The amount of the related party transactions exceeds RMB40 million.
2. **Declaration.** The enterprise is obligated to declare its related party transactions and meets these obligations.
3. **Contemporaneous documents.** The enterprise prepared, maintained, and provided its contemporaneous documents in accordance with the APA regulations.

Duration of the APA

Article 49 provides that an APA generally applies to related party transactions that occur during a three-year to five-year period. These years are consecutive years after the year in which the enterprise filed its formal APA application. The APA process and the audit process run independently of each other. The enterprise's signing of an APA will not affect the tax authorities' transfer pricing tax audit and the tax authorities' adjustments of related party transactions that occur during the year in which the enterprise filed the APA application or in any prior years.

Same or Similar Transactions

The related party transactions in the filing year or in prior years might be the same as or similar to those transactions covered by the APA. The enterprise might be able to apply the APA method to evaluate and adjust the related party transactions that occur during the filing year or prior years. The enterprise will need the tax authorities' approval for this process.

Pre-Filing APA Procedure

Article 50 provides that an enterprise, prior to formally applying for an APA, should declare this intent doing so in written form. The tax authorities are to conduct a pre-filing meeting with the enterprise for the purpose of discussing related issues, the feasibility of the APA, and preparing the "Meeting Minutes of an APA Meeting." The enterprise can conduct a pre-filing meeting on an anonymous basis. Here the Chinese follow the U.S. approach, permitting both unilateral and bilateral APAs:

1. **Unilateral APAs.** An enterprise seeking to establish a unilateral APA is to express its intent in writing to the tax authorities. During the pre-filing meeting, the tax authorities and the enterprise are to discuss these six issues:
   a. The tax years the enterprise and the tax authorities are to cover
   b. Associated parties and the transactions the APA is to cover
   c. The enterprise's business operations in prior years
   d. Functional analysis and risk analysis as to the associated parties in the APA
   e. Whether the enterprise retroactively applied the APA methodologies to resolve tax issues in prior years
   f. Other issues that require explanation
2. **Requesting a bilateral APA or a multilateral APA.** An enterprise might be able to establish a bilateral APA or to establish a multilateral APA. If the enterprise seeks to establish such a bilateral or unilateral APA, the enterprise is to express its intent to do so in writing to both the SAT and the tax authorities in charge. The SAT is to arrange for pre-filing meetings with the enterprise and to discuss, in addition to point (1) just mentioned, these three issues with the enterprise:
   a. The status of the pre-filing meeting applications that the enterprise made to the competent tax authorities of the corresponding country or to the competent tax authorities of the corresponding region involved.

   b. The historical business operations of the enterprise and the related party transactions of the associated parties that are relevant to the APA.
   c. The enterprise is to use proposed pricing principles and calculation methods in developing an APA. The enterprise is to submit these documents to the corresponding tax treaty competent tax authorities.
3. **Reaching an agreement.** The regulations provide for two separate approaches to establishing the APA, depending on whether the enterprise reaches an agreement with the tax authorities through the pre-filing meeting:
   a. The tax authorities and the enterprise might reach an agreement through the pre-filing meeting. In the event that the tax authorities and the enterprise reach such an agreement, the tax authorities are to notify the enterprise, through sending its form "Notice on Formal Negotiation of the APA," to begin formal APA negotiations. The tax authorities are to send this form to the enterprise within 15 days of reaching such an agreement.
   b. The tax authorities and the enterprise might not reach an agreement through the pre-filing meeting. In the event that this failure does take place, the tax authorities are to notify the enterprise through sending its form "Notice on Refusal on the Application of the APA" to deny the application with explanations. The tax authorities are to send this form to the enterprise within 15 days of conclusion of their last meeting.

Filing a "Formal APA Application"

Article 51 provides that the enterprise is to file the "Formal APA Application" with the tax authorities within three months after the enterprise received notification from the tax authorities to begin the formal APA negotiations. An enterprise seeking a bilateral APA or a multilateral APA is to submit the "Formal APA Application" and the "Application for Initiating Mutual Agreement Procedure." The enterprise is to submit those two documents simultaneously to the SAT and to the tax authorities in charge. Here the Chinese authorities follow the U.S. APA approach:

1. **The APA application itself.** The formal written APA application report is to include:
   a. The relevant group organizational chart, company structure, associated party relationships, and related party transactions.
   b. Financial and accounting statements; information on products and information on assets for the prior three years. The assets referred to encompass both tangible assets and intangible assets.
   c. Types of related party transactions involved in the APA and the tax years the APA is to cover.
   d. Allocation of the functions that each relevant associated party performs; allocation of risks that each relevant associated party assumes; the basis of such allocations, such as: establishment, personnel, expenses, assets, and so forth.
   e. The enterprise's applicable transfer pricing, its principles and calculation methods, its functional risk analysis, its comparability analysis, its critical

assumptions, and so forth, where they support the proposed transfer pricing principles and support the method of calculation.
   f. Market conditions, which include future trends and the relevant industry's competition environment.
   g. The scale of annual operations, profit and loss forecasts, and business plans for the years the APA is to cover.
   h. APA-related information (i.e., related party transactions, business operations, and financial information, such as profit level).
   i. The possibility of double taxation.
   j. Any related issues concerning relevant domestic laws, foreign laws, and tax treaties.
2. **Extension.** An enterprise can request an extension for submitting the written APA application with the tax authorities. The enterprise can file the "Extension for Submission of the Formal APA Application" for three special reasons:
   a. The enterprise needs to prepare certain materials in particular.
   b. The enterprise needs to address technical issues regarding materials the enterprise would be submitting, such as translation.
   c. Other nonsubjective reasons.
3. **Documentation.** The enterprise and the tax authorities are to maintain good records of the aforementioned documents and explanations. In addition, the enterprise and the tax authorities are to maintain the documents and materials that could support the proposed transfer pricing principles, the calculation method, and APA eligibility.

Review and Evaluation Process

Article 52 provides that the tax authorities in charge will review and evaluate the application within five months after receiving the enterprise's formal APA application together with related documents and materials. During this review, the tax authorities in charge may ask the enterprise for additional relevant materials in order to draw a conclusion. The tax authorities might need more time for review and evaluation because of special reasons. In the event that the tax authorities have such needs, they are to notify the enterprise through notice (i.e., "Notice on Extended Evaluation for APA Verification and Evaluation"). This extension will not be longer than three months. The review and evaluation of the enterprise's written APA application by the tax authorities in charge will principally include:

1. **Historical business operations.** The tax authorities are to analyze and evaluate documents and materials. These documents and materials reflect the enterprise's operational plans, future trends, and business scope. The focus of these documents and materials is on feasibility analysis, investment budget and results, decisions by the board of directors, and so forth. The tax authorities are to conduct a comprehensive analysis of the relevant information and materials that reflect the enterprise's operational performance. Such relevant information and materials include the enterprise's financials, accounting reports, audit reports, and so forth.

2. **Functions and risks.** The tax authorities are to distinguish between the enterprise's shares and functions, on one hand, and the associated parties' shares and functions, on the other hand. These functions and risks are to include supply, production, transportation, sales, R&D of intangible assets, and the risks that each party assumes as to inventory, credit, foreign exchange, and market.
3. **Comparable information.** The tax authorities are to analyze the domestic comparable pricing information and the overseas comparable pricing information the enterprise provides for the purposes of explaining the material differences between comparable enterprises and APA applicants. The tax authorities should make adjustments to this information accordingly. The tax authorities might not be able to confirm the reasonableness of the comparable transactions or operations. If they are unable to confirm the reasonableness of these operations, the tax authorities are to specifically ask the enterprise to provide additional documents and materials. The purpose of this request is to justify that the enterprise fairly reflects the proposed transfer pricing principles, to justify that the enterprise fairly reflects the related party transactions and economic reality, and to substantiate that the enterprise can support the relevant financial materials and the relevant operational materials.
4. **Critical assumptions.** The tax authorities are to analyze the factors of influence. The tax authorities are to analyze the degree of influence that affects the enterprise's profitability and production. The tax authorities are to undertake this portion of the analysis for the purpose of identifying critical assumptions in order to identify the enterprise's appropriate assumptions for the APA.
5. **Proposed transfer pricing method and calculation method.** The tax authorities are to analyze and evaluate whether and how they accurately could apply the proposed transfer pricing principles and calculation method. This analysis and evaluation pertains to past, current, and future related party transactions as well as to financial and operating results. The tax authorities are to evaluate whether the proposed transfer pricing principles and calculation method satisfy the laws and regulations.
6. **Expected arm's length range of prices or profits.** The tax authorities are to determine the range of prices or profits or that are acceptable to the enterprise and the tax authorities. The parties will need to provide further verification and evaluation as to the comparable price, profit markup, and comparable enterprises' transactions.

Consensus

Article 53 provides two procedures, one approach for unilateral APAs and the other for bilateral and multilateral APAs. In the unilateral APA context, the tax authorities are to further negotiate with the enterprise within 30 days of forming the review and evaluating conclusions for the APA. After the tax authorities and the enterprise reach a consensus, the tax authorities are to submit both the draft APA and the APA evaluation report, level by level, to the SAT for its review and its approval. In the bilateral and multilateral APA context, the SAT is to negotiate with the competent tax authorities of the counterpart country or region. The tax authorities are to prepare the APA draft according to the negotiation memorandum if the tax authorities can achieve consensus. A draft APA is to principally include:

1. **Basic information.** Names, addresses, and relevant basic information about the associated parties.
2. **Related party transactions.** Related party transactions involved in the APA and the years covered.
3. **Comparable data.** Selected comparable prices or transactions, transfer pricing principles, and calculation method.
4. **Terminologies.** Terminologies related to the application of transfer pricing principles and calculation method.
5. **Critical assumptions.** Critical assumptions.
6. **Obligations.** An APA imposes obligations on the enterprise. Such obligations include annual reporting, maintenance of relevant records, a requirement that the enterprise notify the tax authority when critical assumptions change, and so forth.
7. **Legal effects.** Legal effects of the APA; confidentiality of the documents and materials.
8. **Responsibilities.** Clauses as to the responsibilities of both parties.
9. **Revisions.** APA revisions.
10. **Dispute settlement.** Dispute settlement methodology and procedures.
11. **Effective date.** Effective date.
12. **Appendices.** Relevant appendices.

Signatory Authority

Article 54 addresses signatory powers in the unilateral APA context and in the bilateral or multilateral context. In the unilateral APA context, legal representatives or their appointed persons from the tax authority and from the enterprise are to formally sign the APA after these persons have reached a draft agreement. In the bilateral and multilateral APA context, representatives from the SAT and from corresponding competent authorities from other sides or their empowered delegates are to formally sign the bilateral or multilateral APA. Such an agreement process is to take place after the SAT and the competent tax authorities of the counterpart country or region have reached an agreement on the draft bilateral or multilateral APA. The local authorities in charge are to sign the "Implementation Agreement for a Bilateral or Multilateral APA" with the enterprise. The parties are to specify whether they are intending a bilateral APA or a multilateral APA.

Suspension or Termination

Article 55 provides a process under which the enterprise or the tax authorities can suspend or terminate the APA process before the parties sign the APA. The procedure is to apply after the commencement of APA formal negotiation begins. Separate suspension or termination rules apply to a bilateral or multilateral APA. In such a bilateral or multilateral situation, the parties can suspend or terminate the negotiation process, subject to the consultation among the tax authorities of each side. The tax authorities and the enterprise are to return all materials they receive from each other during the negotiations if the parties terminate the negotiation process.

Monitoring

Article 56 establishes a monitoring and administrative system to monitor the execution of the APA. Here the Chinese tax authorities follow the U.S. approach in monitoring the APA:

1. **Annual report.** The enterprise is to maintain relevant documents and materials in order during the APA execution period and not lose, destroy, or remove such items. Such documents and material include accounting books and relevant records. The enterprise is to provide the tax authorities with an annual report as to the execution of the APA, making this report within five months after the tax year-end. The annual report is to include a description of the APA operations and the compliance status as to the APA by the enterprise, including the status regarding all APA requirements. The annual report is to indicate whether the enterprise seeks to revise the APA or to effectively terminate the APA. In the event that certain outstanding issues exist, the enterprise should explain these issues in the annual report with a view toward negotiating with the tax authorities regarding whether the tax authorities and the enterprise should revise or terminate the APA.
2. **Inspection.** During the APA execution period, the tax authorities are to regularly inspect the enterprise's execution of the APA. The tax authorities normally make this inspection every half year. This inspection is to cover:
   a. **Compliance.** Whether the enterprise has abided by the terms and requirements of the APA arrangement
   b. **Operations.** Whether the materials and the annual report being provided by the enterprise for negotiating the APA reflect the enterprise's actual operations
   c. **Correctness.** Whether the materials and calculation method designed to support the transfer pricing method are correct
   d. **Critical assumptions.** Whether the critical assumptions are still valid
   e. **Consistency.** Whether the enterprise's application of the transfer pricing method is consistent with the critical assumptions
3. **Violations.** The enterprise might have violated the APA terms. If the enterprise in fact violated these terms, the tax authorities are to take the necessary steps, possibly to terminate the APA depending on the actual circumstances. The tax authorities are to revoke the APA retroactively to the first year that the APA was in effect if the enterprise hides the facts or the enterprise refuses to comply with APA terms.
4. **Results outside the range.** The enterprise's actual operating results might be outside the range of expected price or profits during the APA execution period. The

tax authorities can seek approval from immediate higher-level authorities to adjust the enterprise's operating results to ensure that the results are within the range of profits or prices, as the agreement specified. If the enterprise has undertaken a bilateral APA or multilateral APA, the foreign tax authorities are to ultimately report these results to the SAT for review and approval through each level of local tax authorities.

5. **Notification.** Substantial changes affecting the APA can arise during the APA execution period. If these changes do occur, the enterprise is to notify the tax authorities, providing this notification within 30 days of these changes taking place. The purpose of the enterprise's notification to the tax authorities is to explain in detail the impacts of these substantial changes on the APA. The enterprise is to attach relevant supporting materials with the notification. There might be situations in which the enterprise cannot report these changes to tax authorities in time because of nonsubjective reasons. The enterprise may request an extension in time to make that notification in that situation. The tax authorities can provide the enterprise with an extension that does not exceed 30 days. The tax authorities are to evaluate the enterprise's written request within 60 days after they receive it. The tax authorities are to take the necessary steps to reflect the enterprise's request. Such changes include the reviewing of the changes, negotiating with the enterprise to revise the APA terms and relevant conditions, or, based on the extent of the impact of such substantial changes on the execution of the APA, taking reasonable steps to revise the APA or terminate the APA. After tax authorities and the enterprise terminate the original APA, the tax authorities may negotiate and sign a new APA with the enterprise in accordance with the chapter's procedures and requirements.
6. **Administrative issues.** The state tax bureau, the local tax bureau, and the enterprise might jointly sign the APA. If this joint signing of the APA occurs, the enterprise is to submit the annual report to both the state tax bureau and the local tax bureau. Then the enterprise is to submit the report regarding substantial changes to both the state tax bureau and the local tax bureau. The state tax bureau and the local tax bureau are to jointly inspect and review the enterprise's execution of the APA.

Renewal

Article 57 provides the procedure under which the enterprise can renew the APA. The APA is automatically invalid after the execution period expires. The enterprise can apply to the tax authorities to renew the APA by filing with the tax authorities an "Application Letter for APA Renewal." The enterprise is to file the "Application Letter for APA Renewal" within 90 days before the existing APA reaches the end of execution period. When the enterprise applies for a renewal, the enterprise should submit reliable evidence showing lack of changes and complete compliance. As to this lack of changes standard, the enterprise is to submit reliable evidence to the tax authorities showing there have been no substantial changes in the facts and in relative environments as described in the existing APA. As to this complete compliance standard, the enterprise is to submit reliable evidence to the tax authorities that the enterprise has been consistently in compliance with the APA terms and conditions. The tax authorities are to determine whether to accept the application. The tax authorities are to send the "Reply Letter for the Application for APA Renewal" to the enterprise, sending this document to the enterprise within 15 days after the tax authorities receive the renewal application. The tax authorities are to review and evaluate the renewal application materials. Further, the tax authorities are to negotiate with the enterprise to redraft the APA if necessary. Finally, the tax authorities are to complete the renewal procedure with the enterprise, doing so at the time and a location codetermined with the enterprise.

SAT Primacy

Article 58 provides that the negotiation of the APA or the execution of the APA can involve tax authorities in two or more areas, whether these areas are different provinces, autonomous regions, municipalities, or cities designated in the state plan, or involving both state tax bureaus and local tax bureaus. In that dual-location situation, the SAT is to organize and coordinate the negotiation of the APA and the execution of the APA. The enterprise can express its intent of the APA in writing directly to the SAT.

Implementation

Article 59 provides that state tax bureaus and local tax bureaus of different places are to implement together the APA arrangement. The tax authorities are to undertake this responsibility if the enterprise and the tax authorities negotiate and sign the APA and the enterprise abides by all terms and requirements of the arrangement.

Confidentiality

Article 60 requires both the tax authorities and the enterprise to keep confidential all the information and materials they obtain during four APA phases: pre-filing, formal negotiation, review, and analysis. The tax authorities and the enterprise are to take meeting minutes of each meeting, to write down the number of copies and the contents of the materials that each party provides, and to have the chief negotiators of both parties sign off.

Use of Data

Article 61 addresses the situation in which the tax authorities and the enterprise fail to reach an APA. In the event that this failure occurs, the tax authorities are not to use nonfactual information they obtain that is related to the enterprise later in the tax audits of the transactions that are covered by the aborted APA. Such nonfactual information includes, but is not limited to, the proposals, reasoning, notions and judgments, and so forth that the tax authorities obtain during the discussion and negotiation phase.

Disputes

Article 62 provides that both parties, the tax authorities and the enterprise, are to resolve any disputes through negotiation if there is any disagreement between them in the execution of the APA. However, the parties might not be able to resolve their disputes through negotiation. In that event, the parties can bring the case to the upper-level tax authorities or ultimately to the SAT, where a bilateral APA or multilateral APA is involved for mediation. The tax authorities must accept the arbitration results or the decision made by the higher-level tax authorities or the SAT. However, the enterprise might still not be able to accept the results of mediation or the decision by higher-level tax authorities or the SAT. The parties should terminate the APA in that situation. Note that the regulations use the terms "mediation" and "arbitration" without delineating the operative differences.

Official Copies

Article 63 provides that the tax authorities are to submit official documents to the SAT, level by level. These official documents pertain to a unilateral APA, an implementation agreement of a bilateral APA or a multilateral APA, or a report of any changes to the APA. The tax authorities are to pursue the documents for records filing within 10 days of signing the APA or agreements with the enterprises or within 20 days as to revising or terminating the APA.

CHAPTER 7: ADMINISTRATIVE GUIDANCE CONCERNING COST SHARING AGREEMENTS

As a general matter, only those countries having tax administrators well versed in transfer pricing and the development of intangibles will look to cost sharing agreements (CSAs). China is such a country, and the tax authorities provide administrative guidance to the CSA process. The reader, in examining this issue, should review the December 2011 U.S. CSA provisions.

Implementation

Article 64 provides a CSA procedure in accordance with this chapter as to the joint development of or acceptance of intangible properties or for the joint provision or the receipt of services. EIT Law Article 41, paragraph 2, and EIT Implementation Rule Article 112 authorize these cost sharing procedures.

Cost Sharing Agreement

Article 65 specifies the rights that a participant has in a CSA. Participants in a CSA are entitled to the beneficial rights of the joint development, to an assignment of intangible properties, or to the participation of service activities. As a result, the participants are to bear the corresponding costs of such activities. The costs that are borne by the associated parties should be consistent with the costs expended by unrelated parties that seek the aforementioned beneficial rights under comparable conditions. Participants to a CSA are not required to pay a royalty for the use of intangible assets the CSA developed or received. In essence, a cost sharing arrangement is in lieu of a royalty arrangement.

Expected Returns

Article 66 provides the enterprise's beneficial rights associated with a CSA. Such beneficial rights involving intangible assets or involving services are to be based on reasonable and measurable returns. The enterprise is to determine these benefits based on reasonable business assumptions and on operational conventions.

Group Activities

Article 67 addresses the issue services in the CSA context. An enterprise can establish a cost sharing arrangement that involves services. A CSA for services is generally applicable to group purchases and to group marketing planning activities.

Cost Sharing Agreement

Article 68 provides that the CSA is to principally include:

1. **Basic information.** The participants' names, country or region of residence, associated party relationships, and the rights and obligations of the agreement.
2. **Content and scope.** The content and the scope of the intangible assets, or the services, that are associated with the CSA. The enterprise is to specify the responsible party to the arrangement and is to specify its responsibilities and tasks relating to R&D or service activities connected with the CSA.
3. **Duration.** The valid duration of the CSA.
4. **Expected benefits.** The methodology and assumptions the enterprise uses for calculating the expected benefits for the participants.
5. **Initial and follow-up investment.** The participants' amount, form, and value determination as to the initial investment and the participant's follow up costs, together with an explanation justifying compliance of the arm's length principle.
6. **Accounting.** The participant's application of the accounting method, together with an explanation of changes to the accounting method.
7. **Entry and exit process.** The procedure and provisions under which participants can join or exit the agreement.
8. **Compensating payments.** The conditions for and provisions for making compensating payments between participants.
9. **Amendment and termination.** The conditions for and provisions for amending or terminating the CSA.
10. **Nonparticipants.** Nonparticipant involvement in the cost sharing provisions.

Level by Level

Article 69 provides that the enterprise seeking a CSA is to submit the CSA to the SAT, level by level, and to record the CSA within 30 days from concluding the CSA. The tax authorities are to report level by level to the SAT for its approval to determine whether the CSA complies with the arm's length principle.

Change in Participants

Article 70 established procedures to reflect changes in participants, or the termination of a CSA that the participants have implemented, and that generate certain assets. The participants are to deal with the preceding issues in accordance with the arm's length principle as follows:

1. **Buy-in payment.** The new participant is to make a reasonable payment for being entitled to benefit from the existing outcome.
2. **Buy-out payment.** The exiting participant is to receive "reasonable compensation" for the transfer of beneficial rights of the existing outcome to other participants.
3. **Change in participants.** The CSA is to adjust all participants' benefits and cost sharing status accordingly to reflect changes in participants.
4. **Distributions.** The CSA is to reasonably distribute the existing outcome when the CSA terminates. The tax authorities have the right to make adjustments where an enterprise fails to deal with the aforementioned situations in accordance with the arm's length principle and, as a result, the enterprise reduces its taxable income.

Compensating Adjustments

Article 71 addresses the compensating adjustment process in the CSA context. During the CSA implementation phase, actual costs that the participants share might not match the actual benefits the participants receive. The CSA should undertake compensating adjustments based on the actual situation in order to match costs and benefits.

Making Adjustments

Article 72 establishes an adjustment process for CSAs in compliance with the arm's length principle:

1. The enterprise can deduct share costs specified in the CSA for the annual tax computation taking place during the CSA effective period.
2. The enterprise's determination of taxable income is to include compensating adjustments for the year in which the CSA makes the adjustments.
3. The enterprise is to treat buy-in payments, buy-out payments, and outcome distributions as a purchase of assets or a disposal of assets. These provisions apply to CSAs involved in intangible properties and apply to the termination of the CSA.

APA Applications

Article 73 provides that the APA and the CSA are not incompatible, according to Chapter 6 of this regulation.

Contemporaneous Documentation

Article 74 provides that an enterprise should prepare and maintain the next eight contemporaneous documents during the CSA enforcement period, documents that are in addition to those prescribed in Chapter 3 of this regulation:

1. **Copies.** Copies of the CSA.
2. **Other agreements.** CSA participants might have reached other agreements for implementing the CSA. The tax authorities are requesting these documents.
3. **Nonparticipants.** Parties that do not participate in the CSA might nevertheless provide outcomes. The tax authorities are requesting the amount or form of the payment that these nonparticipants make for using that outcome.
4. **Participant information.** Information about the participants that join in or exit during the taxable year. Such information includes the name of the joining parties and the exiting parties, their country or region of residence, the associated party relationship, the amount and form of the buy-in payment, and the buy-out compensation.
5. **Amendment or termination.** The enterprise is to provide documents that pertain to the amendment or termination of the CSA. Such statement is to include the enterprise's reasons for the treatment or allocation of the existing CSA.
6. **Cost.** The enterprise is to report the total cost of the CSA and its breakdown arising from the CSA during that current taxable year.
7. **Cost allocation.** The participants are to include cost allocation information during the current taxable year: the amount, the form, and the amount (i.e., the form to which the enterprise the CSA paid allocated costs). The allocation amount reflects the amount for which the CSA paid amounts, together with the allocated costs, the amount, the form, and from whom the cost payments were received.
8. **Expected and actual results.** The enterprise is to reflect a comparison of the expected benefit with the actual results from the CSA. Such amounts are to include the corresponding adjustments made during the current taxable year.

Enforcement Period

The enterprise should be aware of compliance requirements during the CSA enforcement period. During this CSA enforcement period, the enterprise is to file CSA-specific contemporaneous documents with the tax authorities. The deadline for submitting these contemporaneous documents with the tax authorities is before June 20 of the following year for each such taxable year. The enterprise undertaking a CSA is to meet the June 20 contemporaneous documentation filing deadline whether the enterprise's CSA takes the form of an APA or not.

Nondeductible Costs

Article 75 bars the deduction of specific cost allocations where the enterprise initiates its CSA with associated parties:

1. **Purpose and substance.** The CSA does not have a bona fide commercial purpose, or the CSA does not have economic substance.
2. **Arm's length failure.** The CSA does not comply with the arm's length principle.
3. **Unmatched costs and benefits.** The allocation of costs and benefits does not comply with the "cost and income matching" principle.
4. **CSA failure.** The enterprise has not filed the CSA. Or, alternatively, the enterprise has not prepared, maintained, or provided contemporaneous documents to the CSA in accordance with this regulation.
5. **Lack of continuity.** The enterprise has a future period that is less than 20 years from the date at which the enterprise signed the CSA.

CHAPTER 8: ADMINISTRATIVE GUIDELINES CONCERNING CONTROLLED FOREIGN CORPORATIONS

The Chinese government has developed sophisticated rules to monitor controlled foreign corporations (CFCs). The reader is cautioned that such CFC rules apply in other countries, including the United States, Germany, and Canada. The U.S. rules in this regard are much older, going back to 1962.

CFC Defined

Article 76 defines CFCs in this manner: The term "CFCs," as cited in EIT Law Article 45, refers to foreign enterprises where these foreign enterprises are controlled by resident enterprises and/or controlled by individual residents of the PRC. The regulations collectively refer to these owners as "Chinese resident shareholders," which include Chinese resident enterprise shareholders and Chinese resident individual shareholders. The term "CFC" refers to a foreign enterprise established in a country or region in which the effective tax rate is 50% lower than the EIT Law Article 4 paragraph 1 provisions and in which the foreign enterprise does not distribute profits, or in which the foreign enterprise reduces profit distributions without reasonable business needs.

"Controlled" Defined

Article 77 further defines the term "controlled." The term "controlled," as cited in Article 76 of this regulation, refers to the situation in which the enterprise incurs substantial control. The enterprise can incur substantial control through one or more of these facets: shareholding, financing, business, purchase and sales, and so forth. An enterprise can attain control through its shareholding where any single one of the Chinese resident shareholders directly, through a single layer, or indirectly, through multiple layers, holds 10% of the total voting shares of the foreign enterprise in any day of the taxable year, and that all of such Chinese resident shareholders jointly hold more than 50% of the total shares of the foreign enterprise.

Indirect Ownership

The enterprise is to calculate the indirect multiple layer shareholding by a Chinese resident shareholder by multiplying the shareholding percentage for each layer. An intermediary shareholder might own more than 50% of the lower-layer entity. In that more-than-50% intermediary-shareholding situation, the enterprise is to calculate the shareholder percentage of the ultimate shareholders to the lower layer entity by multiplying that amount by 100 percent.

Overseas Investment Report

Article 78 provides that Chinese resident enterprise shareholders are to file an "Annual Report of Enterprise Overseas Investment." This report provides the tax authorities with outbound investment information. Chinese resident enterprise shareholders are to file the "Annual Report of Enterprise Overseas Investment" when they file their annual report.

Tax Authority's Review Process

Article 79 provides that the tax authorities are to gather outbound investment information filed by Chinese resident enterprise shareholders and check on this information. The tax authorities will then issue the "CFC Chinese Resident Shareholder Identity Confirmation Notice" to Chinese resident enterprise shareholders of the CFC. Chinese resident enterprise shareholders might meet the conditions listed in EIT Law Article 45. The tax authorities are to levy tax according to relevant provisions if the Chinese resident enterprise shareholders do meet these EIT conditions.

Deemed Dividend

Article 80 provides that a Chinese resident enterprise shareholder is to include the deemed dividend income from the CFC for the current period by applying this formula:

> The Chinese resident enterprise shareholder's current taxable income is equal to the deemed dividend distribution multiplied by the number of days during which the shares are actually held by the Chinese shareholder, divided by the number of days of the CFC's taxable year multiplied by the proportion of shareholding.

Chinese resident shareholders might hold CFCs through their multilayer shareholding structure. In this multilayering structure, the enterprise is to calculate the proportion of shareholding by multiplying the shareholding percentage of each layer.

Taxable Years

Article 81 addresses the question of different taxable years. A CFC and a Chinese resident enterprise might adopt different taxable year endings. In the situation that multiple taxable years occur, the Chinese resident enterprise is to include the deemed dividend income from the CFC for the Chinese resident enterprise shareholder's taxable year that covers the end date of the CFC's taxable year.

Double Taxation

Article 82 addresses a situation in which the Chinese resident enterprise shareholder's taxable income includes the deemed dividend income for the current period, but a foreign tax authority also taxes that income. The Chinese resident enterprise shareholder might be able to obtain a credit through the EIT Law or tax treaties.

Previously Taxed Income

Article 83 addresses a situation in which, as to a profit distribution, the Chinese resident enterprise has already taxed the income being distributed, in accordance with EIT Law Article 45. In such an event, the Chinese resident enterprise shareholder is to exclude the taxed income distributed for the current period.

Exempt Income

Article 84 exempts deemed dividend income under defined circumstances. The term "deemed dividend income" means the portion of the profits that either are not distributed or are distributed in a lesser manner. The CFC should then distribute this income. A Chinese resident enterprise shareholder can exempt deemed dividend income from its taxable income for the current period if the Chinese resident enterprise shareholder can prove that its CFC is able to satisfy one or more of these three conditions:

1. **Designated location.** The CFC is located in a non– or low–tax-rate country or region that the SAT designates.
2. **Active business activities.** The CFC principally derives income through its active business activities.
3. **Size criterion.** The annual profits of the CFC are no more than RMB5 million.

CHAPTER 9: ADMINISTRATIVE GUIDANCE CONCERNING THIN CAPITALIZATION

The Chinese tax authorities, similar to other tax authorities, are concerned about earning-stripping, or thin capitalization. The reader should note that China uses a unique approach to the thin capitalization provisions.

Nondeductible Interest

Article 85 provides the determination of the nondeductible interest amount when computing taxable income pursuant to EIT Law Article 46. The nondeductible interest expense is equal to the annual interest the enterprise pays to associated parties multiplied by 1 minus the standard ratio divided by the related party debt-to-equity ratio of the enterprise. The Ministry of Finance and the SAT determine the standard ratio. More specifically, the standard ratio is the ratio stipulated by the "Notice of the Ministry of Finance and the State Administration of Taxation on Tax Policy Issues Relating to Deduction Standards for the Interest Payment by Enterprises to Associated Parties."

Related Party Debt to Equity

EIT law Article 46 and EIT Implementation Rules Article 119 define "related party debt to equity" to mean the total debt investment the enterprise receives from associated parties, hereinafter referred to as related party debt investment, versus equity investment. Related party debt investment includes all kinds of debt investment that associated parties guarantee.

Related Party Debt-to-Equity Ratio

Article 86 provides that the related party debt-to-equity ratio is computed as follows: The related party debt-to-equity ratio is the sum of the average related party debt investment for each month in a year divided by the sum of the average equity investments for each month in the year. The average related party debt for each month is equal to one half of the following amount: monthly opening balance of the related party debt investment plus monthly closing balance of related party debt investment. The average equity investment for each month is equal to one half of the following amount: monthly opening balance of the equity investment plus monthly closing balance of the equity investment.

Equity Investment

Equity investment is the amount of the shareholders' equity, as recorded on the balance sheet. The amount of the shareholders' equity might be less than the sum of the paid-in capital plus the capital reserve. In that event, the equity investment is equal to the sum of the paid-in capital and the capital reserve. The sum of the paid-in capital and the capital reserve might be less than the amount of the paid-in capital. In that event, the equity investment is equal to the amount of the paid-in capital.

Interest Expenses

Article 87 defines "interest expenses," as cited in EIT Law Article 46, to include paid interest, guarantee fees, mortgage fees, and other expenses that share the nature of the interest payment where these amounts are directly incurred by debts owed to associated parties.

Nondeductible Interest Expense

Article 88 examines the broad aspects that impact nondeductible interest expenses. As a general matter, when computing taxable income under EIT Law Article 46, nondeductible interest expenses may not be carried forward to the following tax years. Instead, the enterprise is to allocate nondeductible interest expenses among associated parties proportionately according to the interest paid by the enterprise to each associated party. The tax authorities will permit the deduction of interest expense that the enterprise allocates to domestic associated parties where that interest bears a higher effective rate than the tested party. The enterprise is to regard interest the enterprise pays to overseas associated parties, whether directly or indirectly, as a dividend distribution. The enterprise is to pay an additional tax liability, as computed, based on the difference in the income tax rates between dividends and interest. The withholding tax, which already has been paid, is more than the tax computed, is based on deemed dividends, and is not refundable.

Excessive Interest Expense Deductions

Article 89 addresses the treatment of interest expense deductions that are in excess of the standard related party debt-to-equity ratio. An enterprise might claim an interest expense deduction on related party debt investment where that interest expense deduction is in excess of the standard related party debt-to-equity ratio. In that situation, upon the request of the tax authorities, the enterprise is to prepare, maintain, and submit the following contemporaneous documents in addition to preparing the documents prescribed in Chapter 3 of this regulation. The purpose to these documents is to prove that the amount, interest rate, term, financing requirements, debt-to-equity ratios of the related party debt investment, and so forth are all in compliance with the arm's length principle:

1. **Borrowing ability.** Analysis of the borrower's repaying ability and the borrower's crediting ability
2. **Group structure.** Analysis of the group's repaying ability and the group's financing structure
3. **Equity changes.** Explanation of the changes in capital investment, such as changes in the registered capital
4. **Explanations.** Explanation of the nature and purpose of the related party debt investment, together with the market condition when receiving such financing
5. **Currency denomination.** The currency denomination of the related party debt investment, together with the amount, interest rate, term, and financial conditions
6. **Collateral.** The condition of the collateral the enterprise provides
7. **Guarantors.** The condition of the guarantors
8. **Comparative interest rates.** The interest rate of loans having the same type, having the same maturity, and having the same financial conditions
9. **Convertible conversions.** The requirements for converting convertible corporate bonds
10. **Compliance.** Other documents that can prove the enterprise's compliance with the arm's length principle

Failure to Substantiate

Article 90 examines the consequences when an enterprise fails to substantiate that the interest rate complies with the arm's length principle. An enterprise is obligated to prepare, maintain, and provide contemporaneous documents to prove that the amount, interest rate, term, financing requirements, and the debt-to-equity ratios of the related party debt investment conform to the arm's length principle. If the enterprise fails to substantiate that interest rate, it cannot deduct interest expense the enterprise incurred as to related party debt investment that is in excess of the standard ratio when computing taxable income.

"Interest Actually Paid"

Article 91 provides that the term "interest actually paid," in the chapter, refers to interest the enterprise records to reflect relevant costs or expenses on an accrual basis.

Thin Capitalization versus Transfer Pricing

From the standpoint of the tax authorities, transfer pricing takes preference over thin capitalization. This situation can arise because transfer pricing issues can impact related party interest that the enterprise actually paid. If these conflict situations do arise, the tax authorities are to first conduct transfer pricing audit adjustments in accordance with the relevant provisions of Chapter 5 of this regulation.

CHAPTER 10: ADMINISTRATIVE GUIDANCE CONCERNING GENERAL ANTI-AVOIDANCE

As a general matter, tax authorities view tax avoidance separate from transfer pricing. The Hong Kong tax authorities view these provisions together, and China follows the Hong Kong approach. However, China has been slow in implementing these rules.

Anti-Avoidance Audit

Article 92 explores the parameters for the general anti-avoidance audit pursuant to EIT Law Article 47 and EIT Implementation Rules Article 120. The tax authorities have the right to initiate a general anti-avoidance audit for enterprises having any of these five tax avoidance arrangements:

1. **Tax incentives.** Tax incentive abuse
2. **Tax treaties.** Tax treaty abuse
3. **Legal structures.** Abuse of a company's legal form
4. **Tax havens.** Tax avoidance through a tax haven
5. **Other arrangements.** Other arrangements that do not have a bona fide commercial purpose

Substance Over Form

Article 93 provides that the tax authorities are to comprehensively consider the next six substance-over-form factors when determining whether an enterprise has a tax avoidance arrangement:

1. **Form and substance.** The form and the substance of the arrangement
2. **Time period.** The time at which the enterprise is to conclude the arrangement; the execution period for the arrangement
3. **Implementation.** The implementation method of the arrangement
4. **Relationships.** The relationship between each step, or a part of the arrangement
5. **Financial performance.** Changes in the financial performance of each party involved in the arrangement
6. **Tax considerations.** Tax consequences of the arrangement

Restructuring

Article 94 gives the power to the tax authorities to restructure the transaction. The tax authorities have the power to redefine the nature of a tax avoidance arrangement based on business substance. The tax authorities can revoke a tax benefit the enterprise obtained from the tax avoidance arrangement. The tax authorities can, from a tax perspective, deny the existence of the enterprises that fail to provide economic substance, particularly when these enterprises are located in tax havens and result in tax avoidance of their associated parties or unassociated parties.

Audit Methods

Article 95 explains the general anti-avoidance audit process. When the tax authorities begin a general anti-avoidance audit, they are to send a "Notice on Tax Audit" to the taxpayer in accordance with the provisions of the Tax Collection Law and the Tax Collection Law Implementation Rules. The enterprise is to provide documents to the tax authority within 60 days of receiving such a notice to prove that its arrangement has a bona fide commercial purpose. The tax authority has a remedy if the enterprise fails to provide the requested documents to it. The enterprise might fail to provide documents within the specified period, or the enterprise may provide documents, but these documents do not prove its arrangement has a bona fide purpose. In such a situation, the tax authorities are authorized to send a "Special Tax Audit Notice" to the enterprise and make a tax adjustment based on the information the tax authorities have already acquired.

Additional Document Requests

Article 96 provides that when the tax authorities begin a general anti-avoidance audit against the enterprise, they are authorized to require the planner of the tax avoidance arrangement to provide relevant documents and materials pursuant to Tax Collection Law Article 57.

SAT Approval

Article 97 provides that the tax authorities are to report general anti-avoidance audits and adjustments level by level to the SAT for approval.

CHAPTER 11: CORRESPONDING ADJUSTMENTS AND INTERNATIONAL NEGOTIATIONS

China realizes the importance of making corresponding adjustments and undertaking international negotiations. China would make these adjustments through the mutual agreement procedure.

Corresponding Adjustments

Article 98 explains the corresponding adjustment process. One party of a related party transaction might be subject to transfer pricing audit and tax adjustment. In such a situation, the counterparty should be allowed to make corresponding adjustments to avoid double taxation. Such an adjustment might involve an associated party, and the party might be located in a country or region that has entered into a tax treaty with the PRC. In such a situation, the SAT has the power to negotiate with the competent tax authorities of the tax treaty contracting party pursuant to mutual agreement procedures under the tax treaty applicable to the enterprise.

Mutual Agreement Procedure

Article 99 implements the Mutual Agreement Procedure. Corresponding transfer pricing adjustments might involve associated parties in a country or region that entered into a tax treaty with the PRC. In such a situation, the enterprise can file the "Application for Initiating a Mutual Agreement Procedure" with both the SAT and with the competent tax authorities. The enterprise is to provide relevant documents to the tax authorities, including copies of the transfer pricing adjustment notice sent to the enterprise or sent to its associated parties.

Application for Corresponding Adjustment

Article 100 provides that the enterprise seeking a comparable adjustment is to file an application regarding such a comparable adjustment within three years from the date the enterprise or its associated parties receives a transfer pricing adjustment notice from the tax authority. The tax authorities are not to permit the enterprise to file a comparable adjustment application beyond the three-year application period.

Withholding

Article 101 provides for forbearance on withholding when the transfer pricing adjustment involves interest, rental, royalty, and so forth paid by the enterprise to its overseas associated parties. The "tax already withheld is not adjusted any more."

MAP Negotiations

Article 102 examines the MAP negotiating procedure. The SAT can accept a bilateral APA application or accept a multilateral APA application pursuant to Chapter 6 of this regulation. As part of this APA process, the SAT can negotiate with the competent tax authorities for any tax treaty contracting party according to the mutual agreement procedures.

Written Notice

Article 103 examines the MAP notice procedure. The SAT is to issue a written notice to the enterprise, and the tax authorities in charge are to deliver the written notice to the enterprise specifying the result of such a relevant adjustment or mutual agreements.

Excluded Tax Considerations

Article 104 bars the application of corresponding adjustments to these tax issues: i.e., nondeductible interest expense and interest expense deemed a dividend as mentioned in Chapter 9 of this regulation.

CHAPTER 12: LEGAL RESPONSIBILITY

The Chinese tax authorities highlight the taxpayer's obligations during the transfer pricing process. The government specifically addresses compliance failures, the failure to provide documents, and similar situations where the taxpayer might be liable.

Compliance Failures

Article 105 addresses the tax authority's collection powers. The enterprise might fail to submit the annual report to the tax authorities as to related party transactions. Alternatively, the enterprise might fail to maintain contemporaneous documents or other relevant documents pursuant to the Tax Collection Law Article 60 and Tax Collection Law Article 62.

Failure to Provide Documents

Article 106 addresses the enterprise's failure to provide documents. An enterprise might refuse to provide documents as to its related party transactions, such as not providing contemporaneous documentation, and so forth. Alternatively, an enterprise might provide false or incomplete materials or provide untruthful reporting. Tax Collection Law Article 70, Tax Collection Law Implementation Rules Article 96, EIT law Article 44, and EIT Law Implementation Rules Article 115 apply in this instance.

Interest Charge

Article 107 imposes an interest charge when the tax authorities impose a special tax adjustment on the enterprise in accordance with the EIT Law and its Implementation Rules. The tax authorities are to impose an interest charge based on the unpaid tax amounts based on the underpaid tax amount for related party transactions that occur after January 1, 2008. The tax authorities are to charge interest on a daily basis. These are interest expenses:

1. **Interest period.** The interest charging period begins on June 1 of the year following the year in which the enterprise attributes the tax. The interest period continues until the date of the tax payment or tax prepayment.
2. **Interest rate.** The interest is to be 5% plus the basic RMB lending rate. The People's Bank of China publishes the RMB lending rates. The enterprise is to use the RMB lending rate for loans having the same term as for the enterprise's unpaid tax. The enterprise is to use the basic RMB lending rate prevailing on December 31 of the tax year to which the underpaid tax is attributed. The enterprise is to calculate the interest rate based on the above annual rate assuming 365 days per year.
3. **Eliminating the 5% add-on.** The enterprise might be able to pay interest but without adding the 5% add-on. The enterprise can avoid the add-on by providing contemporaneous documents and other relevant documents based on this regulation. Alternatively, the enterprise can avoid the add-on when the enterprise is exempt from the requirement under Article 15 of this regulation as to the preparation of contemporaneous documents, but the enterprise provides other relevant documents based on requirements the tax authorities impose. The provisions in (2) apply if an enterprise believes that it is exempt from the preparation of contemporaneous documents pursuant to Article 15 clause 1 of this regulation, but, during the audit, the tax authorities discover that the actual related party transaction reaches the threshold for the preparation of contemporaneous documents.
4. **Interest deduction.** The enterprise cannot deduct for tax purposes interest paid pursuant to this article.

Advance Tax Payments

Article 108 addresses the treatment of making advance tax payments. An enterprise might make an advance tax payment prior to the tax authority's making a special tax adjustment. In such an event, the enterprise is to determine the tax years to which the tax payment is attributed based on the order of the underpaid tax years when the enterprise receives the tax adjustment notice. The enterprise is to compute the interest amount until the day that the enterprise makes the advance tax payment.

Payment of Underpaid Tax and Interest

Article 109 requires the enterprise to pay the underpaid tax and interest within the certain period prescribed by the special adjustment notice. An enterprise might have difficulty paying the underpaid tax on time because of special reasons. If the enterprise has such difficulty, the enterprise is to file an extension of time for paying the tax. The Tax Collection Law Article 31 and the Tax Collection Law implementation rules Articles 41 and 42 provide for the extension of time. The Tax Collection Law Article 32 applies if an enterprise fails to pay its underpaid tax and interest within the specified time period and the enterprise does not apply for a payment extension.

CHAPTER 13: SUPPLEMENTARY PROVISIONS

The Chinese tax authorities include provisions supplementary to the transfer pricing rules. These provisions address the formalities but restate the documentation requirements.

Priority of Provisions

Article 110 provides that the tax authorities might refer to the relevant provisions in Chapter 5 of this regulation as to the procedures on special tax audit and adjustments other than for the administration of transfer pricing and other than for the administration of APAs.

Joint Investigative Team

Article 111 provides that, during the period of special tax audit and adjustment, all levels of state tax bureaus and local tax bureaus should strengthen communication among themselves. This provision authorizes the state tax bureaus and local tax bureaus to establish a joint investigative team if necessary.

Preservation of Documents

Article 112 directs all tax authorities' personnel to keep and use the documents that the enterprise submitted in accordance with the relevant confidentiality rules, such as the "Provisional Administrative Measures of the SAT on Tax-Related Confidential Information of Taxpayers."[3]

Holidays

Article 113 provides for the treatment of holidays. The last day of the specified period, as prescribed by this regulation, might be a statutory holiday. In that event, the enterprise is to treat the date following the holiday as the last day of the specified period. There might be three consecutive days of statutory holidays within this period of time. In that event, the enterprise can extend the time period by the number of days in the holiday.

Terminology

Article 114 provides that any term such as "more than," "less than," "exceed(s)" certain amounts, and "within," "on," "prior to," or "before" a certain date in this regulation includes the certain amount or the date itself.

Change of Address

Article 115 limits the enterprise's ability to change its address. An audited enterprise might change its business address or the audited enterprise might undergo deregistration during the special tax audit period. Nevertheless, in principle, the tax authorities in charge will not permit the enterprise to change its registration or permit the enterprise to undergo deregulation before the tax authorities close the audit and make their adjustment.

Deadline Postponed

Article 116 postpones the contemporaneous documentation deadline. These provisions might require an enterprise to prepare contemporaneous documents pursuant to Chapter 3 of this regulation as to related party transactions that occur during 2008. The tax authorities have postponed the 2008 contemporaneous documentation deadline to December 31, 2009.

Responsibility

Article 117 provides that the SAT is responsible for the interpretation and amendment of this regulation.

Effective Date

Article 118 provides for the effective date of the Chinese transfer pricing regulations. The regulation is effective as of January 1, 2008. The Chinese authorities invalidated the predecessor provisions at the same time as they promulgated the current provisions. These provisions are obsolete:

- "Administrative Regulations of the State Administration of Taxation concerning Transactions between Associated Enterprises (Trial Version)[4]
- "Notice of the State Administration of Taxation on Amendments to the 'Administrative Regulations concerning Transactions between Associated Enterprises (Trial Version)'"[5]
- "Implementation Rules of the State Administration of Taxation concerning Advance Pricing Arrangements for Transactions between Associated Enterprises"[6]

Different provisions could be effective prior to the SAT's promulgation of this regulation. In that event, this regulation is to prevail.

NOTES

1. For the background of the 25% test in the United States, see Treas. Reg. Sec. 1.6038A-1(c), R. Feinschreiber, *Tax Reporting for Foreign-Owned U.S. Corporations* (New York: John Wiley & Sons, 1992), p. 10.

2. "Notice of the Ministry of Finance and the State Administration of Taxation on Tax Policy Issues Relating to Deduction Standards for the Interest Payment by Enterprises to Associated Parties," Caishui [2008] No. 121.
3. "Provisional Administrative Measures of the SAT on Tax-Related Confidential Information of Taxpayers," Guoshuifa [2008] No. 93.
4. "Administrative Regulations of the State Administration of Taxation concerning Transactions between Associated Enterprises (Trial Version)," Guoshuifa [1998] No. 59.
5. "Notice of the State Administration of Taxation on Amendments to the 'Administrative Regulations concerning Transactions between Associated Enterprises (Trial Version),'" Guoshuifa [2004] No. 143.
6. "Implementation Rules of the State Administration of Taxation concerning Advance Pricing Arrangements for Transactions between Associated Enterprises," Guoshuifa [2004] No. 118.

CHAPTER SIX

Reporting Related Party Transactions in China

THE CHINESE government requires a taxpayer doing business in that country to report related party relationships to the State Administration of Taxation (SAT). The Chinese government developed these reporting forms pursuant to Corporate Income Tax Law Article 43. The SAT requires the taxpayer to submit nine specific documents to the tax authorities on an annual basis:

Form 1—Related Party Relationships
Form 2—Summary of Related Party Transactions
Form 3—Purchases and Sales
Form 4—Services
Form 5—Intangible Assets
Form 6—Fixed Assets
Form 7—Financing
Form 8—Outbound Investment
Form 9—Outbound Payments

Although the SAT requires extensive reporting of outbound investment and payments, the SAT fails to address the treatment of inbound investments and outbound payments. These forms, taken as a group, provide the SAT with data pertaining to transfer pricing, but certain forms, especially Form 8 and Form 9, have a broader purpose not necessarily connected with transfer pricing.

Enterprises that must submit the reporting forms to the SAT include foreign-based resident enterprises. The SAT imposes income taxes according to the taxpayer's accounting books, which include nonresident enterprises that have permanent establishments in China. All of these enterprises are to attach and submit their reporting forms on an annual basis and pay corporate income taxes when they submit their annual reporting forms.

As a preliminary matter, the taxpayer must fill in its full name as reflected on the tax corporate certificate. The taxpayer is to fill in the taxpayer identification number, which is the number of the tax registration certificate number that the tax authorities have verified and issued. The enterprise is to use the company's official stamp, including the taxpayer's identification number. The enterprise is to provide the name of the legal representative, telephone number, and reporting date. The SAT must accept the enterprise's report, reflecting the name of the in-charge tax authorities, the SAT stamp, the signature of the accepting officer, telephone number, and date of the SAT's acceptance. The preparer and the legal representative must each sign and stamp each of the nine related party forms before sending these forms to the SAT.

FORM 1—RELATED PARTY RELATIONSHIPS

The taxpayer, in providing Form 1—Related Party Relationships, is to provide the SAT with this information:

- Name of related party
- Taxpayer identification number
- Country/Region
- Address
- Legal representative
- Type of related party relationship

The SAT provides the taxpayer with further explanations regarding these items. The taxpayer's identification number is the number the taxpayer uses for tax filing in the country or region in which the related party is located. The country or region is the name of the country or region in which the related party is located. The address is the registered address of the related party's actual operation and management, or the residence of the related individuals. The SAT provides the taxpayer with codes for eight separate categories, enumerated A through H, that create the related party relationship with the taxpayer. The taxpayer should fill in more than one relationship code if more than one code is applicable.

The SAT provides a broad array of shareholder relationships as being within the transfer pricing control provisions. The SAT enumerates eight specific related party relationships as discussed in the next sections.

Share Ownership

The SAT uses a 25% ownership threshold that is similar to section 6038A in the United States[1] and similar to the 26% ownership threshold in India. The SAT views parties as being related in under the 25% ownership threshold if one party, directly or indirectly, owns 25% or more of the shares of the other party. The SAT views parties as being related in under the 25% ownership threshold if a third party owns 25% of shares of both the party at issue and the other party.

The party might indirectly own the shares of the other party through an intermediate party. This intermediate party relationship exists so long as the party owns 25% or more of the shares of the intermediate party. In that event, the taxpayer is to calculate the percentage of shares of the other party that is directly owned by the party at issue according to the percentage of shares of the other party that is directly owned by the intermediate party.

Loan Relationships

One party might establish control over the other party by providing an extensive loan relationship to the other party. The SAT excludes independent financial institutions from the loan relationship analysis and from the computations themselves. The SAT provides that a loan relationship constitutes a related party transaction if loans between one party to another party account for 50% or more of the party's paid-in capital; or alternatively, 10% or more of the party's total loans are guaranteed by another party.

Power of Appointment by Controlling the Board

The SAT views the retention of one party's power to control the activities of another party as the presence of a related party relationship. The SAT enumerates four of these related party relationships:

1. The other party might appoint more than half of the senior management personnel of one party, including the board members or managers.
2. The other party might appoint at least one senior board member of one party who has the controlling power over the board.

3. The third party might appoint more than half of the senior management personnel of both parties, including the board members or managers.
4. The third party might appoint at least one senior board member of either party who has the controlling power over the board.

Taking Senior Management Positions

The SAT provides that one party's control over the other party's board indicates control over the other party. The SAT enumerates two of these related party relationships:

1. More than half of the senior management personnel from one party, including board members and managers, take senior management positions of the other party, including board members and managers.
2. At least one senior board member of one party who has the controlling power over the board takes the position of the senior board member of the other party.

Licensing Arrangements Indicate Related Party Relationships

The SAT provides that one party can control the other party because of its control through licensing arrangements. From the standpoint of ascertaining whether parties are related parties or whether the relationship is one of control, the issue becomes whether the production and business operations are determinative, or whether the activities could be carried out in a normal manner only with the licensee from the other party. The lack of choice determines control. Such intangibles include other intangibles, industrial property rights, and proprietary technology.

Control through Purchase and Sale Activities

The SAT provides that one party can control the other party through exercising its control through its purchase and sale activities. One party controls the purchase and sale activities during this control situation.

Offering and Receiving Services Activities

The SAT provides that one party's service activity receives or offers are primarily controlled by the other party.

Catchall Relationships

One party might have effective control of the other party, whether through effective control of the production, operation, or transactions of the other party. Alternatively, both parties might have a shared interest due to another shared relationship. Such shared interest might include common activities not reaching the shareholder percentage stipulated but can arise from both parties' shareholders enjoying generally the same economic interest or with a family or relative relationship enjoying generally the same economic interest.

FORM 2—SUMMARY OF RELATED PARTY TRANSACTIONS

As a preliminary inquiry, Form 2 questions whether:

1. The taxpayer has prepared contemporaneous documentation for the current year pursuant to relevant requirements.
2. The taxpayer is exempt from the contemporaneous documentation preparations for the current year.
3. The taxpayer has a cost sharing arrangement in place for the current year.

Form 2 requires the taxpayer to delineate four primary transaction categories:

- Related party transactions
- Overseas related party transactions
- Domestic related party transactions
- The total amount

The taxpayer is to provide amount and percentage for each such category. Form 2 then requires the taxpayer to delineate its activities into 11 specific activity categories:

1. Purchase of material (products)
2. Sale of material (products)
3. Services income
4. Services disbursement
5. Transfer in of intangibles
6. Transfer out of intangibles
7. Transfer in of fixed assets
8. Transfer out of fixed assets
9. Accrued interest income from financing
10. Accrued interest expense of financing
11. Others

Form 2 is a consolidation of the results from these five forms:

1. Form 3—Purchases and Sales
2. Form 4—Services
3. Form 5—Intangible Assets
4. Form 6—Fixed Assets
5. Form 7—Financing

Because Form 2 is a consolidation, we advise taxpayers to complete Forms 3 through Form 7 before completing Form 2. The interrelationship among the forms is explained next.

1. The columns for purchase of materials and products on Form 2 include these amounts:
   a. The first column of purchase of materials and products in Form 2 is the first item of purchases and sales on Form 3.
   b. The fourth column of purchases of materials and products in Form 2 is the fourth item of purchases and sales on Form 3.
   c. The seventh column of purchase of materials and products in Form 2 is the seventh item of purchases and sales on Form 3.
2. The columns for sale of products and materials in Form 2 include these amounts:
   a. The first column of sale of products and materials on Form 2 is the eighth item of purchases and sales on Form 3.
   b. The fourth column of sale of products and materials in Form 2 is the eleventh item of purchases and sales on Form 3.
   c. The seventh column of sale of products and materials on Form 2 is the fourteenth item of purchases and sales on Form 3.
3. The columns for services income on Form 2 include these amounts:
   a. The first column of services income on Form 2 is the first item on the Services form, Form 4.
   b. The fourth column of services income on Form 2 is the fourth item on the Services form, Form 4.
   c. The seventh column of services income on Form 2 is the seventh item on the Services form, Form 4.
4. The columns for services disbursement on Form 2 include these amounts:
   a. The first column of services disbursement on Form 2 is the eighth item on the Services form, Form 4.
   b. The fourth column of services disbursement on Form 2 is the eleventh item on the Services form, Form 4.
   c. The seventh column of services disbursement on Form 2 is the fourteenth item on the Services form, Form 4.
5. The columns for transfer in of intangible assets on Form 2 include these amounts:
   a. The first column of the transfer in of intangible assets on Form 2 is the first column on the Intangible Assets form, Form 5.
   b. The fourth column of the transfer in of intangible assets on Form 2 is the second column on the Intangible Assets form, Form 5.
   c. The seventh column of the transfer in of intangible assets on Form 2 is the fourth column on the Intangible Assets form, Form 5.
6. The columns for transfer out of intangible assets on Form 2 include these amounts:
   a. The first column of the transfer out of intangible assets on Form 2 is the sixth column on the Intangible Assets form, Form 5.
   b. The fourth column of the transfer out of intangible assets on Form 2 is the seventh column on the Intangible Assets form, Form 5.
   c. The seventh column of the transfer out of intangible assets on Form 2 is the ninth column on the Intangible Assets form, Form 5.

7. The columns for transfer in of fixed assets on Form 2 include these amounts:
   a. The first column of the transfer in of fixed assets on Form 2 is the first column of the Fixed Asset form, Form 6.
   b. The fourth column of the transfer in of fixed assets on Form 2 is the second column of the Fixed Asset form, Form 6.
   c. The seventh column of the transfer in of fixed assets on Form 2 is the fourth column of the Fixed Asset form, Form 6.
8. The columns for transfer out of fixed assets on Form 2 include these amounts:
   a. The first column of the transfer out of fixed assets on Form 2 is the first column of the Fixed Asset form, Form 6.
   b. The fourth column of the transfer out of fixed assets on Form 2 is the second column of the Fixed Asset form, Form 6.
   c. The seventh column of the transfer out of fixed assets on Form 2 is the ninth column of the Fixed Asset form, Form 6.
9. The columns for accrued interest income from financing and accrued interest expense from financing on Form 2 include these amounts:
   a. The fourth column of accrued interest income from financing on Form 2 is the eighth column of the first total of the Financing form, Form 7.
   b. The seventh column of accrued interest income from financing on Form 2 is the eighth column of the second total on the Financing form, Form 7.
   c. The fourth column of accrued interest expense from financing on Form 2 is the seventh column of the first total of the Financing form, Form 7.
   d. The seventh column of accrued interest expense from financing on Form 2 is the seventh column of the second total on the Financing form, Form 7.
10. The term "others" refers to amounts related to those activities other than to the activities just mentioned.

FORM 3—PURCHASES AND SALES

The SAT requires the taxpayer to delineate purchases and sales and to provide these amounts:

1. **Total purchases and sales.** The SAT seeks information concerning domestic and international activities and from related and unrelated activities. The SAT is seeking information as to the annual amount of purchases of tangible goods: raw materials, semifinished goods, materials (products) excluding fixed assets, construction materials, and low-value consumables. Import purchases, domestic purchases, export sales, and domestic sales are each divided between related activities and unrelated activities.
2. **Overseas sales by export trade mode.** The SAT seeks information concerning contract processing and other activities, whether the parties are related or unrelated. The taxpayer is to include the purchasing fees as contract purchasing.

3. **Descriptions of overseas parties to which export sales account for more than 10% of total export sales and the relevant transactions.** The taxpayer is to provide SAT with the name of the overseas related party, the country or region, the amount, the pricing methodology, and notes. This information is required for both related and unrelated parties. "Pricing methodology" refers to one of the following, and the taxpayer is to reflect the pricing method by number: (1) comparable uncontrolled price; (2) resale price method; (3) cost plus method; (4) transactional net margin method; (5) profit split method; other—taxpayer must explain in the notes column.
4. **Descriptions of overseas parties to which payment for overseas purchases accounts for more than 10% of the total overseas purchases and the relevant transactions.** The taxpayer is to provide SAT with the name of the overseas related party, the country or region, the amount, the pricing methodology, and notes. This information is required for both related and unrelated parties. Pricing methodology refers to one of the following, and the taxpayer is to reflect the pricing method by number: (1) comparable uncontrolled price; (2) resale price method; (3) cost plus method; (4) transactional net margin method; (5) profit split method; other—taxpayer must explain in the notes column.

FORM 4—SERVICES

The SAT requires the taxpayer to delineate services income and disbursement for services and to provide these amounts:

1. **Total services transactions.**
2. **Description of overseas parties from which the overseas services income account occurs for more than 10% of the total services income and the respective transactions.** The taxpayer must delineate between related parties and unrelated parties. The taxpayer need take into account the name of the overseas party, the country or region, the amount, the pricing methodology, and notes. Pricing methodology refers to one of the following, and the taxpayer is to reflect the pricing method by number: (1) comparable uncontrolled price; (2) resale price method; (3) cost plus method; (4) transactional net margin method; (5) profit split method; other—taxpayer must explain in the notes column.
3. **Overseas parties to whom the overseas distribution account pertains to more than 10 percent of the total services disbursement and the respective transactions.** The taxpayer must delineate between related parties and unrelated parties. The taxpayer need take into account the name of the overseas party, the country or region, the amount, the pricing methodology, and notes. Pricing methodology refers to one of the following, and the taxpayer is to reflect the pricing method by number: (1) comparable uncontrolled price; (2) resale price method; (3) cost plus method; (4) transactional net margin method; (5) profit split method; other—taxpayer must explain in the notes column.

Form 4 delineates services transactions between services income and disbursement for service. Form 4 also delineates services income activities between income from unrelated parties or income from related parties. Similarly, Form 4 delineates services disbursement activity between disbursements made to unrelated parties and disbursements made to related parties.

FORM 5—INTANGIBLE ASSETS

The SAT would have the taxpayer account for the transfers of intangible assets. Form 5 looks to the direction of the intangible asset transfer, the source of the intangible asset transfer, and the affiliated party nature of the intangible asset transfer:

- The direction of the intangible asset transfer (i.e., whether the transfer is into China or whether the transfer is out of China)
- The source of the intangible asset transfer (i.e., whether the transfer is from overseas sources or whether the transfer is from domestic sources)
- The affiliated nature of the intangible asset transfer (i.e., whether the transfer is with a related party or whether the transfer is with an unrelated party)

The SAT's three inquiries as to the transfers of intangible assets necessitate eight columns mathematically, 23. Then there are two total transaction amount columns, one column for transfer in, and one column for transfer out.

Form 5 requires the taxpayer to specify the nature of the intangible item, whether a "right for use" item or an "ownership" item. The right for use category is subdivided into land use rights, patent rights, nonpatented technology, trademarks, copyrights, and others. The ownership category is subdivided into patent rights, nonpatented technology, trademarks, copyrights, and others.

FORM 6—FIXED ASSETS

The SAT would have the taxpayer account for the transfers of fixed assets. Form 6 looks to the direction of the fixed asset transfer, the source of the fixed asset transfer, and the affiliated party nature of the fixed asset transfer:

- The direction of the fixed asset transfer (i.e., whether the transfer is into China or whether the transfer is out of China)
- The source of the fixed asset transfer (i.e., whether the transfer is from overseas sources or whether the transfer is from domestic sources)
- The affiliated nature of the fixed asset transfer (i.e., whether the transfer is with a related party or whether the transfer is with an unrelated party)

The SAT's three inquiries as to the transfers of fixed assets necessitate eight columns mathematically, 23. Then there are two total transaction amount columns, one column for transfer in, and one column for transfer out.

Form 6 requires the taxpayer to specify the nature of the intangible item, whether a "right for use" item or an "ownership" item. The right to use category is subdivided into buildings; aircraft, trains, ships, machines, and other equipment; equipment, tools, and furniture related to production and operation; transportation vehicles other than aircraft, trains, and ships; electronic equipment; and others. The ownership category is subdivided into buildings; aircraft, trains, ships, machines, and other equipment; equipment, tools, and furniture related to production and operation; transportation vehicles other than aircraft, trains, and ships; electronic equipment; and others.

FORM 7—FINANCING

The SAT requires the taxpayer to determine its debt/equity at the outset of preparing Form 7. This debt/equity ratio is the ratio of debt investment received from related parties from the enterprise divided by the equity received by the enterprise. The SAT requires the taxpayer to determine its debt/equity ratio on a monthly basis. The taxpayer is to determine its debt/equity amount in this way:

- The annual sum of the monthly average debt invested amount from related parties is divided by
- The annual sum of the monthly average equity amounts

The monthly average debt investment amount from related parties is determined in the following manner:

- The book balance of debt investment from related parties determined at the beginning of the month, plus
- The book balance of debt investment from related parties determined at the end of the month, dividing the sum of these amounts by two

The monthly average equity investment is determined in the following manner:

- The book balance of the equity investment at the beginning of the month, plus
- The book balance of the equity investment at the end the month, dividing the sum of these amounts by two

The SAT would have the taxpayer delineate overseas related party debt and domestic related party debt and then delineate between fixed-term financing and other debt. Form 7 requires the taxpayer to provide the SAT with this information:

- Name of overseas related party/Name of domestic related party
- Country or region, the location where the overseas related party is located
- Currency, converted to RMB on the middle exchange rate for RMB on the last day of the taxable year
- Financing-in amount

- Financing-out amount
- Interest rate, the annual interest rate for the financing
- Financing start date and ending date
- Accrued interest expense/interest payable, using accrual accounting, including capitalized interest
- Accrued interest income/interest receivable, using accrual accounting
- Name of guarantor
- Guarantee fee
- Guarantee fee rate

The SAT asks the taxpayer to fill in each fixed-term financing. The SAT asks that the taxpayer not fill in financing-in and financing-out in the same line.

FORM 8—OUTBOUND INVESTMENT

Form 8 is the longest of the nine related party transaction forms, comprising two pages. Form 8 is not a transfer pricing form per se, and the form addresses issues outside of the transfer pricing purview. Form 8 is applicable to PRC tax resident enterprises that own shares on an enterprise located in the foreign country or region. "Foreign enterprises" on this form applies to enterprises incorporated in Hong Kong SAR, Macau SAR, and Taiwan. Form 8 itself addresses nine specific facets:

1. Basic information pertaining to the investment enterprise
2. Basic information pertaining to the invested foreign enterprise
3. Tax rate pertaining to the invested foreign enterprise
4. Profit of the invested foreign enterprise
5. Tax payables of the invested foreign enterprise
6. Shareholders of the invested foreign enterprise
7. Profit and loss statement of the invested foreign enterprise
8. Balance sheet of the invested foreign enterprise
9. Dividend distributions of the invested foreign enterprise

1. Basic Information Pertaining to the Investment Enterprise

Form 8 requires the taxpayer to provide information as to the taxpayer's name, its taxpayer identification number, its registered address, and its legal representative. The taxpayer is to fill out Part I on its own account, excluding the taxpayer's investments.

2. Basic Information Pertaining to the Invested Foreign Enterprise

Form 8 requires the taxpayer to provide information to the SAT concerning the taxpayer's investments. A taxpayer may need to fill out more than one Form 8 if the taxpayer has more than one foreign enterprise.

The taxpayer is to fill out this information:

- Name of the company in which the investment enterprise makes the investment
- Taxpayer identification number of the invested foreign enterprise
- Registered address of the invested foreign enterprise
- Invested foreign enterprise's legal representative
- Operations of the business
- Date on which the business became established
- Address of the legal representative
- Scope of the business, the currency book amount
- Exchange amount for the RMB (using middle rate in exchange rate for the recording currency used in the accounting books to RMB as of December 31 of the taxable year)
- Start and end of the taxable year

In addition to these requests, the SAT asks the taxpayer for information as to total shares of invested foreign enterprises, asking about the total number of shares and the starting or ending date. Similarly, the SAT requests the taxpayer to provide information concerning:

- Shares held by an investment enterprise in invested foreign enterprises, looking at the type of shares
- Start or end date
- Number of shares owned
- Percentage of shares owned

Share types include common shares with voting rights, common shares without voting rights, preferred shares, and other equity capital of a similar nature.

3. Tax Rate Pertaining to the Invested Foreign Enterprise

The SAT seeks to differentiate invested foreign enterprises located in a non–low-tax country or region from invested foreign enterprises located in a low-tax country or region. The SAT itself delineates low-tax and non–low-tax countries or regions.

4. Profitability of the Invested Foreign Enterprise

The SAT seeks to delineate invested foreign enterprises with income exceeding RMB5 million from invested foreign enterprises with income not exceeding RMB5 million.

5. Effective Tax Rate

The SAT is seeking from the taxpayer the effective tax rate of the invested foreign enterprise. The taxpayer is to provide the SAT with this information for each invested foreign enterprise:

- Taxable income
- Income tax actually paid
- Profit after income tax
- Effective tax rate
- Statutory income tax rate of the invested enterprise

6. Information as to All Shareholders of the Invested Foreign Enterprise

The taxpayer is to provide the name of the shareholder, its country or region, its taxpayer identification number, the type of shares, the start and end date, and the percentage of total shares.

7. Annual Profit and Loss Statement of the Invested Foreign Enterprise

The SAT requires the taxpayer to provide this information as to the profit and loss statement:

- Revenues
- Cost (of goods sold)
- Gross profit
- Dividend income
- Interest income
- Rent and royalty income
- Income or loss from the transfer of property
- Other income
- Deductible compensating expenditures
- Rent and royalty expenses
- Interest payments
- Depreciation
- Taxes
- Other deductible items

8. Balance Sheet of the Invested Foreign Enterprise

The SAT requires the taxpayer to provide these balance sheet data:

- Assets or items comprising these assets:
  - Cash
  - Accounts receivable
  - Inventories
  - Other current assets
  - Loans to shareholders and other related parties

- Investments in affiliates
- Other investment affiliates
- Other investments
- Building and other depreciable property
- Land
- Intangible assets
- Total assets
- Liability items comprise:
  - Accounts payable
  - Other current liabilities
  - Loans from shareholders and other related parties
  - Other liabilities
  - Shares
  - Undistributed profits

9. Annual Dividend Distributions of the Invested Foreign Enterprise

The SAT requires the taxpayer to provide information as to distributable dividends from the year, dividends distributed during the year, and the distribution percentage.

FORM 9—OUTBOUND PAYMENTS

The SAT requires the taxpayer to provide this information for each activity:

- Outbound payments for the current year
- Outbound payments to overseas related persons (including amounts accrued and not paid)
- Withholding income tax
- Presence or absence of preferable tax treatment under the tax treaties

The enumerated payments include:

- Dividends (to equity investors)
- Interest (to debt investors)
- Rents (pertaining to tangible assets)
- Royalties (pertaining to patents, nonproprietary technology, trademark payments, copyrights, etc.)
- Trademark payments
- Technology license fees
- Asset transfer expenses

- Commissions (including third-party referrals for suppliers or customers, including handling and kickbacks)
- Design fees (payments for architectural design, construction, system software, etc.)
- Consulting fees
- Training fees
- Management services fees
- Contractor fees
- Construction and installation fees
- Artistic and athletic performance fees
- Certification or testing fees
- Market development fees
- After-sales service fees

NOTES

1. R. Feinschreiber, *Transfer Pricing Handbook* (3rd ed.) (New York: John Wiley & Sons, 2001), Chapters 54–66.

7

CHAPTER SEVEN

Hong Kong Advance Ruling Cases: Taxability of Profits

THE GOVERNMENT of the Hong Kong Special Administrative Region (Hong Kong) has been issuing substantive advance ruling case results since 2000. Hong Kong's Inland Revenue Department issues these advance ruling case results infrequently, issuing just 38 such results during this nearly ten-year interval. This analysis reviews the Inland Revenue Department's taxability of business profits, together with its treatment of expense allocation and transfer pricing, as Hong Kong's advance ruling case process reflects these results.

ADVANCE RULING PROCESS

Hong Kong's Inland Revenue Department designed the Hong Kong advance ruling case results to provide the taxpayer with a defined area of certainty concerning the taxability of business operations. The Inland Revenue Department publishes the advance ruling case results only for general reference, similar to the Internal Revenue Service ruling process in the United States. The department cautions taxpayers not to rely heavily on these advance ruling case results. When the issue becomes the treatment of current tax results, the department will rely on the previously issued ruling only if the factual pattern is the same as in the prior ruling.

Hong Kong's Inland Revenue Department cautions that the Hong Kong government might have changed the relevant tax provisions in the interim after the issuance of the ruling. The department acknowledges that it might have modified its relevant case law interpretation and practice. Further, the department might take a different position than it did in the past if the department believes that the taxpayer is using its tax approach as an avoidance device. More recent rulings reflect the Hong Kong government's strong anti–tax haven response.

Hong Kong's Inland Revenue Department issues these advance ruling case results in a manner that protects taxpayer confidentiality. The department edits the rulings prior to publication and removes identifying information and provides these case results only by ruling number.

The Inland Revenue Department's primary impetus for issuing advance ruling cases is the taxability of profits provision, section 14 of the Inland Revenue Ordinance. The department issued 17 advance ruling cases in this taxability category compared with issuing 38 advance ruling cases in total. The 17 advance ruling cases address various products and trading fact patterns and the treatment of services activities. These taxability of profits provisions frequently address threshold nexus issues and permanent establishment activities.

ADVANCE RULING CASE NO. 4

The taxpayer incorporated its business in Hong Kong on March 31, 1999, for the purpose of trading accessories. This taxpayer maintained a registered office in Hong Kong, effectuating this registered office through a local accounting firm. An Australian enterprise, Company B, was the headquarters of business operations. Mr. A, the sales manager of Company B, was the beneficial owner of the Hong Kong enterprise.

Mr. A. is responsible for negotiating and concluding Company B's purchase contracts. Mr. A's purchasing responsibility applies both to Hong Kong sales and to overseas sales. Mr. A. ordinarily lives in Australia and visits Hong Kong at intervals of about three months.

Company B relies on its local accounting firm to provide documentation of the transactions and to provide other administrative activities. The administrative activities include these activities under Mr. A's direction:

- Preparing purchase orders and sales orders
- Preparing invoices
- Operating bank accounts
- Maintaining accounting records

Company B obtains much of its products from its overseas suppliers. The local accounting firm places its purchase orders with the suppliers and accepts sales orders from Hong Kong. The accounting firm makes the purchase and sales determination under Mr. A's instructions. The suppliers then send its invoices, packing lists, and other documents to Company B's Hong Kong office.

The suppliers deliver the goods to Company B for its sales to local customers and for other offshore customers. Company B keeps the goods in warehouses in Hong Kong. Company B pays the suppliers by letter of credit and receives settlement from its customers by letter of credit.

Company B appointed a People's Republic of China (PRC) agent to act as its agent for selling accessories to a PRC customer. Mr. A negotiates with the PRC customer and with its PRC agent directly for the purpose of securing price, quantity, quality, and shipment. At the same time, Mr. A negotiates with a supplier in Italy for the price, the production schedule, and the delivery of the goods.

The parties operate their trading transactions in this manner:

- Mr. A receives a sales confirmation.
- Mr. A then asks the PRC customer to issue purchase orders to the Hong Kong office directly.
- Mr. A informs the local accounting firm as to the details of the transaction at the same time customer issues the purchase order.
- The local accounting firm then places purchase orders to the Italian supplier, placing that order in accordance with Mr. A's instructions.
- Company B then ships the goods to the PRC customer directly.
- The customer and the supplier settle the transactions on a back-to-back letter of credit basis.
- The local accounting firm sets up the company's back-to back basics.

Hong Kong's Inland Revenue Department, in issuing Advance Ruling Case No. 4, held that Company B's profits that arise from sales to the PRC are onshore profits. These onshore profits are subject to the Hong Kong profits tax pursuant to section 14 of the Inland Revenue Ordinance.

The ruling itself did not provide a rationale for its decision to impose taxation based on the company's onshore activities. We suspect that the department might have viewed the accounting firm's relationship in Hong Kong as creating an agency relationship with the taxpayer. It appears the above-mentioned agency relationship, coupled with the physical presence of the goods in Hong Kong by having a warehouse in Hong Kong, and the presence of the taxpayer's Hong Kong sale activities, created taxable nexus and made the company subject to tax on onshore profits.

ADVANCE RULING CASE NO. 8

The taxpayer incorporated its business in Hong Kong on March 25, 2002, for the purpose of trade in processed fruits and food-related products outside Hong Kong. The company purchases processed fruits and food-related products from Asia, excluding Hong

Kong. The company resells processed fruits and food-related products to customers principally in Europe and other countries, excluding Hong Kong.

The company maintains offices in Taiwan and in Indonesia. Two directors of the company manage its daily operations. The two directors reside in Taiwan and in Indonesia, respectively.

The company has two marketing and procurement officers. The company presently locates these procurement officers in its Indonesia office and aims to recruit additional marketing and procurement officers. The company plans to expand its operations into Thailand. The company plans to locate these additional marketing and procurement officers in its soon-to-be-created Thailand office.

All of the negotiation processes for sales and purchase transactions take place in different countries. The company requires a centralized administrative function to administer and coordinate work performed by employees and directors in these various locations. The company selected Hong Kong as its "centralized administrative office" for the purpose of contributing to the smooth running of the administrative function.

The company plans to set up this office in Hong Kong. The staff of the Hong Kong office is to undertake these activities:

- Issue or accept invoices, but not orders, from a non–Hong Kong customer or supplier.
- The company would make that sale and purchase arrangement on the basis of contracts of sale or purchase that the non–Hong Kong associate already effectuated.
- Arrange for a letter of credit.
- Operate a bank account, and make and receive payments.
- Maintain accounting records.

The company undertook these activities:

- The company intends to enter into purchase contracts with an Indonesian supplier, S Ltd.
- The company intends to enter into sales contracts with a U.S. customer, C Ltd.
- The Taiwanese director located S Ltd. during a business trip to Indonesia.
- The Indonesia director located C Ltd. at a German food exhibition.
- The company followed up the communication between suppliers and the customer outside Hong Kong by e-mail.

The company will arrange for direct shipment from S Ltd. to C Ltd. upon the conclusion of both purchase and sale arrangements. The goods will not pass through Hong Kong. The company will not maintain a stock of merchandise in Hong Kong.

The Hong Kong office will perform these functions:

- Issue or accept invoices
- Arrange for letters of credit
- Operate a bank account

- Make and receive payments
- Maintain accounting records

Hong Kong's Inland Revenue Department determined in Advance Ruling Case No. 8 that it will not tax under section 14 the profits the company derives as to its trading transactions with supplier S Ltd. and with customer C Ltd. In contrast with Advance Ruling Case No. 4, the taxpayer in Advance Ruling Case No. 8 had no nexus to Hong Kong. The goods did not pass through Hong Kong and the activities took place elsewhere.

ADVANCE RULING CASE NO. 9

LC is a life insurance company that offers various life insurance products in the Hong Kong market. LC developed a new life insurance product, X, which is a unit-linked insurance product. X provides the policyholder primarily with life insurance coverage and provides the policyholder with the ability to invest in 12 mutual funds. X is a linked long-term life insurance business under Hong Kong rules.

LC invests policyholder premiums as to X in various investment funds that the policyholder nominates. LC, upon receiving the policyholder's premium, deducts 5% of the premium as its buy-sell charge. LC invests the balance of the premium it receives by buying units in various mutual funds in accordance with the policyholder's instructions.

LC deducts from the policyholder's notational holdings in the investment funds sufficient units to cover the life insurance charge at the beginning of each month. LC determines the life insurance charge by using the same parameters as apply to the company's traditional life products. LC at all times solely owns the investment funds and solely owns all assets in the investment funds, legally and beneficially.

LC permits the policyholder to switch investment funds, making that switch up to a maximum of six times per year without cost. LC imposes a switching charge of 1% for additional changes.

LC might apply an early surrender charge to the policyholder if the policyholder surrenders a policy before its life coverage began. The surrender charge is the life insurance premium that is applicable when the policyholder purchases the coverage. LC expresses the surrender charge as a percentage of the initial surrender charge. The surrender charge diminishes down to zero by the eighth coverage anniversary.

LC receives a premium from policyholders as to the issuance of the product. LC invests the total premium, less the buy-sell charge, in the mutual funds the policyholder nominates. LC derives income from product X by way of the monthly insurance charge and from other charges that LC imposes on the policyholder. LC retains the income from these sources to cover its operating costs and to invest for future liabilities.

The Inland Revenue Department, in Advance Ruling Case No. 9, sought not to impose tax on the insurance income. Instead, the department sought to preclude the deductibility for activities connected with the insurance activities:

- The Inland Revenue Department does not impose tax on LC under section 14 for the income that LC derives by buying, selling, and switching charges as to product X.
- The Inland Revenue Department does not impose tax on LC under section 14 for income derived by way of X's management charge.
- The Inland Revenue Department does not impose tax on LC under section 14 for its income derived from the surrender charge imposed in year 1 through year 8.
- The Inland Revenue Department does not permit a deduction under section 16 for LC's expenses for buying, selling, switching, management, and surrender charges.

ADVANCE RULING CASE NO. 10

The company was in the business of trading bedding products and in trading its related raw bedding materials. The company set up its operations in Hong Kong in 1989. The company maintains offices in Hong Kong and maintains showrooms in Hong Kong. The company's affiliate (Affiliate) in the mainland manufacturers the bedding products.

The company's affiliate is a wholly foreign enterprise, incorporated in the mainland in 1993. China licensed the affiliate to import raw materials and to manufacture bedding products for export and local sale. Affiliate operates an import processing trade owning its factory premises, plant, and machineries. The profits of Affiliate are subject to tax in the mainland.

Here is how the bedding manufacturing process works:

- The company purchases raw materials in Hong Kong.
- The company sells these materials at cost to Affiliate.
- Affiliate processes the raw materials to produce products the company specifies.
- The company sends some supervisors to monitor the manufacturing process in the mainland to ensure production quality.
- Affiliate sells the finished goods at a profit to the company.
- The company sells the finished goods to customers in Hong Kong.
- The company and Affiliate issue invoices to effect the transactions.
- The company and Affiliate make declarations in the import/export forms they present to their customs bureaus.
- The company's trading profits are fully subject to Hong Kong profits.

The company plans to retain its operations in Hong Kong as to its sourcing, purchase of raw material, and the sale of finished products. The company intends to manufacture its products in the mainland. The company intends to execute a processing and assembly agreement with Affiliate, which agreement would be a cost-plus arrangement. The agreement contains three major terms:

1. Affiliate will provide facilities and services to the company to assist and facilitate the company's manufacturing operations in the mainland.
2. The facilities of the plant in the mainland include the use of factory premises, plant, and machines, local labor, and factory utilities.
3. The company will pay and reimburse Affiliate for all the manufacturing costs plus a general service fee.

Affiliate will not furnish the agreement for registration in the mainland. The company and Affiliate will cease to treat both the delivery of raw materials to Affiliate and the furnishing of finished goods to the company as being trading transactions. Instead of reflecting these activities as being separate trading transactions, the company and Affiliate will record these activities as one activity, reflecting the combined results as an internal basis.

After applying the combined results, the parties will no longer prepare invoices to each other. The company and Affiliate will continue to make customs declarations, making those declarations in import/export forms. Both the mainland and Hong Kong customs bureaus will recognize the existence of the import of raw materials and the export of finished goods.

Affiliate continues to operate its bedding products trade in the form of an import processing activity. Affiliate will continue to undertake its processing work for other mainland customers.

Hong Kong's Inland Revenue Department held in Advance Ruling Case No. 10 that the company-affiliate agreement does not cause to license the company to manufacture or to carry out business in the mainland. The Inland Revenue Department held that Affiliate is the manufacturer and that the company is not the manufacturer.

Hong Kong's Inland Revenue Department held that the company derives its profits from trading in Hong Kong. The company is fully subject to section 14 of the Hong Kong profits tax. The Inland Revenue Department rejected the application of the allocation process and held that the trading profits are not subject to allocation.

In Advance Ruling Case No. 10, the company had offices in Hong Kong, had operations in Hong Kong, and had showrooms in Hong Kong. Nexus was not an issue as the company had passed that threshold.

ADVANCE RULING CASE NO. 11

Advance Ruling Case No. 11 appears to describe a reinvoicing structure, a three-party arrangement utilizing a quasi–tax haven (Hong Kong) and two high-taxed countries, South Africa and the United States. X Ltd. was in the business of trading ink products and incorporated the business in Hong Kong on August 24, 2001. S Ltd., a fellow subsidiary, manufactured the goods in South Africa. X Ltd. makes 80% of its sales to related companies, one of which is A Ltd., a fellow subsidiary in the United States.

X Ltd. entered into a master purchase agreement with S Ltd. and enters into master sales agreements with related customers, such as with A. Ltd. The parties make these agreements outside Hong Kong. The enterprise has a holding company that is located in Israel, H Ltd. H Ltd. coordinates the trading transactions and product production. X Ltd. makes all transfer pricing determinations among its subsidiaries, such as X Ltd., and with A Ltd. and S Ltd. X Ltd. prepares X's production plan.

H Ltd. prepares a delivery notice to an individual trading the transaction in Israel for issuance to S Ltd. The individual copies the delivery notice to X Ltd. and to A Ltd. X receives the delivery notice in Hong Kong and prepares a delivery notice to S Ltd. S Ltd. prepares the invoices in South Africa, sends the invoices to Hong Kong, and X receives the invoices to Hong Kong. X Ltd. then prepares the invoices in Hong Kong and sends the invoices to A Ltd. in the United States as to S Ltd.

The parties settle their accounts by remittance to and from X's bank account, which X Ltd. maintains in Hong Kong, taking into account the remittance instructions from Israel. The Inland Revenue Department concluded that the X Ltd. profits arising in or derived from Hong Kong are taxable as to section 14 of the Hong Kong Inland Revenue Ordinance. It appears that the company's activities in Hong Kong necessitated taxability.

ADVANCE RULING CASE NO. 12

A private limited company traded computer commodities, motherboards, chips, and the like. The company incorporated the business in Hong Kong in 2000. The company does have a registered address in Hong Kong, which is the address of the company secretary. The company secretary is an independent service provider that is responsible for annual return filing to the Hong Kong Company Registry. All of the directors of the Hong Kong company are Taiwanese residents. The parent company is T Ltd., a company the Taiwan Stock Exchange lists for trading.

The Hong Kong company does not maintain any office in Hong Kong, nor does it employ any staff in Hong Kong. The Hong Kong company filed a zero tax return for its initial taxable year. The company claimed that it had no trading during the period that began from incorporation and carried forward until December 31, 2000.

The group set up a manufacturing plant in Shenzhen under the name M Ltd. The group sent up this operation in Shenzhen to expand its manufacturing operations and to benefit from the low production overhead on the mainland. The directors of T Ltd. and the directors of M Ltd. are Taiwanese residents. The group does not require the directors to carry out any duties in Hong Kong or to make any decisions for the Hong Kong company in Hong Kong.

The Hong Kong company commenced its business with T Ltd. and with M. Ltd. during the 2001 taxable year. The Hong Kong company has suppliers and customers that are part of the overseas group only. The Hong Kong company holds bank accounts in both Hong Kong banks and Taiwan banks. The T Ltd. staff is responsible for handling the bank transactions on behalf of the Hong Kong company. The staff is authorized to take this banking responsibility. The Hong Kong company does not have its own staff in Hong Kong. T Ltd.'s staff in Taiwan handles the purchases and sales transactions with T Ltd. and M. Ltd.

The owners of the business set up the Hong Kong company as an intermediary to facilitate trading between Taiwan and the mainland. The intermediary arrangement operated in this manner: T Ltd. would source raw materials from suppliers in Taiwan and overseas. M Ltd. would process the raw materials on the mainland.

M Ltd. must import the material it needs in the name of the Hong Kong company. The processing and importation process operates in this manner: M issues purchase orders to the Hong Kong Company. The ultimate purchaser is T Ltd. regarding the purchasing and importation of raw materials.

The Hong Kong company charges a specified markup for the sale of raw materials. The T Ltd. staff in Taiwan, acting on behalf of the Hong Kong company, would confirm and sign the purchase orders the staff received. The T Ltd. staff would prepare the sales invoice and prepare the packing list to M Ltd.

M Ltd. processes and assembles the raw material into finished goods. M Ltd. exports and sells the finished goods that M Ltd. manufactures to the Hong Kong company instead of to T Ltd. directly. T Ltd. then issues purchase orders to the Hong Kong company simultaneously regarding the purchase of the same products. The parties would charge no markup for the sale of finished goods from the Hong Kong company to T Ltd. T Ltd. sells the goods to ultimate customers, including both independent customers in Taiwan and elsewhere.

The Hong Kong company keeps no stock of raw materials or finished materials in Hong Kong. The Hong Kong company delivers the raw material from T Ltd., or from other suppliers, and imports the raw material to Shenzhen directly. The Hong Kong company might ship the finished goods directly from the manufacturing plant in Shenzhen. Alternatively the Hong Kong company might pass through the finished items through Hong Kong for shipment to T Ltd. or to the Hong Kong company's ultimate customers.

The Hong Kong company, besides making sales to T Ltd., makes minor sales to other overseas group companies in Mexico and Japan. The Hong Kong company imposes no markup as to the purchase of raw materials or from the sale of finished goods to the Mexican company. The Hong Kong company charges a prescribed markup for the sale of parts to the Japanese company.

The Hong Kong company books profits it derived from trading transactions that the group companies entered into. The Inland Revenue Department concluded that the purpose of the Hong Kong company is to facilitate trading between Taiwan and the mainland. Profits that the Hong Kong company books are not subject to section 14 of the Hong Kong profits tax. The Inland Revenue Department reached its ruling on the assumption that the operations of the Hong Kong company would remain the same and that the role of the Hong Kong company would follow the contemplated operational transactions.

The Inland Revenue Department failed to conclude that the company had nexus in Hong Kong. It appears that the department was swayed by the company's compliance with the legal and financial formalities that the company had met.

ADVANCE RULING CASE NO. 13

A group of companies having a head office in the United States conducts its operations globally. The group manufactures its products throughout the world and sells its products in over 150 countries. The group comprises four types of entities in various jurisdictions throughout the world: manufacturing entities, distribution entities, marketing entities, and logistical support entities.

None of the manufacturing entities has operations in Hong Kong. The distribution companies are established outside Hong Kong. These distribution companies have no employees in Hong Kong. The manufacturing companies receive orders from the distribution companies and sell the products to the distribution companies. The distribution companies in turn sell its products to the marketing companies.

One marketing company was incorporated in Hong Kong. The Hong Kong marketing company is responsible for the marketing and sale of the group's products in Hong Kong and in the PRC. The group's head office determines the products the company manufactures. The group sets the intergroup selling prices.

The group established Company L in Hong Kong. Company L provides support services to the distribution companies. The logistic companies, including Company L, provide logistical and administrative support to the distribution companies for the purposes of handling procurement and providing supply services.

The group maintains a Web-based international supply system (ISS):

- The group's head office manages the ISS.
- The marketing companies place orders with the distribution companies through this ISS.
- Company L downloads the purchase orders from the ISS as to the Asian marketing purchase orders.
- Company L verifies the details of the purchase orders.
- Company L then consolidates the order into a summary of purchases.
- The distribution companies issue the orders to the manufacturing companies.

Company L then forwards the summary of purchases by e-mail to the respective distribution companies for approval. If applicable, the distribution companies confirm the purchases approval to Company L by e-mail. The group's head office worldwide pricing guidelines determine the acceptance or rejection of the purchase order.

Company L structures the purchase order process:

- Once the head office approves the purchase order, Company L prepares an order form under the name of the distribution company as to purchasing for the manufacturing companies.
- The manufacturing companies confirm the purchase order with Company L via e-mail as to the quantity of goods available for export to the Asian marketing companies.

- Company L then forwards the confirmation of the products available for export to the Asian marketing companies by e-mail to the manufacturing companies.
- Company L then requests the Asian marketing companies to confirm its purchase agreement.

Company L applies this accounts receivable structure:

- Company L prepares pro forma invoices to the Asian marketing companies based on the purchase orders the distribution companies approved and the manufacturing companies confirmed.
- Company L prepares these pro forma invoices under the letterhead of the relevant distribution companies.
- The Asian marketing companies issue purchase orders to the distribution companies upon receipt of the pro forma invoices.
- Company L issues the purchase orders contained in the pro formas.

Company L consolidates the detail transactions of the Asian marketing companies' orders, then forwards these details to the distribution companies via e-mail for approval.

The manufacturing companies ship most of the finished products from them directly to the Asian marketing companies in the region without warehousing the finished products in Hong Kong. The manufacturing companies forward the shipping documents or fax the shipping documents to Company L once they ship the products. Company L issues invoices to the Asian marketing companies under the letterheads of the distribution companies.

On some occasions, the group ships the products to Hong Kong for warehousing. In such circumstances, Company L notifies the Asian marketing companies of the products to be warehoused in Hong Kong. Company L arranges for the shipment of these products. Company L also provides services, including transportation, coordination of customs arrangement and clearance, and visual checking to verify the quantity and package of the products the group imports into Hong Kong. Company L liaises with the suppliers to arrange for the delivery of products to the Hong Kong marketing company for sales to Hong Kong and to the PRC.

Company L maintains all accounting records in connection with the distribution companies' trading activities in the Asia region. This record keeping includes maintaining details of all sales Company L made to the Asian marketing companies and maintaining details of all purchase and sale of raw materials to the manufacturing companies. Company L summarizes and reports the distribution company's accounting transactions to the group treasury center, which is outside Hong Kong.

The distribution companies maintain bank accounts located outside Hong Kong. The group treasury center monitors these bank accounts and fund flows, undertaking these financial activities with Company L. Company L provides the details of the trade receivables and payables to the group treasury center on a monthly basis.

In addition to performing the following activities, Company L undertakes the following activities:

- Company L provides information technology services, including a technology platform and software to enable order processing, stock management, and location processing.
- Company L provides miscellaneous reporting and general communication to customers and management of the distribution companies.

Company L charges a service fee to the distribution companies. The charge is cost plus 5% markup. The Inland Revenue Department, in issuing Advance Ruling Case No. 13, held that the distribution companies carried on its business in Hong Kong through Company L and that the profits that the distribution companies derive from their trading operations with group companies in the Asia region arose in or derived from Hong Kong. The Inland Revenue Department viewed these profits as taxable under section 14 of the Hong Kong profits tax.

The Inland Revenue Department failed to delineate its decision to impose taxation on Country L in contrast with other fact patterns. It is our view that the department reached its taxability decision largely in response to the presence of a Hong Kong marketing company, the presence of a warehouse entity in Hong Kong, and the fact that Company L notifies the Asian marketing companies of the products to be warehoused in Hong Kong.

ADVANCE RULING CASE NO. 16

B is an overseas incorporated bank. B incorporated Company A, its wholly owned subsidiary, in Country X, structured as a limited liability company. Company A has a central management and control in Country X, and does not have any business establishment in Hong Kong. Company A has a branch in London (A-London) that carries on business in London.

The bank provides these services:

- Company A has three business lines: equity derivatives, cash equity sales and trading, and corporate advisory.
- Company B maintains a branch office in Hong Kong (B-HK). Company B principally engages in corporate banking, corporate finance, and mergers and acquisitions.

Company A's equity derivative business consists of these activities: structuring, risk management, and the trading of equity-linked and fund-linked products. Equity-linked and fund-linked products include both listed and over-the-counter financial arrangements. Company A acts as the issuer of these financial products, selling the products to retail banking customers, private banks with European and Asian institutional client bases, financial institutions, and pension funds.

A-London engages B-HK to provide liaison and support services to clients in Asia as to Company A's equity derivative business. Under this liaison and support arrangement, B-HK designates one liaison staff to perform the services. The liaison and support services include five activities:

1. Marketing proposed products to clients
2. Explaining products to clients
3. Dealing with general inquiries and complaints
4. Returning the same inquiries and complaints to A-London
5. Communicating after-sales services requests to A-London

The liaison staff also is involved in providing feedback from clients to Company A. Company A designs the feedback so as to modify the products. Additionally, Company A contacts the private banks and financial institutions to market the products.

The role of the liaison staff is to act as a link between clients and Company A in London. The liaison staff can pass on the client's specific requirements to London for incorporation of these requirements into the structure of the product. The liaison staff in Hong Kong locates and then contacts the clients and communicates negotiations between A-London and the clients.

B-HK is not an agent of A-London and will not hold itself out as agent of A-London. The engagement between B-HK and A-London applies only to the referral of potential investors to A-London. B-HK will not have any power or any authority to conduct transactions on behalf of A-London. B-HK will receive from Company A a fee calculated at a 5% markup on the actual direct and indirect cost B-HK incurs in return for the services B-HK performs.

The Inland Revenue Department concluded in Advance Ruling Case No. 16 that Company A carries on business in Hong Kong through B-HK and that profits arising in Hong Kong or the profits deriving from Hong Kong are subject to tax under section 14. This ruling request addressed only the question of whether Company A carries out business in Hong Kong. The applicant for the ruling did not request or present sufficient information as to whether the Inland Revenue Department has profits arising or deriving from Hong Kong. The department determined that an agency relationship exists notwithstanding the express disclaimer and that an agency relationship can be implied based on the facts at hand.

ADVANCE RULING CASE NO. 19

A company entered into a contract processing agreement with a Chinese party to operate a factory in China, thus creating establishing a China factory. Pursuant to the contract processing agreement, the China party provides labor, factory premises, and water and electric facilities to process the goods for operating the China factory. The Chinese party provides these proceeding inputs in return for receiving processing fees. The company provides raw materials, plant, machines, and the training of workers. The China factory is not initially operational.

After the China factory comes into operation, the company activities in Hong Kong will:

- Complete the sales function
- Purchase raw materials the company would deliver to the factory
- Employ product design

The China factory will be responsible for the processing of the goods. A number of the company's employees will visit the China factory to train the labor and to supervise the production. Some employees work five or six days in the China factory every week.

The Inland Revenue Department determined in Advance Ruling Case No. 19 that the company can apportion its profits arising from the sale of goods processed by the China factory under the contract processing agreement. The profits can be apportioned on a 50/50 basis for Hong Kong profits basis under section 14.

ADVANCE RULING CASE NO. 21

The company is a member of an international group. The group incorporated the company in Country X and registered a branch in Hong Kong (the Branch). In country X, the company imports goods from affiliated companies in Hong Kong and from Country Z. The group set up the Branch to fulfill the requirements that the company's customers impose in Country X. The goal is for the company's customers to manage by themselves the import-related logistics in a more efficient manner.

The company does not maintain any office in Hong Kong other than having a registered address. The company does not have any employees or agents in Hong Kong. The company's staff in Country X carries out the sales transactions. The company's staff in Country X carries out the purchasing transactions with affiliated companies. The computer ordering system bolsters the company's staff in Country X.

The company, by using the Branch, benefits from shorter payment terms from customers under the company–Branch arrangement. But for that arrangement, the parties would rely on local payment terms, which usually would be two to three times longer.

The group purchases goods internally. The product division sets up prices using the resale price method (the market minus method) under the Organisation of Economic Cooperation and Development guidelines.

The company introduces the product in Country X through presenting a product sample and demonstrating the product to potential customers. The company's key account managers and salespeople in Country X will negotiate with customers the price and quantity per product type after they introduce the product. The company confirms the price by fax or e-mail. The company's key account managers in Country X prepare and sign sales contracts on behalf of the Branch.

The company's field application staff will assist customers in the product evaluation until customers agree to the final version and send their purchase orders to the company in Country X. The company applies this field application process only for large volume customers. The company's salespeople then pass on the order information to the company's customer service staff for inputting into the computer ordering system. The computer ordering system automatically generates the purchase order and sends the purchase order to the supplier.

The suppliers then accept the orders. The suppliers then confirm the delivery schedule and input that information to the ordering system. The company's customer service staff then sends the confirmed delivery schedule list to Country X customers by e-mail. The suppliers in Country Z and in Hong Kong will change the order status sign in the computer ordering system to confirm delivery when they complete their orders. The company normally delivers the products by air to the customers in Country X or to their designated factories outside Hong Kong. The Branch usually will not keep a stock of inventory except for storing of certain goods in Country X for some important customers.

The company's financial control team in Country X decides on the credit terms for each customer. The company makes some sales under letter of credit terms. The company's Shared Service Centre (SCT) in Country Z on behalf of the Branch will negotiate the letter of credit with the banks in Hong Kong. The SCT charges a service fee to the Branch for that financial service.

The financial controller of the company in Country X and SCT's accounting manager can operate the Branch's bank account in Hong Kong for receiving customers' money and for making payments. In addition, the financial controller of the company in Country X and SCT's accounting manager have financial control duties and report and handle transaction posting and intercompany and bank reconciliation. The Hong Kong branch books the profits it derives from the sales and purchase transactions it invoiced in its name. SCT enters and keeps the financial accounts and records of the Branch on its behalf.

The Inland Revenue Department under Advance Ruling Case No. 21 held that the profits booked in the accounts of the company's Hong Kong branch are not "arising in nor derived from Hong Kong." As a result, these profits are not subject to tax under section 14(1) of the Hong Kong profits tax.

ADVANCE RULING CASE NO. 23

An international group contains Company B and Company A. The group incorporated Company A in Hong Kong. B is a foreign-based multinational. Company A is a wholly owned subsidiary of Company B. Company B is engaged in the retailing of fashion wares, cosmetics, and accessories principally in European countries and in the United States through its own outlets. Company B appointed Company A as its buying agent to procure overseas suppliers and to source garments in the mainland and in other Asian countries. The garments that Company A procures include knitwear, underwear, woven products, and accessories.

Company A establishes numerous representative offices in various overseas countries to perform its procurement services for Company B. Company A needs to establish these numerous representative offices because of the geographical locations of the overseas suppliers. Company A's representative offices do not have the authority to negotiate, conclude, or execute Company B's sales and purchases. Company B negotiates and concludes the terms of the sales and purchases with its suppliers directly outside Hong Kong. Company B will, once it concludes the contracts, instruct the representative offices to follow up the orders with the suppliers.

Company A receives commission income from Company B for procurement services it rendered outside Hong Kong. Company's commission income is 3% of the freight-on-board value of Company B's purchases. Company A does not employ any staff in Hong Kong. Company A engaged Company C, an affiliated subsidiary in Hong Kong, as its service agent to perform its necessary administrative functions. Company A pays Company C a service fee for the services rendered on the basis of cost plus 5%.

Company A currently maintains a number of representative offices outside Hong Kong. Company A has three representative offices in Shanghai, Beijing, and Guangzhou to perform procurement activities in the mainland. Company A is considering setting up Company D on the mainland to take over the functions that the three representative offices perform.

Company A would completely shut down the Shanghai, Beijing, and Guangzhou representative offices subsequent to the commencement of Company D's operations. Company A would transfer the staff of the three representative offices now stationed on the mainland. The staff would work for Company D going forward.

Company A will enter into a services agreement with Company D outside Hong Kong to engage Company D to perform the procurement services in the mainland for Company B. Under the services agreement, Company A will pay a service fee to Company D for these services that Company D rendered. The fee under the services agreement is based on cost plus 10%.

Company A will continue to receive commission income from Company B on the same basis as before the Company D services agreement. Company A will continue to appoint Company C as its service agent to perform the necessary administrative functions, and will pay its service fee on the same basis as before.

The Inland Revenue Department in Advance Ruling Case No. 23 held that Company A will not be subject to the profits tax on the commission income that Company A derives from the procurement services that Company D renders outside Hong Kong in respect of its participation in the arrangement.

ADVANCE RULING CASE NO. 26

The company is a member of the X Group, whose principal business is the production and trading of chemical products. The Group has production sites in various countries. The company performs its worldwide sales functions in Country B.

The Group incorporated the Company in Hong Kong during 2005–2006. The directors of the company are non–Hong Kong residents. The company is a wholly owned subsidiary of H Ltd., which carries on business in Country A.

The Group has started sourcing chemical S from Country C. The Company's director has a well-established network in sourcing chemical S in Country C. The Group designated the company as X Group's sourcing and sales representative of chemical S.

The company and H Ltd. have entered an agreement under which H Ltd. will handle the purchase and sale of chemical S to its territories, excluding Hong Kong. H Ltd. pays a commission to the company for enabling H Ltd. to derive trading profits in utilizing the director's well-established network in Country C. The company does not maintain any office in Hong Kong, employ any staff in Hong Kong, apply any agent in Hong Kong, or operate any bank account in Hong Kong.

The Inland Revenue Department, in Advance Ruling Case No. 26, held that the company does not carry on business in Hong Kong. The department held that the commissions that the company received pursuant to the commission agreement are not chargeable to the Hong Kong profits tax under section 14. The Commissioner has assumed that the parties would implement the subject arrangement in the way stated in the ruling application and ruling. Section 14 provides that every person who carries on a trade, business, or profession in Hong Kong is subject to the profits tax on profits arising in or derived from Hong Kong. Unofficially, the Inland Revenue Department held that in the present case, the company has no business carried out in Hong Kong to earn the commission in question, making section 14 inapplicable.

ADVANCE RULING CASE NO. 30

The company is an affiliate of Y Group, whose principal business is the production and sale of motors. The company provides administrative services to Y Group in Hong Kong. During 2005–2006, Mr. X became the company's majority shareholder and a director of the company. He has been residing in the PRC. Mr. X has extensive working experience and knowledge concerning a specific type of ship. He has developed a shipping industry business network in the Far East, excluding Hong Kong.

The company and a U.K. firm, R Company, will enter into a services agreement. The services agreement provides that the company will provide marketing research services to R Company. In addition, the services agreement provides that the company will introduce Far East suppliers and customers as to a specific type of ship to R Company in return for receiving service fees.

The company has set up an office in the PRC. Mr. X and the company's staff in Hong Kong will perform all of the services set out in the agreement outside Hong Kong. The staff of the company's Hong Kong office and the Hong Kong director will render none of the services arising from or in connection with the agreement. The staff of the company's Hong Kong office and the Hong Kong director will continue to provide administrative services to Y Group in return for management fees. The management fees are subject to the Hong Kong profits tax.

The Inland Revenue Department, in Advance Ruling Case No. 30, held that the profits that the company derives in the performance of services set out in the agreement will not be chargeable under section 14 under the Hong Kong profits tax.

The ruling presupposes that the Far East, and the Far East Region, does not include Hong Kong. In addition, the ruling presupposes that the company will not subcontract services the company provides under the agreement to Y Group, to the company's affiliates, or to any other third parties.

As a commentary, the Inland Revenue Department provides that under section 14, every person who carries on a trade, business, or profession in Hong Kong is chargeable to profits tax on the profits arising in Hong Kong or derived in Hong Kong. The source of profits in the case of service fee income is the place where the provider performs the services. Unofficially, the Inland Revenue Department provided that, in the present case, the company's profits emanating from the agreement are not chargeable to profits tax because the company performs all relevant services outside Hong Kong.

ADVANCE RULING CASE NO. 34

The company is principally engaged in the distribution of products ("the Products") for a group of companies ("the Group") in Hong Kong and the rest of Asia. The Group incorporated the company in Hong Kong. Factories outside Hong Kong manufacture the Products. The company is contemplating setting up a branch in Country X in Southeast Asia ("the Branch") as part of the Group's business plan to further expand into markets in Asia and in particular Southeast Asia.

The Branch will initially employ 26 personnel: 22 persons in the sales department, 3 persons in the marketing department, and 1 person in the accounting department. The Branch will purchase the Products directly from Group factories at arm's length prices. The Branch will sell the Products to distributors/customers in countries in Southeast Asia based on mutually agreed prices. The Branch's personnel will negotiate purchase and sales contracts, conclude these contracts, and execute these contracts. The Branch's personnel will conduct these activities outside Hong Kong. The Branch in Country X will receive and approve all purchase and sale orders.

The company in Hong Kong will not be involved in the negotiation or the conclusion of the purchase or sale of the Products. In addition, the company in Hong Kong will not be involved in receiving or approving the purchase orders from distributors and customers.

The management of the Group is setting up a bonded warehouse in Country X to provide storage facilities for the Products. Management might first consolidate the Products in the warehouse or ship the Products directly to other countries in Southeast Asia depending on logistics and transportation needs of the distributors and customers in Southeast Asia from time to time.

The Branch will have bank accounts in Country X. The Branch's personnel will handle all payments to factories and receipts from customers through the Country X bank accounts. The Branch's personnel will handle all trade finance arrangements, such as letters of credit, guarantees, and so forth, through the Country X bank accounts.

The company in Hong Kong, to achieve economic efficiency, will provide information technology, finance, accounting, research, and other administrative support to the Branch. The company in Hong Kong will allocate the above-mentioned costs and expenses in providing these services to the Branch for statutory reporting in Country X.

The Inland Revenue Department, in Advance Ruling Case No. 34, held that the profits to be derived from the Branch are offshore sourced. Pursuant to section 14, the Hong Kong Inland Revenue Department will not tax those offshore profits. Under section 14 of the Inland Revenue Ordinance, every person who carries on a trade, business, or profession in Hong Kong is chargeable to profits tax on profits arising in Hong Kong or derived from Hong Kong.

The Inland Revenue Department considers, on an unofficial basis, the Branch in Hong Kong in this case to be a permanent establishment in Country X, where the personnel of the Branch will initiate, negotiate, conclude, and execute the purchase and sales contracts. The Inland Revenue Department views the functions that the company in Hong Kong performs as being ancillary in nature. Accordingly, section 14 does not apply to the Branch's profits.

ADVANCE RULING CASE NO. 35

The company is engaged in the manufacture and sale of printing machinery and manufacture and sale of spare parts for such machinery. The company was incorporated in Country A, and the company manufactures spare parts in Country A. The company, apart from its own manufacture, purchases spare parts from ex–Hong Kong suppliers. The company sells its spare parts to global subsidiaries, which act as distributors in their local markets.

The company employs an independent warehouse manager ("Warehouse Manager") to facilitate the distribution of these products to subsidiaries in the Asia Pacific Region. The company will locate its spare parts in Hong Kong on the premises of the Warehouse Manager.

The Warehouse Manager will undertake to perform these limited functions:

- The Warehouse Manager will neither display information nor provide information regarding the inventory.
- The Warehouse Manager will not communicate with the company's customers.
- The Warehouse Manager will not be involved in any negotiation or conclusion of purchase or sale orders on behalf of the company.
- The Warehouse Manager will merely store the products safely and pack the products for shipment upon instructions from Country A company.

The Company will undertake these functions:

- The company will, in Country A, negotiate directly with third-party carriers for the delivery of spare parts from the Hong Kong stockpile to the customers.

- The company will not maintain any office in Hong Kong in regard to the purchase and sale of spare parts.
- The company will not employ any staff in Hong Kong in regard to the purchase and sale of spare parts.
- The company will not appoint any agent in Hong Kong in regard to the purchase and sale of spare parts.

The company in Country A will negotiate and conclude all spare parts purchases and sales contracts. The company in Country A will handle all paperwork and banking activities relating to purchases and sales.

The Inland Revenue Department, in making its determination for Advance Ruling Case No. 35, held that the company, pursuant to section 14 of the Inland Revenue Ordinance, will not be subject to the profits tax. Under section 14, every person who carries on a trade, business, or profession in Hong Kong is subject to tax on the profits arising in Hong Kong or derived from Hong Kong. The department reached its no-tax conclusion as to the company's profits from the trading of such spare parts located in Hong Kong.

The Inland Revenue Department ruled unofficially that, in this case, the company did not effect any purchases or sales of spare parts in Hong Kong. Section 14 does not apply. The creation of a Hong Kong stockpile at the premises of a third-party Warehouse Manager will not alter the offshore nature of the profits the company derives from the trading of spare parts.

ADVANCE RULING CASE NO. 36

X Group is in the principal business of fish trading. X Group has business operations in various countries, and it bases its management team in Europe. Y Ltd. is a member of X Group. Y Ltd. has been carrying on business in Europe by managing the product requirements of companies within X Group. X Group began sourcing fish in Asian countries and formed the company in order to manage and expand X Group's supplier base in Asia.

An agreement exists between the company and Y Ltd. ("the Agreement"). Pursuant to the Agreement, the company will receive remuneration from Y Ltd. for providing to Y Ltd. sourcing, procurement services, and other services as the agreement spells out. The company will employ local staff in Asian countries where the suppliers are located. The company will use that local staff to perform its services under the agreement. The company will not maintain any office, employ any staff, appoint any agent, or operate any bank account in Hong Kong as long as it has no supplier in Hong Kong.

The Inland Revenue Department, in response to Advance Ruling Case No. 36, held that the Hong Kong government will not tax profits to be derived by the company in providing services under the Agreement under section 14 of the Inland Revenue Ordinance. The ruling presupposes that the company will render no services in Hong Kong and that there is no supplier in Hong Kong.

As to services income, the Inland Revenue Department unofficially held that the source of profits is the place where the company performs the service that gives rise to service fee income. In this case, the government will not impose taxes on profits to be derived by the company from the agreement because the company's relevant services take place outside Hong Kong.

ADVANCE RULING CASE NO. 37

The company is a member of an international group. The group incorporated the company in Country X. The company registered a branch in Hong Kong ("the Branch"). The company imported goods from affiliated companies and sold these goods to customers in Country X. The company set up the Branch to fulfill the customers' requirements in Country X so that the company's customers can manage the import-related logistics by themselves in a more efficient manner.

The company does not maintain any office in Hong Kong other than having a registered address. The company does not employ any employees in Hong Kong nor does it have agents in Hong Kong. Company staff in Country X carry out the sales and purchase transactions. The computer ordering system assists the company's staff. The company benefits by having the Branch to make use of shorter customer payment terms under the arrangement compared with local payment terms, which are usually two to three times longer.

The procurement process works in this manner: The Country X prospective customers issue notice of procurement schedules for which the vendors are to bid. The company prepares for the bidding. The company's key account managers will discuss the price and the product configuration with its Country X customers.

After the bidding process occurs, the company prepares and signs the sales and purchase contracts in the name of the Branch. The company's general manager signs the purchase and sales contracts on behalf of the Branch and the Country X customers.

The sales and purchase contracts provide that the staff of the order desk of the company in Country X will input its customer orders into the ordering system. After that inputting process takes place, the ordering system will automatically generate the purchase orders in the name of the Branch. The ordering system will send these purchase orders to affiliated suppliers. The company sets purchase prices by using the resale price method (or market minus method). The company will not make any purchases from suppliers in Hong Kong.

The suppliers deliver the goods directly to the customers in Country X. The suppliers make the customers' deliveries without transshipping the goods through Hong Kong. The company in Country X monitors the detailed delivery status. The company sends all shipping documents and suppliers' invoices to the company in Country X to input these documents into the ordering system. The company issues customer invoices in the name of the Branch in Country X.

After the company delivers the goods to the customers, the company installs the equipment. The company provides after-sales service for its Country X customers.

The company in Country X decides on credit limits extended to customers. The company makes some of these sales on letter-of-credit terms. The company's finance staff in Country X negotiate the letters of credit with the Branch's bank. The company in Country X monitors and follows up outstanding customer debts.

The company's financial controller located in Country X undertakes the approval payment process. The company's financial controller located in Country X and a shared service center in Country Y make payments to suppliers. The company's financial controller operates the Branch's bank account opened for the trading of goods.

The Branch books the profits it derives from the sales and purchase transactions the Branch invoiced in its name. The service center handles bookkeeping and accounting for the Branch transactions. The company's financial controller in Country X approves these determinations.

The Inland Revenue Department, in examining Advance Ruling Case No. 37, held that the trading profits booked in the accounts of the company's Hong Kong branch do not arise from Hong Kong; nor are these trading profits derived from Hong Kong. As such, these trading profits are not taxable pursuant to section 14(1) of the Inland Revenue Ordinance.

The Inland Revenue Department made material assumptions in making its determination:

- The suppliers and suppliers of the Branch are and will be located outside Hong Kong.
- Associates and companies in Hong Kong within the group will not carry on any business or trading activities on behalf of the Branch or on account of the Branch. This activity includes the preparation of trade documents.
- The existence of the Branch under the arrangement does not form a transaction or scheme or a part thereof contrived to avoid or evade any fiscal liabilities. These anti-avoidance provisions apply to Hong Kong and to other jurisdictions.
- The Branch that books its profits will report the result to the tax administration in Country X. These profits will be subject to tax in Country X under the company's name.

Section 14 of the Inland Revenue Ordinance provides that every person who carries on a trade, business, or profession in Hong Kong is subject to the profits tax on profits arising in Hong Kong or derived from Hong Kong. The department commented unofficially that in this case, the company would not effect any contracts for purchase or sale of the goods in Hong Kong. The Inland Revenue Department held that the company's trading profits are offshore sourced and are not taxed, making section 14 inapplicable.

CHAPTER EIGHT

Hong Kong Transfer Pricing Guidelines

THE INLAND Revenue of Hong Kong issued Transfer Pricing Guidelines—Methodologies and Related Issues on December 2009, as a departmental interpretation and Practice Note No. 46. The Hong Kong Special Administrative Region (SAR) issued the transfer pricing guidelines for the benefit of taxpayers and their tax representatives, thus suggesting that Inland Revenue had preserved other non-public advice for the tax collector itself. Nevertheless, the transfer pricing guidelines were exceedingly clear as to abusive tax schemes and the remedies to these schemes the Inland Revenue would pursue. These guidelines contain the Inland Revenue Department's interpretations and practices in relation to Hong Kong's transfer pricing law as of December 2009.

The Hong Kong December 2009 transfer pricing guidelines follow closely the Organisation for Economic Co-operation and Development (OECD) *Transfer Pricing Guidelines for Multinational Enterprises and Tax Administrations*, as revised earlier in 2009. The audit practices followed by the Inland Revenue Department, as a general matter, do not differ from the transfer pricing methodologies recommended in the OECD guidelines. Nevertheless, there are significant issues of departure from the OECD *Transfer Pricing Guidelines* within the Hong Kong transfer pricing guidelines.

There are five differences between the OECD *Transfer Pricing Guidelines* and the Hong Kong transfer pricing guidelines. The Hong Kong transfer pricing guidelines:

1. Expand the documentation provisions
2. Expand the services provisions
3. Narrow the permanent establishment provisions, compared to the permanent establishment approach in other countries such as India
4. Greatly expand the anti–tax evasion process
5. Greatly expand the profit split method

The Hong Kong transfer pricing guidelines do not interfere with the taxpayer's appellate rights. Taxpayers can make their objections against the Inland Revenue Department's assessments. These taxpayers retain the right of appeal to the Commissioner, to the Board of Review, or to the court. The Inland Revenue Department's Interpretation and Practice Note No. 45 addresses double tax relief pertaining to transfer pricing adjustments.

DOUBLE TAX AGREEMENTS

As background, the Hong Kong Inland Revenue Ordinance determines the transfer pricing provisions in the Hong Kong SAR. In addition to the ordinance, Hong Kong has 25 double tax agreements (DTAs), all of which address transfer pricing issues. The first five DTAs are:

1. Belgium
2. Thailand
3. Mainland China
4. Luxembourg
5. Vietnam

ARM'S LENGTH PRINCIPLE

As a general matter, the Hong Kong transfer pricing guidelines rely on the arm's length principle as a benchmark for transactions for independent enterprises to determine how the enterprise should allocate profits and expenses between associated enterprises. This arm's length principle compares what an enterprise has transacted with its associated enterprise with what a truly independent enterprise would have done in the same or similar circumstances.

The Hong Kong transfer pricing guidelines recognize that the enterprise will distort the tax liabilities of the associated enterprise if transfer pricing did not follow the arm's length principle. These guidelines acknowledge different transfer pricing adjustment procedures for the enterprise in the DTA situation than in other instances. The enterprise is to adjust tax profits paid or payable in the DTA context. Such an adjustment is to reflect the position that would have existed if the Hong Kong government had applied the arm's length principle instead of applying the actual price transacted between the enterprises.

The OECD has endorsed the arm's length principle, as reflected in the Associated Enterprises Article of the OECD Model Tax Convention on Income and Capital, Article 9 of the OECD Model Tax Treaty.[1] The five Hong Kong DTAs have adopted Article 9 and reflect the adjustment process reflected in Article 9.

The OECD Model Tax Treaty reflects the Business Profits Article, or Article 7. The business profits article reflects the concept that transfer pricing principles are equally applicable to transactions between different parts of the enterprise. Thus, the transfer pricing principles apply to the head office, to a permanent establishment, or to different permanent establishments of the same enterprise.

As a general matter, the Hong Kong Commissioner would seek to apply the principles enunciated in the OECD *Transfer Pricing Guidelines for Multinational Enterprises and Tax Administrations* (i.e., the OECD *Transfer Pricing Guidelines*). The Hong Kong Commissioner, however, would exempt herself from the OECD Guidelines when these OECD provisions are incompatible with the express provisions of the Inland Revenue Ordinance.

The Commissioner will consider transactions actually undertaken by associated enterprises except where the economic substance differs from the form of the transaction or where the structure is not one that "commercially rational independent enterprises" would arrange. Having used the term "commercially rational independent enterprises," the Hong Kong transfer pricing guidelines fail to further define the term. The Hong Kong transfer pricing guidelines provide that the Hong Kong tax authorities will accept the use of ranges, such as an interquartile range, in the determination of an arm's length range.

ASSOCIATED ENTERPRISES

As a preview to the arm's length principle as articulated in the Associated Enterprises article, Article 9 of the OECD Model Tax Treaty, Article 9(1) states that the associated enterprise provisions apply in either of two situations where:

1. An enterprise of a Contracting State participates directly or indirectly in the management, control or capital of an enterprise of the other Contracting State, or
2. The same persons participate directly or indirectly in the management, control or capital of an enterprise of a Contracting State and an enterprise of the other Contracting State.

Those associated enterprise provisions apply if, in either case, two enterprises make or impose conditions between themselves as to their "commercial or financial relations." Such "commercial or financial relations" might differ from those relations that the enterprise otherwise might make between independent enterprises.

The enterprise must include the profits of that enterprise and pay tax accordingly if the enterprise otherwise had failed to reflect its profits. The associated enterprises provisions apply if the enterprise had failed to reflect its profits and had failed to accrue these amounts.

The associated enterprises article of the OECD Model Tax Treaty means that, as far as Hong Kong DTAs are concerned, the DTA has the right to adjust upward the profits of an enterprise of that state, where:

- That enterprise participates in the management, control, or capital of an enterprise of the other DTA state pursuant to the parent–subsidiary clause of Article 9(1), or
- The same persons participate directly in the management, control, or capital of that enterprise and an enterprise of the other DTA state pursuant to the common control clause of Article 9(1), and
- The conditions in their relationship differ from the conditions that would have been stipulated between independent enterprises.

The OECD transfer pricing guidelines explain how the taxpayer and the tax collector are to decide and apply "the most appropriate" transfer pricing methodology.

The Hong Kong transfer pricing guidelines, however, articulate the position that the existence of a DTA is not a prerequisite for making transfer pricing adjustments. Where the circumstances warrant, the Inland Revenue Ordinance provides that the Hong Kong Inland Revenue Department will make adjustments to transactions, whether these transactions are domestic or otherwise.

Article 7, "Business Profits," of the OECD Model Tax Treaty also adopts the arm's length principle for transactions between a permanent establishment of DTA state and its head office or other related branches of the other DTA state. Hong Kong's DTAs incorporate Article 7 as to the attribution of profits to a permanent establishment in Hong Kong. This attribution takes the arm's length principle into account. Accordingly, the Hong Kong transfer pricing guidelines apply to Article 7.

Article 9(1) of the OECD Model Tax Treaty specifics that two enterprises are "associated enterprises" with respect to each other if one of the enterprises meets the conditions of Article 9(1). The Hong Kong transfer pricing guidelines give the term "associated enterprises" broad coverage. These guidelines do not specifically address the meaning of "control" but instead refer to an enterprise participating directly or indirectly in the management, control, or capital of the enterprise of the other contracting state, or the same persons participating in both enterprises. Thus, the Hong Kong transfer pricing guidelines contain no threshold to determine control.

APPROPRIATE ADJUSTMENTS

Article 9(2) of the OECD Model Tax Treaty provides for a corresponding downward adjustment to profits to reflect appropriate adjustments to profits made in the other DTA state where this upward adjustment in made under Article (9)(1). The Article 9(2) adjustment seeks to eliminate double taxation that would otherwise arise. Article 9(2) provides that a contracting state includes the profits of the enterprise of the state and taxes the enterprise of the contracting state accordingly. The enterprise in the other contracting state charges the tax in profits. The profits the enterprise includes are profits accrued to the enterprise of the first-mentioned state. These adjustments apply if the conditions made between these two enterprises would have been made between independent enterprises.

In that event, that other state shall make an appropriate adjustment to the amount of tax charged therein on those profits. The parties, in making such adjustment, are to show due regard to other provisions of the tax treaty. The competent authorities of the contracting states are to consult each other if necessary.

The Hong Kong transfer pricing guidelines caution that making the above-mentioned appropriate adjustment is not automatic. The other DTA state makes the adjustment to eliminate double taxation if the DTA state considers the figure of adjusted profits correctly and reflects what the profits would have been on an arm's length basis. In other words, the DTA has to be satisfied that the upward adjustment made by the first-mentioned DTA state is justified both in principle and as regards the amount in terms of Article 9(1).

INLAND REVENUE ORDINANCE AND CASE LAW

Provisions within Hong Kong's Inland Revenue Ordinance together with case law are relevant to transfer pricing. Section 16 of the Inland Revenue Ordinance contains the basic statutory rules affecting the deductibility of expenditures in arriving at assessable profits. In this regard, section 16(1) is specifically attributable to transfer pricing. Section 16(1) restricts the deduction of outgoings or expenses to the extent to which these outgoings or expenses are incurred in the production of assessable profits.

In this regard, as to section 16(1), *Fletcher & Others v. FCT* (1991), there are some minor differences in the United Kingdom and the United States in determining taxable income. Hong Kong follows the U.K. model.[2] A disproportion between the detriment of the outgoing and the benefit of the income may give rise to a need to resolve the problem of characterization of the outgoing for the purpose of section 16(1) by a weighing of the various aspects of the whole set of circumstances. Such a set of circumstances includes the direct and indirect objects and advantages that the taxpayer sought in making the outgoing. The Hong Kong transfer pricing guidelines provide that where that circumstance is so, a "commonsense" or a "practical weighing of all the factors" provides the ultimate answer.

Fletcher & Others v. FCT then provides that consideration might reveal that the taxpayer is to explain the disproportion between outgoing income and relevant taxable income by reference to the independent pursuit of some other objective.[3] Further, the income of parties can be part of the outgoing income, doing so by making reference to the actual production of taxable income or the expected production of taxable income. In that event, it will be necessary to apportion the outgoing income between the pursuit of assessable income and the pursuit of that other objective.

The Hong Kong transfer pricing guidelines provide that the Inland Revenue Department will disallow payments made to an associated enterprise other than at arm's length. The court had denied this deduction on the basis that the taxpayer made this expenditure not for the purposes of the taxpayer's trade but perhaps for the purposes of the recipient's trade (i.e., for other objectives), as referred to in *Fletcher & Others v. FCT.*[4]

The court disallowed as a deduction the price paid to an associated enterprise on the basis of other than arm's length in *Ransom v. Higgs.*[5] The price paid in a transaction dictated by the tax avoidance scheme was not a price paid by the company as a free agent acting from commercial motives in its own interest. Accordingly, the court held that the sum paid was not paid wholly and exclusively for the purposes of the company's trade or business.

Courts have applied the associated company status of the transaction to determine fair value. *Sharkey v. Wernher*[6] articulated this rule, as applied by *Petrotim Securities Ltd. v. Ayers.*[7] In that case, a dealer in stocks and shares sold part of its trading stock to an associated company at a gross undervaluation. The English court took the view that the sale was entirely outside the scope of the company's ordinary trading activities. On the principle established by the other cases, the shares should be treated as having been sold at market value.

A similar decision reached comparable results. In *Skinner v. Berry Head Lands*, the court held that the transaction was so outside the ordinary course of business as to not to represent trading.[8] As a result, the court applied market value to substitute for the actual sales price.

Hong Kong Inland Revenue Ordinance section 17(1)(b) prohibits the taxpayer from deducting any disbursements or expenses as not being money expended for the purposes of producing such profits. Hong Kong does not permit a deduction for expenditures that are not connected with or arising from the trade or business. Implicitly, the exclusion rule has the effect of denying a company a deduction for the payment made for the purposes of the trade or business of the enterprise.

Hong Kong Inland Revenue Ordinance section 17(1)(c) disallows deductions for "any expenditure of a capital nature" or of "any loss or withdrawal of capital." The government can plausibly disallow a payment made to an associated enterprise in appropriate circumstances. The government can disallow the deduction on the basis that the deduction was capital withdrawn from the enterprise carried out in Hong Kong. In other words, the Hong Kong company makes the deduction to support its foreign enterprise.

The Commissioner of Inland Revenue can invoke the provisions of Hong Kong Inland Revenue Ordinance section 61A in the case of abusive profit-shifting transactions. The section 61A ordinance defines the term "transaction" to include any transaction, operation, or scheme, whether such transaction, operation, or scheme is enforceable by legal proceedings or not. Section 61A intends the "transaction" definition to be comprehensive in its scope. The Hong Kong transfer pricing guidelines provide that these transactions include types of transactions, including sales, renting, transfers of rights or interests, licensing, business facilities provisions, and loans, including those among associated enterprises.

The Commissioner of Inland Revenue in Hong Kong can recompute the profits or losses as if the transaction had been at arm's length when section 61A is applicable. Consider as examples *CIR v. Tai Hing Cotton Mill (Development)*[9] and *Ngai Lik Electronics Company Limited v. CIR*,[10] illustrating the Commissioner's power to adjust the profits or losses of the relevant enterprises.

The issue in *CIR v. Tai Hing Cotton Mill (Development)* was the pricing formula for a sale of land that had the effect of giving rise to a tax benefit. The Court of Appeal agreed with the Commissioner that the appraised market value at the date of the transaction should substitute for the non–arm's length price.

The issue in *Ngai Lik Electronics Company Limited v. CIR* was the annual price-fixing arrangement between the company and its associated enterprise. The Court of Final Appeal held that the parties entered into the price-fixing arrangement for the dominant purpose of obtaining a tax benefit for the taxpayer. The Commissioner raised section 61A(2) assessments to counteract the taxpayer's tax benefit. Such an assessment was higher based on the estimate of assessable profits, the amount the taxpayer would have earned if the taxpayer had hypothetically paid an arm's length price for the goods instead of the prices the taxpayer had actually paid pursuant to the price-fixing arrangement.

Hong Kong Inland Revenue Ordinance provides for three sections, in addition to section 61A, which the Commissioner can impose on a resident enterprise of Hong Kong that is not associated with any nonresident enterprise. These sections are section 16(1), section 17(1)(b), and section 17(1)(c). An enterprise might be associated with a nonresident enterprise in the terms of Article 9(1). In that event, the enterprise can apply for double tax relief from the DTA state pursuant to Article 9(2).

The Commissioner can consider requests for an "appropriate adjustment to the amount of tax charged" under Article 9(2) to eliminate double taxation cases in Hong Kong. Such an adjustment might be undertaken as a part of a mutual agreement procedure between the two DTAs. Such an adjustment can mitigate or eliminate double taxation where one tax administration makes a primary upward adjustment as a result of applying the arm's length principle to transactions involving an associated enterprise in the other DTA state.

The Commissioner, when making the "appropriate adjustment," would adjust the profits charged for tax purposes or payable for the Hong Kong enterprise. The Commissioner is to use the adjusted price if she finds this adjusted price is correct in principle and in amount. As a general rule, the Commissioner would grant relief if the DTA state in which the primary adjustment arose arrived at that arrangement based on OECD principles. However, the Hong Kong transfer pricing guidelines caution that the fact that the DTA state has its own domestic transfer pricing rules does not mean that these rules will necessarily reconcile with the OECD transfer pricing guidelines. The parties would have to test this process under the Mutual Agreement Procedure Article. Hong Kong will allow only the amount of the adjustment that meets the arm's length test.

The Commissioner and the competent authority of the other DTA state may take different positions in determining the arm's length conditions. The Commissioner, in applying Article 9(2), is to make such an adjustment only so far as she considers the primary charge by the other DTA state to be justified in principle and in amount. The Hong Kong transfer pricing guidelines warn that the Commissioner will not accept the consequences of an incorrect or arbitrary adjustment by the other DTA state.

PERMANENT ESTABLISHMENT CONSIDERATIONS

The Hong Kong transfer pricing guidelines view the scope of permanent establishment in a narrow manner. The guidelines address DTA issues standing alone; the guidelines fail to address the Hong Kong equivalent of the activities that would be taxed in the United States as income that is effectively connected with a U.S. trade or business—the non-treaty equivalent of a permanent establishment claim.

The Hong Kong transfer pricing guidelines provide a procedure under which Hong Kong is to enforce its attribution rules to determine the profits of a permanent establishment. This guidance governs the Hong Kong's DTAs as to the allocation of taxing rights. As a general matter, it is necessary under Article 7 to attribute profits and expenses to the Hong Kong permanent establishment if the nonresident enterprise has a permanent establishment in Hong Kong. The Hong Kong transfer pricing guidelines provide eight steps to the permanent establishment process:

Step 1. The taxpayer is to identify the "economically significant activities and responsibilities" of the nonresident enterprise undertaken in various places. The guidelines fail to further address the scope of the "economically significant activities and responsibilities" provision.

Step 2. The taxpayer is to postulate the existence of the permanent establishment in Hong Kong.

Step 3. The taxpayer is to identify the "economically significant activities and responsibilities" of the nonresident enterprise undertaken through the permanent establishment in Hong Kong.

Step 4. The taxpayer is to identify the scope, type, value, and timing of the dealings of the permanent establishment.

Step 5. The taxpayer is to determine the character and the structure of the permanent establishment business.

Step 6. The taxpayer is to select the most appropriate transfer pricing methodology for attribution purposes.

Step 7. The taxpayer is to apply the most appropriate transfer pricing methodology, and the taxpayer is to determine the arm's length outcome.

Step 8. The taxpayer is to implement a support process and is to install a review process.

The Hong Kong transfer pricing guidelines provide two main provisions as to the attribution of income and expenditures concerning permanent establishments:

1. Inland Revenue Rules, Rule 5
2. Business Profits Article, Article 7 of the DTAs

The Hong Kong transfer pricing guidelines apply the "functionally separate approach" to determine taxability of the permanent establishment. Using the "functionally separate entity" approach, the Commissioner will treat a permanent establishment as being a separate enterprise as if this enterprise is operating at arm's length, and with permanent establishments in Hong Kong and elsewhere attributing its profits and expenses. The separate entity approach operates to produce the same outcome as would transactions between two enterprises at arm's length.

The Commissioner can assess the profits of the permanent establishment of a nonresident enterprise. The Commissioner, in assessing the profits of the permanent establishment of a nonresident enterprise, can examine the separate sources of profit that the nonresident enterprise has derived from Hong Kong.

A profit is not booked in the permanent establishment in Hong Kong. Nevertheless, the permanent establishment might have to attribute the profit to the permanent establishment of the nonresident enterprise carrying on a business in Hong Kong. The permanent establishment is to reflect these permanent establishment amounts if the enterprise undertakes "economically significant activities or responsibilities" in Hong Kong.

The profit might be generated from "economically significant activities or responsibilities" outside Hong Kong. In that event, the profit will not be attributed to the permanent establishment of the nonresident enterprise in Hong Kong. The presence of "economically significant activities or responsibilities" outside Hong Kong occurs when there is another permanent establishment outside Hong Kong or when the head office undertakes the "economically significant activities or responsibilities."

The Commissioner can attribute profits to the permanent establishment in Hong Kong under Article 7(2). The Commissioner, in making such attribution of profits, is also to consider these functions:

- The significant "people functions" of the permanent establishment
- The key entrepreneurial risk-taking functions of the permanent establishment (i.e., those functions that are relevant to the assumption or acceptance or management of risks)

APPLYING THE ARM'S LENGTH PRINCIPLE

The arm's length principle, as viewed by the Hong Kong tax authorities, requires associated enterprises to charge the same price, royalty, and other fees in relation to a controlled transaction as that which would be charged by independent enterprises in an uncontrolled transaction in comparable circumstances. The arm's length principle, then, represents the closest approximation to the open market and to economic reality. The Hong Kong tax authorities look to a "reasonable allocation of profits and income" standard, so that application of the arm's length principle would produce a "reasonable allocation of profits and income" within a multinational enterprise.

The basis of the arm's length principle, according to the Hong Kong transfer pricing guidelines, is comparative analysis (i.e., a comparison of the conditions made or imposed between associated enterprises in their commercial relations or financial relations with those that would be made between independent enterprises). The OECD transfer pricing guidelines explain the arm's length principle in the following manner, recognizing that OECD member countries should use the arm's length principle as the international standard in determining transfer prices for tax purposes: The arm's length principle is set forth in Article 9 of the OECD Model Tax Convention, which addresses conditions that are made or imposed between the two enterprises in their commercial or financial relations, where these conditions differ from those that would be made between independent enterprises. Article 9 addresses those profits that would have accrued to one of the enterprises but, for reason of those conditions, have not so accrued. Article 9 has the enterprise include the profits of that enterprise and pay tax accordingly.

The "international consensus," according to the Hong Kong transfer pricing guidelines, is the recognition that associated enterprises should treat transactions between them for tax purposes by reference to the profits that would have arisen as if the independent enterprises had executed these transactions.

EXAMPLE 1

The Hong Kong transfer pricing guidelines contain a number of examples to illustrate the points the drafters provide. This example illustrates the arm's length principle in the intercompany loan context. Note two facts before examining the example fact pattern.

1. The term "HIBOR" refers to Hong Kong Interbank Offered Rate.
2. The "group finance company" referred to in the example is an intercompany finance company.

Company HK, a resident in Hong Kong, had previously received a fixed-term third-party loan. The third-party loan bore interest at HIBOR + 1.00%. The loan then had three years to run. Company HK then replaced the third-party loan with a group finance company loan carrying HIBOR + 1.50%, also with three years remaining. The new loan had the same terms as the old loan. The rate of HIBOR plus 1.50% was the market rate at the time Company HK replaced the loan.

The Hong Kong transfer pricing guidelines caution the taxpayer not to rely on the market interest rate at the rate of the transfer. There was "a lack of commercial logic" in replacing a HIBOR + 1.00% rate with a HIBOR + 1.50% rate, with the terms being equal. The Commissioner can adjust interest expense accordingly. ■

FOUR STEPS

The Hong Kong transfer pricing guidelines suggest that the taxpayer undertake a four-step process to implement the arm's length principle:

1. Characterization
   - Characterize the transactions between associated enterprises.
   - Document the characterization.
2. Selection
   - Select the most appropriate transfer pricing methodology.
   - Document the choice of method.
3. Application
   - Apply the most appropriate transfer pricing methodology.
   - Determine the arm's length outcome.
   - Document the application process.
4. Implementation
   - Implement support processes.
   - Undertake a review process.
   - Document the processes.

FUNCTIONAL ANALYSIS

The Hong Kong transfer pricing guidelines relegate functional analysis as being a useful tool in determining comparability between controlled transactions and uncontrolled transactions. Functional analysis, then,

- Assists in assessing the level of comparability present in controlled transactions and uncontrolled transactions
- Assesses the relative contributions of these associated enterprises to these transactions

Functional analysis, according to the Hong Kong transfer pricing guidelines, is an analysis of the functions performed, the assets used, and the risks assumed. Such functions, assets, and risks are assumed by the associated enterprises and by independent enterprises in comparable uncontrolled transactions.

The Hong Kong transfer pricing guidelines caution that functional analysis is not a transfer pricing methodology but a tool that assists in the proper assessment of comparability. The functional analysis process seeks to analyze the functions and risks undertaken by an entity whose transfer pricing is at issue. Functional analysis serves as a basis for identifying potential comparables. Further, functional analysis determines any differences for which adjustments have to be made to permit valid comparisons.

Functional analysis, then, would be useful in assessing:

- The availability of comparables in relation to prices or functions
- The degree of comparability as to the enterprise's uncontrolled transactions, or those transactions undertaken by other enterprises considered as comparables
- The relative weighting of the functions, assets, and risks of each of the associated enterprises to transactions that take place where a transactional profit applies

The Hong Kong transfer pricing guidelines warn the taxpayer about undertaking complex or composite transactions. The guidelines suggest that it is necessary to undertake the functions, assets, and risks separately for each significant combination in complex or composite transactions involving distinctive markets and product/service combinations.

The Hong Kong transfer pricing guidelines recognize that the taxpayer might apply more than one business strategy. In such an event, it will be necessary for the enterprise to perform an analysis of the functions performed, the assets used, and the risks assumed for each business strategy. This separate analysis is necessary because the functions performed, assets used, and risks assumed vary in each market. In *Asia Master Limited v. CIR*, the Court of First Instance observed that it was important to examine the functions and risks of the relevant entities in the transfer pricing study.[11]

COMPARABILITY ANALYSIS

The Hong Kong transfer pricing guidelines declare that "comparability is central to the application of the arm's length principle." The "critical question," then, according to the guidelines, is whether the uncontrolled transaction, which is sought to be compared against the uncontrolled transaction, is indeed comparable.

It is necessary to compare, or benchmark, the actual outcome between independent enterprises that are comparable. The enterprise, in making that comparison, must reconstruct the consideration paid or received under a controlled transaction. The purpose of the reconstruction is to represent the results that might be expected if the associated enterprises had been transacting on an arm's length basis under an uncontrolled transaction. The standard sought by the Hong Kong transfer pricing guidelines might be less than a full and total comparison. In *San Remo Marcaroni Co. v. FCT*, the High Court accepted that the Australian Tax Office had made a bona fide attempt to reconstruct income or determine the arm's length price by relying on customs information and comparable sales.[12]

The Hong Kong transfer pricing guidelines define the term "comparability analysis" to mean the comparison of a controlled transaction with an uncontrolled transaction or transactions. Here the guidelines refer to transactions with no differences and transactions without material differences. Controlled and uncontrolled transactions are comparable if none of the differences between the transactions could materially affect the factor being examined in the methodology. Alternatively, controlled and uncontrolled transactions are comparable if the enterprise can make reasonably accurate adjustments to eliminate the material effects of any such differences.

The Hong Kong transfer pricing guidelines suggest that the search for comparables should not be separated from the comparability analysis itself. Such a search for information as to potentially comparable uncontrolled transactions, as well as the process of identifying comparables themselves, is dependent on prior analysis of the taxpayer's controlled transactions and on the relevant comparability factors.

The Hong Kong transfer pricing guidelines further suggest that a methodical, consistent transfer pricing approach should provide some continuity or linkage in the analytical process. The enterprise should seek to maintain a constant relationship among the various steps in the comparability process:

- The beginning point is the preliminary analysis of the conditions of the controlled transaction.
- The middle point is the selection of the transfer pricing method.
- The final point is the identification of the potential comparables.

DETERMINING COMPARABILITY

The OECD has identified a number of factors the enterprise is to consider in determining comparability and in making adjustments:

- Characteristics of the property or characteristics of the services
- Functions performed, the assets or resources contributed, and the risks assumed
- Contractual terms (i.e., the duration of the agreement, the rights specified, payment options, etc.)
- Economic and market circumstances
- Business strategies, such as market penetration, research and development commitments, market positioning, and so forth

Differences in the specific characteristics of the property or of the services can often explain the differences in their open market value. Comparisons of these features may be useful in determining the comparability of controlled transactions or activities. The Hong Kong transfer pricing guidelines suggest that enterprise focus on the attributes and characteristics that customers value. Such customers value the intangible benefits of design, trademark, and perceived quality.

FUNCTIONS, ASSETS, AND RISKS

The associated enterprises might be transacting on open markets, such as quoted markets for securities, commodities, or financing. In such an event, it may be necessary for the enterprise to conduct only a brief functional analysis. The analysis needs to be more thorough and vigorous in complex cases where intangibles are involved. The Hong Kong transfer pricing guidelines suggest that the enterprise pay particular attention to its structure and organization.

The guidelines delineate the compilation of lists of functions, assets, and risks from the evaluation of the most economically important functions, assets, and risks. The compilation of a list of functions does not, in and of itself, indicate which of the functions is the most significant. In a similar manner, the compilation of a list of functions does not, in and of itself, indicate which functions are economically the most important to the value added by the business activities of the enterprise. The Hong Kong transfer pricing guidelines conclude that the critical part of the analysis is to ascertain:

- Which are the "most economically important" functions, assets, and risks
- How these functions, assets, and risks might be reflected by a comparable price, margin, or profit on the transaction

The Hong Kong transfer pricing guidelines apply an "economic significance" test to evaluate the functions that the enterprise performed. The guidelines caution that while one party might provide a large number of functions relative to the transaction, it is the "economic significance" of these functions that is important for transfer pricing purposes. The guidelines further define "economic significance" for each party in terms of the frequency, nature, and value of the respective parties to the transaction.

EXAMPLE 2

Company HK, a resident in Hong Kong, is a trading enterprise having a portfolio of customers in North America. HK has a team of merchandisers in Hong Kong. HK employs Company F, an associated contract manufacturer located in Country F, to undertake well-defined manufacturing or assembly processes. Company F does not bear any risks associated with currency, inventory, or the selling of the finished goods. Company F does not have any intangible assets, such as patents, trademarks, or designs. Company F's payment terms are based on budgets. The contract between HK and Company F may include a year-end adjustment to reflect any deviation of actual costs from budget.

The Hong Kong transfer pricing guidelines tell us that HK and Company F can set up transfer prices on a cost plus basis. The markups should reflect the relatively low level of risks borne by Company F plus Company F's depreciation costs of the machinery and plant employed. The Hong Kong transfer pricing guidelines describe this amount as being the "opportunity costs of providing the contracted service." ■

EXAMPLE 3

Company HK, a resident in Hong Kong, is a full-fledged distributor in Hong Kong. Company HK performs the same core activity as a wholesaler and marketer having a developed risk profile. Company HK performs value-added activities, such as post-sales services and support, and the maintenance of brands and trade names.

The Hong Kong transfer pricing guidelines suggest that Company HK should consider the risks that it assumes and the extra functions that it assumes when seeking third-party comparable data. The guidelines point out that the above-mentioned factors have a considerable influence on profitability. The guidelines further suggest that the service activities should be separated from sales revenue if feasible, awarding service activities separately rather than relying on data from more integrated businesses that perform sales and service functions. ■

CONTRACT TERMS

The Hong Kong transfer pricing guidelines provide that the contract terms of an arm's length transaction define explicitly or implicitly the way in which independent enterprises divide risks and benefits. The terms and conditions of the proposed agreement influence the ultimate price or margin when independent enterprises negotiate contracts or agreements. Examples of the terms and conditions that may influence the agreed price or margin include:

- Credit and payment terms
- Volume
- Duration of the agreement
- Product liabilities of the parties
- Service liabilities of the parties
- Warranties
- Exchange risk

EXAMPLE 4

Company HK, a resident in Hong Kong, sold the product at the same price to an associated enterprise and to an independent third party. Both the associated enterprise and the independent third party had similar risk profiles. The difference between the associated enterprise and the independent third party is the credit terms. Company HK gave the associated enterprise six months' credit while it gave the independent third party three months' credit.

Prima facie, because of these credit differences, the price charged to the associated enterprise was not at arm's length. The Hong Kong transfer pricing guidelines suggest that Company HK consider the volume of sale, possibly including a bulk discount, to determine whether the transfer of the goods was at arm's length. ■

ECONOMIC AND MARKETING CIRCUMSTANCES

Arm's length prices or margins may vary across different markets, even for transactions involving the same property or the same services. The enterprise, in achieving comparability, must make sure that:

- The markets in which the independent enterprises and associated enterprises operate are comparable.
- The differences do not have a material effect on price or the parties can appropriately adjust the price if there is a material effect on price.

BUSINESS STRATEGIES

The parent company most typically formulates the business strategy of a multinational group. The parent company undertakes this operation after its consultation with its affiliates and its input from them.

The question posed by the Hong Kong transfer pricing guidelines is whether an independent enterprise in similar circumstances might have participated in these business strategies. Then the question becomes the extent of the reward that independent enterprise would expect from that participation.

Market penetration strategies implement the conditions under which parties to the transactions temporarily agree to forgo some portion of the profits. Alternatively, the parties to the transactions incur losses under the market penetration strategy to position themselves for more substantial profits in the future.

Costs might be incurred or profits forgone by an enterprise resulting from a business strategy or policy. The Hong Kong transfer pricing guidelines would then ask which enterprise obtains the benefit from these decisions and the attribution of such costs to such policy or strategy.

The Hong Kong transfer pricing guidelines recognize that independent enterprises will not be prepared to accept strategies or policies that reduce their level of profit for the benefit of another enterprise. Any enterprise accepting additional risks or functions in arm's length transactions would demand an appropriate reward.

As a general matter, it is necessary for the enterprise to prove that a business strategy between associated enterprises is consistent with the arm's length principle. Specifically, it is necessary for the enterprise to establish whether independent enterprises dealing at arm's length in fact:

- Have accepted the terms and conditions of the strategy in the same or similar market circumstances
- Might be expected to have accepted the terms and conditions of the strategy in the same or similar market circumstances

EXAMPLE 5

Company HK, resident in Hong Kong, is a Hong Kong distributor of a computer product that is manufactured by its overseas parent. The overseas parent continues to derive substantial profits. Company HK has not achieved taxable income for many years. Company HK claims that it is pursuing a long-term market penetration strategy. Company HK has to bear all of the costs and risks associated with the long-term market penetration strategy without receiving an additional reward.

The Hong Kong transfer pricing guidelines provide that it is highly unlikely that Company HK is pursuing a valid market penetration strategy unless it can provide contemporaneous documentation supporting its market penetration strategy. However, this example is unrealistic. As a practical matter, the effective tax rate in Hong Kong is much less than that of the country in which the overseas parent manufacturer is located unless the overseas parent manufacturer has net operating losses. Thus, the business strategy determined by the foreign offshore parent would normally be to incur the market penetration study at its own location rather than in Hong Kong. ■

GLOBAL PRICE LISTS

The Hong Kong transfer pricing guidelines address the application of global price lists as a transfer pricing objective. Such global price lists are to specify the prices at which goods or services are sold globally to all purchasers at a particular "level of the market." The guidelines provide that global price lists can be helpful in ascertaining the arm's length price when used with other transfer pricing methodologies.

The Hong Kong transfer pricing guidelines provide that a global price list satisfies the arm's length principle only if the prices meet these conditions:

- The enterprise reviewed the prices using an appropriate arm's length methodology.
- The enterprise applies the global list provisions only in comparable circumstances. Such comparable circumstances apply where the markets are comparable and where the buyers and sellers are performing equivalent functions.
- The enterprise applies the global price list approach to both controlled and uncontrolled dealings.

The Hong Kong transfer pricing guidelines caution that it is difficult for a global list to satisfy these conditions since markets vary by location. The guidelines warn that isolated sales to independent enterprises generally are not sufficient to establish the arm's length nature of a global price list.

ESTABLISHING THE RELIABILITY OF THE DATA

The Hong Kong transfer pricing guidelines specify four factors that would influence reliability of the data:

1. Measurement error arising from differences in definitions, accounting practice, timing, and so forth
2. Departures from perfect market conditions, making economic outcomes indeterminate
3. Unadjusted differences in the circumstances of the transactions involved
4. Differences in the methodologies the enterprises utilize

The Hong Kong transfer pricing guidelines state that the most important factor influencing reliability of the data is the way in which the enterprise deals with material differences in the circumstances surrounding the transactions. Reliability varies between transfer pricing methodologies since different methodologies focus on differing sets of attributes and questions raised in handing material differences.

The enterprise may find it useful to apply multiple methods in resolving difficult or highly contentious cases. Two transfer pricing methods might give the enterprise different answers. One of the transfer pricing methods is likely to be not appropriate to the facts, thus rendering the comparable data not reliable and possibly not comparable. Alternatively, the entrepreneur might have applied one of the transfer price methods incorrectly.

TRANSFER PRICING METHODOLOGIES

The Hong Kong transfer pricing guidelines rely on the OECD *Transfer Pricing Guidelines* regarding transfer pricing methodologies. The OECD guidelines emphasize the importance of comparability analysis and provide detailed descriptions of these various transfer pricing methods. The OECD *Transfer Pricing Guidelines*, like the Hong Kong transfer pricing guidelines, reflect the three "traditional" transfer pricing methods:

1. Comparable uncontrolled method
2. Resale price method
3. Cost plus method

The OECD *Transfer Pricing Guidelines* also discuss two "transactional" profit methods:

1. Profit split method
2. Transactional net margin method

The Hong Kong transfer pricing regulations specify that the profit split method and the transactional net margin method "are also considered" to satisfy the arm's length principle. The Hong Kong transfer pricing regulations, then, implicitly conclude that the traditional transfer pricing methods satisfy the arm's length principle.

In their appendix, the Hong Kong transfer pricing regulations provide details of both the traditional transfer pricing methodologies and the transactional net profit methods. The Hong Kong transfer pricing regulations provide what it terms as a succinct account of these transfer pricing methodologies in *Roche Products Pty Limited v. FCT.*[13]

The Hong Kong transfer pricing regulations caution the reader that the selection of a transfer pricing method always aims at finding "the most appropriate method" for a particular case. These regulations then provide limited guidance in selecting "the most appropriate method." These regulations provide a general rule that the traditional transfer pricing transaction methods are the "most direct means" of establishing whether conditions in the commercial and financial relations are at arm's length.

Having determined the preference for the "most direct means" approach, the Hong Kong transfer pricing guidelines express a preference for traditional transfer pricing methods rather than the transactional profit margin methods where the enterprise can apply each in an "equally reliable" manner. The results are "equally reliable," taking into account the comparability analysis of the controlled transaction under review and the availability of information. The Hong Kong transfer pricing guidelines, in expressing their preference for traditional transfer pricing methods, might reach a different result from the "best [transfer pricing] method."

The enterprise may apply a transactional profit method, either in conjunction with traditional transfer methods or on its own, when the enterprise finds that these transactional transfer methods are more appropriate than traditional transaction methods. The enterprise is to consider comparability analysis, including functional analysis, of the controlled transactions under review and the evaluation of comparable uncontrolled transactions.

The Hong Kong Commissioner accepts the concept that multinational enterprises retain the freedom to apply other transfer pricing methods not described in the OECD *Transfer Pricing Guidelines* to establish prices. The Hong Kong transfer pricing guidelines would apply a prerequisite to the application of other transfer pricing methods (i.e., that the other methods satisfy the arm's length principle). The Hong Kong transfer pricing guidelines specify that the enterprise should not use such other transfer pricing methods in substitution for the OECD-recognized methods where these OECD-recognized methods are appropriate to the facts and circumstances in the case.

The enterprise, in selecting other transfer pricing methods, should support its documentation, including an explanation of why OECD-recognized methods are not appropriate or not workable in the circumstances of the case. The enterprise should indicate why the selected method provides a better solution. The Hong Kong transfer pricing guidelines do not require the counterparty to apply parallel transfer pricing methods.

SOURCES OF PROFITS AND INCOME

The Hong Kong transfer pricing guidelines specify that, as a general matter, the enterprise is to treat profits as being taxed if the enterprise derives the profit from Hong Kong. The enterprise cannot reduce the profits for tax purposes unless the Commissioner is obligated to make an "appropriate adjustment" under the Associated Enterprises Article of the treaty. The Commissioner must be involved in this reduction process for it to apply. In contrast, an enterprise carrying on a trade or business in Hong Kong cannot unilaterally apply any transfer pricing methodology to reduce profits arising in or derived from Hong Kong. The broad guiding principle in deciding the source of profit is to see what the enterprise has done to earn the profits in question and to determine where the enterprise performed the operations in question.

EXAMPLE 6

Company HK, a resident in Hong Kong, purchases finished goods from a subsidiary established in Mainland China. Company HK sells the finished goods to various customers located outside Hong Kong. Company HK undertakes these activities in Hong Kong: It receives orders, places orders, arranges shipment, arranges trade financing, and collects and makes payments. Company HK has higher profits because it paid less in Mainland China. Company HK contends that part of its profits are not taxable, asserting that determination on the basis that Company HK had paid a less-than-market price for the finished goods. Assume that the Mainland China tax authorities have not made any upward adjustment to the subsidiary using the Associated Enterprises Article of the treaty.

The Hong Kong transfer pricing guidelines specify that the source of the trading profits is clearly located inside Hong Kong. The whole of the profits derived by Company HK from the trading profits will be treated as profits subject to taxation. The Commissioner is not obligated to make an "appropriate adjustment" in the absence of an upward adjustment by the counterpart tax official in Mainland China. Accordingly, the Commissioner will reject Company HK's claim. There is no requirement that the counterpart state make adjustments to adjust profits.

Governments apply the transfer pricing rules, in practice, to protect the revenue base of each of the DTA states. The Hong Kong transfer pricing guidelines caution that enterprises should not use transfer pricing rules to achieve double nontaxation of profits or income. Accordingly, the enterprises are not to apply the transfer pricing rules to reduce taxable income undertaken in Hong Kong unless the tax authorities undertake a primary adjustment under the relevant DTA's Associated Enterprises Article. The Commissioner has no obligation to make an appropriate adjustment unless, in such a situation, the Hong Kong tax authorities treat the upward adjustment made as being accepted as correct. ■

EXAMPLE 7

Company HK, a resident in Hong Kong, purchases finished goods from a subsidiary established in Mainland China. Company HK sells the finished goods to various customers located outside Hong Kong. Company HK undertakes these activities in Hong Kong: It receives orders, places orders, arranges shipment, arranges trade financing, and collects and makes payments. The SAT makes an adjustment under the Associated Enterprises Article of the treaty between Mainland China and the Hong Kong SAR on the grounds that Company HK paid less than the market price for the finished goods.

The Hong Kong Commissioner can accept the Mainland China transfer pricing adjustment as being correct in principle and amount. In that event, the Commissioner can make an appropriate adjustment under the Associated Enterprises Article, section 9(2), and Inland Revenue Ordinance (IRO), section 79. ■

ABUSIVE TAX SCHEMES

The Hong Kong transfer pricing guidelines recognize that Hong Kong enterprises often utilize nonresident foreign corporations in the trade context for many valid business purposes. The guidelines further recognize that, in some jurisdictions, the creation of a corporation such as a domestic equity joint venture company might be the only way that a Hong Kong resident enterprise can do business in that jurisdiction (i.e., through an investor or shareholder in the equity joint venture company).

The Hong Kong transfer pricing guidelines recognize that while some nonresident corporations are legally structured without any hidden financial motive, some nonresident corporations are created with tax evasion or tax avoidance as the primary motivation. The guidelines provide such an example: The nonresident corporation often keeps most of the profits; the enterprise pays a small portion of what is left in Hong Kong to the Hong Kong enterprise. The tax scheme involves the creation of an "international business company," often incorporated in a tax-free regime to which the enterprise diverts its profits.

The Hong Kong transfer pricing guidelines point out that enterprises employ a variety of devices to conceal transfers of money or other property to an international business company. The simplest method of diverting profit, according to the Hong Kong transfer pricing guidelines, is by sending skimmed income to the international business company's offshore account. Enterprises use other methods of transferring money offshore, including making use of payments disguised as deductible expenses, such as management fees, consultancy fees, commissions, royalties, and so forth. The enterprise makes these payments to the international business company that is operated from Hong Kong but located in a tax haven jurisdiction.

TRANSFER PRICING SCHEMES

The Hong Kong transfer pricing guidelines point out that perhaps complex tax schemes have evolved from the simple structuring of abusive arrangements that take advantage of the financial secrecy of some foreign jurisdictions and the availability of accounts opened in offshore financial institutions. The enterprise might interpose an international business company without any commercial reason as a tax scheme in these cases:

- The enterprise interposes the international business company to mark up the price upon an alleged sale of goods by a third-party supplier. Then the international business company re-invoices the same goods to the Hong Kong enterprise at a higher price.
- Alternatively, the enterprise interposes the international business company to mark down the price of an alleged purchase of goods from the Hong Kong enterprise. Then the Hong Kong enterprise sells goods at market price.

The international business company can act as an intermediary that marks up the price during the transfer and then re-invoices the Hong Kong enterprise at a higher price. This scheme is known by a variety of names. The structure is called a transfer pricing scheme or a re-invoicing scheme.

EXAMPLE 8

An arrangement took place between Company HK, a resident of Hong Kong, and a nonresident entity, a nonresident company or a nonresident trust. The nonresident entity allegedly sold goods to Company HK at a price that is substantially above market price. Company HK declared profits from the sale of the goods. Nevertheless, the profits from these transactions were lower than the amount that Company HK would have derived if it had purchased the goods directly from third-party purchases.

The arrangement, or the crucial parts of the arrangement, might be a sham. The nonresident entity did not incur any commercial risks and did not incur any value to the goods the nonresident entity had purchased. The Hong Kong transfer pricing guidelines caution that the promoter, or individuals in the nonresident entity operation in Hong Kong, might be acting as agent in relation to that structure. Provisions under section 20, section 61, and section 61A might also be applicable. ■

EXAMPLE 9

An arrangement took place between Company HK, a resident of Hong Kong, and a nonresident entity, a nonresident company or a nonresident trust. Company HK, a Hong Kong entity, allegedly sold goods to a Hong Kong nonresident at a price that is substantially below market price. The nonresident entity in turn allegedly sold the same goods to a third party at market price. Company HK declared its profits from the sale of goods, but the profits were lower than the amount that Company HK would have derived if it had sold the goods at market price to the third party.

The arrangement, or the crucial parts of the arrangement, might be a sham. The nonresident entity did not incur any commercial risks and did not incur any value to the goods the nonresident entity had sold. The Hong Kong transfer pricing guidelines caution that the promoter, or individuals in the nonresident entity operation in Hong Kong, might be acting as agent in relation to that structure. Provisions under section 20, section 61, and section 61A might also be applicable.

In an abusive tax scheme, a nonresident person or a nonresident entity often appears to be the owner of the assets and profits. In fact and in substance, true ownership belongs with the Hong Kong resident enterprise inside Hong Kong.

The Hong Kong transfer pricing guidelines suggest that the enterprise use the comparable uncontrolled price method to test the pricing of purchases or sales compared with tax haven re-invoicing companies that perform no "economically significant functions." The guidelines add that paying for legal fees and other costs of implementing a tax avoidance scheme do not represent the performance of economically significant functions, given that the ultimate third-party buyer receives no value added.

The Hong Kong Commissioner combats such abusive tax schemes. The primary focus of the Commissioner is on the identification and investigation of these tax schemes. Inland Revenue requires disclosure on the part of the taxpayer, including preparation of a statutory form specified by the Board of Inland Revenue under section 86 for the purposes of carrying into effect the provisions in Part IV relating to profits tax. The taxpayer must disclose these matters:

- Transactions for, or with, nonrelated persons (i.e., transactions conducted by agents for nonresident persons)
- Payments to nonresidents for the use of intellectual properties (i.e., payments subject to withholding tax)
- Payments to nonresidents for services rendered in Hong Kong
- Transactions with closely connected nonresident persons

The Hong Kong transfer pricing guidelines provide that the Hong Kong Commissioner can assess profits transferred to an international business company under section 14 or section 20A if the international business company is carrying on a trade or business in Hong Kong. Likewise, the Hong Kong Commissioner can assess profits transferred to a closely connected nonresident enterprise under section 20 to a Hong Kong resident enterprise as if the Hong Kong resident were the agent.

(*continued*)

(continued)

The Hong Kong transfer pricing guidelines provide that an enterprise can disregard the intermediary sale under section 61 if the sale is artificial or fictitious. In such an event, the Hong Kong resident enterprise will be assessed to determine its profits as if there had been no intermediate sale. The Hong Kong Commissioner can counteract the tax benefit accrued to the Hong Kong enterprise under the tax scheme. The Hong Kong tax authorities have the discretionary power given to an Assistant Commissioner under section 61A(2).

The Hong Kong Commissioner interposed the activities of an international business corporation to counteract the substantial reduction in profits tax liability the international business corporation created as to a Hong Kong company. Judge Chua in *Asia Master Limited v. CIR,*[14] at the Court of First Instance, was of the opinion that the Commissioner acted legally in applying section 61 and section 61A in that situation in assessing the profits tax liability of the Hong Kong entity. In *CIR v. Ewig Industries Co. Ltd.*,[15] the District Court disagreed with the approach the Commissioner followed to counteract this type of tax avoidance.

The Hong Kong transfer pricing guidelines address an extreme form of abusive tax schemes (i.e., where the representations of the international business companies could be entirely fictitious). For example, in such a scheme, a Hong Kong resident might record in its accounts transactions with an international business company. In fact, such an international business company has no charter or registration to operate anywhere, and the international business company has no activity in any jurisdiction. The international business company is merely a cyber-company or a legal fiction.

The Hong Kong transfer pricing guidelines provide that these tax scheme activities are clearly subject to the Inland Revenue Ordinance. The Commissioner can establish tax evasion if she can establish the taxpayer's dishonesty or willful intent as to this tax scheme. The Hong Kong transfer pricing guidelines suggest that the taxpayer, when completing a profits return, should make a full and frank disclosure of all material facts relating to the computation of assessable profits in order to avoid the invocation of any penal provisions.

The success of a tax avoidance scheme might be dependent on the Commissioner never finding out the true facts. In that event, such a scheme is more likely to be one of "evasion" rather than "avoidance." Two cases explain the distinction between avoidance and evasion: *R v. Mears*[16] and *Denver Chemical Manufacturing Company v. COT.*[17] ■

TRANSFER PRICING DOCUMENTATION

The Inland Revenue Ordinance does not, in and of itself, require transfer pricing documentation. Section 51C does not expressly require taxpayers to create documents showing compliance with the arm's length principle. Nevertheless, section 51C does require the taxpayer, among other things, to keep records "in sufficient detail." These records are to be in sufficient detail to enable the Commissioner to verify:

- Quantities and values of the goods
- Identities of the sellers or buyers
- Services that result in receipts and payments

The Hong Kong transfer pricing guidelines, "for obvious reasons," encourages taxpayers to engage in transfer pricing documentation. If enterprises are documenting their transfer prices, as a matter of good practice, these enterprises should apply the same management principles that would govern the process of evaluating a business decision applicable to a similar level of complexity and importance.

The Hong Kong Commissioner makes clear that she does not intend to require enterprises carrying on business in Hong Kong to incur disproportionate compliance costs. Nevertheless, she requires the enterprise to draw up their accounts fairly and honestly. The Hong Kong Commissioner may call on the enterprise to justify its transfer price and the amount of its profits and losses reflected for tax purposes in the event she issues an inquiry or holds an audit or investigation. The parameters of what constitutes adequate documentation depend on the nature, size, and complexity of the business or the transaction in question.

The Hong Kong Commissioner, in making an audit or investigation, would require the enterprises in Hong Kong to provide these details:

- Any relevant commercial or financial dealings that fall within section 20, section 20A, section 61, and section 61A.
- The nature, the terms, the prices, and the quantum of relevant transactions. Such transactions include the transactions that form a series of transactions, together with any relevant offsets.
- The method or methods by which it makes use of the nature, terms, and quantum of the relevant transactions. This information is to include any study of comparables the enterprise undertakes.
- The way in which its selection of the transfer pricing method results in arm's length terms and so forth. The enterprise is to reflect the computational adjustment it requires and the method under which it is to calculate the adjustment if the enterprise's selection of the transfer pricing method does not result in arm's length terms. The preceding analysis normally includes an analysis of market data or other information as to third-party comparables.
- The terms of the relevant commercial arrangements between the enterprise with both third parties and with members of the enterprise's group. These arrangements include contemporaneous commercial agreements, including service contracts, distribution contracts, and loan agreements. These arrangements also include any budgets, forecasts, and papers containing information the enterprise relies on in arriving at its arm's length terms, and so forth.

The Hong Kong transfer pricing guidelines provide that the OECD *Transfer Pricing Guidelines* in turn provide guidance as to the type of information that would be useful. Such useful information includes:

- Basic information, including:
  - Information concerning associated enterprises involved in the controlled transactions
  - The transactions at issue

  - The functions performed
  - Information the enterprise derives from independent enterprises engaged in similar transactions
- Information as to the controlled transactions; for example:
  - Its nature and terms
  - Its economic conditions
  - The involvement as to property, product, and service flows
  - Changes in trading conditions
  - Renegotiations of existing arrangements
- Information relating to comparable companies having transactions similar to the controlled transactions.
- Information pertaining to associated enterprises, such as:
  - An outline of the business
  - The structure of the organization
  - Ownership links within the multinational enterprise group
  - Financial results, including the amount of sales and operating results from the last years preceding the transaction
  - The level of the taxpayer's transactions with foreign associated enterprises
- Information as to pricing, business strategies, and special circumstances. Such information would include, for example, factors that would influence the setting of prices or the establishment of any pricing policies for the taxpayer and the whole international group. Such factors would include information regarding the markup on cost, the deduction of related costs from sales prices to end users in the market in which the related foreign parties are conducting a wholesale business, or use of an integrated price or cost policy on a whole combined group basis.
- Information as to the factors that lead to the development of such pricing policies and, where applicable, consistency as to transactional conditions in the open market.
- Explanation of the selection of the transfer pricing method as to the arm's length principle, the application of the transfer pricing method as to the arm's length principle, and the consistency of the transfer pricing method as to the arm's length principle the taxpayer uses to establish its transfer pricing.
- Explanation of the special circumstances concerning any set-off transactions that have an effect on determining arm's length price. This explanation encompasses the details of any particular management strategies or circumstances particular to the type of business that might temporarily alter pricing structures. Such management structures include, for example, market entry, market share, new product development, or, in contrast, defensive strategies.
- Explanation of general commercial conditions and industry conditions.
- Information as to functions the enterprise performed, taking into account the assets the enterprise uses and the risks the enterprise assumes.
- Documents that show the negotiation process as to determining prices as to controlled transactions or revising prices as to controlled transactions.

INTRAGROUP SERVICES ARRANGEMENTS

The term "intragroup services arrangements" encompasses a wide variety of services. Such services broadly include:

- Administrative services
- Technical services
- Financial services
- Commercial services

As a general matter, the Hong Kong Commissioner accepts the basic principles, as defined by the OECD *Transfer Pricing Guidelines*, that pertain to the charging for intragroup services. Two principal issues apply when analyzing intragroup services according to the OECD guidelines:[18]

1. Determining whether a member of the group rendered the service
2. Determining the arm's length charge

The OECD *Transfer Pricing Guidelines* set out the principal conditions when determining whether a member of the group rendered the service. The Hong Kong transfer pricing guidelines partially quote the OECD *Transfer Pricing Guidelines*:

> Under the arm's length principle, the question whether an intra-group service has been rendered when an activity is performed for one or more group members by another group member should depend on whether the activity provides a respective group member with economic or commercial value to enhance its commercial position. This can be determined by considering . . .[19]

The Hong Kong transfer pricing guidelines do take into account the next material from the OECD transfer pricing guide, thus providing the reader with a somewhat obscure commentary:

> whether an independent enterprise in comparable circumstances would have been willing to pay for the activity if performed for it by an independent enterprise or would have performed the activity in house for itself. If the activity is not one for which the independent enterprise would have been willing to pay or perform for itself, the activity ordinarily should not be considered as an intra-group service under the arm's length principle.

The Hong Kong transfer pricing guidelines point out that the OECD transfer pricing guidelines further require the intragroup service entity performing the service to determine which services relate to shareholder activities, which services benefit specific group members, and which services benefit the group as a whole.

The Hong Kong transfer pricing guidelines warn that the enterprise is not to re-charge the cost of shareholder activities unless these costs of shareholder activities are performed by a group company on behalf of the parent company. In that case, the enterprise is to re-charge the cost of the shareholder activity. The next activities normally benefit the parent company in its role of shareholder, and such activities do not benefit the subsidiaries. Nevertheless, what is shareholder activity is a matter of fact but should include:

- Meetings of the parent company's shareholders
- Issuing of shares in the parent company
- Costs of the supervisory board
- Maintaining the share register
- Activities to satisfy statutory reporting requirements of the parent company
- Audit of the parent company

As a general matter, the Hong Kong transfer pricing guidelines provide that services should not be compensated if the parent company provides services for a subsidiary that duplicate what the subsidiary already performs or are otherwise unnecessary.[20]

EXAMPLE 10

A parent company audits the financial statements and the records of an overseas subsidiary. The parent company undertakes the audit to satisfy its own investors and to satisfy legal requirements. The audit duplicates an audit that the overseas subsidiary performed on its own under its own domestic laws. The parent company performed this audit as a steward for its own investments rather than benefiting the overseas subsidiary company. The parent company should bear the cost of the audit. ■

DEDUCTION OF EXPENDITURES PAID FOR INTRAGROUP SERVICES

Under Inland Revenue Ordinance section 16, an enterprise can deduct an expenditure made under an intragroup arrangement and calculated using a specific markup. The Hong Kong transfer pricing guidelines point out that the question of whether the enterprise's expenditure made under the intragroup services arrangement is deductible is a question of fact. Deductibility from a practical and business point of view depends on what the enterprise calculated the expenditure to achieve.

An enterprise can incur an expenditure as to obtaining a supply of goods and services from another associated enterprise under a contract. The enterprise is to characterize such an expenditure by reference to the contractual benefits passing to the enterprise under the contract and by the manner in which those benefits relate to the enterprise's profit-earning activities or business.

The benefits conferred by a service arrangement might provide an objective commercial explanation for the whole of the expenditure made under the service arrangement. Such a service arrangement will suffice to characterize the expenditure as an outgoing or as an expense incurred in the production of taxable profits in the event that the service arrangement does provide such an objective commercial explanation.

There might be situations in which the benefits passing to the associated enterprise under an intragroup service arrangement do not provide an objective commercial explanation for the whole of expenditure. The service arrangement alone, without more, will not suffice to characterize the expenditure in the event that such a lack of commercial explanation event were to occur. In such a case, the enterprise will need to undertake a broader examination of all the circumstances to determine the purposes of the expenditure. This broader expenditure might include an examination of the relationship between the enterprise and the services entity and, depending on the circumstances of the particular case, the manner in which the enterprise and the services entity have dealt with each other, and the taxpayer's purpose, motive, or intention in incurring the expenditure.

The Hong Kong transfer pricing guidelines enunciate three situations in which a services arrangement might not be sufficient to provide an "objective commercial explanation" for the entirety of the expenditure:

1. The service fees pertaining to service arrangement are disproportionate or are grossly excessive in relation to the benefits that the services arrangement provides.
2. The services fees and charges guarantee to the services entity a certain profit outcome, making that guarantee arrangement without providing a "reasonable commercial arrangement."
3. The service fees and charges generate profits in the services entity. The enterprise makes this services and charges determination without showing any clear evidence that the service entity has added value or performed any substantial functions. For example, the enterprise might make this services and charges determination without showing any clear evidence that the service entity has added value when there is no clear separation of the services entity's business activities and those of taxpayer.

DETERMINING THE AMOUNT OF INTRAGROUP CHARGES

The enterprise must determine both the basis of charging and an appropriate margin in determining whether the amount of the charge is in accordance with the arm's length principle. The OECD *Transfer Pricing Guidelines* suggest two principal methods of making the determination as to the basis of charging and the appropriate margin.

The Hong Kong transfer pricing guidelines differentiate between direct charges and indirect charges:

- The enterprise can issue a direct charge, a charge levied by a particular affiliate for a particular service.
- The enterprise can issue an indirect charge by other means, usually through "allocation keys."

The direct charge has the advantage of providing greater transparency, and such a direct charge provides further documentary evidence as to the validity of the charges. The enterprise can ascertain the amount to be re-charged through time sheets, charges to an account, charges to a job code, and so forth.

An indirect charge method applies where, for some reason, including the cost or burden of administrating the charge, the enterprise cannot reliably track the costs it incurs on behalf of one or more associates. The indirect charge method necessitates that the enterprise collect all costs together and share these combined costs among its beneficiaries. The indirect charge process normally requires the enterprise to make estimates of the amounts or approximate the amounts. Enterprises normally make allocations through "keys."

For example, in determining allocation keys, the enterprise can calculate the charges based on head count for human resources costs, or for the number of computer terminals in use for information technology support, and so forth. The OECD *Transfer Pricing Guidelines* provide that the allocation method must be consistent with what a comparable independent enterprise would be prepared to accept.

The scope of intragroup services includes contract manufacturing activities. In such a contract manufacturing case, the group might provide the production enterprise with intensive instruction as to the items to be produced, the quality to be produced, and the quality required. The Hong Kong transfer pricing guidelines provide that such a production enterprise bears low risks. The reader should assume that the enterprise will purchase the entire output, assuming the contact manufacturer meets product quality requirements. The production enterprise could be considered as performing a service in that circumstance and the cost plus method could be appropriate.

An intragroup service entity can be providing services to an associated enterprise. Such a group service entity is obliged to ensure that the intragroup services entity:

- Identifies the services
- Charges for the services
- Charges for the services at arm's length
- Keeps adequate documentation

It is more satisfactory to charge an arm's length cost rather than all relevant costs whether the next situations occur:

- Providing the service is a principal activity of the associated enterprise
- The profit element is significant
- Direct charging is possible as a basis from which to determine the arm's length price

The Hong Kong transfer pricing guidelines provide that an enterprise should include a profit element where one of the next three situations applies:

1. The service entity is engaged in the trade or business of rendering services.
2. The service entity is providing similar services to unrelated parties.
3. The service entity provides the service as one of its principal activities.

SERVICES PROVIDED BY A PERMANENT ESTABLISHMENT

The Hong Kong transfer pricing guidelines provide that the enterprise should include a profit margin where:

- The principal activity of a permanent establishment is to provide specific services to the enterprise
- The providing of services gives a real advantage to the enterprise
- The cost of services is a significant part of the expenses of the enterprise

However, the Hong Kong transfer pricing guidelines provide that there should be no markup where the providing of services is merely part of the general management activity of the enterprise taken as a whole. For example, such an enterprise might have a common system of training for all employees. In that event, the enterprise should treat the costs as being a part of general administrative expenses. The enterprise should allocate these costs on a cost basis among different parts of the enterprise, with proper share being made to the permanent establishment.

The Hong Kong transfer pricing guidelines caution that the enterprise should attribute no profits to a permanent establishment by reason of the mere purchase of the goods or merchandise for the enterprise. No notional profits should accrue to the permanent establishment if the permanent establishment merely purchases goods for the enterprise not in the course of normal business activity.

As a broad basis, the provisions of the Hong Kong Inland Revenue Ordinance and the relevant articles in the DTAs should allow the Commissioner to reallocate profits or adjust deductions. The Commissioner can reallocate profits and adjust deductions by substituting an arm's length consideration for the consideration, if any, stipulated by the resident enterprises and the non-resident enterprises. These allocation and adjustment provisions apply where the Commissioner considers that the resident enterprises and the nonresident enterprises are not dealing at arm's length and where the consideration is not an arm's length consideration.

NOTES

1. OECD, *Transfer Pricing Guidelines for Multinational Enterprises and Tax Administrations*, Chapter IB(i).
2. *Fletcher & Others v. FCT*, (1991), 173 CLR 1, at 18 and 19.
3. Ibid.
4. Ibid.
5. *Ransom v. Higgs*, 50 TC 1 (UK).
6. *Sharkey v. Wernher*, 36 TC 257 (UK).
7. *Petrotim Securities Ltd. v. Ayers*, 41 TC 389 (UK).
8. *Skinner v. Berry Head Lands*, 46 TC 377(UK).
9. *CIR v. Tai Hing Cotton Mill (Development)* [2008], 2 HKLRD 40.
10. *Ngai Lik Electronics Company Limited v. CIR*, FACV No. 29 of 2008.
11. *Asia Master Limited v. CIR*, 7 HKTC 25.
12. *San Remo Marcaroni Co. v FCT*, 43 ATR 53 (Australia).
13. *Roche Products Pty Limited v. FCT*, 70 ATR 703 (Australia).
14. *Asia Master Limited v. CIR*.
15. *CIR v. Ewig Industries Co. Ltd.*, DCTC 7883/2005.
16. *R v. Mears*, 37 ATR 321 at page 323.
17. *Denver Chemical Manufacturing Company v. COT*, 4 AITR 216 at p. 222.
18. OECD, *Transfer Pricing Guidelines for Multinational Enterprises and Tax Administrations*, Chapter VII, section 7.5.
19. Ibid., section 7.6.
20. Ibid., section 7.11.

CHAPTER NINE

9

Hong Kong Challenges Abusive Tax Schemes

THE HONG KONG government is taking action to challenge abusive tax schemes. The government issued its transfer pricing guidelines during December 2009 for the purpose of specifically curtailing the transfer pricing facets of these abusive tax schemes. The Hong Kong government, in promulgating these anti–tax abuse rules, specifically recognizes that taxpayers do design and employ such reinvoicing schemes and similar devices. Some taxpayers have been conjuring up reinvoicing schemes deliberately to confront and to obfuscate transfer pricing head on. The Hong Kong transfer pricing provisions provide significant anti–tax avoidance provisions to counteract these abusive practices through its transfer pricing regime. In this regard, the reader is well advised to examine Chapter 10, Winning Hong Kong's Landmark Transfer Pricing Case, the *Ngai Lik* case.

Transfer pricing guidelines are exceedingly forthright as to abusive tax schemes and the remedies to these schemes the Hong Kong Inland Revenue would pursue. Hong Kong's reaction to these tax schemes is unique. Most other governments go to great lengths to avoid providing full descriptions of the guideposts in which tax havens and other abusive tax schemes operate. These governments fear that they could be giving a road map to ultra-aggressive taxpayers by providing such tax scheme technology. Hong Kong eschews that approach, and its forthright anti–tax haven provisions within the transfer pricing guidelines are a welcome change.

The Inland Revenue of Hong Kong issued its "Transfer Pricing Guidelines – Methodologies and Related Issues" in December 2009. The tax authorities issued this guidance as Departmental Interpretation and Practice Note No. 46. The Hong Kong Special Administrative Region (SAR) issued the guidelines for the information of taxpayers and their tax representatives. It is quite possible, even likely, that the Inland Revenue is providing nonpublic advice to agents in its capacity as tax collector.

MACROECONOMIC ISSUES

The Hong Kong government has been addressing the tax ramifications of the economic crisis of 2008 to 2010. The government has recognized that taxpayers have sought to reposition tax structures to respond to the economic crisis. Both taxpayers and governments have been changing their tax strategies in the current economy. These taxpayer strategies might include reinvoicing sales transactions to shift income to tax-haven jurisdictions and using an intangible holding company to shift profits from high-taxed jurisdictions to low-taxed jurisdictions. Taxpayers are seeking to remedy the shortfall the recession creates to maintain their after-tax revenues by shifting services income from one jurisdiction to another.

Taxpayers are becoming more aggressive in seeking tax relief because of the economic crisis, which is making it increasingly unlikely that businesses can meet stakeholder expectations. Companies, in turn, fear disappointing their stakeholders, but the economic crisis puts pressure on businesses to meet stakeholder expectations. Much of this pressure that companies feel is likely to be financial. Stakeholders place more pressure on the finance department and tax department in particular to achieve better financial results. Tax departments have been seeking to achieve better tax results by paying tax at a lower tax rate, subjecting the company to a lower tax base for which the company pays tax, shifting the income to a lower-tax jurisdiction, or shifting the income to a lower income tax category.

The governments face unpleasant choices. As a general matter, the government is also facing more pressure in response to the economic crisis. The government's revenue needs increase during the economic crises as citizens and residents place more demands on the government. Government revenues decline—especially sources of tax revenues that are based on income. The government faces more demands to cope with financial shortfall, and looks to businesses to fill the gap.

Governments are implementing various tax collection remedies in light of the shortfall. The remedies include:

- Increasing the frequency of tax audits
- Issuing more stringent tax regulations
- Hiring more knowledgeable tax auditors

- Becoming more suspicious of potential tax evaders
- Interfacing with foreign country tax collectors
- Imputing the shareholder's income or profits.

The Hong Kong government is applying each of these remedies, but in various degrees.

Conflicts are likely to increase between taxpayers and governments because of these conflicting objectives. Businesses seek to pay less in taxes, but governments seek to increase tax remedies. The conflict between taxpayers and governments increases because of the economic crisis—there are less tax revenues they can share. Governments and taxpayers have less to offer and have more to lose. Conflict resolution is not in the offing.

ABUSIVE TAX SCHEMES

The Hong Kong transfer pricing guidelines begin their attack on tax haven abuses with a disclaimer, recognizing that Hong Kong enterprises often utilize nonresident foreign corporations in the trade context. The government understands that the taxpayer might need to employ nonresident foreign corporations for business purposes. The guidelines further recognize that, in some jurisdictions, an enterprise's creation of an offshore entity corporation, such as a domestic equity joint venture company, might be the only way that a Hong Kong resident enterprise can do business in that jurisdiction. Such an investor or shareholder would have to become part of such an equity joint venture company.

With those exculpatory provisions aside, the Hong Kong transfer pricing guidelines recognize that while some nonresident corporations are legally structured without any hidden financial motive, some taxpayers create nonresident corporations with tax evasion or tax avoidance as their primary motivation. The guidelines provide such an example: Such a nonresident corporation keeps most of the profits. The enterprise pays a small portion of what is left to the Hong Kong enterprise. The tax scheme involves the creation of an "international business company," a term that the Hong Kong transfer pricing guidelines utilize for an enterprise often incorporated in a tax-free regime to which the enterprise diverts its profits.

The Hong Kong transfer pricing guidelines point out that enterprises employ a variety of devices to conceal transfers of money or other property to an international business company. The simplest method of diverting profit, according to the guidelines, is by sending skimmed income to the international business company's offshore account. Enterprises might be able to use other methods of transferring money offshore, including making use of payments disguised as deductible expenses, such as management fees, consultancy fees, commissions, royalties, and so forth. The enterprise makes these payments to the international business company that is operated from Hong Kong, in fact, but the enterprise structures the entity as being in a tax-haven jurisdiction.

TRANSFER PRICING SCHEMES

The Hong Kong transfer pricing guidelines point out that simple structures have led to more complex tax schemes and abusive arrangements:

- These entities have the tax advantage of claiming financial secrecy in some foreign jurisdictions.
- The availability of accounts that enterprises can open in offshore financial institutions exacerbates the situation.

The enterprise might interpose an international business company without any commercial reason, as are these tax schemes:

- The enterprise interposes the international business company to mark up the price on an alleged sale of goods by a third-party supplier. Then the international business company reinvoices the same goods to the Hong Kong enterprise at a still higher price.
- Alternatively, the enterprise interposes the international business company to mark down the price of an alleged purchase of goods from the Hong Kong enterprise. Then the Hong Kong enterprise sells the goods at market price.

The international business company can act as an intermediary that marks up the price during the transfer and then reinvoices the Hong Kong enterprise at a higher price. This scheme is known by a variety of names. This structure is called a transfer pricing scheme or a reinvoicing scheme.

The Hong Kong transfer pricing guidelines provide two examples, as described next.

Reinvoicing Example 1

An arrangement took place between Company HK, a resident of Hong Kong, and a nonresident entity (i.e., a nonresident company or a nonresident trust). The nonresident entity allegedly sold goods to Company HK, a resident in Hong Kong, at a price that is substantially above market price. Company HK declared profits from the sale of the goods. Nevertheless, the profits from these transactions were lower than the amount that Company HK would have derived if the Company HK purchased the goods directly from third-party purchases.

The arrangement, or the crucial parts of the arrangement, might be a sham. The nonresident entity did not incur any commercial risks and did not add any value to the goods it had purchased. The Hong Kong transfer pricing guidelines caution that the promoter or individuals in the nonresident entity operation in Hong Kong might be acting as agent in relation to that structure. The Hong Kong Revenue Department might apply provisions under section 20, section 61, and section 61A.

Reinvoicing Example 2

An arrangement took place between Company HK, a resident of Hong Kong, and a nonresident entity (i.e., a nonresident company or a nonresident trust). Company HK, a Hong Kong entity, allegedly sold goods to a Hong Kong nonresident at a price that is substantially below market price. The nonresident entity in turn allegedly sold the same goods to a third party at market price. Company HK declared its profits from the sale of goods, but the profits were lower than the amount that Company HK would have derived if it had sold the goods at market price to the third party.

The arrangement, or the crucial parts of the arrangement, might be a sham. The nonresident entity did not incur any commercial risks and did not add any value to the goods the nonresident entity had sold. The Hong Kong transfer pricing guidelines caution that the promoter or individuals in the non-resident entity operation in Hong Kong might be acting as agent in relation to that structure. The Hong Kong Revenue Department might apply provisions under section 20, section 61, and section 61A.

A nonresident person or a nonresident entity often appears in an abusing tax scheme to be the owner of the assets and profits. In fact, and in substance, true ownership belongs with the Hong Kong resident enterprise inside Hong Kong.

LACK OF "ECONOMICALLY SIGNIFICANT FUNCTIONS"

The Hong Kong transfer pricing guidelines suggest that the enterprise use the comparable uncontrolled price method to test the pricing of purchases or sales compared with tax haven reinvoicing companies that perform no "economically significant functions." The guidelines add that the paying for legal fees and other costs of implementing a tax avoidance scheme do not represent the performance of economically significant functions. In other words, Inland Revenue explains that the provision of legal fees and implementation costs provides no benefit or no value added to the ultimate third-party buyer.

HOW THE HONG KONG GOVERNMENT COMBATS ABUSIVE TAX SCHEMES

The Hong Kong Commissioner combats abusive tax schemes. The primary focus of the Commissioner is on the identification and investigation of tax schemes. Inland Revenue requires disclosure on the part of the taxpayer, including preparation of a statutory form specified by the Board of Inland Revenue under section 86 for the purposes of carrying into effect the provisions in Part IV relating to profits tax. The taxpayer must disclose these matters:

- Transactions for, or with, nonrelated persons (i.e., transactions conducted by agents for nonresident persons)
- Payments to nonresidents for the use of intellectual properties (i.e., payments subject to withholding tax)

- Payments to nonresidents for services rendered in Hong Kong
- Transactions with closely connected nonresident persons

The Hong Kong transfer pricing guidelines provide that the Hong Kong Commissioner can assess profits transferred to an international business company under section 14 or section 20A if the international business company is carrying on a trade or business in Hong Kong. The Commissioner also can assess profits transferred to a closely connected nonresident enterprise under section 20 to a Hong Kong resident enterprise as if the Hong Kong resident were the agent.

The Hong Kong transfer pricing guidelines provide that an enterprise can disregard the intermediary sale under section 61 if the sale is artificial or fictitious. In such an event, the Hong Kong resident enterprise will be assessed to determine its profits as if there had been no intermediary sale. The Hong Kong Commissioner can counteract the tax benefit accrued to the Hong Kong enterprise under the tax scheme. Hong Kong tax authorities have the discretionary power given to an Assistant Commissioner under section 61A(2).

The Hong Kong Commissioner interposed the activities of an international business corporation to counteract the substantial reduction in profits tax liability the corporation created as to a Hong Kong company. Judge Chua in *Asia Master Limited v. CIR*,[1] at the Court of First Instance, was of the opinion that the Commissioner acted legally in applying section 61 and section 61A in that situation in assessing the profits tax liability of the Hong Kong entity. In *CIR v. Ewig Industries Co. Ltd.*,[2] the District Court disagreed with this approach the Commissioner followed to counteract this type of tax avoidance.

EXTREME FORMS OF TAX ABUSE

The Hong Kong transfer pricing guidelines address an extreme form of abusive tax schemes (i.e., where the representations of the international business companies could be entirely fictitious). As an example of such a scheme, a Hong Kong resident might record in its accounts transactions with an international business company. In fact, such an international business company has no charter or registration to operate anywhere, and the international business company has no activity in any jurisdiction. The international business company is merely a cybercompany or a legal fiction.

DISTINGUISHING TAX AVOIDANCE FROM TAX EVASION

The Hong Kong transfer pricing guidelines provide that these tax scheme activities are clearly subject to the Inland Revenue Ordinance. The Commissioner can establish tax evasion if she can establish the taxpayers' dishonesty or willful intent regarding this tax scheme. The Hong Kong transfer pricing guidelines suggest that taxpayers, when completing a profits return, should make a full and frank disclosure of all material facts relating to the computation of assessable profits in order to avoid the invocation of any penal provisions.

The success of a tax avoidance scheme might be dependent on the Commissioner never finding out the true facts. In that event, such a scheme is more likely to be one of "evasion" rather than "avoidance." Two cases explain the distinction between avoidance and evasion: *R v. Mears*[3] and *Denver Chemical Manufacturing Company v. COT.*[4]

HOW THE REINVOICING STRUCTURE OPERATES

Typically there are three components to the reinvoicing structure: the manufacturer, the offshore intermediary, and the distributor. All of these entities are related to each other in a tax sense. In extreme situations, the taxpayer might seek to hide this intercompany relationship from the taxing authorities, often a central ingredient to a transfer pricing inquiry:

1. **Manufacturer.** The manufacturing entity typically is located in a high-taxed jurisdiction, producing the goods in question. The manufacturer then sells the goods to the offshore intermediary at an artificially low price. The manufacturer taxes its profits a normal rate of tax for that jurisdiction, but the revenues to the government are small as the manufacturer, having received a low price for the goods, receives little income.
2. **Offshore intermediary.** The offshore intermediary purchases the products from the manufacturing entity at this artificially low price. Then the offshore intermediary sells the products to the distributor entity at an artificially high price. The offshore entity performs few, if any, functions. The offshore entity receives a more than proportionate share of the company's total income, but it pays little, if any, tax in that tax haven jurisdiction.
3. **Distributor.** The distributor, often located in a high-taxed jurisdiction, purchases the products from the offshore intermediary at an artificially high price. The distributor then sells the goods to retail customers at a normal price. The distributor pays its taxes at the normal rate at that jurisdiction, but the government receives little income as the distributor itself receives little income because of the high price it paid for the goods.

Let us consider the cumulative effect of this reinvoicing structure:

- The manufacturer pays little tax. The manufacturer pays at normal tax rate, but, because the income itself is small, the manufacturer has little tax to pay.
- The offshore entity in a tax haven pays little if any tax. The offshore entity has a high income but is not subject to tax in the tax haven.
- The distributor pays little tax. The purchaser pays tax at normal tax rate, but, because the income itself is small, the distributor has little tax to pay.
- The net effect of this reinvoicing structure—taking into account the manufacturer, the offshore entity, and the distributor—is very low tax.

Let us now quantify the reinvoicing fact pattern situation generally, rather than examining Hong Kong specifically. In this fact pattern:

- The manufacturer's jurisdiction imposes a 40% tax rate.
- The offshore jurisdiction imposes a 0% tax rate.
- The distributor's jurisdiction imposes a 35% tax rate.

The group allocates its combined income subject to tax in this manner:

- The manufacturer receives 15% of the combined income subject to tax.
- The offshore entity receives 75% of the combined income subject to tax.
- The distributor receives 10% of the combined income subject to tax.
- The group splits up 100% of the combined income subject to tax.

The cumulative effective tax rate for the reinvoicing example is:

- For the manufacturer: 40% × 15% = 6%
- For the tax haven: 0% × 75% = 0%
- For the distributor: 35% × 10% = 3.5%
- Cumulative tax effect: 6% + 0% + 3.5% = 9.5% effective tax rate

SHIFTING INTANGIBLE PROPERTY: THE TAX PERSPECTIVE

Owners having intangible property might move their intangible property among jurisdictions to claim their own tax advantages, transferring the intangible property to an offshore tax-haven jurisdiction.

Tax collectors, though, are becoming wise to manufacturers' tax-shifting techniques for intangibles.

An owner's transfer of intangible property is often complex, as the transfer involves the interplay of diverse professional tax specialties that address:

- The *transfers* of intangible property between political jurisdictions
- The *direction* of the intangible property transfer
- The *amount* of the intangible property transfer
- Reliance on *related-party contracts* to ascertain intangible property transfers
- Reliance on *economic facets* to ascertain the substance of the intangible property transfers

An owner's first step in structuring the intangible property transfers is to consider various alternatives:

- Licensing agreements, most often reflected as royalty agreements
- Product sales, including changes in price to reflect the intangible property transfer

- Service contracts, including the providing of services as part of the intangible property transfer
- Outright sales of the intangible property

It is important for the owner of the intangible to consider the various roles tax professionals and other professionals play in intangible property transfers, with each of the next parties being "players":

- Legal counsel, who provides an understanding of the patents and contractual arrangements
- Economists, who provide information as to the economic reality of the situation and provide comparative data analysis
- Accountants, who provide record keeping and compliance with government directives
- Tax professionals, who view themselves as uniquely positioned to *value* an intellectual property transfer and as intermediaries among other professionals

Governments are now becoming wise to taxpayer attempts to shift intangible income from one jurisdiction to another. Governments, Hong Kong included, will look at the economic realities of the transfer. Governments are challenging transfer pricing objectives and are:

- Changing their tax audit techniques
- Broadening their audit horizons from local to bilateral to multilateral
- Increasing their databases: transferring databases from government to government, developing common tax audit standards
- Increasing their own knowledge of company transfer pricing aversion techniques and anti–permanent establishment techniques

Taxpayers, despite the governments' increased awareness, are using intangible holding companies to shift profits from intangible property from high-taxed jurisdictions to low-taxed jurisdictions. An enterprise can theoretically set up an intangible holding company in a tax-haven jurisdiction. The ultimate owners of the intangible holding company might use this ownership structure by making use of bank secrecy structures.

These taxpayers might seek to employ such an intangible holding company structure. Here is an example in which holding company structure might work:

- The business creates an offshore related-party entity.
- The business shifts the intangible to the offshore entity.
- The business in a high-taxed country pays a royalty to the company in the tax haven that owns the intangible.
- The business, being in a high-tax jurisdiction, obtains a deduction for the royalty it pays to the tax-haven entity.
- The owner of the intangible, not being in a high-tax jurisdiction, pays little tax when it receives the intangible.

The owner of the intangible might consider the following legal and tax issues that impact the use of the holding company structure. This issue of entitlement to income of the intangible is itself complex, including the legal and licensing issues in the country in which the business does business and in the tax haven in which the enterprise is now located.

Transfer pricing provisions expand the intellectual property concepts. The U.S. transfer pricing regulations apply the more specific intellectual property approach:

- The tax collector can seek "economic substance," which might transcend the contract itself.
- The tax collector can impute the contractual terms where these terms are not part of the contractual agreement, saying "You must have meant that."
- The tax collector can impose a principle on the taxpayer that the alternatives be "realistic alternatives."
- The tax collector can attribute income to the intangible property.
- The tax collector can embed contributions within contractual terms.

NOTES

1. *Asia Master Limited v. CIR*, 7 HKTC 25.
2. *CIR v. Ewig Industries Co. Ltd.*, DCTC 7883/2005.
3. *R v. Mears*, 37 ATR 321 at p. 323.
4. *Denver Chemical Manufacturing Company v. COT*, 4 AITR 216 at p. 222.

10

CHAPTER TEN

Winning Hong Kong's Landmark Transfer Pricing Case

HONG KONG had its first transfer pricing case, *Ngai Lik Electronics Company Limited v. the Hong Kong Commissioner of Inland Revenue*,[1] in 2008. This case sheds light on Hong Kong's judicial process in the transfer pricing context. Most importantly, the case examines sourcing and agency issues before the court addresses transfer pricing issues. We can expect the taxpayer and the Hong Kong Commissioner of Inland Revenue to continue to square off in the years to come.

NGAI LIK LITIGATION

The case at bar has had many gyrations, both in the Hong Kong administrative tax system and in the courts. The Hong Kong Commissioner of Inland Revenue brought an assessment against taxpayer, Ngai Lik Electronics Co. Limited, for five taxable years, 1991–1992 through 1995–1996. The taxpayer contested the Inland Revenue assessment before the Board of Review. The Board dismissed the taxpayer's appeal but stated a case on a question of law for the Court of First Instance in this way: "Whether, on the facts bound by the Board, the Board erred in law by concluding that the Taxpayer and the other participants in the Scheme entered into or carried out the Scheme for the dominant purpose of enabling the Taxpayer to obtain a tax benefit?"

The Court of First Instance dismissed the taxpayer's appeal, and the case went before the Court of Appeal. The Court of Appeal then rejected the taxpayer's appeal,[2] and the taxpayer brought an appeal before the Court of Final Appeal. The Court of Final Appeal allowed the taxpayer's appeal, thus annulling the Commissioner's additional assessments.[3]

HONG KONG'S ADVANCE RULING DETERMINATIONS

The Government of the Hong Kong Special Administrative Region began issuing substantive advance ruling case results in 2000. Hong Kong's Inland Revenue Department issues these advance ruling case results infrequently—approximately four ruling cases per year. Many of these cases address the Inland Revenue Department's taxability of business profits, often together with the department's treatment of expense allocation and transfer pricing. The Inland Revenue Department does disclose the company subject to its review and changes the facts before issuing the rulings to the public. Nevertheless, certain advance ruling determinations may be applicable to the case at bar.

HONG KONG ISSUES TRANSFER PRICING GUIDELINES

The Inland Revenue of Hong Kong issued its "Transfer Pricing Guidelines—Methodologies and Related Issues" in December 2009. Inland Revenue formulated this approach as Departmental Interpretation and Practice Note No. 46. The Hong Kong Special Administrative Region (SAR) issued the transfer pricing guidelines for the information of taxpayers and their tax representatives, thus suggesting that Inland Revenue had preserved other nonpublic advice for the tax collector itself. Nevertheless, the guidelines were exceedingly clear regarding abusive tax schemes and the remedies to these schemes the Hong Kong Inland Revenue would pursue. These guidelines contain the Inland Revenue Department's interpretations and practices in relation to Hong Kong's transfer pricing law as this law stood at date of publication in December 2009.

The Hong Kong December 2009 transfer pricing guidelines follow closely the Organisation for Economic Co-operation and Development (OECD) *Transfer Pricing Guidelines for Multinational Enterprises and Tax Administrations*, as revised earlier in 2009. Inland Revenue has not provided guidance as to whether it will follow the extensive revisions to the OECD *Transfer Pricing Guidelines* promulgated July 22, 2010,[4] including the elevation of the transactional profit split method.[5] The audit practice followed by the Inland Revenue Department, in general, does not differ from the transfer pricing methodologies recommended in the OECD guidelines. Nevertheless, there are significant issues of departure from the OECD guidelines and the Hong Kong guidelines, even with the 2009 OECD guidelines.

Five differences apply between the OECD *Transfer Pricing Guidelines* and the Hong Kong transfer pricing guidelines.[6] The Hong Kong transfer pricing guidelines:

1. Expand the documentation provisions
2. Expand the services provisions
3. Narrow the permanent establishment provisions, compared to the permanent establishment approach in other countries, such as India
4. Greatly expand the anti–tax evasion process
5. Greatly expand the profit split methods

STATUTORY PROVISIONS

The Commissioner of Inland Revenue assessed the taxpayer based on section 61A of the Hong Kong Inland Revenue Ordinance, which provides a remedy to the Commissioner to counter tax avoidance. The ordinance divides section 61A into three parts:

1. Subsection (1) contains both a benefits test and a purpose test:
   - The benefits test would negate "the effect of conferring a tax benefit."
   - The purpose test looks to "the sole or dominant purpose" to obtain a tax benefit.
   - Subsection (1) enumerates seven listed transactions, discussed later.
2. Subsection (2) provides the administrative procedures an assistant commissioner is to follow against the taxpayer.
3. Subsection (3) defines the terms "tax benefit" and "transaction":
   - The term "tax benefit" means the avoidance or postponement of the liability to pay tax or the reduction in the amount thereof.
   - The term "transaction" includes a transaction, operation, or scheme, whether or not such transaction, operation, or scheme is enforceable, or intended to be enforceable, by legal proceedings.

Section 61A(1) enumerates these seven listed transactions to which the Commissioner is to undertake scrutiny:

1. The manner in which the transaction was entered into or carried out
2. The form and substance of the transaction
3. The result, in relation to the operation of this ordinance that, but for this section, would have been achieved by the transaction
4. Any change in the financial position of the relevant person that has resulted, will result, or may reasonably be expected to result from the transaction
5. Any change in the financial position of any person who has, or has had, any connection (whether of a business, family, or other nature) with the relevant person, being a change that has resulted or may reasonably be expected to result from the transaction

6. Whether the transaction has created rights or obligations that would not normally be created between persons dealings with each other at arm's length under a transaction of the kind in question
7. The participation in the transaction of a corporation resident or carrying on business outside Hong Kong.

DETERMINATION BY THE COURT OF FINAL APPEAL

The Court of Final Appeal reached a unanimous determination, reversing the Court of Appeal's decision against the Commissioner.

Justice Ribeiro, in his determination of the case before the Court of Final Appeal as to the interpretation of section 61A to the facts of this case, concluded that three conditions need apply before the Commissioner can exercise her power under section 61A(2) to provide an additional assessment against the taxpayer. These three interlocking conditions are the transaction, the tax benefit, and the dominant purpose:

1. The presence of "a transaction," broadly defined to include an operation or scheme, having been entered into.
2. Such transaction has the effect of conferring a tax benefit on the relevant person—that is, on the taxpayer against whom the section has been invoked—or the transaction would have had but for this section the effect of conferring a tax benefit on the relevant person (i.e., on the taxpayer against whom the section has been invoked).
3. Viewing the transaction through the prism of the seven matters enumerated in section 61A(1)(a) to section 61A(1)(g), it would objectively be included that the transaction was entered into or carried out for the sole or dominant purpose of enabling the taxpayer to obtain a tax benefit.

Justice Ribeiro would have the Commissioner identify "with some precision" the taxpayer's tax benefit. The Commissioner can then examine the transaction in light of the seven enumerated matters to determine whether its sole or dominant purpose is to enable the taxpayer to obtain a tax benefit.

Barrie Barlow represented the taxpayer. Mr. Barlow argued that section 61A was inapplicable to the case at bar because the scheme created no "tax benefit." Ambrose Ho and Joyce Leung, representing the Commissioner, sought to uphold the additional assessments.

THE COMMISSIONER'S DETERMINATION

The Commissioner formulated the scheme as consisting of eight steps:

1. The taxpayer acquired the three British Virgin Island (BVI) companies in around August 1991 to March 1992.

2. Mr. Lam sold Shing Wai Company's business to Shing Wai Co. Limited. in around April 1991.
3. Madame Ting sold Din Wai's business to Din Wai Electronics Limited in around September 1991.
4. The taxpayer set up Ngai Wai Plastic Manufacturing Limited to share Shing Wai Co. Limited's workload in manufacturing parts.
5. The taxpayer executed these master supply agreements:
   - Between Din Wai Electronics Limited and the taxpayer
   - Between Din Wai Electronics Limited and Shing Wai Co. Limited
   - Between Din Wai Electronics Limited and Ngai Wai Plastic Manufacturing Limited
6. The Commissioner treated these mentioned arrangements as being effective April 1, 1992.
7. The parties executed these representative and service agreements:
   - Between Din Wai Electronics Limited and the taxpayer
   - Between Shing Wai Limited and the taxpayer
   - Between Ngai Wai Plastic Manufacturing Limited and the taxpayer
8. The taxpayer adopted this transfer pricing policy after the taxpayer shifted business to the BVI companies:
   - The pricing reflects the setting of the sale price of the finished goods from Din Wai Electronics Limited to the taxpayer.
   - The parties reflect goods sold from Wai Electronics Limited to the taxpayer, reflecting actual quantities of goods ordered and delivered.
   - The parties reflect the granting of additional bulk discounts from Shing Wai Limited and Ngai Wai Plastic Manufacturing Limited to Din Wai Electronics after year-end.

DETERMINATION BY THE BOARD OF REVIEW

The Board of Review accepted the Commissioner's formulation of the scheme and described the tax benefit in this manner: "The effect of the Scheme was to reduce the amount of the profits (manufacturing and trading) of the taxpayer." The scheme reduced the amount of the profits allocated to Din Wai Electronics Limited through Din Wai Electronics Limited to Shing Wai, to Ngai Wai Plastic Manufacturing Limited, and to Shing Wai Limited. The whole of the profits thus allocated would not be taxable to the taxpayer. The scheme had the result of conferring a tax benefit on the taxpayer by reason of the reduction in the amount of the tax as a result of the allocation. The Board of Review concluded that dominant purpose of the taxpayer "and of other participants in the Scheme, was to enable the taxpayer to obtain a tax benefit."

DETERMINATION BY THE COURT OF FIRST INSTANCE

Judge Reyes, speaking for the Court of First Instance, acknowledged that, insofar as the manufacturing profits of Din Wai Electronics Limited, Shing Wai Limited, and

Ngai Wai Plastic Manufacturing Limited arose offshore, these profits were not taxable in Hong Kong. Nevertheless, Judge Reyes upheld the decision by the Board of Review on the basis of findings that:

- The taxpayer had engaged in manufacturing-related activities.
- The pricing mechanism operated by the taxpayer and Din Wai Electronics did not result in arm's length prices being paid by the taxpayer.
- This operated to allocate some of Ngai Lik's assessable profits to Din Wai Electronics, and these profits "could be spread around" through the price setting and discount arrangement between Din Wai Electronics on one hand and on Shing Wai, Shing Wai Limited, and Ngai Wai Plastic Manufacturing Limited on the other hand.

Judge Reyes also took into account the Board's finding in relation to the agency agreements that the 5% that the taxpayer was entitled to charge thereunder "was not enough to cover even the costs of Ngai Lik's disbursements on behalf of the other companies." Judge Reyes stated that "but for the scheme involving after the fact price-setting by accountants, arbitrary additional discounts and low management fees, Ngai Lik's assessable profits (and thus its liability to profits tax) would have been greater." But for the scheme, Ngai Lik presumably would have been charged a lower price (reflecting market profit) for goods supplied by Din Wai Electronics. It would also have earned higher fees for the manufacturing-related services that it provided to the BVI companies. Judge Reyes concluded that the Board of Review was entitled to reach a conclusion that the dominant purpose of the scheme was to enable the taxpayer to obtain a tax benefit.

DETERMINATION BY THE COURT OF APPEAL

The Court of Appeal reviewed the opinion reached by the Court of First Instance. The appellate court had a three-judge panel consisting of Judges Le Pichon, Stone, and Chu. Le Pichon issued an opinion to the case at bar, to which Stone and Chu agreed. The court noted that the Ngai Lik group carried out all of its manufacturing work in mainland China by the three BVI companies. Nevertheless, the taxpayer Ngai Lik Electronics Company Limited had on its payroll a small staff that would order materials as an agent for Shing Wai and Ngai Wai Plastic. The taxpayer had on its payroll a team for sourcing materials on behalf of Din Wai Electronics.

The Court of Appeal noted that the taxpayer prepared and processed purchase orders in Hong Kong. The taxpayer had a storage area for goods and purchased raw materials. If the taxpayer had the goods and raw materials delivered in Hong Kong, the taxpayer would transport the goods and raw materials by trucks owned by the group. The taxpayer made periodic remittances to manufacturing subsidiaries associated to local government corporations.

Based on these mentioned facts, the Court of Appeal upheld the Board of Review's finding that the taxpayer continued its substantial involvement in manufacturing even after the taxpayer relocated the group's production facilities to the mainland in 1987. That substantial involvement gave rise to a "manufacturing element in the taxpayer's profits." Judge Le Pichon thought the taxpayer had reflected this manufacturing element in its financial statements prepared prior to the reorganization.

The Court of Appeal focused on adoption and application of the taxpayer's transfer pricing policy and on the derisory level of management fees, not to mention their nonpayment as between the taxpayer and Din Wai Company. Judge Le Pichon considered the above-mentioned matters to be features of the scheme that did not arise from dealings at arm's length and cannot be explained as a means of minimizing the taxpayer's taxable income. Judge Le Pichon held that it was unnecessary for section 61A purposes to quantify the tax benefit; nevertheless, Judge Le Pichon considered that these facts demonstrated the section 61A benefit: The taxpayer's contribution to the profits of the group dropped from 31.19% in 1991–1992 to 7.19% in 1995–1996. At the same time, the profitability of Shing Wai Hong Kong and the three BVI companies rose accordingly.

Judge Le Pichon then addressed the dominant purpose of the transaction, stating that the scheme was replete with features designed to enable the taxpayer to manipulate and shift its income offshore to its fellow subsidiaries. At the very heart of the scheme was the free hand to rewrite the acquisition cost after the event on an annual basis. The dealings between the taxpayer on one hand and Shing Wai Hong Kong and the three BVI companies on the other hand plainly were not at arm's length. There was a total absence of any commercial reason or other legitimate reason for the transaction. Accordingly, it is hardly surprising that the Board of Review, having considered the various matters set out in section 61A(1), came to the conclusion that "the dominant purpose" of the taxpayer was to confer a tax benefit on the taxpayer.

THE CASE BEFORE THE COURT OF FINAL APPEAL

According to the Court of Final Appeal, the central feature of the tax benefit, as characterized by the Board of Review, was that it had the effect of reducing the amount of the tax payable by the taxpayer by reducing the amount of the profits, both manufacturing and trading, to the taxpayer by the amounts allocated to Din Wai Electronics Limited and through Din Wai Electronics Limited to Shing Wai Co. Limited, to Ngai Wai Plastic Manufacturing Limited, and to Shing Wai Limited.

The Court of Final Appeal sought to identify the scheme, as formulated, with the tax benefit, as so identified. The Court of Final Appeal examined the eight points of the scheme, as formulated by the Commissioner. The Court narrowed significantly the scope of the scheme: "It is obvious that Items (1) to (7) of the Scheme merely give an account of certain steps taken in the reorganization of the taxpayer's business. They do not, in themselves, produce any tax benefit. The Commissioner's case depends on Item (8) of the Scheme" (i.e., the adoption of the transfer pricing policy). The Court of Final Appeal, then, vitiates the heart of the scheme, the use of BVI corporations for mainland operations.

The Board of Review interpreted these facets of the scheme, as conferred by three facets of the taxpayer's transfer pricing policy after the company transferred the business to the BVI companies, per Item 8:

1. The annual exercise of setting the sale price of finished goods from Din Wai Electronics Limited to the taxpayer
2. The number of goods sold from Din Wai Electronics Limited to the taxpayer only recorded in actual quantities of goods ordered and delivered
3. The granting of additional bulk discounts from Shing Wai Limited/Ngai Lik Industrial Holdings to Din Wai Electronics Limited after year-end

DEFICIENCIES IN THE SCHEME AS TO ADDITIONAL ANNUAL BULK DISCOUNTS RECEIVED BY DIN WAI ELECTRONICS LIMITED

The Court of Final Appeal examined the ramifications concerning additional annual bulk discounts as to the tax benefit. Writing for the Court, Justice Ribeiro held that the providing of additional annual bulk discounts "clearly lacks any connection with the Tax Benefit." As formulated by the Commissioner, Ngai Lik's tax benefit was the reduction of the taxpayer's profits by the amount allocated to Din Wai Electronics Limited. The objectionable amount is the price-fixing mechanism that Din Wai Electronics Limited and the taxpayer adopted. The thrust of the Commissioner's complaint is that this price-shifting mechanism enabled the taxpayer to pay to Din Wai Electronics an inflated price for the finished goods, resulting in a corresponding reduction of the taxpayer's taxable income. The taxpayer allocated the profits to Din Wai Electronics Limited, which was outside the purview of the Hong Kong tax authorities. The taxpayer allocated profits away from Ngai Lik, which was taxable in Hong Kong.

The Court of Final Appeal then concluded that the additional annual discount amounts given to Shing Wai (Hong Kong), Shing Wai Limited, and Ngai Wai Plastic Manufacturing Limited to Din Wai Electronics Limited, as referred to Item 8(c) of the scheme, involved different transactions between different parties. The additional annual discounts, according to the Court of Final Appeal, had no impact at all on the taxpayer's profits or its liability to tax. The Court views that the effect of the additional annual discount amounts was to diminish the profits of Shing Wai (Hong Kong), Shing Wai Limited, and Ngai Wai Plastic Manufacturing Limited and to swell the profits of Din Wai Electronics Limited. The Commissioner has viewed the shifting as being artificial. In contrast, the Court of Final Appeal viewed the additional annual discount amounts as having no connection with the tax benefit conferred on the taxpayer by the pricing mechanism and that the Commissioner should not have included the additional annual discount amounts in the scheme.

The Court of Final Appeal then returned to the Board of Review's formulation to consider whether such additional annual discount amounts were the means by which the taxpayer "allocated" profits to Din Wai Electronics Limited, and through Din

Wai Electronics Limited to Shing Wai (Hong Kong), Ngai Wai Plastic Manufacturing Limited, and Shing Wai Limited.

Judge Reyes, writing for the Court of First Instance, had commented that "the profits allocated to Din Wai Electronics as a result of the price-setting mechanism could be spread around among Shing Wai and Ngai Wai Plastic." Judge Le Pichon, writing for the Court of Appeal, commented that the scheme "was replete with features designed to enable the taxpayer's assessable profits to be manipulated and shifted offshore to its fellow subsidiaries."

The Court of Final Appeal commented that the last suggestion is inconsistent with the self-evident effect of the additional discounts, as found by the Board of Review. The other fellow subsidiaries gave these additional discounts to Ngai Wai Plastic Manufacturing Limited. The Court of Final Appeal concluded these additional discounts did not involve Din Wai Electronics passing on to these fellow subsidiaries any amounts that the taxpayer should have declared as part of its taxable profits. The flow of finance was in the opposite direction. The effect of the additional discounts was to diminish the profits of those other fellow subsidiaries and to augment Din Wai Electronics' profits.

Ambrose Ho, representing Hong Kong's Department of Justice, accepted that Item 8(c) of the scheme is irrelevant. Further, aspects of Items (1) through (7), which address the formation of Shing Wai, Shing Wai Limited, and Ngai Wai Plastic and the agreements among those companies, and between those companies, are also irrelevant.

DEFICIENCIES IN THE SCHEME AS TO MANUFACTURING PROFITS

The tax benefit, as contended by the Commissioner, involves the allegation that the effect of the scheme was to reduce the amount of the profits, both the taxpayer's manufacturing income and the taxpayer's trading income, by the amounts that the taxpayer allocated to Din Wai Electronics Limited and through Din Wai Electronics Limited to Shing Wai, to Ngai Wai Plastic Manufacturing Limited, and to Shing Wai Limited. Justice Ribeiro, writing for the Court of Final Appeal, expressed his puzzlement regarding a reference to manufacturing profits in the Commissioner's contention. Justice Ribeiro commented that Item 8(a) and Item 8(b) can be readily understood to be an alleged reduction in the taxpayer's trading profits resulting from the annual price-fixing mechanism but questioned whether that taxpayer had any manufacturing profits to allocate.

Justice Ribeiro continued his attack on the concept that the taxpayer allocated manufacturing profits, stating that if the taxpayer did indeed have manufacturing profits from the source, the scheme does not identify any transaction conferring a tax benefit as to such profits. In contrast, the Commissioner alleged a scheme with a tax benefit that involves manipulation of the prices at which Din Wai Electronics Limited sold the goods to the taxpayer (i.e., transactions that affect the taxpayer's trading profits standing alone).

Justice Ribeiro commented that the Commissioner's reference to manufacturing profits is not a mere slip of the pen. The Board of Review had laid heavy emphasis on the taxpayer earning such manufacturing profits in Hong Kong. The Board took the view that the Commissioner was justified in making the additional adjustments unless the taxpayer could show that it could allocate more than 50% of these profits to its fellow subsidiaries operating on the mainland.

The Board of Review, in addressing the issue of manufacturing profits, noted that, before the scheme, the taxpayer included manufacturing as part of the taxpayer's business. The Board cited the taxpayer's financial statements for the 1988–1990 through 1990–1991 tax years. In contrast, the company treated the entire income (manufacturing income and trading income) as subject to Hong Kong taxation for 1988–1989 and 1989–1990. The taxpayer claimed that slightly more than half of its profits, 50.6%, for 1990–1991 were offshore and not taxable. The taxpayer did much to earn the manufacturing profits in Hong Kong prior to effectuation of the scheme. Since the taxpayer effectuated the scheme, the taxpayer still did much to earn the manufacturing profits allocated to Shing Wai and to the three BVI companies, doing so in Hong Kong.

Hong Kong Inland Revenue's Interpretation and Practice Notes No. 21 generally provided for a 50–50 split as to manufacturing income and trading income but permitted a taxpayer to exclude more than 50% in limited circumstances. The Board of Review, commenting on the case at bar, stated that unless the taxpayer could make good claim for apportionment, which it could make as to 50% of the manufacturing profits as being offshore profits, the best it could hope for was a 50–50 apportionment under the Revenue's Departmental Interpretation and Practice Notes No. 21.

Justice Ribeiro concluded that the Board of Review's approach regarding the 50–50 split as to manufacturing income and trading income directly relates to the manner in which the Commissioner determined the additional tax assessment (i.e., by purporting to treat half of the manufacturing profits of the taxpayer's fellow subsidiaries on the mainland as the taxpayer's profits arising in Hong Kong). Justice Ribeiro then concluded that it is necessary to examine the suggestion that the taxpayer earned such manufacturing profits as a matter of substance.

Section 14 of the Inland Revenue Ordinance provides that the profits of a business that arise offshore are not taxed in Hong Kong, a well-established principle not in dispute. This exemption applies when the taxpayer carries on a business in Hong Kong so long as the profits in question derive from its operations abroad. Section 14(1) of the Inland Revenue Ordinance looks to taxable income "arising in or derived from Hong Kong." Judicial decisions have accepted this allocation approach. Judge Lord Bridge of Harwich noted in *CIR v. Hang Seng Bank Ltd.*[7] that the structure of the section presupposes that the profits of a business may accrue from different sources, some located within Hong Kong, others overseas. Activities in Hong Kong are taxable; the other activities are not taxed in Hong Kong.

Judge Lord Bridge of Harwich noted in *CIR v. Hang Seng Bank Ltd.* that the taxpayer may ensure that the local and offshore businesses are clearly separated by ensuring that the separate businesses of the overseas branch are carried out by a separate company or subsidiary company. Justice Ribeiro commented that this separate entity structure should be borne in mind when considering the respective activities in Hong Kong and its fellow subsidiaries on the mainland.

The Court of Final Appeal, through Justice Ribeiro, then reviewed the source rule issues impacting the case at bar. After the reorganization in 1987, the taxpayer operated manufacturing businesses in the mainland. Din Wai Electronics Limited then sold the finished products to the taxpayer. The taxpayer then sold the finished products to its customers. Justice Ribeiro concluded that "it cannot be in doubt that the relevant manufacturing processes took place outside of Hong Kong." Justice Ribeiro further commented that the profits from these operations would not be chargeable to Hong Kong since the taxpayer would source these activities offshore.

Justice Ribeiro viewed source rules as being a country-by-country determination. Moreover, it is clear that those operations and "those profits were not those of the taxpayer but of its fellow subsidiaries." Those profits were then not within the purview of section 14. The Board of Review's focus was on sourcing and agency activities:

- The taxpayer's activities undertaken in connection with the sourcing of raw materials for use by its fellow subsidiaries in the manufacturing process
- The taxpayer's activities undertaken in connection with other agency services the taxpayer provides

The Board of Review thought that the taxpayer's involvement in the sourcing activity and the agency activity meant that the taxpayer continued to have a manufacturing business and that the taxpayer should treat half of such manufacturing business as arising offshore. Thus, the Board equated the taxpayer's sourcing and agency activities with an involvement in manufacturing. Justice Ribeiro rejected outright the concept that the taxpayer continued to be involved in manufacturing, reaching that conclusion despite the fact that the taxpayer had teams for ordering materials and for sourcing materials as agent, preparing and processing purchasing orders, and had representative and services agreements. Instead, Justice Ribeiro viewed the above-mentioned activities as being trading transactions.

Justice Ribeiro acknowledged that the above-mentioned activities could be described as "involving manufacturing" or as Judge Reyes, speaking for the Court of First Instance, described as "manufacturing-related activities," these activities were at most "ancillary and incidental" to the offshore manufacturing operations. The manufacturing profits arose only on the disposal of the manufactured goods, but the presence of such incidental activities does not provide the basis for locating profits in Hong Kong. Justice Ribeiro viewed the activities as being antecedent activities, activities that do not meet the legal test to determine the source of profits.

Nevertheless, Justice Ribeiro acknowledged that sourcing and agency activities might give rise to taxable income. In this regard, Justice Ribeiro focused on the services incurred pursuant to the representative and service agreements, and according to Judge Le Pichon, was set at a derisory level and was frequently unpaid. Justice Ribeiro then commented that the Commissioner did not identify the underpayment of management or service fees either as part of the scheme or as part of the tax benefit, nor did the Commissioner seek to counteract any tax benefit the taxpayer received for undercharging its sourcing and agency services. Justice Ribeiro viewed the references to the Board of Review and courts below as being "wide of the mark."

DEFICIENCIES IN THE SCHEME AS TO THE RELEVANT YEARS OF ASSESSMENT

Justice Ribeiro challenged timing issues connected to section 61A. The scheme itself connotes the transfer of activities taking place in April 1993 to BVI companies and the adoption of the transfer pricing after the transfer of the BVI companies, meaning that the starting point as to the objectionable transactions took place after April 1993. The Commissioner cannot prevail as to 1991–1992 and 1992–1993 from a time standpoint.

ARE THE SCHEME AND THE TAX BENEFIT STILL VIABLE BASES FOR SECTION 61A ASSESSMENTS?

Justice Ribeiro concluded that the Board of Review's formulation of the scheme and benefit suffered from three serious deficiencies:

1. Item 8(c) of the scheme, relating to annual discounts, is irrelevant.
2. There is no basis for including manufacturing profits as part of the taxpayer's profits, whether in terms of profits deriving from the manufacturer in Hong Kong or by passing along profits to fellow subsidiaries or the profits of the taxpayer's sourcing of agency in Hong Kong.
3. There were timing issues relating to 1991–1992 and to 1992–1993.

Justice Ribeiro then raised two questions:

1. Is there a conceptually viable section 61A scheme if these deficiencies are stripped away from the Board's formulation of the scheme and the tax benefit?
2. Is the Commissioner permitted as a matter of law to proceed on the basis of a pared-down scheme?

Justice Ribeiro concluded affirmatively to the first inquiry, suggesting that Items 8(a) and 8(b) remain, and the tax benefit remains after deleting all references to manufacturing profits and to allocation of profits. This would leave the contention, which, according to Justice Ribeiro, was "always the heart of the case," that the price-fixing arrangement with Din Wai Electronics Limited had the effect of conferring on the taxpayer a tax benefit involving a reduction of taxable income.

Justice Ribeiro then addressed the second inquiry, suggesting that such a de facto amendment is possible providing the amendment is consistent with the findings of the Board of Review, meets the statutory definitions, and does not create unfairness to the taxpayer. Justice Ribeiro viewed this truncated approach as permitting the Commissioner to put the case in alternative ways. Section 61A(2)(a) permits the Commissioner to fashion her assessment as a response to "any part of" a transaction caught by any provision.

IS THERE A "TAX BENEFIT" WITHIN THE MEANING OF SECTION 61A?

Counsel for the taxpayer, Barrie Barlow, contended that, even if the Court strips away the "earlier irrelevances," there was no "tax benefit" within the meaning of section 61A. Mr. Barlow characterized the price-fixing arrangement as being "gratuitous payments" enabling the taxpayer to overstate the cost of acquiring the finished products and therefore to make "unjustified deductions" against the profits arising from their sale to customers. The taxpayer, then, according to Mr. Barlow's approach, understated its taxable income.

Justice Ribeiro rejected Mr. Barlow's approach as to the "gratuitous payments" and "unjustified deductions," suggesting that the payments are not gratuitous payments but reflect payments made in return for goods ordered and delivered. Further, Justice Ribeiro did not accept that such payments were "impermissible deductions." In addition, Justice Ribeiro concluded that excessive prices do not necessarily lead to the disallowance of deductions.

Section 16 of the Inland Revenue Ordinance permits the taxpayer to deduct expenditures to the extent that the taxpayer incurs these expenditures in the production of the taxpayer's profits. Section 17 of the Inland Revenue Ordinance excludes as deductions of disbursements or expenses that the taxpayer does not expend for the purpose of producing such profits. Mr. Barlow took the position that the above-mentioned sections did not require the Commissioner to compare the purchase prices deducted against market prices and to disallow deductions the Commissioner views as excessive. Justice Ribeiro accepted Mr. Barlow's view of these sections, thus precluding the Commissioner from disallowing deductions on the basis that a price paid was not reasonable. Thus, Justice Ribeiro took the position that the taxpayer can deduct all expenses if the taxpayer incurs these expenditures in the production of the taxpayer's profits.

THE NARROWER SCHEME AND THE NARROWER TAX BENEFIT

The case addresses both the narrower scheme and the narrower tax benefit—two different approaches to section 61A:

1. The narrower scheme confines the taxpayer's activities to Item 8(a) and Item 8(b) of the scheme.
2. The narrower tax benefit confines these taxpayer's activities to the taxpayer's trading profits; the benefit ignores references to profits passed on to fellow subsidiaries.

Justice Ribeiro held that, according to findings made by the Board of Review, the taxpayer's payments made pursuant to the narrower scheme were deductible. Following the approach taken by the Court of Final Appeal, the taxpayer did successfully alter its legal liability in the narrower scheme. The taxpayer could claim these deductions that, but for Section 61A, would have the effect of conferring a tax benefit on the taxpayer.

Justice Ribeiro then addressed Lord Hoffmann's determination of the tax benefit in *CIR v. HIT Finance Ltd.*[8] and *CIR v. Tai Hing Cotton Mill (Development) Ltd.*[9] In *CIR v. Tai Hing*, Lord Hoffmann stressed the need to compare the effect of the transaction on the taxpayer's tax liability against its tax liability on some other basis. Lord Hoffmann looked to causation and comparison under section 61A. "If the effect of the transaction is that your liability to tax is less than it would have been on some other appropriate hypothesis, you have had a tax benefit." In *CIR v. HIT Finance*, Lord Hoffmann described the tax benefit as a "difference favourable to taxpayer" based on "his tax liability computed on one basis and his liability computed on a different basis."

The Court of Final Appeal concluded that the Commissioner made an error in not mounting a challenge based on sections 16, 17, 60, and 61A rather than just on section 61A. Justice Ribeiro commented that the Commissioner initially proceeded with all four sections and then later abandoned them but for section 61A.

DOMINANT PURPOSE OF THE NARROWER SCHEME

Justice Ribeiro then sought to assess whether the taxpayer and Din Wai Electronics Limited entered into the price-fixing arrangement with the sole purpose or the dominant purpose of obtaining a tax benefit for the taxpayer. The Court of Final Appeal then examined the seven items listed in section 61A(1)(a) through section 61A(1)(g). Justice Ribeiro noted that sections 61A(1)(a), section 61A(1)(b), and section 61A(c) provide guidance on methodology (i.e., the manner in which the Commissioner is to approach the facts in determining the question of dominant purpose). In contrast, section 61A(1)(d), section 61A(1)(e), section 61A(1)(f), and section 61A(1)(g) point to certain fact classes as possible signposts to the requisite dominant purpose. The Court of Final Appeal went through a point-by-point analysis:

- Section 61A(1)(a) tells us that it is permissible for the Commissioner to look at the genesis of the transaction and at the manner in which the taxpayer implemented the transaction.
- Section 61A(1)(b) tells us that it is permissible for the Commissioner to look beyond the form and substance of the transaction.
- Section 61A(1)(c) requires the Commissioner to assess the fiscal effects of the overall transactions.
- Section 61A(1)(d) and Section 61A(1)(e) require the Commissioner to look at the financial effects of the particular scheme on the taxpayer and on persons

connected with the taxpayer. Under section 61A(1)(d), the scheme might bring about no changes to the taxpayer's financial position while, at the same time, producing a tax benefit. Under section 61A(1)(e), the scheme might involve transactions among group members resulting in an unchanged financial position for the group as a whole but confer a tax benefit on the taxpayer. The hallmark of the tax avoidance is that the taxpayer reduces its tax liability without incurring its economic consequences.

- Section 61A(1)(f) can specify that the scheme might incorporate dealings that are not at arm's length and may suggest that the taxpayer entered into transactions for the dominant purpose of producing a tax benefit for the taxpayer.
- Section 61A(1)(g) can suggest participation in an offshore corporation in the transaction, and might indicate the requisite "dominant purpose."

BOARD OF REVIEW'S APPROACH

The Board of Review emphasized the genesis of the transaction and the manner in which the taxpayer implemented the transaction under section 61A(1)(a), that is, the manner in which the taxpayer entered into and carried out the transaction. The Board regarded the advice given by Ernst & Young (E&Y) was meant as a tax benefit for the taxpayer. Justice Ribeiro thought that this objective as viewed by the Board as being "obviously correct," as the taxpayer achieved this goal by segregating Hong Kong operations and offshore activities to segregate taxable income from nontaxable profits.

In contrast, Justice Ribeiro viewed the statutory purpose of section 61A was not to attack arrangements that the taxpayer has made to secure its tax benefits, especially in situations in which the legislature had intended these benefits to be available to the taxpayer. As Lord Norlan pointed out in *IRC v. Willoughby*,[10] it would be absurd in the context of the relevant anti-avoidance legislation to describe as tax avoidance the acceptance of an offer of freedom from tax that Parliament has deliberately made.

E&Y had provided advice to Ngai Lik, but the advice that E&Y provided did not pertain to the narrower scheme. Justice Ribeiro commented that E&Y never had suggested any annual price-fixing arrangement between Din Wai Electronics Limited and Ngai Lik. In contrast, E&Y suggested that the taxpayer set up a master supply arrangement having a 10% price margin over the cost of purchasing items from the cheapest alternative supplier. The advice that E&Y provided to Ngai Lik, then, was not relevant to paragraph 61A(1)(a).

The Board of Review had considered the manner in which the parties conducted the transaction to be highly significant, not only pursuant to paragraph 61A(1)(a) but also under most of the paragraphs under section 61A for three reasons:

1. The Board thought that the taxpayer continued to have "substantial involvement in manufacturing."

2. The taxpayer had engaged in the "onward allocation of profits" to Shing Wai Co. Limited, Shing Wai Limited, and Ngai Wai Plastic Manufacturing Limited through the system of additional discounts.
3. The taxpayer failed to charge enough for its sourcing and agency activities.

Justice Ribeiro, writing for the Court of Final Appeal, found those conclusions of the Board to be "misdirected."

RIBEIRO'S DOMINANT PURPOSE OF THE NARROWER SCHEME

Justice Ribeiro, while concluding that the above-mentioned conclusions of the Board to be "misdirected," did specify that the findings relating to arm's length transactions are "properly relevant to the Narrower Scheme and to the Narrower Tax Benefit." The Board noted that the taxpayer did not follow the agreement under which the landed cost of each delivery exceeded by more than 10% the costs of an alternative supplier or unless Din Wai Electronics Limited was unable to supply the quantity or quality required. Relying on Mr. Lam's statement that the accounting department determined the price sold by Din Wai Electronics Limited to the taxpayer, the Board stated that this activity points to "manipulation of the amount of profits" transferred from the taxpayer to Din Wai Electronics Limited.

The Board of Review, in examining the Ngai Lik–Din Wai Electronics Limited relationship, accepted payments of 10% more than the costs of alternative supplier as being arm's length. The Board failed to further analyze this cost-plus-10% arrangement as being arm's length—an issue that Justice Ribeiro failed to address. Instead, the Board's focus was not on the agreement itself but on deviations made from this agreement by the accounting department.

The Board of Review found that the taxpayer's profits dropped. The taxpayer's contribution to the profits dropped from 31.19% in 1991–1992 to 7.19% in 1995–1996. Justice Ribeiro found that conclusion by the Board of Review to be relevant in determining the dominant purpose of the narrower scheme, stating that these conclusions "provide a proper basis" for concluding that the taxpayer entered into the price-fixing arrangement with Din Wai Electronics Limited for the dominant purpose of obtaining a tax benefit for the taxpayer.

Justice Ribeiro held that three portions of section 61A(1) are of particular importance to that conclusion:

1. Section 61(A)(1)(d) speaks of changes in the financial position of the relevant person as to the transaction in question.
2. Section 61(A)(1)(e) speaks of changes in the financial position of the relevant person that has any connection with the relevant person as to the transaction in question.
3. Section 61(A)(1)(f) speaks of the creation of rights and obligations that would not normally be created by persons dealing with each other at arm's length under a transaction of the kind in question.

Justice Ribeiro based a conclusion on the fact that because Ngai Lik and Din Wai Electronics Limited had entered into "an ostensibly binding master agreement" that required Ngai Lik to scrutinize Din Wai's Electronics Limited's prices against competing supplier's prices, the price-fixing arrangement superseded the binding master agreement. Ngai Lik's accounting department determined the prices at which Din Wai Electronics Limited sold the finished audio products to Ngai Lik.

Justice Ribeiro commented on Ngai Lik's change in financial position that resulted from the price-fixing arrangement. The arrangement reduced Ngai Lik's profits to the extent that the arrangement inflated Din Wai Electronics Limited's price, producing the tax benefit. Justice Ribeiro criticized the Board of Review for not quantifying the extent of this inflation.

Justice Ribeiro then postulated the changes made by the narrower scheme to the financial position of the group (the group consisted of companies that had a "connection with" the taxpayer within the meaning of section 61A(1)(e)). Justice Ribeiro then concluded that the change in financial position of the group, "significantly, is 'None.'" The path that Justice Ribeiro took would validate all tax haven restructuring, whether to Bermuda, as in the case of Ngai Lik Industrial Holdings Limited, to BVI, as in the case of the other Ngai Lik companies, or to other tax-haven entities. This stance on the part of Justice Ribeiro would put section 61A(1)(e) clearly in conflict with the tax-haven provisions in the Hong Kong transfer pricing guidelines.

Justice Ribeiro looked at an aggregate approach that equates tax-haven entities with taxable entities, providing this aggregate information:

Year	Turnover ($HK million)
1991–1992	454
1992–1993	611
1993–1994	800
1994–1995	875
1995–1996	1,089

The Board of Review found that the taxpayer's contribution of the group profits fell from 31.19% in 1991–1992 to 7.19% in 1995–1996, which, according to Justice Ribeiro, "plainly suggests" that the narrower scheme profits "diverted" profits away from the taxpayer. Justice Ribeiro concluded that "when one asks why the parties entered into the price-fixing arrangement which resulted in group profits being passed from one pocket to another, the irresistible conclusion is that this was done with 'the dominant purpose' of obtaining a tax benefit for the taxpayer." Justice Ribeiro concluded that the Commissioner engaged section 61A, but only as to three tax years from 1993–1994 to 1995–1996. The Commissioner, by virtue of section 61(A)(2), became bound to assess the taxpayer's tax liability. Mr. Barlow, representing Ngai Lik, then argued that the Commissioner misapplied her powers in making the additional assessment claim.

COMMISSIONER'S ASSESSMENT POWER

Section 61A(2) enables the Commissioner to proceed against the taxpayer under two alternative theories:

1. To proceed as if the taxpayer had not entered into the challenged transaction
2. To assess the taxpayer in a manner that the Commissioner considers appropriate to counteract the tax benefit the taxpayer would otherwise obtain

As to the second of the two options, the Commissioner must design an assessment based on a "reasonable postulated hypothetical transaction that produces an assessment designed rationally to counteract the tax benefit." The assessment cannot be raised in some arbitrary amount or arrived at on some basis that is unreasonable or is not rationally related to the tax benefit in question. For example, the Commissioner cannot select an alternative transaction that attracts the highest tax rate. However, the Commissioner can take appropriate steps to counteract the taxpayer's unwarranted benefit, such as disallowing the interest deduction on a borrowing that is in excess of the net proceeds of a loan.

COMMISSIONER'S EXERCISE OF THE SECTION 61A(2) POWER

Justice Ribeiro held that the Commissioner seriously miscarried the exercise of the section 61A(2) power in *Ngai Lik*. The Commissioner sought to treat the whole of the profits of Shing Wai Co. Limited and the three BVI companies as the taxpayer's chargeable profits. The Commissioner then reduced these assessments by half (i.e., assessments that treated half of the profits of the taxpayer's fellow subsidiaries as the taxpayer's assessable profits in Hong Kong).

Justice Ribeiro concluded that these additional assessments (i.e., the entirety of the profits or half the profits) are not based on the first of the two alternatives the Commissioner can select. The Commissioner did not raise these additional assessments based on whether the parties carried out their price-fixing arrangements. Instead, the Commissioner was evidently purporting to exercise the second alternative with a view toward counteracting the tax benefit in question. In other words, the Commissioner was purporting to counteract non–arm's length transactions that had reduced the taxpayer's taxable income.

The Court of Final Appeal concluded that the Commissioner did not reach its objective by raising the additional assessments. The Commissioner could have created an assessment based on the profits that the taxpayer hypothetically could have earned if the taxpayer had purchased the goods at arm's length prices instead of at the prices fixed annually. Instead of applying this approach, the Commissioner raised an assessment equal to half of the profits derived by the taxpayer's fellow subsidiaries from their operations on the mainland. Justice Ribeiro held that is "impossible to see any rational connection between that figure and the excessive prices allegedly paid by the taxpayer to Din Wai Electronics Limited." In short, the additional assessments raised do not counteract the relevant tax benefits.

Justice Ribeiro appeared to be puzzled by the Commissioner's approach. "It appears that" the Commissioner adopted the 50% figure simply on the Revenue's practice concerning the apportionment of profits that are attributable to offshore operations. Nevertheless, Justice Ribeiro contended that the Commissioner failed to properly exercise her section 61A(2) powers in raising the additional assessments. Justice Ribeiro held that the Commissioner miscarried her power.

BOARD'S APPROACH TO THE EXERCISE OF THE SECTION 61A(2) POWER

The Board of Review made its assessment under section 61A(2)(a) rather than under section 61A(2)(b). The Board stated that the taxpayer's manufacturing activities were clearly not wholly offshore. The taxpayer had not made any claim for apportionment and had not made good any claim for apportionment of more than 50% of the manufacturing profits as offshore profits, the onus being on the taxpayer to prove that the assessments appealed against were incorrect or excessive. Unless the taxpayer could make good any claim for apportionment that it might make of the more than 50% the manufacturing profits as offshore profits, the best it could hope for was a 50–50 apportionment under the Revenue's Departmental Interpretation and Practice Notes No. 21.

The Board upheld the additional assessments. Nevertheless, Justice Ribeiro held that "no basis exists for treating any share of the manufacturing profits of the fellow subsidiaries as the taxpayer's assessable profits." Justice Ribeiro further held that "there is a clear mismatch between the Board's approach and the content of the scheme and tax benefit which engages section 61A." The Court of First Instance and the Court of Appeal did not deal with the validity of the Commissioner's exercise of the section 61A(2) power.

DISPOSAL OF THE APPEAL

The Court of Final Appeal terminated the Commissioner's additional assessment for 1991–1992 and 1992–1993. In contrast, for 1993–1994, 1994–1995, and 1995–1996, the Court found section 61A(2) to be relevant and mandatory under the "shall access" terminology. "It follows that since section 61A(1) is engaged in relation to those three years of assessment, the Commissioner ought in principle to carry out her duty under section 61A(2) by raising additional assessments on a proper basis, taking into account the opinion of this Court." Justice Ribeiro provided that such fresh assessments should be aimed at counteracting the tax benefit derived from the price-fixing arrangement for the years in question.

Finally, the Court of Final Appeal acknowledged that there might be difficulties in trying to ascertain what such arm's length prices might have been. One could not expect the exercise to be conducted in great detail or with a high degree of precision. The Court suggested that parties determine a "reasonable estimate of the taxpayer's assessable profits." The Commissioner's aim ought to be to arrive at a figure that assessable profits deriving from dealings at arm's length would at least have attained.

NOTES

1. *Ngai Lik Electronics Company Limited v. the Hong Kong Commissioner of Inland Revenue*, FACV No. 29 of 2008.
2. CACV No. 22 of 2008.
3. Final Appeal No. 29 of 2008 (CIVIL).
4. OECD, *Transfer Pricing Guidelines for Multinational Enterprises and Tax Administrations* (Paris: July 22, 2010).
5. R. Feinschreiber and M. Kent, "What You Need to Know About the Transactional Profit Split Method," *Corporate Business Taxation Monthly* (February 2011):29.
6. R. Feinschreiber and M. Kent, "Hong Kong Issues Transfer Pricing Guidelines," *Corporate Business Taxation Monthly* (March 2010): 17.
7. *CIR v. Hang Seng Bank Ltd.* [1991], 1AC 306 at 318.
8. *CIR v. HIT Finance Ltd.* [2007], 10 HKCFAR 717.
9. *CIR v. Tai Hing Cotton Mill (Development) Ltd.* [2007], 10HKCFAR 704.
10. *IRC v. Willoughby* [1997], 1 WLR 1071 at 1079.

CHAPTER ELEVEN

Transfer Pricing Litigation in India

TRANSFER PRICING has been developing rapidly in India. This rapid development includes the implementation of regulations, audit techniques, and case law. The case law itself is worthy of note. India, unlike most of Asia, is litigious. More cases are on the way.

BACKGROUND

India was a highly regulated economy until 1991, when the country began free market reforms. India is a capital importer, and that fact impacts its tax and trade policy. India attracts direct investments primarily due to its lower labor costs. The country is seeking to protect its tax base, and that fact takes precedence in governmental tax planning rather than seeking equity between taxpayers and the government. The Indian government focuses on transfer pricing as a means of protecting its tax base. Recent case law developments focus on this protectionism. To further implement its tax base concerns, India exempts wholly domestic entities and focuses on international businesses.

India has a number of peculiarities in its tax system. Like the United Kingdom, India uses an assessment year that begins on April 1 rather than determining amounts on a calendar-year basis. India does not use a consolidated return system.

India has other peculiarities in the transfer pricing context. India taxes foreign companies at a higher tax rate than it taxes domestic companies, a rate of more than 41+% for foreign companies compared with a rate of 33+% for domestic Indian companies. India does not require the taxpayer to provide a tax return. Instead, the company's financial statements determine the amount of the corporate tax payable, a procedure that the United Kingdom had used in the past. India imposes double taxation as to royalties and technical fees paid by Indian companies to foreigners.

India requires the taxpayer to maintain contemporaneous documentation. The country has enacted stringent noncompliance penalties, especially for willful negligence. It provides transfer pricing exemptions for small businesses.

TRANSFER PRICING CHRONOLOGY AND ADMINISTRATION

The Income Tax Act of 1961 in India did not address transfer pricing per se, but the government disallowed "excessive payments" that one party makes to a related party. These early excessive payment provisions were based on the "close connection concept." India had sought to curtail the shifting of profits to offshore entities.

India adopted Organisation for Economic Co-operation and Development (OECD) transfer pricing concepts in 2000, and India's Parliament approved transfer pricing legislation in April 2001.The tax authority in India is the Central Board of Direct Taxes (CBDT). The CBDT issued transfer pricing rules in August 2001.

India is an extremely diverse country. It is no surprise that India divides its tax powers geographically and by administrative power. India divides its tax powers in this way:

- CBDT. Direct taxes, including income tax
- Central Board of Excise and Customs. Indirect taxes, including excise duties and customs duties
- Geographic areas, headed by a chief commissioner, commissioners, and assessing officers in five regional locations: Mumbai, Delhi, Bangalore, Chennai, and Kolata
- Transfer pricing officers: one or more in each jurisdiction

Unlike transfer pricing regimes in most other countries, India limits its transfer pricing regime solely to international businesses and exempts wholly domestic Indian businesses. These businesses are within the purview of the transfer pricing provisions:

- Either of the two parties to a transaction where one or both parties are nonresident.
- The transfer pricing provisions do not apply to all-domestic transactions.
- The transfer pricing provisions do not apply between two residents of India.

RELATED PARTIES

India determines related party status by an "Associated Enterprises" concept. That Associated Enterprises concept applies to the following relationships: As a general matter, affiliated status applies to both direct participation and to indirect participation; to management; to control; and to capital. For reference as to the term "affiliated enterprise," see OECD Model Convention Article 8.

Affiliated enterprises status in India can depend on the presence of loans or the presence of equity. Equity holdings of at least 26% cause the relationship to constitute affiliated status. Analogously, Form 5472 in the United States speaks of shareholdings of 25% or more for reporting purposes. Control is determined through the composition of the board of directors. Affiliated enterprise status in India applies because of financial control: providing loans equal to 51% of the assets or providing guarantees equal to 10% of total borrowings.

Affiliated enterprises status in India can result through dependence based on intangibles, such as dependence based on patents, on licenses, or on business or commercial rights. Affiliated enterprises status in India can result through a franchisor/franchisee relationship.

India views the franchisor as the dominant party and views the franchisor as being dominant over each franchisee. As a result, India views the franchisor/franchisee relationship as an affiliated enterprise subject to transfer pricing. Note that Indian companies tend to be in licensee status, and the tax authorities eschew transfer pricing intangibles.

Affiliated enterprises status applies in India through a supply of raw materials.

India treats the providers of raw materials as being affiliated to the users of these raw materials. India, then, recognizes that the raw material provider might have effective influence over the supply of raw materials. The user of the raw materials might purchase 90% of its materials from the raw material supplier, creating an affiliated party relationship. The supplier of the raw materials might influence the price and related conditions of the sale in those circumstances.

Affiliated enterprises status applies in India through the finished product. For example, one party might have "effective influence" over another party as to the sale of a finished product. This provision appears to reflect the manufacturer's domination over its distributors. India might view the manufacturer and its distributors as affiliated enterprises. India might apply the effective influence rule without ascertaining whether the parties are dependent or independent.

Affiliated enterprises status applies in India by virtue of board membership (i.e., when one enterprise appoints more than half of the board members of another enterprise).

In some situations, though, it might be difficult to ascertain whether one party appoints another party. India does not address the indirect control of board members—through attorney, accounting, or banking relationships—in determining affiliated status.

Affiliated enterprises status applies in India because of a relationship of "mutual interest." Note, however, that the term "mutual interest" is vague and might apply to supplier issues, distributor issues, financial issues, and so forth.

TRANSFER PRICING METHOD SELECTION IN INDIA

The transfer pricing method selection criteria in India is based on the most appropriate method (MAM). The MAM is the transfer pricing method that is "best suited to the facts and circumstances." The MAM rule differs from the priority of methods approach used in many countries in Asia, thus raising the likelihood of double taxation. The MAM rule differs from the "best method" rule used in the United States and in other countries.

This is how India's MAM works: The taxpayer and the CBDT are to select a transfer pricing method based on these criteria:

- Nature and class of the transaction
- Class or classes of the associated enterprises
- Availability of data
- Coverage of data
- Accuracy and reliability of data
- Degree of comparability
- Extent to which reliable adjustments can be made
- Assets and risks of the enterprise
- Assumptions used

India permits the taxpayer to apply these transfer pricing methods:

- Comparable uncontrolled price (CUP)
- Resale price method (RPM)
- Cost plus method, including the "normal" gross profit market as adjusted
- Profit split method, based on functions performed, assets employed, and risks assumed, based on reliable external data, in proportion to their relative contributions (India permits the basic return approach)
- Transaction net margin method (TNMM), based on costs incurred, sales effectuated, or assets utilized

India permits taxpayers to use cost sharing procedures, but cost sharing procedures are rarely used in India.

The Indian transfer pricing provisions address the issue of applicable comparable databases. India has widely used databases. The country does not prohibit foreign comparable data, but the tax authorities strongly prefer domestic comparative data. Like the United States, but unlike most of Asia, an Indian taxpayer can look to the two prior taxable years. A case law decision in India permitted the taxpayer to determine the results of one particular tax year standing alone.

As a general matter, countries in Asia and elsewhere permit the taxpayer to develop a range of prices. The reader is forewarned that India does not permit the taxpayer to use such a range of prices. Some countries (e.g., the United States and sometimes Singapore) use the interquartile range concept to narrow the pricing range. India requires an arithmetic mean of prices but then permits a range of 5% from that arithmetic price. The goal in India is to ascertain the one true arm's length price—a transfer pricing approach that other countries had applied in the past.

CONTEMPORANEOUS DOCUMENTATION IN INDIA

Contemporaneous documentation rules in India require the taxpayer to prepare and preserve the following documents. The taxpayer is to prepare documentation by the due date for filing the annual tax return—similar to contemporaneous documentation timing in Japan. India does not require immediate reflection of actual transactions, as the United States and Australia do. The taxpayer need not file contemporaneous documentation with the tax return. The taxpayer must maintain documentation for eight years. The taxpayer is to furnish the documentation within 30 days after the CBDT requests these documents.

A non-Indian company that receives royalties or technical fees from an Indian company is subject to tax in India. In other words, India treats payment as a direct business activity in India rather than being subject to withholding. India's royalty and technical fee approach appears to be taken from the United Nations model tax treaty.

The payment is subject to transfer pricing rules, and both parties are subject to India's documentation rules. The home country might also tax the royalty or technical fee.

India requires the taxpayer to provide three types of documentation to the Indian tax authorities:

1. General information
2. Transaction-specific information
3. Supporting information and documents

These Indian documentation rules are similar in many respects to the U.S. transfer pricing rules.

The Indian transfer pricing documentation rules require the taxpayer to provide general information to the tax authorities. The taxpayer must provide the ownership structure of the Indian entity and indicate the ownership specifics of that particular entity. In addition, the taxpayer is to provide the worldwide ownership structure of the group, including linkages and tax status of each entity. Further, the taxpayer is to describe the business from a business standpoint, including its activities and competition.

The Indian transfer pricing documentation rules require the taxpayer to provide this transaction-specific information to the tax authorities:

- The nature and terms of the transaction, including prices of the transaction
- Functions performed, risks assumed, and assets employed
- Economic and marketing analysis
- Record of uncontrolled transactions, including the use of transaction as in-house comparable
- Comparative analysis
- Transfer pricing methods considered
- Difference adjustments
- Assumptions, policies, and price negotiations
- Adjustment details
- Other information

The Indian tax authorities expect the taxpayer to provide supportive transfer pricing documentation, including market research studies, stock exchange data, and commodity market data, if available. The taxpayer may need to rely on databases in the non-Indian jurisdiction. If so, the taxpayer is to provide that information to the Indian tax authorities. The taxpayer is to provide the tax authorities with its published accounts and financial statements, agreements and contracts, and letters and correspondence impacting transfer pricing. The taxpayer is to provide the tax authorities with the normal documents the company issued under its accounting practice.

The accountant's report plays a significant role in India. The rules require the taxpayer to obtain a transfer pricing report, which is normally prepared by a chartered accountant. The accountant must provide this report to the taxpayer before the taxpayer files its tax return. This disclosure is similar to Form 5472 in the United States and Schedule 25A in Australia. The accountant must certify the taxpayer's proper documentation.

AUDIT PROCEDURES

Two separate governmental parties play a role in a transfer pricing audit in India, the assessing officer (AO) and the transfer pricing officer (TPO). The division between these roles has been before the courts. It is possible that India developed this dual system to limit corruption. The AO has limited powers when the issue pertains to transfer pricing. The TPO, not the AO, takes charge of the case from the government's standpoint. The TPO, having charge of the case, puts in writing its opinion as to the taxpayer's arm's length price. The TPO then sends to the taxpayer its opinion as to the taxpayer's arm's length price. The TPO's letter to the taxpayer is to include its reasons for the redetermination and the application of the method chosen. The taxpayer can challenge the TPO's determination and, if necessary, challenge the TPO's determination in court.

The TPO selects and adjusts the taxpayer's transaction price, based on available information and other material. The TPO is required to issue a notice to the taxpayer, giving the taxpayer the opportunity to show why the TPO should not make the adjustment. The AO then computes the transfer pricing adjustment, computes the taxpayer's total income, and issues a final assessment order to the taxpayer.

India is currently auditing thousands of companies for transfer pricing purposes.

India is increasing the number of transfer pricing audits by 50% per year. The amount of adjustments is increasing 30% per year. The transfer pricing audit process applies only to audits that reach a threshold of 50 million rupees ($1.1 million) per year, based on related party transactions.

Transfer pricing audits in India begin as desk audits. The tax authorities can later expand the audit process. The government and the taxpayer divide the burden of proof. The taxpayer has the burden of proof during the audit process, but the government has the burden of proof in making transfer pricing adjustments. The confidentiality rules apply for audits in India.

The Indian government can request foreign comparables, but the government does not trust foreign comparables without substantiation. India may be using secret comparables—the data the government obtains from other audits—but the burden of proof issue limits the use of secret comparables in making adjustments.

It is important to evaluate India audit issues by industry segment. Services are an important facet transfer pricing issue in India. The CBDT makes frequent adjustments for fulfillment, marketing, research and development, and technical services. India makes very frequent use of the cost plus method because many businesses are service enterprises. The government seeks to impose high markups (i.e., 25% to 40%), thus exacerbating double taxation, as India's trading partners view these services as being low in value. India views research and development activities as being high in value and subjects the taxpayer to a high markup. The TPOs tend to apply market rates for employees as a comparable.

India permits the foreign owner to claim management fees for running its operations in India and to claim a share of common expenses, but the country imposes a benefits test on the foreign owner. India applies internal comparables, relying on product comparability and/or the TNMM in the case of manufacturers. The tax authorities frequently apply the TNMM rather than the resale cost method to a distributor.

PENALTIES

India, like many countries new to transfer pricing, imposes severe transfer pricing penalties. For example, penalties for a transfer pricing adjustment can be a minimum of 100% and a maximum of 300% of the transfer pricing adjustment. However, the taxpayer can avoid the penalty by showing due diligence and good faith. These penalties are stringent, given India's arithmetic mean requirement to determine the transfer price.

India, like the United States, imposes a separate documentation penalty, over and above the transfer penalty, for a taxpayer's failure to maintain or submit documentation in India. The documentation penalty is 2% of the taxpayer's transactions. The penalty applies to information and documents pertaining to the international transaction.

The documentation penalties apply to general business records. The penalty for failure to submit the accountants' transfer pricing report is 100,000 rupees (approximately $2,500).

APPELLATE PROCEDURES

The taxpayer can appeal before the Commissioner of Income Tax (Appeals) CIT(A). The appellate procedure is regional, so that the results might not be consistent on a national basis. Appeals can go to the Income Tax Appellate Tribunal (ITAT), a quasi-judicial authority independent of the revenue authorities, the final fact-finding authority. Then appeals can go to the High Court if the issue is based on the legal issues rather than on facts.

Unique among transfer pricing regimes in Asia, India does not accept the concepts of advance pricing agreements (APAs); nevertheless, the Authority for Advance Ruling (AAR) might serve in essence as a unilateral APA but for the fact that the AAR process does not include valuation issues in its purview. India provides for a tax ruling authority, the AAR. The AAR procedure is available to both residents and nonresidents. The AAR ruling is binding on the taxpayer and on the tax authorities, but taxpayers and the tax authorities have sought to challenge this power.[1]

India set up the AAR, a quasi-judicial body, in 1993, as an alternative dispute mechanism. The AAR procedure can apply to nonvaluation transfer pricing issues, but the AAR process is not limited to transfer pricing issues. High Court judgments take precedence over the AAR ruling.

India makes use of the competent authority procedures when the country is a party to these tax treaties. India's tax treaty network includes the United States and the United Kingdom. India established active double tax avoidance systems in the case of the United States and the United Kingdom in 2003, but it has not applied these tax avoidance systems with other jurisdictions.

The taxpayer should be aware of the negative transfer pricing factors in India. India takes a strong stand against losses, even initial start-up losses. Indian companies are payers of intangible rights, not recipients of intangible rights. As such, to protect its tax base, India takes a strong stand against making payments for intangibles. Further, India imposes exchange control requirements.

India provides investor taxpayers with tax holidays that are designed to increase productivity. Tax holidays benefits do not apply to transfer pricing adjustments. Some taxpayers pump up the markup because of tax holiday, raising the comparable amount to its nonholiday competitors. Taxpayers that use high markups during the holiday period will be stuck with the high markup after the tax holiday period.

As to the AAR ruling in the transfer pricing context, see *Instrumentarium Corporation*, a Finnish company. Instrumentarium had provided a tax-free loan to its affiliate in India at a zero interest rate. This interest rate, quite obviously, was not arm's length. If the Indian subsidiary paid interest as a rate above zero to comply with the arm's length rate precepts, this positive tax rate would diminish taxable income in India. The AAR concluded that it could provide a ruling in 2003 as the issue did not involve valuation. The AAR required Instrumentarium to use the arm's length transfer pricing rate.

TRANSFER PRICING LITIGATION

Transfer pricing litigation began in earnest in India in 2006, with these cases:

- *Sony India (P) Ltd. v. Central Board of Direct Taxes*[2]
- *Central Board of Direct Taxes v. Morgan Stanley & Co. Inc.*[3]
- *Aztec Software & Technology Services, Ltd., v. ACIT*[4]

Sony India v. Central Board of Direct Taxes addressed procedural issues impacting the conflict between the assessment officer (AO) and the TPO. The Indian transfer pricing regulations require the AO to proceed to compute the taxpayer's total income after the TPO makes its transfer pricing determination.

The High Court of Delhi upheld the government's procedure in *Sony India*. The Court held that determination is within the authority of the Central Board of Direct Taxes under Indian law and confirmed that the TPO order does not bind the AO.

Permanent Establishment and *Morgan Stanley*

The tax authorities in India are actively pursuing their potential permanent establishment claims against foreign-based multinational corporations, undertaking this action to protect the Indian tax base. The Indian government's claims against multinational corporations are of two types:

1. The foreign corporation's agency in India is that of a dependent agency rather than of an independent agency; as a result of the dependent agency relationship, the foreign corporation's involvement in India is subject to tax.
2. Even if the foreign-based multinational establishes a subsidiary in India, the foreign-based multinational would again be subject to tax on the basis of permanent establishment precepts.

A multinational corporation doing business in India, then, faces a double risk of permanent establishment exposure, all before addressing transfer pricing exposure. Consider the case of *DIT v. Morgan Stanley & Co.* decided by the Supreme Court of India.[5]

Morgan Stanley is a global investment firm that provides a range of financial services to its clients around the world. The company established a subsidiary in India, Morgan Stanley Advantage Services (MSAS). Morgan Stanley used MSAS to provide "support services" to Morgan Stanley entities outside India.

MSAS is an internal entity and does not directly interact with Morgan Stanley's customer clients. Instead, MSAS directly interacts with members of the Morgan Stanley group. MSAS provides such support services as bookkeeping, accounting, research assistance, and analytics.

From a U.S. perspective, one should note the ambiguous nature of the categorization of the MSAS services in light of section 1.482–9. Thus, it is not certain that the low-valued services provisions under section 1.482–9(b) necessarily would apply to the MSAS fact pattern.

The issue arose as to the applicable transfer pricing method under Indian law to determine the arm's length amount. Morgan Stanley undertook a transfer pricing analysis in India specifically examining MSAS's functions performed. Morgan Stanley was concerned that the Indian tax authorities could make a transfer pricing adjustment and attribute a portion of its overall profits to India.

Morgan Stanley sought a ruling from the appropriate regulatory agency in India, the AAR. The purpose of the ruling was to ensure that the Indian tax authorities would not attribute any portion of the profits of Morgan Stanley to MSAS. The AAR ruled that, once Morgan Stanley remunerated MSAS for the services costs at arm's length rates, the Indian tax authorities could not tax any future benefits. In other words, the AAR rejected a second-tier permanent establishment.

The Indian revenue authorities rejected the AAR ruling, arguing before the Supreme Court of India that they could further attribute a portion of Morgan Stanley's world profits. The Indian revenue authorities asserted that, notwithstanding MSAS receiving arm's length compensation from Morgan Stanley, they could attribute a portion of Morgan Stanley's profit to India.

The Indian Supreme Court rejected the revenue authorities' claim for further profits attributable to India. Commentators close to the scene consider the further attribution theory to remain in other contexts.

Aztec Software

The courts in India had the opportunity to revisit the *Sony India* case with *Aztec Software*. Litigation took place at the ITAT in Bangalore before a five-judge panel, a special bench. Here the court held that the AO must demonstrate tax avoidance before bringing a transfer pricing adjustment. The TPO order did not bind the AO. Subsequent legislation, however, changed the relationship between the AO and TPO. The TPO binds the AO as of June 1, 2007. *Aztec Software* provides that the government has the burden of proof if it seeks a different arm's length price.

Aztec Software addressed the interrelationship between transfer pricing and tax holidays, holding that the transfer pricing provisions apply even when the taxpayer enjoys a tax holiday. Here the TPO rejected the taxpayer's transfer pricing method without providing a basis for this transfer pricing determination. The court criticized the TPO for this lack of analysis. The court in *Aztec Software* did not reach finding as to the most appropriate transfer pricing method. Here the tax authorities applied a single year's data. The court accepted the single-year approach. However, the court addressed the sample size issue, suggesting that a sample size of ten companies might be inadequate.

VODAFONE: HUTCHISON ESSAR ACQUISITION

Vodaphone acquired Hutchison Essar, the fourth largest mobile phone operator in India, paying $10.9 billion in May 2007. The tax authorities in India sought $2.1 billion from Vodaphone as a result of Vodaphone making that purchase of Hutchison Essar shares. The taxpayers expressed two alternative theories to confront the Indian tax authorities:

1. Vodaphone argued that Hutchison Telecommunications International of Hong Kong was the seller of the mobile phone business and that Hutchison Telecommunications International, as the seller, must pay the tax if India prevailed in determining taxability.
2. Vodaphone argued that no tax is payable by anyone because the transaction took place offshore.

This is the Hutchison structure and its ostensible tax consequences: Hutchison Whampoa (the parent company) is based in Hong Kong. Hutchison held its controlling stake in Hutchison Essar through a Mauritius company. The tax authorities in India assert that the Vodaphone-Hutchison transaction is subject to capital gains taxation in India because the assets are in India. The capital gain was $9.6 billion, levied at the 22% rate, an amount of $2.1 billion. The tax authorities in India argue that Vodaphone should have withheld the $2.1 billion and paid the $2.1 billion to India. The Indian Supreme Court held for Vodaphone on January 20, 2012.

NOTES

1. In this regard, see the *Morgan Stanley* case (2007), *infra*.
2. *Sony India (P) Ltd. v. Central Board of Direct Taxes*, High Court of Delhi, WP (C) no. 9594/2005, 288 ITR 52, decision October 10, 2006.
3. *Central Board of Direct Taxes v. Morgan Stanley & Co. Inc.*, High Court of India, 292 ITR 416, 2007.
4. *Aztec Software & Technology Services, Ltd., v. ACIT*, 107 ITD 141, Bangalore SB, 2007.
5. *DIT v. Morgan Stanley & Co.*, 2007 292 ITR 416.

12

CHAPTER TWELVE

PE Issues Impact Indian Transfer Pricing

MULTINATIONAL TAXPAYERS increasingly must address the fact that tax collectors in a myriad of states are developing increasingly sophisticated tax collection strategies. One such strategy of critical importance is the penchant of the tax authorities to investigate potential permanent establishment (PE) activities. If the tax authority can ascertain the presence of these PE activities, it develops a transfer pricing adjustment in favor of itself. Such multinational taxpayers are increasingly facing the risk of extensive double taxation.

One major country making extensive use of ascertaining PE activities and developing transfer pricing adjustments is India. The long arm of the Indian tax authorities extends outward, reaching beyond the geographical confines of the country itself. This long arm often reaches the activities of Indian-based activities taking place abroad as well as those of foreign-based enterprises undertaking activities in India.

Double taxation arises as the U.S. tax authorities also extend outward, imposing taxes on the same income that others would tax. Tax authorities within the United States and foreign countries are also increasing their tax jurisdictions. These long arms of the tax law often reach the activities of non-Indian companies abroad as well as Indian-based activities located outside India.

India, the United States, other treaty partners, and states within the United States seek to impose taxation on the aforementioned activities based on their specific PE concepts, relying when necessary on their aggressive transfer pricing regimes. It is no wonder, then, that the risk of double taxation is an important factor in the ordinary life of a multinational corporation, especially when it involves India or one of its trading partners.

BACKGROUND

The reader is cautioned that significant areas of double taxation exist between India and the United States and between India and other jurisdictions, in part because of the differences in source rules, in part because of aggressive tax enforcement, and in part because India follows the United Nations tax treaty model rather than the Organisation for Economic Co-operation and Development (OECD) model tax treaty. The advance pricing agreement process will alleviate some of these double taxation issues when India puts the advance pricing regime into force.

Prudence would dictate that the multinational taxpayer should undertake the process of aggregating its total effective tax costs, determined on a worldwide basis, taking into account the tax base and tax rate in each jurisdiction. The multinational taxpayer is likely to find that its aggregate tax base, determined on a worldwide basis, is more than 100% of the company's aggregate income. In fact, the multinational taxpayer to likely to find that its aggregate tax income base that involves India and OECD countries is likely to be substantially more than 100% of its aggregate income. As a result, and very importantly, the multinational taxpayer is well advised to address the conflicting tax systems simultaneously from a PE–transfer pricing perspective.

There is a commonplace myth among tax practitioners that "Asians do not litigate." Relying on that idea, some multinational taxpayers make it a point of ignoring Indian tax litigation. As we shall see, nothing could be further from the truth when it comes to Indian tax litigation. We examine more than 20 PE transfer pricing cases promulgated in India during the past years, together with a state case involving an Indian parent company, with a view toward examining current tax PE transfer pricing approaches.

NEXUS, EFFECTIVELY CONNECTED STATUS, AND PERMANENT ESTABLISHMENT

It is hornbook law that a country seeking to impose income taxation on a foreign entity can impose its income tax if the foreign entity has a connection or nexus to the entity. Tax treaties, for the most part, seek to limit this access to taxation by one of the contracting states by imposing a high threshold of effectively connected status that necessitates a PE in that jurisdiction. India is developing an extensive tax treaty network that includes its treaty with the United States and many of its trading partners, including the Netherlands, Canada, Korea, Japan, and elsewhere.

As a start in examining PE issues, the country in which the subsidiary is located might be able to tax the subsidiary because of the subsidiary's activities in the country. But the same country can impose an additional level of tax on the parent company headquartered elsewhere as well as on its subsidiary located in the jurisdiction. The country in which the subsidiary is located can look toward the activities of the parent company and then examine the relationship of the parent company toward the subsidiary. In essence, the country in which the subsidiary is located might be able to tax the parent company based on that parent company–subsidiary relationship.

FOUR FACT-BASED PERMANENT ESTABLISHMENT INQUIRIES

A non-Indian company doing business in India is well advised to examine four facets of the PE process in India: the presence of

1. Direct business activities
2. Agency relationships
3. More-than-stewardship activities
4. Personnel shifts from the parent company to the subsidiary

The non-Indian company doing business in India is well advised to examine the likelihood that the Indian tax authorities will seek a PE determination, based on its Indian-related activities. The Indian tax authorities will then seek to impose the transfer pricing process on the Indian business and on its offshore affiliate. Here is the examination process that we recommend Indian-related businesses undertake to determine their tax exposure:

1. **Presence of direct business activities.** Ascertain whether the direct business activities that the parent company undertakes create a PE in the subsidiary's location. The taxpayer's review of the parent company's direct business activities are a separate inquiry of the subsidiary's operations themselves. Income tax treaties exempt activities that are preparatory to or auxiliary from PE status. The issue of whether these activities are preparatory or auxiliary can be under dispute.
2. **Presence of agency relationships.** Ascertain whether the indirect relationship between the parent company and its subsidiary constitutes an agency relationship that binds the subsidiary to the parent company for PE purposes. The subsidiary can serve as the parent company's agent by negotiating, binding, entering into, or concluding contracts on behalf of the parent company. The taxpayer is well advised to examine the powers that the subsidiary undertakes.
3. **Presence of more-than-stewardship activities.** Ascertain whether the parent company's activities as to the subsidiary go beyond the stewardship level. Stewardship activities themselves are exempt for PE characterization, but the parent company's more-than-stewardship activities on the part of the subsidiary can

create a permanent establishment on the part of the parent company if the parent company performs these more-than-stewardship services.

4. **Presence of personnel shifts among entities.** Ascertain whether shifts of the parent company's personnel to the subsidiary create a permanent establishment. The parent company might have furnished personnel, might continue to payroll the subsidiary, or might take specific responsibility for the work of its employees at the subsidiary's location.

IMPACT OF THE *MORGAN STANLEY* CASE

The Indian tax collector brought suit against Morgan Stanley & Co. Inc., emanating from the claim of the Indian government to tax the U.S.-based Morgan Stanley & Co. Inc. as well as taxing Morgan Stanley's Indian subsidiary. In the case *Morgan Stanley & Co. Inc. v. Director of Income Tax*, Morgan Stanley was successful in India's Supreme Court in Mumbai in July 2007. India's revenue authorities then brought a review petition in India's Supreme Court. India's Supreme Court rejected the revenue authorities' review petition effective January 24, 2008, and ruled in favor of Morgan Stanley. The Court's decision is now final.

The Indian tax authorities claimed Morgan Stanley's operations in India itself caused Morgan Stanley's operations to be subject to tax in India. That claim on the part of the Indian tax authorities was in addition to Morgan Stanley's subsidiary in India that was already subject to tax in India. Morgan Stanley operated its back-office services company in India to take advantage of the differential between wage rates in the United States and in India.

The claim made by the Indian tax authorities was unsuccessful. The Indian Supreme Court rejected the tax authorities' claim because Morgan Stanley's activities in India did not result in having a fixed location in India or a permanent establishment. Morgan Stanley's Indian company did not carry on any business of the U.S. company.

The Indian tax authorities claimed Morgan Stanley's operations in India caused the company to be subject to tax in India because of Morgan Stanley's agency relationship with its Indian subsidiary. The tax authorities asserted that the Indian company incurred such a relationship with its U.S. parent because the Indian company had the authority to negotiate, bind, enter into, or conclude contracts on behalf of the U.S. parent company. The Indian Supreme Court concluded that such agency relationship did not apply to the *Morgan Stanley* facts because the Indian subsidiary did not have the agency authority and did not attempt to exercise such agency powers.

PERMANENT ESTABLISHMENT TRANSFER PRICING LITIGATION IN INDIA

The Indian tax authorities have been taking an aggressive stance on potential PE issues and are making PE claims outside of the transfer pricing context. Although the

Indian tax authorities can rely on conventional transfer pricing analysis, on other occasions the Indian tax authorities can split the profits between the entities with the transfer pricing context.

GALILEO

Galileo International Inc., a U.S. entity, is in the business of maintaining and providing electronic distribution systems to the travel industry in approximately 100 countries. Galileo provides computer reservations distribution services to airlines, hotels, tours, and cabs. Galileo's network connects to its travel agents' computer reservations distribution services through hardwire and computer connections. Galileo had close relationships with two entities in India:

1. Société Internationale de Télécommunications Aéronautiques connected Galileo's master computer system in the United States with travel agents in India.
2. InterGlobe Enterprises Pvt. Ltd. marketed and distributed the computer reservation services to travel agents in India.

The assessing officer (AO) imposed income tax on Galileo under a PE concept, reasoning that Indian travel agents completed their reservations through Galileo's installed hardware. The AO determined that Galileo had a PE in India under Article 5 in the India–U.S. Income Tax Treaty and that income was taxable as business income under Article 7 of that treaty.

The AO held that InterGlobe was a PE in India under Article 5 in the India–U.S. Income Tax Treaty. InterGlobe was independent from Galileo. Nevertheless, the AO rationalized PE status based on these agency-type activities:

- InterGlobe was "economically dependent" on Galileo for its source of business.
- InterGlobe conducted its activities wholly and exclusively for Galileo.
- InterGlobe entered into and concluded contracts on behalf of Galileo.

Galileo appealed the results to the Commissioner of Income Tax (Appeals) [CIT(A)], who held that Galileo in fact had a PE in India because Galileo's computers constituted a fixed place of business through which Galileo carried out its activities. Galileo then appealed the CIT(A) result, this time appealing to the Delhi Income Tax Appellate Tribunal (ITAT).

Galileo argued before ITAT that all of its data processing took place through its master computer system in the United States and that the computers merely displayed the information in India, so that Galileo had no connection in India. ITAT disagreed with Galileo's position as to its activities undertaken. ITAT looked to Galileo's booking of transactions that took place using Galileo equipment in India. ITAT noted the computerized reservation system partially existed in computers installed at subscribers' premises. In fact, Galileo controlled the shifting of computers even within the premises of subscribers. ITAT determined that those Galileo activities constituted a fixed place of business that constituted a PE in India.

ITAT then examined InterGlobe's relationship with Galileo, finding that the relationship was that of dependent agency. InterGlobe had the authority to enter contracts with subscribers, provided specialized services in India, and trained subscribers to use all of the computerized reservation system. InterGlobe was in India exclusively because of its relationship with Galileo, making InterGlobe a dependent agent.

ITAT sought to allocate the functions, activities, and risks in the United States and in India. ITAT, in making that determination, attributed to India 15% of Galileo's revenue based on bookings in India. ITAT, in making that determination, gave credence to the master computer system being outside India and being in the United States.

Galileo paid InterGlobe for the services that InterGlobe rendered to Galileo based on its distribution agreement. ITAT permitted Galileo to deduct the entire payments it had made to InterGlobe as expenses. We suspect that ITAT apportioned expenses to Indian operations and to U.S. operations on a 15%/85% split.

In summary, ITAT applied two separate facets in applying income taxation:

1. The direct activities of the taxpayer, Galileo
2. The indirect activities through the dependent agency relationship between Galileo and InterGlobe

HOTEL SCOPEVISTA

Hotel Scopevista is a hotel management service in India. It entered into an agreement with a foreign contractor under which the contractor was to render "project management services" for the construction of a hotel in India. Hotel Scopevista sought to make payments to the foreign contractor without making withholding payments. Hotel Scopevista, in essence, claimed that those payments are not taxable by India in the hands of the foreign contractor. Hotel Scopevista argued that the ultimate aim of the contractor in providing these services was the construction of the hotel, and the fees were for technical services, which excludes construction activities.

The AO rejected Hotel Scopevista's no-withholding-tax claim, holding that the payment was for management services, not for construction. The AO directed Hotel Scopevista to withhold 20% of the payments to the foreign contractor. Hotel Scopevista appealed to the CIT(A), who sided with the AO and required Hotel Scopevista to withhold the tax.

Hotel Scopevista then appealed again, this time before the ITAT. ITAT focused on the nature of the treaty exemption, stating that the character of the exemption was to shift the activities to a net income basis. The foreign contractor was not otherwise subject to tax in India; ITAT required payments to be made at source.

It appears that the court did not address PE issues, perhaps because the foreign contactor had already left India.

WORLEYPARSONS

WorleyParsons Services, Pty. Ltd. is an Australian company that provides engineering, procurement, and project management services. WorleyParsons entered in a contract with the Gas Authority of India, Ltd. (GAIL) to monitor a pipeline. WorleyParsons requested a ruling as to whether the payments it received from GAIL were in the nature of royalties, or, alternatively, whether the payments that WorleyParsons received were business profits.

WorleyParsons submitted a request to the Authority for Advance Ruling (AAR) seeking to ascertain the applicable tax treatment that WorleyParsons would receive. Based on the preceding facts, WorleyParsons contended that the payments it received were in the nature of PE activities pursuant to the Australia–India Income Tax Treaty taxable as business profits rather than being royalties. WorleyParsons asserted that:

- WorleyParsons performed most of its services in India.
- WorleyParsons' employees were present in India for 165 days.
- Nearly 90% to 95% of the work that WorleyParsons performed pursuant to contract was in India.

The AAR determined that WorleyParsons' technical supervisory services were not in the nature of a royalty but that these technical supervisory services were of the nature of PE that are subject to tax as business profits. The India–Australia Income Tax Treaty uses a "more than six months" time horizon. The AAR appears to have tacked the 165-day period to other time periods to reach the "more than six months" time horizon.

KNOWERX EDUCATION

KnoWerX Education (India) Private Limited was an educational intermediary, collecting exam fees for applicants in India and transmitting these exam fees to foreign institutes. The AAR held that KnoWerX was not obligated to withhold tax payments, the payments were not of a dependent agent, and the payments were not taxed in India.

KnoWerX provided various activities in India: private corporate training, open attendance-based public training, management consulting, publishing, and distribution of educational material. KnoWerX undertook these activities on behalf of professional examination organizations and certification programs. Those professional examination organizations and certification programs had no establishments of their own in India. The professional examination organizations and certification programs undertook these activities in India:

- Hiring other entities to conduct the examinations
- Evaluating answer sheets and awarding certificates outside India

KnoWerX asserted that some of the professional examination organizations and certification programs were tax-exempt in the United States, and thus, those entities would receive no U.S. foreign tax credit benefits. As a result, KnoWerX argued, the professional examination organizations and certification programs would receive no offset under the India–U.S. Income Tax Treaty. The CIT(A) determined that the professional examination organizations and certification programs would be taxable on the receipt of exam fees based on business income.

The AAR held that the examination fees that KnoWerX collected on behalf of the professional examination organizations and certification programs would be taxable. The AAR further determined that the professional examination organizations and certification programs were exempt from U.S. taxation under Internal Revenue Code section 501(c)(6), were liable to pay federal income tax, and, at least explicitly, were eligible to receive the U.S. foreign tax credit.

Nevertheless, the AAR concluded that the relationship between KnoWerX and the professional examination organizations and certification programs was that of independent agent rather than dependent agent. In making that determination as to the independent agency relationship, the AAR noted these facts:

- KnoWerX concluded no contracts between the applicants and the professional examination organizations and certification programs.
- KnoWerX did not maintain stocks of merchandise belonging to the professional examination organizations and certification programs.
- KnoWerX did not secure orders wholly or almost wholly for the professional examination organizations and certification programs, or bind them in the professional examination organizations and certification programs in India.
- There was no financial, managerial, or any other type of participation between KnoWerX and the professional examination organizations and certification programs.

The AAR did not require KnoWerX to withhold taxes from the professional examination organizations and certification programs because of that independent agency relationship, implicitly suggesting that the taxes would be imposed if a dependent agency relationship existed.

ICICI BANK

ICICI Bank is India's second largest commercial bank and the largest private-sector bank in India. In July 2008, the U.S. Ex-Im Bank approved a $250 million delegated authority for Indian infrastructure. India's Ministry of Finance has estimated that India will need more than $500 billion to finance development of its infrastructure.

Prior to that date, ICICI Bank planned to issue floating-rate euro notes. ICICI appointed Moody's Investors Service to provide a rating for these notes. ICICI paid Moody's for rendering that service. ICICI made the payments to Moody's without withholding a portion of the payments. The AO took the approach that ICICI erroneously failed to withhold taxes from its payments to Moody's. ICICI contended that:

- The withholding is inappropriate because Moody's operations are outside India.
- ICICI paid the amounts to Moody's outside India, making withholding impractical.

The AO held that ICICI's payments to Moody's were covered by the technical fee clause under the India–U.S. Income Tax Treaty, and that treaty required withholding at source. ICICI appealed the matter to the CIT(A). ICICI made two arguments:

1. ICICI argued that Moody's was a nonresident in India and no nexus in India, a nexus issue.
2. The income arose in the United States, not in India, a source of income issue.

The CIT(A) rejected ICICI's claim and held that ICICI's payment was covered within the definition of services under the India–U.S. Income Tax Treaty. As a result, the CIT(A) held that ICICI had an obligation to withhold tax pursuant to the treaty.

ICICI appealed the decision by the CIT(A), making that appeal to ITAT in Mumbai. The issue before ITAT was whether Moody's service of providing a credit rating to ICICI was "included services," as defined by the India–U.S. Income Tax Treaty, Article 12. ITAT held that Moody's did not carry on a business or profession in India and that Moody's did not have a PE in India. Accordingly, ITAT held that Moody's was not subject to tax in India under the business profits article of the India–U.S. tax treaty. As a result, ITAT held that ICICI was not responsible for failing to withhold tax on its payments to Moody's.

ZIMMER AG

Zimmer AG, a German company, was a manufacturer of plant and equipment. Zimmer entered into three separate agreements with an Indian company to build a resin manufacturing facility in Halida, India:

1. An equipment supply agreement
2. An engineering and know-how supply agreement
3. A technical supply agreement

The manufacturer paid Zimmer outside India pursuant to the engineering and know-how agreement. Zimmer recognized no liability in India for receiving that payment. The AO held that the payment that Zimmer received from the Indian manufacturer pursuant to the engineering and know-how supply agreement constituted a royalty under Indian law and under the Germany–India Income Tax Treaty. Zimmer appealed the AO's determination. The CIT(A) accepted Zimmer's claim holding that the payment made by the Indian manufacturer to Zimmer was not a royalty. India's tax collector appealed the CIT(A) decision to the ITAT.

ITAT looked at the entirety of Zimmer's relationship with the Indian manufacturer, viewing that relationship as "a composite supply" and the engineering documents as being an integral part of the process. ITAT viewed the transfer of documents to the Indian company as being complete, constituting a transfer of title and interest. ITAT agreed with CIT(A), holding that the payment is not a royalty because the manufacturer purchased the technology from Zimmer on an outright basis.

INTERGRAFICA

Intergrafica Print and Pack, GmbH, a German company, coordinated with MAN Roland Druckmashinen AG, another German company, to supply equipment to Bennett, Coleman & Company in Mumbai. Intergrafica's head office in Germany and its branch office in India arranged for the order and its subsequent supply. Intergrafica allocated 60% of the profit from the commission to the Indian branch office and allocated 40% of the profit from the commission to the home office. However, the AO asserted that all of the operations for the sale and for operations after the sale took place in India and treated all of the profits as taking place in India. Intergrafica appealed the assessing officers' conclusion to the CIT(A).

On appeal, the CIT(A) reviewed the functions that the head office and branch office each performed and determined that the appropriate allocation of profits was 75% to the branch office and 25% to the head office. The CIT(A) noted that the branch office had no authority to approve the contract. Intergrafica then appealed the CIT(A) decision.

ITAT focused on the nature of the home office operations, noting the home office had engineers on its payroll and provided assistance during installation and other times when the branch office so required. The functions of the branch office, according to ITAT, were limited after the end of the warranty period. ITAT accepted Intergrafica's allocation of 60% of the profit from the commission to the Indian branch office and the allocation of 40% of the profit from the commission to the home office.

RANBAXY LABORATORIES

Ranbaxy Laboratories is a multinational company that manufactures and sells pharmaceutical products in India and in 17 associated enterprises. Ranbaxy applied the transactional net margin method (TNMM) for transfer pricing purposes, treating the associated enterprises together as the tested party and treating the profit on sales as the profit level indicator. The net profit margin before tax for the entire group's business is lower than the average net margin before tax of the comparable overseas companies. Ranbaxy asserted that it met the arm's length standard because of that differential in profit margins.

The AO accepted that Ranbaxy's transfer pricing was at arm's length, and the AO did not require an adjustment. The CIT(A) then initiated an action under section 263 of the Indian Income Tax Act, arguing that:

- The AO was to refer the case over to the transfer pricing officer (TPO), which the AO failed to do, to determine whether the transaction was at arm's length.
- Ranbaxy appeared to have used the TNMM incorrectly by combining the results from the associated enterprises operating in diverse conditions as the tested party, while in fact reliable comparative data was available in India.

Ranbaxy argued that it should not be penalized because of the AO's failure to transfer the case over to the TPO. Ranbaxy further argued that the Revenue Department was correct in using the affiliated enterprises as the tested party as their activities are less complex than Ranbaxy's activities.

ITAT looked to the failure of the AO to ascertain an in-house comparable, suggesting that the AO should have ascertained names of the products and quantities of the products Ranbaxy had sold to independent concerns. Further, ITAT was concerned that the AO failed to address the characteristics of the transactions and failed to provide a profile or location for eight of the comparables.

ITAT suggested that the AO should have compared the company's profits with the profit margin of pharmaceutical companies of the same size carrying on similar transactions in India. ITAT implicitly accepted the taxpayer's power to select the tested party but required the taxpayer to provide the relevant information to the taxing authorities unless the comparison data are publicly available. Here ITAT felt that it made sense to view Ranbaxy as the tested party as comparable data were available.

ITAT found that Ranbaxy provided no justification for grouping fundamentally separate and independent transactions carried out at different times and related to different parties. The case is now on appeal before the Delhi High Court. Ranbaxy will contend that the company is applying the "most appropriate [transfer pricing] method."

DEVELOPMENT CONSULTANTS

Development Consultants Pvt. Ltd., an Indian company, had operations in the Bahamas and in the United States through its related entities. The assessment years were 2003–2004 and 2004–2005. The Indian transfer pricing regulations require a company engaged in transfer pricing to file and to furnish an accountant's report to the TPO. Development Consultants failed to furnish its required accountant's report for the assessment years but did file other necessary documents with the TPO during its audit proceedings in 2004–2005.

The TPO adjusted the results during the assessment years. The CIT(A) confirmed the additions to tax that the TPO had made. Development Consultants filed an appeal before ITAT. The issue was whether pricing should be determined on a transaction-by-transaction method, as Development Consultants contended, or be aggregated, at the tax authorities contended.

Before ITAT, the Revenue Department examined the relationship between Development Consultants and its subsidiary in the Bahamas, DCIL. The taxpayer sought to portray DCIL as being an entrepreneur having significant intangibles and argued that Development Consultants should be the tested party. The Revenue Authorities rejected Development Consultants' approach, selected DCIL as the tested party, and applied the resale price method. The Revenue Department, then, viewed DCIL as distributor of services as to its engineering, drawing, and design services, and adjusted the profits for the first of the assessment years. ITAT dispensed with the Revenue Department's assertion that DCIL was a sham company established to avoid taxes.

ITAT then examined Development Consultants' relationship with its U.S. entity. Here, in contrast to the Bahamas situation, ITAT found that the U.S. entity was an entrepreneur that created significant intangibles over the years and accepted Development Consultants as the tested party. ITAT found the transactions to be at arm's length.

ITAT looked at the level of profits that Development Consultants obtained by transferring its employees. Development Consultants used Indian databases to substantiate its profits and was successful with the ITAT.

ITAT then turned its attention to data entry services. DataCore USA, an entrepreneurial company, provided software and back-office work to its customers. DataCore USA uploaded the work to DataCore India, both being subsidiaries of Development Consultants. Development Consultants' profit margins in India were higher than in comparable companies during the related assessment years, and ITAT held that these amounts were all at arm's length.

PERFITTI

Perfitti SPA, an Italian company, owned 100% of Perfitti India Ltd. Perfitti SPA supplied machinery and raw materials to Perfitti India Ltd. The AO asserted that Perfitti SPA's income was taxable in India because Perfitti SPA undertook these activities:

- Perfitti SPA supplied machinery continuously for nearly a year in India.
- Perfitti SPA's managing director and other expatriates received salaries from Perfitti SPA, and Perfitti SPA had total control over the Indian operations.
- Perfitti SPA took orders for the machinery in India for more than a year.
- The prices were not at arm's length and were too high.

The AO did not have Perfitti's global balance sheet nor did the AO have its Italian accounts, but assumed a 20% margin. Perfitti challenged the AO's order and went before the CIT(A). The CIT(A) agreed with Perfitti, deciding that Perfitti had no business connection in India and thus had no permanent establishment. The Revenue Department appealed to ITAT, but ITAT held in favor of Perfitti, finding that:

- The Revenue Department had the onus to establish overinvoicing of the cost of the machinery but had failed to do so.
- The goods were properly shipped to Perfitti India Ltd.
- The Italian company properly shifted the employees to the Indian company.
- The quality control manager and technologists were in India for a short period of time; there was no evidence that Perfitti supervised construction operations; there was no business connection in India; and there was no permanent establishment.

DATA SOFTWARE RESEARCH

Data Software Research Co. (P) Ltd. was an Indian company. Data Software had a branch in the United States. Data Software Research Co. (P) Ltd. had claimed that its profits from the U.S. branch were not subject to tax in India because the United States already had taxed that income. The AO claimed that an Indian resident, such as Data Software Research, is to include all income, from whatever source, and that the India–U.S. Income Tax Treaty permitted India to tax the profits of a U.S. branch.

Data Software Research Co. (P) Ltd. appealed the AO's determination, claiming the inclusion of branch income would result in double taxation. The CIT(A) determined that Data Software Research Co. (P) Ltd. was correct. The Income Tax Department then appealed to ITAT. ITAT determined that Data Software Research Co. (P) Ltd. must compute its worldwide income, including that of its U.S. branch, but that this inclusion does not lead to double taxation because the U.S. branch can apply for a foreign tax credit.

Before ITAT, Data Software Research Co. (P) Ltd. had argued that it had a PE in the United States in the form of a branch company, that the permanent establishment's profits were taxable under U.S. law, and that this income could then not be taxed in India. The Revenue Department argued that the onus of double taxation fell on the United States through its foreign tax credit mechanism.

ITAT recognized that two methods exist to eliminate double taxation: the exemption method and the tax credit method. The Indian government can select between these two elimination methods through the income tax treaty it signs. Relying on Article 25.2(a) of the Income Tax Treaty between India and the United States, ITAT concluded that the AO was correct in determining Data Software Research Co. (P) Ltd. income on a global basis. The U.S. branch could then claim its foreign tax credit.

SNC LAVALIN/ACRES INC.

SNC Lavalin/Acres Inc. was a Canadian-based company having the responsibility of building and setting up the Chamera Hydro Electrical Project in India. The company had a site office in Chamera and established a PE in India. A dispute arose between the company and the AO as to the percentage of profits that were taxable in India. The company first took the position that the entire income from the project was attributable to the PE in India and filed its tax return on that basis. The company later took the position that the income of the project was to be divided between the home office in Canada and the PE in India. The company determined that 19.63% of the income was taxable in India and submitted a letter, not a revised income tax return, to change the initial result.

The AO dismissed the taxpayer's claim, stating that all of the income was from the Chamera project. The taxpayer appealed to the CIT(A). The CIT(A) approved the AO's determination. The taxpayer then appealed to ITAT.

ITAT accepted the taxpayer's letter claim from a procedural standpoint because the AO and the CIT(A) had accepted the taxpayer's approach. Then ITAT addressed the taxpayer's substantive claim.

The initial issue that ITAT had to face was the interpretation of the India–Canada Income Tax Treaty as to the attribution of profits. The taxpayer took the approach that the India–Canada Income Tax Treaty applied the OECD model treaty, thus narrowing scope of attribution of profits concept. The taxpayer treated the home office as a separate functional entity, pointing out that the home office assumed the entire risk, including performance guarantees, and that the home office received all of the contractual proceeds. India's Revenue Department asserted that the "force of attraction" attribution of profits was broader, as the India–Canada Income Tax Treaty applied the UN treaty approach. ITAT agreed with the Revenue Department's approach.

AIRPORT AUTHORITY OF INDIA

The Airport Authority of India is a public sector enterprise that purchased equipment and software from Raytheon, a U.S. company. Raytheon was not involved in operating or maintaining the Airport Authority of India equipment. The Airport Authority of India subsequently entered into two contracts with Raytheon, one for equipment repair and the other for updates and to modify software. The Airport Authority of India then applied for a ruling with the AAR to ascertain whether it must provide for withholding on the payments it made to Raytheon. The Airport Authority of India asserted that its payments to Raytheon are business profits and not subject to withholding.

The parties to the litigation differentiated the consequences of the equipment repair contract and the software maintenance contract. The AAR initially accepted the Airport Authority of India's argument that the amounts it paid to Raytheon in connection with the equipment repair contract were in the nature of business profits, but later the Revenue Department asserted that these activities constituted a permanent establishment.

The AAR determined that the software maintenance contract was in the nature of "fees for included services" and was subject to withholding. The AAR held that Raytheon did not have a PE in India because the equipment repair and software modification activities took place outside India and Raytheon's personnel activities in India were sporadic. The AAR held that the Airport Authority of India had no obligation to withhold payment to Raytheon for equipment repairs but the Airport Authority of

India had the obligation to withhold tax at the 10% rate on the software maintenance and upgrades that the Airport Authority of India paid to Raytheon.

RADHA RANI HOLDINGS

The issue in Radha Rani Holdings (P.) Ltd. was the situs of "control and management" activities and whether the control and management activities took place in Singapore or in India. The company had two shareholders. The Indian resident owned 99% of the company's share capital; the Singapore resident owned 1% of the company's share capital. The Singapore–India Income Tax Treaty potentially applied in this situation.

The AO determined that the company's control and management took place in India exclusively, relying on passport documents that counteracted a board of directors meeting ostensibly taking place in Singapore, and that the 99% Indian shareholder was the source of the corporate funds. The company appealed to the CIT(A). The CIT(A) determined that AO was correct in determining that the entire control and management took place in India. The company then appealed to ITAT.

The taxpayer asserted that the control and management took place exclusively in Singapore, not in India, based on these facts:

- The company's registered office was in Singapore.
- All of the company's board meetings were held in Singapore.
- The company determined its day-to-day administrative and business matters in Singapore.
- The company maintained its statutory books of account in Singapore.
- The company maintained its bank accounts in Singapore.
- The company controlled the operation of its bank accounts in Singapore.
- The Singapore Tax Authority had issued the company a tax residency certificate.
- The company regularly filed its corporate tax returns in Singapore.
- One of the two company directors was a permanent resident and citizen of Singapore.
- The second of two company directors had been a resident of Singapore for three years. That director was not a resident in India during that time period.
- The company raised funds from abroad and made investments from abroad.
- The company made its loan and investment decisions, which were frequent, in Singapore.
- The company undertook stewardship operations to these entities in Singapore.

ITAT examined the meaning of "control and management," viewing control and management as being the head and the brain, as indicated by the board of directors. ITAT took a formalistic approach to the case at hand, as witnessed by these findings:

- ITAT found that all of the company's board of directors meetings took place in Singapore, never in India.

- ITAT concluded that the residence of the directors and the carrying on of day-to-day operations were unimportant.
- ITAT viewed both directors as having equal power even though one shareholder controlled 99% of the shares and the other director controlled 1% of the shares.
- ITAT diminished the importance of physical relationship of the directors, suggesting that the meeting could have taken place by telephone or by video conferencing.
- Further, ITAT viewed Singapore's providing the company with a tax residency certificate as being determinative.

MASHREQ BANK PSC

The India–United Arab Emirates Income Tax Treaty came to the fore in the Mashreq Bank PSC case regarding taxing profits of a permanent establishment. Mashreq Bank PSC was a nonresident banking company headquartered in the United Arab Emirates operating in India through a branch and subject to the PE rules. The AO disallowed some expenses of the branch. The bank appealed this result to the CIT(A), asserting that the bank was entitled to all of its expenses, whether taking place in India or outside India. The CIT(A) determined that domestic Indian law applied to determine the deductibility of the expenses. The bank then appealed to the ITAT.

Citing other sources, ITAT concluded that the location of the expenses determines the deductibility, and tax treaties give the power over taxability to the tax authorities in the jurisdiction in which the taxes are imposed. Each contracting state can apply its own general principles in computing the profits it has a right to tax. In other words, ITAT took the approach that domestic law governs.

MENTOR GRAPHICS (NOIDA) PVT. LTD.

Mentor Graphics (Noida) Pvt. Ltd., an Indian company, was closely related to IKOS, both being engaged in software development. Mentor was engaged in rendering software services to IKOS. IKOS used the software to support IKOS's hardware sold as a package on the open market. Mentor applied the TNMM based on a cost plus markup as the profit level indicator. Mentor used two "screens" to eliminate comparables:

1. The first screen is unusual, filtering out companies having a manufacturing sales to total sales ratio of more than 25% and a trading sales to total sales ratio of more than 25%.
2. The second screen is more common, filtering out companies with different products or functions, related party transactions, low sales, operational losses of more than 10%, and insufficient information.

The cost plus markup for the comparables that Mentor selected was 13.41%. Mentor's own activities had a markup of 11.07%. Mentor claimed the transactions at arm's length based on Income Tax Act section 92C(2), which provides for a variation of plus or minus 5%.

The TPO rejected Mentor's reasoning and the use of data for years other than the year at issue. The TPO rejected some companies as comparables. The TPO then did its own search of comparables and had an average cost plus markup of 26.94%. Mentor had an average cost markup of 24.53% after making adjustments. Mentor appealed the result to the CIT(A). The CIT(A) upheld the TPO's adjustment. Mentor then appealed to ITAT.

ITAT reversed the results provided by the TPO in significant part because the TPO failed to properly assess the level of risk between Mentor and IKOS. Mentor was a captive software development service provider to IKOS. IKOS had most of the business risk, such as contract risk, market risk, credit risk, warranty risk, price risk, and so forth. IKOS owned the intellectual property rights to the intangibles that it provided to Mentor. Further, the TPO had asserted that the companies selected comparables not having any related party transactions, but the facts were otherwise.

MILLENNIUM INFOCOM TECHNOLOGIES LTD.

Millennium Infocom Technologies Ltd., an Indian company, set up Web site leasing servers in the United States. Millennium did not withhold payment it had made to the server owners but claimed these expenses on its tax returns. The AO disallowed the lease payment expense, relying on section 40(a)(i) of the Indian Tax Act, which denies a deduction paid to nonresidents. Millennium appealed this result to the CIT(A). The CIT(A) upheld the AO's finding. Millennium then went before ITAT.

ITAT examined the implications of the India–U.S. Income Tax Treaty as well as changes to Indian domestic law in the context of the Millennium situation.

Millennium successfully sought relief under Article 26(3) of the India–U.S. Income Tax Treaty, which prohibits discrimination against nonresidents. ITAT held the treaty provisions are determinative, and Millennium prevailed against the Revenue Department.

VAN OORD ACZ INDIA

Van Oord ACZ Marine Contractors BV, a Netherlands company, was in the dredging business. It had a subsidiary in India, Van Oord ACZ India, that executed a dredging contract at an Indian port. The Indian subsidiary incurred mobilization and demobilization expenses, primarily for transporting surveying equipment and other plant and machinery from outside India to inside India and from inside India to outside India. The Dutch parent company owned the equipment, and the Indian company used the equipment in its dredging operations. The Dutch parent company reimbursed the Indian subsidiary for these expenses. The parties alluded to the presence of arm's length pricing, but the Indian government did not address the bona fides of the intercompany lease.

The Indian subsidiary did not withhold tax on the reimbursed amounts it paid to its parent company. The Revenue Department ruled that the Indian subsidiary should have withheld tax, and because the subsidiary failed to withhold, the subsidiary could not deduct its dredging mobilization and demobilization costs pursuant to Indian domestic tax law. The Indian subsidiary appealed the Revenue Department's determination and appealed to the CIT(A). The CIT(A) rejected the Indian subsidiary's appeal, and the subsidiary went before ITAT. ITAT rejected the subsidiary's claim.

The subsidiary characterized the payments to its parent company as being a conduit, a reimbursement of actual expenses, causing the subsidiary to earn no profit from that activity. The subsidiary argued that the payments were at arm's length, an issue that the TPO confirmed. Nevertheless, the case did not further dwell on potential transfer pricing considerations. The Revenue Department argued that the parent company had a PE under the India–Netherlands Income Tax Treaty, but ITAT apparently did not address this issue further. ITAT rejected the subsidiary's reimbursement-of-cost approach and determined that the subsidiary should have withheld tax and that the subsidiary could not deduct the reimbursement amounts.

TOKYO MARINE & FIRE INSURANCE CO. LTD.

Tokyo Marine & Fire Insurance Co. Ltd., a Japanese company, established a representative office in India and later entered into a joint venture with IFFCO, an Indian company, IFFCO-Tokyo General Insurance Co. Ltd. in India, for the purpose of underwriting general insurance in India. The Japanese head office paid representative office costs, including expatriate salaries, rent, travel, and legal expenses.

The Revenue Department determined that Tokyo Marine & Fire Insurance Co. Ltd. had a fixed place of business in India that constituted a PE under the India–Japan Income Tax Treaty. Tokyo Marine & Fire Insurance Co. Ltd. appealed to the CIT(A). The CIT(A) set aside the Revenue Department finding and ruled in favor of Tokyo Marine & Fire Insurance Co. Ltd. The Revenue Department then appealed the finding to the Delhi ITAT.

Before ITAT, the Revenue Department, in advocating PE treatment, focused on the rent that Tokyo Marine & Fire Insurance Co. Ltd. had paid, the presence of five expatriates and local staff, and the involvement in the IFFCO contract.

Tokyo Marine & Fire Insurance Co. Ltd. argued that the representative office was only a liaison office, had no authority to conclude contracts on behalf of Tokyo Marine & Fire Insurance Co. Ltd., and the Reserve Bank of India limited the scope of the representative office approval.

ITAT held that the revenue department failed to demonstrate that the representative office was undertaking commercial activities in India beyond the Reserve Bank of India's limitations. Tokyo Marine & Fire Insurance Co. Ltd. conducted its business in India through its joint venture company, which was taxed separately. ITAT ruled against the Revenue Department's approach, relying on Article 5, paragraph 6 of the India–Japan Income Tax Treaty, which provides an exemption of "preliminary or auxiliary" activities, holding that Tokyo Marine & Fire Insurance Co. Ltd. activities were in the nature of "preliminary or auxiliary" activities.

WESTERN UNION MONEY TRANSFER

Western Union Money Transfer, a U.S. company, was engaged in the business of transferring money. Western Union Money Transfer had a liaison office in India and had appointed unrelated agents in India to facilitate its money transfer business. The Revenue Department determined that the company's money transfer activities in India constituted a PE of the U.S. company. Western Union Money Transfer appealed.

ITAT reversed the Revenue Department decision and held that the U.S. company had no PE in India. ITAT concluded that the liaison office was engaged in preparatory and auxiliary activities that the India–U.S. Income Tax Treaty had excluded from PE status. ITAT's conclusion was based significantly on the fact the Indian agents were independent agents. ITAT held that the Revenue Department could tax none of the profits of the U.S. company.

CARGO COMMUNITIES NETWORK

Cargo Communities Network Pte. Ltd. was a cargo facilitator that served as an air cargo portal. Indian agents that were in the business of booking cargo on airlines could subscribe to access to Cargo Communities Network Pte. Ltd., a Singapore company. The access provided the Indian agents with details of the airlines' flight schedules, cargo space availability, and so forth. Cargo Communities Network Pte. Ltd. signed its contracts with Indian agents outside of India. The Indian agents paid their subscription fees to Cargo Communities Network Pte. Ltd. outside of India. The AAR held that the payments that the Indian agents made to Cargo Communities Network Pte. Ltd. were in the nature of royalties and were taxed as such under the India–Singapore Income Tax Treaty.

HYUNDAI HEAVY INDUSTRIES

Hyundai Heavy Industries, Ltd., a Korean company, was in the process of designing, fabricating, and installing equipment, and undertook those activities for an Indian company for a location in India. The revenue authorities assessed the entire profits of the project as being in India and subject to Indian income tax. The Supreme Court held that India cannot tax the non-Indian operations. India was able to tax only the profits related to the installation and commission activities in India.

E. GAIN PVT. LTD.

E. Gain Pvt. Ltd. was an Indian-based captive software service provider, a subsidiary of a U.S. entity. E. Gain Pvt. Ltd. bore no risk emanating from the intercompany transaction; the U.S. parent company bore all the risk from the intercompany transaction. The company, recognizing that it was a captive software provider, charged its parent company at cost plus 5%. The TPO ignored the risk of loss issue, determined that the Indian subsidiary should apply the markup of cost plus 16%, and made an adjustment accordingly. It appears that the TPO relied on a broad base of software companies, some captive, some independent.

ITAT rejected the TPO's analysis and focused instead on functional differences and different levels of risk. The Indian subsidiary in this instance was entitled to a lower cost plus margin because it had a much lower level of risk. ITAT accepted the taxpayer's approach and applied the TNMM.

INFOSYS INTERNATIONAL ACTIVITIES IN NEW YORK STATE

Infosys Technologies Limited is a worldwide Indian-based software development and consulting firm. Infosys operates a self-described "global delivery model" in which Infosys matches small teams of targeted in-country engineers with offshore development centers in India. U.S. wages for engineers were approximately 10 times the amount of Indian wages for engineers in 2000 and 2001, the years under dispute.

Infosys is doing business in New York State and other U.S. locations, as well as in other countries throughout the world. A dispute arose as to Infosys income subject to New York State tax. The New York Administrative Law Judge (ALJ) reached its decision in favor of the New York State's Division of Taxation. The New York Tax Appeals Tribunal affirmed the decision of the ALJ. DTA No. 820669, February 21, 2008.

The initial inquiry before the New York courts was the allocation methods that New York State can apply to determine the amount of Infosys income subject to New York State law:

- Can Infosys develop its own allocation method for purposes of allocating income to New York State, without seeking consent from New York State?
- Must Infosys use New York State's allocation formula for purposes of allocating income to New York State?

The ALJ and the Tax Appeals Tribunal determined that New York's allocation formula applies. The courts reached this decision on procedural grounds, stating that the New York allocation rules were logical and mandatory and that Infosys did not request an exception from the New York allocation method. Infosys's approach, despite its assertion, does not constitute valid "separate accounting."

The second inquiry was the basis on which Infosys was to determine the income subject to allocation:

- Should Infosys determine its taxable income for New York State to be allocated based on its taxable income connected with its U.S. trade or business, as reported on its Form 1120F federal tax return?
- Should Infosys determine its income to be allocated based on its worldwide income, thus disregarding the Form 1120F?

The courts determined that Infosys's allocation to New York State was to be based on its entire worldwide income. The court held that the Form 1120F determination was not specifically relevant to the New York State apportionment issue.

The courts rejected Infosys's approach to apply transfer pricing—comparable profits method—cost plus 7%:

- Courts in the United States and elsewhere prefer an allocation approach rather than transfer pricing because allocation is much easier and more certain than transfer pricing.
- The India–U.S. Income Tax Treaty provides that the treaty does not impact state and local taxes.

A question arose as to how Infosys should determine its receipts factor:

- **Actual charges approach.** An amount based on the actual amounts that Infosys billed to clients for work done within the state and outside the state
- **A formulary approach.** An amount based on a head count ratio or on a days-worked ratio (i.e., a time-spent ratio)

Infosys's gross margin on employee costs in the United States was 42% to 43%. Infosys's gross margin in employee costs was 87%, making Indian operations more profitable. The formula approaches would shift income toward the United States and thus to New York State. The courts concluded that Infosys could not use a "relative values" approach. Infosys was to use the actual amounts invoiced to New York taxpayers, the actual charges approach.

The India–U.S. Income Tax Treaty pertains only to federal taxation, not state taxation. The Infosys result might have been different if Infosys had set up a separate entity for its New York operations. The question remains whether New York State can tax profits in India that result from the New York services.

CHAPTER THIRTEEN

Taxation of Travel Services in India

SABRE INC. (Sabre) successfully defeated the Indian tax authority's claim that a company that pays airline commissions for booking fees in India is a permanent establishment. Sabre rejected the Indian tax authority's claim that the company is subject to tax on its profits in India. Sabre Inc.'s success follows Galileo International Inc.'s similar defeat of the Indian tax authorities. The Sabre and Galileo cases, taken together, provide some useful tax guideposts for the computer reservation services industry and for the travel services industry as a whole.

Both Sabre and Galileo are well-known large players in the competitive world of the global distribution services industry, also termed the computer reservation services industry. Their competitors include other major players, including Amadeus and Worldspan. Both Sabre and Galileo operated in India through InterGlobe, located in Guragon, India. The government of India taxed InterGlobe on their Sabre and Galileo operations, a fact having considerable consequences in both cases.

Both Sabre and Galileo are U.S. entities. Both entities are potentially subject to the 1989 income tax convention between India and the United States. Additionally, both

Sabre and Galileo are potentially subject to the 2002 Competent Authority Agreement between India and the United States.

As tax practitioners, we suspect that, after the Sabre and Galileo cases, other countries are likely to provide their legal authority for imposing taxation on these Internet sales. We suspect that these countries will later be enhancing their audit mechanisms to impose taxation on similar Internet transactions. We also suspect, however, that the mechanism for allocating an appropriate share of the company's income in that country will remain elusive for some time to come, leaving the Sabre and Galileo cases as applicable guidance.

SABRE

The Sabre case before the Delhi Income Tax Appellate Tribunal (ITAT) was first before the lower court, focusing on the government's claim that Sabre's operations in India are subject to tax in India based on a permanent establishment claim. ITAT first examined the taxpayer appeal positions and the tax collector's appeal positions,[1] giving insight into their litigation positions from a permanent establishment perspective:

- The taxpayer argued that the government improperly raised the business connection requirement under section 9(1) of the Indian Income Tax Act, 1961.
- The taxpayer argued that the government erroneously held that the permanent establishment provisions under Article 5 of the India–U.S. Double Tax Avoidance Agreement apply.
- The taxpayer argued that the government grossly erred in holding that the taxpayer has a fixed place permanent establishment in India by virtue of having subscribers in India.

Sabre had a contract with the National Marketing Division (NMD) of Air India and Indian Airlines. The contract made NMD Sabre's distributor in India. The government concluded that this distributor arrangement made NMD Sabre's dependent agent. If the government were proven correct in this assertion, Sabre would be caught into the government's web, having to pay tax on the NMD activities because of that dependent agency relationship.

Sabre paid 60% of the India-generated booking fees to NMD. The taxpayer asserted that its fees to NMD (an unrelated entity) were at arm's length and that the government could attribute no further profits to Sabre in India. The Commissioner of Income Tax (Appeals) [CIT(A)] concluded that, of the total profit earned by Sabre in India, 25% of that profit is attributable to the business activities carried on by its permanent establishment in India.

Sabre contended that the government did not allow or restricted the deduction of expenses connected with the NMD arrangement. Sabre contended that these expenses are legitimate expenses incurred outside India and pertain to the generation of booking fees while computing the profits of these transactions. Sabre further contends that the government erred in ignoring the taxpayer's submissions and in disallowing deductions for home office expenditures. In addition, the taxpayer argued that the government erred as to the taxability of interest.

Government's Claims

The court took cognizance of the government's claims in Sabre. The government claimed that the Deputy Director of Income Tax erred in finding that Sabre's activities in India did not constitute a permanent establishment under Article 5(1) of the India–U.S. Agreement for Avoidance of Double Taxation. The Deputy Director of Income Tax considered the entire income related to the bookings in India as being chargeable in India.

The Deputy Director of Income Tax rejected the audited statements with regard to the booking fee received from Jet Airways by assuming that amount is 60% of the total global booking fees paid by Jet Airways to Sabre. The Deputy Director of Income Tax estimated that 60% of the total global booking fees paid by Jet Airways to Sabre as pertaining to booking originating in India, making that determination without giving Sabre the right to be heard.

The Deputy Director of Income Tax disallowed marketing expenditures attributable to the alleged permanent establishment. The facts of the case should make it evident that the government should have allowed some estimate for expenses against the alleged permanent establishment. Additionally, the government erroneously disallowed data processing expenses and foreign-based head office expenses.

Prior Litigation

ITAT had considered the preceding fact pattern in prior litigation. There ITAT determined that the income was chargeable to tax as Sabre had a business connection in India. ITAT then held that Sabre should treat 15% of the revenue as income accrued or assessed in India under the business connection test.

ITAT held that 15% of the revenue attributable to Sabre as to the bookings made in India should be treated as income accrued or assessed in India. Since Sabre charges €3 per booking, 15% would be €.45, from which Sabre paid €1 per booking, creating a loss, and having no income or profits that are taxed in India.

ITAT held that Sabre had no income or profits that are taxable in India. ITAT held that Sabre had permanent establishment, reaching that determination based on Circular 23, July 7, 1969, and based on the judgment of the Indian Supreme Court in *Morgan Stanley & Co.*[2]

The Indian tax authority pursued the matter before the Supreme Court, contending that ITAT erred in attributing the revenue to India while arriving at a finding that 15% of the revenue be attributable to Sabre in terms of bookings made. The government argued that the criteria, as laid down in the permanent establishment circular as well as the India–U.S. Double Tax Agreement, enumerates the concept of "profits," not of "revenue." The Supreme Court did not accept the government's contentions as to the test to be adopted, which is the attribution of profits and not of revenue.

ITAT questioned whether, having held that Sabre has a business connection in India, how much of that income is subject to tax in India. ITAT then discussed the principle to be followed in apportioning the income tax accruing in India and the income tax accruing outside India. ITAT held that only a part of the reservation order operates and functions in India. The extent of working in India applies only to the extent of channelizing the request and the receiving of the result of the process in India. The major function and database collection as to various airlines and hotels takes place outside India.

ITAT took into consideration the fact that the company's computer in Denver processes various data, such as the schedule of flights, timing, pricing, availability, meal preference, special facilities, and the like. So far as the role of the travel services took place in India, that role concerned desk computers that are merely connected or configured to the extent that the computer can perform a booking function but are not capable of processing the data of all the airlines together at one place.

ITAT was also influenced by what it termed "another important fact" that such functioning requires huge investment and huge capacity, which are not available in the computers installed at the desk of the subscriber in India. On this basis, ITAT formed the opinion that Sabre processes the major part of the work at the host computer in Denver and that the activities in India are only a minor portion of the total effort. Taking into account all of these factors, ITAT was of the opinion that one could reasonably attribute 15% of the revenue accruing to Sabre as to bookings made in India. Sabre incurred major expenses in this endeavor in the United States.

Lack of Applicable Guidelines

ITAT recognized that no guidelines are available regarding how much of the income is reasonably attributable to the operations carried out in India. ITAT would have taxpayers and tax collectors determine the reasonable allocated amounts in each circumstance based on the factual situation prevailing in each case. The taxpayer and the tax collector, in making this allocated amounts determination, would look broadly to factors such as the function performed, assets used, and risks undertaken. The countries can attribute the income between the jurisdictions on the basis of the functions performed, assets used, and risks shared in the two different countries.

ITAT found that the majority of the assets (i.e., the host computer, which has a very large capacity that processes information for all of the participants) are situated outside India. Sabre developed and maintained the computer reservation service as a whole outside India.

ITAT then provides a "but for" and "equal importance" analysis: Income would not exist but for the presence of Sabre in India and the configuration and connectivity being produced in India. Thus, ITAT determined that the initial cause of the generation of income is in India. On the basis of these facts, ITAT attributed 15% of the revenue accruing to the taxpayer as to bookings made in India. ITAT called its determination "reasonable," and the amount as chargeable under section 5(2) of the United States–India 1989 Income Tax Convention between India and the United States and section 9(1) of the Indian Income Tax Act, 1961.

The High Court upheld the approach adopted by ITAT to first arrive at a figure relating to the revenue generated in India and abroad. The High Court concluded that, out of the revenue accrued to the taxpayer as to these bookings, 15% of these amounts should be attributed to India. The result was in keeping in view a "very minor portion" of the activity being carried out actually took place outside India.

ITAT focused its discussion on the relevant consideration, namely, how much of the aforesaid revenues would be attributed to profits. The High Court concluded that ITAT addressed itself to the issue of profits. While giving a finding of fact that 15% of the revenue can be attributed to the activities in India, ITAT had not taken into consideration the commission expenses that Sabre paid to InterGlobe.

The High Court, in the ultimate analysis, followed the Supreme Court in *Hukam Chand Mills Ltd. v. CIT, Bombay.*[3] There the Supreme Court observed that, in the absence of some statutory or other fixed formula, any finding on the question or proportion involves some element of guesswork. The High Court held that the endeavor can only be approximate, and, in the nature of things, there cannot be precision and exactness in the matter. The High Court concluded that as long as the proportion fixed by ITAT is based on relevant material, the High Court should not disturb the finding. The High Court dismissed the government's appeal.

Sabre paid 60% of its receipts, which is far in excess of one third in case of overseas receipts, and 25% of other receipts accrued to Sabre. As a result, no income would be taxable in India. ITAT allowed Sabre's appeal based on the preceding High Court decision.

ITAT in this case followed the prior year ITAT's order and allowed Sabre's appeals. ITAT held that Sabre would not be taxed in India.

GALILEO

Galileo International Inc., a U.S. entity, is in the business of maintaining and providing electronic distribution systems to the travel industry in approximately 100 countries. Galileo provides computer reservations distribution services to airlines, hotels, tours, and cabs. Galileo provides a network that connects to its travel agents' computer reservations distribution services through hardwire and computer connections. Galileo had close relationships with two entities in India:

1. Société Internationale de Télécommunications Aéronautiques connected Galileo's master computer system in the United States with travel agents in India.
2. InterGlobe Enterprises Pvt. Ltd. marketed and distributed the computer reservation services to travel agents in India.

The assessing officer (AO) imposed income tax on Galileo under a permanent establishment concept, reasoning that Indian travel agents completed their reservations through Galileo's installed hardware. The AO determined that Galileo had a permanent establishment in India under Article 5 in the India–U.S. Income Tax Treaty and that income was taxable as business income under Article 7 of that treaty.

The AO held that InterGlobe was a permanent establishment in India under Article 5 in the India–U.S. Income Tax Treaty. InterGlobe was independent from Galileo. Nevertheless, the AO's rationalized permanent establishment status based on these agency-type activities:

- InterGlobe was "economically dependent" on Galileo for its source of business.
- InterGlobe conducted its activities wholly and exclusively for Galileo.
- InterGlobe entered into and concluded contracts on behalf of Galileo.

Galileo appealed the results to the CIT(A). The CIT(A) held that Galileo in fact had a permanent establishment in India because its computers constituted a fixed place of business through which Galileo carried out its activities. Galileo then appealed the CIT(A) result, this time appealing to the Delhi ITAT.

Galileo argued before ITAT that all of its data processing took place through its master computer system in the United States and that the computers merely displayed the information in India, so that Galileo had no connection in India. ITAT disagreed with Galileo's position as to its activities undertaken. ITAT looked to Galileo's booking of transactions that took place using Galileo equipment in India. ITAT noted the computerized reservation system partially existed in computers installed at subscribers' premises. In fact, Galileo controlled the shifting of computers even within the premises of the subscriber. ITAT determined that those Galileo activities constituted a fixed place of business that constituted a permanent establishment in India.

ITAT then examined InterGlobe's relationship with Galileo, finding that the relationship was that of dependent agency. InterGlobe had the authority to enter contracts with subscribers, provided specialized services in India, and trained subscribers to use all of the computerized reservation system. InterGlobe was in India because of its relationship with Galileo exclusively, making InterGlobe a dependent agent.

ITAT sought to allocate the functions, activities, and risks in the United States and in India. ITAT, in making that determination, attributed to India 15% of Galileo's revenue based on bookings in India. ITAT, in making that determination, gave credence to the master computer system being outside India and being in the United States.

Galileo paid InterGlobe for the services that InterGlobe rendered to Galileo based on its distribution agreement. ITAT permitted Galileo to deduct the entire payments it had made to InterGlobe as expenses. We suspect that ITAT apportioned expenses to Indian operations and to U.S. operations on a 15% /85% split.

In summary, ITAT in Galileo used two separate facets in applying income taxation:

1. The direct activities of the taxpayer, Galileo
2. The indirect activities through the dependent agency relationship between Galileo and InterGlobe

INSTALLED HARDWIRE

Galileo and Sabre have different fact patterns as Galileo connected its computers through a hardwire system not present in Sabre. The presence or absence of the physical hardwire connecting the computer to the foreign master computer appears not to bc determinative to the taxability of the global distribution services industry or the computer reservation services industry. Both cases reflect dependent agency relationships, and the presence of a dependent agency appears to determinative.

NOTES

1. ITA No. 2311/Del/08 in assessment year 1999–2000.
2. Morgan Stanley & Co., 292 ITR 406.
3. *Hukam Chand Mills Ltd. v. CIT*, Bombay, 103 ITR 558.

CHAPTER FOURTEEN

Transfer Pricing in Indonesia

INDONESIA WAS one of the earliest countries in Asia to focus on transfer pricing. Indonesia first required enterprises to reflect transfer pricing in 1993. It issued transfer pricing rulings in 2001 and issued a transfer pricing taxation reporting form in 2009.

HISTORICAL BACKGROUND

Indonesia initially had no tax transfer pricing legislation in place, but imposed initial transfer pricing requirements through its issuance of a circular dated March 9, 1993, DGT Circular Letter No. SE-04/PJ.7/1993. The Indonesian government then enacted transfer pricing provisions in Income Tax No.10/1994, Article 18, paragraphs 2 and 3. Indonesia amended the 1984 tax laws in 1994, enacting VAT Law No. 11/1994 Article 2, paragraphs 1 and 2, which coordinates VAT and tax issues.

The Indonesian government issued regulations and rulings in January 2001 as part of its income tax law that was new at the time. The 2001 tax law contains the transfer pricing provisions that are contained in the 1994 statute. The Indonesian government has not yet issued regulations that would fully implement the transfer pricing provisions.

Indonesia's Foreign Investment Law requires foreign owners to utilize a Perseroan Terbates (PT) company. The PT is subject to transfer pricing audits, but domestic Indonesian companies also can be subject to transfer pricing audits.

TRANSFER PRICING CONSIDERATIONS

Indonesia permits enterprises to apply these transfer pricing methods:

- Indonesia authorizes the comparable uncontrolled price method (CUP), which it views as the primary transfer pricing method.
- Indonesia authorizes the cost plus method as an alternative transfer pricing method, but in fact it favors the cost plus method.
- Indonesia permits the taxpayer to use the resale transfer pricing method.
- Indonesia permits the taxpayer to select other transfer pricing methods if the taxpayer cannot determine the transfer price by using traditional transfer pricing methods. Such other transfer pricing methods include the comparable profits method and other return on investment methods.

Indonesia recognizes the importance of product differentiation to determine the transfer pricing method. These differences can include:

- Differences due to geographic markets
- Presence or absence of the distribution chain
- Discount and rebate terms connected to the sale or purchase
- Product quality
- Transportation costs for the item
- Insurance costs

Indonesia relies heavily on the cost plus method. The taxpayer is to ascertain the normal markup from products sold by the taxpayer to unrelated third parties (e.g., in-house comparables) and from products sold by one independent party to another independent party (e.g., external comparables). Indonesia also takes into account commission structures and gross revenue percentages for a similar business.

Special transfer pricing factors apply in Indonesia. The taxpayer in Indonesia must allocate overhead costs in determining costs. In contrast, other countries seeking to apply transfer pricing considerations fail to address the specifics of the cost allocation issues. Thus, for example, the taxpayer in Indonesia must reflect direct labor and direct materials in determining costs. Other countries, for the most part, fail to address the treatment of direct and indirect costs. In Indonesia, the taxpayer is to reflect technological developments in its transfer pricing analysis. The taxpayer is to reflect offers from customers in determining its transfer pricing.

Indonesia has not yet issued transfer pricing documentation requirements. Businesses are to reflect data in domestic Indonesian rupiah and/or United States dollars.

Indonesia is undertaking transfer pricing audits but has not developed a cadre of transfer pricing specialists. As a result, the auditors can address transfer pricing issues together with other tax issues. The auditors can adjust transfer pricing during a tax audit investigation if the auditors determine that the taxpayer used nonmarket rates. The Indonesian tax authorities, not the taxpayer, have the burden of proof in demonstrating nonmarket values.

Indonesia's penalty regime does not focus on transfer pricing per se. Thus, Indonesian law does not provide the taxpayer with specific transfer pricing penalties. Nevertheless, a taxpayer might be subject to a transfer pricing penalty if the tax audit adjustment causes a tax underpayment. A taxpayer can seek to reduce the government's transfer pricing penalties pursuant to the 1994 Tax Law, Article 36, paragraph (1). The taxpayer is to apply to obtain that tax reduction with the relevant tax office, doing so within three months of receiving the assessment letter or tax collection notice.

Indonesia permits the enterprise to undertake an advance pricing agreement (APA). The APA period is limited to two years, and Indonesia does not permit retroactive APAs.

SPECIAL ATTACHMENT

Indonesia has issued a mandatory form to taxpayers as a special attachment. This special attachment is statement of transactions with related parties. The taxpayer is to fill out this form and submit the form together with its corporate annual tax return. The special attachment is one page and comprises four questions, but these four questions in fact comprise 15 inquiries. The four broad categories are:

1. **The company's description in detail.** The request addresses ownership structure, organizational structure, operating aspects (including the functions the company undertakes), and the business environment in detail.
2. **Transactions.** The special attachment looks to transactions with related parties, transactions not influenced by related parties or comparative transactions, pricing policies, and manufacturing cost or acquisition data.
3. **Comparative analysis.** The form requests the company to provide information as to the characteristics of the product being transferred, functional analysis, economic conditions, the terms of transactions, and business strategy.
4. **Determination of fair price.** The form requests the taxpayer's rationale to determine fair price, comparative data impacting the transfer price, and transfer pricing methodologies.

CHAPTER FIFTEEN

Japan's Directive on Transfer Pricing Operations

JAPAN'S NATIONAL TAX AGENCY (NTA) has issued transfer pricing regulations in two parts, both the regulations themselves (the Commissioner's Directive on the Operation of Transfer Pricing) and subsequent examples (the Reference Case Studies on the Application of Transfer Pricing Taxation; hereafter Reference Case Studies). The reader is forewarned that the Japanese transfer pricing regulations are complex compared with transfer pricing regulations in most other countries. Further, the examples address different issues from those issues the regulations raise. As a consequence, this analysis addresses Japan's NTA's transfer pricing regulations standing alone.

BACKGROUND

Japan's NTA amended its Commissioner's Directive on the Operation of Transfer Pricing on June 25, 2007. This directive serves as Japan's Transfer Pricing

Administrative Guidelines in applying the applicable transfer pricing techniques. The Japanese Transfer Pricing Administrative Guidelines take the place of the "Commissioner's Directive on Procedure for Confirmation of Transfer Pricing Methodologies to Determine the Arm's Length Price." The NTA originally issued the guidelines on October 25, 1999. The 2007 Japanese Transfer Pricing Administrative Guidelines address operations that are related to Article 66-4 of the Act on Special Measures Concerning Taxation (i.e., the "Special Taxation Measures of Transactions between Corporations and Foreign-Related Persons"; hereafter referred to as ASMT).

The Japanese Transfer Pricing Administrative Guidelines are extensive, comprising 140 pages in all. These guidelines are themselves 32 pages in size, but the Japanese Reference Case Studies on the Application of Transfer Pricing Taxation that accompany the guideline examples add an additional 108 pages. When comparing the size of these transfer pricing regulations, the Japanese guidelines are second largest in length on a country-by-country basis. Only the United States transfer pricing provisions are lengthier.

The overriding purpose of the Japanese Transfer Pricing Administrative Guidelines is to provide "the proper and smooth enforcement of transfer pricing taxation." As we shall see, some limited instances arose where the Japanese guidelines fail to meet this objective.

The NTA furnished the preceding document in the English language; it is a translation of the original Japanese-language directive. The Japanese-language original is the official text.

REGULATIONS AND THE EXAMPLES—HOW THEY DIFFER

To a large extent, the Reference Case Studies examples cover different transfer pricing issues from what the Japanese Transfer Pricing Administrative Guidelines address. We provide three specific examples. Neither the Japanese Administrative Guidelines nor the Reference Case Studies explain these disparities in focus. The three examples are:

1. **Advance pricing arrangement (APA) procedural issues.** The Japanese Transfer Pricing Administrative Guidelines expend a considerable amount of time and effort on addressing APA procedural issues. In contrast, the Japanese transfer pricing examples, the Reference Case Studies, put little of their attention to these APA procedural issues.
2. **Cost contribution agreements (CCAs).** The Japanese Transfer Pricing Administrative Guidelines devote considerable space to CCAs. In contrast, the Reference Case Studies devote comparatively little space to CCAs.
3. **Residual profit split.** The Japanese Transfer Pricing Administrative Guidelines devote comparatively little attention to the residual profit split transfer pricing approach. The Reference Case Studies, in contrast, devote considerable space to the residual profit split approach.

OPERATION OF THE JAPANESE TRANSFER PRICING ADMINISTRATIVE GUIDELINES

The Japanese NTA organizes the Japanese Transfer Pricing Administrative Guidelines in this manner:

- Chapter 1: Definitions and Basic Policies
- Chapter 2: Examination
- Chapter 3: Points to Note in Calculating Arm's Length Prices
- Chapter 4: Treatment of Foreign Transferred Income
- Chapter 5: Advance Pricing Arrangements (APAs)

CHAPTER 1: DEFINITIONS AND BASIC POLICIES

Chapter 1, Definitions and Basic Policies, comprises:

- 1-1 Definition of Terms, 29 terms in all
- 1-2 Basic Policies
- 1-3 Use of Reference Case Studies

1-2 Basic Policies

Japan's NTA enumerates three basic policies. As a general matter, Japan's NTA expects the taxpayer to properly manage its transfer pricing tax operations, taking into consideration that the Japanese transfer pricing system is based on arm's length principles. The basic policies place heavy reliance on the APA process itself. The three basic policies are:

1. **The comparative process.** Japan's NTA will closely examine whether the prices that the taxpayer fixed for foreign-related transactions are equal to the prices that the taxpayer normally fixed for uncontrolled transactions. Japan's NTA might find that problems exist as to these transactions. If Japan's NTA does find that these problems do occur, the taxpayer is to make the effort to collect information regarding the market and its business. The taxpayer is to facilitate the provision of documents for these objectives:
   a. **Methods:** The tax authority's appropriate examination as to the taxpayer's selection of the transfer pricing methods
   b. **Comparable transactions:** The tax authority's appropriate examination as to the taxpayer's selection of comparable transactions
   c. **Adjustments:** The tax authority's appropriate examination as to the taxpayer's making the adjustments for differences
2. **The importance of predictability.** Japan's NTA is seeking to ensure the predictability of what the corporation achieves and is seeking to recognize the proper and smooth enforcement of transfer pricing taxation. To fulfill these objectives, the

taxpayer is to undertake the APA process where the corporation submits an APA request regarding the calculation of methodologies for the arm's length price and is to include the specific details of that APA request. The taxpayer is to submit the APA request based on the contents of the mutual agreement related to the APA request if such an agreement applies.

3. **Reliance on OECD principles.** It is important for the tax authorities of each country to share an understanding of transfer pricing for the purposes of resolving international double taxation issues that transfer pricing taxation causes. In light of this objective, Japan's NTA is to conduct an examination or is to conduct an APA review in an appropriate manner by referring to the Organisation for Economic Co-operation and Development (OECD) transfer pricing guidelines as necessary.

1-3 Use of Reference Case Studies

The "Reference Case Studies on Transfer Pricing Taxation" is the supplement to Japan's Transfer Pricing Administrative Guidelines. The Reference Case Studies examine 26 factual patterns. Most notably, the Reference Case Studies tend to point the taxpayer toward the residual profit split method in situations in which other taxing regimes might have reached a different result.

The taxpayer is to make use of the Reference Case Studies in order to assist the proper administration of transfer pricing taxation. At the same time, the taxpayer should be mindful that other cases exist as well as those cases described in the Reference Case Studies that, although similar, might be treated differently for transfer pricing purposes because these cases are based on different preconditions.

CHAPTER 2: EXAMINATION

Japan's Transfer Pricing Administrative Guidelines contain 25 specific examination principles:

- 2-1 Examination Policies
- 2-2 Points To Consider when Conducting Examinations
- 2-3 Examination of Attachment for Information on Foreign-Related Persons
- 2-4 Documents To Be Inspected at Time of Examination
- 2-5 Points To Note in Applying the Estimation Clause or the Rules of Inquiry and Inspection to Third Parties in the Same Trade
- 2-6 Loans
- 2-7 Corporations Not in the Financial Business
- 2-8 Providing of Services
- 2-9 Providing of Services Incidental to the Original Business Activities
- 2-10 Treatment of Intra-group Services
- 2-11 Intangible Properties the Examination Is To Consider

- 2-12 Contribution to the Formation, Maintenance, or Development of Intangible Properties
- 2-13 Transactions for Licensing Intangible Property
- 2-14 Cost Contribution Arrangement (CCA)
- 2-15 Treatment of Cost Contribution Arrangements
- 2-16 Points To Consider in Relation to Cost Contribution Arrangements
- 2-17 Use of Existing Intangible Property in Cost Contribution Arrangements
- 2-18 Documents To Be Inspected at the Time of the CCA Examination
- 2-19 Transfer of Money for Price Adjustments and So Forth
- 2-20 Consideration Calculated by Foreign Tax Authority
- 2-21 Relationship with APA Requests
- 2-22 Transfer Pricing Taxation and the Classification Domestic/Foreign Source Income
- 2-23 Relationship with Thin Capitalization Provisions
- 2-24 Relationship with Withholding Tax Provisions
- 2-25 Relationship with the Consumption Tax Provisions

2-1 Examination Policies

As a general matter, the taxpayer should take the preceding foreign-related transactions into account. The purpose of this analysis is for the taxpayer to correctly ascertain whether any problem exists in the transaction subject to transfer pricing taxation. Japan's NTA plans to examine each case carefully in the examination process rather than providing a careful review, bearing in mind the circumstances of each transaction. The Japanese Transfer Pricing Administrative Guidelines impose three specific examination policies on the international taxpayer:

1. **Variations from customary margins.** Japan's NTA plans to examine whether the taxpayer's gross profit margin or the taxpayer's operating margin that arise from the taxpayer's foreign-related transactions is excessively low compared with other transactions. Japan's NTA plans to compare these transactions with transactions the taxpayer undertakes with unrelated persons in a similar market and that are similar in quantity, market level, and other respects.
2. **Low profit margins.** Japan's NTA plans to examine whether the taxpayer's gross profit margin or the taxpayer's operating margin, which margin arises from the taxpayer's foreign-related transactions, is excessively low compared with the taxpayer's gross profit margin or excessively low compared with the taxpayer's operating margin as to other unrelated persons who are engaged in the same category of business. Japan's NTA is to examine the similarity in quantity, market level, and other respects as to the taxpayer's operations.
3. **Functional analysis.** Japan's NTA plans to examine whether the taxpayer's profit that arises from the taxpayer's foreign-related transactions is relatively low compared with the foreign-related person's profit arising from the same or similar nonrelated transactions. Japan's NTA would make this determination in light of

the functions the corporation performs or the risks the corporation assumes or the foreign-related person undertakes as to these foreign-related transactions.

Note that the Australian Tax Office uses a similar transfer audit approach to the three methods in the Japanese Transfer Pricing Administrative Guidelines.

2-2 Points To Consider when Conducting Examinations

Japan's NTA is to examine foreign-related transactions on the basis of the final tax return the taxpayer submitted and on other materials or data that Japan's NTA collected through examinations. This statement, standing alone, would appear to authorize Japan's NTA to select secret comparables, at least as a beginning point when considering bringing a transfer pricing audit against a taxpayer.

Japan's NTA is seeking to determine whether the taxpayer applied arm's length prices. Prior to Japan's NTA's examination as to the arm's length determination issue, the NTA is to conduct other facets of the tax examination. This examination includes the next two methods to determine whether any problems exist regarding transfer pricing taxation, the goal being to ensure that the Japanese NTA conducts these examinations effectively.

1. **Profit margins.** Japan's NTA would verify whether the profit margin of the foreign-related transaction under examination is within the profit margin range of the uncontrolled transactions. Japan's NTA would make this profit margin determination in the same business category and for transactions that are substantially similar to the foreign-related transactions in terms of quantity, market level, and other respects. Japan's NTA terms this process as applying "transactions deemed comparable with the foreign-related transaction."
2. **Average values.** Japan's NTA can use the average value of the consideration or the profit margin for the foreign-related transactions, or for the transactions deemed comparable with foreign-related transactions. The Japan's NTA can make this average value determination during a reasonable length of time, before and after such taxable year, or a consolidated taxable year. The Japan's NTA can use this average value technique if it is inappropriate for the Japan's NTA to examine the price of inventory and so on as to the foreign-related transactions. Japan's NTA would make this average value determination inappropriately based only on information for each relevant year, or consolidated taxable year, due to considerable changes in prices reflecting changes in public demand, product life cycle, or other such factors.

2-3 Examination of Attachments for Information on Foreign-Related Persons

A corporation that conducts foreign-related transactions must attach Form 17-(3), "Information on Foreign-Related Persons," to its final tax return. Alternatively, the taxpayer is to provide sufficient information on its Form 17-(3). Japan's NTA urges the corporation to submit Form 17-(3) and to revise the information that the corporation provided when changes occur. Further, Japan's NTA urges the corporation to obtain the most accurate information on the particulars of the transaction.

2-4 Documents to Be Inspected at the Time of Examination

Japan's NTA expects the taxpayer to provide broad categories of documents in the event of audit. In such examinations, Japan's NTA should ascertain whether any transfer pricing problem exists. Japan's NTA is to obtain information as to the actual circumstances of the foreign-related transaction from documents, books and records, and other materials (referred to in 2-4 as "documents").

1. **Capital relationship.** Documents that contain the capital relationship of the corporation, and of each foreign person, together with the business details:
   a. **Capitalization and business documents.** Documents that contain the capital and the business relationship between the corporation and its affiliate(s).
   b. **Business history.** Documents that contain the history pertaining to the major shareholders of the corporation and to the foreign-related person, together with any changes in position.
   c. **Financial records.** Financial documents, or financial statements and reports, as to the business details of the corporation, together with corresponding documents for the foreign-related person.
   d. **Product lines.** Documents that list the major product lines of the corporation and of the foreign-related person. The documents are to include the transaction price, the selling markets, and the market size for each such product.
   e. **Results and characteristics.** Documents that contain the results and the characteristics of each business, the special circumstances during each taxable year, and other details of the business and the foreign-related person.
2. **Calculations.** Documents that the corporation uses for the calculation of arm's length prices:
   a. **Selection of comparables.** Documents that contain the corporation's selection of comparable transactions, together with the details of these comparable transactions.
   b. **Combining transactions.** In some cases, the corporation might calculate arm's length prices by reflecting more than one transaction as a single transaction. In the event that the corporation does make that calculation, the corporation is to provide documents that report the details of each such original transaction on the basis of which the corporation makes the calculation.
   c. **Transfer pricing rationale.** Documents that contain the reasons for adopting arm's length price and that include any other document the corporation prepared for calculating arm's length prices.
   d. **Adjustments.** The corporation might make adjustments as to determining comparable transactions. In the event that the corporation does make such

adjustments, the corporation is to provide documents that contain the adjustment method and the reason for making such adjustments.

3. **Foreign-related transactions.** Documents that contain details of the foreign-related transactions:
   a. **Contracts.** The contracts themselves, or, alternatively, documents that contain the content of these contracts.
   b. **Pricing policy.** The pricing policy (i.e., the documents that contain the details of price negotiations between the person and the foreign-related person).
   c. **Strategies.** Documents that contain the details of the corporation's business strategies or the foreign-related person's business strategies as to these foreign-related transactions.
   d. **Financial statements.** Documents that contain the corporation's profit and loss statement with regard to foreign-related transactions, or documents that contain the foreign-related person's profit statement with regard to the foreign-related person's profit and loss statement.
   e. **Functions.** Documents that contain the functions the corporation or the foreign-related person performed as to foreign-related transactions, or the risks that the corporation or the foreign-related party assumed as to foreign-related transactions.
   f. **Intangible properties.** Documents that contain the details of the corporation's intangible properties for conducting foreign-related transactions, or documents that contain the details of the foreign-related person's intangible properties for conducting foreign-related transactions.
   g. **Inventory.** Documents that pertain to inventory markets and so forth relating to the foreign-related transactions.
   h. **Inventory details.** Documents containing inventory details and so on related to the foreign-related transactions.
   i. **Closely connected transactions.** The corporation is to provide the details of transactions that are "closely connected with" the foreign-related transactions.
4. **Additional material.** Other documents:
   a. **Accounting standards.** Manuals and so on that contain the corporation's accounting standards details or contain the foreign-related person's accounting standards details.
   b. **Transfer pricing details.** Documents that contain the details of the transfer pricing examinations or APA, that details the foreign tax authorities conducted as to the foreign-related person.
   c. **Documents prepared by the foreign-related person.** The foreign-related person might prepare a document, pursuant to the rules of the foreign-related person's jurisdiction, which require the foreign-related person to prepare appropriate documents for supporting the effectiveness of the system (i.e., the Documentation Rules). The foreign-related person must provide any such prepared document.
   d. **Additional documents.** Other documents, as necessary.

2-5 Points to Note in Applying the Estimation Clause, or the Rules of Inquiry and Inspection to Third Parties in the Same Trade

Japan's NTA might request the corporation to present or submit documents, books, records, or copies. Section 2-5 refers to this request as "documents prescribed in Paragraph 7." Japan's NTA can request the corporation to provide these documents "without delay." ASMT Article 66-4 applies if the corporation in fact fails to provide the Paragraph 7 documents without delay. Such a delay could cause the taxpayer to be subject to Paragraph 7, the Estimation Clause, or the delay could cause the taxpayer to be subject to Paragraph 9, the Rules of Inquiry and Inspection to Third Parties in the Same Trade. These three points are to be noted in applying these delay rules:

1. **The "without delay" standard.** When Japan's NTA requests the corporation to present or submit the Paragraph 7 documents, Japan's NTA is to explain to the corporation that ASMT Paragraph 7 or ASMT Paragraph 9 would apply if the corporation fails to present or submit these documents without delay. Japan's NTA is to record the fact that it provided this explanation to the corporation and is to record the manner in which the corporation presents or submits the documents after receiving such explanation from Japan's NTA.
2. **Timing issues impacting the "without delay" standard.** Japan's Transfer Pricing Administrative Guidelines do not directly address the scope and timing of the "without delay" standard. Instead, Japan's Administrative Guidelines provide that Japan's NTA will determine whether the corporation furnished, presented, or submitted the Paragraph 7 documents, doing so "without delay," in light of the time period "normally required" for such a corporation to submit or present such documents.
3. **Selecting comparative transactions.** The corporation might select an uncontrolled transaction for comparative purposes, pursuant to ASMT Directive 66-4(2)-1, as recognized by applying the provisions of ASMT Article 66-4(9). In the event that the taxpayer might make such a selection of the uncontrolled transaction, Japan's NTA should inform the corporation about the content of the comparable transaction and should inform the corporation as to the method of making an adjustment for such differences. After Japan's NTA provides such an explanation to the corporation, it is to pay attention to the Article 163 provisions, the Confidentiality of Staff provisions within the Corporate Tax Act. Japan NTA should then record the making of that explanation to the corporation.

2-6 Loans

The taxpayer should note these two points when Japan's NTA examines intercompany loans:

1. **Interest-free loans.** Corporate Tax Act 9-4-2 addresses loans the corporation makes to its subsidiary without charging interest to this subsidiary. The taxpayer

is to treat these transactions as being legitimate transactions under the transfer pricing tax provisions.

2. **Maturity date.** The corporation might not know the maturity of a foreign-related transaction. In that event, the corporation is to reasonably calculate the period of the loan in light of the purpose of the loan.

2-7 Corporations Not in Financial Businesses

Japan's NTA might conduct examinations on lending and borrowing activities of a foreign-related person. Japan's NTA can undertake this examination approach in cases where neither party is engaged in lending or investment activities as a core business. Similarly, Japan's NTA can undertake this examination approach in cases where ASMT Directive 66-4(6) is not applicable. In such examination situations, Japan's NTA is to examine the appropriateness of the interest applied to the lending or borrowing. Japan's NTA is to treat the interest rate, being calculated as described next, as the arm's length interest rate:

1. **Normal interest rate.** The interest rate that would normally apply to the loan. This normal rate assumes that the lender involved in the foreign-related transaction made the loan from an unrelated bank under similar conditions in terms of currency, borrowing date, and borrowing period.
2. **The "funds involved" provisions.** The interest rate that would normally be earned in the funds involved in the foreign-related transaction. This analysis presupposes that these funds were invested in government securities or the like under "similar conditions." Japan's NTA is to measure "similar conditions" in terms of currency, transaction date, and transaction period. The provisions in (2) do not apply when the interest rate is set in (1) above.

Note that the presence or absence of a loan's conditional relationship with the foreign-related transaction is not relevant when the interest rate is set forth in (1) above. The presence or absence of a loan's conditional relationship with the foreign-related transaction is not relevant where the bank and/or other lender makes the loan in the foreign-related transaction under "similar conditions," as set forth in (1).

2-8 Providing of Services

Note these two points when examining the providing of services:

1. **Intangible issues.** In some cases, the provider of services might be using intangible properties in providing services. Nevertheless, such a provider of services does not include the consideration for using intangible services in establishing a price for providing these services. Japan's NTA might examine whether the provider of services uses intangible properties when that provider of services provides such services. Nevertheless, Japan's NTA views the providing of services and the use of intangible properties as being conceptually distinct. The taxpayer needs to

consider whether the intangible properties that the service provider provides when rendering services correspond to the intangible properties as set forth in ASMT Directive 66-4(2)-3-(8). Further, the taxpayer needs to consider what effect the providing of services has on the service recipient's activities and functions.

2. **Services in conjunction with property transfers.** In some cases, the provider of services might render its services in conjunction with the transfer and so on as to the transfer of tangible assets or to intangible properties. The provider of services might value the consideration of tangible property and intangible property in the price of such transfers and so on as to such properties.

2-9 Providing Services Incidental to the Original Business Activities

ASMT Directive 66-4(6)-5 applies to the service provider's providing incidental services to the corporation's original business activities with the foreign-related person. In cases where ASMT Directive 66-4(6)-5 does not apply, Japan's NTA should examine whether the consideration for rendering such services is appropriate, assuming the gross cost for rendering such services is an arm's length price.

Japan's NTA defines "incidental services" in this manner: Services that are incidental to the original business activities means the services rendered by the service provider, whether the service provider renders these services incidentally, or whether these services are related to the original business activities of the corporation or a foreign-related person. These preceding definitional provisions apply so long as the recipient is not principally engaged in providing services. As an example of a taxpayer subject to the incidental services provisions, a corporation imports products from its foreign subsidiary and provides technical guidance regarding the manufacturing facilities of the foreign subsidiary.

Japan's NTA defines the "gross cost" for providing services. This gross cost includes, as a rule, the direct expenses related to the services themselves but also includes indirect expenses. "Indirect expenses" include the general and administrative expenses of the department in charge or any assisting department. The taxpayer is to calculate these expense amounts in accordance with reasonable distribution standards.

As a rule, Japan's NTA judges whether the taxpayer provides incidental services based on the taxpayer's underlying purpose of rendering such services. Nevertheless, the taxpayer is not to treat the gross cost incurred in providing services as the arm's length cost if either of two situations apply:

a. **Considerable portion.** The cost that the taxpayer incurs for providing services accounts for a considerable portion of the corporation's or the foreign-related person's costs or expenses for the taxable year during which the service provider renders such services.

b. **Use of intangible properties.** The taxpayer uses intangible properties for providing services or for similar reasons. For that reason, it is inappropriate for the taxpayer to treat the gross cost, which would include intangible costs, as the consideration for services standing alone.

2-10 Treatment of Intragroup Services

Japan, similar to Singapore and the United States, focuses heavily on intragroup services:

- **Commercial value standard.** Japan's NTA applies the "transactions having commercial value" standard for intragroup services. As such, all transactions having commercial value between a corporation and its foreign-related persons come within the scope of these provisions. Japan's NTA is to conduct transfer pricing examinations bearing in mind that these services have commercial value: services regarding management, finance, business, and administration (see the following list). The intragroup services could apply where corporation performs such services for the foreign-related person or where the foreign-related person performs such services for the corporation. The intragroup services could apply where the foreign-related person would need to acquire such services from unrelated persons by paying consideration for these services itself. Alternatively, the foreign-related persons could perform these activities by themselves if the corporation does not perform these activities by themselves in its ordinary course of business.
- **Intragroup services.** These include:
  - Planning and/or coordination
  - Budgeting and/or budgetary control
  - Accounting, tax, and/or legal services
  - Credit management and/or factoring
  - Operation, maintenance, and/or computer network management
  - Cash flow supervision and/or solvency
  - Investing and/or raising of funds
  - Interest management and/or exchange rate risks
  - Assistance as to production, purchase, distribution, and/or marketing
  - Recruiting and/or staff training
- **Staffing and equipment.** The corporation might continuously maintain staff and equipment, where that staff and equipment are ready to perform services for foreign-related persons, doing so on request and at any time. In such case, maintaining this state of readiness is itself a service. As a result, Japan's NTA can examine these services during transfer pricing examinations, conducting these examinations based on the respective conditions.
- **Foreign-related persons and duplication of services.** Foreign-related persons might acquire some services from unrelated persons or the foreign-related persons might perform such services for themselves. Such services that the corporation duplicates for the foreign-related persons do not have "commercial value." The corporation is not to include such duplicate services in the foreign-related transactions. Exceptions apply when the duplication of services is only temporary or where the corporation undertakes the duplication to reduce the risk of a wrong business decision.
- **Stewardship.** Services that the corporation performs in its capacity of being the parent company for the foreign-related person that pertain to intragroup services do not have commercial value. The corporation is not to include these activities as

foreign-related transactions. This treatment applies to activities such as the meeting of shareholders of the parent company or complying with legislative-based reporting requirements. These activities are not the type of activities that foreign-related persons would acquire from unrelated persons by payment or activities the foreign-related persons would perform for themselves if the corporation did not perform these activities by themselves. The taxpayer is to determine if the activities have commercial value or not, whether the taxpayer includes these activities in the activities the parent company performs in its capacity as shareholder, or whether the taxpayer is monitoring the services included as intragroup services.

2-11 Intangible Properties the Examination Is To Consider

Japan's NTA is to determine under audit how intangible properties contribute to the income of the corporation or of the foreign-related persons. Japan's NTA is to comprehensively consider properties such as the following ones that have material value and serve as a source of income:

a. **Patents and trade secrets.** Patents and trade secrets the corporation or the foreign-related person derives from technical innovation.
b. **Know-how.** Know-how that employees derive from experience together with human resources, the corporation or the foreign-related person derives from business activities such as management, front-office operations, production, research and development (R&D), and sales promotion.
c. **Other functions.** Production processes, negotiation procedures, development, distribution, and financing networks.

Japan's NTA is to determine whether the intangible property of the corporation or the intangible property of the foreign-related person serve as a source of income. In this case, it is possible for Japan's NTA to identify a corporation that, without having intangible properties, serves as a source of income among corporations engaging in the same category of business as the foreign-related transaction and having similar markets and scales of operation. Japan's NTA is to make a comparison based on the profit margin or similar indices of the foreign-related transactions of the corporation or of the foreign-related person and profit margin of the corporation without having such intangible properties. Japan's NTA is also to examine the activities, functions, and so forth in relation to the creation of the intangible properties of the corporation or of the foreign-related person. See note 2–8(1) regarding the relationship between the provider of services and provider of intangible properties in cases where the taxpayer uses intangible properties when providing services.

2-12 Contribution to the Formation, Maintenance, or Development of Intangible Properties

When Japan's NTA examines licensing transactions that pertain to intangible properties, Japan's NTA is to take into account the legal ownership of the intangible properties and also take into account the degree of contribution the corporation or the foreign-related person makes to the activities for the formation, maintenance, or development of the intangible property. In assessing the degree of the contribution to the activities for the formation, maintenance, or development of the intangible property, Japan's NTA is to comprehensively take into account the functions that the corporation or the foreign-related person performed. These functions include, for example, decision making, the rendering of services, the bearing of costs, and risk management.

Japan's NTA is to evaluate the extent of the contributions that each party makes. Japan's NTA is to assess the contribution made by a corporation as being low when the corporation or the foreign-related person bears the cost of formation and so on of the intangible properties that are expected to be the source of income.

2-13 Transaction for the Licensing of Intangible Property

There might be situations in which either a corporation or a foreign-related person is using the intangible property owned by either of them without having an agreement concerning its use. In that event, the parties are to calculate the arm's length amount of this transaction as a licensing arrangement except in situations in which the transaction is a transfer transaction.

The parties are to determine the commencement date of the licensing of the property from one of three dates: the date when the parties concerned provided the intangible property, the date when the use of intangible property began, or the date at which the party recorded the profit. The parties, in establishing a commencement date, might want to consider examples of transactions between nonrelated parties.

2-14 Cost Contribution Arrangement (CCA)

A cost contribution arrangement (CCA) is a contract to share the costs that the parties require. The activities giving rise to these costs must be necessary to achieve a common purpose. Such common purpose can include the development of a specific intangible property. These activities include R&D taking place between the contracting parties, known as participants. The purpose of engaging in a CCA is to obtain the interest of the outcome yielded from activities such as from R&D. The taxpayer is to determine that interest in accordance with the proportion to the total amount of the expected benefit the participant expects. The participant expects its proportion of the benefit to increase or decrease by the new outcome that activities such as R&D create.

These relationships fall under the CCA definition:

- **Contract.** A contract takes place to share the costs that participants require for the development of the manufacturing technology between the corporation and the related person.
- **Expected benefit.** The participants would then use the expected proportion of benefit, calculated on the basis of the expected benefit that the participants would enjoy through the sale of the new products the corporation and the foreign-related person would manufacture.

- **Technology.** This CCA makes reference to the manufacturing technology concerned, doing so to obtain the interest of the new intangible property that the participants yield from the development of manufacturing technology.
- **Cost determination.** The participants are to make that cost determination in accordance with the costs that the participants are to share.

2-15 Treatment of the CCA

CCAs include:

1. **Adjustments.** CCAs include adjustments made to the cost contribution amount.
2. **Acquisitions of CCA interests.** CCAs include the acquisition of a CCA interest, such as a buy-in payment, that the corporation and the foreign-related person conclude.
3. **Measures of benefits.** CCAs include cases where the CCA recognizes the expected proportion of benefit to be excessive compared with an appropriate portion.

Sections 2-16 and 2-18 determine the participant's proportion. The corporation cannot deduct the excessive amount for tax purposes because this excessive amount exceeds the arm's length price.

As a general matter, a cost that the corporation shares must treat this cost in accordance with the corporate tax laws and regulations. Consider the treatment of entertainment expenses and so forth. The corporation incurs R&D activities, but these R&D activities constitute entertainment. Pursuant to ASMT Article 61-4(3), the corporation can deduct the amount of shared entertainment expenses based on the proper expected proportion of the benefit and subject to expense limitation rules of ASMT Directive 61-4(1)-23(1), "Methods of the Expenditure of Entertainment Expenses and So Forth." This same procedure applies to the calculation of nondeductible expenses.

2-16 Points To Consider in Relation to the CCA

Japan's NTA is to examine whether the amount of cost contribution is appropriate when a corporation concludes a CCA with a foreign-related person. Japan's NTA is to take these points into consideration:

a. **Range of activities.** Whether the participants clearly define the range of activities, such as R&D, and provide the content concretely and in detail.
b. **Expected benefits.** Whether all participants are expected to enjoy benefit of the CCA directly by using the outcome the participants yield for themselves as to R&D activities.
c. **Research and development.** Whether each participant has determined the amount of cost to be shared by allocating the total amount of costs required for R&D activities. The participants are expected to allocate the proportion of the costs and benefits, based on estimated benefits.

d. **Estimation measures.** The participants can estimate benefits by using the sales amount, the gross margin amount, the operating profit amount, the volume of production or sales, and so forth. In some cases, it will be difficult for Japan's NTA to estimate these benefits. Japan's NTA permits participants to estimate the outcome that these activities yield, such as through R&D.
e. **Benefits and functions.** Whether Japan's NTA reviews the expected proportion of benefits in accordance with the functional standards that the NTA itself created.
f. **Expected and realized benefits.** A difference can occur between the participants' expected proportion of benefits and the realized proportion of benefits. This difference can be significant. The "proportion of benefits realized" means the proportion of increased earnings or decreased costs for each participant. The "proportion of benefits utilized" is based on the outcome the participants yielded as to activities such as R&D compared with the total realized benefit that each party receives.
g. **New entrants.** There might be situations in which a participant joins the CCA as a new entry or a party leaves the CCA. The presence of intangible property might be more relevant in that situation, whether the participants evaluate the intangible property at the time of new entry or withdrawal. Japan's NTA should consider whether the new participant pays for its buy-in payment or whether the participant shares the payment in proportion to the payments made by other participants.

2-17 Use of Existing Intangible Property in the CCA

Existing intangibles are treated in a different manner from the acquisition or development of the intangible. A participant might use such an existing intangible property for activities such as R&D within the CCA. The procedure discussed herein does not apply when the participant acquires or develops intangible property through the CCA.

Japan's NTA is to examine whether the participant who owns the existing intangible property has received the arm's length royalty or whether the participant has developed the cost share, assuming the participant has shared such amount. This procedure does not apply when a participant recognizes the transfer of the intangible property to other participants. Nor does this procedure apply when the participant acquires or develops intangible property through the CCA.

A corporation might conduct development activities and so forth by itself in relation to activities such as R&D within the CCA framework. Additionally, the realized benefit of the foreign-related participant might markedly exceed the foreign-related participant's expected benefits. In these situations, Japan's NTA must examine whether the corporation uses the existing intangible property for activities such as R&D. The points in the principal clause for conducting development apply for purposes of this examination.

2-18 Documents To Be Inspected at the Time of CCA Examination

Japan's NTA is to obtain accurate information as to actual circumstances of the foreign-related transaction from documents and from other items listed in Section 2-4 in examinations. When Japan's NTA applies CCA techniques, Japan's NTA should determine whether there are any transfer pricing taxation problems by requesting that the taxpayer submit CCA documents. Such CCA documents describe the scope and content of the R&D activities. These documents include:

1. **Documents prepared at closing.** Documents that the participants prepared at the time of concluding a CCA:
   a. **Basic documents.** Documents that describe the name, address, capital relations, description of the business, and other information as to the participants.
   b. **Negotiation documents.** Documents that describe the details or the negotiation or consultation that led to the participant's conclusion of the agreement.
   c. **Benefit sharing.** Documents that describe the method of calculating the expected proportion of benefits and the reason why the participants use such a method.
   d. **Accounting standards.** Documents that describe the participant's accounting standard for calculating the amount of the costs being shared and the expected benefit.
   e. **Adjusted amounts.** Documents that describe the details of adjusting the amount of costs shared in the case where there is a difference between the realized proportion of benefit and the expected proportion of benefit.
   f. **Valuation details.** Documents that describe the valuation details as to the intangible property and so on, in cases where any new participation or a withdrawal takes place.
   g. **CCA details.** Documents that describe the CCA details in relation to the modification of contractual terms and conditions; the revision of the CCA; or the termination of the CCA.
2. **Documents prepared after closing.** Documents prepared after the conclusion of the CCA:
   a. **Participant cost breakdown.** Documents that describe the total amount of the cost and the breakdown for activities such as R&D; the costs shared by each participant and the calculation process.
   b. **Differences between expected benefits and actual benefits.** Documents that describe the extent of the difference between the expected benefit proportions and the realized benefit proportions; providing this information as to activities such as R&D.
   c. **Share participation.** Documents that describe the change in the share of each participant in the intangible property and so forth. The participants form the CCA through activities such as R&D. The participant is to include changes through the valuation method as to the intangible property and so forth that the participants form through activities such as R&D.
3. **Additional documents.** Other documents include:
   a. **Intangible property.** Documents that describe the content of the intangible property; details of calculating the royalty in cases where an intangible property is used in activities such as R&D.
   b. **Nonparticipants.** Documents that describe the name, address, and other particulars of those who are scheduled to make use of the outcome for the activities such as R&D, but where such parties do not participate in the CCA.

2-19 Transfer of Money for Price Adjustment and So Forth

Japan's NTA will closely examine cases where a corporation transfers money back and forth with a foreign-related person nominally for the purposes the pricing adjustment. Japan's NTA retains this priority whether the corporation and the foreign-related party in fact make this adjustment for adjusting transfer prices or not.

2-20 Consideration Calculated by Foreign Tax Authority

Since the laws of Japan apply in computing arm's length prices only in Japan, the taxpayer should not necessarily assume that a foreign tax authority would view transfer pricing taxation in Japan as its determination of the arm's length price. A mutual agreement between the countries and taxpayers might change the situation (i.e., creating a common approach in determining arm's length pricing).

2-21 Relationship with APA Requests

The Japanese tax authorities clarify the APA process:

1. **No interruption.** An APA request does not interrupt the tax examination.
2. **Tax examinations are separate.** Japan's NTA cannot use the documents it received from the corporation as an applicant for the APA unless the corporation gives its consent for the use of such materials.

2-22 Transfer Pricing Taxation and the Classification of Domestic/Foreign Source Income

Japan's NTA might apply Article 69(1) of the Foreign Tax Act within the Corporation Tax Act at the same time as Japan's NTA examines the corporation's transfer pricing taxation. Japan's NTA calculates the creditable amount of foreign tax after deciding whether the increased income that arises through the transfer pricing audit is domestic source or is foreign source. Japan's NTA applies Domestic Source Income provisions of Article 138 of the Corporation Tax Act and applies the Details of the Scope of Domestic Source Income provisions of Article 140 of the Corporation Tax Act, inclusive.

2-23 Relationship with Thin Capitalization

Japan's NTA might apply the Special Rules for Interest on Indebtedness Pertaining to Foreign Controlled Stockholders, ASMT Article 66-5, together with applying transfer pricing taxation in tax examinations. In that event, the taxpayer cannot apply the portion of the interest on borrowed funds that exceeds the arm's length price when calculating the interest on borrowed funds.

2-24 Relationship with Withholding Tax

In some cases, as a result of a tax examination, Japan's NTA might identify any difference for the purpose of levying the corporation tax as to the amount of interest or the amount of royalty the corporation paid to the foreign-related person and the arm's length price. Such a difference does not affect the interest or the amount of royalty subject to withholding tax. Treaties with some countries do not permit reduced tax rates in those circumstances.

2-25 Relationship with Consumption Tax

As a general matter, transfer pricing taxation covers the application of the Corporate Tax Act and other laws related to corporation tax. A transfer pricing tax audit does not affect the calculation of consumption tax.

CHAPTER 3: POINTS TO NOTE IN CALCULATING ARM'S LENGTH PRICES

Chapter 3 provides for seven specific points in making adjustments for these differences:

- 3-1 Method for Adjusting Differences
- 3-2 Selection of Comparable Transactions for Foreign-Related Transactions with Use of Intangible Properties
- 3-3 Calculating Arm's Length Prices for Some Comparable Transactions
- 3-4 Treatment of Common Expenses in the Profit Split Method
- 3-5 Treatment of the Residual Profit Split Method
- 3-6 Selling and General Administrative Expenses in Applying the Transactional Net Margin Method
- 3-7 Points To Note Concerning the Treatment of Taxation by Estimation

3-1 Method for Adjusting Differences

The taxpayer can adjust differences between a foreign-related transaction and a comparable transaction. The taxpayer can make the adjustment by applying the method described below according to the circumstances of each case. The taxpayer can adjust for the differences if it is objectively clear that such differences would have an impact on:

- ASMT Article 66-4(2) item 1(a) as to the calculation of the consideration
- ASMT Article 66-4(2) item 1(b) and ASMT Article 66-4(2) item 1(c) as to the determination of the profit margin
- ASMT 39-12(8) item 2 of the Cabinet Order and ASMT 39-12(8) item 3 of the Cabinet Order on the calculation of the percentage, by the same method given in ASMT Article 66-4(2) item 2(a)

As to adjusting these four differences:

1. **Trade terms.** The trade terms for one transaction might be free on board (FOB) and the trade terms for the other transaction might be cost, insurance, and freight

(CIF). When that difference applies, the taxpayer is to add or deduct the amount of freight or insurance from the consideration of the comparable transaction.

2. **Payment period.** There might be a difference between the foreign-related transaction and a comparable transaction as to the period of payment. When that time period exists, the taxpayer is to add or deduct the amount of interest that accrues during that period as to consideration of the comparable transaction.
3. **Discount or rebate.** The trade terms for a comparable transaction might specify the discount or rebate according to the quantity of the transaction. In that event, the taxpayer is to use the consideration that results from the application of the terms, such as the discount or the rebate of the comparable transactions as to the quantity of the foreign-related transaction.
4. **Function and risk.** In some cases, there might be differences as to function or as to risk. In such an event, the taxpayer is to measure the extent of such function or risk by the amount of expenses the parties incur as to the foreign-related transaction and the comparable transaction. The taxpayer is to adjust that difference using the percentage of the amount of the above-mentioned expenses to total sales, or to sales cost, that relate to foreign-related transaction and the comparable transaction.

3-2 Selection of Comparable Transactions for Foreign-Related Transactions with the Use of Intangible Properties

A corporation or a foreign-related person might engage in foreign-related transactions involving the use of intangible properties pursuant to ASMT Directive 66-4(2)-3. In that situation, the taxpayer should consider the similarity of intangible properties in terms of type, scope, mode of use, and so forth when selecting comparable transactions.

3-3 Calculating Arm's Length Prices for Some Comparable Transactions

The taxpayer can apply a mean of prices or a mean of margin profits from comparable transactions if such comparable transactions are so similar. ASMT Directive 66-4(2)-3 describes the factors that make comparable transactions so similar.

3-4 Treatment of Common Expenses in the Profit Split Method

Japan's NTA applies a "reasonable factors" approach for common expenses in splitting profits. The term "common expenses" means cost of sales, together with general, administrative, and selling expenses incurred in connection with both the foreign-related transaction and with other expenses. Japan's NTA permits the taxpayer to treat the costs of goods (cost of sales) as an expense that the taxpayer could treat as a general expense. Note that many other countries, including the United States, directly tie the cost of goods sold to the product being sold rather than treating this amount as an expense.

The taxpayer might include common expenses (i.e., the cost and expenses of the corporation or its foreign-related person) for purposes of determining the profit to be split pursuant to ASMT Directive 66-4(4)-1. The taxpayer is to divide the costs and expenses in accordance with the proportion of reasonable factors. The taxpayer is to regard the reasonableness of these factors in light of the content of the transactions and the nature of these expenses. The taxpayer is to take into account such factors as sales, cost of sales, value of the assets the taxpayer uses for these transactions (i.e., the number of employees involved in the transactions, etc.). The taxpayer calculates the common expenses based as above when it calculates the factors the taxpayer is to use for attributing profits to be split. The OECD permits multinational enterprises and tax administrations to address common expenses in a similar manner. See OECD, *Transfer Pricing Guidelines for Multinational Enterprises and Tax Administrations*, July 2010 2.124–2.126.

3-5 Treatment of the Residual Profit Split Method

The profit split method pertains to "ordinarily gained profit" obtained from "the profit to be split" where unrelated persons do not possess these material intangibles. When the taxpayer applies the residual profit split method, as prescribed in ASMT Directive 66-4(4)-5, the taxpayer is to calculate this profit split amount based on profit indices. Such profit indices include ratios, such as the ratio of operating profit to the value of the business assets or the ratio of operating profit to the sales of the corporation. Such analysis does not include a corporation that has material intangible assets. The prerequisite for applying the residual profit split method is that the taxpayer must be engaged in the same category of business as the foreign-related person and the company the corporation applies for comparative must be similar in market size or scale of operation to the foreign-related person. The OECD permits multinational enterprises and tax administrations to address residual analysis in a similar manner. See OECD, *Transfer Pricing Guidelines for Multinational Enterprises and Tax Administrations*, July 2010 2.121–2.123.

3-6 Selling and General Administrative Expenses in Applying the Transactional Net Margin Method

The Japanese Transfer Pricing Administrative Guidelines define the term "selling and general administrative expenses for selling the inventory concerning the foreign-related transaction" to contain the direct cost of selling and the indirect cost of selling in computing arm's length prices using the transactional net margin method. Costs can arise from both foreign-related transactions and from other transactions. In such an event, the taxpayer is to divide these costs according to a rational ratio in light of the contents of both transactions and the nature of such expenses. Such a ratio might include, for example, sales, cost of sales, value of assets, and the number of employees, according to the format of the individual transaction.

3-7 Points to Note Concerning the Treatment of Taxation by Estimation

The Japanese tax authorities recognize that transfer pricing is not an exact science and that some transfer pricing facets can be time-consuming. As a result, the Japanese tax authorities permit the taxpayer to undertake estimation techniques:

1. **Estimation methods.** The taxpayer might apply the estimation method set forth in ASMT Cabinet Order Article 39-12(12) item 1. When the taxpayer does apply this method, the taxpayer is to apply ASMT Directive 66-4(4)-1 through ASMT Directive 66-4(4)-5 inclusive with the matters or things being the same but altered when necessary. The taxpayer is to allocate in principle the operating profit or a corresponding sum to the corporation and to foreign-related persons by splitting the profit according to factors provided. The operating profit or the corresponding sum arise from business involving foreign-related transactions according to financial documents that describe the consolidated assets and the profit and loss situation of the business group to which the corporation and the foreign-related person belong.
2. **Operating profit.** Note that, in some cases, the taxpayer might not separate the operating profit when the operating profit arises from business involving foreign-related transactions, measured according to consolidated financial statements. In that event, the taxpayer can apply an estimation approach, calculating the operating profit arising from the business involving foreign-related transactions. The taxpayer can allocate the operating profit by proportion of (b) to (a):
   a. **Degree of contribution.** Factors that are sufficient to estimate the degree of contribution of the business group to the generating of the operating profit from the business group, including businesses involving foreign-related transactions.
   b. **Factors.** Factors, among those factors specified in (a), above, that are sufficient to estimate the degree of contribution made by the business involving such foreign-related transactions.
3. **Manner of applying the estimation method.** When the taxpayer applies the estimation method set forth in ASMT Article 39-12(12) Cabinet Order item 4, the taxpayer is to apply ASMT Directive 66-4(5)-1 with the matters or things being the same but altered when necessary.

CHAPTER 4: TREATMENT OF FOREIGN TRANSFERRED INCOME

Three specific provisions apply to the treatment of foreign transferred income:

- 4-1 Treatment of the Refund of Foreign Transferred Income
- 4-2 Treatment of the Refund of Foreign Transferred Income with Corresponding Adjustment
- 4-3 Treatment of Amounts Refunded to Foreign-Related Persons with Corresponding Adjustment

4-1 Treatment of the Refund of Foreign Transferred Income

A corporation might have submitted a refund request pursuant to ASMT Directive 66-4(8)-2, but the corporation did not receive all or part of the refund stated in that document by the scheduled date. Japan's NTA will determine whether the corporation's refund application is appropriate, examining whether there is any reasonable reason for not providing a refund. The corporation might inquire about the form of the document prescribed in ASMT Directive 66-4(8)-2; Japan's NTA is to inform the corporation that it can use the "Application for Refund of Foreign Transferred Income."

4-2 Treatment of the Refund of Foreign Transferred Income with Corresponding Adjustment

The foreign tax authority might have imposed tax on a foreign-related person under a system that corresponds to transfer pricing taxation. The tax authorities might reduce the corporation's taxable income by reason of corresponding adjustment based on a mutual agreement. The corporation might have remitted the entire amount reduced to the foreign-related person. The corporation cannot deduct the remitted amount from its taxable income.

4-3 Treatment of Amounts Refunded to Foreign-Related Persons with Corresponding Adjustment

The corporation might be able to reduce its taxable income by reason of its corresponding adjustment based on mutual agreement. Such a corporation might possibly remit the entire amount so related to the foreign-related person within a reasonable period or remit part of the amount so related to the foreign-related person within a reasonable period. Such a corporation is to request a correction to its tax return pursuant to the provisions of Article 7(1) of the Act on Special Provisions for the Enforcement of Income Tax Conventions, "Special Measures for Correction in the Case of Agreement Based on Income Tax Convention Concerning the Amount of Compensation for Transactions."

The corporation is to report the next particulars in writing, using the Notification Regarding Refund of Foreign Transferred Income with Corresponding Adjustment, appended Form 7. The corporation is to submit this notification to the District Director or submit this document to the Regional Commissioner in the case of a corporation the regional tax bureau handles. The foreign-related person is to treat the amount to be refunded as an account payable.

The corporation is to provide this information:

a. Name of the corporation
b. Place of tax payment
c. Name of the representative
d. Name and location of the foreign-related person
e. Scheduled date of the refund

f. Amount of the refund, together with the amount in foreign currency in the case of transactions in foreign currencies
g. Method of refund

The amount that the corporation reports as a refund as to a transaction in foreign currency is to be the yen equivalent. The corporation is to determine the yen equivalent in accordance with the provision of the Corporate Tax Act Directive 13-2-1-2, "Transactions in Foreign Currencies and Yen Conversions by the Accrued Calculation Method." The corporation is to include its gross revenue or loss in the taxable year on the day in which the refund falls (i.e., the difference between the "Transactions in Foreign Currencies and Yen Conversions by the Accrued Calculation Method" and the yen equivalent converted by using the foreign exchange buying and selling rate on the day of the refund).

CHAPTER 5: ADVANCE PRICING ARRANGEMENTS

Japan's Transfer Pricing Administrative Guidelines address these issues pertaining to APAs agreements:

- 5-1 APA Policies
- 5-2 Filing Request for the APA
- 5-3 Documents the APA Applicant Is To Attach
- 5-4 Translation of Attached Documents
- 5-5 Revision of APA Requests
- 5-6 Forwarding APA Requests and So On
- 5-7 Taxable Years To Be Confirmed
- 5-8 Amendments to APA Requests
- 5-9 Withdrawal of APA Requests
- 5-10 Pre-Filing Consultations
- 5-11 Review of APA Requests
- 5-12 Mutual Consultations Relating to an APA
- 5-13 Coordination of the RTB Division in Charge, the NTA, and the Office of Mutual Agreement Procedures
- 5-14 In the Case where an APA and the Performance of an APA Process Are Not Appropriate
- 5-15 Notification of the Results on an APA Review
- 5-16 Effect of the APA
- 5-17 Submission of Reports
- 5-18 Treatment of Reports
- 5-19 Compensating Adjustments
- 5-20 APA Revisions
- 5-21 APA Cancellations

5-1 APA Policies

The purpose of the APA policy is to ensure the predictability of transfer pricing taxation for corporations and to assist the proper and smooth enforcement of transfer pricing taxation. In light of that objective, the tax authorities are to conduct APA reviews in a manner that is balanced, accurate, and swift, according to the complexity and importance of each case, while paying full consideration to ensure taxing rights of Japan.

Corporations are eligible to initiate appropriate pre-filing consultations in order to improve the convenience of the APA procedure and to expedite the APA procedure.

5-2 Filing Requests for the APA

Japan, like most other countries that have an APA process, treats the APA process in a formal manner:

- **Eligibility.** Corporations are eligible to file APA requests relating to some or all foreign-related transactions. The corporation is to file the APA request with the District Director. Alternatively, corporations are eligible to file the APA requests with the Regional Commissioner of the Regional Taxation Bureaus (the RTB Commissioner) in cases where these corporations are within the jurisdiction of the RTB Large Enterprise Examination Division under the Ministry of Finance Ordinance No. 49 of 1949 who has the responsibility for the corporation's returns.
- **Timing requirements.** In requesting an APA, the applicant is to file the request for the APA as to the transfer pricing method by filing Form 2. This document becomes the APA request. The applicant is to file the APA request for each address in the country with the District Director having a precinct RTB. The applicant is to undertake this process by the prescribed due date for filing final tax returns. The applicant can extend this process by securing an extension pursuant to the provisions of Article 75-2 of the Corporation Tax Act, Special Rules for Extending the Due Date by Filing Final Returns. The date in question is the first taxable year of the taxable years that the applicant is requesting confirmation with Japan's NTA.
- **Multiple copies.** The Japanese government requires taxpayers to meet specific multiple copy requirements:
  - The applicant in general is to file the APA request in duplicate.
  - However, the applicant is to file the APA request in triplicate when a tax authority requests that Japan's NTA pursue mutual agreement procedures.
  - The applicant is to file the APA request in triplicate if the applicant is a corporation handled by the RTB Large Enterprise Examination Division.

- However, if the applicant filing the APA request is a corporation handled by the RTB Large Enterprise Examination Division, the applicant is to file such an APA request in quadruplicate when a tax authority requests that Japan's NTA pursue mutual agreement procedures. See cases 5–3, 5–8, and 5–9.

5-3 Documents the APA Applicant Is to Attach

The District Director is to ask the APA applicant to submit these documents with the APA request:

a. **Outline of the transactions.** Documents that describe the outline of the transactions the District Director is to confirm, and the organizations to confirm these transactions.
b. **Transfer pricing methods.** Documents that describe the transfer pricing method that the applicant seeks to confirm with the District Director, and the specific details thereof, and an explanation as to why the method is the most reasonable.
c. **Business and economic conditions.** Documents that describe the business and economic conditions essential to the APA and the continuation of the APA, hereinafter referred to as "critical assumptions."
d. **Detailed explanation of the transactions.** Documents that provide a detailed explanation of the transactions the applicant would seek the District Director to confirm, including the cash flow considerations and the currencies involved.
e. **Direct and indirect relationships.** Documents that reflect direct or indirect relations and relations under substantial control with the foreign-related person pertaining to transactions the applicant seeks to confirm with the District Director for the APA. Japan's Transfer Pricing Administrative Guidelines call this party an "applicable foreign-related person."
f. **Functions.** Documents that pertain to the functions the APA applicant performs in transactions that the applicant seeks to confirm with the District Director, and documents that pertain to the functions the applicable foreign-related person performs in transactions that the applicant seeks to confirm with the District Director.
g. **Internal data.** Operating and accounting information for the prior three years for the APA applicant and the applicable foreign-related person. The APA applicant can provide alternative information, such as future business plans; business projections suffice if the APA applicant is seeking the District Director confirm a relatively new product or business and data, if data for the prior three years are not available.
h. **Prior audits, taxation, and litigation.** Documents that describe any transfer pricing examinations, appeals, lawsuits, and so forth where these documents pertain to applicable foreign persons, and the details of past taxation in the country where the foreign persons are located.
i. **Additional data.** Documents Japan's NTA would require so that the APA applicant can concretely examine the transfer pricing method. These documents include the results of the APA application for the transfer pricing method that the

applicant requested in seeking confirmation from Japan's NTA for the preceding three years.

In addition to requesting the documents set forth in items (g) and (i), above, the RTB in charge shall require the APA applicant to submit documents for the two possible years if Japan's NTA finds it impossible to conduct a proper APA review in using the documents for three taxable years. Japan's NTA, in making that determination, is to consider factors such as the life cycle of the products involved and is to consider the nature of the transactions the APA applicant seeks to confirm with Japan's NTA.

5-4 Translation of Attached Documents

Japan's NTA can request APA applicants to submit Japanese translations if any of the documents the APA applicants submit are written in foreign languages.

5-5 Revision of APA Requests

The Corporation Examination Group within the Tax Office, the group in charge of corporate tax, or the RTB Large Enterprise Examination Division is to check the content of the APA request and documents as prescribed in Section 5-3. The APA applicant might have submitted documents containing misstatements or deficiencies. In that event, the Corporation Examination Group or the RTB can ask the APA applicant to revise the APA request.

5-6 Forwarding of APA Requests and So On

The Corporation Examination Group within the Tax Office shall promptly forward two sets of the APA request documents it received from the APA applicant to RTB Corporation Tax Division. If the APA applicant requests a mutual agreement procedure, the Corporation Examination Group within the Tax Office is to promptly forward three sets of the APA request documents it received from the APA applicant to the RTB Corporation Tax Division.

The RTB Corporate Tax Division, upon receiving two sets of the APA request documents from the APA applicant, shall promptly provide one of these two sets to the NTA Corporation Tax Division. If the APA applicant seeks a mutual agreement procedure, the Corporate Tax Division, upon receiving three sets of the APA request documents from the APA applicant, is to promptly provide two of these three sets to the NTA Corporation Tax Division.

If the APA applicant requests a mutual agreement procedure, the NTA division in charge shall forward one set of the APA request documents to the NTA's Office of Mutual Agreement Procedures.

5-7 Taxable Years to Be Confirmed

Japan's NTA can confirm the applicant's results taking place between three to five taxable years.

5-8 Amendments to APA Requests

An APA applicant might submit documents that pertain to the amendments of the APA that the APA applicant has filed with Japan's NTA. In the event that the APA applicant submits such amendment documents, the Corporation Examination Group of the Tax Office or the RTB Large Examination Division shall process such amendment request in accordance with the provision of Section5-5 and 5-6.

5-9 Withdrawal of APA Requests

An APA applicant might submit documents that pertain to the withdrawal of the APA that the APA applicant has filed with Japan's NTA. In the event that the APA applicant submits such withdrawal documents, the Corporation Examination Group of the Tax Office or the RTB Large Examination Division shall process such withdrawal request in accordance with the provision of Sections 5-5 and 5-6.

5-10 Pre-Filing Consultations

The Japanese tax authorities require the taxpayer to meet specific pre-filing requirements before seeking a consultation with the government:

1. **Pre-filing procedure.** An APA applicant can request a pre-filing consultation with the RTB. The RTB in charge shall accede to requests made by corporations for a pre-filing consultation. The NTA division in charge, in principle, is to attend such consultations. The NTA division in charge includes the Office of Mutual Agreement Procedures in the case of consultations with an APA with mutual agreement.
2. **Procedure for facilitating APA requests.** The Japanese tax authorities are mindful that APA applicants request pre-filing consultations to make APA procedures more convenient for corporations, and request pre-filing consultations to expedite APA procedures. As a result of these objectives, the RTB division in charge, including the NTA division in charge involved in pre-filing consultations, focus on streamlining the APA request process for the APA and to facilitate APA requests after their review. The RTB division in charge, including the NTA division in charge involved in pre-filing consultations, shall pay attention to these points when meeting with corporations:
   - **Necessary procedures.** Matters that are necessary to APA procedures. Such procedures include guidelines on the preparation of the attached documents the APA applicant submits with the APA requests and deadlines for submission. The Japanese tax authorities are to explain these guidelines at the time of the pre-filing consultations.
   - **Foreign-related transactions.** The Japanese tax authorities will extend the effort to provide the effort that the APA applicant would require in order to correctly ascertain the details of the foreign-related transactions that are the subject the consultation. The Japanese tax authorities will extend the effort to enable

the corporation concerned to make an appropriate judgment as to whether to apply for an APA and make an appropriate judgment as to the kind of application the corporation is to make.

3. **Pre-filing discussions.** During the pre-filing consultation process, the RTB division in charge is to discuss issues and information that fall within the scope of the documents the corporation requesting the consultation presents or submits. The APA applicant might fail to present or submit documents required for the pre-filing consultation. In that event, the RTB division in charge shall explain to the APA applicant why it cannot hold such a pre-filing consultation.
4. **Failure to provide documents.** There might be a situation in which the APA applicant fails to attach the Section 5-3 documents, as specified, as part of an APA request. If the APA applicant fails to provide the above-mentioned documents, the Japanese tax authorities shall inform the taxpayer that it cannot conform the APA request pursuant to the provisions of Sections 5-15(4) and 5-15(5). However, situations might arise in which there are adequate grounds for the APA applicant not to submit certain documents by the APA submission deadline at a pre-filing consultation where these documents are specified in 5–3. In such an instance, the RTB division in charge shall not be required to apply the provisions of 5–15(4) and 5–15(5). The delay provides the APA applicant with an extension for a period "deemed ordinarily necessary" for the preparation of such documents. The procedure is different when the APA applicant requires an extended period of time, termed the "submission grace period." In such a case, the RTB in charge is to specify the submission grace period to the corporation requesting the pre-filing consultation. The RTB in charge is to explain to the APA applicant that in principle the RTB has deferred the APA review for the duration of that grace period.

5-11 Review of APA Requests

The RTB division in charge is to evaluate the APA request in this manner:

1. **Commencing the APA review.** The RTB division in charge is to commence the APA review promptly upon its receipt of the APA request. The RTB division in charge is to conduct the review in a balanced manner that is appropriate to the complexity and difficulty of the case, while endeavoring to process the request correctly and swiftly. The NTA division in charge will additionally be involved in the APA review as necessary. The NTA recognizes that cooperation of the APA applicant is essential for the NTA to process the APA review swiftly. As such, the NTA is promoting a better understanding to the APA applicant as to the importance of such cooperation.
2. **APA review is not an examination.** The RTB division in charge is in principle to perform APA reviews in accordance with provisions of 2–1 and 2–2 and otherwise prescribed in Chapter 2 and in Chapter 3. Such APA reviews do not constitute an examination or inspection of the taxpayer's books and records regarding corporation tax.

3. **Inadequate documentation.** The documents prescribed in 5–3 might not be sufficient for APA purposes in all circumstances. The RTB division in charge should explain to the APA applicant the deficiencies in the APA submitted application, and request that the APA applicant submit these additional documents. In order to expedite the APA review process, the RTB division in charge is to set a deadline for the submission of such additional documents. The RTB division in charge is to set a deadline that is reasonable in view of the circumstances of the APA applicant in light of the period the APA applicant would need to prepare such documents.
4. **Amending the APA request.** The RTB division in charge might request the APA applicant to amend its APA requests in the case where the division concludes the transfer pricing method that the APA applicant requested is not the most reasonable method.
5. **Role of the NTA.** The NTA division in charge is to request the RTB division in charge to report on the status of the APA review process as necessary.

5-12 Mutual Consultations Relating to the APA

The Japanese tax authorities have separate requirements for unilateral APAs and bilateral APAs, and address foreign tax authorities' prior requests.

1. **Unilateral APAs.** Situations can occur in which the APA applicant has requested that the Japanese tax authorities agree to accept a unilateral APA, and the APA applicant has not filed a request with the Japanese tax authorities for a mutual agreement procedure for the APA. In such situations, the RTB division in charge is to provide information the APA applicant requires to appropriately decide what kind of request the APA applicant is to make. The Japanese tax authorities can confirm that the APA applicant intends to request an APA with the mutual agreement procedure. If the APA applicant proceeds with this procedure, the Japanese tax authorities are to recommend that the applicant request mutual consultation in order that the APA applicant can avoid double taxation and to ensure tax predictability.
2. **Prior request filed by foreign tax authority.** The RTB division in charge is to recommend the prompt requesting of a pre-filing consultation, or that the corporation file an APA request, in the situation in which the corporation or the foreign-related person already filed an APA request with a foreign tax authority.
3. **Application for mutual consultation.** An APA applicant must take an additional step if the APA applicant requests the mutual agreement procedure from the RTB division in charge. The RTB division in charge is to request the APA applicant to file an Application for Mutual Consultation, prescribed in the "Commissioner's Directive on Mutual Agreement Procedures (Administrative Guidelines)" issued on June 25, 2001.[1]

5-13 Coordination among the RTB Division in Charge, the NTA, and the Office of Mutual Agreement Procedures

An APA applicant might request a mutual agreement procedure pertaining to the APA. If that situation occurs, the RTB division in charge, the NTA division in charge, and the Office of Mutual Agreement Procedures are to consult with each other as necessary.

The RTB division in charge is to complete its APA review and then present its opinions pertaining to the APA request to the Office of Procedures through the National Tax Office division in charge. The Office of Mutual Agreement Procedures is to forward the contents of thc mutual agreement to the RTB division in charge and then to the NTA division in charge.

5-14 In the Case where the APA and the Performance of the APA Process Are Not Appropriate

When the Japanese tax authorities conduct APA reviews, these tax authorities are to properly handle these reviews as prescribed in (1) or (2) in order to ensure the proper and smooth enforcement of transfer pricing taxation:

1. **Inappropriate APAs.** Situations can arise in which an APA is inappropriate. In such a situation, the RTB division in charge is to request the APA applicant to correct the APA request. The RTB division in charge is to make this determination after its consultation with the NTA division in charge (including the Office of Mutual Agreement procedures in the case of an APA with mutual agreement). The APA applicant might fail to make such a correction. In the event the APA applicant fails to make such a correction, the Japanese taxing authorities are to provide the APA applicant with an explanation that an APA is not possible. The content of a pre-filing consultation might fall within (a) below. The Japanese taxing authorities are to explain the next details to the corporation requesting the pre-filing consultation:
    a. **Inappropriate attempt to reduce the tax burden.** The facts indicate that the APA applicant could reduce the Japanese tax burden without reasonable economic grounds as a result of a transaction that the APA applicant sought to confirm with the Japanese taxing authorities. Such a transaction could be a form that unrelated parties do not ordinary undertake.
    b. **Failure to submit information.** The failure of the APA applicant to submit information necessary for the APA review or otherwise fail to provide necessary cooperation that would hinder an APA.
2. **Inappropriate continuation of the APA process.** A procedure applies to situations such as the following when the commencement of the APA review or the continuation of an APA review is inappropriate. The RTB division in charge is to consult with the NTA division in charge, including the Office of Mutual Agreement Procedures in the case of an APA with mutual agreement. The Japanese tax authorities are to provide the APA applicant with an explanation that they are deferring the APA process until the time that the commencement or recommendation of the APA review is possible.
    a. **Similarity based on prior reassessment.** The APA applicant might file an APA request for transactions that are similar to those transactions involving reassessment based on transfer pricing taxation. In such a situation, it is necessary

for the Japanese tax authorities to conduct an APA review following adjudication of an appeal or finalization of a decision or a judgment regarding such assessment.

b. **Improper coordination with the mutual agreement procedure.** In some cases, an APA applicant might file an APA request and might file a request for a mutual agreement procedure in respect of foreign-related transactions other than transactions that the APA applicant seeks to confirm. In such a situation, it is necessary for the Japanese tax authorities to conduct an APA review for these transactions following a mutual agreement.

c. **Need to confirm transactions.** In some cases, it might be necessary for the Japanese tax authorities to conduct an APA review after the Japanese tax authorities confirm these transactions. The Japanese tax authorities might not be able to ascertain the actual circumstances of the business operations just from the documents, such as for future business plans and business projections, as prescribed in the parenthetical clause to Section 5-3(g).

5-15 Notification of the Results of the APA Review

The Japanese tax authorities provide the taxpayer with a complex notification process.

1. **Receipt of notification.** The RTB division in charge might receive notification of a mutual agreement from the Office of Mutual Agreement Procedures, doing so via the NTA division in charge. After the RTB division in charge receives this notification, and after the RTB division in charge suitably processes the APA request, the RTB division in charge is to promptly notify the district director that they have made the APA confirmation based on the results of the agreement. The RTB division in charge is to request the APA applicant to correct the application if necessary according to the results of the agreement.
2. **Failure to receive mutual agreement notification.** The RTB division in charge might not receive notification of a mutual agreement from the Office of Mutual Agreement Procedures, doing so via the NTA division in charge. After the RTB division in charge receives this notification, the RTB division in charge is to ask the opinion of the APA applicant regarding whether the APA applicant is to withdraw its APA request or to seek an APA without having a mutual agreement (i.e., through unilateral APA). The RTB division in charge is then to process the APA request in accordance with the provisions of Section 5-9, 5-12(3), or 5-15(4).
3. **Failure to file for a mutual agreement.** The RTB division in charge might conclude, after its review of the applicant's APA, that the corporation's transfer pricing method is the most reasonable selection. If the APA applicant has not filed for a mutual agreement procedure, the RTB division in charge is to promptly forward an APA notice to the district director.
4. **Wrong selection of transfer pricing method.** The RTB division in charge might conclude, after its review of the applicant's APA, that the corporation's selected transfer pricing method is not the method that is the most reasonable.

Alternatively, the APA applicant might fail to submit the documents set forth in Section 5-11(3), or the RTB division in charge determines that it cannot conduct the APA review in accordance with the provisions of Section 5-14(1). In such situations, the RTB division in charge shall, in consultation with the NTA division in charge, including the Office of Mutual Agreement Procedures in the case of APA request with mutual agreement, promptly inform the district director that APA confirmation is not possible.

5. **Intraoffice coordination.** The district director might receive a notice set forth in Section 5-15(1), 5-15(3), or 5-15(4) from the RTB division in charge. In the event that the district director does receive such a notice, the district director is to send a notice for or against the APA, as applicable, to the APA applicant. The district director is to use Form 3, Notification of Confirmation of Method of Calculation of Arm's Length Prices, or Form 4, Notification that Method of Calculation of Arm's Length Prices Cannot be Confirmed.

5-16 Effect of the APA

The corporation might have received a notice of APA confirmation as set forth in Section 5-15(5), and such a corporation might file tax returns that comply with the content of the APA for the confirmed taxable years. Such a corporation is termed a "confirmed corporation." The district director is to treat the foreign-related transactions, hereinafter referred to "confirmed transactions," as having been conducted at arm's length.

In some situations, a taxable year to be confirmed has already lapsed at the time of confirmation. If this situation occurs, an amended return submitted by the confirmed corporation to confirm the return filed for the taxable year will comply with the content of the APA requirement. Such an amended return is not treated as a "return filed foreknowing that corrections should be made" as prescribed in Article 65(5), Additional Tax for Deficient Returns, of the Act on General Rules for National Taxes.

5-17 Submission of Reports

The district director requests that confirmed corporations submit their reports with the following information, submitting this report no later than the prescribed date for filing tax returns. This date pertains to confirmed transactions pertaining to each taxable year confirmed (hereinafter referred to as a "confirmed taxable year,") or within the period specified by the district director. The APA applicant is to file this report in duplicate in the case of corporations handled by the RTB Large Enterprise Examination Division and in triplicate in the case of all other corporations. The APA applicant is to submit this information:

a. **Compliance statement.** A statement that the confirmed corporation files tax returns that comply with the contents of the APA.
b. **Income statement data.** Profit or loss data of the confirmed corporation, and profit or loss data of the applicable foreign-related person that relate to the confirmed

transactions. In cases where it is necessary, the parties to the APA are to take the content of the APA into account.

c. **Fluctuations.** Statement of the fluctuations, if any, of the material and economic conditions based on the fluctuations that the APA has taken into account.
d. **Adjustments.** Statement of the adjustments made by the confirming corporation, as provided in Section 5-19, in cases where the results of the confirmed transaction do not comply with the contents of the APA.
e. **Financial and accounting data.** Financial and accounting data for the confirmed corporation and financial and accounting data for the applicable foreign-related person for the confirmed taxable years.
f. **Additional information.** Other relevant information that helps the tax authorities determine whether the confirmed corporation files tax returns that comply with the contents of the APA.

5-18 Treatment of Reports

The Japanese tax authorities recognize that the report might have continuing value to the tax administrations as well as to multinational enterprises.

1. **Ordinary processing.** A confirmed corporation might submit the report prescribed in Section 5-17. In the event that the confirmed corporation does submit this report, the Examination Group Corporation of the Tax Office or the RTB Large Enterprise Examination Division are to process the report in accordance with Section 5-5 or 5-6.
2. **Evaluation of the report.** The RTB division in charge is to evaluate the report submitted and to determine whether the confirmed corporation complies with the contents of the APA. This report corresponds to corporate tax examinations. The RTB division in charge is to explain that relationship to the confirmed corporation at the time it reviews the report. This report review might indicate that the APA applicant has not filed a return that complies with the contents of the APA, and that the APA applicant has understated the amount of income. In that event, the RTB division in charge is to explain to the confirmed corporation that it needs to submit an amended application.
3. **Voluntary filing.** Note that the confirmed corporation might voluntarily file an amended return pursuant to the provisions of Section 5-19(2)(b). The confirmed corporation might file the amended return voluntarily if it detects such an understatement before the RTB in charge knew of the report review. The RTB division in charge might have known of the report review on account of visitation of the corporation by officials of the RTB division in charge for the purpose of report review or for indicating such an understatement. The RTB division in charge does not treat such an amended return as corresponding to a "return filed foreknowing that corrections should be made" as prescribed in Article 65(5), Additional Tax for Deficient Returns, as part of the Act on General Rules for National Taxes. The RTB division in charge is to judge whether a return corresponds to a "return

filed foreknowing that corrections should be made." The RTB in charge is to make this determination in the basis of the Administrative Guidelines, "Treatment of Additional Tax for Understatement and Return After the Due Date" issued on July 3, 2000.[2]

4. **Intraoffice coordination.** The RTB division in charge is to report the results of the report review to the NTA as required. The RTB division in charge is to forward the results to the Office of Mutual Agreement Procedures via the NTA division in charge where the parties reach a mutual agreement.

5-19 Compensating Adjustments

Certain tax authorities recognize that the multinational enterprise and the tax administrations might need to make compensating adjustments to fully reflect transfer pricing adjustments.

1. **Adjustment process.** The confirmed corporation might make adjustments the district director requires to comply with the contents of the APA in its financial statements. In the event that the confirmed corporation makes these adjustments, the district director is to regard these adjustments as legitimate transactions for transfer pricing purposes.
2. **Request for compensating adjustments.** The RTB division in charge is to request that the confirmed corporation make compensating adjustments pertaining to the APA in this way:
   a. **Correction of taxable income.** The confirmed corporation is to correct its taxable income on its final return. The confirmed corporation is to correct its taxable income where the confirmed corporation had understated its income due to an inconsistency between the actual transaction and the results of applying the confirmed transfer pricing method before the confirmed corporation filed its final tax returns.
   b. **Filing amended returns.** The confirmed corporation is to promptly file amended tax returns in a case when it turns out that the confirmed corporation understated its income in its tax returns. This procedure applies to confirmed taxable years. The procedure reflects an inconsistency between the actual transaction and applying the confirmed transfer pricing method after filing its final tax returns.
   c. **Mutual agreement implications.** A mutual agreement might cover the APA (i.e., a bilateral APA). In the event that such an agreement exists, the confirmed corporation can correct the taxable income on the final returns based on the mutual agreement concerning adjustments. The confirmed corporation can make these adjustments if it turns out that income in the financial statements pertaining to the confirmed taxable years is overstated. Such overstatement can arise due to a difference between the actual transaction and the results of applying the confirmed transfer pricing method. This difference takes place after the closing date for financial statements and before filing final tax returns.

d. **Overstatements.** A mutual agreement might cover the APA (i.e., a bilateral APA). In the event that such an agreement exists, the confirmed corporation can file a request to correct the tax return, as prescribed in Article 7(1) of the Act on Special Provisions for Enforcement of Income Tax Conventions. That procedure pertains to the mutual arrangement concerning compensating adjustments. The confirmed corporation can apply this compensating adjustment approach if it turns out that the confirmed corporation overstated its income due to a difference between the actual transaction and the results of applying the confirmed transfer pricing method in the tax returns. This procedure takes place after the confirming corporation files final tax returns that pertain to the confirmed taxable years.

5-20 APA Revisions

The confirmed corporation might file a request to revise the APA where material differences can arise in a situation that would cause material differences to business and economic conditions that are essential to the continuation of the APA in each of the confirmed taxable years. In such a situation, the district director is to process and receive the revisions to the APA and process these revisions in accordance with its relevant provisions of Section 5-1 to 5-19, inclusive.

5-21 APA Cancellations

The Japanese tax authorities acknowledge that there are situations in which the government can cancel the APA procedure.

1. **Cancellation process.** The district director can cancel the APA under narrowly defined circumstances. The RTB division in charge is to forward a notice to the district director concerning that cancellation. The cancellation applies to taxable years subsequent to the year in which the applicable incident incurred as to (a), (b), or (c). The cancellation applies retroactively as to (d):
   a. **Failure to revise.** A confirmed corporation fails to submit a request for a revision as prescribed in Section 5-20 even when material differences arise.
   b. **Failure to comply.** A confirmed corporation fails to comply with the contents of the APA in its tax returns.
   c. **Failure to submit.** A confirmed corporation fails to submit the report, as prescribed in Section 5-17, or the report contains material errors.
   d. **False statements.** Any of the facts on which the Japanese tax authorities have relied for the APA but are revealed to be false; or the APA request contains material errors.
2. **Intra-agency coordination.** The RTB division in charge is to consult with the NTA division in charge when necessary before the RTB division in charge forwards a notice of cancellation under Subparagraph (1).
3. **Intervening mutual agreement.** Subparagraph (1) might apply to an APA that is covered by a mutual agreement. In such an event, the RTB division in charge is to consult with the Office of Mutual Agreement Procedures via the NTA division in charge. The RTB division in charge is to forward a notice to cancel the APA

after the RTB division in charge receives a notification of another subsequent mutual agreement that cancels the former mutual agreement.

4. **Intra-agency notification.** The district director is to cancel the APA upon its receipt of a notice from the RTB division in charge. The district director is to send to the confirmed corporation appended Form 5, Notification of Cancellation of Confirmation of Method of Calculation of Arm's Length Prices.

5-22 APA Renewal

A confirmed corporation can file a request to renew the APA. The district director is to process this request pursuant to provisions Section 5-1 through 5-21. The confirmed corporation is to file an APA renewal request with the precinct district director, in principle by the day before the commencement of the taxable years to be confirmed.

5-23 Applying the Transfer Pricing Method to Tax Years Prior to the Confirmed Years

An APA applicant might intend to apply the requested transfer pricing method for years prior to the taxable years to be conformed. This procedure also applies to consolidated taxable years, if they are applicable. The APA applicant is to accompany the APA request with a request for a mutual agreement. The parties must regard the confirmed transfer pricing method as being the most appropriate method even for the years prior to the confirmed taxable years. The parties are to process the APA request in accordance with the provisions of Section 5-15, 5-16, 5-19, and 5-21.

5-24 Application of Transactions between the Head Office and Branches

The head office of a corporation might be located outside Japan. In such a situation, the foreign tax authority in the country where the head office of the corporation is located might request the commencement of a mutual agreement. Such a mutual agreement can be based on a request corresponding to the APA as to transactions between the head office or branch offices in foreign countries and the branch office in Japan that conducts business. These provisions are set forth in CTA Cabinet Order Article 176(1), item 7. The Japanese tax authorities are to take necessary measures in accordance with provisions 5-1 through 5-23.

5-25 Treatment of the Corporation's Entry into the Consolidated Corporation Group

A multinational enterprise can enter into a consolidated group. This is the joining process:

1. **Joining the affiliated group.** An APA applicant might become a member of a consolidated group when the consolidated group files an APA request. In that

situation, the district director is to request that the consolidated corporation promptly submit its requisite form (i.e., Form 6, Application for Continuation of APA after Entry into Consolidated Corporation Group). The APA applicant is to submit its form in duplicate with the RTB Commissioner or in triplicate if the consolidated parent corporation requests a mutual agreement. Alternatively, the APA applicant is to submit the form in triplicate with the district director or in duplicate if the consolidated parent corporation requests a mutual agreement.

2. **Filing requirements.** The consolidated parent corporation, as set forth in Subparagraph (1), might submit Form 6 to the precinct district director. In that event, the precinct district director is to send a copy of Form 6 to the district director who governs the district in which the concerned corporation's head office or main office is located. The Examination Group Corporation of the Tax Office or the RTB Large Enterprise Division is to handle the case in accordance with the provisions of Section 5-5 and 5-6. The NTA division in charge is to send a copy of Form 6 to the Office of Mutual Agreement procedures when the concerned corporation requests a mutual agreement.
3. **Consolidated filing.** The consolidated parent company might be submitting Form 6. In that situation, the Commissioner's Directive on the Operation of Transfer Pricing with Regard to Consolidated Corporations, issued on April 28, 2005, Section 5-1 to 5-25 inclusive, is to apply to the APA as to the concerned corporation. This procedure assumes that the consolidated parent corporation sent this request to the precinct district director pursuant to the Commissioner's Directive on the Operation of Transfer Pricing with regard to Consolidated Corporations, Section 5-2.

NOTES

1. Document ID: Office of Mutual Agreement Procedures 1–39.
2. Document ID: Corporation Tax Division 2–9, etc.

16

CHAPTER SIXTEEN

Selecting the Arm's Length Price in Japan

IN JAPAN, the taxpayer's selection of the arm's length price is an important facet of its transfer pricing regime. The arm's length price selection in Japan is particularly onerous because the transfer pricing provisions contain two specific factors:

1. The complexity of Japan's transfer pricing regime itself, the most complex across Organisation for Economic Co-operation and Development (OECD) and non-OECD members, except for the United States, as Japan places a high priority on method selection
2. The Japanese transfer pricing method selection criteria, which delineate three broad transaction categories:
   a. The traditional transaction methods themselves
   b. Methods that are "equivalent to" the traditional transaction methods
   c. Methods that are "equivalent to" the methods that are "consistent with" the traditional transaction methods

BACKGROUND

The National Tax Agency (NTA) of Japan issued its Transfer Pricing Administrative Guidelines in 2001 and amended these Administrative Guidelines to reflect 2007 litigation. The NTA, to supplement these Administrative Transfer Pricing Guidelines, issued its Reference Case Studies on the Application of Transfer Pricing Taxation (hereafter Reference Case Studies). These "cases," or, more technically "examples," provide an analysis of many transfer pricing issues a multinational taxpayer might face, 26 examples in all:

1. Section 1—Selection of the method of calculation of arm's length price, 9 such situations
2. Section 2—Points to note concerning the application of methods as to the calculation of arm's length price, 15 situations
3. Section 3—Advance pricing arrangements, 2 situations

DEMONSTRATING THE SELECTION OF ARM'S LENGTH PRICE

The Reference Case Studies specifically examine nine method selection examples within Section 1:

- Case 1: Comparable uncontrolled price method
- Case 2: Resale price method
- Case 3: Cost plus method
- Case 4: Methods consistent with the comparable uncontrolled price method
- Case 5: Methods equivalent to methods that are consistent with the cost plus method
- Case 6: Use of the transactional net margin method
- Case 7: Use of the contribution profit split method
- Case 8: Use of the residual profit split method
- Case 9: Adjustments for differences

SELECTION OF THE METHOD OF CALCULATION OF ARM'S LENGTH PRICE

The Reference Case Studies first examine selection of the method of calculation of arm's length price:

1. Comparable uncontrolled price
2. Resale price method
3. Cost plus method

4. Methods consistent with the comparable uncontrolled price method
5. Methods equivalent to methods consistent with the cost plus method
6. Transactional net margin method
7. Contribution profit split method
8. Residual profit split method
9. Adjustment for differences

CASE 1: USE OF THE COMPARABLE UNCONTROLLED PRICE METHOD

The schematic of the business relations is:

- Japanese corporation P is a distributor of Products A and B.
- Corporation P established Corporation S in Country X ten years before to distribute Product A.
- Corporation P purchases Product A and purchases Product B to different intermediaries.
- Corporation P sells Product A to S, a foreign-related person.
- S sells Product A to 200 third-party retailers.
- Corporation P sells Product B to T, a third party.
- T sells Product B to third-party wholesalers.

Functions and Activities

Company P classifies Product A differently from Product B in terms of model numbers, but both products are similar in terms of properties, construction, functions, and so forth.

The functions performed by:

- Company P in the sale of Product A to Company S
- Company P in the sale of Product B to Company T

are:

- The purchase of the inventory of Product A
- The purchase of the inventory of Product B

and:

- The sale of the Product A inventory to Company S
- The sale of the Product B inventory to Company T

Note that the phraseology in the Reference Case Studies is misleading. The Reference Case Studies refer to "the sale of these inventories to Company S and Company T," thus erroneously suggesting that Company P is selling both Product A and Product B to Company S and Company T.

Company P engages in no unique activities. Further, there are no differences in function between the sale of the product A inventory to Company S and the sale of the product B inventory to Company T. Neither the sale of the Product A inventory to Company S nor the sale of the Product B inventory to Company T makes use of trademarks or other functions.

Note the lack of contract differences between the sale of the Product A inventory to Company S and the sale of the Product B inventory to Company T:

- Both transactions have the same market level (e.g., wholesale or retail).
- Both transactions have substantially the same volume.
- The terms of the contracts for both transactions are the same as to delivery terms, payment terms, product warranties, and conditions for returns.
- The transaction price differs between Product A and Product B.

Treatment of Case 1 Facts for Transfer Pricing Taxation Purposes

Japan's Act on Special Measures Concerning Taxation (ASMT) provides that traditional transaction pricing methods have preference in selecting an arm's length price.[1] The examination of Case 1 facts produces these findings:

- Product A and Product B are of the same type of product in terms of properties, construction, functions, and so forth despite the fact the Company P classified the products into different product categories.
- Both Company S and Company T are wholesale traders, selling products to retailers in Country X. There are no differences in market level between these two transactions.
- The two transactions have the same volume and have the same contract terms. There are no differences in the volume of the goods or transactional contract terms.
- Company P has the same business strategies toward Product A and toward Product B.
- There were no differences in Company P's role and functions as to these transactions. The parties made no use of intangible properties.
- Both Company S and Company T are located in Country X. As such, the market conditions are the same. There are no government regulations on Product A or Product B.

Selection of the Method for Determining the Arm's Length Price

The NTA would have the taxpayer first determine traditional transaction methods to determine the arm's length price. The NTA would apply the comparable uncontrolled price method[2] to the sales of inventories of Product A that Company P sells to Company S and the sales of Product B that Company P sells to Company T, treating these transactions as being comparable transactions.

Explanation of the Comparable Uncontrolled Price Method

Part 1. As a general matter, the NTA requires the taxpayer to select a "reasonable method" that is in "keeping with the particular facts" and in compliance with the requirements that law lays down. Such a taxpayer, when selecting the method of calculation of the arm's length price, must first consider the applicability of the traditional transaction methods. Such traditional transaction methods include methods equivalent to the traditional transaction methods. The taxpayer is to explain the difference in the "explanation" section.

The judgment as to the applicability of the traditional transaction methods must conform to the specific facts. The taxpayer can rely on an internal comparable transaction or on an external comparable transaction based on:

1. Internal information, such as materials concerning transactions in which the corporation is engaged, or with foreign-related persons, together with
2. Corporate information, such as financial statements
3. Database information, such as financial data on corporations
4. External information, such as information from industry associations

Public information includes the last three of the preceding four categories.

Six ASMT Directives become relevant:

1. ASMT Directive 66-4(2)-1: Significance of Comparable Transactions
2. ASMT Directive 66-4(2)-2: Treatments of Debits and Credits of Tangible Properties
3. ASMT Directive 66-4(2)-3: Factors to Consider when Selecting Comparable Transactions
4. ASMT Directive 66-4(2)-4: Treatment of Monetary Lending or Borrowing
5. ASMT Directive 66-4(2)-5: Treatment for the Providing of Services
6. ASMT Directive 66-4(2)-6: Treatment of Licensing of Intangible Properties

The third ASMT, ASMT Directive 66-4(2)-3, Factors to Consider when Selecting Comparable Transactions, is most specifically relevant as to the comparable uncontrolled price method, especially through examining the factors contained on that list.

Foreign-related transaction might involve intangible properties. In the event that the foreign-related transaction does involve intangible properties, the taxpayer should consider comparability based particularly on ASMT Directive 66-4(2)-3-(8), Intangible Properties Used by the Seller or Buyer. Administrative Guideline 3-2 specifies that in such intangible property cases, the taxpayer is to consider the similarity of the intangible property in terms of type, scope, mode of use, and so forth when selecting comparable transactions.

Part 2. The taxpayer is to consider the application of the traditional transaction methods. When the taxpayer does consider the application of the traditional transaction methods, the Reference Case Studies suggest that it is "often comparatively simple" to determine whether internal comparable transactions engaged in by a corporation or by a foreign-related person qualify as comparable transactions, as described in Part 1 above, because the corporation or the foreign-related person will have the information on these transactions.

In contrast, the Reference Case Studies suggest that cases can exist where the taxpayer does not have sufficient information to make a comparability judgment. Such a taxpayer may need to rely on publicly available information pertaining to external comparable transactions engaged in by a corporation and third parties other than foreign-related parties.

In some cases, the resale price method or the cost plus method uses the profit margin calculated from gross sales of comparable transactions. In situations in which the taxpayer determines the gross profitability of those transactions, it is often not possible to obtain sufficient information concerning transactions deemed comparable with the foreign-related transactions. This failure is due to differences in the systems for the disclosure of corporate financial data in different countries in these cases:

- When applying the resale price method when the foreign-related person is the buyer of the inventories involved in a foreign-related transaction
- When applying the cost plus method when the foreign-related person is the seller of inventories in foreign-related transactions

The Reference Case Studies caution that the taxpayer might not have the access to the data required to examine comparability from financial data at the individual enterprise level on the basis of publicly available data. These data might not be available in cases where an enterprise does business in a number of segments unless the taxpayer can extract financial data as to a specified segment from the overall data.

The Reference Case Studies thus recognize that it might not be possible for the taxpayer to apply the traditional transaction methods, especially where the taxpayer cannot obtain the information it requires to determine whether transactions qualify as comparable transactions in applying the traditional transaction methods. The Reference Case Studies state that the taxpayer should undertake the following procedure:

- The method of application might be consistent with traditional transaction methods, ASMT Article 66-4(2), Item 1(d).
- Other methods prescribed in the ASMT Cabinet Order, or methods equivalent to such methods under Item 2(b), above.
- See Part 3 and Part 4, below, regarding methods consistent with the traditional transaction methods.
- See the following cases prescribed in the ASMT Cabinet Order:
  - Case 6—transactional net margin method
  - Case 7—contribution profit split method
  - Case 8—residual profit split method

The Reference Case Studies recommends that the taxpayer verify the validity of the results of its calculations using these transactions as necessary, doing so to identify transactions having a certain degree of comparability. The Reference Case Studies would apply these verification rules even where the taxpayer cannot select comparable transactions for the application of the traditional transaction methods and when the taxpayer determines the arm's length price by a method other than the traditional transaction methods.

Part 3. The Reference Case Studies recognize that the taxpayer might apply the traditional transaction methods. The Reference Case Studies recognize legal provisions that are consistent with each of the traditional transaction methods. These methods are considered to leave the way open to employing reasonable methods suited to the content of the transactions. This rule contains a proviso that these methods do not diverge from the concept behind the traditional transaction methods.

The Reference Case Studies recognize that there may be cases in which the taxpayer cannot easily find comparable foreign-related transactions when applying the traditional transaction methods as prescribed by law. The Reference Case Studies do recognize, though, that there are instances in which it is possible to select comparable transactions by using "reasonable similar methods of calculation." These reasonable similar methods of calculation can focus on the various forms of these transactions, or the taxpayer can determine the arm's length price by adopting "reasonable transactions" as comparable transactions.

The Reference Case Studies recognize that the above-mentioned transfer pricing methods allow a wider choice of comparable transactions than do the traditional transaction methods. As a result, the taxpayer must consider comparability, bearing in mind the possibility of applying these transfer pricing methods in a manner consistent with the traditional transaction methods.

The Reference Case Studies provide five examples of transfer pricing methods that are "consistent with" the traditional transaction methods:

1. Cases can apply in which the taxpayer cannot find uncontrolled transactions that are comparable with foreign-related transactions. The taxpayer can apply the arm's length price based on "objective and practical" indicators. Such objective and practical indicators include commodity exchange prices or other market prices, for example.
2. Cases can apply in which the purchaser of inventories in a foreign-related transaction sells its inventories to an unrelated person by initially selling the inventory to a related person. The taxpayer can apply the resale method. The taxpayer can determine the selling price of the buyer to the related person after deducting a "normal profit" when applying the resale price method, Reference Case Studies Case 2. This normal profit is based on the price of inventories sold to an unrelated person and then by calculating the arm's length price for the foreign-related transaction on this basis.
3. Cases can apply in which the buyer of inventories in a foreign-related transaction manufactures a product or other goods using those inventories and then sells these goods to an unrelated person. The taxpayer can determine the arm's length price after deducting the cost of the manufacture of these products. In making this determination, the taxpayer is to exclude the amount of consideration it receives for inventories in the foreign-related transaction. The taxpayer is to take

into account its profit that is commensurate with the manufacturing functions of these products. The taxpayer is to make that determination in addition to taking into account the normal profit in determining the application of the resale price method from the selling price of the products sold to the unrelated person.

4. Cases can apply in which a company sells its own products as a set, with the company purchasing products from another company and selling them to a related person. The taxpayer can calculate the arm's length price through a parallel use of the comparable uncontrolled price method (CUP; Case 1) or the cost plus method (Case 3).
5. Cases can apply in which the taxpayer has multiple comparable transactions where these transactions are deemed to be similar in light of the factors that ASMT Directive 66-4(2)-3 prescribes. The taxpayer can calculate the arm's length price using the average values of price, profit margin, or a similar indicator in these transactions.

Administrative Guideline 3-3 permits the taxpayer to use the average price or profit margin or similar amount of these transactions when calculating the arm's length price in the case of multiple comparable transactions deemed to be equivalently similar. The next table illustrates inventory sales transactions and equivalent transactions.

Priority of Methods for Calculating the Arm's Length Price

	Category 1		
Category	**Inventory Sales Transactions**	**Equivalent Transactions**	**Remarks**
1	Traditional transaction methods	Equivalent to traditional	Precedes 2, 3
1	CUP	Equivalent to CUP	Precedes 2, 3
1	Resale price method	Equivalent to CUP	Precedes 2, 3
1	Cost plus method	Equivalent to RP	Precedes 2, 3
	Category 2		
Category	**Inventory Sales Transactions**	**Equivalent Transactions**	**Remarks**
2	Methods consistent traditional	Methods consistent traditional	No difference
2	Methods consistent with CUP	Methods consistent with CUP	No difference
2	Methods consistent with RP	Methods consistent with RP	No difference
2	Methods consistent with CP	Methods consistent with CP	No difference
	Category 3		
Category	**Inventory Sales Transactions**	**Equivalent Transactions**	**Remarks**
3	ASMT Cabinet order	Other equivalent methods	No difference
3	TNMM	Methods equivalent to TNMM	No difference
3	Methods equivalent to TNMM	Methods equivalent to TNMM	No difference
3	Contribution PS method	Equivalent to PS contribution	No difference
3	Comparable PS method	Equivalent to PS comparable	No difference
3	Residual PS method	Equivalent to PS residual	No difference

Part 4. Japan does not permit a relaxation of the comparability requirements for comparable transactions when applying the traditional transaction methods as to

ascertaining methods that are consistent with the traditional transaction methods. The ASMT Directive 66-4(2)-3 as to the similarity of factors does not negate the comparability requirements. The taxpayer cannot use transactions that do not meet these comparability requirements as being comparable transactions when applying methods that are consistent with the transaction methods.

Part 5. The Reference Case Studies find it necessary to draw taxpayers' attention to these points: The underlying purpose is the acquiring of information concerning the grounds for determining the transaction prices and other ordinary transaction prices. The taxpayer must consider this information together with information on other matters, including the functions performed by the counterpart foreign-related parties as to these transactions.

The tax authorities need this information to ensure the "smooth and proper administration of transfer pricing taxation." The tax authorities are concerned with the validity of the transfer price, as various factors determine that price. These points apply:

- The taxpayer, upon the request from the tax authority, must promptly present or submit the books of account or other documents that the tax authority requires to calculate the arm's length price that the taxpayer selected when calculating the arm's length price. If the taxpayer fails to meet the preceding compliance requirement, the tax authority has the power to estimate the taxpayer's taxation, undertaking this action pursuant to ASMT Article 66-4(7) and ASMT Article 66-4(9).
- Taxpayers are obligated to acquire the books of account and other documents kept by foreign-related persons, as the tax authority requires, to calculate the arm's length price in transfer pricing examinations. Taxpayers are to promptly present or submit the materials that the tax authority requests, in order to calculate the arm's length price. Such taxpayers will be considered having met the conditions for applying the estimated tax amount requirements.

The tax authorities can inspect documents and other materials, as set forth in Administrative Guidelines 2-4, that form the basis of the taxpayers' final tax returns. The tax authorities can request the submission of the necessary materials if the results that the taxpayer produces are not found by the tax authorities to be the arm's length price. The tax authorities are to take care to fully explain to the taxpayer the reasons why the results found by the tax authorities are not the arm's length price. The tax authorities are to explain the details of the adjustments rather than presenting the taxpayer with examination findings with a view toward achieving the taxpayer's understanding.

Part 6. Taxpayers should make efforts to ascertain whether comparable transactions do exist in applying the traditional transaction methods, and should extend the effort to acquire "regular information" to the extent that this information is "normally available," and should take this information into consideration.

Taxpayers are to undertake the process of selecting comparable transactions in applying the traditional transaction methods. Certain constraints can apply in compiling the necessary information. Such constraints include the lack of publicly available information, and the location of the information being overseas.

The Reference Case Studies provide an analysis of the "typical steps" in the process of selecting comparable transactions. Nevertheless, despite determining these steps as being "typical," the Reference Case Studies treat this process as being mandatory.

Comparable Transaction Process

The Japanese tax authorities enumerate data the multinational enterprise or the tax administration will need in undertaking the comparable transaction process:

- Transactions deemed comparable with foreign-related transactions:
  - Internal information—materials of the corporation or on the foreign-related person on these transactions
  - External information—corporate databases
  - External information—industry information for business associations, and so forth
  - External information—other information
  - Information the tax authorities obtain from questioning and inspection of other companies in the same line of business, ASMT Article 66-4, Paragraph 9
- Uncontrolled transactions—Are the transactions between unrelated parties?
- Availability of data—Are price data or are the data for calculating the profit margin available for each transaction?

Typical factors the taxpayer is to consider:

- **Type of inventory, the content of the services, and so forth.** Are the physical characteristics of the inventories and the nature of the services involved in the same or similar foreign-related party transactions?
- **Market level.** Are we concerned about a retailer or wholesaler, or a primary or secondary wholesaler?
- **Volume and time of transactions.** Do the transactions differ in volume or differ in timing?
- **Contract terms.** Are there any differences in terms of trade, payment terms, conditions for returns, or conditions regarding contract renewal?
- **Functions performed and risks assumed by the buyer or by the seller.** Are there any differences in the functions of the seller or of the buyer? These differences could include research and development (R&D), marketing, after-sales service, and so forth.
- **Intangible properties the seller or the buyer uses.** Are intangible properties used by the seller or by the buyer in these transactions?
- **Business strategy and the timing of the market entry of the seller or of the buyer.** Are there any differences in terms of business strategy? "Business strategy" means the policy toward market development and penetration. Are there any differences in terms of the timing of market entry?

- **Status of government regulation and markets.** Are there any differences in governmental regulation (i.e., price regulation), market size, competition, and so forth affecting prices and profit margins?
- **Special circumstances.** Are there any special circumstances that dictate that transactions might not be regarded as comparable, such as a bankruptcy situation?

The final result is to achieve comparable transactions.

CASE 2: USE OF THE RESALE PRICE METHOD

Consider the next fact pattern that leads to the conclusion that the resale price method is the applicable transfer pricing method.

Transaction Itself

Here are basic facts:

- Foreign-related person P purchases raw materials and so forth in Country X.
- Foreign-related person P manufactures product A in Country X.
- Foreign-related person P sells product A to Japanese corporation S as being the sole import agent.
- Japanese Corporation S sells product A to about a dozen third-party companies as agents.

Comparable Transaction

Here is the information as to the comparable transaction:

- Independent third parties purchase raw materials and so forth in Country X.
- Independent third parties manufacture Product B in Country X. The schematic prepared by the Reference Case Studies erroneously refers to Product A rather than to Product B at this phase of the schematic.
- Independent third parties sell Product B to Japanese Corporation T as being the sole import agent.
- Japanese Corporation T sells Product B to third parties as agents.

Additional Facets of the Transactions

Here are the additional facets as to the transactions:

- Japanese Corporation S is a distributor of Product A in Japan.
- Corporation P, located in Country X, is Company S's parent company.
- Corporation P manufactures and distributes Product A in Country X.
- Company S imports product A as Company P's sole import agent.

- Company S sells Product A to some ten third-party agents in Japan.
- Company S does not engage in unique or original advertising or sales promotion activities.
- Company S does not make use of its own trademarks or of such other properties in its distribution activities.

State of the Japanese Market

Approximately a dozen manufacturers make products that compete with Product A, and these manufacturers have entered the Japanese market. Five of these manufacturers are sole import agents and file financial statements that are openly accessible. These sole import agents provide additional information, including information from the companies' Web sites, and market researchers publish analysis as well.

The taxpayer reviews the preceding materials and determines that Company T is a reseller of products imported from a third-party foreign manufacturer to third-party agents in Japan. Company T does not engage in any other business. Company T sells Product B, which is a product similar to Product A in terms of its properties, construction, and function. The taxpayer found that Company T is similar to Company S in terms of sales, market level, and sales functions, such as advertising, sales promotion, after-sales service, packing, and delivery. The taxpayer found that Company T does not use its own trademarks or other such properties in its distribution activities.

Applicability of the Traditional Transaction Methods

The Japanese tax authorities give preference to the traditional transaction methods when selecting the method of calculation of the arm's length price pursuant to ASMT Article 66-4(2), Item 1. An examination of comparable transactions, made in accordance with ASMT Directive 66-4(2)-1, ASMT Directive 66-4(2)-3, and other relevant provisions, produced these findings:

- The resale price method might potentially be viable, among the traditional transaction methods, because Company S resells Product A that Company S purchases from third parties. Company S has access to the financial data to apply the resale price method from publicly available information pertaining to Company T.
- Product B, imported from a third party from Company T and sold by Company T to agents in Japan, is strongly similar to Product A. Company T is generally similar to Company S in terms of its functions as a reseller, the scale of the transactions, market conditions, and so forth.

Section of the Method of Calculating the Arm's Length Price

The taxpayer found that it can use similar Product B, imported from a foreign third party, as a comparable transaction to Product A that Company S buys from Company P. Based on this situation, the taxpayer found that, among the traditional transaction methods, it is appropriate to apply the resale price method to Company S pursuant to

ASMT Article 66-4(2), Item 1(b) to calculate the arm's length price. Here S was the buyer of inventories involved in the foreign-related transaction. See the explanation to Case 1 regarding notes to consider when applying the applicability of the traditional transaction methods, including methods equivalent to the transaction methods, and in judging whether transactions correspond to comparable transactions.

CASE 3: USE OF THE COST PLUS METHOD

In this case, the taxpayer found, after considering the applicability of the traditional transaction methods, that the cost plus method was appropriate.

- Japanese Corporation P purchases Product A and Product B.
- Japanese Corporation P then separately sells Product A and Product B.
- Japanese Corporation P's sales of Product A are to foreign-related person S, located in Country X.
- Japanese Corporation P's sales of Product B are to third-party T, an agent, in Country X.
- Foreign-related party S, having purchased Product A from Japanese Corporation P, then sells Product A to approximately 200 third-party retailers.
- Third-party T, having purchased Product B from Japanese Corporation P, then sells Product B as agent to third-party retailers.

Explanation of the Activities

These are business activities that the companies undertake:

- Japanese Corporation P is a distributor of Product A and Product B.
- Japanese Corporation P established Corporation S in Country X as a subsidiary ten years ago to distribute Product A.
- Company P sells Product A to Company S.
- Company S then sells Product A to approximately 200 third-party retailers located in Country X.
- In the same time frame, Company P sells Product B to agent T, a third-party company located in Country X.
- Company T sells Product B to retailers located in Country X.
- Product B has a somewhat different specification from Product A, but the two products are similar in terms of properties, construction, function, and so forth.
- The volume of Product A that Japanese Corporation P sells to foreign-related person S is about the same as the volume of Product B that Japanese Corporation P sells to third-party T as agent.
- Japanese Corporation P performs the same functions for Product B as for Product A: purchasing Product A, selling Product A to foreign-related party S, purchasing Product B, selling Product B to third-party T as agent.

- Japanese Corporation P is not engaged in unique activities.
- Japanese Corporation P does not use trademarks or other such properties.
- Japanese Corporation P performs the same functions for the sales transaction with Company S as with the sales transaction with Company T.
- The terms and conditions are identical except as to price:
  - P's sales of Product A to Company S
  - P's sales of Product B to Company T
- The terms and conditions of the preceding sales contracts are identical as to delivery terms, payment terms, product warranties, and return conditions.

Treatment of the Cost Plus Method

The Japanese transfer pricing provisions give preference to the traditional transfer pricing methods when selecting an arm's length price pursuant to ASMT Article 66-4(2), Item 1, or an examination of comparable transactions in accordance with ASMT Directive 66-4(2)-1 and Directive 66-4(2)-3 and other relevant provisions.

- Product A and Product B have similar properties, constructions, functions, and so forth, and are deemed to be similar inventories.
- Company S and Company T are both wholesale traders, selling products to retailers in Country X. There are deemed to be no differences in the market level concerning P's sales to Company S and P's sales to Company T.
- The two transactions are substantially the same in volume and in contract terms.
- There are no differences in Company P's business strategies toward Product A and Product B.
- There are no differences in P's role and functions as to these transactions.
- The parties make no use of intangible properties.
- The market conditions are the same as both Company S and Company T arc located in Country X.
- There are no governmental regulations on Product A or Product B.

The taxpayer determined that Company P's sale of Product B to Company T could be used as the comparable transaction for the sale of Company P's sale of Product A to Company S. The seller of the inventories involved foreign-related transactions. The taxpayer looked to traditional transaction methods to determine the arm's length price and determined that it was appropriate to apply the cost plus method to Company P pursuant to ASMT Article 66-4(2), Item 1(c). See the explanation for Case 1 as to the points to note regarding the applicability of traditional transaction methods, including methods that are equivalent to the traditional transaction methods, in judging whether transactions correspond to comparable transactions.

CASE 4: METHODS CONSISTENT WITH THE COMPARABLE UNCONTROLLED PRICE METHOD

Case 4 examines the situation in which the taxpayer considered applying the traditional transaction methods or methods equivalent to the traditional transaction methods but determined that it could not do so.

Nevertheless, the taxpayer found that it was appropriate to apply a method that is "consistent with" the comparable uncontrolled price method or is "consistent with" a method that is consistent with the comparable uncontrolled price method. Case 4 describes two such situations, a sale of inventories fact pattern and a loan transaction fact pattern.

Schematic

The schematic for the inventory fact pattern indicates:

- Company S, in Country X, a foreign-related person to Japanese Corporation P, supplies raw material "a" to Japanese Corporation P in Japan.
- Japanese Corporation P, a manufacturer and distributor of Product A, obtains raw material "a" from related party S in Country X, manufactures Product A, and sells Product A to third-party agents in Japan.
- Japanese Corporation P previously established Company S in Country X ten years ago as a subsidiary to supply raw material "a" for Product X.
- Company S sells its entire output of raw material "a" to Japanese Corporation P.
- Japanese Corporation P manufactures Product A and sells Product A to third-party agents in Japan.
- Japanese Corporation P receives no supplies of raw material "a" from any source except from Company S.
- Raw material "a," which contains Product A, is sold worldwide on the commodity exchanges.
- The commodity exchanges reflect a quoted price for raw material "a."

Applicability of Traditional Transaction Methods

Japanese transfer pricing gives preference to the traditional transaction methods when selecting a method of calculation that gives rise to the arm's length price pursuant to ASMT Article 66-4(2), Item 1. An examination of comparable transactions the taxpayer undertakes in accordance with ASMT Directive 66-4(2)-1 and ASMT Directive 66-4(2)-3 and other relevant provisions produces these findings:

- Japanese Company P receives no supply of raw material "a" except from Company S.
- Company S supplies its entire output of raw material "a" to Japanese Company P.
- It is therefore not possible to find any comparable transactions in applying the comparable uncontrolled price method.

- It also was not possible to find any comparable transactions from publicly available information in applying the comparable uncontrolled price method.
- It is not feasible to apply the resale price method in this situation because Company P performed the manufacturing function in producing Product A from raw material "a."
- Of the three traditional transaction methods, one possible option would be to apply the cost plus method to Company S. The comparable transactions in such a case would be the uncontrolled transactions in Country X. The taxpayer cannot apply the cost plus method because Japanese Company P and Company S cannot obtain sufficient information to adjust for such differences. Company S would have needed to adjust for profit margin differences for the gross profit on sales.

Based on the foregoing analysis, the taxpayer determines that it could not apply the traditional transaction methods. The taxpayer then considers the application of methods that are "consistent with" the traditional transaction methods as prescribed in ASMT 66–4(2), Item 1(d). The taxpayer concluded that worldwide transactions are present on commodity exchanges, that there exists a market price for raw material "a," and that the taxpayer could apply the CUP after adjusting for differences in particular transaction terms, such as for transportation costs, to calculate the arm's length price. See ASMT Article 66-4(2), Item 1(d).

Explanation

At the outset, the reader should consider the applicability of the traditional transaction methods, including methods equivalent to the traditional transaction methods, and in judging whether the transactions correspond to comparable transactions, as reflected in the explanation of Case 1. If there are no transactions that exist between unrelated persons that are comparable to the foreign-related transaction and the taxpayer cannot apply the traditional transaction methods, it might be possible to apply a method that is "consistent with" the traditional transaction methods. Objective and realistic indicators of variables may exist, such as market prices (e.g., the quoted market price in this instance). These methods may be available using these transactions as comparable transactions in order to calculate the arm's length price.

Money-Lending Transactions

The schematic indicates that these transactions have taken place:

- Japanese Corporation P lends funds to foreign-related person S in Country X.
- The Japanese Corporation P–foreign-related person S loan is for ten years at 3% interest per annum.
- Bank T loans funds to Bank T at a 0.7% spread.
- Both Japanese Corporation P and foreign-related person S manufacture and sell Product A.
- There are no bank transactions.
- Japanese Corporation P is manufacturer and distributor of Product A.

- Company S, a subsidiary of Japanese Corporation P, manufactures and distributes Product A.
- Both Japanese Corporation P and Company S manufacture and distribute Product A.
- Neither Japanese Corporation P nor Company S engages in money laundering or in similar activities.
- Company S is doing well, and Company S has no need for support from Japanese Company P.

Past Fundraising Activities

Japanese Corporation P extended a loan to Company S seven years ago, denominated in Country X's currency, to fund Company S's investment in the expansion of S's manufacturing capacity. Japanese Corporation P funded its loan to Company S from Japanese Corporation P's funds on hand. This loan was for 10 years, bearing an interest rate of 3%.

Neither Japanese Corporation P nor Company S is engaged in money-lending transactions with related persons apart from financial institutions. Company S had never previously borrowed from banks or from similar institutions. As a result, there is no prospect that either the Japanese Corporation P or Company S could obtain information concerning spreads.

Japanese Corporation P previously took out a long-term loan from its main bank, Bank T. Bank would have loaned the funds to Japanese Corporation P to fund the loan to foreign-related Company S at a 0.7% spread. Japanese Corporation P and Company S could obtain swap data from a financial services provider. The financial data provider provided information to Japanese Corporation P and to Company S that the interest swap rate involving Country X's currency for the ten-year time period would be 5%.

The Reference Case Studies define the "spread" as the interest rate corresponding to the profit that a financial institution can expect to earn. The spread includes the portion corresponding to the administrative expenses of the financial institution and the portion corresponding to the credit risk of the borrower. The "swap rate" of an interest rate swap indicates the level of the long-term interest rate that is exchangeable for the short-term interest rate, as indicated by the international financial markets.

Applicability of Methods that Are Equivalent to the Traditional Transaction Methods

Japanese transfer pricing provisions give preference to the taxpayer's use of methods that are equivalent to the traditional transaction methods pursuant to ASMT Article 66-4(2), Item 2, when the taxpayer selects an arm's length price for the money-lending transaction between Japanese Corporation P and Company S. An examination of comparable transactions pursuant to ASMT Directive 66-4(6)-4 and ASMT Directive 66-4(2)-3 and other relevant provisions produces these findings:

- Given the information available, the taxpayer is unable to find comparable transactions to apply a method that is equivalent to the CUP or to a method that is equivalent to the cost plus method.

- It was impossible to apply the methods prescribed in ASMT Directive 66-4(6)-4 as Company S had no bank loans.
- The taxpayer was unable to obtain information as to the interest rate that a lender would apply where the company had taken out a loan from a bank or similar institution under the same terms and conditions.

Selection of the Arm's Length Price for Interest Rate Spreads

The calculation of interest rate was:

- Japanese Corporation P had determined the bank loan.
- The bank could provide spread information as to Corporation P.
- The taxpayer is to determine the arm's length price using the interest rate pursuant to Administrative Guideline 2-7(1) and ASMT 66-4(2), Item 2(b), methods equivalent to methods consistent with the comparable uncontrolled price method.
- The arm's length price is the interest rate for the money-lending transactions between Japanese Corporation P and Company S.
- The arm's length rate is 5.7%, the objective interest rate of 5% plus the 0.7% spread.

Explaining the Arm's Length Interest Rate Determination

As a general matter, see Case 1 for such transfer pricing analysis that concerns the applicability of traditional transaction methods. This analysis includes methods equivalent to the traditional transaction methods and pertains to the judging whether transactions correspond to comparable transactions.

There might be situations in which the taxpayer cannot find any transactions with unrelated persons that are comparable to foreign-related transactions, and, for that reason, the taxpayer cannot apply the traditional transaction methods. In that situation, it might be possible for the taxpayer to calculate the arm's length price by a transfer pricing method that is "consistent with" the traditional transaction methods or a transfer pricing method that is "equivalent to" a method that is "consistent with" the traditional transaction methods that use such transactions as the comparable transaction. The prerequisite for applying the "consistent with" method or the "equivalent to" method is the existence of "objective and realistic indicators" pertaining to market prices or similar variables, such as the market interest rate, as in the present case.

The taxpayer is to use the next four-step procedure for calculating the arm's length price for money-lending transactions by corporations by themselves providing that they do not engage in the money-lending business:

1. The taxpayer is to begin with the principle transfer pricing methods pursuant to ASMT Directive 66-4(6)-4, pertaining to methods that are equivalent to the CUP or to the cost plus method. Such amount is the actual interest rate on the transaction. If the taxpayer cannot apply this method, the taxpayer is to proceed with step 2.
2. The taxpayer is to apply the transfer pricing methods set forth in the note to ASMT Directive 66-4(6)-4, the method using the borrower's bank lending rate

(i.e., the market interest rate). If the taxpayer cannot apply this method, the taxpayer is to proceed with step 3.

3. The taxpayer is to apply the transfer pricing method set forth in Administrative Guidance 2–7(1), the method of using the bank financing rate of the lender (i.e., the market interest rate). If the taxpayer cannot apply this method, the taxpayer is to proceed with step 4.
4. The taxpayer is to apply the transfer pricing method set forth in Administrative Guidance 2–7(2), the method of using the investment return on government bonds and so forth of the lender (i.e., the market interest rate).

The interest rate that this methodology provides is the same regardless of whether the lender provides the loan through its funds at hand or through borrowed funds. The situation might exist where a financial transaction occurs under the same terms and conditions and under the same currency. In that situation, there is no fundamental need to allow for differences due to markets because the level of interest rates in each financial market is mostly the same.

CASE 5: METHODS CONSISTENT WITH THE COST PLUS METHOD

If the taxpayer determines that it cannot apply a transfer pricing method that is "equivalent to" the traditional transaction methods, the taxpayer can apply a transfer pricing method that is "consistent with" the cost plus method. The fact pattern for Case 5 is:

- Japanese Corporation P is engaged in the manufacture of Product A and the sales of Product A and part "a."
- Japanese Corporation P undertakes sales relationships with foreign-related person S in Country X and with third-party T in Country X.
- Japanese Corporation P sells part "a" to foreign-related person S in Country X and third-party T in Country X.
- Japanese Corporation P provides maintenance services to foreign-related person S and maintains and inspects production facilities for foreign-related person S.
- Foreign-related person S manufactures Product A and sells Product A to third parties.
- Third-party T manufactures Product B and sells Product B to third parties.

The additional facts pertaining to Case 5 are:

- Japanese Corporation P established Company S ten years ago in Country X as a subsidiary to manufacture Product A and distribute Product A.
- Company S buys part "a" from Japanese Corporation P, which Japanese Corporation P manufactures.

- Company S combines part "a" with other parts to produce Product A for sale to third parties in Country X.
- Japanese Corporation P sells part "a" to Company T, a third party located in Country X.
- Company T purchases part "a" from Japanese Corporation P.
- Company T combines part "a" with other parts to manufacture Product B for sale to third parties in Country X.
- The providing of services is not a "core business" to Japanese Corporation P.
- Japanese Corporation P sells part "a" to Company A and to Company T at the same price.
- The market level, transaction terms, and transaction volumes for part "a" are the same.

Services Transactions

Japanese Corporation P performs two functions for Company S. Japanese Corporation P provides three engineers from its manufacturing division, for a total of two months per year, to maintain and inspect Company S's facilities to manufacture Product A and to train Company S's equipment operators. The maintenance, inspection, and other services that Japanese Corporation P undertake through its three engineers are not independent. However, the maintenance, inspection, and other services do not make use of Japanese Corporation P's manufacturing know-how and so forth. Company S does not provide any consideration to Japanese Corporation P for the maintenance, inspection, and other services.

Neither Japanese Corporation P nor Company S engages in similar services transactions with unrelated parties. Furthermore, the taxpayer is unable to find similar services transactions between unrelated parties.

Applicability of the Traditional Transaction Methods for the Sale of Part "a"

The Japanese transfer pricing provisions give preference to the traditional transaction methods when selecting an arm's length price pursuant to ASMT Article 66-4(2), Item 1. The taxpayer undertakes an examination of comparable transactions in accordance with ASMT Directive 66-4(2)-1, ASMT Directive 66-4(2)-3, and other provisions. The taxpayer finds that there are no problems from the point of view of transfer pricing taxation arising from the CUP as to the sale of part "a." Japanese Corporation P and Company C use the sale of part "a," using as a comparable transaction Japanese Corporation P's sale to Company T.

Applicability of "Equivalent Methods"

The Japanese transfer pricing provisions give preference to the traditional transaction methods, and to method equivalent, when selecting an arm's length price pursuant to ASMT Article 66-4(2), Item 2. An examination of comparable transactions in accordance with ASMT Directive 66-4(6)-5, ASMT Directive 66-4(6)-3, and other relevant provisions produce these findings:

- The taxpayer is unable to find any comparable transactions as to methods that are equivalent to the CUP or to the cost plus method as to Japanese Corporation P because the scope of the information is limited.
- Due to the content of the transaction, the taxpayer found it unfeasible to apply a transfer pricing method that is equivalent to the resale price method.

Applying the Services Method

The taxpayer determined that the providing of services by Japanese Corporation P to Company S was incidental to Japanese Corporation P's core business, which is the sale of part "a," and that the cost of providing the services did not account for a significant portion of Japanese Corporation P's costs in the taxable year in which the services activities took place. Japanese Corporation P made no use of intangible properties in providing services.

Based on the preceding facts, the taxpayer rejected the use of the cost plus method. Instead, the taxpayer found it appropriate to apply a transfer pricing method that is "consistent with" the cost plus method (i.e., by applying the final cost of services provision as being the arm's length price pursuant to Administrative Guidance 2–9).

The final service cost is the sum of:

- Salaries, bonuses, and retirement expenses during the dispatch period
- Engineers' travel, transport, and accommodation costs
- Other costs to dispatch the engineers
- Indirect costs allocated on a reasonable basis, such as the general expenses of the division concerned and associated divisions

The reader should review the explanation for Case 1 as to the applicability of the traditional transaction methods, including methods that are "equivalent to" the traditional transaction methods, and in judging whether the transactions correspond to comparable transactions. The reader should review the explanation for Case 1 as to the traditional transaction methods, including methods that are "consistent with" the traditional transaction methods.

ASMT Directive 66-4(6)-5 addresses transfer pricing methods that are "equivalent to" the comparable uncontrolled method or a method that is "equivalent to" the cost plus method for services transactions. The application of the cost plus method necessitates a markup in the expenses required to provide the services. Nevertheless, it generally will be difficult for the taxpayer to find "comparable transactions" among the uncontrolled transactions as services transactions that are incidental to the corporation's core business. Thus, the Reference Case Studies recognize that there may some cases where the ASTM Directive provides transfer pricing methods the taxpayer cannot apply. As a result, pursuant to Administrative Guideline 2-9, the final services cost might include the cost without markup for the expenses required.

Administrative Guideline 2-9 provide that the final service cost is not the arm's length price if:

- The services activities are "not incidental to" the core business
- The cost of providing the services "does not" account for a significant proportion of the cost or expenses of a corporation of a foreign-related business
- The taxpayer uses intangible property in providing services

These provisions would suggest that the taxpayer consider other calculation methods in this instance.

The Reference Case Studies, in applying the second of these three tests, makes use of the term "does not" in reference to the costs or expenses involved. As transfer pricing practitioners, we suggest that the Reference Case Studies contain an error, and that "does" is the word that the Reference Case Studies would require.

The next four points specify the differences as to whether the final services costs can be treated as the arm's length price where these costs are incidental to the core business between the corporation and the foreign-related business:

1. ASMT Directive 66-4(6)-5 requires the taxpayer to ascertain whether there are comparable transactions for applying a transfer pricing method that is equivalent to the CUP or whether the transfer pricing method is equivalent to the cost plus method. If the answer is no, the final cost might be equal to the arm's length price depending on subsequent steps in this analysis. If the answer is yes, ASMT Directive 66-4(6)-5 does not treat that final cost as the arm's length price.
2. Administrative Guideline 2-9 requires the taxpayer to consider whether, in light of the purpose for the services, the providing of services is "incidental to" the company's core business. If the answer is yes, the final cost is equal to the arm's length price, subject to the results in step 3 and step 4. If the answer is no, ASMT Directive 66-4(6)-5 does not treat that final cost as the arm's length price.
3. Note (a) to Administrative Guideline 2-9 requires the taxpayer to ascertain whether the cost of providing the services does account for a significant proportion of the costs or expenses of the corporation or the foreign-related person. If the answer is yes, Administrative Guideline 2-9 note (a) does not treat that final cost as the arm's length price. If the answer is no, the cost of the services does not account for a significant portion of the costs and expenses, and the final cost is equal to the arm's length price, pending the results of step 4.
4. Note (b) to Administrative Guideline 2–9 requires the taxpayer to ascertain whether the taxpayer uses intangibles in providing services. If the answer is yes, Administrative Guideline 2-9 note (b) does not treat the final cost as the arm's length price. If the answer is no, the taxpayer did use intangibles in providing services, and the final cost is equal to the arm's length price.

The Reference Case Studies caution that a corporation might engage in an inventory transaction and a services transaction, both with a foreign-related person. In that event, the taxpayer should consider that transfer pricing issues can apply to both situations.

CASE 6: TRANSACTIONAL NET MARGIN METHOD

In the case at hand, the taxpayer considered the applicability of the traditional transaction methods. The taxpayer determined that it could not apply the traditional transaction methods in this instance. The taxpayer then ascertained that it could obtain comparable transactions that would enable it to apply the transactional net margin method, making the transactional net margin method appropriate. The taxpayer then considered the applicability of transfer pricing methods that are "equivalent to" the traditional transaction methods and determined that the transactional net margin method was appropriate as being "equivalent to" the traditional transaction methods.

Case 2 considers two situations in which the transactional net margin method might be appropriate: the first addresses the sale of inventories; the second addresses the licensing of intangible properties.

Sale of Inventories

Consider this fact pattern:

- Japanese Corporation P purchases raw materials and so forth in Japan.
- Japanese Corporation P established Company S in Country X ten years ago to distribute Product A.
- Japanese Corporation P manufactures Product A in Japan.
- Japanese Corporation P sells Product A to foreign-related party S in Country X.
- Foreign-related party S, in Country X, purchases Product A from Japanese Corporation P.
- Foreign-related party S, in Country X, sells Product A to a dozen or so third-party companies as agents in Country X.
- Japanese Corporation P manufactures Product A using its original technology it developed through its R&D process.
- Company S does not engage in any advertising or sales promotion activities.
- Country X does require that companies disclose financial data, but Country X does not require the company to disclose cost items.
- Japan does require the company to disclose operating income.

Potential Applicability of the Traditional Transaction Methods

The Japanese transfer pricing provisions give preference to the traditional transaction methods to determine the arm's length price. ASMT Article 66-4(2), Item 1, provides that the taxpayer must examine comparable transactions in accordance with ASMT Directive 66-4(2)-1, ASMT Directive 66-4(2)-3, and other relevant provisions. These findings are:

- Product A, which Japanese Corporation P manufactured and sold to Company S, is a product that utilizes Japanese Corporation P's technologies resulting from its R&D activities.

- The taxpayer was unable to find comparable transactions from the available data in applying the CUP or the cost plus method to Japanese Corporation P.
- Company S was not engaged in original advertising or in sales promotion activities.
- Company S has no intangible properties that provide a source of income.
- See Cases 10 to 15 regarding the relationship between intangible properties and sources of income.
- It was not possible to ascertain gross profit on sales, or cost of sales, from publicly available information in Country X.
- The taxpayer was unable to obtain the information it would need to adjust the differences affecting the ratio of gross profit to sales.
- As a result, the taxpayer could not find comparable transactions to apply the resale price method to Company S.

Methods that Would Substitute for the Traditional Transaction Methods

The taxpayer found that it could not apply the traditional transaction methods. The taxpayer considered applying methods that are "consistent with" the traditional transaction methods, as prescribed by ASMT Article 66-4(2), Item 1(d), and other methods prescribed in the ASMT Cabinet Order, with these results. The taxpayer was unable to find comparable transactions in applying methods that are consistent with the traditional transaction methods. It was possible for the taxpayer to identify comparable transactions for Company S from publicly available information based on the operating margin. As a result, it was deemed to be appropriate in this case to calculate the arm's length price by applying the transactional net margin method to Company S pursuant to ASMT Cabinet Order, Article 39-12(8), Item 2.

Transactional Net Margin Method and the Profit Split Method

The reader should examine the examination process applicable to Case 1, including traditional transaction methods, including methods "equivalent to" methods consistent with the traditional transaction methods. The transactional net margin method calculates the arm's length price by selecting comparable transactions for one of the counterparts to the transaction concerned. There may be, however, cases in which the profit split method is more appropriate, based on the corporation's role and functions, in order for the taxpayer to calculate arm's length price based on the contributions of both the corporation and the foreign-related person to generate profit.

Transactional Net Margin Method

These factors apply to the transactional net margin method:

- The transactional net margin method is a comparison of net incomes. Taxpayers might apply the transactional net margin method to calculate the arm's length price for foreign-related transactions. They can focus on the level of operating income from these foreign-related transactions. When considering the application of the transactional net margin method, taxpayers need to consider the similarity of factors listed in ASMT Directive 66-4(2)-3 when selecting comparable transactions.

- The comparable uncontrolled cost method compares the prices of goods themselves and requires the taxpayer to apply strict similarity or homogeneity of inventories. In contrast, the resale price method or the cost plus method focuses on gross profit on sales. These traditional methods require the taxpayer to determine whether those activities are similar, as performed by the buyer and by the seller.
- Differences in products tend to affect prices. Differences in functions tend to affect the profit margin (i.e., the gross profit on sales). However, many knowledgeable practitioners view the operating margin as being less susceptible to the effects of such differences. Nevertheless, the taxpayer might find that such transactions may be usable as a source of comparability with transactional net margin method transactions. The taxpayer might reach that conclusion even where the comparability that traditional transaction methods would require is not available.
- The Japanese tax authorities introduced the transactional net margin method for fiscal 2004. Taxpayers can apply the method for taxable years commencing in or after April 1, 2004.

Profit Split Method

The Japanese transfer pricing methodology provides for three specific profit split methodologies:

1. **The contribution profit split method.** See Case 7 for an example of the contribution profit split method.
2. **The comparable profit split method.** The comparable profit split method is a method of reasonably allocating the profits to be split. The taxpayer is to use the proportionate allocation of profits that correspond to the profits to be split between unrelated entities. Such uncontrolled transactions are engaged in conditions that are consistent with the foreign-related transactions when applying the profit split method pursuant to ASMT Directive 66-4(4)-4.
3. **The residual profit split method.** See Case 8 for an example of the residual profit split method.

Profit Split Method and the Transactional Net Margin Method

The Japanese transfer pricing provisions treat the transactional net margin method and the profit split method as being of equal importance. Neither of the two methods has more importance than the other in deciding which transfer pricing method to apply.

As a general matter, the Japanese transfer pricing provisions view transfer pricing taxation as a system of taxation concerning transactions between a corporation and a foreign-related person. The Japanese transfer pricing provisions suggest that the taxpayer should pay attention to whether the profit arising from a foreign-related transaction is commensurate with the roles and function of each party to the transaction. Pursuant to Administrative Guideline 2-1(3), the taxpayer is to indicate whether it has problems concerning transfer pricing taxation.

The Japanese transfer pricing provisions require the taxpayer to select "the most reasonable" transfer pricing method, making that determination in keeping with the actual situation in each particular case. The taxpayer must consider this point when making the selection.

Licensing Activities

The Reference Case Studies provide this scenario concerning the licensing of patents and manufacturing know-how:

- Japanese Corporation P manufactures and sells Product A in Japan.
- Japanese Corporation P established foreign-related person S as a subsidiary to manufacture and distribute Product A.
- Japanese Corporation P manufactures Product A through applying its own original R&D technologies.
- Japanese Corporation P licenses patents and manufacturing know-how to foreign-related person S in Country X, using Japanese Corporation P's own technologies.
- Foreign-related party S purchases raw materials.
- Foreign-related party S licenses patents and manufacturing know-how from Japanese Corporation P.
- Foreign-related party S manufactures Product A in Country X.
- Forcign-related party S sells Product A to third parties in Country X as agents.
- No trading of inventories takes place between Japanese Corporation P and Company S.
- Company S has no R&D operations.
- Company S licenses Japanese Corporation P's technology to manufacture Product A.

Treatment of the License for Transfer Pricing Purposes

The Japanese transfer pricing provisions give preference to the traditional transaction method and to transfer pricing methods that are "equivalent to" these methods when the taxpayer selects an arm's length price. The taxpayer would apply ASMT Article 66-4(2), Item 2, in examining comparable transactions in accordance with ASMT Directive 66-4(6)-6, ASMT Directive 66-4(2)-3, and other relevant provisions. This analysis produced these findings:

- The patents and know-how that Japanese Corporation P licensed to Company S are Japanese Corporation P's original R&D technologies.
- Based on the information available, it is not possible for the taxpayer to find comparable transactions for applying a transfer pricing method that is "equivalent to" the CUP or to a method that is "equivalent to" the cost plus method to Japanese Corporation P.

- The taxpayer was unable to apply a method that is "equivalent to" the resale price method given the content of the transaction.

Finding a Method to Substitute for the Traditional Transaction Methods

In this situation, the taxpayer found that it was impossible to apply a transfer pricing method that was "equivalent to" the traditional transaction methods. Further, the taxpayer found that it was impossible to apply methods that are "equivalent to" methods that are "consistent with" the traditional transaction methods. The taxpayer considered applying the transfer pricing methods prescribed in ASMT Article 66-4(2), Item 2(b), and other methods prescribed in the ASMT Cabinet Order, and obtained these results:

- The taxpayer was unable to identify comparable transactions in seeking to apply the "equivalent to" methods that are "consistent with" the arm's length results.
- The taxpayer can obtain operating margins on comparable transactions from publicly available information that are comparable with manufacturing and sales transactions that Company S undertakes.
- The taxpayer could be able to calculate the arm's length price indirectly, doing so by calculating the "normal profit" that is "commensurate with" Company S's functions operating margin.
- The taxpayer could then treat Company S's residual profit in excess of the normal profit amount as being the consideration for licensing of patents and manufacturing know-how.
- The taxpayer can apply the preceding indirect arm's length approach by directly calculating the consideration for licensing intangible properties between Japanese Corporation P and Company S.
- In this particular case, the taxpayer found it appropriate to calculate the arm's length price by applying a transfer pricing method that is "consistent with" the transactional net margin method as applied to Company S, pursuant to ASMT Cabinet Order Article 39-12(8), Item 4.

Explanation for the Transactional Net Margin Method Determination

The reader should review the explanation to Case 1 as to the applicability of the traditional transaction methods and the applicability of transfer pricing methods that are "equivalent to" the traditional transaction methods.

It may be possible for the taxpayer to apply the transactional net margin method and to indirectly calculate the amount of consideration for the furnishing of intangible properties. The taxpayer might be able to apply this approach when the corporation furnishes intangible properties to a foreign-related person through the licensing of patents or of similar property. The taxpayer can calculate the normal profit that is "commensurate with" the functions of the foreign-related person and then treat the residual profit of the foreign-related person as the excess amount.

It is possible for the taxpayer to apply this profit split approach if the foreign-related person engages in the same category of business as that of the foreign-related transaction. It is possible for the taxpayer to apply this profit split approach if the corporation has comparable manufacturing functions or sales functions to other corporations in similar markets of a similar size. This procedure does not apply to corporations that have material intangible properties. This method of calculating the arm's length price is "a method that is equivalent to" a transfer pricing method that is "consistent with" the transactional net margin method.

The case at hand is premised on the license of intangible properties under contract. This situation can apply even if Japanese Corporation P and Company S do not have an agreement between them. The taxpayer might be able to apply the intangible arrangement if the facts and circumstances would deem a license to be created based on the actual state of the transactions, pursuant to Administrative Guideline 2-13.

The transactional net margin method is a method of calculating the arm's length price by selecting comparable transactions. These comparable transactional net margin transactions would involve one or the other counterparts to the underlying transaction. There may be cases in which the profit split method is a more appropriate method that is the transactional net margin method in determining the arm's length price. The method selection depends on the contribution of the corporation and the foreign-related party to the generation of profit, determined in light of the roles and functions of the corporation and the foreign-related party.

CASE 7: CONTRIBUTION PROFIT SPLIT METHOD

In the case at hand, the taxpayer considered the applicability of the traditional transaction methods and found that it could not apply the traditional transaction methods. The taxpayer determined that the profit split method was appropriate.

First Application of the Contribution Profit Split Method

The first application of the contribution profit split method is shown next.

- Japanese Corporation P purchases raw materials and other items in Japan.
- Japanese Corporation P manufactures Product A in Japan.
- Japanese Corporation P established Company S in Country X ten years before.
- Japanese Corporation P sells Product A in Japan.
- Japanese Corporation P sells part "a" to foreign-related person S in Country X.
- Foreign-related person S combines part "a" with other parts to produce Product A.
- Foreign-related person S manufactures Product A in Country X.
- Foreign-related person S sells Product A to third-party agents in Country X.
- Foreign-related person S has no R&D operations.
- Foreign-related person S does not engage in original advertising or sales promotion activities.
- Foreign-related person S does not use its own trademark or other properties in its distribution activities.

Other Conditions of the Transfer

Company S sells Product A to third parties located in Country X. However, two other corporations manufacture products that are similar to Product A and sell these products in Country X. These two corporations are manufacturing subsidiaries whose parent companies are located outside Country X. The market for such products in Country X is an oligopoly of these three companies. These two companies have similar products as Product A.

Product A has an equal share of the market compared with these two companies. Product A is almost the same as the similar products of the same companies in terms of product and price. In Japan, only one corporation manufactures and sells a product similar to Japanese Corporation P's Product A. Transactions involving the similar product are controlled transactions.

Inapplicability of the Traditional Transaction Methods

The Japanese transfer pricing provisions give preference to traditional transfer pricing transaction methods when the taxpayer selects an arm's length price pursuant to ASMT Article 66-4(2), Item 1. ASMT Directive 66-4(2)-1, ASMT Directive 44-4(2)-3, and other relevant provisions produce these findings:

- Regarding Japanese Corporation P, one corporation is manufacturing and selling a product that is similar to Product A in Japan. All transactions involving that product are controlled transactions. As a result, based on the information available, it is not possible for the taxpayer to identify comparable transactions in seeking to apply the CUP or the cost plus method.
- Regarding Company C, the transactions of the two companies deal in similar products, but they are controlled transactions. As a result, the taxpayer cannot find comparable transactions in applying the resale price method to Company S's sales transactions.

Substituting for the Traditional Transaction Methods

The taxpayer cannot apply the traditional transaction methods in the present case. The taxpayer considered applying methods that are "consistent with" the traditional transaction methods, as prescribed by ASMT Article 66-4(2), and other methods, as prescribed by the ASMT Cabinet Order. The taxpayer was unable to find comparable transactions in applying methods that are "consistent with" the traditional transaction methods. The taxpayer then considered it appropriate in this case to calculate arm's length amount pertaining to foreign-related transactions between Japanese Corporation P and Company S by applying the profit split method.

The taxpayer was unable to identify any comparable transactions in applying the transactional net margin method. Neither Japanese Corporation P nor Company S had material intangible property. As a result neither party could apply the residual profit split method.

Explaining the Selection of a Transfer Pricing Method

The reader should note that Case 1 addresses the applicability of the traditional transfer pricing transaction methods, including methods that might be considered as methods "equivalent to" the traditional transaction methods, and for judging whether these transactions correspond to comparable transactions. There might be situations in which it is difficult for the taxpayer to find comparable transactions due to the state of the market, such as the existence of an oligopoly. A taxpayer might be better off in that situation in using the contribution profit split transfer pricing method but without seeking to use comparable transactions as the method of arm's length price. The contribution profit split method might be the method that is "more appropriate." The taxpayer cannot apply the residual profit split method if neither the corporation nor the related person has material intangible properties. The reader should see the explanation to Case 8 to determine whether the residual profit split method is compatible.

The issue in applying the contribution profit split method can be the selection of factors the taxpayer is to use. The taxpayer is to make use of the factors that are suited to estimating the extent of the contribution to the profit that is to be split, depending on the content of the foreign-related transaction. These factors might include, for instance, the amount of the expenses incurred, such personnel costs, and the amount of capital the corporation or the foreign-related person employ pursuant to ASMT Directive 66-4(4)-2.

For instance, in applying the contribution profit split method, the taxpayer might consider if the function the taxpayer ordinarily performs (e.g., in manufacturing or in distribution) contributes to the generation of profit. In such a case, it would be logical for the taxpayer to use the human resource expenditures and depreciation expenses that reflect that function.

Financial Institutions with International Operations

Japanese Corporation A is a financial institution having international operations in Country X and in Country Y:

- Japanese Corporation A does business with foreign-related person XA in Country X.
- Japanese Corporation A does business with foreign-related person YA in Country Y.
- Japanese Corporation A, foreign-related person XA, and foreign-related person YA all engage in derivative transactions as a single group.
- Japanese Corporation A markets derivative products to customers.
- Japanese Corporation A takes orders from customers.
- Japanese Corporation A, a front-end company, creates, develops, and markets derivative products to meet customer demands.
- Foreign-related person XA provides Japanese Corporation A with pricing these derivative products.
- Foreign-related person XA, according to Japanese Corporation A's request, engages in interbank market transactions.

- Foreign-related person XA engages in trading operations, including revenue and risk management concerns as to all financial products that foreign-related person XA handles.
- Foreign-related person YA is a party to contracts with customers, according to customer needs, and engages in trading operations.

Determination of Transfer Pricing Methods

The Japanese transfer pricing provisions give the taxpayer preference to transfer pricing methods that are "equivalent to" the traditional transfer pricing methods when the taxpayer selects an arm's length price pursuant to ASMT Article 66-4(2), Item 2. An examination of comparable transactions pursuant to ASMT Directive 66-4(6)-5, ASMT Directive 66-4(2)-3, and other provisions produces these findings:

- The taxpayer was unable to ascertain comparable functions as to front-end operations, marketing, and trading, as the taxpayer dispersed these functions among related parties through services transactions with unrelated parties.
- Given the data available, the taxpayer was unable to identify uncontrolled transactions in the same or similar category of business that Japanese Corporation A, foreign-related person XA, and foreign-related person YA undertook with the same terms of service provision.
- The taxpayer was not able to find any comparable transactions in applying methods that are equivalent to the traditional transaction methods.

Selection of a Transfer Pricing Method that Determines the Arm's Length Price

In this particular case, the taxpayer found that it could not apply a transfer pricing method that is "equivalent to" the traditional transaction methods. The taxpayer considered applying transfer pricing methods that are "equivalent to" transfer pricing methods that are "consistent with" the traditional transaction methods pursuant to ASMT Article 66-4(2), Item 2(b), and to other transfer pricing methods that are "equivalent to" other methods, as prescribed in the ASMT Cabinet Order. The taxpayer determined:

- The taxpayer was unable to find comparable transactions to the application of a transfer pricing method that is "equivalent to" a transfer pricing method that is "consistent with" the traditional transaction methods.
- The taxpayer concluded that the Japanese Corporation A performed its operations as a single set of functions concerning the sale of derivative products to customers by the business group as a unit.
- Based on the foregoing, the taxpayer found it appropriate to apply the profit split method by apportioning the profit that arose from Japanese Corporation A, foreign-related person XA, and foreign-related person YA.

- The taxpayer was to apportion the combined profit "according to the level of each foreign-related person's contribution."
- The taxpayer found no comparable transactions in considering whether to apply the transactional net margin method.

Explaining the Choice of Transfer Pricing Method

The reader should consider that the explanation to Case 1 discusses the applicability of traditional transaction methods, including transfer pricing methods that are "equivalent to" traditional transaction methods, and in judging whether the transactions correspond to comparable transactions.

Transactions might be highly integrated and might be global in nature. The company's functions can be dispersed among a corporation and foreign-related persons that do business together cooperatively as a single unit. In such situations, it is difficult for the taxpayer to determine the revenues of each of the related persons by means of a transfer pricing method that is equivalent to the traditional transaction methods. In such situations, the taxpayer should consider applying transfer pricing methods that are "equivalent to" methods "consistent with" the traditional transaction methods, as prescribed by ASMT Article 66-4(2), Item 2(b), and to methods that are "equivalent to other methods," as prescribed in the ASMT Cabinet Order.

The taxpayer will find that the application of transfer pricing methods that are consistent with the traditional transaction methods is difficult for the same reasons as applying methods that are "equivalent to" the traditional transaction methods. The taxpayer, then, needs to consider the application of a transfer pricing method that is "equivalent to" the profit split method or a transfer pricing method that is "equivalent to" the transaction net margin method. In the case of transactions such as those described in this case, however, it is generally appropriate for the taxpayer to apply a transfer pricing method that is "equivalent to" the profit split method. The taxpayer, in applying the profit split method, can allocate the profit arising from the overall transactions to each of the operations concerned according to their contributions. This method would be a transfer pricing method that is "equivalent to" the contribution profit sharing method. This profit split method might be feasible due to the frequent infeasibility of finding comparable transactions when applying the transactional net margin method.

CASE 8: RESIDUAL PROFIT SPLIT METHOD

In the case at hand, the taxpayer found that it could apply the traditional transaction transfer pricing methods. The taxpayer reached this determination after considering the applicability of the traditional transaction methods, including methods that are "equivalent to" the traditional transaction methods. Here the taxpayer found the residual profit split approach to be appropriate because the corporation and the foreign-related person create intangible properties through R&D, sales promotion, and other activities that serve as a source of income.

The business relationships are:

- Japanese Corporation P purchases raw materials and other items.
- Japanese Corporation P manufactures Product A in Japan.
- Japanese Corporation P sells Product A.
- Japanese Corporation P established foreign-related person S as a subsidiary ten years ago to manufacture and distribute Product A.
- Japanese Corporation P and foreign-related person S manufacture Product A using original technologies that result from Japanese Corporation P's R&D activities.
- Japanese Corporation P supplies part "a" to foreign-related person S in Country X.
- Part "a" is a core part that aggregates original technologies that Japanese Corporation P produces.
- Foreign-related person S combines part "a" with other parts to manufacture Product A.
- Foreign-related person S manufactures Product A based on original technologies that Japanese Corporation P furnishes to foreign-related person S.
- Japanese Corporation P licenses patents and manufacturing know-how to related-person S in Country X.
- Foreign-related person S manufactures Product A in Country X.
- Foreign-related person S sells Product A to approximately 200 third-party retailers.
- Foreign-related person S has no R&D operations.
- Foreign-related person S has numerous sales representatives.
- Foreign-related person S engages in original advertising and sales promotion activities that foreign-related person S targets to retailers and to end consumers.

Product A has achieved a certain market share in Country X. Product A achieved this market share because of:

- Product A's unique technical performance
- Strong product recognition
- A well-developed network of retailers, built up through advertising and sales promotion activities
- Foreign-related person S selling Product A at a stable price

Traditional Transaction Methods and Methods "Equivalent to" Traditional Transaction Methods

The Japanese transfer pricing provisions give preference to traditional transaction methods and to methods "equivalent to" transaction methods for purposes of ascertaining the arm's length price pursuant to ASMT Article 66-4(2). An examination of comparable transactions in accordance with ASMT Directive 66-4(2)-1, ASMT

Directive 66-4(6)-6, ASMT Directive 66-4(2)-3, and other provisions produced these findings:

- Japanese Corporation P licensed patents and know-how to foreign-related person S. Japanese Corporation P created these patents and know-how as original technologies emanating as a result of its R&D activities.
- Japanese Corporation P manufacturers part "a" as a result of these original technologies.
- Based on the information available, the taxpayer found it impossible to find any comparable transactions for purposes of applying the CUP or any equivalent method.
- Based on the information available, the taxpayer found it impossible to find any comparable transactions for purposes of applying the cost plus method or any equivalent method.
- The hallmark of transfer pricing taxability then becomes the delineation between a "corporation engaging solely in basic activities" and a corporation that exceeds this basic activities threshold.
- In this case, a "corporation engaging solely in basic activities" is a corporation that:
  - Performs basic manufacturing activities
  - Performs basic sales activities
  - Engages in the same category of business as that of the foreign-related transaction
  - Is of a similar scale as the basic manufacturing or sales activities
  - Is active in a similar market
  - Has no intangible properties that contribute to generating profit
- Foreign-related person S, due to advertising and sales promotion activities, does its business by "employing a better-developed network of retailers" and by "enjoying higher product recognition" compared with "a corporation engaging solely in basic activities."
- In the present case, the business has strong product recognition, well-developed retailer networks, original technologies, and low manufacturing costs, all of which differ from a "corporation engaging solely in basic activities."
- Based on the information available, the taxpayer found it impossible to find any uncontrolled transactions that took place under the same conditions as the transactions in which foreign-related person S was engaged.
- Based on the information available, the taxpayer found it impossible to identify comparable transactions in applying the resale price method to foreign-related person S.

Selection of Substitute Methods

The taxpayer determined that it was unable to find transfer pricing methods that constitute traditional transaction methods or methods that are "equivalent to" the traditional transaction methods. The taxpayer then considered applying transfer pricing methods that are "consistent with" the traditional transaction methods, as prescribed in ASMT Article 66-4(2), Item 1(d), ASMT Article 66-4(2), Item 2(d), and the ASMT Cabinet Order. The taxpayer obtained these results:

- The taxpayer was unable to find comparable transactions in applying transfer pricing methods that are "consistent with" the traditional transaction methods.
- The taxpayer was unable to find comparable transactions in applying transfer pricing methods that are "equivalent to" methods that are "consistent with" the traditional transaction methods.
- The taxpayer then sought to contrast the operations under review with a corporation that engages in basic activities: The intangible properties that Japanese Corporation P creates through its R&D activities plus the foreign-related person S's advertising and sales promotion serve as a source of income for Japanese Corporation P and for the foreign-related party's foreign-related transactions. Cases 10 to 15 examine the relationship between intangible properties and the source of income.
- Based on the preceding analysis, the taxpayer found that the residual profit split method was appropriate to determine the company's arm's length price, making that determination pursuant to ASMT Cabinet Order Article 39-12(8), Item 1, and ASMT Directive 66-4(4)-5.
- The taxpayer was unable to find comparable transactions in applying the transactional net margin method.

Explanation

The explanation to Case 1 examines the points to note when considering the applicability of the traditional transaction methods, including transfer pricing methods that are "equivalent to" the traditional transaction methods. The explanation to Case 1 examines points to note in the case of the use of intangible properties in foreign-related transactions. It examines transfer pricing methods that are "consistent with" the traditional transaction methods, including those transfer pricing methods that are "equivalent to" methods that are "consistent with" the traditional transaction methods.

The presence of intangible properties typically puts their users in an "economically competitively advantageous position" compared with corporations that engage solely in basic activities, making this delineation based on the originality, individuality, and uniqueness of the intangible property holders. It is often difficult for the taxpayer to select comparable transactions for foreign-related transactions that involve such properties. The taxpayer might choose the residual profit split method pursuant to ASMT Directive 66-4(4)-5, particularly in cases where the corporation and the foreign-related persons have material intangible properties.

CASE 9: ADJUSTMENT FOR DIFFERENCES

Schematic of the business relations is:

- Japanese Corporation P is a distributor of Product A.
- Japanese Corporation P previously established foreign-related person S in Country X as a subsidiary to distribute Product A.

- Japanese Corporation P purchases Product A.
- Japanese Corporation P sells Product A to two persons in Country X: foreign-related person S and third-party T.
- Foreign-related person S in turn sells Product A to approximately 200 third-party retailers.
- Third-party T in turn sells Product A as agent to third-party retailers.
- Japanese Corporation P had been selling Product A through third-party agent T before Japanese Corporation P established foreign-related person S.
- Japanese Corporation P has two sales channels in Country X: through foreign-related person S and through third party T. (As a note of caution, the schematic refers to "Third-party T." The discussion refers to Company Y, but the schematic itself does not reflect a "Company Y.")

Japanese Corporation P's Transactions with Foreign-Related Person S

Japanese Corporation P's transactions with foreign-related person S and with third-party T are virtually identical in terms of market level, volume, and terms, except:

1. Delivery terms
   a. The delivery terms with foreign-related person S are CIF (price including cost, insurance, and freight).
   b. The delivery terms with third-party T are FOB (free on board).
2. Payment period
   a. The payment period for transactions with foreign-related person S is 30 days.
   b. The payment period for transactions with third-party T is 90 days.
3. The usance rate—the rate changed for credit—in both cases is 5%.

Transfer Pricing Taxation

One option the taxpayer faces for transfer pricing taxation purposes is to adjust for the differences from Japanese Corporation P's sale to foreign-related party S, on one hand, and Japanese Corporation P's sale to third-party T, on the other hand, taking into account the fact that these two transactions are highly comparable. The differences in delivery terms and in settlement terms have an impact on both transactions. It is possible for the taxpayer to adjust for differences in the delivery terms by adding freight and insurance premiums to the transaction price with Company T: Company T purchase price + freight + insurance premiums. It is possible for the taxpayer to adjust for differences in settlement terms by calculating the interest component for Company T to match the terms for foreign-related party S. The taxpayer can apply this formula:

$$\text{Company T transaction price}/\{1+0.05\times(90\text{days}/365\text{days})\}\times\{1+0.05\times 30\text{days}/365\text{days})\}$$

In this case, the taxpayer can adjust for the consideration for the sale of Product A by Japanese Corporation P to Company T after adjusting for this difference to provide the arm's length price.

Explanation

Differences can arise in this case, as well as others, as to the price or profit margin in applying transfer pricing methods. Differences can pertain to transactions between a foreign-related transaction, on one hand, and uncontrolled transactions the taxpayer selects as comparable transactions, on the other hand. These transfer pricing methods pertain to the traditional transaction methods and the transactional net margin method, including methods "equivalent to" the traditional transaction methods and methods that are equivalent to the transactional net margin method.

The taxpayer might still be able to use these transactions as comparable transactions in calculating the arm's length price providing that the taxpayer can make adjustments for these differences. For reference to this procedure, see ASTM Article 66-4(2); ASMT Cabinet Order 39-12, paragraph 6 to 8; and ASMT Directive 66-4(2)-1.

The taxpayer adjusts these differences in order to ensure that the uncontrolled transactions the taxpayer chooses as potential comparable transactions can serve as reasonable comparable transactions. The differences that the taxpayer is to adjust for are to be those differences that "objectively clearly effect" the amount of the consideration, as specified in Administrative Guideline 3-1, second paragraph. These differences do not include everything that potentially could give rise to "differences in the amount of consideration." In this regard, see the Takamatsu High Court, October 13, 2006, and finally adjudicated by the Japanese Supreme Court on April 10, 2007, as to the dismissal of the final appeal.

The comparability of the transactions themselves becomes problematical if the taxpayer cannot disregard the differences between a foreign-related transaction and comparable transactions based on profit or on profit margin.

NOTES

1. ASMT Article 66-4(2), Item 1, ASMT Directive 66-4(2)-1, ASMT Directive 66-4(2)-3.
2. ASMT Article 66-4(2), Item 1(a).

17

CHAPTER SEVENTEEN

Applying Japanese Intangible Transfer Pricing Methods

THE JAPANESE tax authorities reissued the Reference Case Studies in the Application of Transfer Pricing Taxation (hereafter Reference Case Studies) following the 2007 Japanese Supreme Court decisions. These Reference Case Studies specifically examine 26 "cases," or examples. Six of these 26 cases specifically address intangible transfer pricing issues, which is our present focus. The Japanese tax authorities examine an array of intangible issues across the wide spectrum of intangible properties:

- Research and development (R&D) and marketing activities as being intangible property, Case 10
- Distribution channels and quality control know-how as being intangible property, Case 11
- Human resource business activities as being intangible property, Case 12
- Contributions to create, maintain, and develop intangible properties, Case 13
- Delineating creation-only intangibles, Case 14
- Determining when loans of employees create intangible property, Case 15

A taxpayer might be engaged in a situation in which its intangible activities go beyond the specific transfer pricing intangible examples. Such a taxpayer should seek to ascertain the commonalities that would apply to all of the Japanese intangible transfer pricing based on these six cases.

CASE 10: INTANGIBLES CREATED BY R&D AND MARKETING ACTIVITIES

A taxpayer can create intangible properties through its R&D and marketing activities. The schematic of business relations indicates these relationships:

- Japanese Corporation P purchases raw materials and purchases other items.
- Japanese Corporation P manufactures Product A in Japan and sells Product A.
- Japanese Corporation P had established foreign-related person S in Country X ten years ago as a subsidiary to manufacture and distribute Product A.
- Japanese Corporation P makes Product A by using technologies it develops from its R&D technologies.
- Part "a" is an unspecified core part that aggregates Japanese Corporation P's original technologies.
- Japanese Corporation P sells part "a" to foreign-related person S in Country X.
- Japanese Corporation P sells part "a" for product A to foreign-related person S in Country X and licenses to foreign-related person S in Country X its patents and know-how for manufacturing Product A.
- Japanese Corporation P created the above-mentioned technologies as result of its R&D activities.
- Japanese Corporation P licenses patents and manufacturing know-how to foreign-related person S in Country X.
- Foreign-related person S manufactures Product A in Country X and sells Product A to approximately 200 third-party retailers.
- The licensing contract between Japanese Corporation P and foreign-related person S provides that Japanese Corporation P will provide technical assistance to foreign-related person S.
- Foreign-related person S combines part "a" with other parts to manufacture Product A.

Functions and Activities of the Corporation and the Foreign-Related Person

Japanese Corporation P has created an efficient manufacturing process. Japanese Corporation P founded that manufacturing process based on the manufacturing know-how that it built up through its R&D activities. Foreign-related person S benefits from Japanese Corporation P's technical assistance. That technical assistance covers the entire spectrum of the manufacturing processes, including foreign-related party person S's same efficient manufacturing method. Foreign-related person S achieves a low manufacturing cost similar to that of Japanese Corporation P.

Japanese Corporation P plans large-scale global advertising and undertakes this advertising to promote the company's image. Persons in many countries recognize Japanese Corporation P's name and logo. Japanese Corporation P plans large-scale global advertising to advertise Product A in the media, including television, magazines, and the Internet. Product A makes use of Product A's strong recognition.

Foreign-related person S has no R&D operations. Foreign-related person S's manufacture of Product A is based on Japanese Corporation P's technologies that Japanese Corporation P originates and furnishes. Foreign-related person S, however:

- Has numerous sales representatives
- Engages in a variety of sales promotion activities targeted at retailers and at end customers
- Has a considerable number of client retailers
- Has formed a well-developed retail network

Product A has acquired a certain market share in Country X thanks to its:

- Unique technical performance
- Strong product recognition
- Well-developed retail network, built up through its advertising and sales promotion

Product A sells at a largely stable price.

Treatment of the Intangibles for Transfer Pricing Taxation Purposes

The taxpayer found that Japanese Corporation P or foreign-related person S was involved in these three foreign-related transactions:

1. Japanese Corporation P developed original technologies and manufacturing know-how.
2. Foreign-related person S developed strong product recognition, whether by brand or by trademark.
3. Foreign-related person S developed a strong retail network.

Japanese Corporation P created these intangible properties through the following activities:

- Japanese Corporation P's R&D activities
- Japanese Corporation P's planned large-scale activities
- Foreign-related person S's sales promotion activities

Product A has secured a certain market share because of:

- Its unique technical performance
- Strong product recognition
- A well-developed retail store network
- A stable price

From a cost standpoint, foreign-related person S achieved a low cost of manufacture based on Japanese Corporation P's manufacturing know-how.

Japanese Corporation P and foreign-related person S, taken together, do more than basic activities. Taken together, Japanese Corporation P and foreign-related person S are engaged in these additional activities:

- Original R&D
- Advertising
- Sales promotion activities

These intangible properties serve as Japanese Corporation P and foreign-related person S's source of income. This above-mentioned material takes place within section 2 of the Reference Case Studies on the Application of Transfer Pricing Taxation. Cases 10 through 15 within section 2 illustrate the treatment of intangible properties. These cases do not describe the preconditions necessary to selecting a specific method of calculating the arm's length price.

Explaining the Treatment of Intangible Properties

A taxpayer, when considering the level of profit attributable to the corporation or to the foreign-related person, needs to ascertain the nature of the profit from which the profit arises. In particular, the taxpayer must consider the nature of the intangible properties of the corporation of the foreign-related person.

The Japanese transfer pricing provisions define intangible properties for transfer pricing purposes as "copyrights, industrial properties prescribed by Basic Directive 20-1-21, and other things having material value, such as customer lists and networks," pursuant to ASMT Directive 66-4(2)-3. Nevertheless, the taxpayer must consider "proper consideration" as to the content of the foreign-related transactions, the activities and functions of the corporations and foreign-related persons, market conditions, and so forth when the taxpayer judges whether that something has "material value" as intangible property.

When the Japanese tax authorities conduct tax examinations, they need to examine a wide range of factors in the intangible context:

- The Japanese tax authorities will need to examine the sources of income that have material value.
- The Japanese tax authorities will need to comprehensively consider whether these intangible properties are in fact involved in foreign-related transactions.

- Pursuant to Administrative Guideline 2-11, clause 1, the Japanese tax authorities need to determine whether the intangibles create sources of income.

  The Japanese tax authorities are to consider three sources of income:

1. The Japanese tax authorities may categorize the following as intangible properties as being related to technical innovation: patents, trade secrets, and so forth, created as a result of technical innovation.
2. The Japanese tax authorities may categorize the following as intangible properties relating to human resources: know-how created through the experience of employees and other human resources in management, front-end operations, production, R&D, sales promotion, and other business activities.
3. The Japanese tax authorities may categorize the following as intangible properties relating to human resources: production processes, negotiation procedures, and trading networks related to development, sales, financing, and similar activities.

The first clause of Administrative Guideline 2-11 does not provide new definitions of intangible property. Instead, owing to the complexity and the diversity of transactions involving intangible properties, the first clause of Administrative Guideline 2-11 categorizes intangible properties according to their form. The purpose of this analysis is to examine, from various perspectives, the relationship between intangible properties and the profit that a corporation derives.

The taxpayer is to consider whether the intangible properties of the domestic corporation or of the foreign-related person serve as a source of income. It might be possible for the taxpayer to identify for comparative purposes a corporation without having intangible properties serving as a source of income for other corporations of a similar size doing business in the same category of business as the foreign-related transaction and being active in a similar market. In undertaking this process, it is necessary for the taxpayer to:

- Compare the level of factors, such as the profit margin of the foreign-related transactions of the corporation or of the foreign-related person, but without having such intangible properties.
- Fully analyze the activities and functions involved in the creation of intangible properties of the corporation or the foreign-related person. Such activities and functions relate to R&D and advertising in the present case, pursuant to Administrative Guideline 2-11, clause 2.

Administrative Guideline 3-5 identifies procedures for selecting a corporation for the purposes of undertaking the selection process. The basic criteria are to select corporations that do not have intangible properties that provide the source of income, do business in the same business category, are active in the similar market, and are of the similar size as a foreign-related transaction. The transfer pricing provisions do not require the taxpayer to seek rigorous comparability in selecting such corporations because the information that is obtainable is just one factor for determining whether these intangible properties serve as a source of income.

The taxpayer can apply the residual profit split method if it finds that the intangible properties of the corporation or of the foreign-related person serve as a source of income compared with a corporation that is engaging solely in basic activities. It might not be possible to apply the traditional transaction methods in that instance, including transfer pricing methods that are "equivalent to" the traditional transaction methods.

There are two stages in applying the residual profit split analysis:

1. Determine the portion of the income that is attributable to the basic activities:
   - Determine the amount corresponding to the profit normally arising from an uncontrolled transaction without having the benefit of material intangible properties.
   - Apportion that income to the corporation and to the foreign-related person, respectively.
2. Apportion the residual amount according to the value of the material intangible properties of the corporation or of the foreign-related person pursuant to ASMT Directive 66-4(4)-5.

Almost all enterprises engage in some kind of action or effort to, for instance, reduce costs and engage in advertising activities. It might not be possible for the taxpayer to immediately judge that material intangible properties must serve as a source of income simply on the basis of such action or effort, making that comparison with corporations that engage solely in these basic activities.

The Japanese transfer pricing provisions make reference to the Organisation for Economic Co-operation and Development (OECD) transfer pricing provisions as well as those of the United States. The reader is cautioned that the OECD and U.S. references are no longer current. The OECD Transfer Pricing Guidelines are from 1996, and the U.S. transfer pricing guidelines are reflected in section 1.482-4(b).

Comparisons of the Definitions of Intangible Properties

The Japanese, United States, and OECD provisions provide these intangible property categories:

- ASMT Directive 66-4(2)-3(8)
  - Copyrights
  - Patents, utility models, designs, trademarks
  - Patent, utility model, design, and trademark licenses, and so on
  - Creations that are repeatedly usable in production or other operations (production-related systems employing original ideas or methods, secrets, and other knowledge and designs, etc.) having special value, including know-how, production systems embodied in the plans or drawings of the machinery and facilities, and designs
  - Customer lists, distribution channels
  - Other things having material value

- OECD Transfer Pricing Guidelines
  - Paragraph 6.2—patents, trademarks, trade names, designs, and models.
  - Literary and artistic property rights, know-how, trade secrets.
  - Paragraph 6.3—computer software.
  - Paragraph 6.4—marketing intangibles (trademarks, trade names, customer lists, distribution channels, and unique names, symbols, or pictures that have an important promotional value.
  - Paragraph 6.5—know-how and trade secrets are proprietary information or knowledge that assists or improves a commercial activity.
  - Know-how represents what a manufacturer cannot know from a mere examination of the product and mere knowledge of the progress of the technique.
  - Know-how may include secret processes or formulas or other secret information concerning industrial, commercial, or scientific experience that is not covered by patent.
- U.S. Treasury Regulations 1.482–4(b)
  - An "intangible" is an asset that comprises any of the following items, and has substantial value independent of the services of any individual:
    - Patents, inventions, formulas, processes, designs, patterns, or know-how
    - Copyrights and literary, musical, or artistic compositions
    - Trademarks, trade names, or brand names
    - Franchises, licenses, or contracts
    - Methods, programs, systems, procedures, campaigns, surveys, studies, forecasts, estimates, customer lists, or technical data
    - Other similar items (an item is considered to be similar to those items just listed if the item derives its value not from its physical attributes but from its intellectual content or from other intangible properties)

CASE 11: DISTRIBUTION CHANNELS AND QUALITY CONTROL KNOW-HOW

Case 11 contains a fact pattern that involves distribution channels and know-how during a 20-year interval:

- Japanese Corporation P manufactures Product A in Japan.
- Japanese Corporation P sells Product A to third parties in Japan.
- Japanese Corporation P sells Product A to third parties in other countries.
- Twenty years ago Japanese Corporation P established foreign-related party S in Country X as a subsidiary to manufacture Product A.
- Foreign-related party S procures raw materials and other items.
- Japanese Corporation P sells part "a" to foreign-related party S.
- Foreign-related party S sells product A to Japanese Corporation P.
- Japanese Corporation P sells product A in Japan and throughout the world.
- The production of Product A consists of typical process inventory operations.

- Japanese Corporation P and foreign-related party S incur fixed costs for a large proportion of the manufacture, enabling Japanese Corporation P and foreign-related party S to benefit from economies of scale.
- Japanese Corporation P undertook detailed market research to identify the most promising markets.
- In implementing the preceding study, Japanese Corporation P established sales branches in countries around the world.
- Japanese Corporation P does business through agents in countries where it does not have its own marketing operations.
- A corporation engaging solely in basic activities would have limited global distribution channels.
- Japanese Corporation P's business group has a large global market share compared with a corporation engaging in basic activities. The group has more broadly developed its global distribution channels.
- Japanese Corporation P's business group's marketing and sales promotion division leads the development of business strategies that are suited to market needs in each country.

Functions and Activities of Foreign-Related Party S

Foreign-related party S has two divisions, a separate quality control division and a separate manufacturing division. More than 10% of the entire workforce is engaged in quality control activities (i.e., checking products and inspecting product lines in order to maintain the quality of Product A). Foreign-related party S's quality control division has accumulated know-how on dealing with and solving the quality control problems that have arisen in the course of its manufacturing experience. The quality control division has independently developed inspection techniques and testing equipment. The quality control division checks quality and production lines at each of the key stages of production. Based on that know-how, the quality control division rectifies any problems that occur during manufacturing.

Foreign-related party S's unique quality control setup dramatically increases its inspection efficiency. This unique quality control setup reduces the cost of manufacture by reducing foreign-related party S's spoilage. This unique quality control setup reduces product complaints from end users concerning Product A. Product A has acquired a reputation for reliability, and foreign-related party S has achieved a superior sales position.

Treatment for Transfer Pricing Taxation Purposes

At the outset, the taxpayer sought to differentiate its distribution functions from those of a corporation having basic activities standing alone. As to the foreign-related transactions in this case:

- Japanese Corporation P attained high sales through its global distribution channels (i.e., Japanese Corporation P obtained higher profits as a percentage of sales increases because of the high fixed costs in the cost of manufacture).

- Japanese Corporation P achieved a superior sales position because it reduced its spoilage loss in the cost of manufacture and achieved a lower incidence of faults due to foreign-related party S's original quality control know-how.
- This superior sales position served as a source of income for Japanese Corporation P and foreign-related party S's foreign-related transactions when compared with a corporation engaging solely in business activities.

Explanation

The reader should review the explanation to Case 10 concerning the treatment of transfer pricing taxation of intangible properties. The reader should recognize that, as a general matter, corporations ordinarily have some kind of distribution channels, even when these corporations engage solely in basic activities.

The reader should further recognize that the corporation typically engages in distribution channels and quality control, and the corporation cannot deem these activities to be a source of income as to foreign-related transaction compared with a corporation engaging solely in basic activities. However, the reader should recognize that while the corporation typically engages in distribution channels and quality control, the corporation can deem these activities to be a source of income in a foreign-related transaction if the distribution channels are broader and unique, or when quality control know-how is more unique than corporations engaging solely in business activities.

CASE 12: KNOW-HOW ACCUMULATION THROUGH HUMAN RESOURCE BUSINESS ACTIVITIES

Enterprises might accumulate know-how through the business activities of its employees and other human resources. Case 12 examines this accumulation of know-how as intangible properties:

- Japanese Corporation P manufactures production facilities in Japan.
- Japanese Corporation P sells these production facilities.
- Since the owners of Japanese Corporation P established that company, Japanese Corporation P has been engaged in the planning, design, procurement, construction, and maintenance of various types of production equipment in Japan and around the world.
- Japanese Corporation P established foreign-related person S 10 years ago as a subsidiary for the purpose of entering into contracts and to implement construction facilities in Country X.
- Japanese Corporation P provides services to foreign-related person S such as management guidance.
- Foreign-related person S, with the support of Japanese Corporation P, won an order for a large-scale production facility.
- Foreign-related person S's business has steadily grown.

- Foreign-related person S now operates this large-scale production facility, which foreign-related person S completed five years before under contract.
- Japanese Corporation P provides services to foreign-related person S in Country X.
- Foreign-related person S manufactures production facilities in Country X.
- Foreign-related person S sells these production facilities, presumably only in Country X.
- Foreign-related person S provides construction and provides operating control of the production facilities to a third party, presumably only in Country X.

Functions and Activities of the Corporation and of the Foreign-Related Person

The functions and activities regarding the information gathering and the receipt of orders are:

- Japanese Corporation P has information-gathering operations, including from its branches and offices all over the world, allowing it to gather and accumulate information for planning the construction of production facilities around the world.
- Japanese Corporation P's information-gathering operations enable it to learn of plans for the construction of a large-scale production facility in Country X ahead of other competitors.
- Japanese Corporation P's overseas sales representatives have developed good relations with clients, providing know-how as to sales negotiations and the analysis of project profitability through the company's production and sale of production facilities to date.
- Foreign-related person S makes maximum use of Japanese Corporation P's advantages and know-how.
- Foreign-related person S, working in collaboration with the staff involved in the design, equipment procurement, and construction at Japanese Corporation P, ultimately won an order after intensive negations with a client in Country X.

The functions and activities relating to construction and to operation control over the facilities are:

- Japanese Corporation P makes use of the original know-how and trading networks it developed to date by its staff in various departments in regard to the production and sale of production facilities as to:
  - Making decisions as to the design of production facilities
  - Selection and procurement of equipment
  - Formulation of construction plans
  - Selection of construction contractors
  - Construction management
  - Other activities

- Japanese Corporation P has assisted foreign-related person S with the operation, control, and maintenance of the large-scale facilities, doing so since foreign-related person S completed the facilities.
- Japanese Corporation P provided this assistance to foreign-related person S through Japanese Corporation P's experience to date in providing after-sales service.

Details of the business decisions that Japanese Corporation P made as to foreign-related person S are:

- Foreign-related person S communicates with the staff members at Japanese Corporation P who are involved in overseas business, design, equipment procurement, construction, and operation control.
- Foreign-related person S takes orders from clients after obtaining advice from Japanese Corporation P.
- Foreign-related person S receives necessary instructions from Japanese Corporation P.
- Foreign-related person S responds to inquiries.
- Foreign-related person S obtains materials from Japanese Corporation P regarding construction work.

Treatment of the Activities for Transfer Pricing Taxation Purposes

Japanese Corporation P provides foreign-related person S with services that relate to information gathering and enable negotiations to take place as to foreign-related person S's construction of major production facilities in Country X. Japanese Corporation P provides foreign-related person S with services as to business decisions and risk management concerning the design, construction, and operation control over such facilities. The taxpayer determined that these above-mentioned services affect foreign-related person S's business profitability and that foreign-related person S depends on these independent business services.

Foreign-related person S engaged in business that was related to large-scale production facilities in Country X. In engaging in that business endeavor, foreign-related person S has the business judgment and risk management know-how regarding the production facility business as to:

- Contact employees in the course of Japanese Corporation P's production and sales facilities around the world
- Interface with Japanese Corporation P's informational network
- Participate in negotiating procedures and trading network as to the receipt of orders, placement of orders for equipment, construction, control, and so forth

Foreign-related person S furnishes these strengths as being an integrated whole, in conjunction with the above services, to enable foreign-related person S to pursue the above projects. In light of the preceding results, the taxpayer found that the next activities serve as a source of income in foreign-related person S's foreign-related transactions:

- The know-how that Japanese Corporation P's employees developed from past business experience
- Japanese Corporation P's information network
- Negotiation procedures
- Trading network
- Other activities

Explanation

Case 12 examines the interrelationship between services transactions and intangible transactions. For services transactions, the taxpayer must consider the impact of intangible properties if the taxpayer makes use of intangible properties in the treatment of services. In this regard, see Administrative Guideline 2-8(1).

The taxpayer should note the presence or absence of certain conditions if the taxpayer investigates whether intangible properties would apply to services when the taxpayer provides know-how, and so forth, to an enterprise that accumulates its employees' accumulated business activities or makes use of the trading network or negotiation procedures. The two items are conceptually distinct:

- The providing of services
- The use of intangible properties

The taxpayer should consider whether a use is also reflected as intangible property listed in ASMT 66-4(2)-3-(8) or whether the service is provided by the service provider when the taxpayer provides such services. The taxpayer is to consider the impact of providing these activities and functions of the corporation when the taxpayer receives services in accordance with Administrative Guideline 2-8(1) note. A taxpayer should consider undertaking a wide range of options when investigating transactions as to the intangible properties' contribution to income pursuant to Administrative Guideline 2-11.

Administrative Guideline 2-11 addresses the tax examination procedure the taxpayer should undertake in determining the intangible contributions to the corporation or to the foreign-related person. The taxpayer is to consider the properties that have material value as a source of income and should comprehensively consider:

- Patents and trade secrets the taxpayer derives from technical innovation
- Know-how that the taxpayer derives from the experience of employees and by other human resources through business activities such as management, front office operations, production, R&D, and sales promotion
- Production processes, negotiation procedures, development networks, distribution networks, and financing networks

Note that Administrative Guideline 2-11 applies regarding intercompany services, and in applying intangible properties in cases where the taxpayer applies such services.

The Japanese tax authorities view know-how as being a material valuable intangible property if they find that the know-how accumulated by a corporation through its employees' business activities:

- Are furnished organizationally by a corporation to a foreign-related person
- Functions as a material element in the foreign-related person's business activities
- Serves as a source of income in the foreign-related transaction compared with the cases of a corporation that engages solely in business activities

CASE 13: CONTRIBUTIONS TO CREATE, MAINTAIN, AND DEVELOP INTANGIBLE PROPERTIES

The schematic of business relations indicates:

- Japanese Corporation P is a manufacturer and distributor of Product A.
- Ten years ago, Japanese Corporation P established foreign-related party S in Country X as a subsidiary to manufacture and distribute Product A.
- Japanese Corporation P purchases raw materials and other items.
- Japanese Corporation P has a patent.
- Japanese Corporation P manufactures and sells Product A.
- Foreign-related party S buys part "a" from Japanese Corporation P.
- Foreign-related party S has a patent.
- Foreign-related party S manufactures Product A in Country X.
- Foreign-related party S sells Product A to several third-party agents.
- Japanese Corporation P and foreign-related party S make Product A using Japanese Corporation P's original technologies and R&D activities.
- Part "a" is a core part that aggregates Japanese Corporation P's original technologies.
- Japanese Corporation P sells part "a" to foreign-related party S.
- Foreign-related party S combines part "a" with other parts to produce Product A.

Functions and Activities of the Corporation and the Foreign-Related Person

Japanese Corporation P's R&D division initiated the development of product A. Nevertheless, foreign-related party S also has a product development division, having approximately 10 researchers. The product development division undertook part of the development work. Both Japanese Corporation P and foreign-related party S have continued to pursue R&D since Japanese Corporation P launched Product A, undertaking these efforts so as to improve product performance.

Japanese Corporation P and foreign-related party S formulate R&D strategy, allocate specific fields of responsibility, manage the R&D progress, and make decisions as to the continuation or discontinuation of activities. Japanese Corporation P assesses the researchers' performance under the supervision of its R&D managers. Japanese Corporation P's R&D staff supervises foreign-related party S's product development operations.

Foreign-related party S notes that Product A has shown a sales increase due to its unique technical performance. Foreign-related party S has achieved a certain market share for Product A in Country X. The price for Product A in Country X is stable.

Japanese Corporation P and foreign-related party S aggregate Product A's original technologies resulting from their R&D. Japanese Corporation P patents its aggregate original technologies in Japan. Foreign-related party S patents its aggregate original technologies in Country X.

Treatment of the Patent Activities for Transfer Pricing Taxation Purposes

In this case, the patents result from R&D that both Japanese Corporation P and foreign-related party S undertake. In some situations, the corporation might be engaging solely in basic activities, but such is not the case here. Product A's resulting technical performance emanates from the source of income for both Japanese Corporation P and foreign-related party S.

In this case both Japanese Corporation P and foreign-related party S registered the patents for Product A in their own respective names. Nevertheless, differences exist as to the efforts that Japanese Corporation P and foreign-related party S expended in conjunction with these patents as to the activities involved in their creation, maintenance, and development. Japanese Corporation P undertook the greater part of the R&D activity, decision making as to development, and risk management. Foreign-related party S performed only some of the R&D work. Accordingly, pursuant to Administrative Guideline 2-12, it is appropriate to account for the extent of the contributions to income, focusing these activities and functions to create, maintain, and develop patents for Product A that Japanese Corporation P and foreign-related party S undertake.

Explanation

The reader should review the explanation to Case 10 as to the treatment of intangible properties. The legal ownership of the intangible properties and the parties contributing to their creation, maintenance, and development are not necessarily the same. As a result, there is need to consider not only the ownership of the intangible properties but also the extent of the contributions to their creation, maintenance, and development when considering the extent of the contributions to the income from these intangible properties.

Pursuant to Administrative Guideline 2-12, it also becomes necessary for the taxpayer to account for the functions and so forth that the corporation or foreign-related person undertakes in decision making and in R&D risk management, as well as for the actual providing of services and the burden of costs. In this context, "decision making" refers to judgmental and decision-making elements, including the formulation and direction of concrete development strategy and preparatory work, such as information gathering. "Risk management consists of the comprehensive identification of risks inherent in activities, such as the creation of intangible properties, and the management of these risks in an integrated fashion through overall and continued control of progress."

CASE 14: A COMPANY BEARING ONLY THE COST OF CREATION OF THE INTANGIBLE PROPERTIES

This case illustrates the relationship between the cost burden, on one hand, and the contribution to create, maintain, and develop intangible properties, on the other hand, in the case that the foreign-related person bears a portion of the R&D cost that the corporation incurred.

The schematic of the business relations is:

- Japanese Corporation P purchases raw materials and other items.
- Japanese Corporation P manufactures part "a."
- Japanese Corporation P sells part "a" to foreign-related person S in Country X.
- Japanese Corporation P owns patents.
- Japanese Corporation P licenses patents and manufacturing know-how to foreign-related party S in Country X.
- Foreign-related person S pays Japanese Corporation P toward its R&D costs.
- Japanese Corporation P manufactures and sells Product A in Japan.
- Foreign-related party S manufactures and sells Product A in Country X to several third-party agents.
- Japanese Corporation P 10 years previously established foreign-related person S in Country X as a subsidiary to manufacture and distribute product A.
- Japanese Corporation P and foreign-related person S produce Product A using Japanese Corporation P's original technologies resulting from its R&D technologies.
- Part "a" is a core part that aggregates Japanese Corporation P's original technologies.
- Japanese Corporation P sells part "a" to foreign-related person S for the purposes of manufacturing Product A.
- Japanese Corporation P licenses patents and manufacturing know-how, the original technologies that result from Japanese Corporation P's R&D, to foreign-related person S for the production of Product A.
- Foreign-related person S combines part "a" with other parts to manufacture Product A.

Functions and Activities of the Corporation and the Foreign-Related Person

Product A is an outcome of Japanese Corporation P's activities. Japanese Corporation P, together with foreign-related person S, has seen sales increases for Product A because of its unique technical performance. Foreign-related person S has secured a certain market share for Product A in Country X, where Product A sells for a largely stable price.

Foreign-related person S produces Product A based on Japanese Corporation P's original technologies. Foreign-related person S has no R&D technologies, and does not engage in R&D activities. Foreign-related person S does bear part of Japanese Corporation P's R&D activities to improve Product A quality and improve the product line. Japanese Corporation P undertakes its complete decisions on R&D strategy and risk management without foreign-related person S's involvement. Japanese Corporation P registers all the patents from its R&D, and foreign-related person S has no patents.

Treatment of the Structure for Transfer Pricing Purposes

Japanese Corporation P and foreign-related person S manufacture Product A by using Japanese Corporation P's original R&D technologies. In contrast to cases in which a corporation is engaging solely in basic activities, Japanese Corporation P and foreign-related person S's original technical performance was found to serve as a source of income in the case of Japanese Corporation P and foreign-related person S.

Here foreign-related person S bears part of the R&D cost:

- to improve the quality of Product A, which foreign-related person S produced using previously created original technologies, and
- to improve the product line.

Nevertheless, foreign-related person S had no divisions involved in R&D and plays no role in the R&D. Thus, Japanese Corporation P's R&D activities contribute to the creation, maintenance, and development of intangible properties. Foreign-related person S's contribution to the creation, maintenance, and development of intangible properties is low.

Explanation

The reader should examine the transfer pricing treatment of intangible properties in the Explanation to Case 10. Administrative Guidelines specify that it is necessary for the taxpayer to take into account the role played and the function performed in decision making, the providing of services, the funding of costs, and risk control toward the creation, maintenance, and development of the intangible properties. The taxpayer should make this analysis when considering the extent of the contribution to the creation, maintenance, and development of intangible properties.

In the case at hand, the party's involvement in R&D activity does not coincide with the parties bearing the cost of the R&D. It is not possible for the taxpayer to simply treat the cost borne by foreign-related person S as its contribution to the erection, maintenance, and development of intangible properties. If the taxpayer were only to consider the bearing of the cost of creation, maintenance, and development of intangible properties when determining the source of income, that level of contribution is low. Foreign-related person S contributed only part of the original R&D cost, nothing further.

In this case, it might be appropriate to apply the residual profit split method, assuming the foreign-related person had separate material intangible properties. Even in such a case the simple bearing of costs without performing an R&D function would not constitute a factor for splitting residual profit. The taxpayer would have to take into consideration the calculation of basic profit in the same matter as other general expenses.

See Case 22 (in Chapter 18) for the factors for splitting residual profit.

CASE 15: INTANGIBLE PROPERTIES FOR EMPLOYEES ON LOAN

This case illustrates the corporation's contribution where that corporation lends employees to a foreign-related person at the time the employees transfer intangibles to the foreign-related person.

The schematic of the business relations is:

- Japanese Corporation P purchases raw materials.
- Japanese Corporation P manufactures Product A in Japan.
- Japanese Corporation P sells Product A to third-party retailers in the Japanese market.
- Japanese Corporation P had established foreign-related S in Country X 10 years ago as a subsidiary to distribute Product A.
- Japanese Corporation P lends employees to foreign-related person S in Country X.
- Japanese Corporation P uses its original technologies and R&D activities to create Product A.
- Foreign-related person S purchases raw materials and so forth.
- Foreign-related person S manufactures Product A in Country X.
- Foreign-related person S sells Product A to approximately 200 third-party retailers in Country X.

Functions and Activities of the Corporation and the Foreign-Related Person

In the past, Japanese Corporation P used to sell Product A to foreign-related person S. Currently, foreign-related person S manufactures Product A by sourcing all of its raw materials and other supplies locally within Country X. Japanese Corporation P lends 10 employees to foreign-related person S. Five of these employees are responsible for production engineering. Five of these employees are responsible for marketing and sales promotion. Details of these employee transfers follow.

- The production engineering loan employees are engaged in the development of production technologies in Japanese Corporation P's technology division. The production engineering loan employees have advanced knowledge and technology development experience. Japanese Corporation P lends these employees to foreign-related person S to provide foreign-related person S with access to Japanese Corporation P's know-how. Foreign-related person S has achieved a low cost of manufacture through efficient manufacture through foreign-related person S's improvements in its production engineering division The cause for improvement is the guidance that the Japanese Corporation P provided and the use of Japanese Corporation P's manufacturing know-how.
- Foreign-related person S's production division employs local employees as well as making use of Japanese Corporation P's five loan employees. The local employees

perform auxiliary work and do not have a particularly high level of technical knowledge.

- Japanese Corporation P's employees lent to foreign-related person S's production division communicate frequently with Japanese Corporation P by e-mail and by fax in the course of their work. These employees requested materials from fellow researchers in Japanese Corporation P's technology development division to obtain advice.
- The employees who are on loan to the marketing and sales area have no advanced marketing knowledge or sales knowledge. These employees perform routine work under the direction of local employees in foreign-related person S's marketing and sales promotion division.

Treatment of the Loan Arrangement for Transfer Pricing Taxation Purposes

Foreign-related person S is able to achieve more efficient manufacturing and is able to achieve a lower manufacturing cost as a result of the guidance that foreign-related person S received from the production engineers on loan from Japanese Corporation P.

As a result, the taxpayer found that Japanese Corporation P's manufacturing know-how serves as a source of income in foreign-related person S's foreign-related transactions compared with a taxpayer that engages solely in basic activities. In this particular case, this manufacturing know-how resulted from Japanese Corporation P's past activities in developing production technologies. Japanese Corporation P furnished this know-how to foreign-related person S through its loan of its employees.

In contrast, the loan employees that Japanese Corporation P furnished to foreign-related person S for marketing and sales promotion have yet to acquire advanced ability and knowledge of sales and marketing through their work at Japanese Corporation P. As a result, the transfer of marketing and sales promotion employees did not cause Japanese Corporation P to transfer marketing and sales promotion intangibles to foreign-related person S.

Explanation

The taxpayer should review Case 10 as to the transfer pricing treatment of intangible properties. The parent company is to receive a transfer pricing benefit from the creation, maintenance, and development of these intangible properties if:

- The parent company lends its employees to a foreign subsidiary
- The parent company's employees created, maintained, and developed these intangible properties for the benefit of the subsidiary
- These intangible properties serve as a source of income in comparison with a corporation engaging solely in basic activities

CHAPTER EIGHTEEN

18

Japanese Profit Split Transfer Pricing Methods

THE JAPANESE taxing provisions provide a strong preference to the traditional transfer pricing transaction methods. Nevertheless, despite that strong preference, the Japanese transfer pricing provisions in fact favor the profit split method when the enterprise is unable to apply the traditional transfer pricing transaction methods. We consider seven profit split transfer pricing examples, a significant percentage of the 26 examples overall:

1. Case 16: Applying the Profit Split Method to a Series of Foreign-Related Transactions
2. Case 17: Excluding Transactions from the Profit Split Method
3. Case 18: Calculation of the Profit to Be Split
4. Case 19: Differences in Labor Costs Impact the Residual Profit Split Method
5. Case 20: Treatment of Market Fluctuations
6. Case 21: Calculation of Basic Profit
7. Case 22: Factors for Splitting the Residual Profit

CASE 16: APPLYING THE PROFIT SPLIT METHOD TO A SERIES OF FOREIGN-RELATED TRANSACTIONS

In the case at hand, the business undertakes a series of foreign-related transaction situations. The taxpayer determines that it is appropriate to aggregate multiple foreign-related persons when it applies the profit split method.

Schematic of the Business Relationships

Here is the fact pattern that explains the business relationships:

- Japanese Corporation P purchases raw materials.
- Japanese Corporation P manufactures Product A and Product B.
- Japanese Corporation P sells Product A.
- Japanese Corporation P sells Product B.
- Japanese Corporation P sells part "a" (a core part) and licenses patents and manufacturing know-how to three related parties: foreign-related person SX, foreign-related person SY, and foreign-related person SZ.
- Foreign-related person SX manufactures Product A.
- Foreign-related person SX sells Product A to third-party retailers in Country X.
- Foreign-related person SY sells semifinished Product "b" to foreign-related person SX.
- Foreign-related person SZ manufactures Product B.
- Foreign-related person SZ sells Product B to third-party retailers in Country Z.

Activities of the Business of the Corporation and of the Foreign-Related Persons

Japanese Corporation P is a manufacturer and a distributor of Product A and of Product B. Japanese Corporation P has a number of subsidiaries:

- Foreign-related person SX manufactures Product A and distributes Product A in Country X.
- The Reference Case Studies reflect a situation in which foreign-related person SY manufactures Product A and distributes Product A in Country Y. The government provides a diagram that does *not* reflect SY's manufacture of Product A, *nor* does it reflect the distribution of Product A in Country Y.
- Foreign-related person SZ manufactures Product B and distributes Product B in Country Z.
- Japanese Corporation P, foreign-related person SX, and foreign-related person SZ produce Product A and produce Product B using Japanese Corporation P's original research and development (R&D) technological activities.

Summary of the Foreign-Related Transactions

Foreign-related person SX in Country X purchases part "a" from Japanese Corporation P. Part "a" is a core part that aggregates Japanese Corporation P's original technologies.

Foreign-related person SX manufactures Product A using licensed patents and manufacturing know-how. Japanese Corporation P created these original technologies as a result of its R&D activities. Foreign-related person SX has insufficient production capacity, and, as a result, purchases semifinished Product "b" from foreign-related party SY to produce Product A. Foreign-related party SX sells Product A to third-party retailers in Country X through its own sales division.

Foreign-related person SY in Country Y purchases part "a" from Japanese Corporation P. Foreign-related person SY, using licensed patents and manufacturing know-how from Japanese Corporation P, manufactures semifinished Product "b." Foreign-related person SY needs semifinished Product "b" to manufacture Product A. Foreign-related person SY sells Product "b" entirely to related party SX.

Foreign-related person SZ in Country Z purchases part "a" from Japanese Corporation P. Foreign-related person SZ, using licensed patents and manufacturing know-how from Japanese Corporation P, manufactures Product B. Foreign-related person SZ sells Product B to third-party retailers in Country Z through its own sales division. Product B differs from Product A in several respects, including shape, use, and sales channel.

Functions and Activities of the Corporation and of the Foreign-Related Persons

The sales of Product A and the sales of Product B are increasing because of their original technical performance. Foreign-related person SX and foreign-related person SZ have acquired a certain market share respectively in Country X and in Country Z for Product A and Product B. Foreign-related person SX and foreign-related person SZ sell Product A and Product B at a largely stable price.

Foreign-related person SX, foreign-related person SY, and foreign-related person SZ have no R&D operations. Japanese Corporation P originates and furnishes Product A, semifinished Product "p," and Product B based on its original technologies.

Foreign-related person SX and foreign-related person SZ each have numerous sales representatives and actively engage in sales activities. Foreign-related person SX and foreign-related person SZ each engage in large-scale advertising and sales promotion activities. Those sales, advertising, and sales promotion activities put them in a superior sales position compared with corporations engaging in basic activities in each of these countries. Note that SY, in selling its entire output of semifinished Product "b" to Company SX, does not engage in any of the above-mentioned sales activities.

Treatment of the Profit Split for Transfer Pricing Taxation Purposes

The taxpayer had considered the applicability of the traditional transaction methods and methods "equivalent to" the traditional transaction methods. The taxpayer was unable to find comparable transactions for the sale of part "a" and for the licensing of patents between Japanese Corporation P and foreign-related corporation SX. See Case 1 as to the applicability of the traditional transaction methods, including method "equivalent to" the traditional transaction methods. The taxpayer considered applying transfer pricing methods that are consistent with the traditional transaction methods, the methods that are equivalent to them, other methods prescribed in the Act on Special Measures Concerning Taxation (ASMT) Cabinet Order, and methods equivalent to them. The analysis of these methods yielded these results:

- The taxpayer was unable to find comparable transactions for applying transfer pricing methods that are consistent with the traditional transaction methods. The taxpayer was unable to find transfer pricing methods that are equivalent to them. See Case 1 as to methods that are "consistent with" the traditional transaction methods, including methods that are "equivalent to" methods consistent with the traditional transaction methods.
- The taxpayer found the application of the residual profit split method to be appropriate as to Japanese Corporation P and foreign-related person SX. The intangible properties served as a source of income compared to cases where a corporation engages solely in basic activities. The same result applies regarding the applicability of the traditional transaction methods and methods equivalent to the traditional transaction methods in the case of transactions between Japanese Corporation P and foreign-related person SY, and between Japanese Corporation P and foreign-related person SZ.
- The taxpayer considered that it was reasonable to consider as a single unit owing to their constituting a series of foreign-related transactions relating to the manufacture of Product A sold to foreign-related party SX:
  - The sale of Product A
  - The licensing of patents and know-how between Japanese Corporation P and foreign-related person SY
  - The sale of semifinished Product B between foreign-related person SY and foreign related person SX
- Given these circumstances, the taxpayer found it appropriate to calculate the arm's length price by applying the residual profit split methods of Japanese Corporation P, foreign-related person SX, and foreign-related person SY from the transactions among these three companies in this case. The taxpayer, when applying the residual profit split method, allocated only the basic profit to foreign-related person SY as foreign-related person SY did not have material intangible properties.
- The sale of part "a" between Japanese Corporation P and foreign-related person SZ and the licensing of patents and know-how are transactions involving Product B. Because Product B is a different product from Product A, it is necessary to consider the transaction separately from transactions between Japanese Corporation P and foreign-related person SX.
- The taxpayer found that Japanese Corporation P's and foreign-related person SZ's intangible properties were a source of income in the foreign-related transactions between Japanese Corporation P and foreign-related person SZ compared with cases of a corporation that engages solely in basic activities. The taxpayer found it appropriate to calculate the arm's length price by applying the residual profit split method to the transactions between the two companies. See Case 1 as to the

applicability of the traditional transaction methods, including methods "equivalent to" the traditional transaction methods.

Explanation

Example 16 seeks to examine whether the taxpayer is to combine a series of transactions (i.e., chain transactions) between multiple foreign-related persons within the scope of the profit split method. The taxpayer is to determine whether, for instance, this series of transactions constitutes a series of transactions involving a single product. The taxpayer might find that a series of foreign-related transactions are not conducted at an arm's length price. That fact will affect the calculation of the profit to be split that arises from the foreign-related transactions. As a rule, it is necessary for the taxpayer to consider the related transactions as a whole even though these transactions are "sandwiched in" between these uncontrolled transactions. Case 17 explores an exception to that rule.

The taxpayer is to consider only the basic profit when the taxpayer includes transactions in a series of foreign-related transactions within the scope of the application of the profit split method where these transactions do not have material intangible properties. The taxpayer might be performing arm's length price calculations, as a rule, for individual arm's length transactions. Nevertheless, the taxpayer might be able to calculate the arm's length price by taking into consideration transactions belonging to the same product group. It might be deemed reasonable to calculate the arm's length price for these same units. Alternatively, it might make sense for the taxpayer to undertake the sale of a part for the production and licensing of related manufacturing know-how as a single package. It could be deemed reasonable to calculate the arm's length price as being a single unit, pursuant to ASMT Directive 66-4(3)-1. This provision states that the taxpayer can treat multiple foreign-related transactions as a single unit where this result is reasonable from the point of view of calculating the arm's length price.

The goal is to consider which transaction units the taxpayer can consider as being reasonably used to calculate the arm's length price according to law. The taxpayer might apply the profit split method due to the absence of comparable transactions in seeking to apply the traditional transaction methods.

CASE 17: EXCLUDING TRANSACTIONS FROM THE PROFIT SPLIT METHOD

Case 17 illustrates how a taxpayer that takes foreign-related transactions into account at an ordinary transaction price precludes the profit split method where there is a series of foreign-related transactions.

The summary of the business relations schematic follows.

- Japanese Corporation P is a manufacturer and distributor of Product A.
- Japanese Corporation P has established two subsidiaries:
  1. Foreign-related person SX in Country X. Japanese Corporation P establishes foreign-related person SX to manufacture Product A in Country X.

2. Foreign-related person SY in Country Y. Japanese Corporation P establishes foreign-related person SY to manufacture Product A in Country Y.

- Japanese Corporation P establishes Product A resulting from its R&D original technologies.

Japanese Corporation P's business relations are:

- Several third parties supply raw materials to Japanese Corporation P.
- Japanese Corporation P manufactures and sells Product A.
- Japanese Corporation P sells part "a" to foreign-related person SX.
- Japanese Corporation P licenses patents and manufacturing know-how to foreign-related person SX.

Foreign-related person SX's business relations are:

- Foreign-related person SX buys part "A" from Japanese Corporation P.
- Foreign-related person SX licenses patents and manufacturing know-how from Japanese Corporation P.
- Foreign-related person SX sells Product A to foreign-related person SY.
- Foreign-related person SX sells Product A to several third-party sole agents.

Foreign-related person SY's business relations are:

- Foreign-related person SY purchases Product A from foreign-related person SX.
- Foreign-related person SY sells Product A to a dozen or so third-party agents.

Several third-party sole agents' business relations are:

- Several third-party sole agents purchase Product A from foreign-related person SX.
- Several third-party sole agents sell Product A to a dozen or so third-party agents.

Sale of part "a" and the licensing of patents and manufacturing know-how involve:

- Part "a" is a core part that aggregates Japanese Corporation P's original technologies and part of Product A.
- Japanese Corporation P sells part "a" to foreign-related person SX.
- Japanese Corporation P licenses patents and manufacturing know-how to foreign-related person SX for the manufacture of Product A.
- Japanese Corporation P licenses patents and manufacturing know-how that emanate from Japanese Corporation P's original R&D technologies.
- Foreign-related person SX combines part "a" with other parts to manufacture Product A.
- Foreign-related person SX exports Product A to Company SY in Country Y and exports Product A to third-party sole agents in several other countries.

- Foreign-related person SX does not sell Product A in Country X.
- Foreign-related person SX exports Product A as foreign-related person SX's sole agent to a dozen of its third-party agents in Country Y.
- The volume of Product A that foreign-related person SX sells does not materially differ from the volume of Product A that foreign-related person SY sells to the sole agents in other countries. The parties set the selling price in the same way, and there is no marked difference in the sales price between Country Y and other countries.

Functions and Activities of the Corporation and the Foreign-Related Persons

Product A is an outcome of Japanese Corporation P's R&D activities. Japanese Corporation A's original technical performance has increased Product A's sales. Product A has secured a certain market share in Country Y and in other countries. Product A sells at a largely stable price in these countries.

Foreign-related person SX has a technological development division of about ten engineers. Foreign-related person SX performs some of the development for Product A and contributes to achieving Product A's original technologies and performance in conjunction with Japanese Corporation P's R&D. Foreign-related person SX has a sales function, which is simply a marketing effort directed to sole agents in each country. Foreign-related person SY has a sales function, which is simply reselling Product A.

Profit and Loss Situation at Foreign-Related Person SY

Economic levels are similar in the region in which foreign-related person SY and several other countries are located. Foreign-related person SY and the sole agents in other countries are almost the same in terms of scale and the category of business, and the profit margins for each are around 3% to 4%. This profit level is approximately the same (4%) as among enterprises in the same industry in these countries.

Treatment for Transfer Pricing Purposes

The taxpayer considered the applicability of the traditional transaction methods and the applicability of methods that are "equivalent to" the traditional transaction methods. The taxpayer was unable to find such comparable transactions. See Case 1 as to the applicability of the traditional transaction methods, including transfer pricing methods that are "equivalent to" these transfer pricing methods. The taxpayer then considered other transfer pricing methods prescribed in the ASMT Cabinet Order and other methods that are equivalent to them. The results were:

- The taxpayer was unable to find any comparable transactions for applying transfer pricing methods that are "consistent with" the traditional transaction methods and transfer pricing methods that are "equivalent to" them. See Case 1 as to transfer pricing methods that are "consistent with" the traditional transaction methods, including transactions that are "equivalent to" methods that are "consistent with" the traditional transaction methods.

- The taxpayer then looked to the level of "basic activities" and sought to compare a corporation engaging solely in such basic activities. The taxpayer determined that Japanese Corporation P and foreign-related corporation SX undertook intangible properties as a source of income in their foreign-related transactions. As to Japanese Corporation P and foreign-related person SX, the taxpayer found it appropriate to calculate the arm's length price by applying the residual profit split method. There are no problems from the standpoint of transfer pricing taxation as to the treatment of related persons of foreign-related person SX and foreign-related person SY:
  1. The parties similarly set transactions between foreign-related person SX with unrelated persons, sole agents, in other countries.
  2. The foreign-related person SY profit level was the same as the industry average, approximately the same as that of unrelated persons in other countries in which foreign-related person SX engages in similar transactions.
- As a result, it was possible for the taxpayer to apply the residual profit split method only to Japanese Corporation P and foreign-related person SX, standing alone. As such, it was possible for the taxpayer to exclude transactions between foreign-related person SX and foreign-related person SY from the scope of the profit split method.

Explanation

When a taxpayer seeks to apply the profit split method, a series of foreign-related transactions between related persons might not occur at the arm's length price. This factor will affect the calculation of the profit to be split arising from the foreign-related transactions. These facts make it necessary for the taxpayer in principle to also consider transactions between the corporation and the foreign-related person and between foreign-related persons being "sandwiched in" between uncontrolled transactions.

The enterprise need not include such "sandwiched in" transactions within the scope of profit splitting, even if the enterprise engages in a series of foreign-related transactions. For instance, there might not be any transfer pricing taxation problems in light of a comparison of average profit levels in the industry. Alternatively, the transactions might be of low value, so that they would have little impact on the calculation of the profit to be split that is arising from the foreign-related transaction. Administrative Guideline 2-1, Administrative Guideline 2-2, and other relevant provisions provide the decision as to what to do in such cases.

CASE 18: CALCULATION OF THE PROFIT TO BE SPLIT

Case 18 illustrates the calculation of profits to be split when the taxpayer applies the profit split method. The summary of the schematic of the business relations follows.

- The ultimate determination of the profit to be split depends on two related entities, Japanese Corporation P and foreign-related person S.

- Japanese Corporation P is a manufacturer and distributor of Product A, which Japanese Corporation P sells in Japan.
- Japanese Corporation P established foreign-related person S ten years ago in Country X as a subsidiary to manufacture and sell Product A in Country X.

Schematic of Business Relations Pertaining to Japanese Corporation P

The Japanese corporation has a variety of business relationships, including manufacture, sale, purchasing, and licensing:

- Japanese Corporation P is engaged in the manufacture of Product A.
- Japanese Corporation P is engaged in the sale of Product A to approximately 300 third-party retailers.
- Japanese Corporation P purchases raw materials.
- Japanese Corporation P licenses patents and manufacturing know-how to foreign-related person S.
- Japanese Corporation P supplies part "a" to foreign-related person S.

Schematic of Business Relations Pertaining to Foreign-Related Persons

A foreign-related person has a number of business relationships, including these:

- Foreign-related person S obtains a license of patents and manufacturing know-how from Japanese Corporation P.
- Foreign-related person S receives a supply of part "a" from Japanese Corporation S.
- Foreign-related person S purchases Product B from a third-party manufacturer.
- Foreign-related person S sells Product B to several third-party users.
- Foreign-related person S manufactures Product A.
- Foreign-related person S sells Product A to approximately 200 third-party retailers.

Functions and Activities of the Corporation and the Foreign-Related Persons

The Japanese corporation and foreign-related persons have a number of functions and activities, including:

- Japanese Corporation P and foreign-related person S manufacture Product A by using Japanese Corporation P's original technologies and R&D activities.
- Part "a" is a core part that aggregates Japanese Corporation P's original technologies.
- Japanese Corporation P sells part "a" for Product A to foreign-related person S.
- Foreign-related person S engages in various sales promotion activities.
- Foreign-related person S's various sales promotion activities employ numerous sales representatives.

- Foreign-related person S advertises on a large scale in Country X.
- Foreign-related person S has secured a certain market share for Product A in Country X thanks to the unique technical performance of the product itself, Product A's strong product recognition, and a well-developed retail store network, built up by advertising and sales promotion.
- Foreign-related person S sells Product A at a largely stable price.

Japanese Corporation P's Divisions and Operating Profits

Internally, Japanese Corporation P is organized in this manner:

- A production division that manufactures part "a" for use in Product A
- An R&D division
- A sales division for marketing Product A domestically
- A general administrative division

Japanese Corporation P's profit and loss data are:

Sales of Product A	200
Sales of part "a"	35
Royalties received	5
Total sales and royalties	240
Cost of goods sold for Product A	95
Cost of goods sold for part "a"	25
Total cost of goods sold	120
Gross profit on sales	120
Product A selling expenses	48
Part "a" selling expenses	2
R&D cost	25
Administrative expenses	15
Total selling and administrative expenses	90
Net operating expenses	30

Foreign-related person S's profit and loss data are:

Sales of Product A	110
Sales of Product B	500
Total sales	610
Purchases of part "a"	35
Other costs of Product A	10
Purchases of Product B	480
Royalties paid	5
Total cost of sales	530
Gross profit on sales	80

Product A selling expenses	15
Product B selling expenses	5
Administrative expenses	10
Total selling and administrative expenses	30
Net operating expenses	50

Treatment for Transfer Pricing Taxation Purposes

The taxpayer considered the applicability of the traditional transfer pricing transaction methods and considered applying methods that are "equivalent to" the traditional transfer pricing transaction methods. The taxpayer was unable to find any comparable transactions for any of the foreign-related transactions as to part "a" and to licensing of patents and know-how. As a result, the taxpayer was unable to apply traditional transfer pricing transaction methods or methods that are "equivalent to" the traditional transfer pricing transaction methods. See Case 1 as to the applicability of the traditional transaction methods and of methods that are "equivalent to" the traditional transfer pricing transaction methods. The taxpayer considered applying transfer pricing methods that are "consistent with" the traditional transaction methods, considered applying methods that are "equivalent to" the traditional transfer pricing transaction methods, and considered applying other methods prescribed in the ASMT Cabinet Order.

The next step in the transfer pricing process is for the taxpayer to compare its activities with a corporation engaging solely in basic activities. Japanese Corporation P and foreign-related person S have intangible properties that serve as a source of income in foreign-related transactions. In the current case, because of Japanese Corporation P's and foreign-related person S's intangible activities, it was appropriate to calculate the arm's length price by applying the residual profit split method.

The taxpayer then determined the amount of operating income by extracting profit and loss on foreign-related transactions from the overall profit and loss attributable to Japanese Corporation P and foreign-related person S. The taxpayer determines the profit to be split for the purposes of the residual profit split method.

Japanese Corporation P's Profit and Loss from the Foreign-Related Transactions

The taxpayer seeks to calculate the profit and loss on foreign-related transactions that emanate from Japanese Corporation P's entire profit and loss. The taxpayer divided Japanese Corporation P's manufacturing division into:

1. Gross profit related to part "a," with part "a" being destined for foreign-related person S:

Sales of part "a"	35
Cost of goods sold for part "a"	25
Net amount	10

2. Gross profit related to Product A, with Product A being destined for domestic sales:

Sales of Product A	200
Cost of goods sold for Product A	95
Net amount	105

The taxpayer then apportions Japanese Corporation P's R&D division expenses to the part "a" activities and to the Product A activities based on appropriate criteria. The taxpayer is to exclude apportionment expenses that are directly allocable. The Reference Case Studies on the Application of Transfer Pricing Taxation (hereafter Reference Case Studies) eschews the use of the sales amount for part "a" to foreign-related person S of 35 because the sale is a controlled transaction. Instead, the Reference Case Studies are more comfortable with an apportionment based on the sales of Product A to Japanese customers of 200 and sales to Country X of 110 by foreign-related person S as being the applicable criteria.

The taxpayer then addresses the apportionment of selling and administrative expenses. It is appropriate that the taxpayer link those selling and administrative expenses to the gross profit relating to part "a" and to the gross profit relating to Product A as to Product A's expenses of 48 and part "a" selling expenses of 2. The taxpayer proportionally apportions the shared expenses on the basis of a reasonable criterion, such as cost of goods sold:

Japanese Corporation P's cost of goods sold for part "a" destined for foreign-related Party S 25

Japanese Corporation P's cost of goods sold for Product A destined for the Japanese Market 95

Japanese Corporation P's profit and loss computations on foreign-related transactions are:

- The R&D cost after apportionment of expenses is:
  - Total cost R&D cost to be apportioned is 25.
  - The formula is sales to Country X of 110 divided by the sum of the sales to Country X of 110 plus the sales of 200 to Japanese customers.
  - The mathematical computation is 9.

$$25 \times \{110/(110+200)\}$$

- The administrative expenses after apportionment of expenses are:
  - Total administrative expense to be apportioned is 25.
  - The formula is the cost of goods sold to Country X of 25 divided by the sum of the cost of goods sold to Country X of 25 plus the cost of goods sold to the Japanese market of 95.

- The mathematical computation is 3.

$$15\times\{25/(25+95)\}$$

Japanese Corporation P's total net profit on foreign-related transactions is:

- Sales of part "a" 35
- Part "a" cost of goods sold (25)
- Royalties received 5
- R&D cost (after apportionment) (9)
- Part "a" selling expenses (2)
- Administrative expenses (after apportionment) (3)
- Net income 1

Foreign-Related Person's Profit and Loss on Foreign-Related Transactions

The taxpayer seeks to apply the profit split method to foreign-related corporation S's foreign-related transactions. The taxpayer must calculate the profit and loss attributable to the Product A business division and apportion any expenses paid jointly with the Product B business division according to reasonable criteria. Foreign-related person S's administrative expenses are 10. The Reference Case Studies would oppose the use of the purchases ratio as an apportionment method in this particular case, such as by adding the purchases for part "a" of 35 plus other costs of 10 and then dividing that amount by the cost of purchasing Product B of 480. The Reference Case Studies would oppose the use of the cost of purchasing as being inappropriate, as it would include controlled transactions. The Reference Case Studies suggested that the taxpayer use a variable, such as the ratio of selling expenses to each business division. This ratio is the ratio of Product A expenses of 15 to the ratio of Product B expenses of 5.

The apportionment of administrative expenses is:

- Total administrative expenses are 10.
- The apportionment formula is: Product A expenses are 15, divided by the sum of the Product A expenses of 15 and the Product B expenses of 5.
- The result is 8.

$$10\times\{15/(15+5)\}$$

Foreign-related corporation's profit and loss on foreign-related transactions are:

- Sales of Product A 110
- Purchases of part "a" (35)
- Other costs of Product A (10)
- Royalties paid (5)
- Product A selling expenses (15)
- Administrative expenses (8)
- Net operating income 37

Explanation

When a taxpayer calculates the profit to be split, the taxpayer must first calculate the expenses linked to revenue, including the cost of goods sold and proportion of selling and administrative expense. The taxpayer needs to calculate indirect (shared) expenses by apportioning the expenses based on what is considered to be the "most reasonable criteria" based on Administrative Guideline 3-4. The Reference Case Studies view as inappropriate the inclusion of the cost of goods sold of a subsidiary that purchases from its parent company and of expenses whose proportionate allocation are subject to arbitrary change. Adjustments may be made if the accounting categories for profit and loss differ from that of the corporation and the foreign-related person.

CASE 19: DIFFERENCES IN LABOR COSTS IMPACT THE RESIDUAL PROFIT SPLIT METHOD

Case 19 illustrates the application of the residual profit split method in situations in which the cost of foreign manufacture is lower than the cost of domestic manufacture. Here the taxpayer transferred the production operations to a foreign country where the foreign labor costs are lower than in the case of domestic manufacturing.

The schematic of the business relations before the transfer of manufacturing operations is:

- Japanese Corporation P manufactures Product A at an 80 manufacturing cost.
- Japanese Corporation P sells Product A to foreign-related person S in Country X.
- Foreign-related person S sells Product A to third parties at a 100 sales amount.

The schematic of the business relations after the transfer of manufacturing operations is:

- Japanese Corporation P manufactures and sells Product A.
- Japanese Corporation P licenses patents and manufacturing know-how to foreign-related party S.
- Foreign-related person S manufacturers and sells Product A.
- Foreign-related person S's cost of manufacture is 45.
- Foreign-related person S sells Product A to third parties at a 100 sales amount.

Summary of Business Corporation and the Foreign-Related Person Relationships

The Japanese business corporation and foreign-related parties have these relationships:

- Japanese Corporation P established foreign-related person S ten years ago in Country X as a subsidiary to distribute Product A.
- Japanese Corporation P used to sell Product A domestically to third parties using foreign-related person S as an intermediary.

- Foreign-related person decided to switch to local production in Country X five years ago due to lower labor costs in Country X and other lower expenses in Country X.
- Japanese Corporation P transferred its operations in Japan to foreign-related person S in Country X.
- Japanese Corporation P and foreign-related person S made Product A by using Japanese Corporation P's original technologies resulting from its R&D activities.
- After transferring its production facilities overseas to foreign-related person S, Japanese Corporation P licensed to foreign-related person S Japanese Corporation P's patents and manufacturing know-how.
- Foreign-related person S procures raw materials locally in Country X to produce Product A, basing Product A on Japanese Corporation P's technologies.
- Foreign-related person S then sells the Product A output to third parties in Country X.

Functions and Activities of the Corporation and of the Foreign-Related Person

Product A is an outcome of Japanese Corporation P's R&D activities. Foreign-related person S has increased the sales of Product A in Country X due to Product A's original technical performance. Foreign-related person S has achieved a certain market share and a largely stable price for Product A in Country X.

Foreign-related person S has no R&D operations. Foreign-related person S's manufacturing of Product A is based on technologies originating and furnished from Japanese Corporation P. Foreign-related person S has traditionally engaged in large-scale advertising and promotional activities as a distributor. Foreign-related person S's marketing and promotional activities have put the company into a more competitive sales position due to the strong product recognition of its products and its large distribution channels.

The change in the profit and loss situation before and after the transfer of production operations was:

- Japanese Corporation P's cost of manufacture for Product A was 80 before Japanese Corporation P transferred the manufacturing operations to foreign-related person S.
- Foreign-related person S's cost of manufacture for Product A became 45 after Japanese Corporation P transferred the manufacturing operations to foreign-related person S.
- The combined profits of Japanese Corporation P and foreign-related person S were 20 before Japanese Corporation P transferred the manufacturing operations to foreign-related person S.
- The combined profits of Japanese Corporation P and foreign-related person S became 55 after Japanese Corporation P transferred the manufacturing operations to foreign-related person S.
- There was no change in the selling price of Product A in Country X before and after the transfer of production operations.
- There were no other changes to the production operations.

Treatment for Transfer Pricing Taxation Purposes

The taxpayer considered the potential applicability of transfer pricing methods that are equivalent to the traditional transaction methods but was unable to find comparable transactions. The reader should consider applying Case 1 regarding the applicability of methods that are "equivalent to" the traditional transaction methods and to the methods that are "equivalent to" methods that are "consistent with" the traditional transaction methods. The taxpayer considered applying transfer pricing methods that are "consistent with" the traditional transaction methods and applying methods that are "equivalent to" other methods the ASMT Cabinet Order prescribed. The taxpayer obtained these results:

- The taxpayer was unable to find comparable transactions in applying transfer pricing methods that are "consistent with" the traditional transaction methods.
- Both Japanese Corporation P and foreign-related person S have intangible properties:
  - Product A's unique technical performance, founded in Japanese Corporation P's technical capacities
  - Product A's strong product recognition and distribution channels built up by foreign-related person S's advertising and sales promotion activities
- Both Japanese Corporation P and foreign-related person S create sources of income as to their respective foreign-related transactions when compared with a corporation engaging solely in basic activities.
- The taxpayer concluded that it was appropriate to calculate the arm's length price by applying the residual profit split method.
- The low level of labor costs in Country X is one factor that has an impact on foreign-related person S's operating margin. Pursuant to Administrative Guideline 3-5, foreign-related person S takes this low level of profit factor into account for comparative purposes by selecting a corporation that similarly receives the benefit of labor costs in the process of calculating foreign-related person S's basic profit when applying the residual profit split method.

Explanation

The cost of manufacture decreases compared with domestic Japanese production when the taxpayer transfers the production operations to Country X, the foreign-related person's country, where labor costs and other expenses are lower. The reduction in manufacturing cost is externally generated by Japanese Corporation P's business group as a result of a business decision. Profits will increase after the transfer of operations to the extent that the business reduces its manufacturing costs. This situation would apply if the business can sell the product of the same quality and brand as before the transfer of the production operations at approximately the same volume and approximately the same price.

A taxpayer normally undertakes activities and know-how to maintain quality, brand, selling price, and volume and to improve production efficiency. The profit that the enterprise associates with the transfer of production operations will be tied together by interrelated combinations of internal factors and external factors, such as labor. It will be difficult for the taxpayer, when applying the profit split method, to distinguish these factors from the profits to be split.

A corporation might engage only in basic manufacturing operations in a country with relatively low costs in an uncontrolled transaction context. The transfer pricing in that situation is the price assigned that enables profit to be commensurate with the function to be secured. Other corporations in similar markets and business categories enjoy the benefits of low labor costs. Even if the corporation enjoys the benefit of lower labor costs as a result of transferring the business operations, the corporation will obtain comparable benefits that are the level of profit that are "commensurate with" the basic manufacturing activities (i.e., the benefits that unrelated parties would assume by unrelated parties performing the manufacturing functions under the same economic conditions). The business can take into account the difference in labor costs before and after the transfer of production operations by selecting an appropriate comparable corporation pursuant to Administrative Guideline 3-5 for the purposes of calculating the basic method when applying the residual profit split method.

The taxpayer, in seeking to apply the residual profit the taxpayer first takes into account the basic profit amount to be split. The taxpayer could apportion this income to the foreign corporation and to the foreign-related person according to respective contributions.

CASE 20: TREATMENT OF MARKET FLUCTUATIONS

Case 20 examines application of the residual profit split method when the enterprise features market features and market fluctuations that impact the profits of the corporation or the foreign-related person.

The schematic of the business relations for Japanese Corporation P is:

- Japanese Corporation P purchases raw materials.
- Japanese Corporation P manufactures Product A in Japan.
- Japanese Corporation P sells part "a" to foreign-related person S.
- Japanese Corporation P licenses patents and manufacturing know-how to foreign-related person S.

The schematic of the business relations for foreign-related person S is:

- Foreign-related person S licenses patents and manufacturing know-how from Japanese Corporation P.
- Foreign-related person S purchases part "a" from Japanese Corporation P.
- Foreign-related person S manufactures Product A in Country X.
- Foreign-related person S sells Product A to several third parties (i.e., agents and wholesalers).

The business issues confronting Japanese Corporation P and foreign-related person S are:

- Ten years ago, Japanese Corporation P established foreign-related person S in Country X as a subsidiary to manufacture and distribute Product A.
- Japanese Corporation P and foreign-related person S produce Product A using Japanese Corporation P's original technologies and R&D.
- Part "A" is a nondescript core part that aggregates Japanese Company P's original technologies.
- Japanese Corporation P sells part "a" to foreign-related person S.
- Japanese Corporation P licenses to foreign-related person S patents and know-how for the manufacture of Product A.
- Foreign-related person S combines part "a" with other parts to manufacture Product A.
- Foreign-related person S sells Product A to a number of third-party agents in Country X.

Functions and Activities of the Corporation and the Foreign-Related Person

Product A is the outcome of Japanese Corporation P's R&D. Japanese Corporation P and foreign-related person S have caused Product A's sales to increase because of unique technical performance. Foreign-related person S achieved a certain market share in Country X.

Foreign-related person S has a technology development division that consists of about 10 engineers. Foreign-related person's technology development division performed some of the development for Product A. That effort contributed to achieving Product A's unique technical performance in conjunction with Japanese Corporation P's R&D. Foreign-related person S does not engage in original advertising or sales promotion activities. Foreign-related person S does not use its own trademark in marketing.

Marketing Conditions

The Product A industry, to which Japanese Corporation P belonged, is known for being subject to severe global fluctuations. The Japanese Corporation P's group takes these fluctuations in demand into account in determining its regular cycle of business profits. In practice, this business cycle takes place over a ten-year interval considering the foreign-related person's actual operating margin and the operating margins of corporations in the same industry in Japan, the world, and databases of corporate data.

The industry's average profit level in Country X is higher than the world average. This difference is attributable to the market price for Product A in Country A being somewhat higher than international profitability due to governmental price regulation.

Treatment for Transfer Pricing Taxation Purposes

The taxpayer considered the applicability of the traditional transaction methods and considered the methods "equivalent to" the traditional transaction methods. The taxpayer was not able to find any comparable transactions, and the taxpayer was not able to apply these transfer pricing methods. See Case 1 as to the application of the traditional transaction methods, including those methods "equivalent to" the traditional transaction methods. The taxpayer considered applying transfer pricing methods that are "consistent with" the traditional transaction methods, and considered methods that are "equivalent to" these transfer pricing methods. The taxpayer considered methods that are prescribed in the ASMT Cabinet Order and transfer pricing equivalent to them. The taxpayer achieved these results:

- The taxpayer concluded that it would be appropriate to apply the residual profit split method.
- Both Japanese Corporation P and foreign-related person S have intangible properties that serve as a source of income as to their foreign-related transactions compared with a corporation engaging solely in basic activities.
- Three factors could potentially impact foreign-related person S's operating margin:
  1. Intangible properties the Japanese Corporation P and foreign-related person S create, including foreign-related person S's R&D activities.
  2. Fluctuations in demand arising from cyclical changes in market conditions. The average profit margin in the industry follows the same trend in Japan, in Country X, and in the world. Corporations belonging to the same industry typically enjoy the same margin.
  3. The level of the market prices in Country X. The industry's average profit margin in Country X is comparatively high compared with the global level. It is thought that the other companies in Country X might enjoy this high profit level.
- When the taxpayer applies the residual profit split method, pursuant to Administrative Guideline 3-5, the taxpayer is to select a corporation in Country X for comparative purposes where the taxpayer considers this experience to be similar. This comparison could affect the impact of fluctuations in demand and the level of market prices in the calculation of foreign-related person S's basic profit.

Explanation

Fluctuations in demand, market prices, and the effect on profit levels arising from the peculiarities of the market would have a similar impact on corporations doing business in the same market. When the taxpayer applies the residual profit split method, the taxpayer is to reflect the impact of the fluctuations in demand, in market prices, and in the features of the market, such as customer preferences and government regulation. The taxpayer is to select an appropriate corporation pursuant to Administrative Guideline 3-5, providing that the company provides financial data for the same period.

CASE 21: CALCULATION OF BASIC PROFIT

Case 21 examines the selection of corporation to calculate the basic profit normally earned between unrelated parties without the presence of material intangible properties. The schematic of the business relations is described in this section.

Japanese Corporation P

The Japanese corporation has these activities:

- Japanese Corporation P purchases raw materials.
- Japanese Corporation P manufactures and sells Product A.
- Japanese Corporation P licenses patents and manufacturing know-how to foreign-related person S.
- Japanese Corporation P sells part "a" to foreign-related person S.

Foreign-Related Person S

The foreign-related person has these activities:

- Foreign-related person S licenses patents and manufacturing know-how from Japanese Corporation P.
- Foreign-related person S purchases part "a" from Japanese Corporation P.
- Foreign-related person S manufactures and sells Product A.
- Foreign-related person S sells Product A to approximately 200 third-party retailers.

Business of the Corporation and the Foreign-Related Person

The history of the relationship between the Japanese Corporation and the related person is explained next.

- Ten years ago, Japanese Corporation P established foreign-related person S in Country X as a subsidiary to manufacture and distribute Product A.
- Japanese Corporation P and foreign-related person S make Product A using Japanese Corporation P's original technologies from its R&D activities.
- Part "a" is an unspecified core part that aggregates Japanese Corporation P's original technologies.
- Japanese Corporation P sells part "a" for Product A to foreign-related person S.
- Japanese Corporation P licenses to foreign-related person A patents and manufacturing know-how for the manufacture of Product A.
- Japanese Corporation P created the original know-how as a result of its R&D activities.
- Foreign-related person S combines part "a" with other parts to manufacture Product A.
- Foreign-related person S sells Product A to about 200 third-party retailers in Country X.

- Foreign-related person S has seen a sales increase due to its technical performance.
- Foreign-related person S has acquired a certain market share of Product A in Country X.
- Foreign-related person S sells Product A at a largely stable price in Country X.
- Foreign-related person S has no R&D operations and depends on the original technology that Japanese Corporation P furnished.
- Foreign-related person S enjoys a superior sales position thanks to its strong product recognition and large distribution channels.
- Foreign-related person S created these distribution channels through its large-scale original advertising and sales promotion activities.

Treatment for Transfer Pricing Taxation Purposes

The taxpayer sought to apply the traditional transaction methods and sought to apply methods that are "equivalent to" the traditional transaction methods, but the taxpayer was unable to find these comparable transaction methods. As such, the taxpayer was unable to apply the traditional transaction methods or methods that are "equivalent to" the traditional transaction methods. The reader should examine Case 1 as to the applicability of the traditional transaction methods, including methods that are "equivalent to" the traditional transaction methods and methods that are "consistent with" these traditional transaction methods. The taxpayer sought to apply methods prescribed in the ASMT Cabinet Order and achieved these results:

- The taxpayer was unable to find comparable transactions that are "consistent with" the traditional transaction methods and comparable transactions that are "equivalent to" the traditional transaction methods.
- The taxpayer found that Japanese Corporation P has intangible properties and is a source of income to Japanese Corporation P as to foreign-related transactions.
- The taxpayer found that foreign-related person S has intangible properties and is a source of income to foreign-related person S as to foreign-related transactions.
- As a result, the taxpayer deemed it appropriate to calculate the arm's length price by applying the residual profit split method.
- When applying the residual profit split method, it is necessary for the taxpayer to calculate the residual profit that arises from material assets by allocating the basic profit to Japanese Corporation P and to foreign-related person S from the profit to split from foreign-related transactions.
- The taxpayer must calculate the basic profit allocated to Japanese Corporation P and to foreign-related person S.
- The taxpayer, in calculating the basic profit allocated to Japanese Corporation P, needs to calculate the basic profit amounts using corporate financial data that exclude corporations with material intangible assets but are in the same industry as Japanese Corporation P (i.e., the manufacture and distribution of part "a," being active in similar markets, and being of a similar size).

- The taxpayer, in calculating the basic profit allocated to foreign-related person S, needs to calculate the basic profit amounts using corporate financial data that exclude corporations with material intangible assets but are in the same industry as foreign-related person S (i.e., the manufacture and sale of Product A, being active in similar markets, and being of a similar size).

Explanation

The taxpayer is to begin with the profit to be split. Then the taxpayer is to calculate and deduct the basic profit from the profit to be split when applying the residual profit split method. The taxpayer is to calculate the basic profit based on the profit indicators. The taxpayer is to express the profit indicator, for example, as the ratio of operating income to business assets or to the sales of the corporation. The taxpayer is to determine the profit indicator for a corporation that is in the same category of business as the foreign-related transaction involving the corporation and the foreign-related person, is active in a similar market, and is of a similar size, excluding corporations with material intangible properties. Pursuant to Administrative Guideline 3-5, such a corporation is termed a comparable corporation.

The taxpayer is to judge the validity of such profit indicators based on the individual circumstances, making that comparison through a process of selecting a more comparable corporation. The taxpayer can use figures at the corporate level, not at the transaction level, from publicly available data if the taxpayer can ensure sufficient comparability.

The taxpayer is to select a comparable corporation from corporations that do not have material intangible properties, where the corporations are in the same category of business as the foreign-related transaction involving the corporation and the foreign-related person, is active in a similar market, and is of a similar size. Appropriate criteria for selecting the comparable company include:

- Industry code
- Goods traded in
- Market level (wholesale or retail, etc.)
- Overseas sales ratio
- Size of sales
- Scale of facilities (tangible fixed assets)
- Number of employees
- Existence of intangible fixed assets
- Level of R&D costs
- Advertising expenses

The taxpayer is to exclude corporations not operating under normal business conditions, such as corporations that are bankrupt.

The term "basic profit" is the amount that corresponds to the profit normally earned from uncontrolled transactions without having material intangible properties pursuant to ASMT Directive 66-4(4)-5. This financial data applies to corporations engaging in comparatively simple manufacturing and sales activities.

The comparable corporations the taxpayer selects in order to calculate the basic profit should follow the preceding steps. The taxpayer, however, should bear in mind the existence of certain limitations on the availability of data, such as the absence of publicly available information and the location of information overseas.

Typical Selection Criteria for Comparable Corporations

The Japanese tax administration describes the typical selection criteria for comparable corporations:

1. Corporations in the same business category—identified based on industry code in the corporate database.
2. Exclude controlled transactions (i.e., corporations engaging in transactions that cannot be regarded as being uncontrolled)—determined according the proportion of related transactions.
3. Exclude corporations active in different markets—determined according to country, market level, and overseas sales ratio.
4. Exclude corporations of different sizes—determined according to the scale of the business in terms of sales, expenses, and assets.
5. Exclude corporations having material intangible properties—determined according to the existence of intangible properties and the level of R&D costs.
6. The result, after making those exclusions, is comparable corporations.

Ideally, the taxpayer should select as many comparable corporations as possible in order to calculate basic profit as long as the taxpayer can ensure comparability.

CASE 22: FACTORS FOR SPLITTING THE RESIDUAL PROFIT

Case 22 illustrates an instance in which the taxpayer can use expenditures in each period—creation, maintenance, and development of intangible properties—as factors for splitting residual profit.

Schematic for Japanese Corporation P

The Japanese corporation undertakes these activities:

- Japanese Corporation P buys raw materials.
- Japanese Corporation P manufactures and sells Product A.
- Japanese Corporation P sells part "a" to foreign-related person S.
- Japanese Corporation P licenses patents and manufacturing know-how to foreign-related person S.

Schematic for Foreign-Related Person S

The foreign-related person undertakes these activities:

- Foreign-related person S buys part "a" from Japanese Corporation P.
- Foreign-related person S licenses patents and manufacturing know-how from Japanese Corporation P.
- Foreign-related person S manufactures Product A in Country X.
- Foreign-related person S sells Product A to approximately 200 third-party retailers.

Summary of the Business of the Corporation and the Foreign-Related Person

The Japanese corporation and the foreign-related person have these business activities:

- Ten years ago, Japanese Corporation P established foreign-related person S in Country X as a subsidiary to manufacture and distribute Product A.
- Japanese Corporation P and foreign-related person S manufacture Product A using Japanese Corporation P's original technologies and R&D activities.
- Part "a" is a nondescript core part that aggregates Japanese Corporation P's original technologies.
- Japanese Corporation P sells part "a" for Product A to foreign-related person S.
- Japanese Corporation P licenses patents and manufacturing know-how for the manufacture of Product A.
- Japanese Corporation P creates original technologies from its R&D.
- Foreign-related person S combines part "a" with other parts to manufacture Product A.
- Foreign-related person S sells Product A to about 200 third-party retailers in Country X.
- Foreign-related person S engages in large-scale advertising through television commercials, magazine advertisements, and other media in Country X.
- Japanese Corporation P's and foreign-related person S's manufactured Product A acquires a certain market share in Country X due to its strong product recognition, to its unique technical performance, and to foreign-related person S's advertising activities.
- Product A sells at a largely stable price.

Information Relevant to the Creation of These Intangible Properties

The Japanese Corporation and the foreign-related person undertake these functions:

- Japanese Corporation P continues to engage in R&D on Product A. This research includes R&D that did not ultimately lead to deliverables. Japanese Corporation P

does not keep its R&D expenditures separate for management accounting purposes as to its individual patents and manufacturing know-how.
- Foreign-related person S's advertising activities concern Product A. Foreign-related person S's advertising activities concerning Product A are deemed to contribute to the creation of intangible properties in foreign-related person S's marketing.
- According to Japanese Corporation P's past profit and loss statements, Japanese Corporation P's expenditures as to its R&D activities approximate 7% of sales for each period.
- According to foreign-related person S's past profit and loss statements, foreign-related person S's advertising costs approximate 8% of sales for each period.

Treatment for Transfer Pricing Taxation Purposes

The taxpayer sought to apply the traditional transaction methods and to apply methods that are "equivalent to" the traditional transaction methods, but the taxpayer was unable to find such comparable transactions. The reader should see Case 1 as to the applicability of the traditional transaction methods, including methods that are "equivalent to" the traditional transaction methods. The taxpayer considered transfer pricing methods that are "consistent with" the traditional transaction methods, considered transfer pricing methods that are "equivalent to" these traditional transaction methods, and considered "other methods" as the ASMT Cabinet Order prescribed. The taxpayer obtained the following results.

The taxpayer compared its operations with a corporation engaging solely in basic activities. The intangible properties that Japanese Corporation P R&D activities creates and that foreign-related person S advertising activities create serve as sources of income as to Japanese Corporation P's and foreign-related person S's foreign-related transactions. Based on these facts, the taxpayer applied the residual profit split method.

Pursuant to ASTM Directive 66-4(4)-5 note, the Japanese transfer pricing provisions permit the taxpayer to allocate the residual profit to Japanese Corporation P and to foreign-related person S based on the expenses expended by the two companies as to the development of material intangible properties. The amount that Japanese Corporation P and foreign-related person S expend each fiscal year was deemed to be the appropriate factor for splitting residual profit. The taxpayer cannot identify the creation of individual patents, manufacturing know-how, and individual properties employed in marketing. Further, the amount of expenses expended on the creation of intangible properties is largely constant each term.

Explanation

The residual profit split operates in this manner:

1. The taxpayer allocates the residual profit split to Japanese Corporation P and to foreign-related person S according to the extent of the contribution that Japanese Corporation P and foreign-related person S make toward the residual profit,

obtained through the extent of the contribution of intangible properties to residual profit. Consequently, according to ASMT Directive 66-4(4)-1 and ASMT Directive 66-4(4)-5, the taxpayer uses the value of the material intangible properties to serve as a source of income for splitting the residual profit.

The taxpayer, in measuring the extent of the contribution of intangible properties, need not consider the absolute value of the intangible properties that Japanese Corporation P or foreign-related person S possesses. Instead, the proportions of the relative values of the respective parties' intangible properties can suffice. ASTM Directive 66-4(4)-5 note provides that "allocation based on the value of the material intangible properties according to the amount of the expenses expended on development of the material intangible properties is allowed as a reasonable method of allocation." The taxpayer might be able to avail itself of other measurement techniques, such as the use of expenses expended in each period that reflect the creation, maintenance, and development of intangible properties, as well as the use of the acquisition cost of the intangible properties.

2. Often it is difficult for the taxpayer to individually identify the expenses relating to the creation, maintenance, and development of patents and manufacturing know-how through R&D activities. It is especially difficult for the taxpayer to individually identify the expenses in cases where the taxpayer uses the acquisition cost as the split factor. Furthermore, the value of the intangible properties might decline with the passage of time. In the event that this decline does take place, it is necessary for the taxpayer to estimate in a reasonable and objective manner the period during which the individual tangible properties are likely to sustain their value.
3. The focus, in applying the residual profit split, might be, for instance, on the activities to create, maintain, and develop intangible properties. In situations in which the focus is on the activities to create, maintain, and develop intangible properties, it is reasonable for the taxpayer to allocate residual profit using the amount of expenses in each period that are associated with activities as the split factor. This approach presupposes that the taxpayer performs these activities continuously. In addition, this approach presupposes that the expenses in each period associated with these activities are comparatively stable.

It might be detrimental for the taxpayer to use the expenses in each period as being the split factor. The results might be detrimental, for example, if the taxpayer incurs large fluctuations in the amount of the expenditures concerning activities to create, maintain, or develop intangible properties in each period. In that situation, it might be possible for the taxpayer to use the average amount of expenditures during a reasonable period as a basis of the residual profit split. Alternatively, it might be possible for the taxpayer to use the sum of the expenditures in a reasonable period of years, allocated according to a certain number of years, as the basis for the residual profit split.

There might be situations in which the taxpayer uses the amount of expenditures in each period as the split factor, the taxpayer has reasonably determined the split factor, and the taxpayer has appropriately calculated the proportions of the relative values of the material intangible properties. In such an event, the taxpayer should treat the profit split method as being appropriate even if the split factor is relatively small in proportion to the amount of the residual profit.

4. The taxpayer can use the "amount of expenses expended" to create the intangible properties as the factor for splitting the residual profit. If the taxpayer is to apply the "amount of expenses expended" approach as the method for splitting the residual profit, the taxpayer is to identify related expenses among expenses such as:
   a. Intangible properties the taxpayer uses in manufacturing activities, such as patents and manufacturing know-how: expenses related to the R&D division and the manufacturing division
   b. Intangible properties the taxpayer uses in marketing activities, such as brands, trademarks, distribution channels, and customer lists; expenses related to advertising, sales promotion, and marketing divisions
   c. Intangible properties the taxpayer uses other than for manufacturing activities and marketing activities (i.e., for know-how regarding business judgment, risk management, financing, and marketing); expenses related to planning operations, finance, front-office divisions, and other divisions that perform such activities

   These expenses are "closely connected" to the activities to create material intangible properties.

5. The calculation process the taxpayer uses for the residual profit split method is:
   a. Japanese Corporation P's profit or loss from foreign-related transaction is 40
   b. Foreign-related person S's profit or loss from foreign-related transaction is 60
   c. Japanese Corporation P's basic profit (after calculation) is 8
   d. Foreign-related person S's basic profit (after calculation) is 12
   e. Factors for splitting the residual profit:
      i. Split factor for Japanese Corporation P: R&D activities 80%
      ii. Split factor for foreign-related person S: advertising activities 20%
   f. Calculation of the profit to be split:
      i. Japanese Corporation P's profit or loss from foreign-related transaction 40
      ii. Foreign-related person S's profit of loss from foreign-related transaction 60
   g. Calculation of basic profit:
      i. Basic profit for Japanese Corporation P 8
      ii. Basic profit for foreign-related person S 12
      iii. Residual profit – to be allocated 80
   h. Allocation of residual profit:
      i. R&D activities 80%
      ii. Advertising activities 20%
      iii. Residual profit applicable to Japanese Corporation P 80 × 80% = 64
      iv. Residual profit applicable to foreign-related person S 80 × 20% = 16
      v. Results of the profit split:
      vi. Results of the profit allocation after splitting: Japanese Corporation P 8 + 64 = 72
      vii. Results of the profit allocation after splitting: foreign-related person S 12 + 16 = 28

19

CHAPTER NINETEEN

Japanese Guidelines Address Diverse Transfer Pricing Issues

THE JAPANESE transfer pricing regulations address a number of diverse issues as part of the case examples. These examples address:

- Case 23: Determining whether Services Provide Commercial Value
- Case 24: Multiple Year Considerations
- Case 25: Establishing the Target Profit Margin
- Case 26: Critical Assumptions

CASE 23: DETERMINING WHETHER SERVICES PROVIDE COMMERCIAL VALUE

The schematic of the business relations specifies:

- Japanese Corporation P manufactures and sells Product A.
- Ten years ago, Japanese Corporation P established three companies as subsidiaries to produce and to distribute Product A in their respective countries:
    - Foreign-related person SX in Country X
    - Foreign-related person SY in Country Y

  - Foreign-related person SZ in Country Z
  - Japanese Corporation P provides services to foreign-related person SX, to foreign-related person SY, and to foreign-related person SZ
- The S companies procure all of their parts and raw materials locally to produce and sell Product A in their respective countries.
- Japanese Corporation P has a unit that has responsibility for various operations concerning the S group.

Japanese Corporation P

Japanese Corporation P provides these services to the S group:

a. Japanese Corporation P determines the human resource policy at the S group and interviews candidate directors at the S group.
b. Japanese Corporation P manages business operations at the S group through weekly teleconferencing.
c. Japanese Corporation P checks draft budgets the S group prepared and provides instructions on amendments if these instructions are problematic from the standpoint of business operations.
d. Japanese Corporation P compiles monthly financial and production and sales management data as to what the S group requires to produce internal reports.
e. Japanese Corporation P checks the consolidated report data sent by the S group and provides instructions on amendments if they contain minor numerical errors.
f. Japanese Corporation P accompanies its internal auditors when the corporation performs business audits and prepares written instructions as to business improvements.
g. Japanese Corporation P accompanies the auditors of the outside accounting firm to audit Japanese Corporation P's consolidated results. The S group requests that a different accounting firm perform an audit due to legislation in Country X.
h. Japanese Corporation P audits the S group compliance with environmental legislation and guidance on rectifying problem areas.
i. Japanese Corporation P checks contracts that the S group entered into with unrelated persons. Japanese Corporation P answers the S group's legal queries.
j. Japanese Corporation P develops and maintains computer systems for dealing promptly with product complaints. The computer system connects Japanese Corporation P with the S group online.
k. Japanese Corporation P provides judgment on financing fresh capital investment for the S group. Japanese Corporation P provides risk analysis of financing fresh capital investment for the S group. Japanese Corporation P arranges the financing of fresh capital investment for the S group.
l. Japanese Corporation P serves as a liaison regarding consultations on operational matters from the S group. There are no actual instances of these consultations taking place.

m. Japanese Corporation P supports the development of the S group relations with key clients, the negotiations of transaction term, and so forth.
n. Japanese Corporation P provides contract negotiations and decision making as to the S group main contracts and fulfills the terms of those contracts.

Treatment for Transfer Pricing Taxation Purposes

The taxpayer can determine whether each of the preceding services that Japanese Corporation P provides to foreign-related person S has commercial value. The taxpayer is to make the commercial value determination by considering the commercial value criteria specified in Administrative Guideline 2-10. Administrative Guideline 2-10 provides for:

1. Whether foreign-related person S would have to pay consideration for another person to perform these services
2. Whether foreign-related person S would have to perform these services itself if Japanese Corporation P had not provided these services

The fact pattern in this example does not provide sufficient facts to determine whether each service has commercial value. In practice, the taxpayer would need to undertake a more detailed investigation. Nevertheless, the Reference Case Studies on the Application of Transfer Pricing Taxation (hereafter Reference Case Studies) suggest that the services falling into categories (d), (e), and (g) do not have commercial value. Those services arise from Japanese Corporation P's position as shareholder. In contrast, the Reference Case Studies suggest that the other enumerated services would often be judged to have commercial value. The taxpayer should provide proper consideration to Administrative Guideline 2-10. This consideration includes determining whether such activities correspond to the activities that the provider of services performed in its capacity as a shareholder:

Explanation

All of the transactions between Japanese Corporation P and the foreign-related corporation S that have commercial value correspond to foreign-related transactions. The taxpayer is to treat transactions as having commercial value if the subsidiary is a foreign-related person that:

- Receives managerial, financial, operational, or administrative services from its parent company
- Had to obtain such services from an unrelated person for payment of a consideration
- Undertook the providing of the services itself, if the parent company had not provided such services

A corporation might routinely maintain personnel resources, facilities, and similar resources that are capable of providing services. The corporation might retain these resources to provide services, as and when necessary, in response to requests by foreign-related persons. The maintenance of such resources is equivalent to the providing of services.

A subsidiary might receive services from an unrelated person, or the subsidiary might engage in such services for itself, even if the parent company provides the same services to the subsidiary. Those services are duplicate services. The term "duplicate services" excludes instances where such duplication is considered to be temporary or where the duplicated services are deemed to be procedural double-checks to reduce the risks associated with errors in business judgment. Such duplicate services have no commercial value, and these duplicate services are not treated as foreign-related transactions.

The same situation for duplicate services also applies to shareholder activities. Services that the shareholder undertakes as a parent company in its capacity as a shareholder of the subsidiary provide no commercial value, and these shareholder services are not treated as foreign-related transactions. This treatment applies to activities undertaken by the parent company for its general meeting of shareholders, or to prepare its financial reports in accordance with the Securities and Exchange law.

As a general matter, the decision is to be made as to whether services have commercial value by making that determination according to the respective circumstances pursuant to Administrative Guideline 2-10. The decision can then be made as to whether the activities of the parent company correspond to the shareholder activities—for instance, an oversight of a subsidiary deemed to be providing services.

A taxpayer calculates arm's length services provisions pursuant to Administrative Guideline 2-10, the Treatment of Intra-Group Services. The taxpayer is to examine transfer pricing methods that are "equivalent to" the comparable uncontrolled price method and to examine methods that are "equivalent to" the cost plus method (i.e., methods that are "equivalent to" the traditional transaction methods pursuant to Act on Special Measures Concerning Taxation [ASMT] Directive 66-4(6)-5). The taxpayer is to mark up the services expenses as required. However, the services that the taxpayer provides may be incidental to the core operations of the corporation of the related person. In that event, it might be possible for the taxpayer to use the final cost of services as the arm's length price pursuant to Administrative Guideline 2-9. The reader should see Case 5.

A company that provides services with commercial value to the subsidiary might employ the parent company's intangibles. If that situation applies, it is necessary to the taxpayer to consider whether it includes the portion of the intangibles in the consideration for such services pursuant to Administrative Guideline 2-8. If the taxpayer excludes these intangibles, it is necessary for the taxpayer to access the business activities of the subsidiary to which the intangible assets are used. After the taxpayer contributes activities, it might not be possible to shift the intangible from the taxpayer to the contributors.

The taxpayer is to contribute these intangible activities for the purpose of calculating the consideration each party makes to these activities. The taxpayer is to take the parent's core business into account and to ensure the parent's business has appropriately allocated this income.

CASE 24: MULTIPLE-YEAR CONSIDERATIONS

Case 24 illustrates the calculation of the arm's length price in a multiyear situation that reflects changes in market conditions. The schematic reflecting this situation is shown next for Japanese Corporation P and foreign-related person S in Country X.

Japanese Corporation P

Japanese Corporation P undertakes these activities:

- Japanese Corporation P is a manufacturer and distributor of Product A.
- Japanese Corporation P purchases raw materials and other items.
- Japanese Corporation P sells part "a," a nondescript part, to foreign-related person S in Country X.
- Japanese Corporation P licenses patents and manufacturing know-how to foreign-related person S in Country X.

Foreign-Related Person S

Foreign-related person S undertakes these activities:

- Foreign-related person S in Country X purchases part "a" from Japanese Corporation P.
- Foreign-related person S in Country X licenses patents and manufacturing know-how from Japanese Corporation P.
- Foreign-related person S is a manufacturer of Product A.
- Foreign-related person S sells product A as agent to several third parties.

Foreign-Related Transactions

Over a 10 year interval, Japanese Corporation P and foreign-related person S undertook these activities:

- Ten years ago, Japanese Corporation P established foreign-related person S in Country X as a subsidiary to manufacture and distribute Product A.
- Japanese Corporation P and foreign-related person S manufacture Product A using Japanese Corporation P's original research and development (R&D) technologies.
- Part "a" is a nondescript part that aggregates Japanese Corporation P's original technologies.
- Japanese Corporation P sells part "a" for Product A to foreign-related person S.
- Japanese Corporation P creates its patents and manufacturing know-how as a result of its R&D activities.
- Japanese Corporation P licenses its patents and know-how to related-person S for the manufacture of Product A.

- Foreign-related person S combines part "a" with other parts to Product A.
- Foreign-related person S then sells Product A to several third-party agents in Country X.
- Foreign-related person S has increased its sales of Product A as a result of Japanese Corporation P's unique technical performance as to Product A.
- Foreign-related person S has acquired a certain market share in Country X.
- Foreign-related person S has no R&D functions and does not engage in original advertising or sales promotion activities.

Market Conditions for Product A

Product A is part of a broader industrial category, termed "Product A industry." The Product A industry to which the Japanese Corporation P's group belongs is known for its large global swings in demand. Company profits follow a cyclical pattern, subject to fluctuations in demand. Foreign-related corporations' actual operating margins and the operating margins of corporations in Product A industry have exhibited a regular cycle over the past ten years according to a database of Country X corporate data.

A comparison has taken place between foreign-related person S's operating margin and the average operating margin of the corporations in the Product A industry. This operating margin comparison indicates that, on a single-year basis, foreign-related person S's operating margin is generally higher than the industry average in each year. Foreign-related person S's operating margin is similarly higher than the industry average for the past ten years.

Country X requires corporations to provide financial data disclosure, but this financial data disclosure system does not require corporations to reflect cost data. Japan does require the corporations to disclose these costs as part of operating income in these reports.

Treatment for Transfer Pricing Purposes

Foreign-related person S's operating margin generally exceeds the operating margin level in the industry as a whole in individual years, and the average for multiple years over the past ten years, despite being affected by cyclical fluctuations in market demand.

These fluctuations present problems for the taxpayer from the point of view of the transfer pricing taxation of foreign-related taxation of foreign-related transactions between Japanese Corporation P and foreign-related person S, pursuant to Administrative Guideline 2-2(2).

The taxpayer sought to ascertain the applicability of traditional transaction methods and sought to ascertain the applicability of methods that are "equivalent to" these traditional transaction methods. The taxpayer had sought a method of calculation of the arm's length price as to these transactions. The taxpayer, however, was unable to find these applicable data for comparable transactions.

The reader should see Case 1 as to the applicability of the traditional transaction methods, including methods that are "equivalent to" the traditional transaction methods. The taxpayer considered applying transfer pricing methods that are "consistent with" the traditional transaction methods, considered applying transfer pricing methods that are "equivalent to" these methods, considered applying other transfer pricing methods prescribed in the ASMT Cabinet Order, and considered applying other transfer pricing methods that are "equivalent to" these methods. The taxpayer obtained these transfer pricing results:

- The taxpayer was unable to find comparable transactions in applying transfer pricing methods that are "consistent with" the traditional transaction methods and was unable to find transfer pricing methods that are "equivalent to" the traditional transaction methods.
- It is possible for the taxpayer to find comparable transactions by using foreign-related person S's operating margin, where these transaction have comparatively simple functions, and when the taxpayer can obtain these data from publicly available information.
- The taxpayer applied the transactional net margin method, including methods that are "equivalent to" the transactional net margin method, in this case.
- In this case, corporations in the same industry and in the same market in Country X experience the same demand cycle. As a result, it was not necessary for the taxpayer to take special account of the demand cycle when applying the transactional net margin method. The taxpayer can calculate the arm's length price for each year, providing the taxpayer chooses the appropriate comparable transactions and applies comparable financial data for the same period.

Explanation

The taxpayer is to consider these possible problems from the transfer pricing taxation point of view. The taxpayer is to consider the existence of this analysis or otherwise from multiple perspectives according to the specific circumstances of individual transactions. At the same time, the taxpayer should be mindful of the items listed in Administrative Guideline 2-1, the State of Allocation of Profits between the Corporation and the Foreign-Related Person. The taxpayer should undertake this process in such a manner as not to impede an efficient tax audit pursuant to Administrative Guideline 2-2.

For an example of such an approach, take the case where the taxpayer finds it inappropriate to examine foreign-related transactions by considering information on individual taxable years standing alone. For a second example, take the case where the taxpayer finds it inappropriate to examine foreign-related transactions for taxable years owing to considerable fluctuations in prices of inventory assets, such as commonly occurring changes in demand or changes in the product life cycle. In such cases, the taxpayer is to treat the average consideration as being acceptable for the foreign-related transaction or transactions deemed comparable with the foreign-related transaction. Alternatively, the taxpayer is to treat the average consideration as being acceptable as to the foreign-related transaction or transactions deemed comparable with the foreign-related transaction.

The taxpayer is to take the preceding analysis into account for transactions that take place during a "reasonable period" before and after the taxable year or the consolidated taxable year. The taxpayer is to treat such an amount as a base, and take this amount when considering whether there are any transfer pricing taxation problems pursuant to Administrative Guideline 2-2(2). This same treatment applies to the provisions of Administrative Guideline 2-2(1).

There might be situations in which there are considerable price fluctuations in a foreign-related transaction context but prices of transactions are deemed comparable with the foreign-related transactions remaining at a constant level. Alternatively, there might be fluctuations of these prices in a different manner compared with the foreign-related transaction. In those situations, it is necessary for the taxpayer to consider whether it has any transfer pricing taxation problems. The taxpayer can use a variable, such as average consideration or profit margin for the foreign-related transaction and for transactions the taxpayer would deem comparable with foreign-related transactions in multiple years.

In the present case, multiple transactions that are deemed comparable with the foreign-related transaction exhibit largely the same price fluctuations as a foreign-related transaction. The taxpayer need undertake no special consideration in this instance, given the market cycle for the foreign-related transaction. The taxpayer is to consider the life cycle of the product involved in a foreign-related transaction and in the life cycle of products involved in the transactions if the taxpayer can identify that data from publicly available information.

The taxpayer might make use of average consideration or profit margin in multiple years. The taxpayer, in helping to determine whether there are transfer pricing problems, must calculate the arm's length price, on a tax-assessed basis, only for such taxable years found to be problematic in light of transfer pricing taxation, as prescribed in ASMT Article 66-4 if these problems exist.

CASE 25: ESTABLISHING THE TARGET PROFIT MARGIN

The facts in Case 25 reflect the setting of a profit range for an advance pricing agreement (APA) applicant.

The schematic of the business relations is:

- Japanese Corporation P purchases raw materials and other supplies.
- Japanese Corporation P manufactures Product A.
- Japanese Corporation P sells Product A to foreign-related person S.
- Foreign-related person S sells Product A to a dozen or so third-party agents.
- Ten years ago, Japanese Corporation P established foreign-related party S in Country X as a subsidiary to distribute Product A.
- Japanese Corporation P manufactures Product A using Japanese Corporation P's original technologies that emanate from Japanese Corporation P's R&D activities.

- Foreign-related person S has been increasing its sales of Product A due to Japanese Corporation A's market performance and has acquired a certain market share in Country X.
- Foreign-related person S does not engage in original advertising or in sales promotion activities.
- Product A is part of the Product A industry.
- Japanese Corporation P's business group belongs to the Product A industry.
- The Product A industry is subject to major global swings in demand, which cause the company profit situations to reflect large cyclical fluctuations.

Advance Pricing Agreement Procedure

Japanese Corporation P and foreign-related person S filed advance pricing agreement (APA) applications with mutual agreement to the tax authorities in both countries.

Both Japanese Corporation P and foreign-related person S considered the selection of transfer pricing methods for purposes of the APA. The parties determined that Japanese Corporation P manufactured Product A using Japanese Corporation P's original technologies that result from Japanese Corporation P's R&D activities. The parties were unable to find comparable transactions in applying the traditional transaction methods to Japanese Corporation P, and the parties did not apply the traditional transaction methods.

Foreign-related person S has no intangible properties that could serve as a source of income in foreign-related transactions. Nevertheless, it was not possible for foreign-related person S to acquire the information that it would need from information publicly available in corporate databases to select comparable transactions in applying the traditional transaction methods. As a result, foreign-related person S could not apply the traditional transaction methods. See Case 1 as to the applicability of the traditional transfer pricing transaction methods, including transfer pricing methods that are "equivalent to" the traditional transaction methods. Therefore, Japanese Corporation P and foreign-related person S considered applying transfer pricing methods that are "consistent with" the traditional transaction methods and considered applying other methods prescribed in the ASMT Cabinet Order. Japanese Corporation P and foreign-related person S had these results:

The taxpayer could find comparable transactions for the purpose of applying the transactional net margin method to foreign-related person S. Foreign-related person S's use of the transactional net margin method is appropriate due to its having relatively simple functions. Japanese Corporation P's selection of comparable transactions is appropriate for APA purposes.

It is appropriate in this case to incorporate the effects of the business cycle in the target profit margin range because there is a large cycle of profit fluctuations among companies in the Product A industry to which Japanese Corporation's business group belongs. The taxpayer must attach critical assumptions in the APA application in cases of extreme changes in conditions, such as those conditions that exceed normal fluctuations in the Product A industry. Case 26 addresses the setting of critical assumptions.

Explanation

Here is how the Japanese tax authorities apply the APA program:

1. APAs consist of a district tax office director's or a similar official's advance confirmation of the taxpayer's method of calculating an arm's length price for foreign-related transactions. Governments perform APAs in response to taxpayer applications to ensure the predictability of transfer pricing taxation by taxpayers.

   Japan adopted the APA system in 1987; it was one of the first countries in the world to adopt the APA system.

   A taxpayer that receives a confirmation from the government as to the APA application might file a tax return that corresponds to the APA in the taxable year. In that event, the taxpayer is to treat the transaction to be confirmed as having occurred at the arm's length price. A taxable year that the government is to confirm might have elapsed at the time of the APA. In that event, the taxpayer might submit an amended return. The taxpayer might submit the amended return to the confirmed corporation to make the return filed for the year in question comply with the context of the APA. The filing of an amended return is not treated as corresponding to "a return foreknowing that corrections should be made," as described in Article 65(5), Additional Tax for Deficient Returns, within Administrative Guideline 5-16 of the Law on General Rules for National Taxes.

   Transactions that the government is to confirm relative to the return are not subject to transfer pricing examination because of the APA. The preceding situation applies in cases where the taxpayer files the return in question for the taxable year concerning the confirmation of the APA process.
2. The taxpayer is to calculate the arm's length price as part of the APA process. The taxpayer is to calculate the arm's length price using the information the corporation obtains. For example, the corporation can obtain information:
   - On internal comparable transactions that the corporation or its foreign-related person engage in
   - About external comparable transactions based on publicly available information from sources as corporate databases
   - From applying the profit split method using internal information from the corporation and the foreign-related person

   As to external comparable transactions, the taxpayer must ensure comparability by considering other data available as well as information from corporate databases.

   In APA evaluations, the taxpayer is to consider matters set forth in Administrative Guideline 2-1 and Administrative Guideline 5-11(2). As the same time, the taxpayer should bear in mind that the government can request the submission of materials enabling the government to confirm the state of income allocation between the corporation and the foreign-related person. This governmental power is not premised on the APA's application of the profit split method.

   The Regional Tax Bureau (RTB) division in charge is to finish its evaluation of an APA application as part of the mutual agreement process. When the RTB completes this evaluation, it is to communicate its opinion to the Office of Mutual Agreement Procedures through the National Tax Agency division in charge. The Office of Mutual Agreement Procedures is then to convey this opinion to the APA applicant corporation.

3. An APA is a means of forecasting the APA applicant's future profit from a foreign-related transaction. There are cases in which the taxpayer can set up an APA using a fixed range of profit margin, such as an interquartile range, rather than using a specific level (i.e., a specific point) in order to ensure the predictability of the taxpayer's transfer pricing taxation. Transfer pricing treatment that includes such a range will naturally differ from examinations that would require calculation of an arm's length price at a specific point in order to determine the amount of income in past taxable years. When a taxpayer does establish such a range of prices, there may be cases in which it is appropriate for the taxpayer to use a range of prices consisting of all comparable transactions as well as applying interquartile range.

   In Japan, a taxpayer can set up an APA unilaterally (i.e., without mutual agreement confirmation). The Japanese tax authorities can provide confirmation using only the upper limit or the lower limit of the respective ranges according to whether the corporation to be verified is a foreign-related person or is an APA applicant. The interquartile range is normally the range the taxpayer obtains by dividing the profit margins, or other such indicators, of the comparable transactions into four categories in descending order, then excluding the upper quarter and the lower quarter.

4. The taxpayer can establish the target profit range in two ways:
   a. When the taxpayer verifies the data for each year to be confirmed, the taxpayer is to update the data pertaining to the profit margins of comparable transactions using the most up-to-date data to establish the range of target profit. This computation is a means of establishing the range of the target profit margin, using the average of the profit margins as to the comparable transactions in each year to be confirmed. The taxpayer is to update these profit margins to include data for the latest period by adding data for the corresponding taxable year to be confirmed and removing the data for the oldest period. This method enables the taxpayer to use data corresponding to the year of the foreign-related transaction, to use comparable APA transactions, and to incorporate fluctuations in market conditions into the target profit range. The taxpayer might not apply this method. If the taxpayer does use this method, however, it is necessary for the taxpayer to take into consideration the fact that the target profit margin is not determined until the profit margin data for the comparable transactions to be updated becomes available. It is possible that the range of the target profit margin can become skewed. This problem can arise if the comparable transactions the taxpayer uses at the time of the APA cease to exist.
   b. The taxpayer can use a fixed period relating to comparable transactions to establish the target profit margin. This approach is a method of establishing the profit margin range as the target, based on the average profit margin

during a fixed period for comparable transactions, together with fixing and applying the range over the entire period of the taxable years to be confirmed. Taxpayers generally apply this transfer pricing method when fluctuations in business conditions are not particularly great and when taxpayers predetermine the range of the target profit margin.

CASE 26: CRITICAL ASSUMPTIONS

Case 26 addresses the appropriateness of attaching material commercial or economic conditions to the APA. The schematic of the business relations is:

- Japanese Corporation P purchases raw materials.
- Japanese Corporation P manufactures Product A.
- Japanese Corporation P sells Product A to foreign-related person S.
- Foreign-related person S sells Product A to a dozen or so third-party agents.
- Ten years ago, Japanese Corporation P established foreign-related party S in Country X as a subsidiary to distribute Product A.
- Japanese Corporation P manufactures Product A using Japanese Corporation P's original technologies that emanate from Japanese Corporation P's R&D activities.
- Foreign-related person S has seen sales increases for Product A because of Japanese Corporation P's unique performance and R&D.
- Foreign-related person S has secured a certain market share of Product A in Country X.
- Foreign-related person S does not engage in advertising or in sales promotion activities.

Market Conditions

Product A and similar products are susceptible to sharp fluctuations in market prices worldwide. The profits for Product A and for similar products fluctuate considerably, depending on fluctuations in market prices. Further, the specifications of the best-selling products change rapidly in this industry. The accounting system in Country X is currently undergoing major revision. Taxpayers expect future extensive amendments to the Country X accounting system.

Status of the APA Application

Japanese Corporation P and foreign-related person S apply to the tax authorities of the two countries for an APA. Both Japanese Corporation P and foreign-related person S seek to apply mutual agreement procedures. Both Japanese Corporation P and foreign-related person S would apply the transactional net margin method to foreign-related person S as the means of calculating the arm's length price. These APA applications were appropriate in content in terms of the selection of the transfer pricing method to calculate the arm's length price, the choice of comparable transactions, and so forth.

Treatment for Transfer Pricing Taxation Purposes

In this case, there is a possibility that foreign-related person S's actual profit margin in the future might substantially fluctuate in the event of large fluctuations in market prices or changes in the specifications of the products traded. If these substantial fluctuations occur, it is considered inappropriate for the taxpayer to use the arm's length price, in unmodified form, that the taxpayer has confirmed with the government based on the current situation.

Moreover, the method that foreign-related person S applies to calculate its profit margin might undergo change as a result of changes to its accounting system. Foreign-related person S's actual profit margin might diverge from the results calculated based on the details foreign-related person S submitted for the APA request. As a result of this divergence, there is risk that Japanese Corporation P and foreign-related person S could no longer determine whether the actual value conforms to the content of the APA.

In this case, Japanese Corporation P and foreign-related person S need to attach the business or economic conditions for the APA and for confirmation with the tax authorities to guard against such a situation occurring in taxable year. Such conditions might include:

1. Foreign-related person S's sales will not diverge substantially from present circumstances.
2. The portfolio of foreign-related person S's goods traded will not change substantially.
3. There shall be no substantial changes in X's accounting system.

Explanation

A taxpayer concludes the APA process when the taxpayer finds that the transfer pricing methodologies are reasonable, based on the method of calculating the arm's length price in future years, in light of the business situation concerning past and present foreign-related transactions.

Unforeseeable changes in material circumstances can arise in the taxable year the government is to confirm. Such unforeseeable changes could include substantial changes in market prices. In the event that such changes in circumstances could occur, the taxpayer must change the conditions on which the taxpayer relies. In such circumstances, it is no longer appropriate to continue the APA in unmodified form. For this reason, the taxpayer should set up its critical assumptions (i.e., the material and business conditions essential to the APA). The taxpayer should attach documents describing these conditions with the APA document request pursuant to Administrative Guideline 5-3(c).

It is difficult for the taxpayer to exhaustively predetermine the factors that might affect the continuation of an APA. For that reason, it is common for the taxpayer to attach generic conditions to the APA request. Such a general condition could include, for example, the requirement that there should be "no material changes in business conditions or in economic conditions." Similarly, the general condition could include, for example, "the requirement that they have made no specific fundamental changes in the functions performed by the related parties or the assets they have utilized." However, the parties may need to attach more specific conditions in some cases, such as to preclude a change beyond a certain range in exchange rates. The taxpayer might provide such a proviso in order to make clear whether a situation corresponds to the conditions established as critical assumptions.

Changes might occur in the changes the critical assumptions prescribe. In the event that such changes occur, it is necessary for the taxpayer to consider its calculation of the arm's length price as to the situation in question. As a rule, the confirmed corporation will have to apply for an amendment of the APA pursuant to Administrative Guideline 2-10. This amendment process is mandatory. The failure to apply for an application invalidates the APA from the taxable years in which the situation arose pursuant to Administrative Guideline 5-21(1)(a).

In the case of an APA that has a mutual agreement, the tax authorities must initiate the mutual agreement procedure and take into account an agreement the tax authorities reached on a method of calculating the arm's length price that differs from the initial method.

The confirmed corporation is to enter and submit a report for each taxable year. That report is to provide a "statement of changes" to changes to business conditions or to economic conditions, based on whether the government provides the taxpayer with the APA pursuant to Administrative Guideline 5-17.

20

CHAPTER TWENTY

Malaysia Advance Ruling Guidelines

MALAYSIA PERMITS a taxpayer to secure an advance tax ruling in many fact patterns. The advance ruling process is important to U.S. businesses doing business in Malaysia as well as for Malaysian businesses doing business in the United States because the two countries have no income tax treaty except for a shipping and air transportation treaty signed April 18, 1989. The Malaysian prime minister announced the advance tax ruling concept as part of the 2007 budget, effective January 1, 2007. The Inland Revenue Board Malaysia (IRBM) promulgated the specific advance rulings guideline procedure on February 14, 2008.[1]

As we shall see, Malaysia's advance tax ruling process puts taxpayers in an uncertain position from a transfer pricing standpoint. At the outset, Malaysia's advance process does not encompass bilateral advance pricing agreements. Further, Malaysia's advance pricing process possibly might not encompass unilateral advance pricing agreements. Nevertheless, a matched unilateral advance pricing agreement, if permitted by the Malaysian tax authorities, would be an appropriate transfer pricing alternative for Malaysian businesses doing business in the United States and for U.S. businesses doing business in Malaysia.

GENERAL FACETS OF THE ADVANCE RULING PROCEDURE IN MALAYSIA

As a general matter, Malaysia's advance ruling procedure is designed to interpret and apply the income tax provisions pursuant to Malaysia's primary tax law, the Income Tax Act 1967.[2] Any taxpayer can request such an advance ruling. A foreign party can request such a ruling if the party is represented by local counsel.[3] The IRBM intends that the issuance of an advance ruling will achieve these objectives:[4]

- To ensure clarity and certainty of the tax treatment
- To provide consistency in the application of the income tax law
- To promote tax compliance
- To minimize disputes between the IRBM and the taxpayer

The Income Tax Act 1967 empowers the Director General Inland Revenue (DGIR) to provide an advance ruling on behalf of the taxpayer.[5] Upon the taxpayer's request, the DGIR can rule as to how the provisions of the act would apply to the person and to the arrangement for which the taxpayer seeks a ruling. The Income Tax Act 1967 empowers the minister of finance to provide for the scope and procedure as to the advance ruling and to provide fees associated with the advance ruling.[6] The advanced ruling procedure is retroactive to January 1, 2007.[7]

The DGIR issues the advance ruling to the taxpayer interpreting how the IRBM is to apply a proposed arrangement pursuant to the Income Tax Act 1967. The scope of the advance ruling procedure in Malaysia is narrow, limited only to the class of activities that constitute "proposed arrangements."[8] This chapter examines the scope of "proposed arrangement" factors.

As a general matter, an advance ruling is binding on the taxpayer.[9] In contrast, the DGIR can withdraw the ruling under specific circumstances.[10] The advance ruling comprises these facets:[11]

- The ruling must pertain to the circumstances that in turn pertain to the ruling provisions contained in the Income Tax Act 1967.
- The ruling must be binding on the taxpayer.
- The ruling applies only to the taxpayer's taxable year.
- The ruling applies only as to the proposed arrangement specified in the advance ruling.

BINDING NATURE OF AN ADVANCE RULING

The advance ruling does not serve as a precedent for other cases. The ruling automatically lapses if the taxpayer fails to carry out the arrangement stipulated in the ruling by the end of the ruling's time period. The ruling is subject to any qualifications stated in the ruling, but otherwise the ruling is binding on the DGIR.[12] The guidelines enumerate four situations in which the advance ruling will not be binding in the DGIR:[13]

1. The advance ruling will not be binding on the DGIR if the arrangement that the taxpayer carries out is materially different from the arrangement specified in the ruling itself. This "materially different" exclusion encompasses situations in which the transactions, as materialized, differ from the arrangement specified in the advance ruling in such a way that the provisions in the Income Tax Act 1967, as stated in the advance ruling, no longer apply to such transactions or no longer can be applicable to such transactions.[14]
2. The advance ruling will not be binding on the DGIR if the taxpayer made a material omission or misrepresentation in the application of the advance ruling or in connection with the application of the advance ruling.[15]
3. The advance ruling will not be binding on the DGIR if the DGIR made an assumption as to a future event or another matter that is material to the advance ruling where that assumption subsequently proves to be incorrect. The taxpayer should recognize that the ruling request process limits itself to assumptions stipulated in writing in the promulgation of the ruling.[16]
4. The advance ruling will not be binding on the DGIR if the DGIR stipulates conditions on the taxpayer and the taxpayer fails to satisfy any one of these stipulated conditions.[17]

The advance ruling guideline provides specific terms that apply through the guideline in various contexts.[18] The guideline defines the term "arrangement" in a broad manner to include "any scheme, contract, agreement, plan, or undertaking," whether such an arrangement is enforceable or not.[19] Such an arrangement includes all the steps and transactions that carry the arrangement into effect. The guideline requires, for the DGIR to approve the ruling, that the taxpayer propose an arrangement that the taxpayer seriously contemplates.[20] The guideline defines the term "seriously contemplated" to mean a "concerted effort" and a defined course of action, whether this action is unilateral or otherwise, to undertake the arrangement in the near future. The guideline fails to define the term "near future."

SCOPE OF THE ADVANCE RULING REQUEST

The prerequisite for requesting an advance ruling is that the issues that would be addressed in the ruling require a determination of the income tax laws. The advance ruling guideline cautions that an advance ruling request is not to seek information as to what the law already provides or a question of fact.[21] For example, an advance ruling request is not designed to render a decision as to whether a person is a resident.

The prerequisite for requesting an advance ruling is that the taxpayer "seriously contemplates" the proposed arrangement for implementation in the near future.[22] The taxpayer is precluded from requesting the advance ruling on a whim or before the taxpayer has adequate documentation concerning the transaction contemplated. The taxpayer must put forward relevant documentation as evidence to indicate that the taxpayer seriously contemplated the arrangement.

Malaysia basic income tax law itself permits a taxpayer to obtain an advance ruling, indicating how any provision in the tax law would apply to the taxpayer's proposed arrangement.[23] The DGIR will issue an advance ruling only if the taxpayer seriously contemplates the arrangement and the arrangement exists in fact.

The DGIR can provide other restrictions of the advance ruling procedure. The DGIR will not provide an advance ruling if the matter sought by the taxpayer pertains to a provision in the Income Tax Act 1967 that would authorize or require the DGIR or the Minister of Finance to undertake these activities:

- Impose a penalty, or remit a penalty
- Remit tax due and payable
- Approve an application
- Inquire as to the correctness of any tax return or of any other supplied by any person
- Prosecute any person
- Recover any debt owing by any person

CIRCUMSTANCES IN WHICH MALAYSIA TAX AUTHORITIES WILL NOT ISSUE AN ADVANCE RULING

The DGIR has no obligation to respond favorably to each advance ruling. The DGIR will reject requests to provide an advance ruling in these ten circumstances:[24]

1. The DGIR will reject requests to provide an advance ruling if the taxpayer has already effectuated the arrangement at the time that the taxpayer filed the ruling request or before the DGIR issued the advance ruling.[25] The DGIR will not issue an advance ruling for a completed transaction or a series of transactions as to an arrangement made significantly in advance.
2. The DGIR will reject requests to provide an advance ruling if the application for the advance ruling is frivolous, vexatious, or based on hypothetical situations.[26]
3. The DGIR will reject requests to provide an advance ruling if the issue raised in the advance ruling would require the DGIR to interpret foreign law. The DGIR will reject requests for an advance ruling if the issue is being dealt with or should be dealt with by the competent authorities of the tax treaty, the agreement for the avoidance of double taxation.[27]
4. The DGIR will reject requests to provide an advance ruling if an advance ruling already exists as to how the relevant portions of the Income Tax Act 1967 apply to the taxpayer and to the arrangement, and the taxpayer makes a request for an advance ruling on the same arrangement that relates to the same period or the taxable year.[28]

5. The DGIR will reject requests to provide an advance ruling if an arrangement is the subject of an audit or an investigation as to how any provision of the Income Tax Act 1967 applies to a taxpayer and that taxpayer requests an advance ruling on a similar arrangement.[29]
6. The DGIR will reject requests to provide an advance ruling if the DGIR requests that the taxpayer provide additional information, but the taxpayer fails to provide full information concerning the application to the DGIR.[30]
7. The DGIR will reject requests to provide an advance ruling if the advance ruling would require the DGIR to provide an opinion as to generally accepted accounting principles or an opinion as to commercially accepted practices.[31]
8. The DGIR will reject requests to provide an advance ruling if the matter on which the advance ruling is sought involves an advance pricing arrangement or a tax avoidance scheme.[32] The authors question whether the DGIR intends to preclude an advance pricing agreement as an "advance pricing arrangement." It appears to us that the terms "advance pricing arrangement or a tax avoidance scheme" refer to nefarious activities rather than to an attempt to avoid double taxation.
9. The DGIR will reject requests to provide an advance ruling if the matter is prospective, addressing proposed legislation (i.e., an interpretation of a provision in the Income Tax Act 1967 that has not been enacted).[33] For example, the DGIR will reject requests for an advance ruling if a provision addresses budget proposals, or addresses rules or regulations that the government has not enacted. Nevertheless, a taxpayer may seek a written technical confirmation from the DGIR, a procedure separate from the advance ruling guideline, in the case of those rules or regulations.
10. The DGIR will reject requests to provide an advance ruling if in the matter, in the DGIR's opinion, it would be unreasonable for the DGIR to make an advance ruling in view of the resources available to the DGIR.[34] Such a situation can occur, for example, if the request for an advance ruling pertains to a highly technical and sophisticated arrangement or to a technology or product to which the DGIR is not yet familiar.

CIRCUMSTANCES IN WHICH THE DGIR CAN DECLINE TO ISSUE AN ADVANCE RULING

In addition to the preceding ten situations in which the DGIR will reject requests to provide an advance ruling, the DGIR may generally decline an application for an advance ruling in these four circumstances:[35]

1. The DGIR may generally decline requests to provide an advance ruling if the matter on which the taxpayer requests an advance ruling is purely a question of fact.[36] Such a "purely a question of fact" situation can arise, for example, as to the determination of the commencement date of a housing developer's project.
2. The DGIR may generally decline requests to provide an advance ruling if the correctness of the advance ruling would depend on the making of assumptions, whether these assumptions pertain to a future event or to any other matter.[37]

3. The DGIR may generally decline requests to provide an advance ruling if the matter on which the ruling is sought is the subject of an appeal, whether this appeal is in relation to the taxpayer or to any other person.[38]
4. The DGIR may generally decline requests to provide an advance ruling if the taxpayer has outstanding debts to the DGIR pertaining to prior advance ruling applications.[39]

NOTICE REQUIREMENTS

The DGIR has the power to decline to make an advance ruling or not make an advance ruling. In such a case, the DGIR is to notify the applicant in writing at the earliest possible time. The DGIR is to provide the reasons why the DGIR did not make an advance ruling or declined to make an advance ruling.[40]

ADVANCE RULING APPLICATION PROCEDURE

The advance ruling application procedure addresses these specific processes:[41]

- Eligible parties
- Application
- Information requirements
- Applicant's withdrawal of an advance ruling request

As a general matter, any person may apply for an advance ruling as to how a provision of the Income Tax Act 1967 would apply to the person, or the prospective person, as the case may be.[42] In general, any person may apply for an advance ruling as to any particular arrangement that falls under the purview of the advance ruling. The advance ruling process is available to both companies already in existence and companies that are not yet in existence, but the application process differs between them to some extent.

A taxpayer that is already in existence must apply for the advance ruling on its own behalf.[43] For example, the taxpayer includes a company that has already been incorporated in Malaysia. The taxpayer, at its option, *may* employ the services of an approved tax agent or a certified revenue lawyer, both of whom practice their profession in Malaysia. Such an approved tax agent or a certified revenue lawyer can complete the advance ruling application form and prepare the advance ruling application for submission to the DGIR on behalf of the client. The person responsible for the advance ruling application form must sign the form. The responsible person includes, by way of example, a company director or a partner in a partnership. Note that this process is optional on the part of a business incorporated in Malaysia but mandatory on the part of the foreign enterprise.

Two or more persons can jointly make an advance ruling application. The joint application, by way of example, includes a group of companies in the same group, and includes partners in a partnership.[44] The "person responsible" for each participant to the joint ruling application must sign the return before the entity submits its return to the DGIR.

Two scenarios limit the taxpayer's application for the advance ruling:

1. A taxpayer might not be in existence at the time the taxpayer files an advance ruling request with the DGIR.
2. The entity might be foreign.

In either of these two scenarios, the representative of the taxpayer must be an approved tax agent or a certified revenue lawyer where such person practices its profession in Malaysia.[45] A representative acting on behalf of the taxpayer must forward a letter of authority that authorizes the representative to act on the taxpayer's behalf. The representative must fill out the details in the application.

ADVANCE RULING APPLICATION FORM

The taxpayer applying for an advance ruling must furnish the next information to the DGIR:[46]

- A complete description as to all facts relevant to the arrangement.[47] This description includes all of the taxpayer's factual assumptions in regard to the arrangement and includes the names, addresses, business activities, and other relevant particulars as to all parties to the arrangement.
- The tax issues that the taxpayer requests the DGIR consider.[48]
- The provisions under the Income Tax Act 1967 that relate to the following in the advance ruling application, that is:[49]
  - the appropriate case law
  - published commentaries, if any, and
  - legal reasons that support the taxpayer's interpretation of the applicable sections
- Information that states the stance or opinion on the tax treatment that should be accorded to the proposed arrangement for which the advance ruling is sought. The taxpayer should identify the relevant provisions in the Income Tax Act 1967 that are applicable.[50]
- Information that provides the commercial or reasons for the arrangement, if applicable.[51]
- Copies of all documents, identifying all the relevant parts or passages.[52]
- Information as to the taxable years to which the advance ruling application relates.[53]
- A statement to the DGIR identifying whether the applicant has made a previous advance ruling request on the same or a similar arrangement.[54] If the applicant made such an advance ruling, the applicant is to state the advance ruling application and the reference number of the advance ruling issued by the IRBM.

INFORMATION REQUEST REQUIREMENT

The DGIR needs to receive sufficient information from the applicant to complete its review in granting an advance ruling. The DGIR has the right to request further relevant information or to carry out an on-site inspection in instances where the applicant provided insufficient information.[55] The DGIR also has the right to waive any requirements it would otherwise need in filling out the application. The DGIR can waive these requirements if it is the DGIR's opinion that it would be unreasonable to request information for which the applicant has no means of providing or information for which the applicant has no access.[56]

A person who has submitted an advance ruling application can withdraw the application before the DGIR issues its advance ruling. A person seeking to withdraw its advance ruling application can do so by forwarding such a notice to the DGIR in writing.[57] A person who withdraws its application for an advance ruling remains liable to pay all fees incurred up to the time the DGIR receives a notice of withdrawal.[58] A person seeking to withdraw its advance ruling application must acknowledge this requirement in filing the withdrawal request.[59]

ISSUANCE OF THE ADVANCE RULING

The guideline on advance rulings provides that the DGIR is to notify the applicant for the advance ruling that the DGIR has in fact issued such a ruling. In addition, the DGIR is to notify the applicant as to the additional fees the applicant must pay in relation to the advance ruling. The DGIR will issue the advance ruling to the applicant only when the applicant pays all fees payable.[60]

The guideline on advance rulings provides that the DGIR will issue an advance ruling to the applicant that specifies:[61]

- That it is issued pursuant to section 138B of the Income Tax Act 1967[62]
- The identity of the persons requesting the ruling, the applicable provisions within the Income Tax Act 1967 subject to the advance ruling, and the arrangement sought by the applicant[63]
- How the provision in the Income Tax Act 1967 applies to the person requesting the ruling and to the arrangement sought by the applicant[64]
- The number of taxable years for which the advance ruling applies[65]
- The material assumptions the DGIR makes about a future event or other matters[66]
- The conditions, if any, that the DGIR imposes[67]

The DGIR, in developing the advance ruling, might request additional information from the applicant. The DGIR, at its option, can issue an advance ruling based on assumptions it makes if the applicant cannot provide the necessary information. The DGIR is to make such assumptions that are appropriate, but the DGIR can decline to make an advance ruling if the applicant provides insufficient information.[68]

The advance ruling process expects that the applicant and the IRBM will undertake prior consultations. The purpose of the collaborative process is to clarify that the applicant provides an advance ruling application.[69] The IRBM is not obligated to disclose the decisions it makes within the applicant's advance ruling process at any time before the DGIR issues the advance ruling.

The recipient of an advance ruling may apply in writing to extend the application of the ruling beyond the taxable year indicated in the advance ruling.[70] The taxpayer must file a request to extend the period for which the advance ruling is applicable, doing so within three months prior to the end of the period or taxable year specified in the advance ruling or at any other period the DGIR approves. The arrangement might be essentially the same as the arrangement specified in the advance ruling. In the event that the arrangement is essentially the same, the applicant may request to the DGIR that it apply the same interpretation of the Income Tax Act 1967 prospectively to another period or to another taxable year.

The guideline on advance rulings contains an exculpation clause for typographical errors and/or other minor errors. Such errors, if they were to occur in the DGIR's advance ruling issued to the applicant, do not adversely affect the advance ruling or make the advance ruling void if these errors do not in any way alter the way the provision of the Income Tax Act 1967 applies in the advance ruling.[71]

A taxpayer that files an advance ruling application is still obligated to comply with the obligations under the Income Tax Act 1967. For example, the taxpayer is obligated to file its tax return within the stipulated tax frame for compliance before the taxpayer filed its advance ruling application.[72] The DGIR's issuance of an advance ruling to an applicant does not change any powers the DGIR has to make or amend tax assessments under the Income Tax Act 1967.

ADVANCE RULING FINALITY AND DISCLOSURE

When the DGIR issues an advance ruling, that advance ruling is final. The advance ruling is final, whether it is applicable to the taxpayer or not. The DGIR will not entertain any correspondence or inquiry after it issues the advance ruling.[73] The taxpayer cannot appeal the ruling. However, the taxpayer has the choice not to carry out the proposed arrangement if an advance ruling is disadvantageous to the taxpayer. The taxpayer must comply with the advance ruling if the taxpayer chooses to effectuate the proposed arrangement. Although the advance ruling is final, the taxpayer can object to the tax treatment under the normal Income Tax Act 1967 procedures.[74]

A taxpayer that receives an advance ruling has an obligation to disclose the following information in the preparation of its annual tax return:[75]

- The existence of an advance ruling[76]
- Whether the taxpayer has complied with the advance ruling or not[77]
- Whether the taxpayer made material changes to the arrangement made in the advance ruling[78]

The advance ruling guideline fails to address certain timing issues. For example, the disclosure provisions fail to address issues such as the fact that the taxpayer must reflect the existence of the ruling in the taxable year in which the DGIR issues the ruling, but the provision does not indicate whether the taxpayer must reflect advance rulings in prior years. The DGIR can enforce the disclosure provision by penalties that it can impose for noncompliance with the advance ruling.

THE DGIR CAN WITHDRAW THE ADVANCE RULING

The DGIR retains the right to withdraw an advance ruling at a time after it issues the ruling to the applicant. The DGIR can withdraw the advance ruling request because of changes in the tax laws based on differing court decisions.[79] Nevertheless, the withdrawal provisions are open-ended, permitting the taxpayer to withdraw the request under a wide variety of circumstances independent of court decisions.

The DGIR is to effectuate the withdrawal of an advance ruling issued to an applicant by means of issuing a notice of withdrawal to the applicant. The DGIR is prohibited from withdrawing the advance ruling on a prospective basis and beyond a date at which the taxpayer is reasonably expected to receive a notice of withdrawal.[80]

A taxpayer might have effectuated the arrangement provided for in the advance ruling before the DGIR withdraws the ruling. In the event that the taxpayer has proceeded accordingly, the taxpayer can follow the advance ruling until the end of the period stated in the ruling. However, the taxpayer might not have effectuated the arrangement at the time that the DGIR issues the taxpayer a notice of withdrawal. The arrangement then is prospective, and the taxpayer cannot obtain a tax advantage from the advance ruling.[81] The proceeding withdrawal process enables an applicant that undertakes an arrangement in reliance of an advance ruling may bind the DGIR for the reminder of the period. However, the DGIR will not be bound by the advance ruling if the DGIR withdraws an advance ruling before the applicant enters into the arrangement.

SITUATIONS IN WHICH THE ADVANCE RULING CEASES TO APPLY

When the DGIR issues an advance ruling to an applicant, this ruling will be binding on the applicant and on the DGIR,[82] subject to the provisions subject to the binding nature of an advance ruling[83] and the withdrawal of an advance ruling by the DGIR.[84] An advance ruling ceases to apply in situations in which any provision of the Income Tax Act 1967 repeals or amends the subject of the ruling. This cessation takes place if the repeal or amendment of that provision in the Income Tax Act 1967 alters the way in which the tax law applies. The cessation of the advance ruling takes place from the date of repeal or the amendment becomes effective.

FEE STRUCTURE

An applicant must pay a fee to secure an advance ruling from the DGIR. The fees will be based on each applicant's requesting an advance ruling, including for each applicant requesting the advance ruling.[85] The DGIR imposes these fees on the applicant as a debt due to the government of Malaysia.

The fee structure begins with an application fee of RM500 ($150 USD) upon application and is nonrefundable. This fee takes into account the amount of time the DGIR would need to accede to the request.[86] In addition, the DGIR imposes a further fee of RM150 ($45) per hour or part thereof after the first four hours, including the time that DGIR spends in consulting with the applicant.[87] Moreover, the taxpayer must reimburse the DGIR for its professional advice the DGIR obtains with consent of the applicant[88] and for any other reasonable costs the DGIR incurs.[89] In any event, the DGIR will at all times ensure that it makes every effort to minimize the fees payable.

An applicant that withdraws its application for an advance ruling remains liable for all fees incurred on behalf of the applicant up to the time in which the applicant receives a letter from the DGIR acknowledging the withdrawal.[90] The DGIR may waive any fees payable by an applicant for an advance ruling request, except for the nonrefundable application fee of RM500.[91] The DGIR can provide the waiver at its own discretion.

INTERNAL PROCEDURE

The DGIR will normally address an advance ruling request in the order in which the request is received. The DGIR intends that it will issue the advance ruling within a stipulated time frame of 60 days from the date the applicant submits the application. The DGIR expects to meet this 60-day time period provided the applicant submits the relevant information together with the request and that the DGIR does not need further consultations with the applicant.[92] The DGIR is to advise the applicant if any unusual delay is foreseen.

All information in the advance ruling is confidential. The DGIR will not publish the advance ruling in any form.[93] There may be situations in which there are similarities of common concern including the applicant and other taxpayers. The DGIR may produce a public ruling to address these issues in the event that there are issues of common concern.

NOTES

1. LHDN.01/35/42/51/122/3, February 14, 2008.
2. Guideline on Advance Rulings, section 1.
3. Guideline on Advance Rulings, section 10.4; Guideline on Advance Rulings, section 1.
4. Guideline on Advance Rulings, section 1.
5. Guideline on Advance Rulings, section 2.1.
6. Guideline on Advance Rulings, section 2.2.

7. Guideline on Advance Rulings, section 1, section 2.3.
8. Guideline on Advance Rulings, section 5.2, section 6.2.
9. Guideline on Advance Rulings, section 4.1.
10. Guideline on Advance Rulings, section 13.
11. Guideline on Advance Rulings, section 1.
12. Guideline on Advance Rulings, section 4.1.
13. Guideline on Advance Rulings, section 4.2.
14. Guideline on Advance Rulings, section 4.2a.
15. Guideline on Advance Rulings, section 4.2b.
16. Guideline on Advance Rulings, section 4.2c.
17. Guideline on Advance Rulings, section 4.2d.
18. Guideline on Advance Rulings, section 5.
19. Guideline on Advance Rulings, section 5.1.
20. Guideline on Advance Rulings, section 5.2.
21. Guideline on Advance Rulings, section 6.1.
22. Guideline on Advance Rulings, section 6.2.
23. Income Tax Act 1967, section 138B; Guideline on Advance Rulings, section 6.3.
24. Guideline on Advance Rulings, section 7.
25. Guideline on Advance Rulings, section 7a.
26. Guideline on Advance Rulings, section 7b.
27. Guideline on Advance Rulings, section 7c.
28. Guideline on Advance Rulings, section 7d.
29. Guideline on Advance Rulings, section 7e.
30. Guideline on Advance Rulings, section 7f.
31. Guideline on Advance Rulings, section 7g.
32. Guideline on Advance Rulings, section 7h.
33. Guideline on Advance Rulings, section 7i.
34. Guideline on Advance Rulings, section 7j.
35. Guideline on Advance Rulings, section 8.
36. Guideline on Advance Rulings, section 8a.
37. Guideline on Advance Rulings, section 8b.
38. Guideline on Advance Rulings, section 8c.
39. Guideline on Advance Rulings, section 8d.
40. Guideline on Advance Rulings, section 9.
41. Guideline on Advance Rulings, section 10.
42. Guideline on Advance Rulings, section 10.1.
43. Guideline on Advance Rulings, section 10.2.
44. Guideline on Advance Rulings, section 10.3.
45. Guideline on Advance Rulings, section 10.4.
46. Guideline on Advance Rulings, section 10.5.
47. Guideline on Advance Rulings, section 10.5a.
48. Guideline on Advance Rulings, section 10.5b.
49. Guideline on Advance Rulings, section 10.5c.
50. Guideline on Advance Rulings, section 10.5d.
51. Guideline on Advance Rulings, section 10.5e.
52. Guideline on Advance Rulings, section 10.5f.
53. Guideline on Advance Rulings, section 10.5g.

54. Guideline on Advance Rulings, section 10.5h.
55. Guideline on Advance Rulings, section 10.6.
56. Guideline on Advance Rulings, section 10.7.
57. Guideline on Advance Rulings, section 10.8.
58. Guideline on Advance Rulings, section 15.2.
59. Guideline on Advance Rulings, section 10.8.
60. Guideline on Advance Rulings, section 11.1.
61. Guideline on Advance Rulings, section 11.2.
62. Guideline on Advance Rulings, section 11.2a.
63. Guideline on Advance Rulings, section 11.2b.
64. Guideline on Advance Rulings, section 11.2c.
65. Guideline on Advance Rulings, section 11.2d.
66. Guideline on Advance Rulings, section 11.2e.
67. Guideline on Advance Rulings, section 11.2f.
68. Guideline on Advance Rulings, section 11.3.
69. Guideline on Advance Rulings, section 11.4.
70. Guideline on Advance Rulings, section 11.5.
71. Guideline on Advance Rulings, section 11.6.
72. Guideline on Advance Rulings, section 11.7.
73. Guideline on Advance Rulings, section 12.1.
74. Income Tax Act 1967, section 99.
75. Guideline on Advance Rulings, section 12.2.
76. Guideline on Advance Rulings, section 12.2a.
77. Guideline on Advance Rulings, section 12.2b.
78. Guideline on Advance Rulings, section 12.2c.
79. Guideline on Advance Rulings, section 13.1.
80. Guideline on Advance Rulings, section 13.2.
81. Guideline on Advance Rulings, section 13.3.
82. Guideline on Advance Rulings, section 14.
83. Guideline on Advance Rulings, section 4.
84. Guideline on Advance Rulings, section 13.
85. Guideline on Advance Rulings, section 15.1.
86. Guideline on Advance Rulings, section 15.1a.
87. Guideline on Advance Rulings, section 15.1b.
88. Guideline on Advance Rulings, section 15.1ci.
89. Guideline on Advance Rulings, section 15.1cii.
90. Guideline on Advance Rulings, section 15.2.
91. Guideline on Advance Rulings, section 15.3.
92. Guideline on Advance Rulings, section 16.
93. Guideline on Advance Rulings, section 17.

21

CHAPTER TWENTY-ONE

Malaysia Transfer Pricing Guidelines

THE GOVERNMENT of Malaysia adopted its Transfer Pricing Guidelines on July 2, 2003.[1] These transfer pricing parameters loosely follow the Organisation for Economic Co-operation and Development (OECD), *Transfer Pricing Guidelines for Multinational Enterprises and Tax Administrations* but provide innovative examples and other guidance. This guidance specifically addresses foreign-based multinationals in the Malaysian context. We also examine Malaysia's advance ruling process effectively promulgated January 1, 2007, the specific advance rulings guideline procedure promulgated on February 14, 2008, and the limitations on that advance ruling process from a transfer pricing standpoint.

INTRODUCTORY PROVISIONS

Transfer pricing in Malaysia generally pertains to the pricing of cross-border transfers of goods, services, and intangibles.[2] The Malaysia Transfer Pricing Guidelines address leasing only in passing; they fail to address intercompany loans and borrowing. The guidelines themselves are 31 pages in length. The Malaysia Transfer Pricing Guidelines, while acknowledging that transfer pricing can apply to transactions between associated enterprises within the same country, address only transactions between associated enterprises within a multinational business where one enterprise is subject to tax in Malaysia and the other enterprise is located overseas.[3]

The Malaysia Transfer Pricing Guidelines would apply to the taxpayer by analogy as to transactions between a permanent establishment (PE) and to the company's head office or other related branches. The guidelines hypothetically treat the PE as a distinct and separate enterprise (i.e., an entity separate from its head office or other related branches).[4]

The Malaysia Transfer Pricing Guidelines provide a discussion of the arm's length principle, the concept of comparability, and the factors that determine comparability. The guidelines provide special considerations for intangible property and for intragroup services. Nevertheless, the guidelines expend half its time examining arm's length methodologies.

MALAYSIAN TRANSFER PRICING PROCEDURE

The audit division of Malaysia's Inland Revenue Board is responsible for the Transfer Pricing Guidelines. As a general matter, the Malaysian tax law[5] empowers the Director General to disregard transactions where the Director General believes these transactions have the direct or indirect effect of altering the taxpayer's tax incidence.[6] Malaysian tax law gives broad powers to the Director General:

- The Director General can alter the taxpayer's tax incidence as the Director General sees fit to counteract the effects of these transactions.
- The Director General has the power to disregard transactions where the Director General believes that these transactions were not at arm's length.[7]
- The Director General can invoke transfer pricing provisions in the above-mentioned situations.
- The Director General can make necessary adjustments to revise the liability or impose the tax liability on the persons concerned.

Non–arm's length dealings include transactions between persons one of whom has control over the other. In addition, non–arm's length dealings include transactions between persons both of whom are controlled by some other person.[8] "Control" refers to both direct control and indirect control.[9] The Malaysian income tax statute interprets the terms "related companies" and "related company" as "companies in the same group," doing so initially in the contexts of holding companies and subsidiary companies.[10] The Malaysia Transfer Pricing Guidelines provide that two enterprises are associated enterprises with respect to each other if:[11]

- One of the enterprises participates directly or indirectly in the management, control, or capital of the enterprise, or
- The same persons participate directly or indirectly in the management, control, or capital of the enterprise.

APPLICATION OF THE ARM'S LENGTH PRINCIPLE

As a general principle, the Malaysian Transfer Pricing Guidelines state that, ideally, transfer pricing should not differ from the prevailing market price. When business dealings take place between connected persons, these dealings might not always reflect the dynamics of market forces as would be expected if such transactions were carried out by independent enterprises.[12]

The Inland Revenue Board of Malaysia (IRBM), similar to other tax administrators, has the duty to ensure the multinational taxpayer adopts reasonable transfer pricing methodologies. IRBM's overriding goal is to make sure that the Malaysian subsidiaries are paying their fair share of tax. The Malaysian taxpayer must be able to provide adequate documented proof to the IRBM to support its transfer pricing policies.[13] The Malaysian Transfer Pricing Guidelines, promulgated in 2003, view multinational corporations as having offshore headquarters rather than having a Malaysian base. Given the advances in the Malaysian economy, these provisions may prove to be self-limiting.

The Malaysian Transfer Pricing Guidelines seek to provide all multinational businesses with this information:[14]

- Information concerning Malaysian legislation
- Transfer pricing methodologies that the IRBM would accept
- Administrative regulations, including the types or records or documentation that the IRBM expects from taxpayers involved in transfer pricing arrangements

MALAYSIA'S TRANSFER PRICING REGIME

The Malaysian Transfer Pricing Guidelines, unlike the United States transfer pricing regime, do not require the taxpayer to select the best transfer pricing method. Instead, the Malaysian Transfer Pricing Guidelines permit the taxpayer to select from various transfer pricing methodologies, doing so "with the ultimate aim of arriving at an arm's length transfer price."[15] The IRBM intends that the Malaysian Transfer Pricing Guidelines, which the IRBM reviews from time to time, will assist multinational taxpayers in meeting two objectives at the same time:

1. To assist multinational taxpayers in their efforts to determine transfer prices that are consistent with the arm's length principle and, at the same time
2. To comply with Malaysian tax laws and IRBM administrative requirements

The IRBM can adjust the taxpayer's transactions regarding:[16]

- The sale, purchase, or lease of tangible assets
- The provision of services
- The transfer, purchase, or use of intangible assets

- The lending and borrowing of money
- Other transactions that affect the enterprise's profit or loss

As a general matter, the governing standard of the Malaysian Transfer Pricing Guidelines is the OECD *Transfer Pricing Guidelines*.[17] The OECD guidelines rely on the arm's length principle. The Malaysian Transfer Pricing Guidelines contain methodologies and supporting rationale based on the OECD's arm's length principle.

The Malaysian Transfer Pricing Guidelines contain examples that are strictly for illustrative purposes.[18] The taxpayer must examine the facts and circumstances of each case before deciding on the applicability of the transfer pricing methods described.

The IRBM has adopted the arm's length transfer pricing approach, which is internationally accepted as the preferred basis for determining the transfer price of a transaction between associated parties.[19] The IRBM's acceptance of the arm's length approach is consistent with its objective of minimizing the possibility of double taxation.

As a definitional matter, the "arm's length price" is the price that the taxpayer would determine if such transactions were made between independent entities under the same or similar circumstances. A transfer price is acceptable under the arm's length principle if all transactions between related parties are at arm's length.

A taxpayer, in applying the arm's length principle to a multinational corporation, should focus its attention on the nature of the transactions between two associated entities and dealings between a PE and its head office. The transfer pricing process treats each member of an affiliated group as if it were a separate entity rather than as an inseparable part of a single unified business.

COMPARABILITY AND TRANSFER PRICING

The Malaysian Transfer Pricing Guidelines specify that the taxpayer must undertake a comparability analysis as a prerequisite in applying all transfer pricing methodologies that conform to the arm's length principle.[20] This comparability analysis involves comparing conditions in a controlled transaction with those transactions that take place between independent parties. The IRBM deems transactions to be comparable if there are no material differences between the transactions being compared or, alternatively, if the taxpayer can make reasonably accurate adjustments to eliminate any differences that take place as to the transactions.

These factors are the focus in a comparability analysis:[21]

- Circumstances surrounding the commercial and financial relations between associated enterprises
- Processes involved
- Economic performance, such as profits and margins
- Factors that influence the economic performance

The taxpayer must undertake a comparability analysis even when dealing with sophisticated products or with high-tech products, such as computer software, or where the activities involve consultancy services or engineering services. The guidelines specifically address the factors that a taxpayer should consider in a comparability analysis.

Comparability Factors

The Malaysian Transfer Pricing Guidelines specify that the taxpayer is to compare prices or is to compare profit margins. The taxpayer is to make this comparison between controlled transactions and uncontrolled transactions.[22] The similarity of product characteristics is more relevant in comparing prices than it is in comparing profit margins. The taxpayer, in applying the comparable uncontrolled price (CUP) method, compares product characteristics. The taxpayer makes this physical comparison more in this instance than it does for other transfer pricing methods. The taxpayer can compare these characteristics:

- Physical characteristics, including physical features, quality, and the volume of property supplied[23]
- Nature and extent of the services it provides[24]
- Form of the transaction and type of property the taxpayer provides in the case of intangible property[25]

Functional Analysis

The taxpayer must undertake a functional analysis in determining the comparability of its transactions.[26] Functional analysis involves the determination as to how the business is to divide up its functions, assets (including tangible property), and risks. The division impacts the parties involved in the transaction under review.

The taxpayer, in undertaking the functional analysis, is to compare specific functions. Those functions include product design, manufacturing, marketing, advertising, and research and development. The taxpayer, in comparing such functions, is to consider the:

- Assets employed, such as plant and machinery
- Nature of such assets employed, such as age and market value
- Use of intangibles

The taxpayer must consider a variety of risks, such as:

- Market risks
- Financial risks, including exchange risks
- Risks associated with the success or failure of the research and development that the multinational enterprise undertakes

The Malaysian Transfer Pricing Guidelines warn that a functional analysis itself does not determine the arm's length result of a controlled transaction; instead, the functional analysis itself should form the basis upon which the taxpayer is to identify comparables.

The Malaysian Transfer Pricing Guidelines provides that the taxpayer should analyze contractual terms as part of its functional analysis.[27] The contractual agreement would normally define the allocation of responsibilities, risks, and benefits between enterprises. A transaction's terms and conditions might influence the price of the transfer or the margin, including, among other things:

- Credit or payment terms
- Volume of sales or purchases
- Warranty terms

A comparability study should take into account how in practice the conduct of the associated parties conforms to the terms of the contract. The study should ascertain how the terms and conditions would influence transactions made between independent enterprises.

The taxpayer is to take economic circumstances into account where these economic circumstances will affect prices charged or profits earned in controlled transactions and in uncontrolled transactions.[28] Such economic circumstances include:

- Geographic location of the market
- Size of the market
- Availability of substitute goods and services
- Extent of governmental intervention (i.e., whether the government controls the goods being compared)
- Timing of the transactions

The taxpayer is to take business strategies into account in determining comparability. Such business strategies include:[29]

- Innovation and new product development
- Degree of diversification
- Market penetration strategies
- Selection of distribution channels
- Market level
- Location

The taxpayer, in making this comparability analysis, may need to consider whether independent enterprises in the same circumstances would have adopted the same strategies. The taxpayer would then evaluate what awards would be expected from this behavior.

TRANSFER PRICING ALTERNATIVES

The Malaysian Transfer Pricing Guidelines permit the taxpayer to select from two transfer pricing alternatives:[30] traditional transfer pricing methods and other transfer pricing methods, also called transactional profit methods. The traditional transfer pricing methods comprise the CUP method, the resale price method, and the cost plus method. Other transfer pricing methods include the profit split method and the transactional net margin method (TNMM).

The Malaysian Transfer Pricing Guidelines reiterate that the taxpayer has the right to choose any transfer pricing method or any combination of the methods. The Malaysian Transfer Pricing Guidelines do warn, however, that the taxpayer's emphasis in selecting the transfer pricing method should be on arriving at an arm's length price. Accordingly, the Malaysian Transfer Pricing Guidelines, similar to the OECD guidelines, provide that the taxpayer is to use transactional profit methods only when the taxpayer cannot reliably apply traditional transfer pricing methods or when the taxpayer cannot apply traditional transfer pricing methods at all.

As a general matter, the Malaysian Transfer Pricing Guidelines indicate that the IRBM prefers taxpayers to select a transfer pricing method that requires the fewest adjustments. Such a method should provide the most reliable measure of an arm's length result and should reduce the scope and nature of future disputes. The selection of the transfer pricing method depends heavily on the availability of data. The Malaysian Transfer Pricing Guidelines request taxpayers to consider in selecting the "most appropriate [transfer pricing] method":

- The degree of "actual comparability" when the taxpayer makes comparisons with transactions between independent parties
- The completeness and accuracy of the data as to the uncontrolled transaction
- The reliability of the assumptions the taxpayer makes
- The data might be inaccurate or the assumptions might be incorrect (The issue becomes the extent to which the adjustments are affected.)

COMPARABLE UNCONTROLLED PRICE TRANSFER PRICING METHOD

The Malaysian Transfer Pricing Guidelines provide that the CUP method is ideal only if:[31]

- Comparable products are available.
- The taxpayer can make reasonably accurate adjustments to eliminate material product differences.

The CUP method involves the direct price comparison for a transaction of a similar product between two independent parties.[32] The CUP method is the most direct way of ascertaining the arm's length price. The Malaysian Transfer Pricing Guidelines warn that the taxpayer will have to consider other transfer pricing methods if the taxpayer cannot adjust material product differences to give the taxpayer a reliable measure of an arm's length result.[33]

The taxpayer contemplating the use of the CUP transfer pricing method is to undertake a comparability analysis.[34] As a general matter, an uncontrolled transaction is comparable to a controlled transaction for purposes of the CUP method if the taxpayer meets one of these two conditions:[35]

1. There are no differences between the transactions being compared, or between the enterprises undertaking these transactions, or these differences could not materially affect the price in open market.[36]
2. The taxpayer can make reasonably accurate adjustments to eliminate the effects of these differences.[37]

A multinational corporation can use the CUP method to determine its transfer price by using this process:[38]

1. The multinational taxpayer must first identify all of the differences between its product and the independent manufacturer's product.
2. The multinational taxpayer then determines whether these differences have a material effect on price.
3. The multinational taxpayer adjusts the price of products the independent manufacturer sells to reflect these differences and arrive at an arm's length price.

The taxpayer, in undertaking a comparability analysis under the CUP method, should undertake the following facets:

- The taxpayer needs to consider product characteristics, such as the physical features of the product and the quality of the product.
- Is the product in the form of services? In that event, the taxpayer is to provide the nature and extent of such services.
- Is the product sold? In that event, the taxpayer is to compare the product at the same points in the production chain.
- The taxpayer needs to consider product differentiation, which takes place in the form of patented features, such as trademarks, design, and so forth.
- The volume of the sales might impact the amount charged. In that event, the taxpayer is to take sales volume into account.
- Seasonal fluctuations and other changes in market conditions might impact the timing of the sale. In that event, the taxpayer is to take into account these seasonal fluctuations and other changes in market conditions.
- The taxpayer should take into account whether the costs of transport, packaging, marketing, advertising, and warranty are included in the deal.
- The taxpayer should take into account whether the economic conditions are the same in which the taxpayer sells its products.

COMPARABLE UNCONTROLLED COST TRANSFER PRICING EXAMPLE

Company A, a multinational corporation, sells its product to two customers:

- Company A sells 70% of its product to an overseas associated company, Company B, at price of 100 per unit.
- Company A sells 30% of its product to a local independent enterprise, Company C, at a price of 150 per unit.

Company A's products are the same, whether the product is sold to Company B or to Company C. Company A can consider the sales to Company C as being a comparable uncontrolled transaction. Company A must undertake a functional analysis of Company B and Company C to determine any differences that might exist. Company A will need to adjust for these differences if they exist.

Company A will need to make adjustments to account for market conditions since Company B and Company C are located in different countries. Company A will need to make adjustments to account for product quality discounts since the sales volume to Company B and Company C are not the same. For example, Company A can apply the CUP method using the unit price of 150 as a comparable arm's length price assuming Company A can make reasonably accurate adjustments to eliminate the material effects of these differences. ■

RESALE PRICE TRANSFER PRICING METHOD

The Malaysian Transfer Pricing Guidelines provide that the resale price transfer pricing method is the most appropriate transfer pricing method when the company's final transaction in the distribution chain is with an independent distributor.[39] The utility of the resale price method depends on how much the company added to value or the extent of the reseller's alteration before the product is resold or the time lapse between the time the company purchases the product and its outward sale. The resale price method is more difficult for the taxpayer to apply if:

- The product has gone through a number of processes and the time lapse is too long, causing market conditions to have changed before the company sells the product
- The reseller contributes substantially to the creation of an intangible property or the maintenance of an intangible property that is attached to the product

The beginning point in determining the resale price method is the price at which a company purchases the product from an associated enterprise and then the company resells the product to an independent enterprise.[40] The company, in determining the resale price, is to reduce from the resale amount an appropriate gross margin (i.e., the resale price margin). The appropriate gross margin is the amount from which the reseller would seek to recover its selling expenses and other operating expenses. The taxpayer, in determining its appropriate gross margin, is to do so in light of the functions it performs, taking into account the assets it uses and the risks it assumes to make an appropriate profit. The taxpayer is to obtain the arm's length price for the original transaction between associated enterprises by subtracting that gross margin and by adjusting other costs associated with the product, such as customs duties.

A taxpayer can reflect a resale price adjustment in this manner: The arm's length price is the resale price less the resale price multiplied by the resale price margin. The resale price margin is the sales price less the purchase price, all divided by the sales price. The resale price margin must be comparable to margins earned by other interdependent enterprises performing similar functions, bearing similar risks, and employing similar assets.

The focus of the resale price method is the resale price margin. The taxpayer should establish its resale price margin from comparable transactions between the reseller involved in the controlled transaction and other independent parties. If those transactions do not exist, the taxpayer can determine the resale price margin from the sales of other resellers in the same market. The taxpayer can expect the resale price method to vary according to the reseller's value added. The contribution to value added depends on the reseller's level of activities.

A taxpayer, in undertaking a comparability analysis as to the resale transfer pricing method, is to view an uncontrolled transaction as being comparable if the taxpayer meets one of these two conditions:[41]

1. There are differences in the transactions being compared, or, alternatively, if these differences do exist, the differences do not materially affect the resale price margin in the open market.[42]
2. The taxpayer can make reasonable adjustments to eliminate the material effects of these differences.[43]

The next factors might influence the resale price margin when the taxpayer conducts the comparability analysis:[44]

- The taxpayer should seek to ascertain the functions that the reseller performs or the activities the reseller performs, together with the risks the reseller undertakes. For example, the taxpayer should seek to ascertain whether the reseller is merely a forwarding agent or, in contrast, is a distributor who assumes full responsibility for advertising the product by risking its own resources in these activities.[45]
- The taxpayer should seek to ascertain how the reseller employs similar assets in controlled transactions and in uncontrolled transactions through a developed distribution network.[46]
- The resale price method allows broader product differences than does the CUP method. Nevertheless, product similarities are still significant to some extent, particularly when the taxpayer assigns a high value or unique intangibles to the product.[47]

- The taxpayer, in applying the resale price margin, might use an independent enterprise in a comparable transaction. If the taxpayer uses such a comparable transaction, the taxpayer should take into account differences in the way the business is managed as an indicia of profitability.[48]
- There might be a time lapse between the original purchase of the product and the resale of the product. A longer time lapse may give rise to changes in the market, exchange rates, cost, and so forth.[49]
- The resale price might depend on whether the manufacturer gives the reseller exclusive rights to resell the products.[50]
- The taxpayer might need to take accounting practices into account to ensure that the cost components are the same in arriving at the same gross margins for controlled transactions as for uncontrolled transactions.[51]

RESALE COST TRANSFER PRICING EXAMPLE

Taxpayer A is a multinational corporation that is not located in Malaysia. Taxpayer A has two distributors:

- Taxpayer A distributes its products to B, a distributor reseller and A's subsidiary in Malaysia.
- Taxpayer A distributes its products to D, a distributor reseller in Malaysia.

The products that A sells to D are lesser in quality than the products that A sells to B. Taxpayer A undertakes a functional analysis and finds that Company B and Company D perform the same functions, and both are resellers in the same market. Although there are quality product differences between the products that B sells compared with products that D sells, the differences in margins are not material even though a comparison based on price would be material.

A sells its products to B for 7.6 per unit. B sells the product to C, an independent party, for 8.0 per unit, so that B has a total income of 0.4 per unit. A has a gross profit ratio of 10% in its sales to D. A must adjust its selling price to B to reflect the same margin A used in its sales to D (i.e., 10%). A's arm's length resale cost amount to B is 7.2 per unit, 8 minus 10% of 8. As a result of this analysis, A must reduce in price to B from 7.6 to 7.2. ■

COST PLUS TRANSFER PRICING METHOD

The Malaysian Transfer Pricing Guidelines view the cost plus transfer pricing method as applying in the following circumstances:[52]

- A manufacturer sells its semifinished goods to associated parties.
- Different companies in a multinational group have concluded joint facility arrangements.

- The manufacturer is a contract manufacturer.
- A member of the controlled group provides services.

The taxpayer is to begin with the supplier's cost in applying the cost method in the case of the transfer of products between associated parties. The supplier then is to add an appropriate markup to this cost to determine the price that the supplier should be charging the buyer under the cost plus method.[53]

The taxpayer ideally should establish the appropriate markup by referring to the markup that the same supplier earns from uncontrolled sales to independent parties. Transactions having similar characteristics are more likely to be found among sales of product by the same supplier than among sales by other suppliers. The taxpayer might not be able to find transactions having these similar characteristics. In the event that the taxpayer is unable to find these comparables, the taxpayer may determine the appropriate markup by relying on independent parties operating independently.

There might be material differences between controlled transactions and uncontrolled transactions that could affect the gross profit markup. In that event, the taxpayer must make appropriate adjustments to the gross profit markup earned in the uncontrolled transaction.

The cost plus allocation formula applies in this matter: The arm's length price is cost plus the cost amount multiplied by a markup. The cost plus markup is equal to the sales price less costs, all divided by the cost amount. The cost plus markup amount is to reflect markup amounts earned by independent parties performing comparable functions, bearing similar risks, and using similar assets.

The cost plus method that the taxpayer uses to determine costs and accounting policies should be consistent with and comparable between controlled transactions and uncontrolled transactions, determined over time as to the particular enterprise.[54] The cost plus method refers to the aggregate direct and indirect costs of production, as a taxpayer would apply these amounts in applying absorption costing. The taxpayer might be able to take additional costs into account if the taxpayer can justify these costs and if the consideration of these costs would result in a more accurate estimate of the appropriate cost plus margin. The taxpayer, in computing costs, must do so in accordance with generally accepted principles or with normal accounting standards in Malaysia.

A taxpayer undertaking a comparability analysis should recognize that an uncontrolled transaction is comparable to a controlled transaction if the transaction meets one of the two conditions:[55]

1. There are no differences between the transactions being compared, or, alternatively, the differences between the transactions being compared or between the enterprises undertaking these transactions do not materially affect the cost plus markup in the open market.[56]
2. The taxpayer can make reasonably accurate adjustments to eliminate the material effects of such differences.[57]

The taxpayer, in undertaking the comparability analysis for cost plus purposes, should take into account the similarity of functions, risks assumed, contractual terms, market conditions, business strategies, and any adjustments the taxpayer must make to account for the effects of differences in the aforementioned factors between controlled and uncontrolled transactions.[58] As with the resale price method, for purposes of the cost plus method, the fewer adjustments the taxpayer needs to make the better in determining product differences.

COST PLUS TRANSFER PRICING METHOD EXAMPLE

A is a foreign multinational. B is Malaysia's subsidiary. C is an independent enterprise. B manufactures electrical components and exports these electrical components to A. A sets the electrical components, and B fulfills A's requirements. B purchases all raw materials from C at price of 20 per unit. B's total cost per unit of the manufactured product is 80 per unit. B sells the product to A at a price of 100 per unit. A similar but unassociated manufacturing company sells its product to an independent company having a markup of 40%.

B's gross profit is this: Sales to A are 100, purchases are 20, manufacturing costs are 50, and overheads are 10, making total costs 80. B's gross profit is 100 minus 80, or a gross profit of 20. A's product is an extensively customized product, meaning that there are no product comparables. Nevertheless, the taxpayer can use the 40% markup from the same company as a comparable to determine the arm's length price because the other company performs the same functions, bears similar risks, and uses similar assets as does Company B. The arm's length price of the electrical component that B sells to A should be B's costs of 80 plus a 40% markup of 32 (e.g., 40% of 80, or 32). The cost amount then becomes 80 plus 32, or 112 in total. As a result, B must increase its price to A of 12, 112 minus 100.

■ ADDITIONAL TRANSFER PRICING METHODS

Although the Malaysian Transfer Pricing Guidelines state that "it is the prerogative of the taxpayer to choose from the various methodologies laid out with the ultimate aim at arriving at an arm's length transfer price,"[59] the guidelines then say that the taxpayer is to consider the transactional profit margin methods only when the taxpayer cannot apply the traditional transfer pricing methods.[60] The guidelines, then, view the transactional profit margin methods as "last resort" methods that take into account profits that arise from particular transactions that take place among associated enterprises that are compared to the profits arising from comparable transactions between independent enterprises.

The IRBM takes a strong stance against global formulary apportionment, stating that the global formulary apportionment is arbitrary and that it could not reliably approximate arm's length conditions. The term "global formulary apportionment" refers to a transfer pricing method that applies a predetermined, mechanistic formula, normally based in a combination of costs, assets, payroll, and sales undertaken, to allocate the global profits of a multinational enterprise among associated enterprises in different countries.

PROFIT SPLIT TRANSFER PRICING METHOD

The Malaysian Transfer Pricing Guidelines provide that the profit split method provides an alternative transfer pricing method where the taxpayer cannot identify comparable transactions between independent parties. The taxpayer might not be able to identify comparables when the transactions are very interrelated and the taxpayer cannot evaluate these transactions separately. The profit split method is based on the concept that the taxpayer can equitably divide profits earned in a controlled transaction between associated parties involved in the transaction according to the functions that each entity performs.

The taxpayer, in arriving at an arm's length price, is to value the contributions that each associated entity makes to the transactions. The taxpayer assesses the transaction based on how independent enterprises under the same circumstances would expect to split the profits between them. Under the Malaysian Transfer Pricing Guidelines, this analysis would normally involve making comparisons with independent enterprises that have entered into joint ventures.

The Malaysian Transfer Pricing Guidelines recognize two approaches for estimating the division of profits, whether these profits are projected or actual. These methods are the residual profit approach and the contribution analysis approach. The guidelines caution that the residual profit approach and the contribution analysis approach are not necessarily exhaustive or mutually exclusive.

The Malaysian Transfer Pricing Guidelines permit the taxpayer to apply the residual profit split approach as a last resort method, which creates rather than resolves a plethora of ambiguities. There are two stages of dividing profits under the residual profit split approach:[61]

1. The taxpayer apportions the combined profit according to basic returns assigned to each party in the transaction. The taxpayer is to base the basic returns based on the basic functions that each party performs. The taxpayer is to ascertain its basic returns by reference to market returns obtained by independent parties in similar transactions. The basic return, then, does not generally account for the return that a taxpayer would generate through any unique and valuable assets owned by the participants.
2. The taxpayer allocates the remaining profit and loss, doing so in reference to how independent parties in similar circumstances would have divided such residuals.

The Malaysian Transfer Pricing Guidelines permit the taxpayer to apply the contribution analysis approach as a last resort.[62] Under the contribution analysis approach, the taxpayer would divide the combined profits based on the relative value of functions, or contributions, that each party performs. The Malaysian contribution analysis approach in many ways is analogous to the U.S. cost sharing approach. The taxpayer, in determining the relative value of a contribution, might need to focus on:

- The degree of each party's contribution, such as the providing of services and capital invested
- The relative comparison or percentage and market data assigned

Unlike the residual profit approach, the contribution analysis approach does not allocate basic returns to each of the parties to the transaction before the taxpayer undertakes the profit split. As a general matter, the taxpayer is to combine the operating profit. The taxpayer can consider combining a split of gross profits when the taxpayer lacks expense data that it would otherwise apply to controlled transactions. The taxpayer would then deduct expenses after making the gross profit allocation.

RESIDUAL ANALYSIS EXAMPLE

X, Y, and Z are companies that are located in different countries.

- X manufactures the major component. X designs and manufactures the major components of a high quality electrical product. X sells its products to Y.
- Y manufacturers the final component. Taking the components that Y received from X, Y further develops these components and manufactures them into the final component. Y then exports the final product to Z, an independent distributor.
- Z is a distributor.

The profit and loss statements for Company X and for Company Y are:

	X	Y
Sales	100	300
Purchases	15	100
Manufacturing cost	20	35
Gross profit	65	165
R&D	20	15
Other operating expenses	15	10
Net profit	30	140

In this case, the final product is a unique product for which there is no comparable. There are, however, several companies that carry out similar functions to X and Y involving semifinished products and final products, but of a lower quality. The average net markups for these independent companies are 30% as to the type X situation and 20% as to the type Y situation.

The taxpayer is then to select the transfer pricing method. The taxpayer cannot apply the CUP transfer pricing method in this instance because of the uniqueness of the final product. In this instance, there are insufficient data and information to apply the cost plus method. The resale price method is inappropriate because the product has undergone a substantial transformation at the Y level. The taxpayer, after affirmatively rejecting the three traditional transfer pricing methods, adopts the profit split method using the residual approach.

Under the example provided by the Malaysian Transfer Pricing Guidelines, the taxpayer combines the total profit for X and Y, analogous to the computation of combined taxable income for DISC purposes:[63]

Total sales	300
Cost of goods sold (X)	35
Cost of goods sold (Y) excluding purchases	35
Gross profit	230
R&D	35
Operating profit	25
Net profit	170

Next, the taxpayer determines the basic return, using the predetermined external data for X and Y, 30% and 20%, respectively, based on cost of goods sold plus other operating expenses. The basic return to X is 30% of cost of goods sold plus other operating expenses. Cost of goods and operating expenses for X are 35 plus 15, 50 in total, so that 30% of this amount is 15.

The calculation of the basic return to Y has to take into account that the cost of goods sold for comparable companies has included the purchase price for the semifinished product. The basic return for Y, as previously stated, is 20%. The basic return for Y is a function of the transfer price (i.e., 20% of the cost of goods sold minus the purchase price), adding the operating expenses and the arm's length transfer price (TP). The taxpayer does determine this amount directly. Instead, the formula for the basic return becomes 20% of (35 + 10 + TP) or 9 + 0.2TP.

The next step is to determine the residual profit split, which is the net profit minus the sum of the return to X and the return to Y. The net profit, as previously stated, is 170. The sum of the return to X of 15 and the return to Y of 9 + 0.2TP is stated as 170 – (15 + 9 + 0.2TP), which can be simplified as 146 – 0.2TP.

The example assumes that in this instance R&D is a reliable indicator of X's and Y's relative contribution of an intangible asset. In that event, X and Y determine R&D in this manner:

	X	Y	Total
R&D	20	15	35
Ratio	57%	43%	100%

Next we determine the residual profit for X and for Y:

For X: 57% of (146 – 0.2TP) = 83.22 – 0.114TP
For Y: 43% of (146 – 0.2TP) = 62.78 – 0.086TP

We can determine the net profit for X:

The basic return to X is 15.
The residual return to X is 83.22 – 0.114TP.
The total return to X is therefore 98.22 – 0.114TP.

We can determine the net profit for Y:

The basic return to Y is 9 + 0.2TP.
The residual return to Y is 62.78 – 0.086TP.
The total return to Y is therefore 71.78 + 0.114TP.

Now we adjust the X and Y transfer price:

We begin with a no-profit determination for X: sales are 100, purchases are 15, and operating expenses are 15, having deductions of 30, and leaving an intercompany price of 70. These amounts do not reflect R&D, as the taxpayer is to take R&D into account after the completion of this analysis. We next adjust the intercompany price of 70 in the following manner: X's adjusted sales price (transfer price) is 70 plus the X's adjusted net profit, which is 70 + 98.22 – 0.114TP or 168.22 – 0.114TP. TP is then 168.22 / 0.114TP, or 151. As a result, the arm's length adjustment is 51, and the adjusted sales amount is 151.

The adjusted net profit becomes:

	X	Y
Sales	100	300
Arm's length adjustment	51	
Adjusted sales	151	
Purchases	15	100
Adjustment		51
Adjusted purchases		151
Manufacturing cost	20	35
Gross profit	65	165
Adjusted gross profit	116	114
R&D	20	15
Other operating expenses	15	10
Net profit	30	140
Adjusted net profit	81	89

TRANSACTIONAL NET MARGIN METHOD

The TNMM uses a margin method, as do the resale cost method and the cost plus method. The TNMM, however, examines the net profit margin, in this case relative to an appropriate base, such as costs, sales, or assets the multinational corporation attains from a controlled transaction.[64] As with the cost plus or resale price methods, the taxpayer should preferably derive its margin from comparable uncontrolled transactions between the same taxpayer and independent parties (i.e., in-house comparables). In situations in which an in-house comparable might not exist, the taxpayer may refer to the net profit margin that would have been earned in comparable transactions by an independent enterprise.

The taxpayer seeking to apply the TNMM must undertake a functional analysis of the associated enterprise to determine comparability. Unlike gross margins or prices, various factors significantly influence net margins other than products or functions. Such factors include competitive position, varying cost structures, differences in cost of capital, and the like. The Malaysian Transfer Pricing Guidelines emphasize that the taxpayer should confine the TNMM to cases in which the functions have a high degree of similarity so as to eliminate the effects of those other factors.

TNMM EXAMPLE

The Malaysian Transfer Pricing Guidelines provide this example that illustrates the TNMM:

X is a distributor located in Malaysia; Y is a manufacturer located overseas. X is a subsidiary of Y. Y manufactures computers. Y sells its computers to X and to other associated distributors in different countries. Company Y trademarks its goods. Company X sells Company Y trademarked computers and provides technical support to all its customers. X's trading account is:

Sales	100,000
Cost of goods sold	90,000
Gross income	10,000
Operating expenses	15,000
Net loss	(5,000)
Margin	–5%

The fact pattern assumes that the taxpayer cannot apply the CUP method. There are no reliable adjustments the taxpayer can make to account for differences with similar products in the market. The taxpayer does not use the resale price method, as it is unable to obtain a comparable measure of gross margin due to differences in accounting practice among independent distributors. The taxpayer adopts the TNMM, applying the net profit return on sales. The taxpayer determines that the net profit margin to sales earned in a comparable transaction by an independent enterprise is 5%.

X then makes these adjustments: X's net profit should be 5% of its 100,000 sales, or 5,000. X is to restate its cost of goods sold from 90,000 to 80,000. X's income would then reflect its sales of 100,000, cost of goods sold of 80,000, and operating expenses of 15,000, for a profit of 5,000. ■

INTANGIBLE PROPERTY

The Malaysia Transfer Pricing Guidelines, following the OECD guidelines, provide that intangible property includes both marketing intangibles and trade intangibles.[65]

- In general, intangible property includes patents, know-how, inventions, trademarks, brand names, copyrights, registered designs, franchises, licenses, literary and artistic property rights, and other similar items. The taxpayer would value that intangible property for its intellectual content or its intangible content.
- The term "marketing intangibles" refers to trademarks and trade names, for example.
- The term "trade intangibles" refers to patents that the taxpayer creates through risky and costly R&D, for example.

The Malaysia Transfer Pricing Guidelines provide that the taxpayer can undertake the transfer of intangibles between associated parties in this manner:[66]

- By outright sale; or by transfer for consideration, by gift, or by capital contribution[67]
- In the form of a lease, or a license, where the royalty is paid to the owner[68]

Intangibles, by their nature, are essentially unique products.[69] The taxpayer must address special considerations regarding these intangibles. These special considerations are discussed next.

1. The taxpayer is to ascertain whether the intangible in fact exists. The Malaysia Transfer Pricing Guidelines caution that marketing activities that comprise market research, product promotion, and so forth do not necessarily result in the creation of a business asset.[70] Similarly, not all R&D expenditures lead to the production of a trade intangible. Such expenditures might be current expenditures. The functional analysis of these activities establishes their comparability.
2. When a taxpayer transfers intangibles, the taxpayer must evaluate the terms of the agreement between transferor and transferee. Such an agreement would normally indicate:[71]
   - Whether the transfer of the intangible is an outright sale or whether the transfer of the intangible is a licensing agreement for the royalties to be paid.
   - If the transfer of the intangible is a royalty to be paid, the taxpayer needs to ascertain the basis of payment.
   - The taxpayer needs to ascertain whether the price of the product being transferred includes compensation for the use of intangible property. In the event that the product being transferred includes compensation for the use of intangible property, the taxpayer must ascertain whether other businesses provide royalties or other payments for the technology in relation to the same product.
   - The taxpayer needs to ascertain how the marketer is compensated if the transfer of the intangible is a marketing intangible where the legal owner undertakes marketing activities.

The Malaysia Transfer Pricing Guidelines provide that the arm's length principle, the concept of comparability, and the basis of selecting the most appropriate method all apply to intangibles as they do to tangible property.[72] The taxpayer is to undertake the following facets as part of its comparability analysis:

- The taxpayer is to ascertain the expected benefits from the intangible property, undertaking this analysis for controlled transactions and uncontrolled transactions.[73]
- A special rule applies in the case of a patent. In such cases, the taxpayer is to ascertain the:[74]
  - Nature of the patent
  - Duration of the patent
  - Nature of the patent laws in relevant countries
  - Value of the final product that is attributable to the patent
- A special rule applies to marketing intangibles such as trademarks. The Malaysian Transfer Pricing Guidelines require the taxpayer to ascertain the value that the trademark adds by taking into account:[75]
  - Consumer acceptability
  - Geographic significance
  - Market share
  - Sales volumes
- The Malaysian Transfer Pricing Guidelines acknowledge that the taxpayer will find it difficult to find comparable uncontrolled transactions. Accordingly, the Malaysian Transfer Pricing Guide provides that Malaysia taxpayers frequently use the profit split transfer pricing method. The taxpayer, in determining comparability or relative value of the contributions of each party, must ascertain the amount, nature, and incidence of the costs that the taxpayer incurred in developing or maintaining the intangible property under review.[76]

TRANSFER PRICING SERVICES REGULATIONS

The Malaysian Transfer Pricing Guidelines acknowledge that most multinational corporations provide for a wide range of services for intragroup use. Such services include technical aid and know-how. The parent or other service companies within the multinational group initially bears these costs but recoups them from other associated companies through some intragroup arrangement.[77] The Malaysian Transfer Pricing Guidelines view the intragroup services as providing two subissues:[78]

1. Whether a party within the group provides services to another party in the group[79]
2. Whether the intragroup charges for the service provided are at arm's length[80]

The Malaysian Transfer Pricing Guidelines recommends that the taxpayer take into account these factors in determining whether the taxpayer rendered the applicable services:[81]

- Whether the activity of one group member provides the other group member with economic value or commercial value.
- Whether an independent enterprise in comparable circumstances would be willing to pay for or perform such activities in house for itself.
- The taxpayer needs to address the possibility of duplicate services. The taxpayer cannot charge for duplicate services undertaken by one member where these services merely duplicate a service that another group member is performing for itself. The taxpayer cannot pay for services being performed for such other group member by a third party.
- The taxpayer should avoid accounting for incidental benefits. A taxpayer might be providing incidental benefits to associated enterprises that arise out of the activities or services meant for other members of the multinational corporation. The taxpayer should not take these intragroup services into account for that particular enterprise.

The Malaysian Transfer Pricing Guidelines do not specifically address transfer pricing methods in the services context. Instead, the taxpayer is to apply the transfer pricing methods otherwise applicable to transfers of tangibles.[82] The taxpayer is to undertake a functional analysis of the various group members to establish the relationship between the relevant services and the activities and performances of the members.

DOCUMENTATION

The taxpayer is required to keep sufficient records for the purposes of providing necessary records to the Director General to ascertain income or loss from the business.[83] The taxpayer must keep these records for a period of seven years.[84] The taxpayer must keep records pertaining to Malaysia in Malaysia itself.[85] For this purpose, records include books of account, invoices, vouchers, receipts, and other documents necessary to verify entries in any books of account.[86]

As a general matter, it will be advantageous to the taxpayer to adhere to the next documentation and record-keeping requirements for transfer pricing purposes. Adherence with the documentation and record-keeping requirements reduces the risk of a tax audit and subsequent adjustments.[87] The Director General has the power to engage in tax audits and make subsequent adjustments according to whether the Director General views them as being reasonable transfer prices.

The taxpayer has no obligation to submit transfer pricing documents with its return forms. In contrast, the taxpayer should make these documents available to the IRBM when the IRBM requests these forms. The taxpayer must keep its relevant documentation in English or in Malay, or translate these documents into English or into Malay.[88] The taxpayer is to translate the documents at the time that the taxpayer establishes the transfer price. The translation is to include particulars as to the transaction.

The Malaysian Transfer Pricing Guidelines provide a list of documents that the taxpayer must retain.[89] The guidelines indicate that this list is not exhaustive, nor do the guidelines intend to apply this list to all types of businesses. Instead, the taxpayer is to maintain documents that are applicable in the taxpayer's circumstances. The taxpayer must be prepared to provide additional information or documentation to the IRBM not contained in the list but that might become relevant in determining the arm's length price.

The documentation requirements are reflected in three parts:

1. Company details
2. Transaction details
3. Determination of the arm's length price

The Malaysian Transfer Pricing Guidelines require the taxpayer to retain three types of company details:[90]

1. Ownership structure of the company, showing linkages between all entities within the multinational group[91]
2. The company organization chart[92]
3. Operational aspects of the business, including details of the functions the company performs[93]

The Malaysian Transfer Pricing Guidelines require the taxpayer to retain seven types of transaction details:[94]

1. The taxpayer is to provide a summary of transactions with other entities in the same multinational group. The taxpayer is to indicate the name and address of each entity within the group with whom the taxpayer and the member have entered into the international transaction. The taxpayer is to specify the type of transaction (e.g., purchase of raw material or fixed assets, sale of finished goods, the borrowing of money, and so forth).[95]
2. The taxpayer is to provide a summary of the preceding transactions when conducted with independent parties or information the taxpayer derives from independent enterprises engaged in similar transactions or businesses.[96]
3. The taxpayer is to provide the economic conditions taking place during the time of the transactions.[97]
4. The taxpayer is to provide to the IRBM the terms of the transactions in which the taxpayer was engaged. The taxpayer is to provide, when applicable, contractual agreements with associated parties in regard to:[98]
   - Technical assistance fees
   - Management fees
   - Marketing fees
   - Recruitment fees
   - Other services that the taxpayer provides
   - Royalties payable
   - Purchase or rental of equipment or other assets
   - Handling charges

- Loans
- Allocation of overhead expenses or other specific expenses, such as promotional expenses or advertising expenses borne by the foreign entity
- Other payments the taxpayer makes to overseas associates

5. The taxpayer is to specify its transfer pricing policy over the seven-year period.[99]
6. The taxpayer is to provide a breakdown of its manufacturing costs.[100]
7. The taxpayer is to provide its product price list to the IRBM.[101]

The Malaysian Transfer Pricing Guidelines provide that the taxpayer is to retain this information about its transfer price:[102]

- The taxpayer is to specify the pricing methodology it adopts, showing the IRBM how the taxpayer derives its arm's length price.[103]
- The taxpayer is to specify its functional analysis, taking into account all risks that the taxpayer assumes and the assets the taxpayer employs.[104]
- A comparability analysis might result in a range of arm's length outcomes. In the event that there is a range of arm's length outcomes, the taxpayer is to provide documents relating to these outcomes. The taxpayer is to provide its rationale in selecting the particular arm's length range.[105]

MALAYSIA ISSUES ADVANCE RULING GUIDELINES

Malaysia now permits a taxpayer to secure an advance tax ruling in many fact patterns. The advance ruling process is important to U.S. companies doing business in Malaysia as well as for Malaysian companies doing business in the United States because the two countries have no income tax treaty except for a shipping and air transportation treaty signed April 18, 1989. The Malaysian Prime Minister announced the advance tax ruling concept as part of the 2007 budget, effective January 1, 2007. The IRBM promulgated the specific advance rulings guideline procedure on February 14, 2008.[106]

As we shall see, Malaysia's advance tax ruling process puts taxpayers in an uncertain position from a transfer pricing standpoint. At the outset, Malaysia's advance process does not encompass bilateral advance pricing agreements. Further, Malaysia's advance pricing process possibly might not encompass unilateral advance pricing agreements. Nevertheless, a matched unilateral advance pricing agreement, if permitted by the Malaysian tax authorities, would be an appropriate transfer pricing alternative for Malaysian companies doing business in the United States and for U.S. companies doing business in Malaysia.

GENERAL FACTS ABOUT THE ADVANCE RULING PROCEDURE IN MALAYSIA

As a general matter, Malaysia's advance ruling procedure is designed to interpret and apply the income tax provisions pursuant to Malaysia's primary tax law, the Income

Tax Act 1967.[107] Any taxpayer can request such an advance ruling. A foreign party can request such ruling if the party is represented by local counsel.[108] The IRBM intends that the issuance of an advance ruling will achieve these objectives:[109]

- Ensure clarity and certainty of the tax treatment
- Provide consistency in the application of the income tax law
- Promote tax compliance
- Minimize disputes between the IRBM and the taxpayer

The Income Tax Act 1967 empowers the Director General Inland Revenue (DGIR) to provide an advance ruling on behalf of the taxpayer.[110] Upon the taxpayer's request, the DGIR can rule as to how the provisions of the act would apply to the person and to the arrangement for which the taxpayer seeks a ruling. The Income Tax Act 1967 empowers the Minister of Finance to provide for the scope and procedure as to the advance ruling and to provide fees associated with the advance ruling.[111] The advance ruling procedure is retroactive to January 1, 2007.[112]

The DGIR issues the advance ruling to the taxpayer interpreting how the IRBM is to apply a proposed arrangement pursuant to the Income Tax Act 1967. The scope of advance ruling procedure in Malaysia is narrow, limited only to class of activities that constitute "proposed arrangements."[113] This chapter examines the scope of "proposed arrangement" factors.

As a general matter, an advance ruling is binding on the taxpayer.[114] In contrast, the DGIR can withdraw the ruling under defined circumstances.[115] The advance ruling comprises these areas:[116]

- The circumstances that pertain to the ruling provisions contained in the Income Tax Act 1967.
- The ruling must be binding on the taxpayer.
- The ruling applies only to the taxpayer's taxable year.
- The ruling applies only to the proposed arrangement specified in the advance ruling.

BINDING NATURE OF AN ADVANCE RULING

The advance ruling does not serve as a precedent for other cases. The issued ruling automatically lapses if the taxpayer fails to carry out the arrangement stipulated in the ruling by the end of the ruling's time period. The ruling is subject to any qualifications stated in the ruling, but otherwise the ruling is binding on the DGIR.[117] The guidelines enumerate four situations in which the advance ruling will not be binding on the DGIR:[118]

1. The advance ruling will not be binding on the DGIR if the arrangement that the taxpayer carries out is materially different from the arrangement specified in the ruling itself. This "materially different" exclusion encompasses situations in which the transactions, as materialized, differ from the arrangement

specified in the advance ruling in such a way that the provisions in the Income Tax Act 1967, as stated in the advance ruling, no longer apply to such transactions or no longer can be applicable to such transactions.[119]

2. The advance ruling will not be binding on the DGIR if the taxpayer made a material omission or misrepresentation in the application of the advance ruling or in connection with the application of the advance ruling.[120]
3. The advance ruling will not be binding on the DGIR if the DGIR made an assumption as to a future event or another matter that is material to the advance ruling where that assumption subsequently proves to be incorrect. The taxpayer should recognize that the ruling request process does limit itself to assumptions stipulated in writing in the promulgation of the ruling.[121]
4. The advance ruling will not be binding on the DGIR if the DGIR stipulates conditions upon the taxpayer, and the taxpayer fails to satisfy any one of these stipulated conditions.[122]

The advance ruling guideline provides specific terms that apply through the guideline in various contexts.[123] The guideline defines the term "arrangement" in a broad matter to include "any scheme, contract, agreement, plan, or undertaking," whether such arrangement is enforceable or not.[124] Such arrangement includes all the steps and transactions that carry the arrangement into effect. The guideline requires, for the DGIR to approve the ruling, that the taxpayer propose an arrangement that the taxpayer seriously contemplates.[125] The guideline defines the term "seriously contemplates" to mean a "concerted effort and a define course of action, whether this action is unilateral or otherwise, to undertake the arrangement in the near future." The guideline fails to define the term "near future."

SCOPE OF THE ADVANCE RULING REQUEST

The prerequisite for requesting an advance ruling is that the issues that would be addressed in the ruling require a determination of the income tax laws. The advance ruling guideline cautions that an advance ruling request is not to seek information as to what the law already provides or a question of fact.[126] For example, an advance ruling request is not designed to render a decision as to whether a person is a resident.

The prerequisite for requesting an advance ruling is that the taxpayer "seriously contemplates" the proposed arrangement for implementation in the near future.[127] The taxpayer is precluded from requesting the advance ruling on a whim or before the taxpayer has adequate documentation concerning the transaction contemplated. The taxpayer must put forward relevant documentation as evidence to indicate that the taxpayer seriously contemplated the arrangement.

Malaysia basic income tax law itself permits a taxpayer to obtain an advance ruling, indicating how any provision in the tax law would apply to the taxpayer's proposed arrangement.[128] The DGIR will issue an advance ruling only if the taxpayer seriously contemplates the arrangement contemplated and the arrangement exists in fact.

The DGIR can provide other restrictions of the advance ruling procedure. The DGIR will not provide an advance ruling if the matter sought by the taxpayer pertains to a provision in the Income Tax Act 1967 that would authorize or require the DGIR or the Minister of Finance to undertake these activities:

- Impose a penalty or remit a penalty
- Remit tax due and payable
- Approve an application
- Inquire as to the correctness of any tax return or of any other information supplied by any person
- Prosecute any person
- Recover any debt owing by any person

Circumstances in which Malaysia Tax Authorities Will Not Issue an Advance Ruling

The DGIR has no obligation to respond favorably to each advance ruling. The DGIR will reject requests to provide an advance ruling in these ten circumstances:[129]

1. If the taxpayer has already effectuated the arrangement at the time that the taxpayer filed the ruling request or before the DGIR issued the advance ruling.[130] The DGIR will not issue an advance ruling for a completed transaction or a series of transactions as to an arrangement made significantly in advance.
2. If the application for the advance ruling is frivolous, vexatious, or based on hypothetical situations.[131]
3. If the issue raised in the advance ruling would require the DGIR to interpret foreign law. The DGIR will reject requests for an advance ruling if the issue is being dealt with or should be dealt with by the competent authorities of the tax treaty, the agreement for the avoidance of double taxation.[132]
4. If an advance ruling already exists as to how the relevant portions of the Income Tax Act 1967 apply to the taxpayer and to the arrangement, and the taxpayer makes a request for an advance ruling on the same arrangement that relates to the same period or the taxable year.[133]
5. If an arrangement is the subject of an audit or an investigation as to how any provision of the Income Tax Act 1967 applies to a taxpayer and that taxpayer requests an advance ruling on a similar arrangement.[134]
6. If the DGIR requests that the taxpayer provide additional information, but the taxpayer fails to provide full information concerning the application to the DGIR.[135]
7. If the advance ruling would require the DGIR to provide an opinion as to generally accepted accounting principles or an opinion as to commercially accepted practices.[136]
8. If the matter on which the advance ruling is sought involves an advance pricing arrangement or a tax avoidance scheme.[137] The authors question whether the DGIR intends to preclude an advance pricing agreement as an "advance pricing arrangement." It appears to us that the terms "advance pricing arrangement or a

tax avoidance scheme" refer to nefarious activities rather than to an attempt to avoid double taxation.

9. If the matter is prospective, addressing proposed legislation (i.e., an interpretation of a provision in the Income Tax Act 1967 that has not been enacted).[138] For example, the DGIR will reject requests for an advance ruling if a provision addresses budget proposals or addresses rules or regulations that the government has not enacted. Nevertheless, a taxpayer may seek a written technical confirmation from the DGIR, a procedure separate from the advance ruling guideline, in the case of those rules or regulations.
10. If in the matter, in the DGIR's opinion, it would be unreasonable for the DGIR to make an advance ruling in view of the resources available to the DGIR.[139] Such a situation can occur, for example, if the request for an advance ruling pertains to a highly technical and sophisticated arrangement or to a technology or product with which the DGIR is not yet familiar.

Circumstances in which the DGIR Can Decline to Issue an Advance Ruling

In addition to the preceding ten situations in which the DGIR will reject requests to provide an advance ruling, the DGIR may generally decline an application for an advance ruling in these four circumstances:[140]

1. If the matter on which the taxpayer requests an advance ruling is purely a question of fact.[141] Such a situation can arise, for example, as to the determination of the commencement date of a housing developer's project.
2. If the correctness of the advance ruling would depend on the making of assumptions, whether these assumptions pertain to a future event or to any other matter.[142]
3. If the matter on which the ruling is sought is the subject of an appeal, whether this appeal is in relation to the taxpayer or to any other person.[143]
4. If the taxpayer has outstanding debts to DGIR pertaining to prior advance ruling applications.[144]

Notice Requirements

The DGIR has the power to decline to make an advance ruling or not make an advance ruling. In such a case, the DGIR is to notify the applicant in writing at the earliest possible time. The DGIR is to provide the reasons why the DGIR did not make an advance ruling or declined to make an advance ruling.[145]

ADVANCE RULING APPLICATION PROCEDURE

The advance ruling application procedure addresses these specific processes:[146]

- Eligible parties
- The application

- Information requirements
- The applicant's withdrawal of an advance ruling request

As a general matter, any person may apply for an advance ruling as to how a provision of the Income Tax Act 1967 would apply to the person, or to the prospective person, as the case may be.[147] As a general matter, any person may apply for an advance ruling as to any particular arrangement that falls under the purview of the advance ruling. The advance ruling process is available to both companies already in existence and companies that are not yet in existence, but the application process differs between them to some extent.

A taxpayer that is already in existence must apply for the advance ruling on its own behalf.[148] For example, the taxpayer includes a company that has already been incorporated in Malaysia. The taxpayer, at its option, *may* employ the services of an approved tax agent or a certified revenue lawyer, both of whom practice their profession in Malaysia. Such an approved tax agent or a certified revenue lawyer can complete the advance ruling application form and prepare the advance ruling application for submission to the DGIR on behalf of the client. The person responsible for the advance ruling application form must sign the form. The responsible person includes, by way of example, a company director or a partner in a partnership. Note that this process is optional on the part of a business incorporated in Malaysia but mandatory on the part of the foreign enterprise.

Two or more persons can jointly make an advance ruling application. The joint application, by way of example, includes a group of companies in the same group, and includes partners in a partnership.[149] The "person responsible" for each participant to the joint ruling application must sign the return before the entity submits its return to the DGIR.

Two scenarios limit the taxpayer's application for the advance ruling:

1. A taxpayer might not be in existence at the time the taxpayer files an advance ruling request with the DGIR.
2. The entity might be foreign.

In either of these two scenarios, the representative of the taxpayer must be an approved tax agent or a certified revenue lawyer where such person practices its profession in Malaysia.[150] A representative acting on behalf of the taxpayer must forward a letter of authority that authorizes the representative to act on the taxpayer's behalf. The representative must fill out the details in the application.

ADVANCE RULING APPLICATION FORM

The taxpayer applying for an advance ruling must furnish this information to the DGIR:[151]

- A complete description as to all facts that are relevant to the arrangement.[152] This description includes all of the taxpayer's factual assumptions in regard to the arrangement and includes the names, addresses, business activities, and other relevant particulars as to all parties to the arrangement.

- The tax issues that the taxpayer requests the DGIR consider.[153]
- The provisions under the Income Tax Act 1967 that relate to these items in the advance ruling application:[154]
  - Appropriate case law
  - Published commentaries, if any
  - Legal reasons that support the taxpayer's interpretation of the applicable sections
  - The stance or opinion on the tax treatment that should be accorded to the proposed arrangement for which the advance ruling is sought. The taxpayer should identify the relevant provisions in the Income Tax Act 1967 that are applicable.[155]
  - The commercial or other reasons for the arrangement, if applicable.[156]
  - Copies of all documents, identifying all the relevant parts or passages.[157]
  - Information as to the taxable years to which the advance ruling application relates.[158]
  - A statement identifying whether the applicant has made a previous advance ruling request on the same or similar arrangement.[159] If the applicant made such an advance ruling, the applicant is to state the advance ruling application and the reference number of the advance ruling issued by the IRBM.

INFORMATION REQUEST REQUIREMENT

The DGIR needs to receive sufficient information from the applicant to complete its review in granting an advance ruling. The DGIR has the right to request further relevant information or to carry out an on-site inspection in instances where the applicant provided insufficient information.[160] The DGIR also has the right to waive any requirements the DGIR would otherwise need in filling out the application. The DGIR can waive these requirements if it is the DGIR's opinion that it would be unreasonable to request information for which the applicant has no means of providing or information to which the applicant has no access.[161]

A person who has submitted an advance ruling application can withdraw the advance ruling application before the DGIR issues its advance ruling. A person seeking to withdraw its advance ruling application can do so by forwarding such a notice to the DGIR in writing.[162] A person who withdraws its application for an advance ruling remains liable to pay all fees incurred up to the time the DGIR receives a notice of withdrawal.[163] A person seeking to withdraw its advance ruling application must acknowledge this requirement in filing the withdrawal request.[164]

ISSUANCE OF THE ADVANCE RULING

The advance ruling guideline provides that the DGIR is to notify the applicant for the advance ruling that the DGIR has in fact issued such a ruling. In addition, the DGIR is to notify the applicant as to the additional fees the applicant must pay in relation to the advance ruling. The DGIR will issue the advance ruling to the applicant only when the applicant pays all fees payable.[165]

The advance ruling guideline provides that the advance ruling is to specify:[166]

- That the DGIR issued the ruling pursuant to section 138B of the Income Tax Act 1967.[167]
- The identity of the persons requesting the ruling and the applicable provisions within the Income Tax Act 1967 that are subject to advance ruling and the arrangement sought by the applicant.[168]
- How the provision in the Income Tax Act 1967 applies to the person requesting the ruling and to the arrangement sought by the applicant.[169]
- The number of taxable years for which the advance ruling applies.[170]
- The material assumptions the DGIR makes about a future event or other matters.[171]
- The conditions, if any, that the DGIR imposes.[172]

The DGIR, in developing the advance ruling, might request additional information from the applicant. The DGIR, at is option, can issue an advance ruling based on assumptions it makes if the applicant cannot provide the necessary information. The DGIR is to make such assumptions that are appropriate, but the DGIR can decline to make an advance ruling if the applicant provides insufficient information.[173]

The advance process expects that the applicant and the IRBM will undertake prior consultations. The purpose of the collaborative process is to clarify information the applicant provides in the advance ruling application.[174] The IRBM is not obligated to disclose the decisions it makes within the applicant's advance ruling process at any time before the DGIR issues the advance ruling.

The recipient of an advance ruling may apply in writing to extend the application of the ruling beyond the taxable year indicated in the advance ruling.[175] The taxpayer must file a request to extend the period for which the advance ruling is applicable, doing so within three months prior to the end of the period or taxable year specified in the advance ruling or at any other period the DGIR approves. The arrangement might be essentially the same as the arrangement specified in the advance ruling. In the event that the arrangement is essentially the same, the applicant may request to the DGIR that it apply the same interpretation of the Income Tax Act 1967 prospectively to another period or to another taxable year.

The advance ruling guideline contains an exculpation clause for typographical errors and/or other minor errors. Such errors, if they were to occur in the DGIR's advance ruling issued to the applicant, do not adversely affect the advance ruling or make the advance ruling void if these errors do not in any way alter the way the provision of the Income Tax Act 1967 applies in the advance ruling.[176]

A taxpayer that files an advance ruling application is still obligated to comply with the obligations under the Income Tax Act 1967. For example, the taxpayer is obligated to file its tax return within the stipulated tax frame for compliance before the taxpayer filed its advance ruling application.[177] The DGIR's issuance of an advance ruling to an applicant does not change any powers the DGIR has to make or amend tax assessments under the Income Tax Act 1967.

ADVANCE RULING FINALITY AND DISCLOSURE

When the DGIR issues an advance ruling, that advance ruling is final whether the advance ruling is applicable to the taxpayer or not. The DGIR will not entertain any correspondence or inquiry after the DGIR issues the advance ruling.[178] The taxpayer cannot appeal the ruling. However, the taxpayer has the choice not to carry out the proposed arrangement if an advance ruling is disadvantageous to the taxpayer. The taxpayer must comply with the advance ruling if the taxpayer chooses to effectuate the proposed arrangement. Although the advance ruling is final, the taxpayer can object to the tax treatment under the normal Income Tax Act 1967 procedures.[179]

A taxpayer that receives an advance ruling has an obligation to disclose this information in the preparation of its annual tax return:[180]

- The existence of an advance ruling[181]
- Whether the taxpayer has complied with the advance ruling[182]
- Whether the taxpayer made material changes to the arrangement made in the advance ruling[183]

The advance ruling guideline fails to address certain timing issues. For example, the disclosure provisions fail to address issues such as the taxpayer must reflect the existence of the ruling in the taxable year in which the DGIR issues the ruling, but the provision does not indicate whether they must reflect advance rulings in prior years. The DGIR can enforce the disclosure provision by penalties that the DGIR can impose for noncompliance with the advance ruling.

THE DGIR CAN WITHDRAW THE ADVANCE RULING

The DGIR retains the right to withdraw an advance ruling at any time after the DGIR issues the ruling to the applicant. The DGIR can withdraw the advance ruling request because of changes in the tax laws based on differing court decisions.[184] Nevertheless, the withdrawal provisions are open-ended, permitting the taxpayer to withdraw the request under a wide variety of circumstances independent of court decisions.

The DGIR is to effectuate the withdrawal of an advance ruling issued to an applicant by means of issuing a notice of withdrawal to the applicant. The DGIR is prohibited from withdrawing the advance ruling on a prospective basis. The DGIR also is prohibited from withdrawing the advance ruling beyond a date at which the taxpayer is reasonably expected to receive a notice of withdrawal.[185]

A taxpayer might have effectuated the arrangement provided for in the advance ruling before the DGIR withdraws the ruling. In the event that the taxpayer has proceeded accordingly, the taxpayer can follow the advance ruling until the end of the period stated in the ruling. However, the taxpayer might not have effectuated the arrangement at the time that the DGIR issues the taxpayer a notice of withdrawal. The arrangement then is prospective, and the taxpayer cannot then take advantage of the advance ruling.[186] The proceeding withdrawal process enables an applicant that undertakes an arrangement in reliance of an advance ruling to bind the DGIR for the remainder of the period. However, the DGIR will not be bound by the advance ruling if the DGIR withdraws an advance ruling before the applicant enters into the arrangement.

SITUATIONS IN WHICH THE ADVANCE RULING CEASES TO APPLY

When the DGIR issues an advance ruling to an applicant, this ruling will be binding on the applicant and on the DGIR,[187] subject to the provisions subject to the binding nature of an advance ruling[188] and the withdrawal of an advance ruling by the DGIR.[189] An advance ruling ceases to apply in situations in which any provision of the Income Tax Act 1967 repeals or amends the subject of the ruling. This cessation takes place if the repeal or amendment of that provision in the Income Tax Act 1967 alters the way in which the tax law applies. The cessation of the advance ruling takes place from the date the repeal or amendment becomes effective.

FEE STRUCTURE

An applicant must pay a fee to secure an advance ruling from the DGIR. The fees will be based on each applicant's requesting an advance ruling, including the request for each applicant requesting the advance ruling.[190] The DGIR imposes these fees on the applicant as a debt due to the government of Malaysia.

The fee structure begins with an application fee of RM500 ($150 USD) upon application that is nonrefundable. This fee takes into account the amount of time the DGIR would need to accede to the request.[191] In addition, DGIR imposes a further fee of RM150 ($45) per hour or part thereof after the first four hours, including the time that DGIR spends in consulting with the applicant.[192] Moreover, the taxpayer must reimburse the DGIR for its professional advice the DGIR obtains with consent of the applicant[193] and any other reasonable costs the DGIR incurs.[194] In any event, the DGIR will at all times ensure that it is making every effort to minimize the fees payable.

An applicant that withdraws its application for an advance ruling remains liable for all fees incurred on its behalf up to the time at which the applicant receives a letter from the DGIR acknowledging the withdrawal.[195] The DGIR may waive any fees payable by an applicant for an advance ruling request, except for the nonrefundable application fee of RM500.[196] The DGIR can provide the waiver at its own discretion.

INTERNAL PROCEDURE

The DGIR will normally address an advance ruling request in the order in which it receives the request. The DGIR intends that it will issue the advance ruling within a stipulated time frame of 60 days from the date the applicant submits the application. The DGIR expects to meet this 60-day time period provided the applicant submits the relevant information together with the request and that the DGIR does not need further consultations with the applicant.[197] The DGIR is to advise the applicant if any unusual delay is foreseen.

All information in the advance ruling is confidential. The DGIR will not publish the advance ruling in any form.[198] There may be situations in which there are similarities of common concern including the applicant and other taxpayers. In the event that there are issues of common concern, the DGIR may produce a public ruling to address these issues.

NOTES

1. Garis Panduan Pindahan Harga.
2. Malaysia Transfer Pricing Guidelines, chapter 1.
3. Malaysia Transfer Pricing Guidelines, chapter 3.1.
4. Malaysia Transfer Pricing Guidelines, chapter 3.2.
5. Income Tax Act 1967, subsection 140(1).
6. Malaysia Transfer Pricing Guidelines, chapter 4.2.
7. Income Tax Act 1967, section 140.
8. Income Tax Act 1967, subsection 140(6).
9. Income Tax Act 1967, section 139; Malaysia Transfer Pricing Guidelines, chapter 4.3.1.
10. Income Tax Act 1967, subsection 2(4); Malaysia Transfer Pricing Guidelines, chapter 4.3.1.
11. Malaysia Transfer Pricing Guidelines, chapter 4.3.2.
12. Malaysia Transfer Pricing Guidelines, chapter 1.
13. Malaysia Transfer Pricing Guidelines, chapter 1.
14. Malaysia Transfer Pricing Guidelines, chapter 2.
15. Malaysia Transfer Pricing Guidelines, chapter 2.
16. Malaysia Transfer Pricing Guidelines, chapter 3.3.
17. Malaysia Transfer Pricing Guidelines, chapter 3.4.
18. Malaysia Transfer Pricing Guidelines, chapter 3.5.
19. Malaysia Transfer Pricing Guidelines, chapter 4.1.
20. Malaysia Transfer Pricing Guidelines, chapter 5.1.
21. Malaysia Transfer Pricing Guidelines, chapter 5.2.
22. Malaysia Transfer Pricing Guidelines, chapter 6.1.
23. Malaysia Transfer Pricing Guidelines, chapter 6.1(a).
24. Malaysia Transfer Pricing Guidelines, chapter 6.1(b).
25. Malaysia Transfer Pricing Guidelines, chapter 6.1(c).
26. Malaysia Transfer Pricing Guidelines, chapter 6.2.1.
27. Malaysia Transfer Pricing Guidelines, chapter 6.2.2.
28. Malaysia Transfer Pricing Guidelines, chapter 6.3.1.

29. Malaysia Transfer Pricing Guidelines, chapter 6.3.2.
30. Malaysia Transfer Pricing Guidelines, chapter 7.1, chapter 7.2.
31. Malaysia Transfer Pricing Guidelines, chapter 7.3.1.
32. Malaysia Transfer Pricing Guidelines, chapter 7.3.2.
33. Malaysia Transfer Pricing Guidelines, chapter 7.3.1.
34. Malaysia Transfer Pricing Guidelines, chapter 7.3.3.
35. Malaysia Transfer Pricing Guidelines, chapter 7.3.3(a).
36. Malaysia Transfer Pricing Guidelines, chapter 7.3.3(a)(i).
37. Malaysia Transfer Pricing Guidelines, chapter 7.3.3(a)(ii).
38. Malaysia Transfer Pricing Guidelines, chapter 7.3.3(b).
39. Malaysia Transfer Pricing Guidelines, chapter 7.4.1.
40. Malaysia Transfer Pricing Guidelines, chapter 7.4.2.
41. Malaysia Transfer Pricing Guidelines, chapter 7.4.3(a).
42. Malaysia Transfer Pricing Guidelines, chapter 7.4.3(a)(i).
43. Malaysia Transfer Pricing Guidelines, chapter 7.4.3(a)(ii).
44. Malaysia Transfer Pricing Guidelines, chapter 7.4.3(b).
45. Malaysia Transfer Pricing Guidelines, chapter 7.4.3(b)(i).
46. Malaysia Transfer Pricing Guidelines, chapter 7.4.3(b)(ii).
47. Malaysia Transfer Pricing Guidelines, chapter 7.4.3(b)(iii).
48. Malaysia Transfer Pricing Guidelines, chapter 7.4.3(b)(iv).
49. Malaysia Transfer Pricing Guidelines, chapter 7.4.3(b)(v).
50. Malaysia Transfer Pricing Guidelines, chapter 7.4.3(b)(vi).
51. Malaysia Transfer Pricing Guidelines, chapter 7.4.3(b)(vii).
52. Malaysia Transfer Pricing Guidelines, chapter 7.5.1.
53. Malaysia Transfer Pricing Guidelines, chapter 7.5.2.
54. Malaysia Transfer Pricing Guidelines, chapter 7.5.3.
55. Malaysia Transfer Pricing Guidelines, chapter 7.5.4 (a).
56. Malaysia Transfer Pricing Guidelines, chapter 7.5.4 (a)(i).
57. Malaysia Transfer Pricing Guidelines, chapter 7.5.4 (a)(ii).
58. Malaysia Transfer Pricing Guidelines, chapter 7.5.4 (b).
59. Malaysia Transfer Pricing Guidelines, chapter 2.
60. Malaysia Transfer Pricing Guidelines, chapter 7.6.
61. Malaysia Transfer Pricing Guidelines, chapter 7.6.1(i).
62. Malaysia Transfer Pricing Guidelines, chapter 7.6.1(ii).
63. IRC section 994(a)(2). See R. Feinschreiber and M. Kent, *Export DISC Handbook* (2008), p. 146.
64. Malaysia Transfer Pricing Guidelines, chapter 7.6.2.
65. Malaysia Transfer Pricing Guidelines, chapter 8.1.
66. Malaysia Transfer Pricing Guidelines, chapter 8.2.
67. Malaysia Transfer Pricing Guidelines, chapter 8.2(i).
68. Malaysia Transfer Pricing Guidelines, chapter 8.2(ii).
69. Malaysia Transfer Pricing Guidelines, chapter 8.3.
70. Malaysia Transfer Pricing Guidelines, chapter 8.3(i).
71. Malaysia Transfer Pricing Guidelines, chapter 8.3(ii).
72. Malaysia Transfer Pricing Guidelines, chapter 8.4.
73. Malaysia Transfer Pricing Guidelines, chapter 8.4(i).
74. Malaysia Transfer Pricing Guidelines, chapter 8.4(ii).

75. Malaysia Transfer Pricing Guidelines, chapter 8.4(iii).
76. Malaysia Transfer Pricing Guidelines, chapter 8.4(iv).
77. Malaysia Transfer Pricing Guidelines, chapter 9.1.
78. Malaysia Transfer Pricing Guidelines, chapter 9.2.
79. Malaysia Transfer Pricing Guidelines, chapter 9.2(i).
80. Malaysia Transfer Pricing Guidelines, chapter 9.2(ii).
81. Malaysia Transfer Pricing Guidelines, chapter 9.3.
82. Malaysia Transfer Pricing Guidelines, chapter 9.4.
83. Malaysia Transfer Pricing Guidelines, chapter 10.1.
84. Income Tax Act 1967, paragraph 82(1)(a).
85. Income Tax Act 1967, subsection 82(7).
86. Income Tax Act 1967, subsection 82(9).
87. Income Tax Act 1967, section 140.
88. Malaysia Transfer Pricing Guidelines, chapter 10.2.
89. Malaysia Transfer Pricing Guidelines, chapter 10.3.
90. Malaysia Transfer Pricing Guidelines, chapter 10.3(A).
91. Malaysia Transfer Pricing Guidelines, chapter 10.3(A)(i).
92. Malaysia Transfer Pricing Guidelines, chapter 10.3(A)(ii).
93. Malaysia Transfer Pricing Guidelines, chapter 10.3(A)(iii).
94. Malaysia Transfer Pricing Guidelines, chapter 10.3(B).
95. Malaysia Transfer Pricing Guidelines, chapter 10.3(B)(i).
96. Malaysia Transfer Pricing Guidelines, chapter 10.3(B)(ii).
97. Malaysia Transfer Pricing Guidelines, chapter 10.3(B)(iii).
98. Malaysia Transfer Pricing Guidelines, chapter 10.3(B)(iv).
99. Malaysia Transfer Pricing Guidelines, chapter 10.3(B)(v).
100. Malaysia Transfer Pricing Guidelines, chapter 10.3(B)(vi).
101. Malaysia Transfer Pricing Guidelines, chapter 10.3(B)(vii).
102. Malaysia Transfer Pricing Guidelines, chapter 10.3(C).
103. Malaysia Transfer Pricing Guidelines, chapter 10.3(C)(i).
104. Malaysia Transfer Pricing Guidelines, chapter 10.3(C)(ii).
105. Malaysia Transfer Pricing Guidelines, chapter 10.3(C)(iii).
106. LHDN.01/35/42/51/122/3 February 14, 2008.
107. Guideline on Advance Rulings, section 1.
108. Guideline on Advance Rulings, section 10.4; Guideline on Advance Rulings, section 1.
109. Guideline on Advance Rulings, section 1.
110. Guideline on Advance Rulings, section 2.1.
111. Guideline on Advance Rulings, section 2.2.
112. Guideline on Advance Rulings, section 1, section 2.3.
113. Guideline on Advance Rulings, section 5.2, section 6.2.
114. Guideline on Advance Rulings, section 4.1.
115. Guideline on Advance Rulings, section 13.
116. Guideline on Advance Rulings, section 1.
117. Guideline on Advance Rulings, section 4.1.
118. Guideline on Advance Rulings, section 4.2.
119. Guideline on Advance Rulings, section 4.2a.
120. Guideline on Advance Rulings, section 4.2b.
121. Guideline on Advance Rulings, section 4.2c.

122. Guideline on Advance Rulings, section 4.2d.
123. Guideline on Advance Rulings, section 5.
124. Guideline on Advance Rulings, section 5.1.
125. Guideline on Advance Rulings, section 5.2.
126. Guideline on Advance Rulings, section 6.1.
127. Guideline on Advance Rulings, section 6.2.
128. Income Tax Act 1967, section 138B; Guideline on Advance Rulings, section 6.3.
129. Guideline on Advance Rulings, section 7.
130. Guideline on Advance Rulings, section 7a.
131. Guideline on Advance Rulings, section 7b.
132. Guideline on Advance Rulings, section 7c.
133. Guideline on Advance Rulings, section 7d.
134. Guideline on Advance Rulings, section 7e.
135. Guideline on Advance Rulings, section 7f.
136. Guideline on Advance Rulings, section 7g.
137. Guideline on Advance Rulings, section 7h.
138. Guideline on Advance Rulings, section 7i.
139. Guideline on Advance Rulings, section 7j.
140. Guideline on Advance Rulings, section 8.
141. Guideline on Advance Rulings, section 8a.
142. Guideline on Advance Rulings, section 8b.
143. Guideline on Advance Rulings, section 8c.
144. Guideline on Advance Rulings, section 8d.
145. Guideline on Advance Rulings, section 9.
146. Guideline on Advance Rulings, section 10.
147. Guideline on Advance Rulings, section 10.1.
148. Guideline on Advance Rulings, section 10.2.
149. Guideline on Advance Rulings, section 10.3.
150. Guideline on Advance Rulings, section 10.4.
151. Guideline on Advance Rulings, section 10.5.
152. Guideline on Advance Rulings, section 10.5a.
153. Guideline on Advance Rulings, section 10.5b.
154. Guideline on Advance Rulings, section 10.5c.
155. Guideline on Advance Rulings, section 10.5d.
156. Guideline on Advance Rulings, section 10.5e.
157. Guideline on Advance Rulings, section 10.5f.
158. Guideline on Advance Rulings, section 10.5g.
159. Guideline on Advance Rulings, section 10.5h.
160. Guideline on Advance Rulings, section 10.6.
161. Guideline on Advance Rulings, section 10.7.
162. Guideline on Advance Rulings, section 10.8.
163. Guideline on Advance Rulings, section 15.2.
164. Guideline on Advance Rulings, section 10.8.
165. Guideline on Advance Rulings, section 11.1.
166. Guideline on Advance Rulings, section 11.2.
167. Guideline on Advance Rulings, section 11.2a.
168. Guideline on Advance Rulings, section 11.2b.

169. Guideline on Advance Rulings, section 11.2c.
170. Guideline on Advance Rulings, section 11.2d.
171. Guideline on Advance Rulings, section 11.2e.
172. Guideline on Advance Rulings, section 11.2f.
173. Guideline on Advance Rulings, section 11.3.
174. Guideline on Advance Rulings, section 11.4.
175. Guideline on Advance Rulings, section 11.5.
176. Guideline on Advance Rulings, section 11.6.
177. Guideline on Advance Rulings, section 11.7.
178. Guideline on Advance Rulings, section 12.1.
179. Income Tax Act 1967, section 99.
180. Guideline on Advance Rulings, section 12.2.
181. Guideline on Advance Rulings, section 12.2a.
182. Guideline on Advance Rulings, section 12.2b.
183. Guideline on Advance Rulings, section 12.2c.
184. Guideline on Advance Rulings, section 13.1.
185. Guideline on Advance Rulings, section 13.2.
186. Guideline on Advance Rulings, section 13.3.
187. Guideline on Advance Rulings, section 14.
188. Guideline on Advance Rulings, section 4.
189. Guideline on Advance Rulings, section 13.
190. Guideline on Advance Rulings, section 15.1.
191. Guideline on Advance Rulings, section 15.1a.
192. Guideline on Advance Rulings, section 15.1b.
193. Guideline on Advance Rulings, section 15.1ci.
194. Guideline on Advance Rulings, section 15.1cii.
195. Guideline on Advance Rulings, section 15.2.
196. Guideline on Advance Rulings, section 15.3.
197. Guideline on Advance Rulings, section 16.
198. Guideline on Advance Rulings, section 17.

22

CHAPTER TWENTY-TWO

New Zealand Transfer Pricing Developments

NEW ZEALAND issued transfer pricing guidelines as an appendix to the *Tax Information Bulletin*, Vol. 23, no. 10 (October 2000), doing so as a guide to section GD 13 of New Zealand's Income Tax Act 1994. Earlier transfer pricing provisions go back to the Income Tax Act 1976, section 22. The New Zealand transfer pricing guidelines specifically address documentation and intangibles issues in detail as well as examining services and cost sharing issues.

Most recently, New Zealand's current transfer pricing focus, as of May 14, 2008, addressed four issues related to transfer pricing: royalties, business restructuring, private equity, and intangible asset impacts. New Zealand transfer pricing is quite advanced, given the country's population. Thus, for example, New Zealand has a fully developed advance pricing agreement (APA) program, completing 31 APAs as of March 31, 2008, and having 6 APA applications in progress.

NEW ZEALAND TRANSFER PRICING GUIDELINES

The New Zealand transfer pricing guidelines are 79 pages in length and comprise these areas:

- Introductory material
- Arm's length principle
- Pricing methods: theoretical and practical considerations
- Principles of comparability
- Practical application of arm's length principles
- Documentation: statutory considerations and the Inland Revenue's approach
- Intangible property
- Cost contribution arrangements
- Changes from the draft guidelines

INITIAL DEVELOPMENTS

New Zealand follows closely the Organisation for Economic Co-operation and Development (OECD) *Transfer Pricing Guidelines for Multinational Enterprises and Tax Administrations.* New Zealand's Inland Revenue initially followed the OECD transfer pricing rules in their entirety during the development of the New Zealand transfer pricing guidelines. The New Zealand transfer pricing guidelines do not differ substantially from the OECD's view on any point, but the New Zealand transfer pricing guidelines elaborate on intangibles and documentation beyond the OECD guidelines. The New Zealand transfer pricing guidelines, then, should be read as supplementing the OECD guidelines rather than superseding them. The OECD guidelines will form the basis for resolving transfer pricing disputes under the mutual agreement articles of New Zealand's double tax agreements.

New Zealand's Inland Revenue has issued documentation guidelines that fill the void in the OECD regulations. New Zealand reserves the right to make its own decisions when the OECD so permits. New Zealand has done so in the case of documentation, for example, staking out its own position. The New Zealand transfer pricing guidelines specify that documentation plays a key role in determining whether the Inland Revenue is likely to review taxpayers' transfer pricing in detail.

The purpose of the New Zealand transfer pricing guidelines is to:

- Provide guidance as to the factors that the parties should consider in determining whether an amount constitutes an arm's length price
- Determine how these factors might affect a transfer pricing analysis

In addition to reliance on the OECD, the New Zealand transfer pricing rules make specific reference to guidelines issued by the Australian Tax Office and to guidelines issued by the U.S. Internal Revenue Service. The New Zealand transfer pricing guidelines state that there should be no conceptual transfer pricing differences between the U.S. rules and the Australian rules. Nevertheless, the range of comparables and the scope of transfer pricing adjustments in Australia and the United States might differ from those in New Zealand.

These New Zealand transfer pricing provisions go back to 2000. The New Zealand Inland Revenue, or the taxpayer, as the case may be, might be able to claim that New Zealand can ignore Australian rules or U.S. rules issued subsequent to 2000, arguing that Australia or the United States diverged from the New Zealand rules after that point.

The New Zealand transfer pricing guidelines warn the taxpayer not to make corresponding adjustments or deductions directly on their tax returns. New Zealand's tax law requires the taxpayer to use the actual transaction price unless the transfer pricing rules substitute an alternative price. The foreign tax administration's substitution of an alternative price is insufficient for New Zealand's purposes.

ARM'S LENGTH PRINCIPLE AND THE PRICING METHODS

The New Zealand transfer pricing guidelines focus on "market forces" as being the essential pricing determinant. An example determines this pricing analysis in a two-party context, using the "combined profit" of both parties as a starting point. New Zealand accepts five specific transfer pricing methods:

1. Comparable uncontrolled price (CUP) method
2. Resale price method
3. Cost plus method
4. Profit split method
5. Comparable profits methods

The profit split transfer pricing method typically refers to operating profit, but in some circumstances the parties can split profits based on gross profits rather than on operating profit. The parties can split the profits based on an "economically valid basis" approximating the division of profits that would have been anticipated and reflected in agreement made at arm's length.

The New Zealand transfer pricing guidelines and legislation do not establish an explicit hierarchy for the transfer pricing methods. The New Zealand Inland Revenue looks to the transfer pricing method that will "provide a more reliable result" than others. Inland Revenue equates the comparable profits method as used in the United States as being equivalent to the OECD's transactional net margin method. Note that the availability of data is frequently an issue in New Zealand, given the small market in the country, and this fact may impact the taxpayers' choice of pricing method as well as the use of foreign entities as tested parties.

As to the real-world constraints that impact transfer pricing, the New Zealand transfer pricing guidelines focus on two areas:

1. Identifying as a benchmark an independent firm that is as close as possible
2. Identifying and adjusting differences between the product or functions of the multinational firm from the product or functions of the benchmark firm

The New Zealand transfer pricing guidelines recognize real-world constraints imposed on manufacturers, as opposed to distributors, in seeking such a comparable independent firm.

The New Zealand transfer pricing guidelines appear to be enamored with the profit split transfer pricing method, speaking of a split based on an economically valid basis, approximating the division of profits that the parties would have anticipated, and reflected in an agreement made at arm's length. The New Zealand transfer pricing guidelines speak of the profit split method in the context of the ownership and division of intangible property.

BASICS OF THE TRANSFER OF INTANGIBLE PROPERTY

In economic terms, the New Zealand transfer pricing guidelines refer to intangible property as something that an entity owns; tangible property is something that enables the entity to earn more from a particular activity than the entity could earn if the entity did not own the property. The issue becomes the delineation between the use of the term "intangible" in the economic sense as opposed to in the legal sense. The New Zealand transfer pricing guidelines refer to that term in the economic sense but refer to legal ownership positions.

The New Zealand transfer pricing guidelines, like the OECD guidelines, delineate two types of intangible property:

1. Manufacturing intangibles
2. Market intangibles

The New Zealand transfer pricing guidelines emphasize the importance of ascertaining to which party the intangible's return should accrue. As a general matter, the returns should accrue to the party that created the intangible, typically the party that paid for the creation of the intangible. Thus, the retailer might use the cost plus method to determine the arm's length price that it created as to the intangible. The manufacturer might use the resale price method to determine the arm's length price created as to the intangible.

The New Zealand transfer pricing guidelines, in discussing intangible property, focus on risk and reward in the legal context. The development of intangible property involves some degree of risk for the party bearing that risk. The firm undertaking that risk as to intangible property would expect to be compensated for that risk. Ultimately, it will be the legal ownership of property concerned that determines which party benefits directly from the exploitation of the property. The compensation to the party that risks the development of the intangible depends on whether the creator of the intangible is the legal owner of that property or not. The legal ownership of the intangible property determines the property that benefits directly from the intangible property.

Two situations apply to the treatment of the creator of intangible property, depending on the legal ownership of that intangible property:

1. The creator of the intangible property would benefit directly from the intangible property, directly accruing any gains that arise as a consequence, if the creator of the intangible property is entitled to legal ownership of the intangible.
2. The creator of the intangible property that is not the legal owner of the intangible property would expect to be compensated for the costs and the risks it had undertaken as to this intangible. The owner of the intangible property would expect to provide compensation to the creator of the intangible property for the costs and risks that the creator of the intangible property undertook. The form of the compensation from the owner of the intangible property to the creator of the intangible property could be in the form of remuneration for services.

The New Zealand transfer pricing guidelines view the ownership of the intangible property as being entirely with the legal owner of the intangible property, most typically the foreign parent company that established the brand in its home country. The New Zealand Inland Revenue expects the foreign parent company to compensate the New Zealand subsidiary in one of two ways if the New Zealand subsidiary builds up its brand:

1. A share of the legal ownership of the brand name
2. Direct compensation

At arm's length, an independent party would expect something in return for incurring costs and risks. The New Zealand transfer pricing guidelines provide these examples of this return:

- By reducing the price of inventory sold by the foreign manufacturer to the New Zealand subsidiary
- Reimbursing the New Zealand subsidiary on a cost plus basis

PROFIT SPLIT METHOD AND THE JOINT OWNERSHIP OF INTANGIBLE PROPERTY

As a practical matter, more than one party to the transaction might own the intangible property. Consider the case of a foreign party that develops its technology elsewhere, imports the technology to New Zealand, and the New Zealand subsidiary develops its own brand name. Both parties in this instance would be creating valuable intangible property. The parties then need to ascertain:

- The total value that is attributable to the intangible property
- How the parties are to allocate the intangible property

It is rarely feasible to ascertain benchmark rates for these intangibles. Instead, the New Zealand Inland Revenue in essence recommends that taxpayers apply the profit split method. The parties then would:

- Determine the aggregate profit from the transaction.
- Divide this aggregate profit from the transaction between the parties on their relative economic contributions.

PROFIT SPLIT METHOD

The New Zealand transfer pricing guidelines refer to the OECD profit split methods as applicable in New Zealand:

- Residual profit split approach
- Contribution analysis approach

The New Zealand transfer pricing guidelines distinguish between the profit split methods and global formulary apportionment. The guidelines argue that global formulary apportionment "is determined without considering what the parties are actually contributing."

RESIDUAL PROFIT SPLIT ANALYSIS

The New Zealand transfer pricing guidelines favor the residual profit split analysis if the parties are to split profits. The residual profit split involves these processes:

- The first step in applying the residual profit method is to utilize a basic return, doing so to both the manufacturer and the retailer, based on what return independent firms would provide, such as by applying the cost plus method.
- The second step looks to the residual amount, which is the excess return over and above the basic return rate. The parties would then divide this amount, based on the parties' relative contribution to the intangible property. This profit split process involves judgment as to what factors contribute to the residual profit and their relative contributions of these factors, making this process a "somewhat subjective measure."

The New Zealand transfer pricing guidelines acknowledge that, as far as the profit split method is concerned, "there are difficulties in applying this method in practice" and taxpayers need to be aware, therefore, that not all jurisdictions will readily accept the determination of an arm's length price based on the profit split method.

TRANSACTIONAL NET MARGIN METHOD

The New Zealand transfer pricing guidelines provide that the transactional net margin method (TNMM) is considered, in international practice, along with the profit split method, to be a method of last resort. Nevertheless, the New Zealand transfer pricing guidelines provide that information constraints may dictate the TNMM as the only practicable approach in many cases. Further, the New Zealand transfer pricing guidelines provide that intangible property in the production process may further complicate the issue. A TNMM based on some cost base (excluding the transfer price) may, therefore, be an appropriate way to determine the basic return for the manufacturer's functions.

Both members of a multinational may own valuable intangible property. The valuation of this intangible property may make the application of the transactional methods or the TNMM methods impractical. The New Zealand transfer pricing guidelines conclude that it may be appropriate to consider applying the profit split method in such circumstances.

MARKET PENETRATION TECHNIQUES

New Zealand's Inland Revenue may apply a number of factors in evaluating a taxpayer's claim that it is following a strategy, such as a market penetration strategy, that temporarily decreases profits in return for higher long-term profits:

- Inland Revenue could examine the conduct of the parties to determine whether that conduct is consistent with the party's professed business strategy. Inland Revenue could expect the party undertaking a market share strategy to use unusually intensive marketing and advertising efforts along with that market share strategy.
- Inland Revenue could examine the market penetration strategy to ascertain whether the strategy is consistent with the taxpayer bearing the costs of that strategy.
- Inland Revenue could examine whether there is a plausible explanation that the business strategy will produce a return that is sufficient to justify its costs within a period of time that would be acceptable in arm's length arrangements.

AUSTRALIA'S FOUR-STEP PROCESS TO ASCERTAIN THE ARM'S LENGTH APPROACH

New Zealand's Inland Revenue views with favor the four-step process developed by the Australian Tax Office (ATO) to determine arm's length prices:

1. Understand the cross-border dealings between the associated enterprises in the context of the taxpayer's business.
2. Select the transfer pricing methodology or methodologies.
3. Apply the transfer pricing methodology or methodologies.
4. Determine the arm's length outcome. Implement support processes. Install review processes to ensure adjustments for material changes.

DOCUMENTATION

The New Zealand transfer pricing guidelines emphasize the importance of documentation in the transfer pricing process and provide the taxpayer with broad general parameters and nothing more. The New Zealand transfer pricing guidelines contain no explicit statutory requirement to prepare and maintain transfer pricing documentation. Thus, the New Zealand transfer pricing guidelines fail to provide specific guidance, as would the U.S. transfer pricing provisions, leaving instead extensive discretion on the part of the New Zealand taxpayer. The New Zealand taxpayer is not expected to prepare levels of documentation that are disproportionate to the amount of tax revenue at risk in their transfer pricing transactions.

At a minimum, Inland Revenue would expect the taxpayer to provide this documentation:

- An identification of the cross-border transactions for which the taxpayer has transfer pricing exposure
- A broad functional analysis of the taxpayer's operations so as to identify the taxpayer's functional functions being performed
- An estimation of the business risk of not undertaking and documenting a more detailed transfer pricing analysis
- An estimation of the costs of complying with the transfer pricing rules

New Zealand does *not* apply the contemporaneous documentation concept but approaches the contemporaneous documentation concept in many respects. Inland Revenue considers that a taxpayer should, as far as practicable, seek to collect and retain documentation that is:

- Existing at the time that the taxpayer was developing or implementing any arrangement that might raise transfer pricing issues, or
- Brought into existence *close to the time* the transaction occurs.

DOCUMENTATION AND THE BURDEN OF PROOF RULE

The New Zealand statutory provisions address the burden of proof shifting in the transfer pricing context. The price determined by the taxpayer is the arm's length price unless one of these conditions applies:

- The Commissioner can determine "a more reliable measure" of the arm's length amount than the measure of the arm's length amount determined by the taxpayer.
- The taxpayer does not cooperate with the Commissioner's administration of the transfer pricing rules.

A taxpayer electing not to prepare transfer pricing documentation leaves itself exposed on two counts:

1. It is more likely that Inland Revenue will examine the taxpayer's transfer pricing in detail if the taxpayer has not prepared its documentation.
2. Inland Revenue can substitute, as a result of this examination, an alternative arm's length amount for the one that the taxpayer adopts. The taxpayer's lack of documentation will make it difficult for the taxpayer to rebut Inland Revenue's substitution.

Inland Revenue views adequate documentation as being the best evidence that the taxpayer can produce to demonstrate that it has complied with these documentation rules. A taxpayer's failure to prepare and provide transfer pricing documentation, coupled with Inland Revenue's ability to demonstrate a more reliable measure of the arm's length amount, can cause the taxpayer to be subject to penalty. New Zealand has two specific penalties:

1. The taxpayer's failure to exercise reasonable care brings with it a 20% penalty.
2. The taxpayer's gross carelessness brings with it a 40% penalty.

INLAND REVENUE SEEKS TO ASCERTAIN THE RISKS TO THE REVENUE

The New Zealand transfer pricing guidelines provide that the primary determinant as to whether Inland Revenue will examine the taxpayer's transfer price in detail is the extent to which Inland Revenue perceives that the transfer prices present a "risk to the revenue." Inland Revenue is likely to conclude that a taxpayer's transfer pricing practices constitute a low revenue risk if the taxpayer can establish to Inland Revenue that it has set its prices in accordance with the arm's length principle and has documented how it determined these prices. In that event, Inland Revenue's role would then be one of monitoring the results.

The New Zealand transfer pricing guidelines view the documentation process as having two parts:

1. Part A considers the amount and quality of the documentation that the taxpayer should prepare and maintain to meet its statutory requirements.
2. Part B considers the Inland Revenue's transfer pricing enforcement strategy and considers the tools that Inland Revenue has available for obtaining and applying information if Inland Revenue is to examine the taxpayer's transfer prices in more detail.

Inland Revenue expects the taxpayer to consider the trade-off between the cost of compliance and the risk that Inland Revenue will audit the taxpayer's transfer prices and adjust the results. A taxpayer's determination of the arm's length price will be more persuasive in the face of an inquiry by Inland Revenue if the taxpayer's analysis is sound and is supported by good-quality documentation. Inland Revenue is likely to use a taxpayer's documentation, or the lack of it, as an important factor in determining whether the taxpayer's transfer prices present a risk to the revenue and whether they should receive further attention. Inland Revenue does not expect taxpayers to prepare levels of documentation that are disproportionate to the amount of tax revenue at risk in their transfer pricing transactions.

Inland Revenue rates these six factors as suggesting low risk when it comes to transfer pricing:

1. An APA exists.
2. The company provides actively negotiated prices, based on third-party pricing.
3. The company provides a strong economic and commercial basis.
4. The company is very cooperative.
5. The documents clearly support the most reliable method and are available.
6. The company provides an excellent compliance record.

RETENTION OF RECORDS

A New Zealand taxpayer must keep records for these time periods:

- Seven years after the tax year for which these records apply
- Three additional years if the Commissioner requests the extension

New Zealand taxpayers should extend the record retention period in these circumstances:

- In the case of long-term contracts
- In the case of licenses and similar arrangements

New Zealand normally requires the taxpayer to maintain the documents in New Zealand, and in English. The taxpayer can request the Commissioner to keep some records outside New Zealand or to maintain these records in a language other than in English.

TRANSFER PRICING IN COUNTRIES WITHOUT A DOUBLE TAX AGREEMENT

New Zealand Inland Revenue will look more closely at transactions with countries in which New Zealand does not have a tax agreement. Transactions with low-tax jurisdictions are particularly subject to Inland Revenue scrutiny. New Zealand might enforce exchange of information provisions when available. It may therefore be prudent for the taxpayer to prepare higher-quality documentation when the transactions involve nontreaty countries.

Taxpayers should consider the three-part delineation:

1. **Transactions with treaty countries.** Inland Revenue's normal scrutiny applies.
2. **Transactions with nontreaty countries, not low-tax jurisdiction countries.** Inland Revenue applies heightened scrutiny.
3. **Transactions with nontreaty countries, with low-tax jurisdiction countries.** Inland Revenue applies much higher scrutiny.

A nonresident parent company might dictate the transfer price to the New Zealand subsidiary. Such a subsidiary might have limited, if any, documentation that would demonstrate why its transfer prices comply with the arm's length principle. In that event, the Inland Revenue might have recourse to the documentation held by the nonresident parent if the Inland Revenue reviews the taxpayer's transfer pricing.

Inland Revenue acknowledges that taxpayers might face difficulties obtaining information from foreign-related parties that the taxpayers would normally not encounter if Inland Revenue required the taxpayers to produce only their own documents because:

- The subsidiary lacks control.
- Accounting standards and legal documentation requirements might differ.
- Prudent management might not suggest that the taxpayer keep these documents.
- The cost and expense of translating and producing these documents might be prohibitive.

Section 21 of the Tax Administration Act 1994 relates to payments the taxpayer makes for acquisitions made from a related foreign party. The taxpayer has an obligation to provide information as to that payment within 90 days of receipt from the Commissioner's request. If the taxpayer fails to comply with the Commissioner's request, the taxpayer then could not use that information in evidence in judicial proceedings.

The Inland Revenue does not intend, as a matter of course, to use non–publicly available information in an attempt to substitute that information as an alternative measure of the arm's length amount. It appears that the New Zealand Inland Revenue does not use secret comparables as an evidentiary standard but will use these secret comparables in ascertaining which taxpayers could be most responsive to transfer pricing adjustments.

INTANGIBLE PROPERTY AUDITS

Intangible property may be more problematic to audit than tangible property because it is difficult to apply intangible comparables and because multinational enterprises may structure their arrangements in ways different from independent firms. Functional analysis is critical in determining the real nature of the property being transferred because it seeks to identify:

- The owner of the intangible
- The factors that have led to the creation of intangible value
- The location as to where the rewards to that intangible accrue

The quest for comparables becomes paramount in the intangible property context. One such comparability approach is to compare the return to a manufacturing function that incorporates equivalent intangible property, a cost plus approach. The taxpayer may find that when using internal (or in-house) comparables, the transfer of the same property to an independent third party, if available, could provide a valuable source of information. It might not always be practicable to ascertain comparables directly. Inland Revenue cautions that it may be better to apply no comparable than to apply a patently wrong comparable. The profit split method requires a less rigorous determination of comparables than do other transfer pricing methods. As an alternative, taxpayers should consider valuing reliable projections of cash flow.

TRADE INTANGIBLES AND MARKETING INTANGIBLES

The OECD, like New Zealand, delineates two broad categories in intangible property: trade intangibles and marketing intangibles. The OECD guidelines are the basis behind the New Zealand rules:

1. A trade intangible arises from risky and costly research and development. The developer can create marketing intangibles for a substantially lower cost through the use of trademarks and trade names. In contrast, developing and maintaining marketing intangibles can become more costly.
2. Trade intangibles are associated with the production of goods. In contrast, marketing intangibles are associated with the promotion of goods and services.

3. A company's use of a patented trade intangible may result in a monopoly for the product. In contrast, competitors that can differentiate the marketing intangible can enter the market if they can differentiate the products.
4. Any legal rights for the trade intangible, such as for a patent, are likely to have a limited life. The use for which a company can apply the trade intangible determines the value of the trade intangible. In contrast, a marketing intangible may have an indefinite life if the company properly maintains the marketing intangible. A marketing intangible may have a very limited life unless the company incurs current marketing expenditures. The value of the marketing intangible will quickly evaporate if the company eliminates its marketing intangible efforts. Such a marketing intangible would then have little or no inherent value. It would then be inconsistent with the arm's length principle for that inactive marketing intangible to earn anything beyond a nominal return.

The New Zealand transfer pricing guidelines recognize that the boundary between trade intangibles and marketing intangibles might become blurred in many instances. As such, the New Zealand transfer pricing guidelines deemphasize this classification and instead emphasize the awareness of the factors that lead to the creation of value for intangible property of different natures.

ASCERTAINING THE ARM'S LENGTH AMOUNT FOR INTANGIBLE PROPERTY

The New Zealand transfer pricing guidelines recognize that there are inherent difficulties in ascertaining the arm's length amount for intangible property:

- It may be difficult to discern the precise nature of a transaction. Thus, a transaction might represent a number of components, both tangible and intangible, which are bundled together.
- The intangible property might have a special character that complicates the search for comparables. This special character might make it difficult for the taxpayer or the tax authorities to determine the comparables.
- Multinational businesses may adopt structures that are different from the structures of independent firms. For example, the multinational firm might transfer intangible property to an affiliated party that the multinational firm might not transfer to an independent firm.

ASCERTAINING THE OWNERSHIP OF INTANGIBLE PROPERTY

As a general matter and as a rule of thumb, the party that owns the intangible property initially bore the risks and expenses of the risks associated with its development, whether the party incurs these risks and expenses directly or indirectly through recompensing another entity undertaking work on its behalf. The owner of that property is entitled to all of the income that the property generates.

The initial owner of the intangible may choose to transfer some or all the rights to exploit the intangible. The initial owner should impose an arm's length charge for the transfer of these rights. The transferee would then be entitled to the income that is attributable to the transferred rights.

There might be situations in which the party that developed the intangible property does not acquire ownership of the property. The legal owner of the intangible property nevertheless would be the owner of the property even though the legal owner of the property did not contribute to its development. The developer non-owner of the intangible property can expect to receive arm's length consideration for its development services either through:

- Cost reimbursement, together with a profit component
- Lump-sum compensation, including a profit component

FACTORS IN ASCERTAINING THE NATURE OF INTANGIBLE PROPERTY

The New Zealand provisions follow the OECD rules in focusing on factors that ascertain the nature of intangible property:

1. The expected benefits from the intangible property. A net present value computation might be appropriate to determine the expected benefits.
2. The terms of the transfer. The terms of the transfer include:
    - The exploitation of rights that the transfer contains
    - The exclusive or nonexclusive character that the transfer contains
    - Any restrictions on the use the transfer reflects
    - Any limitations in the transfer as to the geographic area in which the transferee can exploit the intangible
3. The stage of the development of the intangible in the market in which the intangible is to be exploited:
    - Extent of any capital investment
    - Extent of any start-up expenses
    - Extent of any development work required
    - Necessary government approvals
    - Necessary authorizations
    - Necessary licenses
4. Rights to receive updates, revisions, or modifications of the intangible.
5. The uniqueness of the intangible property, and the period for which the property remains unique. This uniqueness of the intangible includes:
    - Degree of protection that the property affords under the laws of relevant countries

- Value of the process in which the property contributes to the final product

6. The duration of the license, contract, or other agreements, together with any termination rights or negotiation rights.
7. Any economic liability risks or product risks the transferee assumes.
8. Collateral and business relationships:
   - Existence of any collateral transactions taking place between the transferee and the transferor
   - Extent of any collateral transactions taking place between the transferee and the transferor
   - Existence of a business relationship taking place between the transferee and the transferor
   - Extent of a business relationship taking place between the transferee and the transferor
9. The functions that the transferee performs, including any ancillary or subsidiary services.

TERMS AND CONDITIONS OF THE INTANGIBLE PROPERTY TRANSFER

There can be various conditions for transferring the intangible property. Two of the most common conditions for the transfer include:

1. An outright sale of the intangible
2. A licensing arrangement for the rights pertaining to intellectual property

The New Zealand transfer pricing guidelines warn that it may be difficult to monitor the conditions for the transfer of the intangible. For example, it might be difficult to differentiate between a transfer of an intangible and a supply of a product or service that benefits from the intangible.

The treatment of embedded intangibles is an area of potential confusion. Such embedded intangibles include tangible property that carries the rights to use a trade name or trademark. This embedded intangible situation arises where the manufacturer sold the intangible to a related distributor.

The taxpayer needs to address a number of issues when dealing with the transfer of tangible property that includes an intangible element, such as a trademark:

- The taxpayer should consider whether the taxpayer has actually transferred the intangible rights. For example, the transfer of branded goods from one party to another typically does not involve the transfer of intangible rights.
- If the taxpayer has already transferred an intangible right, the taxpayer should then consider whether it should value that right separately from the intangible property. The taxpayer may need to consider the available comparable data and

the available transfer pricing methods. In addition, the taxpayer might need to consider industry-specific factors in determining the value of the intangible.

VALUING INTANGIBLE PROPERTY

The valuation of the intangible property might be uncertain when the transferor transfers the intangible property. One question to consider is whether the tax administrations can properly review the transfer price by reference to a form of arrangement that differs from the arrangement the taxpayer adopted.

The New Zealand transfer pricing guidelines take the approach that the parties to the transfer will share the risks and rewards when they transfer that intangible property. The structure of the arrangement may involve the sharing of the market, credit, country, and other risks between the parties. The form of the transaction rarely controls the transaction; substance over form controls. The central issue should be whether the taxpayer assumes an allocation of rewards, including the royalty rate, which is consistent with the risks that the taxpayer assumes. Functional analysis is paramount.

In New Zealand, the Inland Revenue will, in evaluating the transfer price, need to benchmark its analysis against an objective external standard. Yet the taxpayer's arrangement may be unique. The Inland Revenue might need to look to the arrangements that independent enterprises might make in comparable circumstances. Thus, Inland Revenue might inquire as to whether the associated enterprises made adequate projections, taking into account all feasible reasonable developments, making this determination without resorting to hindsight.

The taxpayer's documentation is crucial, documenting why the taxpayer structured the transaction as it has. The taxpayer needs to document how it determined the components of that price. The taxpayer should make this determination in reference to what independent parties in similar circumstances would have done.

The question then arises as to whether a small country, such as New Zealand, should automatically accept a multinational enterprise's royalty rate that the other countries accept. New Zealand Inland Revenue might inquire as to whether the empirical royalty rate is the stated royalty rate and as to whether the markets are sufficiently similar, taking into account the economics of the situation.

NON-OWNER'S MARKETING ACTIVITIES

An enterprise that does own the trademarks or trade names might undertake to promote the product through its marketing activities. A question then arises as to how the owner of the trade names and trademarks should compensate the marketer for promoting these products. A second-tier question then arises as to whether the owner of the trade names and trademarks should compensate the marketer as being a service provider or, alternatively, as sharing in any additional return attributable to the marketing intangible.

A distributor having its own marketing activity would expect to share in the potential benefits of these activities. However, the distributor might not be able to justify an extra return. Consider these cases:

- The distributor might have a long-term distribution contract for the trademarked product. In that event, the distributor may benefit directly from its investment in developing the value of the intangible because of its turnover and market share.
- There would be no justification for a distributor to receive any additional margin relative to an independent distributor unless a distributor bears expenditures beyond what an independent distributor with similar rights would bear.

It is important to consider the extent to which the distributor is bearing real risk compared with the risk that an independent firm in the market would bear. A controlled distributor might bear relatively greater risk than comparable independent firms. In that event, the controlled distributor is entitled to receive a greater margin from its activities.

The analysis should consider the impact of the marketing activities with the price of the tangible product. For example, the foreign manufacturer might undercharge the New Zealand subsidiary for the product it receives, but the New Zealand marketer might be incurring excessive expenses. The transfer price for the product and the expenses can be viewed together, compensating one for the other.

APPLYING THE PROFIT SPLIT METHOD TO INTANGIBLE PROPERTY

The New Zealand transfer pricing guidelines provide that, in many cases, taxpayers will face difficulties in identifying reliable comparables on which to base a sound transfer pricing analysis. Nevertheless, it will be very important to identify that the independent transaction used as a benchmark is truly comparable. Taxpayers may need to examine alternative approaches for performing this analysis.

One option that is available to taxpayers is the use of the profit split method. According to the New Zealand transfer pricing guidelines,

> a key feature of the profit split method is that it requires a less rigorous application of comparables than is required for analysis under any other methods. The downside of this, however, is that because the method tends to be more subjective in application than the other methods, it can increase the potential for disagreement between taxpayers and Inland Revenue over what transfer pricing are appropriate.

The New Zealand transfer pricing guidelines provide that "the profit split method might be a *useful alternative approach*" (emphasis added) for providing an analysis. In stark contrast, the OECD Guidelines provide that "the profit split *may be relevant* although there may be practical problems in its application" (emphasis added). Despite the OECD's cautious approach to the profit split method, New Zealand's Inland Revenue "considers the profit split method could represent a useful tool."

INTANGIBLE PROPERTY PLANNING

The taxpayer and the tax administration face special difficulties when addressing intangible property, especially in determining the arm's length price for that intangible. The taxpayer may have undertaken complex arrangements. As such, the taxpayer and the tax administration will find it difficult to ascertain comparable transactions. As to the question of ascertaining comparable transactions, one party to the transaction might not have contributed intangible property to the transaction. In that event, then, the most straightforward analysis is to test the party that did not provide the intangible.

It is important to look to the costs of maintaining the intellectual property. A subsidiary might be bearing the cost of this maintenance, but an independent party might not have to bear these costs.

The analysis of the intangible property may depend on a subjective judgment, especially when applying the profit split method. The taxpayer and tax administration may have limited resources to ascertain reliable comparables. In finding these comparables, the taxpayer should ensure that each party to the transaction obtains a return that is broadly consistent with the functions performed, assets employed, and risks assumed as to the transaction involving the intangible.

It might be appropriate to value intellectual property based on realistic projections of future benefits. It is then necessary to determine arm's length royalty rates to discount future benefits to present value.

A company undertaking marketing activities might not own the marketing intangible. The owner of the intangible needs to compensate the non-owner for undertaking these marketing activities. That compensation needs to be commensurate with what independent entities would charge given the rights and obligations under the marketing arrangement.

CHAPTER TWENTY-THREE

23 Philippine Transfer Pricing Regulations

THE REPUBLIC OF THE PHILIPPINES is in the process of developing transfer pricing regulations. The Philippine Department of Finance, Bureau of Internal Revenue (BIR), issued a draft of these transfer pricing regulations on June 21, 2006. Despite expectations to the contrary, the BIR has not issued final regulations as of July 2012.

The National Internal Revenue Code of 1997, section 50, raises transfer pricing responsibilities. The BIR designed the Philippine transfer pricing regulations to address the section 50 considerations. Section 50 addresses the determination of true taxable income, the methods for verifying and applying the arm's length standard, and the maintenance of necessary documents. The BIR addressed the draft transfer pricing regulations to its internal revenue officers rather than to the enterprise.

SCOPE OF THE PHILIPPINE PROVISIONS

The Philippine transfer pricing regulations are comprehensive, and, as a general matter, follow the Organisation for Economic Co-operation and Development (OECD) principles:

Section 1. Scope
Section 2. Authority of the Commissioner to allocate income and deductions
Section 3. Definition of terms
Section 4. Scope and purpose of review
Section 5. Limits to allocation
Section 6. Arm's length standard
Section 7. Comparability analysis
Section 8. Arm's length pricing methodologies
Section 9. Best transfer pricing method
Section 10. Application of advance pricing arrangements in avoiding and resolving transfer pricing disputes
Section 11. General rules in the determination of taxable income in specific situations
Section 12. Documentation

PHILIPPINE-SPECIFIC PROVISIONS

The Philippine 2006 draft of the transfer pricing provisions, if enforced, would impose specific provisions at variance with the OECD provisions.

Control

The draft Philippine transfer pricing provisions would impose a broad definition of "control" so as to include any type of control, direct or indirect, whether legally enforceable or not, and however exercisable or exercised. Section 3 would impose a reality test as to the control: "It is the reality of the control that is decisive, not the form or mode of its exercise."

Most important, the draft Philippine transfer pricing provisions would impose a 30% shareholding test to impose control. "A control is said to exist if one entity holds not less than 30 percent of the outstanding shares entitled to vote of a corporation." The draft Philippine transfer pricing provisions would impose a presumption of control requirement, specifying that a presumption of control arises if the enterprise arbitrarily shifts income or deductions.

Controlled Taxpayers

The draft Philippine transfer pricing provisions would give the BIR broad powers over the enterprise in a tax audit review. These measures would provide the BIR with "special scrutiny" over the enterprise. At the same time, the draft Philippine transfer pricing provisions would lower the threshold as to modifying "true taxable income" to modifications the enterprise made "either by inadvertence or design."

Divergence of Interests and Contract Terms

The draft Philippine transfer pricing provisions would give specific recognition to the importance of the "divergence of interests" between independent parties and that such divergence between unrelated parties would ensure that these parties would ordinarily seek to hold each other to the terms of the contract. The BIR recognizes that the parties will ignore or modify contract terms after the fact only if it is in the interests of both parties to do so. The drafters then recognize that the same divergence of interests might not exist in the case of associated enterprises. Accordingly, as to the conduct of these associated parties, the drafters provide that "it is important to examine whether the conduct of the parties conform to the terms of the contract," or "whether the parties' conduct indicates that the contractual terms have not been followed or are a sham."

Profit Split Method

The draft Philippine transfer pricing provisions in Section 8 portray the profit split method as the splitting of the profits between "involved associated enterprises" on an "economically valid basis." This economically valid basis would approximate the enterprise's anticipated division of profits of that enterprise. The draft Philippine transfer pricing provisions envision the enterprise splitting profits on the basis of the "relative contribution of each member." Nevertheless, the draft provisions seek to apply the residual profit split method.

In-House Comparables

The draft Philippine transfer pricing provisions express a clear preference for in-house comparables rather than external comparables. Thus, for example, as to the comparable uncontrolled price method, the cost plus method, and the resale price method, the draft Philippine transfer pricing provisions emphasize that transactions having "similar characteristics are more likely found among sales of products/services by the same supplier than among sales of other suppliers."

Best Transfer Pricing Method

The draft Philippine transfer pricing provisions look to the "most reliable measure" of an arm's length result. Section 8 provides the specifics of these transfer pricing methods. The draft Philippine transfer pricing provisions assert that the traditional transfer pricing methods are preferable to other transfer pricing methods. Nevertheless, the draft Philippine provisions provide that "neither the BIR nor the taxpayer is held to the hierarchy of methods specified in Section 8 of these Regulations."

Documentation

The BIR is conscious the taxpayers might face compliance and administrative costs in keeping adequate documentation. In response to these considerations, BIR imposes a "reasonable assessment" standard. "Taxpayers are only required to prepare and obtain documents necessary to allow a reasonable assessment of whether they have complied with the arm's length principle."

24

CHAPTER TWENTY-FOUR

Singapore Implements Advance Pricing Arrangement Procedure

THE INLAND REVENUE AUTHORITY OF SINGAPORE (IRAS) implemented Singapore's advance pricing arrangement (APA) procedure on October 20, 2008, through the issuance of a supplementary circular. This detailed APA procedure implements Section 6 of Singapore's transfer pricing guidelines that the IRAS had issued on February 23, 2006. As a general matter, Singapore permits a Singapore taxpayer to undertake an APA in one of two forms:[1]

1. The taxpayer can enter into an APA that is a unilateral arrangement involving the taxpayer and the IRAS standing alone.
2. The taxpayer can enter into a bilateral agreement or a multilateral agreement that involves agreement between Singapore and one or more of its tax treaty partners.

Two specific APA facets of the Singapore APA procedure are particularly relevant to U.S. taxpayers:

1. The United States and Singapore do not have an income tax treaty (except for airlines). As such, the Singapore and the United States cannot form a bilateral APA.

Nevertheless, such a taxpayer might choose to consider implementing a matched unilateral APA agreement.

2. The Singapore supplementary circular does not permit a taxpayer to enter into a roll back in the case of unilateral APAs.

OBJECTIVES OF THE SUPPLEMENTARY CIRCULAR

The IRAS issued the supplementary APA circular to achieve three specific objectives:[2]

1. To provide the taxpayer with the considerations and procedures that the taxpayer should observe as an APA applicant. This APA application process involves these two steps:
   a. The filing of the APA application by the taxpayer and the acceptance by the IRAS of the APA application.
   b. The discussion and agreement by or among the competent authorities concerned.
2. To address the circumstances under which the IRAS may allow an APA applicant's request for the APA to "roll back" and apply to roll-back years.
3. To set out the circumstances that would warrant the IRAS from discontinuing the APA process that the taxpayer initiated.

WHAT THE SUPPLEMENTARY CIRCULAR PROVIDES

Singapore's APA procedure, as specified in the supplementary circular, contains these parts:

- Considerations for facilitating acceptance of the APA application by the IRAS and discussions of APA application with the taxpayer
  - Pre-filing of the APA application
  - Formal APA submission
  - APA review and negotiation
- The APA roll back
- Discontinuation of the APA process
  - Nonsubmission of the APA application after expiration of specified time frames
  - Insufficient level of support efforts during the APA process
  - Absence of communication as to complete information
- Effective date
- Inquiries

MINIMUM INFORMATION REQUIREMENTS

Singapore's APA procedure specifies the minimum information the IRAS will accept for the pre-filing meeting and for submitting the formal APA application:

- The taxpayer's name, address, tax identification number, and contact details
- The letter of authorization from the taxpayer to its tax advisors or other representatives the taxpayer engages for purposes of the APA application
- A statement indicating whether the proposed APA application is a unilateral APA, a bilateral APA, or multilateral APA
- The nature of the covered transaction, and how these transactions relate to the overall business activities of the enterprise involved
- The covered transactions entities and detailed organized chart
- The covered period, including any roll-back period
- An overview of the next points by the covered entities during the proposed APA period:
  - Functions undertaken
  - Assets employed
  - Risks assumed
- An analysis of how the functions the covered entities undertake, the assets the covered entities employ, and the risks the covered entities assume have changed. This comparison is based on the period prior to the commencement of the proposed APA.
- The transfer pricing methodology chosen and the reasons why the taxpayer selected that transfer pricing method.
- The transfer pricing analysis, including these items where applicable:
  - Taxpayer's choice of the tested party
  - Profit level indicator
  - Screening criteria the taxpayer suggests for comparables and the database the taxpayer uses, as suggested at the pre-filing meeting
  - Transfer pricing adjustments the taxpayer may need, as suggested at the pre-filing meeting
  - Arm's length result, as suggested at the pre-filing meeting
- The critical assumptions under which the proposed APA will operate.

CONSIDERATIONS FOR ACCEPTING THE APA

The IRAS specifies that the APA process is a voluntary process and that the taxpayer must initiate the APA process for it to occur. In this regard, then, the Singapore APA initiation process is more akin to that of the U.S. APA process rather than that of the APA process in Australia. The initiation of the APA process in Singapore does not suspend any examination or enforcement process that the IRAS might conduct.[3]

The IRAS cautions that when initiating the APA process, the taxpayer would have recognized the advantages of seeking an APA with one or more competent authorities. The IRAS cautions regarding the advantages of seeking an APA with one or more competent authorities are curious in that a taxpayer might elect to have a unilateral APA—which does not directly involve competent authorities—rather than having bilateral APA or a multilateral APA. The IRAS suggests that it is in the interest of the taxpayer to take steps "to provide well for the APA process."[4]

The IRAS warns that, while an APA provides many advantages, the taxpayer should not underestimate the obligations and effort on its part to see the APA process to its fruition. These efforts might prove a highly time-consuming and costly exercise not only to the taxpayer but also to competent authorities concerned.[5]

When embarking on an APA, the IRAS recommends that the taxpayer be ready to fully cooperate with the competent authorities concerned, doing so to support their consideration of the APA application. This cooperation requires, among other things, the taxpayer's readiness to dedicate sufficient resources throughout the APA process to provide:[6]

- Swift, accurate, and good-quality analysis of the issues that arise or might arise
- Responses and clarifications to queries raised by competent authorities in the APA process

The taxpayer needs to dedicate resources to the APA process. In addition to having those dedicated resources, the taxpayer should "take appropriate active steps" beginning with the commencement of its APA preparation to maximize:

- The acceptance of the APA application by the IRAS
- Productive discussion and agreement by and/or among the competent authorities concerned

The IRAS observes, however, that a taxpayer that avails itself of the APA facility might not always appreciate the extent of the resources and efforts the taxpayer needs to effectuate this APA process.[7]

The supplementary circular states that it is critical that a taxpayer contemplating availing itself of the APA facility fully understand the obligations and efforts required on its part in this regard. Based on its experience in processing APA applications, particularly APA applications that involve agreement with another competent authority, the IRAS believes that, in such circumstances, the taxpayer should observe certain requisites and procedures to enhance the chances of a successful APA process. The supplementary circular explains the requisites and procedures the taxpayer should observe in order to support the APA process well.[8]

PRE-FILING APA PROCESS

The supplementary circular defines an APA as a determination, made in advance, of an appropriate set of criteria to ascertain the transfer prices of a specified period of time, the "proposed covered period." The pre-filing APA process addresses both the timing of the APA process and duration of the APA. An example indicates that the IRAS will accept an APA having a five-year period. The IRAS suggests a six-month time frame in applying for the APA before the inception of the proposed covered period. This APA turnaround time is quite short compared with that of the United States and Australia.

The supplementary circular contains an example in which the proposed APA covered period begins September 1, 2009, and ends August 31, 2014, suggesting that the taxpayer strive to submit the APA application no later than March 1, 2009.[9]

The IRAS suggests that the taxpayer contact the IRAS early in the submission of the APA application to initiate a pre-filing meeting. The purpose of the pre-filing meeting is to initiate a pre-filing meeting, before the pre-filing meeting between the taxpayer and the IRAS to discuss the proposed APA application.[10] The IRAS recommends that the taxpayer's first pre-filing meeting with the IRAS should preferably take place at least three months before the taxpayer intends to submit an APA application with the IRAS and/or another competent authority. This three-month delay is designed to allow sufficient time for:

- The IRAS to consider information provided by the taxpayer relevant to the feasibility of the APA application
- The IRAS to seek further details from the taxpayer relevant to the feasibility of the APA application
- The taxpayer to prepare and respond to any additional information required

Returning to the example in which the proposed APA covered period begins September 1, 2009, and ends August 31, 2014, and the taxpayer would submit the APA application by March 1, 2009, the first taxpayer–IRAS pre-meeting should take place no later than December 1, 2008. It is not uncommon for taxpayers and the IRAS to have more than one pre-filing meeting. Because more than one meeting is likely, the taxpayer should provide adequate lead time for the first pre-filing meeting and for any subsequent pre-filing meetings, as appropriate. The taxpayer should take into account the potential complexities surrounding the transactions covered by the APA.

The taxpayer should provide certain minimum information to the IRAS to facilitate constructive discussion pertaining to the proposed APA during the first pre-filing meeting. The taxpayer should provide this information to the IRAS at least one month before the first pre-filing meeting.[11] The minimum information requirements are discussed above.

The taxpayer and the IRAS intend that the purpose of the first pre-filing meeting is to address the material aspects of taxpayer's proposed APA application face-to-face. Accordingly, the IRAS imposes a unique but obvious requirement: that the taxpayer's representatives have good in-depth business knowledge and processes in relation to:[12]

- APA covered transactions
- Oversight responsibilities of the taxpayer's tax matters to participate in the first pre-filing meeting
- Any subsequent pre-filing meeting, upon request

It is usual for the tax professional to request its tax agent to attend pre-filing meetings with the taxpayer.

Three time periods precede the APA covered period:[13]

1. The taxpayer is to provide certain minimum information to the IRAS one month before the taxpayer and the IRAS have the pre-filing APA meeting.
2. The first pre-filing meeting between the taxpayer and the IRAS is to take place at least three months before the taxpayer intends to submit an APA application.
3. The taxpayer should submit the APA application six months before the proposed covered period is to begin.

A normal process during the pre-filing meeting is for the IRAS to request clarification or additional information from the taxpayer so that the IRAS can better assess the proposed APA application. During this pre-filing meeting, the IRAS will provide preliminary comments to the proposed APA application. These preliminary comments will include suggestions to the taxpayer (e.g., steps the taxpayer can undertake to culminate the APA process). The first pre-filing APA meeting, then, should help the IRAS and the taxpayer identify critical focus areas (e.g., where the IRAS and the taxpayer will require additional information, documentation, and analysis.)[14]

The IRAS discourages "anonymous" involvement on the part of tax professionals. Tax professionals had contacted the IRAS on some occasions. The IRAS does not encourage anonymous requests but will meet on that basis if the tax professional can demonstrate that there are sound reasons to do so.

The IRAS cautions the taxpayer that the lack of crucial information is likely to place severe limitations on the APA for that taxpayer. This lack of information is likely to impair the validity of any views that the IRAS provides incident to a meeting on a proposed APA. These "anonymous" meetings do not constitute pre-filing APA applications. The taxpayer, then, is strongly advised to engage the IRAS, doing so without masking its identity, if the taxpayer is serious about applying for an APA.[15]

FORMAL APA SUBMISSION PROCEDURES

The IRAS might agree during the pre-filing meeting with the taxpayer that the appropriate next step is to submit an APA application. The supplementary circular implies that the IRAS will provide a deadline to the taxpayer in submitting the APA application. This deadline might be reasonable as the IRAS is acting on data that might become stale quickly. That time period is not less than six months before the first day of the proposed covered period. The taxpayer should undertake "active steps" to submit its APA application no longer than the specified date. The IRAS can extend these time periods.[16]

A specific rule applies to bilateral APAs and to multilateral APAs. There the taxpayer should submit its APA application at the same time to both the IRAS and to the competent authorities of the relevant foreign tax jurisdictions. The APA application deadline for the foreign jurisdiction may be earlier than the six months that applies in Singapore. In that event, the taxpayer should submit its APA application concurrently to the IRAS and to the foreign tax jurisdiction at the same earlier date. The taxpayer is forewarned that failure to meet this timing requirement may cause the IRAS to reject the taxpayer's APA application.[17]

The APA application the taxpayer submits should include all of the key information components in the main transfer pricing circular. The IRAS needs at least three hardbound copies of the APA submission and one soft copy of the submission. Filing a complete and comprehensive APA submission is instrumental in speeding up the APA review and negotiation process.[18]

APA REVIEW AND NEGOTIATIONS: CONSIDERATIONS AND REQUIREMENTS

The IRAS will further evaluate the contents of the APA application upon its receipt of the APA application from the taxpayer. The IRAS might then seek further clarification from the taxpayer if necessary.[19]

The IRAS has agreed to inform the taxpayer within one month of the IRAS's receipt of the taxpayer's application as to the IRAS's acceptance of the APA application or otherwise.[20] The taxpayer should be aware of these situations:

- The IRAS might agree to accept the taxpayer's APA application. In the case of a bilateral APA or a multilateral APA, in the event that the IRAS does accept the APA application, the taxpayer has limited resources. The IRAS will proceed to contact the competent authorities of the relevant foreign jurisdictions to initiate the APA review and negotiation process.
- The IRAS might decline to accept the taxpayer's APA application. If the IRAS does decline the taxpayer's APA application, the IRAS would then fully explain the grounds for declining the request.

The IRAS and the other competent authorities concerned have the discretion to accept or reject an APA application. Nevertheless, without reserving the power to accept or reject the APA application, the IRAS is unlikely to decline the APA application if the taxpayer has complied with the requisites and procedures pertaining to pre-filing and submission of the APA application mentioned in the preceding paragraphs. The IRAS can, however, express its reservations on the appropriateness of the APA application during its pre-filing discussions with the taxpayer.[21]

The supplementary circular provides information to taxpayers concerning the scope of the IRAS's acceptance of the APA application. A taxpayer that makes an APA application should note that acceptance of the APA application does not mean the IRAS has accepted the specific facts of the APA application. In other words, the IRAS can accept the taxpayer's APA application without necessarily accepting in its entirety the taxpayer's proposed transfer piecing methodology or other variables (e.g., arm's length range, etc.) put forth in the APA application. The IRAS reserves the right to propose alternative methodologies, whether doing so on its own or in consultation with a treaty partner in a bilateral APA situation or a multilateral APA situation.

The IRAS also can request an expansion or restriction to the proposed APA even after the taxpayer formally submits the APA application.[22]

The IRAS, in the course of the APA review and the negotiation process, might find it necessary to request additional information from the taxpayer. Such additional information can include different levels of segmental data related to the APA covered transactions if the taxpayer did not previously provide this information. The IRAS warns that the taxpayer's "full cooperation and proactive support" in providing the requisite information to the IRAS is critical to the success of the APA process.

The supplementary circular provides that the IRAS is "committed to do its best" to expedite the APA review and the negotiation process. Nevertheless, the time taken by the taxpayer to respond to further information and clarification requested by the IRAS is also critical in determining the pace of progress of the APA review and the negotiation process. The taxpayer should take proactive steps to share with the IRAS any new facts and information that are likely to affect the outcome of the APA process.[23]

A special IRAS APA procedure applies to bilateral APAs and to multilateral APAs. As part of this APA procedure, the IRAS and/or its negotiation partners may require the taxpayer and/or its covered entities to submit additional information in response to queries raised by the competent authorities of the foreign tax jurisdictions concerned. The taxpayer is obligated to inform the IRAS when the taxpayer receives such queries from the relevant foreign competent authorities. The taxpayer should simultaneously submit to the IRAS any information submitted to the foreign competent authorities. The taxpayer should update the IRAS on a timely basis on the discussions of any meetings that the taxpayer and/or covered entities of the APA might hold with the relevant foreign authorities.[24]

The IRAS implicitly takes the position that the taxpayer will not be part of the APA review process nor the APA negotiation process. The IRAS, for its part, will also keep the taxpayer regularly updated on the outcome of the APA review process and the negotiation process.[25] Taxpayers should be cautious of the "updated on the outcome" phraseology in the supplementary circular as this term may connote the desire on the part of the IRAS to remove the taxpayer from the negotiation process altogether as if the treaty partners were part of mutual agreement procedure negotiations.

APA ROLL-BACK

The supplementary circular points out that the taxpayer, in some instances, may request an APA for a covered period to apply to certain prior years. This retroactive request is referred to as a "roll-back."[26]

The IRAS will consider the taxpayer's request to apply the APA to roll-back years only for bilateral APAs and multilateral APAs. The IRAS will consider the taxpayer's request based on:[27]

- The merits of the taxpayer's request
- That there are "no significant changes" to the facts and circumstances during the roll-back period
- That the transfer pricing methodology remains current to these earlier time periods

The taxpayer is expected to maintain relevant documents to substantiate the above facts. As a general manner, the IRAS might accept a roll-back period of up to two years prior to the proposed APA covered period.

Taxpayers outside of Singapore as well as taxpayers in Singapore itself are cautioned that the IRAS will *not* consider requests for the APA to apply to roll-back years in the case of unilateral APAs.[28] The supplementary circular failed to provide a rationale for that unilateral APA limitation.

DISCONTINUATION OF THE APA PROCESS

The IRAS will discontinue the APA process for a number of reasons, including when:

- The taxpayer does not submit the APA application after the expiration of specified time frame
- The taxpayer does not provide a sufficient level of support during the APA process
- There is an absence of communication or complete information

The IRAS stresses strongly that the success of the APA process:

- Is a highly time-consuming and resource-consuming process for the IRAS
- Requires the taxpayer to "consistently demonstrate full cooperation and active support efforts" throughout the entire APA process

The IRAS expects the taxpayer to "act in good faith with the IRAS" throughout the APA process. Similarly, the IRAS expects the taxpayer to be forthcoming in providing "complete and reliable information" relating to the APA application. This information includes any communication the taxpayer may have with the relevant foreign competent authorities and includes any information provided to the relevant foreign competent authorities. The IRAS may consider discontinuing the APA where these elements seem to be absent or are not forthcoming during any part of the APA process.[29]

The IRAS provides a number of examples of the circumstances that would warrant the IRAS's discontinuing the APA process. These examples illustrate the approach the IRAS would take in these circumstances.[30]

NONSUBMISSION OF THE APA APPLICATION

The IRAS expects that where the IRAS and the taxpayer have agreed, during a prefiling meeting, that the appropriate next step is for the taxpayer to submit an APA application, the taxpayer would take active steps to submit the APA application, doing so no later than the agreed specified application date unless the IRAS extends the application date. If the taxpayer does not submit the APA application by the specified application date, the IRAS is entitled to consider the taxpayer as not longer interested in pursuing the APA application process.[31] The supplementary circular does not address the procedure under which the taxpayer can seek to extend the APA extension date.

The IRAS provides taxpayers with a rule of thumb to assuage the taxpayer's continued interest in the APA application. The IRAS will consider a taxpayer as having no further interest in pursuing the APA application if the IRAS does not receive further information from the taxpayer regarding the application within six months from the date of the most recent pre-filing meeting.[32]

INSUFFICIENT LEVEL OF SUPPORT DURING THE APA PROCESS

The IRAS is likely to need to request additional information and other support from the taxpayer during the APA review process and the negotiation process. In this regard, the IRAS expects to receive full cooperation and proactive support from the taxpayer on a timely basis. The IRAS expects the taxpayer to provide to the IRAS accurate, good-quality information and analysis in response to the IRAS's information requests.[33]

As part of the APA review process, the IRAS seeks to agree with the taxpayer on the expected time frame by which the taxpayer should submit the additional information that the IRAS seeks. The IRAS will consider the taxpayer as having withdrawn from the APA process if the taxpayer fails to respond to information requests by the specified time frame and the information requested by the IRAS remains outstanding for an extended period of time.[34] The IRAS, as a rule of thumb, will consider the APA process as having been discontinued by the taxpayer if the taxpayer fails to provide requisite information to the IRAS within three months after the agreed expected time frame by which the IRAS is due to receive the information.[35]

ABSENCE OF COMMUNICATION

The IRAS evaluates the APA application based on the specific facts and information the taxpayer furnishes to the IRAS in the APA application. The taxpayer has an obligation to provide any relevant and material facts or information to the IRAS on a timely basis. These relevant and material facts or information are those items that would affect the outcome of the APA on a timely basis.[36]

The next example illustrates the materiality of the communications requirement. The taxpayer and/or the covered entities in a bilateral APA or multilateral APA can communicate with the relevant foreign competent authorities concerned, or the taxpayer and/or the covered entities in a bilateral APA or multilateral APA can provide them with additional information in response to their queries. Such information being transferred is likely to affect the outcome of discussions between the competent authorities. As a result, the supplementary circular requires the taxpayer to update the IRAS, on a timely basis, about the details of all such communications with the foreign relevant competent authorities concerned. The IRAS reserves the right to discontinue the APA process if it is subsequently determined that the taxpayer failed to provide material information to the IRAS and this information could have affected the outcome of the APA.

The IRAS can consider the timeliness for pre-filing and the timeliness of the formal application on a fresh basis. The taxpayer can express a wish to resume the APA process or seek to discuss the same APA application. The taxpayer can treat the application as if it were a new APA application subject to acceptance by the IRAS. The IRAS may take into account its prior experience in assessing the acceptability of the new application. The IRAS reserves the right to accept the new APA application. If the IRAS were to accept the new APA application, the IRAS will process this application and prioritize the application relative to other cases that the IRAS might already be processing. In this regard, the IRAS will treat unilateral, bilateral, and multilateral APA applications in the same manner.[37]

EFFECTIVE DATE

The IRAS will apply the administrative guidance provided in the supplementary circular to APA requests made on or after October 20, 2008. The taxpayer might have difficulty in applying the administrative guidance for a prior period before October 20, 2008. The IRAS will consider these taxpayer requests on a case-by-case basis.[38]

NOTES

1. Supplementary Administrative Guidance on Advance Pricing Arrangements, October 20, 2008, Sec. 1.
2. Supplementary Administrative Guidance on Advance Pricing Arrangements, October 20, 2008, Sec. 2.
3. Supplementary Administrative Guidance on Advance Pricing Arrangements, October 20, 2008, Sec. 3.
4. Supplementary Administrative Guidance on Advance Pricing Arrangements, October 20, 2008, Sec. 4.
5. Supplementary Administrative Guidance on Advance Pricing Arrangements, October 20, 2008, Sec. 5.
6. Supplementary Administrative Guidance on Advance Pricing Arrangements, October 20, 2008, Sec. 6.
7. Supplementary Administrative Guidance on Advance Pricing Arrangements, October 20, 2008, Sec. 7.
8. Supplementary Administrative Guidance on Advance Pricing Arrangements, October 20, 2008, Sec. 8.
9. Supplementary Administrative Guidance on Advance Pricing Arrangements, October 20, 2008, Sec. 9.

10. Supplementary Administrative Guidance on Advance Pricing Arrangements, October 20, 2008, Sec. 10.
11. Supplementary Administrative Guidance on Advance Pricing Arrangements, October 20, 2008, Sec. 11.
12. Supplementary Administrative Guidance on Advance Pricing Arrangements, October 20, 2008, Sec. 12.
13. Supplementary Administrative Guidance on Advance Pricing Arrangements, October 20, 2008, Sec. 13.
14. Supplementary Administrative Guidance on Advance Pricing Arrangements, October 20, 2008, Sec. 14.
15. Supplementary Administrative Guidance on Advance Pricing Arrangements, October 20, 2008, Sec. 15.
16. Supplementary Administrative Guidance on Advance Pricing Arrangements, October 20, 2008, Sec. 16.
17. Supplementary Administrative Guidance on Advance Pricing Arrangements, October 20, 2008, Sec. 17.
18. Supplementary Administrative Guidance on Advance Pricing Arrangements, October 20, 2008, Sec. 18.
19. Supplementary Administrative Guidance on Advance Pricing Arrangements, October 20, 2008, Sec. 19.
20. Supplementary Administrative Guidance on Advance Pricing Arrangements, October 20, 2008, Sec. 20.
21. Supplementary Administrative Guidance on Advance Pricing Arrangements, October 20, 2008, Sec. 21.
22. Supplementary Administrative Guidance on Advance Pricing Arrangements, October 20, 2008, Sec. 22.
23. Supplementary Administrative Guidance on Advance Pricing Arrangements, October 20, 2008, Sec. 23.
24. Supplementary Administrative Guidance on Advance Pricing Arrangements, October 20, 2008, Sec. 24.
25. Supplementary Administrative Guidance on Advance Pricing Arrangements, October 20, 2008, Sec. 25.
26. Supplementary Administrative Guidance on Advance Pricing Arrangements, October 20, 2008, Sec. 26.
27. Supplementary Administrative Guidance on Advance Pricing Arrangements, October 20, 2008, Sec. 27.
28. Supplementary Administrative Guidance on Advance Pricing Arrangements, October 20, 2008, Sec. 28.
29. Supplementary Administrative Guidance on Advance Pricing Arrangements, October 20, 2008, Sec. 29.
30. Supplementary Administrative Guidance on Advance Pricing Arrangements, October 20, 2008, Sec. 30.
31. Supplementary Administrative Guidance on Advance Pricing Arrangements, October 20, 2008, Sec. 31.
32. Supplementary Administrative Guidance on Advance Pricing Arrangements, October 20, 2008, Sec. 32.

33. Supplementary Administrative Guidance on Advance Pricing Arrangements, October 20, 2008, Sec. 33.
34. Supplementary Administrative Guidance on Advance Pricing Arrangements, October 20, 2008, Sec. 34.
35. Supplementary Administrative Guidance on Advance Pricing Arrangements, October 20, 2008, Sec. 35.
36. Supplementary Administrative Guidance on Advance Pricing Arrangements, October 20, 2008, Sec. 36.
37. Supplementary Administrative Guidance on Advance Pricing Arrangements, October 20, 2008, Sec. 37.
38. Supplementary Administrative Guidance on Advance Pricing Arrangements, October 20, 2008, Sec. 38.

CHAPTER TWENTY-FIVE

Singapore Transfer Pricing Consultation Process

THE INLAND REVENUE AUTHORITY OF SINGAPORE (IRAS) provided taxpayers with a Transfer Pricing Consultation study on July 30, 2008, revising the study on August 6, 2008 (the study). The 2008 study implements the February 2006 Transfer Pricing Guidelines Circular.[1] The IRAS issued the study primarily to buttress the documentation facets of the Transfer Pricing Guidelines Circular. This study explains how the IRAS carries out its transfer pricing "Consultation." Note that an IRAS "consultation" can result in a full-fledged tax audit plus professional advice provided *by* the Singapore tax authorities *to* the taxpayer.

BACKGROUND

The IRAS issued its Transfer Pricing Guideline Circular in February 2006, doing so to provide guidance to Singapore taxpayers on applying the arm's length principle.[2] The IRAS guidelines provide Singapore taxpayers with key concepts and with guiding principles, with the purpose of preparing and maintaining adequate documentation. The principal objective of preparing and maintaining transfer pricing documentation is to place the taxpayer in a position in which the taxpayer can readily demonstrate that it has "exerted reasonable efforts" to ensure that its transfer prices are consistent with the arm's length principle.[3] Section 4 in the 2006 circular provides specific documentation guidelines.

The IRAS has formalized its consultative process with Singapore taxpayers in its issuance of the study.[4] The IRAS will apply the consultation process to its taxpayers with taxpayers it selects. The IRAS's rationale in issuing the study is "to further help taxpayers comply with the arm's length principle in related party transactions." The IRAS intends to achieve three objectives as part of this consultative process. The IRAS will:

1. Assess the taxpayer's transfer pricing risks
2. Review the taxpayer's transfer pricing documentation
3. Provide recommendations to the taxpayer for managing risks

OBJECTIVES OF THE TRANSFER PRICING CONSULTATION

The IRAS imposes three objectives on the taxpayer:

1. To exert "reasonable efforts" to undertake sound transfer pricing analysis
2. To ascertain arm's length pricing
3. To demonstrate that the taxpayer has undertaken those efforts

Despite the IRAS's general expectations as to taxpayer behavior, the IRAS will monitor the taxpayer's ease of compliance and the taxpayer's level of compliance with the guidelines.[5]

The Transfer Pricing Consultation is a process designed for the IRAS to encourage taxpayers to further assist and advise the taxpayers as to the guidelines themselves and to the potential risks that the IRAS and the taxpayer identify. The IRAS states that the Transfer Pricing Consultation has two objectives:[6]

1. To assess the level of compliance with the transfer pricing guidelines[7]
2. To identify potential areas in which the IRAS can further facilitate and advise taxpayers as to good transfer pricing practices[8]

ISSUANCE OF THE TRANSFER PRICING QUESTIONNAIRE

The IRAS is in the process of sending questionnaires to selected taxpayers that have a significant number of related party transactions or appear to have a significant number of related party transactions.[9] The IRAS is focusing primarily on transactions with overseas parties. The IRAS is looking at the volume of transactions over time. However, the consultation fails to provide guidance as to the level that would constitute a "significant amount" to engender the IRAS's involvement with a taxpayer.

The taxpayer must provide the following transfer pricing information to IRAS through a questionnaire:[10]

- The principal activities of the business and a detailed description of the business's products or services
- The group of affiliated entities and other entities
- The types of transfer pricing methods the company determines; the taxpayer must provide the values of all transactions with each related party
- A detailed extent of the documentation the taxpayer obtains, pursuant the Annex G of the guidelines

The IRAS is to evaluate the taxpayer's response to the questionnaire. Based on these taxpayer responses, the IRAS will then determine whether it should undertake a transfer pricing consultation for the taxpayer.[11]

TRANSFER PRICING CONSULTATION

The transfer pricing consultation process entails the IRAS's field office visit to the taxpayer. The stated purpose of the field office visit is to:[12]

- Provide a better understanding of the taxpayer's business
- Provide a physical review of the documentation, if necessary

Based on this field office review, the IRAS might (or might not) decide to proceed with a transfer pricing consultation with a taxpayer. If the IRAS does proceed with a transfer pricing consultation with a taxpayer, the IRAS will seek written information for the taxpayer as to a number of matters.[13]

- After the IRAS reviews the taxpayer's responses to the questionnaire, the IRAS may require the taxpayer to provide additional information or clarification to those responses.
- The IRAS can request that the taxpayer provide copies of documents, such as contracts or agreements.
- The taxpayer can indicate a proposed date at which IRAS officers will come to the taxpayer's business premises.
- The IRS can provide to the taxpayer the contents of the taxpayer's presentation during the field office visit.

The IRAS consultation rules set parameters for the IRAS's visit to the taxpayer's facilities. The taxpayer is to make available the relevant personnel to make a presentation on:[14]

- The business structure of the business
- The activities and mode of operations of the business
- Explanations as to how certain factors in its business or industry affect the business's operating results

In particular, the taxpayer is to provide these explanations to the IRAS as to its business operations:

- The related party transactions in detail
- How the business prices these transactions
- How the business prices its transactions compared with transactions with unrelated parties

The IRAS reserves for itself the power to review the manner in which the company prepares and maintains its documentation and the contents of the documentation being prepared.

The IRAS is to provide the taxpayer with its opinion as to the following issues based on the IRAS's findings:[15]

- Whether the taxpayer's documentation is adequate and timely.
- Any reservations the IRAS might have regarding the taxpayer's transfer pricing methodology.
- The IRAS is to review the taxpayer's transfer pricing risk and provide an assessment of that risk, taking into account the commercial realism of the company's business results and the quality of the company's documentation.
- The IRAS is to provide advice to the taxpayer as to how the taxpayer can improve its documentation or methodology.

The transfer pricing consultation is "a process designed to further facilitate taxpayer's compliance with the transfer pricing guidelines."[16] Nevertheless, the taxpayer's transfer pricing might deviate significantly from the IRAS's opinion of arm's length pricing. In that event, the IRAS will express its position and will "make arrangements with the taxpayer to review the issue at an appropriate time."

The transfer pricing consultation process is designed to push the taxpayer toward tax preparation and self-review. Accordingly, the taxpayer with significant related party transactions should ensure that it has a system in place to prepare and maintain adequate and timely transfer pricing documentation, doing so to demonstrate compliance with the arm's length principle.[17] The taxpayer can use Annex G of the 2006 guidelines as a general checklist of the usual types of information as to such documentation. The taxpayer can use this information to help prepare its documentation or conduct a self-review of its documentation. Taxpayers and others can reach the IRAS at ctmail@iras.gov.sg or call 63513367 in Singapore.

TRANSFER PRICING QUESTIONNAIRE

The IRAS provides the Singapore taxpayer with a sample questionnaire but reserves the right to change the format and contents of the questionnaire from time to time or to customize the form for specific taxpayers. The IRAS is to indicate the taxable year of the entity. The taxpayer is to provide this information to IRAS:

1. Principal activities of the business.
2. Detailed description of the business's products or services.
3. Ultimate holding company, including its country of incorporation.
4. Immediate holding company, including its country of incorporation.
5. Chart of accounts for the group of companies to which the company belongs, from and including the ultimate holding company to the direct and indirect subsidiaries and associated companies of the company and other related companies. The chart is to include companies with which the company entered related party transactions.
6. The taxpayer is to indicate its sales to unrelated parties, specifying the currency the taxpayer uses.
7. The taxpayer is to indicate its sales to related parties, specifying the name of each related party, the country or domicile, the description of the goods or services provided, and the amount of applicable currency.
8. The taxpayer is to indicate its purchases to unrelated parties, specifying the currency the taxpayer uses.
9. The taxpayer is to indicate its purchases from related parties, specifying the name of each related party, the country or domicile, the description of the goods or services provided, and the amount of applicable currency.
10. The taxpayer is to indicate its other income and gains from related parties, specifying the name of each related party, the country or domicile, the description of the goods or services provided, and the amount of applicable currency.
11. The taxpayer is to indicate its other income and losses from related parties, specifying the name of each related party, the country or domicile, the description of the goods or services provided, and the amount of applicable currency.
12. The IRAS seeks information as to transfer pricing inquiries in other jurisdictions, including audit and tax adjustments in any foreign tax jurisdiction. The taxpayer is to provide the details of the affected transactions, current status and issues, and action taken by the related party.
13. The taxpayer is to indicate the extent of the company's documentation in Annex G, specifying the noncompliance, partial compliance, or completion as to each category:
    - General information concerning the group:
        - Worldwide organizational structure
        - Group's line of business and so forth
        - Group's business models and strategies
        - Principal business of each party
        - Business relationships or related parties
        - Consolidated financial statements
    - Information as to each related party in Singapore:
        - General information
        - Entity's line of business and so forth
        - Entity's business models and strategies
        - Entity's functions, risks, and assets

    - Entity's financial statements
  - Transactions between the company and all related parties:
    - All transactions taking place with related parties
    - The party's contracts and agreements
    - The party's segmented financial accounts
  - Transfer pricing analysis:
    - Taxpayer's choice of tested party, and the reasons why the taxpayer made that choice
    - Comparables the taxpayer uses and the company's screening criteria
    - Taxpayer's comparability analysis
    - Taxpayer's adjustments to achieve comparability
    - Transfer pricing method the taxpayer selects and the taxpayer's rationale in making that decision
    - Computation of the taxpayer's arm's length price or margin
    - The taxpayer's reasons for selecting the arm's length range

14. The tax preparer must sign and date the Questionnaire, affirming that information the tax preparer provides is true and complete.

NOTES

1. For background concerning the Transfer Pricing Guidelines Circular, see R. Feinschreiber and M. Kent, "Transfer Pricing in Singapore," *Corporate Business Taxation Monthly* (November 2007): 35.
2. Inland Revenue Authority of Singapore Transfer Pricing Consultation, 2008, sec. 1.1.
3. Inland Revenue Authority of Singapore Transfer Pricing Consultation, 2008, section 1.2.
4. Inland Revenue Authority of Singapore Transfer Pricing Consultation, 2008, section 1.3.
5. Inland Revenue Authority of Singapore Transfer Pricing Consultation, 2008, section 2.1.
6. Inland Revenue Authority of Singapore Transfer Pricing Consultation, 2008, section 2.2.
7. Inland Revenue Authority of Singapore Transfer Pricing Consultation, 2008, section 2.2(a).
8. Inland Revenue Authority of Singapore Transfer Pricing Consultation, 2008, section 2.2(b).
9. Inland Revenue Authority of Singapore Transfer Pricing Consultation, 2008, section 3.1.
10. Inland Revenue Authority of Singapore Transfer Pricing Consultation, 2008, section 3.2.
11. Inland Revenue Authority of Singapore Transfer Pricing Consultation, 2008, section 3.3.
12. Inland Revenue Authority of Singapore Transfer Pricing Consultation, 2008, section 4.1.
13. Inland Revenue Authority of Singapore Transfer Pricing Consultation, 2008, section 4.1.
14. Inland Revenue Authority of Singapore Transfer Pricing Consultation, 2008, section 4.2.
15. Inland Revenue Authority of Singapore Transfer Pricing Consultation, 2008, section 4.3.
16. Inland Revenue Authority of Singapore Transfer Pricing Consultation, 2008, section 4.4.
17. Inland Revenue Authority of Singapore Transfer Pricing Consultation, 2008, section 5.1.

CHAPTER TWENTY-SIX

Singapore Transfer Pricing Guidelines

THE INLAND REVENUE AUTHORITY OF SINGAPORE (IRAS) issued an IRAS Circular, The Transfer Pricing Guidelines, on February 23, 2006. The guidelines themselves are 38 pages in length, and emanate from long-standing provisions in the Singapore tax law.[1] The guidelines themselves are cohesive and comprehensive but they are brief, touching on many salient transfer pricing issues. Nevertheless, these guidelines do not address many of the arcane issues in which the U.S. tax authorities and its trading partners are now enmeshed. As we shall see, however, the guidelines fail to flesh out certain facets of the cost plus method and to consider practical database issues impacting comparables for the residual profit split method.

The IRAS conceptualizes the presence of "independent commercial prices," and views the lack of independence between related parties as potentially leading to the setting of prices that deviate from these independent commercial prices. The IRAS abides by the arm's length principle and believes that this arm's length principle is the most appropriate standard to determine transfer prices of related parties. Nevertheless, the IRAS recognizes that tax authorities worldwide are stepping up their audit efforts to verify compliance with the arm's length principle.

Transfer pricing provisions in Singapore depend on the presence of related parties. The IRAS's Section 2.2 speaks of control as the determinant of related party status. The IRAS defines a related party in this matter: "A related party, in relation to any other entity, means any other entity who, directly or indirectly, by that entity, or where both entities, directly or indirectly, are under common control of a common entity." However, after creating the linkage between control and related party status, the IRAS fails to define the parameters of "control" activities or status.

The IRAS transfer pricing guidelines contain four operative provisions:

1. Arm's length principle
2. Documentation
3. Mutual agreement procedures
4. Advance pricing agreements

KEY CONCEPTS AND ARM'S LENGTH PRINCIPLES

Singapore's tax legislation does not contain a specific provision stipulating the use of the arm's length principle for related party transactions. Nevertheless, the IRAS rendition of the arm's length principle contains key concepts and guiding principles of their own, beginning with the Organisation for Economic Co-operation and Development (OECD) transfer pricing guidelines and model tax convention. The IRAS, then, speaks of "market forces" driving the "terms and conditions" that would "reflect the true economic value of the contributions made by each party in the transaction."[2]

The IRAS recognizes that it may be difficult to apply the arm's length principle in certain circumstances, especially when certain business structures and arrangements are complicated and unique. The taxpayer would rarely encounter comparables in that situation. Business secrets and confidential information will compound the comparability issues.

Accordingly, the IRAS recognizes that transfer pricing is not an exact science and that it requires judgment. The IRAS then recommends that taxpayers adopt a pragmatic approach in determining arm's length pricing. Unlike in many other countries, in Singapore, the taxpayer is not expected to adhere rigidly to a defined set of rules to establish the arm's length price. The taxpayer can depart from or complement the approaches in the circular if by doing so the taxpayer aids in determining the arm's length price.[3] Nevertheless, the IRAS appears to mandate specific documentation guidance.[4] The taxpayer is likely to find that it is difficult to apply the requirements of Annex G, item (d)(iv) (i.e., details of adjustments necessary to achieve comparability and the reasons for these adjustments).

The IRAS put the taxpayer as having the best position to perform "a robust and comprehensive transfer pricing analysis" to determine the arm's length price.[5] The IRAS expects the taxpayer to "exert reasonable efforts" to undertake a sound transfer pricing analysis and to demonstrate that the taxpayer has performed that analysis.[6] A taxpayer that undertakes these obligations will be considered prima facie as having met the arm's length determination. The circular reflects the IRAS's openness to discussions with taxpayers.

THREE-STEP APPROACH

The IRAS applies a three-step approach in applying the arm's length principle:[7]

1. Conduct a comparability analysis (i.e., identification of independent parties that serve as the benchmark for comparable transactions).
2. Identify the appropriate transfer pricing method and tested party.
3. Determine the arm's length results.

The IRAS expects the taxpayer to apply "an element of judgment" in the transfer pricing analysis. Contrary to the transfer pricing approach taken by many jurisdictions, the IRAS specifically provides that "the recommended steps are neither mandatory or prescriptive."[8] The IRAS, then, expects the taxpayer to present its transfer pricing analysis logically and persuasively.

The IRAS recognizes that the arm's length principle can be based on a comparison of prices or on comparison of margins, comparing independent transactions with related party transactions. In this regard, the IRAS views the comparative analysis as taking place between such activities as the provision of goods, services, or intangible property.[9]

COMPARISON OF ECONOMICALLY SIGNIFICANT FUNCTIONS

The IRAS believes that a comparison of economically significant functions performed, assets used, and risks assumed is an essential transfer pricing ingredient to the transfer pricing mechanism.[10] In this regard:

- Functions include a broad base of activities. These activities include, but are not limited to, such activities as design, research and development, manufacturing, distribution, sales, marketing, logistics, advertising, financing, and the like.[11]
- The IRAS would have the taxpayer, in determining assets employed, include assets the taxpayer has not yet employed. Such assets would include the plant and equipment and valuable intangibles. It appears that the IRAS would expect the taxpayer to include assets being constructed, such as plant, into the assets employed computation. The IRAS apparently does not expect the taxpayer to determine the current value of these assets. Instead, the IRAS expects the taxpayer to reflect the age of these assets.[12]
- The IRAS would have the taxpayer assess and appraise risks on a broad basis. Such risks would include market risks, financial risks, research and development failures, foreign exchange risks, and credit risks.[13]

The IRAS states that the taxpayer is to take into account a broad range of commercial and economic circumstances in determining arm's length prices:[14]

- The taxpayer is to reflect basic economic circumstances, including the availability of substitute goods and circumstances.[15]
- The taxpayer is to reflect government policies and regulations. These policies specifically include price controls and national insurance costs.[16]
- The commercial and economic circumstances provisions address business strategies. (Market penetration is a different matter, and the IRAS provides for market penetration separately.) The IRAS views business strategies broadly to include innovation, new product development, diversification, risk aversion, and political changes.[17]
- The IRAS takes into account the taxpayer's market penetration, market share expansion plans, or market defense strategies. The taxpayer seeking IRAS approval as to its market strategy must demonstrate that the strategy is temporary. Further, the taxpayer must demonstrate that it undertook the market development approach, which reduces short-term profits, in anticipation of higher long-term profits. Following the OECD guidelines, the IRAS does not use the term "marginal costing" in this context. The IRAS expects the taxpayer to demonstrate that an independent party would have taken the same actions.[18]

COMPARABLE UNCONTROLLED PRICE METHOD

The IRAS follows the OECD guidelines and favors the comparable uncontrolled price method (CUP) as being the most direct method.[19] The IRAS looks to a high degree of comparability,[20] in terms of type, physical characteristics, quality and quantity transacted, undertaken in similar market or economic conditions.[21] The IRAS permits the taxpayer to make use of internal or external comparables:

- The IRAS provides an external comparable CUP example in which an unrelated party sells a commodity product to other parties.[22]
- The IRAS provides an internal comparable CUP example in which a seller of computer disk drives sells the drives to a subsidiary and, for comparison, sells them to an unrelated company.[23]

TRANSFER PRICING METHOD SELECTION

The IRAS, in following the OECD guidelines, expresses in theory that the traditional transaction methods would provide a more direct comparison of independent party transactions and in theory would be superior to the profit-based profit methods.[24] However, the IRAS, as a matter of practice, moves toward the U.S.-sponsored best method approach, stating that the IRAS does not have a specific preference for any one transfer pricing method. The IRAS does, however, look critically at the availability and quality of data, the accuracy of the adjustments, and the method that limits necessary adjustments.

The interquartile range is a U.S. concept, designed to limit the scope of acceptable transfer pricing ranges. The OECD does not make use of the interquartile range. The IRAS permits the taxpayer to make use of the interquartile range but does not specifically require its use.[25]

Resale Price Method

The IRAS, similar to the OECD guidelines, favors the resale price method or the cost plus method if the taxpayer's activities make the CUP method infeasible. The resale method is potentially viable if the taxpayer buys the product from a related party and sells the product to an independent party. The starting point in the transfer pricing analysis is to begin with the price that the reseller receives from the independent party. The taxpayer then reduces from the price received from the independent party the amount of the comparable gross margin or resale price margin to arrive at the intercompany sales price. The resale price margin includes the reseller's operating costs plus a reasonable profit based on the functions the reseller performs.[26]

The IRAS permits the taxpayer to apply the resale price method under either of two bases:[27]

1. The taxpayer determines the resale profit through comparing independent resale transactions (in-house comparables).
2. The taxpayer applies the resale profit in reference to the profit an independent party would make through its sales to its unrelated parties (external comparables).

The IRAS provides an example of the in-house comparable but does not provide an example of an external comparable.[28] The IRAS states that the resale price method is most appropriate where the reseller adds little value to the properties.[29] The greater the value that the reseller adds, such as through complicated assembly or assembly with other products, the more difficult it is for the reseller to apply the resale price method. Nevertheless the IRAS phraseology "complicated assembly or assembly with other products" gives the reseller more flexibility than other tax jurisdictions provide as to the resale price method.

Cost Plus Method

The cost plus method determines the markup obtained by a supplier that transfers property, typically manufactured property, to a related purchaser or provides services to a related purchaser. The IRAS views the cost plus method as being most useful when semi-finished items are sold between related parties or when the related party transaction involves the provision of services.[30] As tax practitioners, we view the IRAS approach regarding the cost plus method as being too narrow. For example, the cost plus method should be the best method for suppliers of finished widgets to be used in a broader manufacturing process as well as for producers of semi-finished goods.

The IRAS visualizes "costs" as reflecting:[31]

- Direct costs, such as the cost of raw materials
- Indirect costs, such as depreciation, repair, and maintenance that can be allocated among several products
- Operating expenses, such as supervisory, marketing, general, and administrative expenses

Apparently, the IRAS would exclude rent, utilities, property tax, and similar expenses in determining "cost" for purposes of the cost plus method. We view labor costs as a direct cost, although the IRAS guideline refers only to raw materials in the determination of cost.

Annex D provides a cost method example that differs from cost plus examples in other jurisdictions. The fact pattern describes an external comparable, but the same analysis could be undertaken using internal comparables. Internal comparables would apply if the manufacturing entity sells its goods to independent parties and sells the same goods to members of the controlled group.[32]

Annex D describes a situation in which the manufacturer of pharmaceutical products located in Singapore essentially performs the role of contract manufacturer to its foreign-based parent, which invented the drug and is the only manufacturer. There is one comparable for transfer pricing purposes, an unrelated Singapore manufacturer in the pharmaceutical industry that manufactures a different drug as contract manufacturer to several independent principals.

Profit Split Method

The IRAS views the profit split method as "particularly useful" when the transactions are so highly interrelated that they cannot be evaluated separately or where the parties have unique intangible assets.[33] The IRAS views the profit split method as having two steps:

1. Identifying the profit to be split.
2. Splitting the profit by reference to the contributions of the parties to the transaction. The party identifies its contributions by taking into account:
   - Functions that the party performs
   - Assets of the party
   - Risks that the party assumed

The IRAS would have the taxpayer value its contributions (functions, assets, and risks) valued as far as possible by reference to independent data. As tax practitioners, we have recommended to the Internal Revenue Service (IRS) and Treasury Department in formal meetings in Washington, D.C., and Atlanta to adopt an alternative approach relying on in-house comparables based on equivalent parameters as to the parties involved rather than relying on independent data. The IRAS's view, with which we disagree, is that the relative value of the contribution of each party is often more difficult to quantify when one attempts to divide the profit directly.[34]

The IRAS states that the income to be split is normally the operating profit. Nevertheless, the taxpayer can split that gross profit and then deduct the expenses incurred by each party or expenses attributable to each party.

The IRAS identify two types of profits to be split:

1. Total profit from the arrangement.
2. A residual amount that cannot be easily assigned to one party or the other. Such a residual amount is typically associated with high-value and unique intangibles.

The IRAS provides two methods for splitting profits:

1. Residual analysis approach
2. Contribution analysis approach

According to the IRAS, the residual analysis approach splits total profit from the transaction in two stages. In the first stage of the analysis, each party is allocated a "basic return" determined using comparable data for the readily identifiable functions, such as manufacturing, distribution, service provision, and so forth.[35] The taxpayer would presumably make reference to independent data at this stage of the analysis, but the IRAS is not totally clear on this point. This basic return analysis leads to the taxpayer's uncertainty, as the rate of return is most typically a range rather than a certain amount. The first step in the analysis should exclude the return generated by unique and valuable assets. As tax practitioners, we find the delineation between unique and valuable assets, on one hand, and ordinary assets, on the other hand, difficult to apply.

The IRAS would have the taxpayer divide the remaining profits after taking into account the profits attributable to the basic return. The remaining profit, then, is attributable to the unique assets. The taxpayer would then allocate the remaining profit between the parties based on their relative contributions as to the creation of such assets. The IRAS would then have the taxpayer divide these residual profits, taking into consideration how independent parties have divided such residual profits in similar circumstances. As tax practitioners, it is our belief that such comparable data are often not available, in large measure because competitors would not reveal and publicly quantify their unique property–ordinary property delineation. The IRAS recommends that taxpayers use the residual profit split method in cases where the profit split is appropriate.

The IRAS permits the taxpayer to use the contribution analysis approach, but the IRAS does not favor that transfer pricing method. Under the contribution analysis approach, the taxpayer would divide the total profit earned by the parties from a related party transaction based on each party's contribution to that profit. The IRAS disfavors the contribution analysis approach as it is "often more difficult to quantify" when the taxpayer attempts to divide the profit directly. The IRAS presupposes that the taxpayer would resort to comparable data in the residual analysis approach but not in the contribution analysis approach, and favors the residual analysis approach on that basis. We respectfully favor the contribution analysis approach rather than the residual analysis approach in situations in which the profit split method is appropriate.

The IRAS Circular, the Transfer Pricing Guidelines, provides a complex example illustrating the profit split method: the residual profit split approach. A Singapore manufacturing company developed an original microprocessor. This Singapore company holds the patent for manufacturing technology and owns a foreign manufacturing subsidiary. The example presupposes that there is just one comparable for similarly situated wholesalers in that industry. There is just one comparable for similarly situated contract manufacturers (here handphone contract manufacturers) in that industry, with all parties excluding intangibles. In our view, the IRAS articulated the residual profit method; but it is our view that as a general matter, the database that the IRAS presupposed is often unrealistic.

Transactional Net Margin Method

The transactional net margin method (TNMM) compares net margins, comparing the independent entities based on an appropriate base, such as costs, sales, or assets.[36] The TNMM as found in the OECD guidelines is quite similar to the U.S. comparable profits methods, but the results of these methods differ in some situations. The TNMM is similar to the resale method and the cost plus method in many respects.[37] The IRAS suggests that the taxpayer account for differences in the efficiency in plant and machinery, management and personnel capabilities, competitive position, and the like to produce reliable measures of arm's length margins.[38] The IRAS's approach is theoretically sound but, in our view, is difficult to apply, often limiting the taxpayer's choice of the TNMM. In the United States, as a matter of practice, the IRS often ignores those limiting factors in all but the largest transfer pricing transactions.

Annex F provides the taxpayer with a helpful example. The taxpayer in this instance cannot account for the differences with similar products in the market and, accordingly, the taxpayer does not apply the CUP method. One such difference is the presence or absence of warranty functions, and the taxpayer has no information concerning the cost differential. The TNMM is then the best transfer pricing method, relying on net margins. The example uses a cost markup approach.

TRANSFER PRICING DOCUMENTATION

The IRAS's Transfer Pricing Guidelines provide limited documentation guidelines compared with those in the United States. According to the IRAS, the taxpayer's goal is to "exert reasonable efforts to undertake a sound transfer pricing analysis." The IRAS expects the taxpayer to demonstrate that it has performed this transfer pricing analysis and has retained records to demonstrate that it conformed to the arm's length principle.[39]

The IRAS does not impose detailed documentation requirements on the taxpayer. Instead, the IRAS expects the taxpayer to demonstrate that it has exerted reasonable efforts to ensure that its transfer prices are consistent with the arm's length principle.[40] The IRAS expects the taxpayer to provide sufficient details and on a timely basis.[41]

The IRAS had expressed in its Transfer Pricing Guidelines its concern with the taxpayer's compliance and administrative costs affecting transfer pricing documentation.[42] The IRAS threshold is the amount of documentation that a taxpayer can prepare or maintain to enable the IRAS to provide a reasonable assessment of whether the taxpayer has complied with the arm's length principle.[43] The IRAS, unlike the United States in mandating compliance with Forms 5471 and 5472, seeks a balance as to how extensive the documentation should be. The balance should be between the taxpayer's need to show compliance with the arm's length principle and the taxpayer's administrative costs. On one hand, then, the taxpayer is not expected to go to such great lengths to make documentation costs disproportionate to the amount of tax revenue at risk. On the other hand, the taxpayer must keep documentation for complex and significant related party transactions.

The IRAS does not impose specific documentation requirements on the taxpayer, viewing the documents submitted as specific to the taxpayer's industry.[44]

Many countries impose specific penalties on taxpayers that do not provide the necessary documentation. Singapore, however, does not provide for any documentation-specific penalties.[45] Instead, the IRAS can impose penalties under other tax provisions regarding the taxpayer's failure to provide and obtain documentation.

The IRAS suggests two reasons why a taxpayer should keep adequate documentation:[46]

1. To discharge its burden of proof
2. To apply for assistance under the mutual agreement procedures

The IRAS does not require the taxpayer to submit documentation at the time the taxpayer files its tax return. The IRAS provides instead that the taxpayer maintain its transfer pricing documentation as long as there is a possibility of being subject to transfer pricing examinations or the taxpayer can be involved in a mutual agreement procedure.[47]

Annex G provides guidance as to the documentation requirements. In a broad context, the IRAS requires the taxpayer to provide documentation as to the group as a whole, each party in Singapore, details of transactions between each Singapore entity with its related parties, and the transfer pricing analysis itself.

The general information about the group involves details as to the organizational structure, linkages, line of business, regulatory conditions, and business relationships. The general information grouping also requires the taxpayer to ascertain business activities and functions and to prepare financial statements as well as providing business models and strategies, past, present, and future. In our view, the IRAS requirement that the taxpayer provide linkages and business relationships leads to uncertain results because of the uncertainty of these terms.

The IRAS expects the taxpayer to provide information about each related entity in Singapore. The IRAS asks for detailed information about the entities' business models and strategies, past, present, and future. This requirement differs from the preceding requirement as it requires detailed information.

The IRAS expects taxpayers to provide detailed information between the Singapore entity and related parties. This documentation includes contracts or agreements, if any, that show the terms of the transaction. In addition, the IRAS expects the taxpayer to provide segmented accounts and to provide explanations regarding the assumptions that give rise to the segmented information.

The IRAS expects taxpayers to develop its transfer pricing analysis, including the choice of the tested party and the taxpayer's reasons for making that choice. Then the IRAS expects the taxpayer to provide details regarding the comparables and provide the screening criteria for choosing the comparables. Having the preceding information, the IRAS expects the taxpayer to provide a comparability analysis of the related party transactions and the comparables.

The IRAS expects the taxpayer to make adjustments that the taxpayer finds necessary to achieve comparability and then to provide the details and reasons for making those adjustments—an impossible task for all but the largest enterprises. The taxpayer is to choose a transfer pricing method, identify the pricing method to the IRAS, and substantiate why that method is most appropriate. The IRAS expects the taxpayer to determine the arm's length price or margin, showing detailed computations and assumptions. The taxpayer can determine the arm's length range but must furnish details and reasons to reflect its determination and the use of that range.

MUTUAL AGREEMENT PROCEDURES

Singapore makes use of double taxation mutual agreement procedures (MAPs), including transfer pricing issues. Singapore has at least 50 comprehensive tax treaties in force, of which the United States is not included. The IRAS permits the taxpayer to apply for an MAP and to withdraw from the process. Further, the taxpayer can withdraw from the agreed outcome.[48] The IRAS expects the taxpayer to comply with the documentation requirements when pursuing an MAP.[49] The IRAS is not obligated to accept an MAP request; the IRAS requires the taxpayer to provide documentation, comply with time limits, and demonstrate that double taxation is almost certain.[50]

A taxpayer being subjected to transfer pricing adjustments with its transactions and with a related party is to notify the requisite tax authorities to activate the MAP.[51] The taxpayer must notify the IRAS in writing, describing the situation.[52] The IRAS warns the taxpayer not to, under any circumstances, unilaterally make claims for corresponding adjustments or file amended tax returns but to notify the IRAS instead.[53] The IRAS undertakes to meet with the taxpayer within four weeks after the IRAS receives the request.[54] The MAP process between competent authorities is a governmental process, but the IRAS recognizes that taxpayers are stakeholders in the MAP process and endeavors to regularly update them on competent authority consultations and timing.[55]

ADVANCE PRICING AGREEMENTS

The IRAS provides for bilateral and multilateral APAs.[56] Taxpayers need not seek an APA but can do so in recognition of their commercial needs. The Singapore taxpayer has recourse to the MAP process if the IRAS rejects its APA request. The IRAS issues APAs having a three- to five-year period and permits a one- to two-year roll back. Quite curiously, the IRAS requests that the taxpayer seek meetings with the relevant tax authorities in the case of unilateral or bilateral APAs.[57] Such meetings are essential for a bilateral APA but are quite unusual for a unilateral APA unless the party is seeking matched unilateral APAs. The IRAS treats the APA process in an analogous manner to an MAP in treating the APA process like a government-to-government negotiation, which ultimately may be unduly restrictive.

COMMENTS

The taxpayer has much to look forward to in its transfer pricing process in Singapore. For a U.S. taxpayer or for a taxpayer in a country that follows the OECD transfer pricing provisions, many of the IRAS provisions will be familiar ground.

NOTES

1. Singapore Income Tax Act, Sec. 53 and 33; see L. Lim, S. Timms, and B. Savic, Chapter 18, in R. Feinschreiber (ed.), *Transfer Pricing International: A Country-by-Country Guide* (New York: John Wiley & Sons, 2000).
2. IRAS Circular, Transfer Pricing Guidelines, Sec. 3.1.4.
3. IRAS Circular, Transfer Pricing Guidelines, section 3.1.8(i).
4. IRAS Circular, Transfer Pricing Guidelines, Annex G.
5. IRAS Circular, Transfer Pricing Guidelines, section 3.1.8(ii).
6. IRAS Circular, Transfer Pricing Guidelines, section 3.1.8(iii).
7. IRAS Circular, Transfer Pricing Guidelines, section 3.2.2.
8. IRAS Circular, Transfer Pricing Guidelines, section 3.2.3.
9. IRAS Circular, Transfer Pricing Guidelines, section 3.2.4.2(a)(ii).
10. IRAS Circular, Transfer Pricing Guidelines, section 3.2.4.2(b).
11. IRAS Circular, Transfer Pricing Guidelines, section 3.2.4.2(b)(iii).
12. IRAS Circular, Transfer Pricing Guidelines, section 3.2.4.2(b)(iv).
13. IRAS Circular, Transfer Pricing Guidelines, section 3.2.4.2(b)(v).
14. IRAS Circular, Transfer Pricing Guidelines, section 3.2.4.2(c).
15. IRAS Circular, Transfer Pricing Guidelines, section 3.2.4.2(c)(i).
16. IRAS Circular, Transfer Pricing Guidelines, section 3.2.4.2(c)(ii).
17. IRAS Circular, Transfer Pricing Guidelines, section 3.2.4.2(c)(iii).
18. IRAS Circular, Transfer Pricing Guidelines, section 3.2.4.2(c)(iv).
19. IRAS Circular, Transfer Pricing Guidelines, section 3.2.5.1(a)(ii).
20. IRAS Circular, Transfer Pricing Guidelines, section 3.2.5.1(a)(iii).

21. IRAS Circular, Transfer Pricing Guidelines, section 3.2.5.1(a)(iv).
22. IRAS Circular, Transfer Pricing Guidelines, Annex A.
23. IRAS Circular, Transfer Pricing Guidelines, Annex B.
24. IRAS Circular, Transfer Pricing Guidelines, section 3.2.5.3.
25. IRAS Circular, Transfer Pricing Guidelines, section 3.2.6.1.
26. IRAS Circular, Transfer Pricing Guidelines, section 3.2.5.1(b)(ii).
27. Ibid.
28. IRAS Circular, Transfer Pricing Guidelines, Annex C.
29. IRAS Circular, Transfer Pricing Guidelines, section 3.2.5.1(b)(v).
30. IRAS Circular, Transfer Pricing Guidelines, section 3.2.5.1(c)(i).
31. IRAS Circular, Transfer Pricing Guidelines, section 3.2.5.1(c)(iv).
32. IRAS Circular, Transfer Pricing Guidelines, section 3.2.5.1(c)(ii).
33. IRAS Circular, Transfer Pricing Guidelines, section 3.2.5.2(a)(i).
34. IRAS Circular, Transfer Pricing Guidelines, section 3.2.5.2(a)(v).
35. IRAS Circular, Transfer Pricing Guidelines, section 3.2.5.2(a)(iii).
36. IRAS Circular, Transfer Pricing Guidelines, section 3.2.5.2(b)(i).
37. IRAS Circular, Transfer Pricing Guidelines, section 3.2.5.2(b)(ii).
38. IRAS Circular, Transfer Pricing Guidelines, section 3.2.5.2(b)(ii).
39. IRAS Circular, Transfer Pricing Guidelines, section 4.1.
40. IRAS Circular, Transfer Pricing Guidelines, section 4.3.1.
41. IRAS Circular, Transfer Pricing Guidelines, section 4.3.2.
42. IRAS Circular, Transfer Pricing Guidelines, section 4.3.3.
43. IRAS Circular, Transfer Pricing Guidelines, section 4.3.3(a).
44. IRAS Circular, Transfer Pricing Guidelines, section 4.4.1.
45. IRAS Circular, Transfer Pricing Guidelines, section 4.3.3(b).
46. IRAS Circular, Transfer Pricing Guidelines, section 4.3.3(c).
47. IRAS Circular, Transfer Pricing Guidelines, section 4.3.3(d).
48. IRAS Circular, Transfer Pricing Guidelines, section 5.3.3.
49. IRAS Circular, Transfer Pricing Guidelines, section 5.4.3.2.
50. IRAS Circular, Transfer Pricing Guidelines, section 5.3.5.
51. IRAS Circular, Transfer Pricing Guidelines, section 5.4.1.1.
52. IRAS Circular, Transfer Pricing Guidelines, section 5.4.1.2.
53. IRAS Circular, Transfer Pricing Guidelines, section 5.4.1.3.
54. IRAS Circular, Transfer Pricing Guidelines, section 5.4.2.1.
55. IRAS Circular, Transfer Pricing Guidelines, section 5.4.4.2.
56. IRAS Circular, Transfer Pricing Guidelines, section 6.1.
57. IRAS Circular, Transfer Pricing Guidelines, section 6.6.1.2.

CHAPTER TWENTY-SEVEN

Singapore Transfer Pricing Guidelines for Related Party Loans and Services

THE INLAND REVENUE AUTHORITY OF SINGAPORE (IRAS) issued Transfer Pricing Guidelines for Related Party Loans and Related Party Services on February 23, 2009. As background, the IRAS had issued draft supplementary guidelines for related party loans and services on October 21, 2008. The draft supplementary guidelines were subject to public comment. The IRAS took these comments into account in finalizing the Transfer Pricing Guidelines for Related Party Loans and Related Party Services.

The loan guidelines and the services guidelines supplement the February 23, 2006, transfer pricing guidelines. The supplementary guideline circular addresses these issues:

- Interest-free loans
- The 5% markup on costs applied in the services context
- No-markup services provided by one service provider to another service provider

All citations, except as noted, pertain to the Transfer Pricing Guidelines for Related Party Loans and Related Party Services that the IRAS issued on February 23, 2009.

The IRAS believes that the arm's length principle is the "most appropriate standard" to determine the transfer prices for related party transactions.[1] As such, the IRAS abides by this arm's length principle. The IRAS recognizes that the arm's length principle should apply to all related party transactions. Nevertheless, despite this affirmation of the arm's length principle, the IRAS recognizes that "a mechanical application" of the arm's length principle could give rise to difficulties and concerns for businesses. The IRAS recognizes that, in some cases, the conduct of a comprehensive analysis for the purpose of demonstrating compliance with the arm's length principle might not be practical. As such, the IRAS will allow practical alternatives to the arm's length principle to assist taxpayers with complying with the principle.

The IRAS is increasingly concerned about the increased level of cross-border related party transfers. The IRAS points out that most tax authorities, implicitly including itself, focus on these cross-border related party transactions, doing so to ensure that the transactions do not erode their tax bases. The IRAS warns that a tax authority that makes a transfer pricing adjustment concerning cross-border related party transactions may cause double taxation to the taxpayer. The IRAS then suggests that the taxpayer having related party transactions establish arm's length transfer pricing policies and maintain adequate documentation to minimize the incidence of double taxation.[2]

TRANSFER PRICING GUIDELINES FOR RELATED PARTY LOANS

As a general matter, the Singapore loan guidelines provide that an entity that undertakes a loan made to a related entity should charge the related entity for the use of funds at a rate that reflects an arm's length rate of interest. The arm's length rate is the rate of interest that an independent party would charge to the recipient under similar circumstances. In other words, the arm's length rate of interest is the interest rate that the lender of the funds would charge to provide funds to borrowers that are independent of the lender.[3]

Such a related party loan includes a loan in which a related party lends money, in one form or another, irrespective of whether the party makes the loan through a written agreement or afterward.[4] Such a related party loan includes credit facilities or intercompany balances that arise from the normal course of sales or services. The credit balance provision applies to services that are "left uncollected over a substantial period of time," the time period beyond which a third party creditor would typically allow.

TWO LOAN CATEGORIES

The Singapore loan guidelines delineate two types of related party loans:[5]

1. A related domestic loan that takes place between a domestic party that lends to a related domestic entity or, alternatively, a domestic party that borrows from a related domestic entity

2. A related cross-border loan that takes place between a domestic party that lends to a related foreign entity or, alternatively, a domestic party that borrows from a related foreign entity

A "domestic entity" means any business entity that is incorporated in Singapore or registered in Singapore and is carrying on a business in Singapore.

Domestic Loan Provisions

The Singapore loan provisions postulate that, in adhering to the arm's length principle, an entity that makes a loan to another related entity or otherwise becomes a creditor of another related entity should charge the related entity for the use of funds at a rate that reflects an arm's length rate of interest.[6] The Singapore loan provisions define the arm's length rate of interest in the case of loans as the rate of interest that should have been charged between independent parties under similar circumstances at the time the evidence arose.[7] The IRAS defines the arm's length rate of interest as "the interest rate that a lender of the funds would charge to provide funds to borrowers that are independent of the lender."

As to the treatment of related domestic loans, the IRAS recognizes that it currently had been common practice for entities to extend interest-free loans, or to receive interest-free loans, or for entities to extend or receive interest-bearing loans at rates that are not supported by transfer pricing analysis to or from other related entities. In the past, the IRAS had not strictly required entities making these loans to adopt an arm's length procedure to determine the rate of interest. The IRAS has now agreed to accept this prior non–arm's length practice as to domestic loans. Nevertheless, the IRAS will accept this non–arm's length practice only to related party domestic loans and then only where the lender is not in the business of borrowing and lending funds. The final loan guidelines would restrict the amount to any interest expense claimed by the lender on such loans, where applicable.[8]

During the review process following the issuance of the proposed loan regulations, taxpayers expressed their concern that the IRAS requirement regarding applying arm's length methodology to all related party loans would result in complications for these taxpayers and would result in increased compliance cost. These taxpayers requested that the IRAS continue with the current practice of restricting the interest expense claimed as a proxy to the arm's length principle.[9]

The IRAS reviewed the taxpayers' suggestion. At the outset, it was the view of the IRAS that the arm's length principle is the correct and most appropriate standard for determining the rate of interest in related party loans. Interest adjustments applied at the lending entry level may serve as a proxy to the arm's length principle under certain circumstances. Nevertheless, the interest adjustment is not a perfect proxy and may address concerns of revenue leakage partially under certain other circumstances for domestic purposes vis-à-vis a case where arm's length methodology is applied.[10] The IRAS provides as an example the fact that the limit on the tax deduction is of minimal impact if the lending entity does not incur interest expense.

The IRAS sought to take into account the taxpayers' feedback and other considerations. The IRAS agreed to facilitate the efforts of domestic taxpayers in complying with the arm's length standard by continuing the current practice of making adjustments on lenders that make loans to related entities that are interest-free or otherwise at interest rates that are not supported by transfer pricing analysis.[11] The IRAS will apply this practice only to domestic loans, and where the lender concerned is also not in the business of borrowing and lending funds, such as through banks or other financial institutions or finance and treasury centers.

International Loan Provisions

The Singapore loan guidelines take a stronger stance in enforcing arm's length pricing in the case of related cross-border loans than they do for related domestic loans. The IRAS recognizes that some domestic lenders may have extended loans to foreign-related entities and that these loans may be tax-free or at interest rates not supported by transfer pricing analysis. These domestic lenders may need time to restructure the loans to reflect commercial conditions and obtain an arm's length rate of interest.[12]

Here the IRAS would enforce the arm's length rule, but only after a two-year transition period beginning January 1, 2009. The IRAS has recognized that some domestic lenders might have extended loans to foreign-related entities on an interest-free basis or otherwise at interest rates that the transfer pricing analysis does not support. Beginning January 1, 2011, the IRAS would require all cross-border loan arrangements to reflect arm's length conditions.

The Singapore loan guidelines recognize that the observance of the arm's length standard is part of Singapore's tax treaty obligations and that the arm's length standard is the internationally adopted standard. As such, the loan guidelines warn the taxpayer that chooses to extend interest-free cross-border loans to related parties or extend interest-bearing cross-border loans not supported by transfer pricing analysis to related parties. These taxpayers should then recognize these loans might be subject to higher risk of unresolved disagreements when these loans are subject to transfer pricing audits and adjustments.[13] Thus, double taxation is more likely to result.

FACTS AND CIRCUMSTANCES TO DETERMINE COMPARABILITY ANALYSIS

The Singapore loan guidelines provide nine nonexclusive comparability factors to determine the arm's length rate:[14]

1. Nature and purpose of the loan
2. Market conditions at the time the loan is granted
3. Principal amount of the loan, duration of the loan, and terms of the loan
4. Currency in which the loan is denominated
5. Exchange risks that the lender or borrower bears

6. Security that the borrower offers
7. Guarantees connected with the loan
8. Borrower's credit standing
9. Interest rate prevailing at the situs of the lender, or prevailing at the situs of the borrower, for comparable loans between unrelated parties

The Singapore loan guidelines, in determining the interest rate, specifically prefer the comparable uncontrolled price (CUP) method for loans. The IRAS favors the CUP method because of its conceptual superiority compared with other methods and because it is often found to be the most suitable method of loan transactions.[15] Nevertheless, a taxpayer can select a different transfer pricing method for its loans if the taxpayer believes this other method to be more appropriate. In addition, the taxpayer needs to maintain documentation to justify why that method is more suitable.

The IRAS suggests that the taxpayer rely on a suitable reference rate for comparability purposes. The IRAS suggests two reference rates and permits the taxpayer to apply other rates:

- Singapore Interbank Offered Rate (SIBOR)
- London Interbank Offered Rate (LIBOR)
- Prime rates offered by banks
- Special rates quoted by banks for similar loans

The taxpayer can make adjustments to the reference rate, based on the outcome of the comparability analysis the taxpayer undertakes, to arrive at the appropriate arm's length rate or a range of rates.[16]

TRANSFER PRICING GUIDELINES FOR RELATED PARTY SERVICES

The Singapore services guidelines address the application of the arm's length principles to related party services, here termed "intragroup services within a group of companies or businesses." The Singapore services guidelines recognize that related parties within a group would arrange for a wide array for services to one or more members of the group.[17] Such services may include, for example, these activities:

- Administrative services
- Technical services
- Financial services
- Commercial services
- Management services
- Coordination services
- Control functions

The Singapore services guidelines do not address other services activities that the taxpayer might view as profit-center activities. Such noneligible activities include:

- Sales activities
- Leasing activities
- Engineering activities
- Manufacturing activities

The Singapore services guidelines apply certain of the arm's length principles only on a prospective basis.[18]

The first order of business, from the standpoint of the Singapore services guidelines, is to ascertain whether one party provided services to another party. However, the services guidelines fail to provide such an established set of strict criteria to determine whether one party provided services to another. The IRAS recognizes that it is not possible to establish a set of strict criteria to determine if an activity amounts to a service provided.[19] Instead, the taxpayer is to look to the surrounding facts and circumstances. Generally accepted considerations apply to determine whether one company in fact provided services to another company.

As a general matter, one party provides services to another when the provider of services receives benefits from these activities or, alternatively, when the provider of the services expects to receive benefits from such activities. Services are considered to have taken place when there is a reasonable expectation or intention of providing services conferred or received, even if the expected service does not eventually materialize.[20]

The benefit that a party receives or provides must have economic or commercial benefit such that an independent party would expect to receive or pay for that service. The benefit must be identifiable and capable of being valued. Hence, the benefit must be sufficiently direct and substantial. No service is considered to have been provided if the benefit to be derived from an activity is not what an independent party in comparable circumstances would be willing to pay for or to carry out for itself.[21]

The Singapore services guidelines recognize that it is common for a parent company, or for a designated entity within a group of companies, to undertake activities that benefit the group as a whole. Such centrally performed entities can include, for example, administrative functions, financial functions, and personnel functions. The central thrust of Singapore's service provisions are activities that an independent party would be willing to pay for, or to perform for itself.[22]

As a general matter, a taxpayer views a service as having been provided when the taxpayer meets an identified need of the related party or a group of related parties by performance of these services by another related party. An independent party would have either engaged the services of a third party or performed the activities itself to fulfill the need. Consequently, although the performance of an activity confers a benefit to a related party that has no need for such activity, then no services are deemed provided. When the benefit is too remote, no service is deemed provided.[23]

DIRECT CHARGING VERSUS INDIRECT CHARGING OF SERVICES

The Singapore services guidelines delineate both the direct charge method and the indirect charge method. The service provider can adopt the direct charge method or the indirect charge method, as the service provider determines:[24]

- **Direct charge method.** Under the direct charge method, the service provider would identify clearly the actual work the service provider performs, the costs that the service provider expended, and the basis of making that charge. The Singapore services guidelines prefer the direct charge method in charging for related party services because the direct charge method facilitates the tax authorities' review and examination. Nevertheless, the services guidelines favor the direct charge method only in the context of providing specific services, such as, in an example in the services guidelines, in conducting a market survey for a particular product developed by a related party. The prerequisite for applying the direct charge method is where the beneficiary of the services and the costs incurred for the performance of the services are usually identifiable.[25]
- **Indirect charge method.** The indirect charge method entails the use of an appropriate apportionment basis or allocation key to charge or to bill for services provided.[26] Such apportionment basis or allocation key includes, for example, gross sales, income, or receipts, loans and deposits, staff numbers, floor area, and asset size. The IRAS recognizes that it might not be practical for taxpayers to adopt the direct charge method for all related party services to the members belonging to the same group or to services performed specifically for individual recipients. The IRAS suggests that accounting services, for example, would be better accounted for under the indirect charge method to approximate the charges.

The central ingredient in applying the indirect charge method is the selection of the apportionment basis or the allocation key. The services guidelines imply that the service provider must select an apportionment basis or allocation key that is appropriate. This selection of the allocation key depends on the nature and use of the services.[27]

As a general matter, the most appropriate allocation key is the method that most accurately reflects the share of the benefits the beneficiary receives or expects to receive. The services guidelines acknowledge that the taxpayer selects the allocation key and that that choice is largely a question of judgment. The services guidelines expect the taxpayer to use judgment to demonstrate that it has undertaken in choosing the allocation key.

The IRAS is prepared to accept the allocation key that the taxpayer adopts so long as the allocation key meets these criteria:

- The allocation key must be reasonable.
- The allocation key must be founded on sound accounting principles.

- The taxpayer applies the allocation key consistently year to year throughout the group unless there are very good reasons for failing to do so.

ASCERTAINING THE ARM'S LENGTH FEE

After the service provider determines which charging method is appropriate, the next step is to determine the arm's length fee for services the service provider provides. This remuneration should be in accordance with the arm's length principle, based on a comparability analysis with an independent party.[28] The services guidelines suggest that the taxpayer undertake this analysis from the perspective of both the service provider and the recipient of the services. This charge is the amount that a service provider would charge an independent party, taking into account the service provider's costs and the amount than the recipient is willing to pay for that service. The parties are to consider what the service provider would have otherwise paid to independent parties for similar services under similar circumstances.[29]

The taxpayer is to be guided by what services guidelines term "important considerations," such as these, when determining the appropriate transfer pricing method:

- Nature of the transaction
- Availability of the data
- Quality of the data

This services analysis is directly applicable to related party services.

Notwithstanding this services analysis, however, the services guidelines indicate that CUP and the cost plus methods are most often the most appropriate choices for determining the arm's length fee for related party services.[30]

ROUTINE SERVICES AND THE 5% MARKUP

The services guidelines refer to "a common practice [in Singapore] among parent companies or group service companies to charge a 5% markup on costs incurred for providing certain routine support services." The services guidelines postulate that the service provider provides these services for the purposes of business convenience and efficiency, centralizing these routine support services within the parent company or a group service company. The services guidelines provide three such nonexclusive examples: the performance of accounting services, of payroll services, and of certain other management or administrative functions. The services guidelines then acknowledge that related companies might, in practice, based on their own business considerations, provide intragroup services to one another even when these services activities are beyond routine services.[31]

The issue as to whether a 5% cost markup conforms to the arm's length principle depends on three facets:

1. The exact nature the service provider provides
2. The actual or reasonably expected benefits the service provider provides to the recipient of the service
3. A detailed analysis of what an independent party would have been willing to pay for a similar service under similar circumstances

The IRAS is prepared to accept the current 5% markup for certain routine support services as a reasonable arm's length charge for these services on the proviso that the service provider, in providing these routine support services, does not also offer these routine support services to an unrelated party. The objective of the IRAS is to facilitate taxpayers' compliance with the arm's length standard while maintaining a high level of adherence to the arm's length principle, based on industry norms. The services guidelines accept the practicality that performing a proper transfer pricing comparability analysis for every type of service would greatly increase the administration and compliance for the taxpayer and would increase the administration costs of evaluating them.

The IRAS is prepared to accept the current 5% markup adopted for certain routine support services as a reasonable arm's length charge for such services. The IRAS is willing to make this determination to facilitate taxpayers' compliance with the arm's length standard while maintaining a high level of adherence to the arm's length principle. The IRAS requires, for the 5% cost markup to apply, that these routine support activities that the service provider offers to its related party are not also provided to an unrelated party.[32]

A taxpayer, in charging routine support services at a 5% markup, needs to take into account all costs for this purpose that are directly related or indirectly related to the services performed. The direct costs include, for example, materials consumed and labor expended to render these services. The indirect costs include, for example, overheads, depreciation, and telecommunication expenses that the department provides to the department providing these services.[33]

The Singapore services guidelines provide Annex A, which lists routine support services that companies commonly provide on an intragroup basis across many industries. The IRAS can modify or expand the list of routine services in the future. These routine support services do not generate a significant arm's length markup. This list is nonexhaustive, but the taxpayer must follow the existing list of routine services.[34] The list includes:

- Accounting and auditing services, including maintenance of accounting records, preparation of financial statements based on such records, ensuring authenticity and reliability of accounting records, and so forth, including the performance of operational and financial audits.
- Accounts receivable and accounts payable services, including the collation and verification of data pertaining to accounts receivable and accounts payable, undertaken for the purposes of financial reporting, aging, billing, soliciting payments from customers, payment to vendors, procurement, and so forth.
- Budgeting services, including the compilation of data for preparing budget estimates, reports, and so forth.

- Computer support services, including providing technical services and troubleshooting support services in relation to the usage of computer hardware, computer software, maintenance of intellectual property software, and so forth.
- Database administration services, including the general maintenance of computer databases, including data storage, but excluding analytic services performed on stored data.
- Employee benefits services, including the administration of employee compensation and benefit plans, such as health care, life insurance, dental, employee incentive compensation, profit sharing plans, and so forth; and including the coordination with external parties, such as hospitals, insurers, and so forth to implement such benefit plans.
- General administrative services, including the performance of clerical and administrative functions, such as data entry, photocopying, scanning of materials, scheduling of appointments, word processing, file maintenance, and so forth.
- Legal services, including the providing of legal services by in-house legal counsel.
- Payroll services, including the compilation and verification of employees' time worked and employee claims for reimbursable expenses to compute salaries, commissions, and reimbursements. Payroll services include the payment of paychecks and arranging credit of such payments into employees' bank accounts.
- Public relations services and corporate communications, including the handling of internal and external communications relating to corporate policies.
- Purchasing services, including the procurement of goods and services based on organization requirements or based on standards.
- Staffing and recruiting services, including the management of staffing requirements, performance issues, and staff welfare in the organization or group and the implementation of recruitment plans, such as publicizing open positions and candidate screening, and so forth.
- Tax services, including the preparation of various tax returns, computations, refund claims, and responses to inquiries for submission to the tax authorities, the processing of tax payments, and so forth.
- Training and employee development services, including the management and implementation of employee training and development programs.

The draft of services guidelines included purchasing services, including the procurement of goods and services based on organization requirements or based on standards. The final services guidelines exclude the purchasing services category.

The IRAS is prepared to consider adding additional services on further review where taxpayers view that certain of these intragroup services are routine support services but are not included in this routine support list. The IRAS's acceptance of a 5% markup for routine services provides taxpayers with an alternative to having service providers undertake a detailed transfer pricing analysis. These service providers might have undertaken a detailed transfer pricing analysis that supports the charging for services at different markups other than 5%. In the event that this difference occurs, the service provider should adopt that alternative markup. Once the taxpayer adopts the arm's length markup, the taxpayer should apply this markup consistently year after year throughout the group until there are material changes to the circumstances or to the services that the service provider provides. These service providers should regularly review the markup they have adopted to make sure that the markup continues to reflect arm's length conditions in their situations.[35]

COST POOLING CONTRACTS

The IRAS has developed a virtually new and quite useful transfer pricing technique termed "cost pooling."[36] Taxpayers can apply this cost pooling technique to certain routine services expenditures that occur among related parties with the corporate group. Cost pooling arrangements differ in numerous respects from cost contribution arrangements (or cost sharing arrangements) that taxpayers enter into primarily to develop intangible assets. Regrettably, the Singapore services guidelines fail to distinguish between cost pooling arrangements and cost sharing arrangements.

Taxpayers that have exceptional circumstances might find it mutually beneficial to enter into a cost pooling contract among members of the corporate group.[37] The cost pooling contract enables members of the corporate group to share in the costs of routine support services for the common use of the group to meet a common need of the members. The cost pooling arrangement allows the members of the corporate group to pool resources together in order to acquire services that meet these parameters:

- A party to the cost pooling contract must have a reasonable expectation of benefiting from or must actually benefit from the services for which costs are being shared.
- Contributions by related parties to the costs of providing the services must be made in proportion to the nature and extent of the expected benefits that each party receives.
- Each party's share of the costs in the cost pooling arrangement must be borne in the form of cash or by other monetary contributions.

The proposed services guidelines had provided that the arrangement must be necessary for the corporate group to function effectively. The final services guidelines eliminate this requirement.

Additional pooling requirements are:[38]

- The arrangement is to acquire services that are not the principal activities of the corporate group.
- The arrangement is not intended to be a profitable exploit of the corporate group.
- The arrangement must address mutual benefit among members of the group.
- The party to the arrangement must reasonably expect to benefit from the shared services or actually benefit from the shared services.

- The party to the arrangement must determine the contribution as to the costs of providing the service in proportion to the expected benefits that each party receives.
- Each party must bear the share of its costs in the form of cash or other contributions, and nothing else.
- To satisfy the arm's length principle, each participant's share of the costs must be consistent with the costs to which an independent party would have agreed under comparable circumstances, given the benefit the participant would have expected to derive from the services being provided.

The services guidelines provide specific parameters for the allowance of the cost pooling arrangement:[39]

- The arrangement must be termed a proportionate share of the cost of the services.
- The arrangement can be determined on a prospective basis.
- The arrangement is to be determined with no element of markup.
- The service provider that offers its services to its related parties does not offer these same services to unrelated parties.
- The service provider, in providing these services to related parties is not the principal activity for which the service provider is to undertake. The term "principal activity" is based on facts and circumstances, based on a 15% threshold.
- These provisions apply to Annex A services.
- The taxpayer provides sufficient documentation to show that the parties intended to pool their resources to share costs, doing so before the service provider performs the services.

The services guidelines require the taxpayer to maintain adequate documentation to support the cost allocation as being arm's length. The services guidelines require the taxpayer to maintain adequate documentation to demonstrate the sharing of expected benefits arising from providing these services. The proposed services guidelines were concerned about the taxpayer's risk of double taxation and suggested that the taxpayer retain the following documentation:[40]

- Description of the type of services provided
- Rationale for selecting a specific cost method
- Nature of the related parties' contributions
- Anticipated benefits
- Calculation details

STRICT COST PASS-THROUGH

Singapore's services guidelines address two separate procedures to aggregate and distribute services costs:

1. The cost pooling arrangement addresses the aggregation of costs by a party within the group that provides the services to the group as a whole.

2. The strict pass-through arrangement addresses the aggregation of costs by a third-party provider that provides the services to the group as a whole.

A group service provider might occasionally arrange and pay for services from third-party providers. A third-party provider can undertake this service on behalf of the related parties in the group, but the third party can be independent from the related party or can be related to that party. A third-party service provider or a related party service provider might have already charged the members an arm's length markup for their services. In the event that the provider has already charged the members for these costs, it may be appropriate for the group service provider to pass on these costs without incurring further markup. The parties are to pass on the costs without markup if the group service provider is merely the paying agent, and the group service provider itself does not act to enhance the value of these services.

The IRAS is prepared to accept that these costs may be charged without a markup to the related party for whose benefit the services are provided. These costs must meet the next preconditions:[41]

- The costs are the legal liabilities or the contractual liabilities of the related party.
- The group service provider is merely the paying agent, and the service provider does not itself act to enhance the value of such services.

Singapore's services guidelines provide an example of the strict cost pass-through method.[42] Assume that a group service provider incurs expenses on behalf of a related party to pay for the costs of engaging a third-party firm to provide various corporate secretarial services for its related party. The parties can identify the costs as legal or contractual liabilities of the party itself. The group service provider is the paying agent. The group service provider can pass on these costs to the related party, doing so without markup.

Singapore's services guidelines provide that the group service provider is to ensure an arm's length markup for its own aggregate costs of providing the services.[43] This markup is to be reflective of the nature of the services rendered by the service provider and the extent of the value-added amount that benefits the participants who receive these services. The aggregate costs that related parties incur should include its own costs incurred, if any, in facilitating the purchase of services from third-party service providers or from related party service providers. Returning to the prior example, assume that the group service provider used its own resources to arrange, select, and liaise in having the third-party firm provide corporate secretarial services. In that event, the group service provider should charge this cost to its related parties at an arm's length markup.[44]

DOCUMENTATION

The main transfer pricing circular highlights the importance of documentation. Documentation is important for loan and services transactions, and the taxpayer should refer to the main transfer pricing circular for guidance on appropriate documentation.[45]

NOTES

1. Transfer Pricing Guidelines for Related Party Loans and Related Party Services, 1.2.
2. Transfer Pricing Guidelines for Related Party Loans and Related Party Services, 1.3.
3. Transfer Pricing Guidelines for Related Party Loans and Related Party Services, 2.1.
4. Transfer Pricing Guidelines for Related Party Loans and Related Party Services, 2.1.1.
5. Transfer Pricing Guidelines for Related Party Loans and Related Party Services, 2.1.2.
6. Transfer Pricing Guidelines for Related Party Loans and Related Party Services, 2.1.3.
7. Transfer Pricing Guidelines for Related Party Loans and Related Party Services, 2.1.4.
8. Transfer Pricing Guidelines for Related Party Loans and Related Party Services, 2.1.5.
9. Transfer Pricing Guidelines for Related Party Loans and Related Party Services, 2.1.6.
10. Transfer Pricing Guidelines for Related Party Loans and Related Party Services, 2.1.7.
11. Transfer Pricing Guidelines for Related Party Loans and Related Party Services, 2.1.8.
12. Transfer Pricing Guidelines for Related Party Loans and Related Party Services, 2.1.9.
13. Transfer Pricing Guidelines for Related Party Loans and Related Party Services, 2.1.10.
14. Transfer Pricing Guidelines for Related Party Loans and Related Party Services, 2.2.2.
15. Transfer Pricing Guidelines for Related Party Loans and Related Party Services, 2.2.3.
16. Transfer Pricing Guidelines for Related Party Loans and Related Party Services, 2.2.4.
17. Transfer Pricing Guidelines for Related Party Loans and Related Party Services, 3.1.1.
18. Transfer Pricing Guidelines for Related Party Loans and Related Party Services, 3.1.2.
19. Transfer Pricing Guidelines for Related Party Loans and Related Party Services, 3.2.1.
20. Transfer Pricing Guidelines for Related Party Loans and Related Party Services, 3.2.2.
21. Transfer Pricing Guidelines for Related Party Loans and Related Party Services, 3.2.3.
22. Transfer Pricing Guidelines for Related Party Loans and Related Party Services, 3.2.4.
23. Transfer Pricing Guidelines for Related Party Loans and Related Party Services, 3.2.5.
24. Transfer Pricing Guidelines for Related Party Loans and Related Party Services, 3.3.2.
25. Transfer Pricing Guidelines for Related Party Loans and Related Party Services, 3.3.3.
26. Transfer Pricing Guidelines for Related Party Loans and Related Party Services, 3.3.4.
27. Transfer Pricing Guidelines for Related Party Loans and Related Party Services, 3.3.5.
28. Transfer Pricing Guidelines for Related Party Loans and Related Party Services, 3.3.6.
29. Transfer Pricing Guidelines for Related Party Loans and Related Party Services, 3.3.7.
30. Transfer Pricing Guidelines for Related Party Loans and Related Party Services, 3.3.8.
31. Transfer Pricing Guidelines for Related Party Loans and Related Party Services, 3.3.9.
32. Transfer Pricing Guidelines for Related Party Loans and Related Party Services, 3.3.10.
33. Transfer Pricing Guidelines for Related Party Loans and Related Party Services, 3.3.11.
34. Transfer Pricing Guidelines for Related Party Loans and Related Party Services, 3.3.12.
35. Transfer Pricing Guidelines for Related Party Loans and Related Party Services, 3.3.13.
36. Transfer Pricing Guidelines for Related Party Loans and Related Party Services, 3.3.14.
37. Transfer Pricing Guidelines for Related Party Loans and Related Party Services, 3.3.15.
38. Transfer Pricing Guidelines for Related Party Loans and Related Party Services, 3.3.16.
39. Transfer Pricing Guidelines for Related Party Loans and Related Party Services, 3.3.16.
40. Transfer Pricing Guidelines for Related Party Loans and Related Party Services, 3.3.16.
41. Transfer Pricing Guidelines for Related Party Loans and Related Party Services, 3.3.18.
42. Transfer Pricing Guidelines for Related Party Loans and Related Party Services, 3.3.18.
43. Transfer Pricing Guidelines for Related Party Loans and Related Party Services, 3.3.19.
44. Transfer Pricing Guidelines for Related Party Loans and Related Party Services, 3.3.19.
45. Transfer Pricing Guidelines for Related Party Loans and Related Party Services, 4.1.

CHAPTER TWENTY-EIGHT

28

South Korea Transfer Pricing

TAXPAYERS IN Korea are facing the increasing wrath of their tax authorities, in part because of increasing regulations in Korea and in part because of the breathtaking transfer pricing developments in Asia as a whole.[1]

BACKGROUND

At the outset, the reader should note that the transfer pricing process in Korea is well established and sophisticated; it is the second oldest transfer pricing regime in Asia after Japan. Furthermore, Korea is a member of the Organisation for Economic Co-operation and Development (OECD), the only such country in Asia after Japan, as of the mid-2010s. As a legal matter, Korean transfer pricing is based on the Law for the Coordination of International Tax Affairs and on a presidential enforcement decree promulgated in 2006. The Korean approach provides that "substance" takes precedence over "form," and provides for intergroup service deductions. These provisions address the advance pricing agreements (APAs) program, provide for cost contribution agreements, and provide for an increasing role for Korea's tax collector, the National Tax Service (NTS).

RELATED PARTY TRANSFER PRICING RELATIONSHIPS IN KOREA

The Law for the Coordination of International Tax Affairs (LCITA) gives the tax authorities these powers to undertake the following to achieve arm's length pricing:

- The power to adjust the transfer price based on an arm's length price
- The power to determine or recalculate a resident's taxable income when the transfer price of the Korean company and its foreign counterpoint are below the arm's length price or are above the arm's length price

Related party transfer pricing relationships in Korea are based on two precepts: the presence of stock ownership or, alternatively, the presence of economic interest and control, both of which are termed special relationships. There are two ways in which stock ownership related party transfer pricing relationships apply in Korea. The first method of stock ownership is having direct ownership (i.e., to have 50% ownership of one party over the other party). The second method of stock ownership is having indirect ownership, that is, 50% ownership through a *johap* (partnership) or trust.

Korea's LCITA provides for two types of these "special relationships":

1. Equity ownership test
2. Substantial control test

Equity Ownership Test

There are four facets of the equity ownership test:

1. A foreign company owns, directly or indirectly, 50% or more of the voting shares of a Korean company.
2. A Korean company owns, directly or indirectly, 50% or more of the voting shares of a foreign company.
3. A corporation, or an individual, owns, directly or indirectly, 50% or more of the voting shares of a foreign company.
4. A corporation, or an individual, owns, directly or indirectly, 50% or more of the voting shares of the Korean company.

Substantial Control Test

There are two facets of the substantial control test:

1. Substantial control exists if one transaction party (Company A) substantially controls the "business policy" of the other transaction party (Company B), or vice versa, at the time they share the same interest.
2. Substantial control exists if the third party controls the "business policy" of both Company A and Company B, and, at the same time, both transaction parties have the same interest.

COMPUTATION OF INDIRECT OWNERSHIP

The South Korean transfer pricing provisions place a strong emphasis on direct ownership in ascertaining control relationships.

Example 1

- Company A owns a 50% or more stake in Company B.
- Company B owns a certain percentage of shares in third Company C.
- B's equity ratio in C would constitute the ratio that Company A indirectly owns in Company C.

Indirect ownership applies to determine control in Korea in the more-than-50% situation. The taxpayer determines indirect ownership on a pro rata basis. Consider a situation in which A owns a 50% or more stake in B. B has X% of the shares in C. B's equity ratio in C is A's indirect ownership in C. For example: A owns a 60% stake in B. B has a 70% stake in C. B's equity ratio in C is A's indirect ownership in C, 60% × 70%, or 42%.

Example 2

- Company A owns less than a 50% stake in Company B.
- B owns a certain percentage in the shares of a third company, Company C.
- A is then considered to own Company C to the extent of the ratio computed by multiplying Company A's equity ratio in Company B by Company B's equity ratio in Company C.

Indirect ownership applies to determine control in Korea in the less-than- 50% situation. The taxpayer determines indirect ownership on a pro rata basis.

Consider a situation in which A owns a less-than-50% stake in B. B has X% of the shares in C. A is considered to own a portion of C based on a ratio computed by A's equity ratio in B multiplied by B's equity ratio in C. For example, A owns a 40% stake in B. B has an 80% stake in C. A's indirect ratio in C is A's 40% stake in B × 80% for B's stake in C, or 32%.

ECONOMIC INTEREST AND CONTROL

Related party relationships in Korea arise through economic interest and control. This economic interest and control arise through any of these situations:

- A majority of executives or employees are shifted from one entity to another within three years.
- Fifty percent of one business relies on transactions with the other party.

- Fifty percent of the funds come from one business to another.
- A business provides 50% or more of its intangible assets to the other party. The regulations fail to address the overall worth of these intangibles.

Korea provides for "substantial control" in addition to the equity ownership test. The "substantial control" provisions apply if one party controls the business policy of the other party and, at the same time, the parties share the same interest. Alternatively, the "substantial control" provisions apply if a third party controls the business policy of both parties and, at the same time, the parties share the same interest.

TRANSFER PRICING METHOD ALTERNATIVES

Korea's Law for the Coordination of International Tax Affairs and its decree permit the taxpayer to apply any of these five transfer pricing methods:

1. Comparable uncontrolled price (CUP) method
2. Resale minus method
3. Cost plus method
4. Profit split method
5. Transactional net margin method (TNMM)

Note that Korea previously permitted the Berry method (gross profit divided by operating expenses) as a transfer pricing method.

The overall pricing concept in Korea is to ascertain the arm's length price, a price that the parties establish or could expect to establish in a "normal transaction" between independent enterprises without having a "special relationship."

The taxpayer must apply these transfer pricing methods in order—a limited "strict priority" requirement. Korea does not apply the "best method" selection process but instead requires the taxpayer to select the "most reasonable method applicable to the situation." Prior law required the taxpayer to demonstrate that a specific transfer method listed at a higher level than the intended transfer pricing method will not work in the taxpayer's particular circumstances. Current law results in three transfer pricing priorities before addressing the "most reasonable method applicable to the situation" priorities:

Preference 1: CUP

Preference 2: Other traditional transfer pricing methods: resale minus method and the cost plus method

Preference 3: Transactional net profit methods: the profit split method and the TNMM

Comparable Uncontrolled Price Method

The CUP method evaluates the arm's length price by comparing the price that an independent uncontrolled person under the same or similar circumstances, in terms of trade conditions or volume, would set for goods identical to those in question.

Resale Price Method

The taxpayer can apply the resale price method when a manufacturer sells its products to a related person, and the related person resells the same product to an unrelated third party, with the related party undertaking no further processing. The resale price method permits the taxpayer to adjust the transfer price between related parties by subtracting an appropriate markup amount from the price that the related reseller charges for the product to unrelated third parties.

Cost Plus Method

The taxpayer can, in principle, apply the cost plus method where the manufacturer sells its products to a related party, and where the related party adds value to the product by processing the product further to sell to unrelated parties. The taxpayer in such cases applies the arm's length price amount as the price of the refined goods, less the actual costs of further processing, together with an appropriate markup on such costs.

Profit Split Method

The taxpayer determines the arm's length price by taking the sum of the profits the related parties earn and then allocating these profits in proportion to the respective contribution by each party toward profits utilized.

Transactional Net Margin Method

The taxpayer evaluates the arm's length price by first seeking an independent third company that is similar to the company at issue in terms of business operations and the nature of its business. Then the taxpayer subjects this independent third company to functional and analysis comparability analysis. The taxpayer then estimates the income earned by the third company based on these three ratios:

1. Profits to assets
2. Operating profits to turnovers
3. Profits to equity

The taxpayer then estimates these results to evaluate the income and profits of the related parties and then, if necessary, to adjust the income and profits of the related parties. An example: If in a certain segment of electronics sales the normal profit in sales is 13% to 15%, the related parties could claim profits in that range with an explanation why it is using the higher or lower range.

If the Korean government finds that the transfer price is too high or too low, it can apply these remedies: The government can compel the taxpayer to treat this adjustment as a dividend. Alternatively, the government can compel the taxpayer to treat this adjustment as a capital contribution. If amounts may be due as a result of this adjustment procedure, the taxpayer must pay interest on these amounts on an arm's length basis.

The Korean tax authorities apply economic criteria in transfer method selection. Thus, the level of comparability between transactions with the related party and transactions with unrelated parties must be high, there must be sufficient data as to the comparable independent party, and the economic assumptions must reflect the actual economic situation of the parties in comparing independent transactions with related party transactions.

Korea focuses on the degree of comparability. The taxpayer is to evaluate its circumstances based on the functions performed, the risks assumed, the types and characteristics of the goods and services, the economic environment of the market, and the degree of change in economic conditions.

INFORMATION REQUESTS AND DOCUMENTS

As a general matter, the business must file results of its transfer pricing items with the tax authorities. The government can request additional documents from the business.

The Korean business must include these transfer pricing items on its tax return:

- Summary of intercompany transactions
- Profit and loss statement for each foreign-related party
- Declaration of its applicable transfer pricing methods

The Korean government can request these documents in a transfer pricing audit:

- Copies of sales contracts between the Korean company and foreign counterparts
- Price list(s) for the products at issue
- Company organization chart reflecting the functions of each department
- Schedule of manufacturing costs for the party in question
- Intercompany pricing policy
- Equity relationships of the parties

Korean tax authorities can request the foreign-company documentation pertaining to the related party as part of its transfer pricing audit. The NTS frequently makes this request. The tax authorities typically accept foreign comparables. However, the taxpayer must prove that the data submitted are comparable to the company under review.

Specific Documents and Timing

Korea's NTS can request the taxpayer to submit detailed transfer pricing documentation, as the LCITA requires, through a formal information request or through a tax audit. These documents include:

- Documents that would support the taxpayer's transfer pricing policy, including intercompany agreements, product price lists, segmented income statements, statements of transfer pricing policy, the transfer pricing study, and so forth
- Other documents regarding intragroup services and cost sharing agreements

The taxpayer is to submit the requested documents to the NTS within 60 days after the NTS requests these documents.

The taxpayer might be able to claim a 60-day extension from the timing requirement.

If the taxpayer fails to submit the documentation the NTS requests, the taxpayer may be faced with penalties of up to 30 million won for each issue of noncompliance as well as for its failure to submit documents at a later date.

Additional Documentation Requirements

Korea increased documentation requirements on December 16, 2006, issuing three new forms:

Form 1 Transfer Pricing Methods for Intangibles
Form 1-2 Transfer Pricing for Intra-Group Services
Form 1-3 Declaration of Transfer Pricing Method

As a general matter, the documentation forms in Korea look to the applicant (the Korean party) and to the overseas related party, the applicant's business, the representatives, both as to the applicant and to the overseas related party. The forms then require the taxpayer to specify a transfer pricing method and the reason(s) for selecting that method.

Transfer Pricing Methods for Intangibles, Form 1, requires the taxpayer having an intangible to provide the date of licensing agreement, the licensing payment, and the lump-sum payment. The taxpayer is to specify the royalty rate and the basis of the royalty. Form 1 requires the taxpayer to provide specific information as to outright sale of intangible assets in Korea:

- Date on which the taxpayer sells the intangible asset
- Monetary amount of the transfer
- Valuation method for ascertaining the transfer amount

Transfer Pricing for Intra-Group Services, Form 1-2, requires the taxpayer to specify four points:

1. Nature of the services
2. Taxpayer's main business
3. Type of service
4. Basis on which the amount is determined

Declaration of Transfer Pricing Method, Form 1-3, requires the taxpayer to declare its transfer pricing method and provide a brief explanation of the transfer pricing method the taxpayer selects for tangible goods, intangibles, and services. The taxpayer need not submit Form 1-3 if its overall transaction volume is 5 billion won or less for goods or 500 million won or less for services. The taxpayer need not submit Form 1-3 if the individual transaction volume with each foreign affiliate is 1 billion won or less for goods or 100 million won or less for services.

The taxpayer must submit Form 8 to specify the related parties with which it engages in transactions and the amount of these transactions. The taxpayer must submit Form 8-2, the Summary of Foreign Affiliate Income Statements, when the NTS requires the taxpayer to submit a summary of international transactions. In such a situation, the taxpayer must also submit to the NTO a summary of income statements of the foreign-related parties. The taxpayer need not submit the Form 8-2 to the NTS if the transaction volume with each relevant foreign affiliate is 1 billion won or less for goods or 100 million won or less for services. The taxpayer need not resubmit Form 8-2 details to the NTS if the taxpayer submitted the summary and financials as required under the Korean Corporate Income Tax Law.

TRANSFER PRICING AUDITS

The NTS is more likely to examine taxpayers for transfer pricing purposes when the tax returns indicate a clear pattern of tax evasion or when the taxpayer's statute of limitations is going to run out. However, a regular tax audit can include transfer pricing.

The NTS uses two audit approaches to transfer pricing: on-site audits and desk audits.

In Korea, the burden of proof in a tax assessment generally is on the tax authorities. But the law shifts much of that burden of proof to the taxpayer in a transfer pricing audit. The taxpayer has the obligation to demonstrate that its transfer price is reasonable.

The NTS has its own transfer pricing experts. The NTS has an international tax division, and that international tax division has a transfer pricing team of experts.

The NTS has its own database. The NTS makes use of the country's customs data and value-added tax (VAT) data, and makes use of secret comparables. The taxpayer may be able obtain more detail from the NTS database in some situations, which sometimes permits the taxpayer to obtain the components of the secret comparables.

Korea requires the taxpayer to retain documentation. The NTS can impose penalties on businesses that do not provide those requested documents. As a general matter, the NTS gives the business 60 days to respond to the documentation request. The tax authorities might, at their discretion, give the taxpayer another 60 days to comply. If the taxpayer then fails to comply with the government's documentation request, the tax authorities may impose a penalty of 30 million won. The taxpayer can appeal the government's determination.

PERMANENT ESTABLISHMENT, COMPETENT AUTHORITY, AND ADVANCE PRICING AGREEMENTS

Korea has been focusing more attention on possibly bringing permanent establishment issues claims. In this regard, the NTS is challenging representative offices or liaison offices. The NTS might claim that these offices are doing substantial business activity in Korea.

Korean treaties provide for competent authority relief. Alternative dispute resolution and compromises between tax authorities and the taxpayer are the norm. Korean taxpayers rarely litigate transfer pricing issues.

APAs are becoming commonplace in Korea. Korea began its APA program on January 1, 1997, and has years of experience with APAs, but Korean taxpayers rarely used APAs until recently. Korea's APA procedure is versatile and permits roll-backs. Korea now permits a three-year roll-back for unilateral APAs and a five-year roll-back for bilateral APAs. The NTS is seeking to reduce the time period for APA negotiations, now two years and three months for bilateral APAs and one year and six months for unilateral APAs. Korea does not charge for setting up an APA.

As of the end of 2008, the NTS received 172 APA requests and concluded 106 cases. The NTS negotiates most frequently with the United States, Japan, and Switzerland. We expect that NTS APAs with China will be increasing rapidly. Most NTS negotiations involve these industries: semiconductor/LCD, pharmaceutical, consumer products, and luxury goods. Sixty percent of APAs pertain to the transfer of tangible goods, but royalty and service transactions are increasing.

THIN CAPITALIZATION AND TAX HAVENS

Korea has thin capitalization rules that can impact its transfer pricing policies. Debt is limited to three times the amount of equity. Korea treats excessive debt payments as dividends.

Korea has an anti–tax haven regime. By definition, a tax haven is country that has an effective tax rate of 15% or less. Korea apparently views Hong Kong and

Singapore as not being tax havens, as those effective tax rates are slightly above the 15% threshold. In addition, Korea exempts from its anti–tax haven regime businesses doing active business operations that take place in the tax haven. These tax haven rules apply to shareholders that have 20% or more ownership. The tax haven rules do not apply to companies having annual income of 100 million won or less.

APPLYING THE "MOST REASONABLE METHOD" STANDARD TO DETERMINE ARM'S LENGTH PRICE

Korea applies a "most reasonable method" standard in evaluating the selection of the transfer price. The NTS is to determine the arm's length price based on the "most reasonable method" that applies to a particular situation. The method that the transfer pricing process determines to be the "most reasonable method" can be one of many: the comparable uncontrolled method, the resale price method, the cost plus method, or "any other" transfer pricing method.

The NTS sets out three criteria under which it is to determine whether the taxpayer's transfer pricing selection is the "most reasonable method:"

1. The "level of comparability" between the transactions of related parties and the transactions of independent parties. The NTS specifies that the level of comparability must be high but fails to further define the parameters that would create a high degree of comparability. Nevertheless, the NTS provides the parameters to address "the degree of comparability."
2. The party must have sufficient data as to a comparable independent party. This second "most reasonable method" criteria might presuppose that the taxpayer can rely on just one comparable. The NTS does not address the sufficiency of the data that the party must use in undertaking the comparable.
3. The NTS applies an "actual economic situation" standard to addressing economic assumptions. The economic assumptions that the parties make in comparing the related parties' transactions with the transactions of the independent parties must reflect the actual economic situation of the parties. The NTS fails to further define the parameters for the "actual economic situation."

Korea NTS, having defined the "level of comparability" standard for determining the "most reasonable method" objective for ascertaining the arm's length price, then looks to the issue of comparability itself. The NTS provides three criteria under which it can evaluate the degree of comparability:

1. The party is to look to the functions performed and the risks assumed, as reflected in the conditions and the transactions. Korea's NTS, unlike many other tax jurisdictions, does not look to the assets the taxpayer employs for comparability purposes.

2. The party is to look to the types and characteristics of the goods or services involved for comparability purposes.
3. The party is to examine economic considerations, both the "economic environment" of the market and the "degree of change in market conditions." The NTS fails, however, to further define "economic environment" or the "degree of change in market conditions."

UNDERPAYMENTS AND OVERPAYMENTS

The NTS contemplates that the intercompany price established between a Korean company and a foreign-related party might differ from an arm's length price. Should such an eventuality occur, the NTS states that the Korean company should pay its income tax based on the income the Korean company would report under the arm's length basis. The NTS implicitly contemplates that the Korean company would have reflected a lower income amount, thus expecting the Korean company to pay tax on the higher arm's length basis amount. The NTS does not address the situation in which the Korean government reflected a higher income amount compared with the arm's length basis amount. Based on that absence, the Korean company could then argue that it met its taxing obligations by paying the lower, arm's length amount rather than paying the higher reflected income amount.

SELECTING TRANSFER PRICING METHODS

Korea's transfer pricing law clearly delineates its priority in selecting transfer pricing methods. The Korean taxpayer must consider the integration of its priority rules with the implementation of the "most reasonable method" provisions. The NTS expresses its clear priority in favor of the comparable uncontrolled price method. The taxpayer is to select the comparable uncontrolled price method over any other method if there is a transaction between related parties that is identical to or similar to the transactions between the related parties at issue.

After expressing its preference for the comparable uncontrolled price method, the NTS then expresses its second choice for the traditional transactional methods: the comparable uncontrolled price method, the resale price method, and the cost plus method. These traditional transaction methods have priority over the transactional profits methods. Such transactional profits methods include the profit split method and the TNMM. The NTS contemplates that the taxpayer would use such a transactional profits method only if the traditional methods are "inapplicable." The NTS, however, fails to define the parameters under which a traditional method would be "inapplicable."

The NTS seeks to preclude the possibility of price manipulation interfering in transfer pricing analysis. The parties cannot treat an international transaction between unrelated parties as an arm's length transaction when there is "the possibility of price manipulation." The taxpayer, then, cannot use such transactions as comparables. It is noteworthy that the NTS is, by this approach, expanding its grasp from related party concerns to unrelated parties.

The NTS permits the tax authorities—but not the taxpayer—to employ an arm's length range in order to adjust the taxpayer's taxable income. Two or more uncontrolled transactions determine the arm's length range. The tax authorities must make that tax adjustment based on reasonable values they compute from the transactions they examine.

REPORTING METHODS FOR DETERMINING ARM'S LENGTH PRICE

The taxpayer must disclose to the tax authorities the transfer pricing method the taxpayer uses and the reasons why the taxpayer adopted that transfer pricing method in determining its arm's length price. The taxpayer must reflect the information concerning the transfer pricing selection process in a report the taxpayer submits with its tax return.

The taxpayer must adjust its intercompany price if the intercompany price between the Korean company and its foreign counterpart differs from the transfer price the taxpayer determines when applying the proper method for determining an arm's length price.

ADVANCE PRICING ARRANGEMENTS

Korea is enmeshed in the advance pricing agreement practice. Korea permits a taxpayer to undertake a unilateral APA or a bilateral APA. The NTS employs specific timing requirements that impact the unilateral APA process.

The taxpayer seeking to obtain a unilateral APA should submit an APA application to the NTS by the end of the first fiscal year concerned. The NTS must approve the taxpayer's application before the taxpayer can proceed. The taxpayer's application must include a request to the NTS as to transfer pricing method the taxpayer would undertake to determine the arm's length price.

Both the NTS and the taxpayer are bound by the transfer pricing method that they agree on in their APA. The unilateral APA permits the taxpayer or the government to roll-back the APA to the prior three years. This procedure is a change from the prior years. A taxpayer or the government then could apply a roll-back only on a progressive basis.

The Korea NTS can use the data that the taxpayer submits with its APA application only for the purposes of deciding whether it will grant the APA or not. The NTS permits the taxpayer to withdraw its APA application or to change the particulars of such APA application. The NTS can refuse the APA application or the taxpayer can withdraw its APA application. The NTS will return the data to the applicant in the event of such withdrawal or refusal in order to safeguard the taxpayer's confidentiality rights.

A procedure applies when the taxpayer obtains the APA. The taxpayer, after obtaining the APA, must file an annual report with the NTS. Such an annual report is to show the intercompany price that the parties to the APA have agreed are appropriate, reflecting the transfer pricing method that the parties to the APA have agreed on. The taxpayer is to file its annual report to the government within six months of the annual tax return submission due date.

The NTS provides a mutual agreement procedure (MAP) in the context of the APA system for a bilateral APA. A taxpayer that applies for an APA may request that the NTS invoke an MAP with the competent authorities of the country in which its foreign-related party is a resident under the relevant tax treaty. The MAP process is not obligatory within the APA process. The NTS may grant an APA without undergoing an MAP for the taxpayer's convenience.

A tax return procedure applies after the taxpayer obtains an APA. The taxpayer, after obtaining an APA, may file an amended tax return. The amended tax return is to reflect the change from its prior intercompany price with a related party and is to reflect the price that the APA determined.

Secondary Adjustment

The NTS has a procedure for making adjustments after making the basic audit adjustments. The tax authorities give the foreign-related party a 90-day period during which the foreign-related party may return to the Korean company the amount plus interest accrued up to the point of the return. The secondary adjustment applies in these circumstances:

- The tax authorities have adjusted the transfer price between a Korean company and its foreign-related party based on an arm's length price, *or*
- The tax authorities have increased the taxable income of the Korean company, *and*
- The foreign party has not returned an amount equal to the additional taxable income to the Korean company

The transfer pricing provisions address situations in which the foreign-related party fails to comply with the above-mentioned requirements during the requisite period. In that event, the amount equivalent to the additional taxable income "will be mostly treated as a dividend." The secondary adjustments apply even if the foreign party is a related company of the Korean company other than the shareholder itself.

Corresponding Adjustments

The LCITA and its enforcement decree state that a foreign government, on the basis of an arm's length price, can increase the taxable income of a foreign company, which is an associated enterprise, to its Korean counterpart. The Korean government can correspondingly reduce the taxable income of that Korean company if the foreign government can increase the taxable income to its Korean counterpart. The countries can apply these countervailing adjustments if the two governments have agreed on an arm's length price applicable to the case through an MAP. The taxpayer may apply for a downward adjustment in its taxable income if the countervailing arrangement does apply. The taxpayer is to file a notification of the MAP results with the tax authorities.

Adjustments Made in Regard to a Cost Sharing Agreement

Korean tax law reflects the international standards that the Korea NTS uses to verify the appropriateness of the cost sharing between a resident and its foreign-related party. These cost sharing adjustment principles are new. The NTS appears to limit the concept of a cost sharing agreement to a situation in which a resident of Korea agrees to develop intangible property jointly with its foreign-related party, and where the resident of Korea agrees to share costs and expenses in relation to such development with the foreign-related party. If the cost sharing agreement provisions do apply, the resident of Korea may adjust its tax base based on arm's length price. The shared costs, based on arm's length price, are tax deductible.

SANCTIONS IMPOSED ON FAILURE TO COMPLY WITH THE DATA REQUEST

The LCITA empowers the tax authorities to request from the taxpayer the data the tax authorities would require for adjusting the intercompany price. The tax authorities may extend a 60-day extension if the taxpayer fails to submit the requested data within 60 days without providing any justification. The government can impose penalties on the taxpayer. The taxpayer can appeal within 30 days from the date the government imposes such a penalty.

Thc tax authorities may request these specific data from the taxpayer:

- Copy of the sales contract between the Korean company and its foreign counterpart
- Price list pertaining to the products at issue
- Manufacturing cost schedule for the products at issue
- The company's organizational chart, together with a description of the functions for each department
- Intercompany price policy
- Equity relationship of the group

PENALTIES

As a general matter, the NTS imposes an underreporting penalty, 10% of the additional corporate tax, and requires the taxpayer to maintain contemporaneous documentation.

Effective January 1, 2009, taxpayers that maintain contemporaneous documentation will be granted relief from the underreporting penalty. A taxpayer seeking the penalty waiver should maintain this documentation and should submit this information to the tax authorities within 30 days after the tax authorities request it:

- General description of the company's business, including the analysis of the factors that may affect the price of assets and services
- Information that may affect the transfer price. Such information includes data as to foreign-related parties and their relationship with the taxpayer (i.e., the group organizational structure)
- Documentation that supports the taxpayer's selection of the transfer pricing method the taxpayer reports on its corporate tax return

The NTS will determine whether the taxpayer reasonably determined the arm's length price by applying the next factors:

- The taxpayer is to ascertain data as to the profitability of comparable companies as of the end of the tax year. The data should be representative, and the taxpayer should not willfully exclude the comparable company profitability in order to derive an arm's length price favorable to the taxpayer.
- The taxpayer is to collect and systematically analyze this data in applying the transfer pricing method.
- The taxpayer might select and apply a transfer pricing method different from the transfer pricing method the taxpayer applied in an APA with the NTS during the previous tax year or apply a transfer pricing method selected by the tax authorities during a previous tax audit. In that event, the taxpayer is to provide a valid reason to the NTS specifying the reason why the transfer pricing method differs.

THIN CAPITALIZATION RULES

The Korea NTS has thin capitalization rules with the transfer pricing provisions. These thin capitalization rules come from a recognition that a multinational enterprise might adopt a tax avoidance mechanism, such as where the multinational enterprise decreases the paid-in capital to a subsidiary in Korea while increasing the loans to its subsidiary as much as possible. Such a structure might result in the minimization of the subsidiary's taxable income, a device the taxpayer would achieve through increasing the subsidiary's income tax deduction. The taxpayer, in benefiting from a thin capitalization structure, replaces nondeductible dividend payments with deductible interest payments.

The LCITA and its enforcement decree contain anti–thin capitalization rules to cope with these abuses. The NTS will recharacterize excessive interest payments as dividends, and as such, those payments would lose their interest expense tax deduction. Korea normally limits the deductibility for debt as being three times the amount of equity or six times the amount of debt in the case of financial institutions. The NTS will seek to recharacterize these debt structures in the situation in which a Korean company borrows funds from its controlling shareholders overseas. The NTS will recharacterize the interest on debt that is greater than three times the equity (or six times the equity in case of financial institutions) as dividends.

The NTS will recharacterize money borrowed from an unrelated third party as being borrowed from its controlling shareholders overseas if the controlling shareholders overseas guarantee the funds. The NTS provides this excess interest formula:

A is the debt borrowed from the controlling shareholders overseas or debt that the controlling shareholders overseas guarantee.

B is A's debt, as specified above, less the controlling shareholders' overseas contribution, as paid-in capital × 3 (or × 6 in the case of financial institutions).

The nondeductible interest is the interest and discount payable to the controlling shareholders overseas × B/A.

DEBT UNDER AN ARM'S LENGTH SITUATION

A comparative principle overrides the thin capitalization rule. The thin capitalization rule does not apply, even though the ratio of debt owed to the controlling shareholders overseas to equity exceeds 3:1, if this debt is reasonable compared to the debt from an independent third party. Such debt is excluded from the thin capitalization rules and such debt is deductible.

The NTS specifies that it has adopted the anti–thin capitalization rules from Article 9(1) of the OECD Model Tax Convention. Thus, the debt–equity ratio in the industry will prevail rather than a 3:1 ratio or a 6:1 ratio if the taxpayer meets these requirements.

ANTI–TAX HAVEN RULES

The Korean anti–tax haven provisions look to the unreasonably reserving profits in the tax haven company. In essence, the anti–tax haven provisions override normal Korean tax rules and treat these unreasonably reserving profits as a dividend that is paid out to the Korean company. These anti–tax haven principles apply only if the Korean company invests in a company located in a "tax haven."

The Korean anti–tax haven provisions contain a shareholder percentage requirement, a definition of a "tax haven," an active business requirement, and a size requirement:

- **Shareholder percentage requirement.** The anti–tax haven provisions apply only if the Korean resident or individual owns, directly or indirectly, 20% or more of the voting shares in the foreign company. Civil law determines indirect ownership, which includes family affiliation.

- **Tax rate definition.** The anti–tax haven provisions are designed to regulate a company that has made "overseas investments of an abnormal nature." The NTS applies a quantitative test to ascertain whether the "overseas investments" are of "an abnormal nature" or not. The quantitative test is "an average effective tax rate of 15% or less." The NTS applies the 15% test by examining the actually accrued income in the country of incorporation. The NTS applies this quantitative test for a three-year period but formerly applied the test for a one-year period. The presence of the 15% test is quite important for tax planning as Korea, by virtue of this quantitative test, does not view Hong Kong operations or Singapore operations as being subject to the anti–tax haven provisions.
- **Active business requirement.** The anti–tax haven provisions do not apply if a company operated in a tax haven "actively engages" in its business operations through an office, shop, or factory.
- **Size requirement.** The anti–tax haven provisions do not apply for a company whose actual accrued income is 100 million won or less.
- **Defining the term "actually accrued income."** For purposes of the tax rate definition and for the size requirement, the term "actually accrued income" refers to the net income, before tax, calculated based on the generally accepted accounting principles (GAAP) of the host country. However, the host country's GAAP might be significantly different from Korean GAAP. In this eventuality, the NTS will compute the actually accrued income in that jurisdiction based on the Korean GAAP.

SCOPE OF THE "TAX HAVEN" JURISDICTION

The LCITA and its decree provide that a country that meets either of these conditions is a tax haven:

- A country or an area whose average effective tax rate for the past three years is 15% or less of the actually accrued income of a company incorporated in that jurisdiction. "Actually accrued income" is net income before the imposition of corporate income tax computed based on GAAP.
- The Commissioner of the NTS, with the approval of the Minister of Finance and Economy, can designate a country or area as being a tax haven. The Commissioner is to make its tax haven determination on the basis that these countries impose no taxes or little taxes on a company's actually accrued income. The designation of a tax haven follows the OECD or its member countries' definition of a tax haven.

For purposes of making the tax rate determination to assess whether a jurisdiction is a tax haven, if a company has paid foreign taxes, the company will be deemed to have paid such foreign taxes to the resident state. The term "effective tax rate" is based on this formula:

$$\text{Effective tax rate} = \frac{\text{Tax paid to the resident country} + \text{Foreign taxes paid}}{\text{Net income before corporate income tax}}$$

COMPUTATION OF THE RESERVED INCOME DISTRIBUTED AMOUNT

The taxpayer is to reflect the earned surplus amount as represented on its income statements prepared in accordance with the GAAP of the resident state of the foreign company that is subject to the anti–tax haven system. The taxpayer is to compute the reserved income. The taxpayer can then determine the amount from which it can make the distribution. The taxpayer is to subtract these items from the adjusted amount earned surplus:

- Distribution of earned surplus, based on an appropriation of retained earnings
- Bonuses, severance pay, and other types of outlays, based on the appropriation of retained earnings
- Reserves to be retained under the law of the resident state
- Reserves remaining after the distribution of earned surplus for the year, where these amounts were subject to tax in the previous taxable years

The Commissioner of the NTS will recompute the resident state's GAAP pursuant to the Korean GAAP if the resident state's GAAP is significantly different from the Korean GAAP.

GIFT TAX ON PROPERTY LOCATED OUTSIDE KOREA

Unique among transfer pricing directives, the current Inheritance and Gift Tax Law in Korea imposes a gift tax on certain transfers:

- The donee is domiciled in Korea.
- The donated property is located in Korea.

The Korean tax authorities cannot levy a gift tax if a Korean individual donates a property located offshore to a donee domiciled offshore. The NTS is aware of this nontaxability and recognizes that the foreign country in which the donee is domiciled might not impose a gift tax, a situation the NTS describes as "double nontaxation." The NTS warns taxpayers that Korea is member of the OECD and intends to adopt the "taxation of the donor" principle contained in the OECD Model Double Taxation Convention on Estates and Inheritances and on Gifts. The donor will be subject to the

Korean gift tax under the LCITA and its enforcement decree if a person domiciled in Korea donates offshore property to a person who is domiciled in a foreign country, providing that foreign country does not impose a gift tax on that transfer.

MUTUAL AGREEMENT PROCEDURE

A Korean resident individual, a domestic Korean company, a nonresident Korean individual, or a foreign company with a permanent establishment in Korea can request that the NTS resolve its case through consultation with the competent authorities under an applicable treaty. If the taxpayer does make such a request through the NTS, the Minister of Finance and Economy or the Commissioner of the NTS shall invoke the MAP in these situations:

- Where it is necessary for Korea to consult with foreign competent authorities as to the application of the tax treaty or the interpretation of the tax treaty
- Where a Korean resident is subject to taxation in a foreign country
- Where it becomes necessary for the competent authorities of the two countries to adjust the taxable income of the taxpayer

An invocation of the MAP process delays the appellate process. Once the Commissioner of the NTS invokes the MAP process, the taxpayer can postpone the filing of an appeal with the NTS until the NTS completes the MAP. Additionally, if the governments invoke an MAP under an applicable tax treaty, the governments will postpone tax collection of national and local taxes on a reciprocal basis until they complete the MAP.

INTERNATIONAL TAX COOPERATION

The LCITA and its enforcement decree accept the general principle that income classification under a Korean tax treaty takes priority over income classification under domestic Korean tax law.

The Korean tax authority can request the tax authority of the treaty partner to collect Korean taxes, making that authority pursuant to the LCITA and its enforcement decree, but subject to any limitations the treaty provides. Similarly, the treaty partner might request that the Korean tax authority cooperate in collecting taxes from a Korean resident. In such an event, the Korean tax authority may collect the treaty partner's tax, doing so in accordance with the procedure for the collection of taxes that the National Tax Collection Law provides.

Korean tax treaties permit exchanges of information. The Korean tax authority may exchange tax information with foreign countries with which Korea has entered into these tax treaties. However, the tax treaties might have provisions and other limitations concerning the exchange of tax information provisions.

The LCITA gives wide authority to the Korean tax authorities. The Korean tax authorities can undertake either to:

1. Simultaneously conduct a tax audit with the foreign authorities concerned, pursuant to the convention for cooperation in tax administration with that foreign country, *or*
2. Dispatch Korean tax officials to the foreign country concerned, to conduct a direct tax audit of the company in that country

Korea has entered into bilateral tax treaties with more than 65 countries. These bilateral tax treaties are conventions for the avoidance of double taxation and the prevention of fiscal evasion with respect to taxes on income and capital. These tax treaties, in addition to meeting the primary objective of avoiding international juridical taxation, serve purposes such as promoting the introduction of advance technology and capital from abroad, and encourage business expansion of domestic companies in foreign countries.

NOTE

1. The material in this chapter reflects presentations by Robert Feinschreiber and Margaret Kent to tax professionals in Seoul, Korea, on September 13–14, 2007, and comments made by Henry An at the International Fiscal Association China, Japan, and Korea Tax Conference, May 19–20, 2010, in Seoul, Korea.

29

CHAPTER TWENTY-NINE

Sri Lanka Transfer Pricing

THE SRI LANKA Ministry of Finance promulgated transfer pricing regulations on April 22, 2008, through the issuance of Gazette Order 1546/10. The Gazette Order does not specifically address the effective date of these transfer pricing regulations. Sri Lanka introduced transfer pricing legislation two years earlier, in April 2006. The 2008 transfer pricing regulations implement that statute.

Sri Lanka's transfer pricing regulations are quite brief but they include six annexes that address transfer pricing concerns:

Annex 1: Test of Control—Associated Undertaking
Annex 2: Arm's Length Pricing Methodologies
Annex 3: Appropriate Pricing Methodology—Factors to Consider
Annex 4: Comparability of an Uncontrolled Transaction—Factors to Consider
Annex 5: Prescribed Documentation
Annex 6: Suggested Supporting Documents

ASSOCIATED UNDERTAKINGS

Sri Lanka's transfer pricing provisions apply to transactions between "associated undertakings," which, in essence, are transactions between related parties. The Sri Lanka law treats such an "undertaking" to be an associate of the other party if the first undertaking party participates in the control of the second undertaking party. This undertaking process can be direct or indirect, or can occur through one or more intermediaries. The associated undertaking process necessitates that the first party exercises control over the second party in such a manner or to such an extent that the regulations prescribe.

Sri Lanka's transfer pricing provisions set out conditions that meet Sri Lanka's control test. The reader should be aware that Sri Lanka's control requirements are pervasive, viewing "control" from an operating standpoint as well as from a formalistic viewpoint. Such a "control" standard might encompass relationships that might in general not be viewed as being controlled activities. As a general matter, Sri Lanka's Ministry of Finance views any two undertakings as being associated if, at any time during the previous year, the companies meet any one of the standards for control specified in Annex 1.

ARM'S LENGTH PRICE

Sri Lanka's transfer pricing provisions define the term "arm's length price" to mean a price that applies in uncontrolled conditions between persons other than through associated undertaking. Sri Lanka's Ministry of Finance assumes that market forces determine the terms of the contract when independent undertakings deal with each other. Sri Lanka's Ministry of Finance assumes that the terms of the contract may deviate from open market norms when a transaction is between associated undertakings. Such deviation may give rise to tax leakages owing to the relationship between the parties. The Ministry of Finance views the application of arm's length transfer pricing as a means of removing these distortions.

The Ministry of Finance views the arm's length pricing methods as being the pricing methodologies prescribed by the regulations in the gazette together with the comments by Sri Lanka's Ministry of Finance on the underlying rationale of each methodology. Annex 2 states that Sri Lanka's Ministry of Finance expects the taxpayer to apply the "most appropriate" transfer pricing method. The most appropriate transfer pricing method is the method that:

- Is best suited to the facts and circumstances of each particular transaction
- Provides the "most reliable measure" of arm's length price in relation to the transaction

Annex 3 provides the factors that the taxpayer should consider in selecting a transfer pricing method.

The comparability of an uncontrolled transaction depends on these factors. The taxpayer is to consider an uncontrolled transaction as being a comparable transaction if:

- A difference arises from the transaction but that difference in the transaction will not materially affect the price or cost being charged. Alternatively, comparability can be based on the profit arising from such a transaction in the open market.
- If the taxpayer can make reasonably accurate adjustments to eliminate the material effects of such differences.

Annex 4 provides the factors that a taxpayer should consider in selecting a transfer pricing method.

Sri Lanka's Ministry of Finance provides guidance to the taxpayer in selecting data to evaluate comparability. The taxpayer should obtain data from the same financial year as the year under review in analyzing the comparability of an uncontrolled transaction. Nevertheless, the Sri Lanka transfer pricing regulations contain an overriding provision that permits the taxpayer to submit data from a two-year period preceding the taxpayer's financial year. The taxpayer can take data from those years into account if the taxpayer can establish that such data for such years reveal facts that could have an influence on the determination of transfer prices relative to the transactions the taxpayer is comparing.

DOCUMENTATION

Gazette Order 1546/10 requires a taxpayer that must undertake a transfer pricing analysis must maintain specified information and documents, as specified in Annex 5. The taxpayer must retain these documents for a period of five years after the relevant assessment year. The transfer pricing regulations further prescribe the availability of authentic documents to support the above-mentioned information. Annex 6 contains the suggested documents, which documents include public information.

THRESHOLD FOR APPLYING SRI LANKA TRANSFER PRICING

Sri Lanka's Ministry of Finance, in issuing these transfer pricing regulations, contains a de minimis rule. The threshold is Rs. 100 million, which the taxpayer is to determine by reference to aggregate values, as recorded in the taxpayer's books of account. At the time of this writing, the rate of exchange from the Sri Lanka rupee to the U.S. dollar is 114:1. The small taxpayer might have to retain its documentation to substantiate its small business exemption. Although the Sri Lanka regulations are not clear on this point, it appears that the taxpayer must aggregate transactions in considering whether the de minimis rule applies.

ADVANCE PRICING AGREEMENTS

The transfer pricing regulations permit the taxpayer to enter into an advance pricing agreement (APA). Sri Lanka's Ministry of Finance views the APA as an arrangement that determines, in advance of controlled transactions, an appropriate set of criteria. Such criteria might include the transfer pricing method, comparables and adjustments thereto, and critical assumptions as to future events. The APA applies to the transfer pricing determination for these transactions over a fixed period of time.

The APA is a procedural arrangement between the taxpayer and tax administrations (whether unilateral or bilateral) intended to resolve potential transfer pricing disputes in advance. APAs would provide the taxpayer with some degree of certainty regarding how governments would apply transfer pricing in a given set of circumstances. Thus, the legal consequences of the proposed APA are determined in advance, based on assumptions and facts. The validity of the APA depends on the assumptions and on facts occurring when the actual transactions take place.

The APA provisions provide for both:

- Unilateral arrangements between the Sri Lanka tax administration and the taxpayer. Other tax administrations are not involved in this particular APA.
- Bilateral arrangements in which two or more tax administrations concur in regard to the pricing methodology being adopted.

BURDEN OF PROOF

The Commissioner General of Inland Revenue (CGIR) has the power to call on taxpayers to prove their transactions with associated persons as being arm's length. The taxpayer has the burden of proof. The CGIR can assess the taxpayer if the taxpayer fails to satisfy the CGIR that the terms of the contract are at arm's length.

IMPLEMENTATION

The Sri Lanka transfer pricing regulations apply to both domestic and international transactions. Sri Lanka is a relatively small country. The country's database more likely can be found outside the country.

ANNEX 1: TEST OF CONTROL—ASSOCIATED UNDERTAKING

Gazette Order 1546/10 Annex 1 provides an expansive definition of "control" for transfer pricing purposes, in terms of operational issues. However, the control test provides a narrow definition of "control" from a voting power standpoint. Annex 1 provides nine specific activities that indicate control:

1. Control exists where one enterprise holds, directly or indirectly, shares that carry 50% or more of the voting power in each such undertaking.

2. Control exists where any person or undertaking holds, directly or indirectly, shares that carry 50% or more of the voting power in each such undertaking.
3. The primary lender has control over the borrower. Control exists when loans by one undertaking to another undertaking constitute 51% or more of the book value of the total assets of the other undertaking. Note that provision compares loans compared to assets; this control test does not compare one asset to another. The book value concept presumably does not reflect mark to market adjustments.
4. Primary guarantors are in a control relationship. Control exists when one party guarantees 25% or more of the other undertaking.
5. Directors can cause the undertaking to have control in the first of two situations: Control exists when the same person or persons appoint more than half of the directors or appoint more than half of the members of the governing board.
6. Directors can cause the undertaking to have control in the second of two situations: Control exists when more than half of the directors, or members of the governing board, of each of the two undertakings are appointed by the same person or persons.
7. Contractual relationships can determine the presence of control. Manufacturing activities or the maintaining of business might be "wholly dependent" on an intangible, such as the use of know-how, patents, copyrights, trademarks, licenses, and franchises. Similarly, the presence of other intangible property might determine control. Such intangible property includes other businesses or commercial rights of a similar nature. This intangible property also includes any data, documentation, drawing, or other specification relating to any patent, invention, model, design, secret formula, or process. The threshold for determining control is that the other undertaking is the owner or has exclusive rights as to that intangible. Gazette Order 1546/10 Annex 1 fails to define the term "wholly dependent."
8. Control over raw materials or control over consumables can prove control for transfer pricing purposes. Control exists when one undertaking requires 90% or more of the raw materials and consumables for the manufacturing or processing of goods or articles. Similarly, the undertaking has a controlled relationship when one undertaking supplies the raw materials or consumables, or when one undertaking specifies the raw materials or consumables, or when the prices and other conditions relating to supply influence the undertaking.
9. A catchall provision enables the Ministry of Finance to determine that a control relationship exists between two undertakings if there is "any relationship of mutual interest."

ANNEX 2: ARM'S LENGTH PRICING METHODOLOGIES

Annex 2 specifically addresses five transfer pricing methodologies:

1. Comparable uncontrolled price (CUP) method
2. Resale price method

3. Cost plus method
4. Profit split method
5. Transactional net margin method (TNMM)

Comparable Uncontrolled Price Method

The CUP method applies to property transactions and to service transactions:

- The CUP method compares the price being charged for property being transferred in a controlled transaction to the price being charged for property transferred in a comparable controlled transaction in comparable circumstances.
- The CUP method compares the price being charged for services being transferred in a controlled transaction to the price being charged for services transferred in a comparable controlled transaction in comparable circumstances.

The CUP method is the most direct and reliable way to apply the arm's length principle when it is possible for the taxpayer to locate a comparable uncontrolled transaction. The taxpayer might need to make adjustments to bring the controlled transaction to a comparable base. In the event that the taxpayer must make such adjustments, the extent and reliability of these adjustments will affect the relative reliability of the analysis under the CUP method.

Gazette Order 1546/10 Annex 2 provides a three-step calculation methodology as to the CUP method. The taxpayer is to:

1. Identify the price charged or paid for property transferred. Alternatively, the taxpayer is to identify the price charged or paid for services transferred. This transaction under review is to take place in a comparable uncontrolled transaction or in a number of such comparable uncontrolled transactions.
2. Adjust the price to account for differences, if any, between the transaction and the comparable uncontrolled transaction. Alternatively, the taxpayer is to adjust these amounts between the undertakings entering into such transactions. The taxpayer is to take these adjustments into account when these adjustments would materially affect the price in the open market.
3. Adjust the price to account for these differences. The taxpayer is to use an arm's length amount to make that adjustment to the property transferred or services provided in the transaction.

Resale Price Method

The resale price method addresses a situation in which:

- The first associated enterprise sells the product to the second associated enterprise.
- The second associated enterprise then sells the product to the independent enterprise.

The resale price begins with the amount that the second associated enterprise (the reseller) charges the independent enterprise for the product. In determining the profitability of the second associated enterprise under the resale price method, the second enterprise reduces its gross margin from its sales price of the product it sold to the independent enterprise. The reseller's gross margin represents the amount the reseller would need to cover its selling and other operating expenses, including the reseller's profit. The reseller would make an "appropriate profit" determined in light of the functions the reseller performs, taking into account its assets used and risks assumed.

The residual price for the product, from the standpoint of the reseller, after deducing the gross margin from the sales price to the independent enterprise, is the intercompany sales price between the first associated enterprise and the second associated enterprise. Taxes and levies are included in the residual amount. That residual amount is then the arm's length amount.

Gazette Order 1546/10 Annex 2 provides a five-step calculation methodology as to the resale price method. The taxpayer is to:

1. Identify the price at which it purchases property or services from an associated undertaking and then resells that property to an unrelated enterprise.
2. Reduce such sales price by the amount of normal gross margin accruing to the undertaking or to an unrelated enterprise from the purchase and resale of the same or similar property, or from obtaining and providing the same or similar services. The taxpayer would determine this amount through a comparable transaction or through a number of such transactions.
3. Further reduce the price it had arrived at by the undertaking in connection with the purchase of property or the obtaining of services.
4. Adjust the price so arrived at to take into account functional and other differences, including differences in accounting practices, if any. These differences pertain to the transaction and to comparable uncontrolled transactions, or between the undertakings entering into such transactions. The taxpayer is to take these adjustments into account when these adjustments would materially affect the amount of gross profit margin in the open market.
5. Take the adjusted price into account as being the arm's length price concerning the purchase of the property or the obtaining of services by the enterprise from the associated enterprise.

Cost Plus Method

The supplier of property or services in a controlled transaction transfers the property or services to the related purchaser. The transferor of the property adds an appropriate gross markup to the transferor's cost. Under the cost plus method, the taxpayer adds the appropriate cost plus markup to the taxpayer's original cost. The taxpayer's appropriate cost plus markup takes into account the taxpayer's profit in light of the taxpayer's functions performed and the taxpayer's market conditions. The arm's length price is original cost plus the cost plus markup.

Gazette Order 1546/10 Annex 2 provides a five-step calculation methodology as to the cost plus method. The taxpayer:

1. Determines the direct costs of production and the indirect costs of production the enterprise incurs as to property the taxpayer transfers or services the taxpayer provides to an associated undertaking.
2. Determines the amount of the normal gross profit markup as to these costs. The taxpayer is to determine the normal gross profit markup by using the same accounting norms for comparative purposes. The taxpayer is to determine the normal gross profit markup arising from the transfer of the same or similar property or service by the enterprise, or by an unrelated enterprise, in a controlled transaction or in a number of such transactions.
3. Adjusts the preceding gross profit markup to adjust for functional differences and for other differences. These differences can occur between the transaction and the comparable uncontrolled transactions. These differences can occur between the undertakings entering into such transactions. This difference analysis applies to transactions that could materially affect such profit markup in the open market.
4. Increases its direct costs of production and the indirect costs of production by the adjusted profit markup as determined above.
5. The arm's length price is the sum of the direct costs of production and the indirect costs of production plus the adjusted profit markup, determined in relation to the supply of the property or the provision of services pertaining to the undertaking.

Profit Split Method

The profit split method splits profits between associated enterprises on an "economically valid basis." Such a profit split method uses a "valid" method that approximates the division of profits that the parties would anticipate and reflect in an agreement made at arm's length. The profit split method seeks to eliminate the effect of profits on special considerations made or imposed in a controlled transaction. The taxpayer applies the profit split method by determining the division of profits that independent enterprises would have expected to realize from engaging in the transaction or transactions.

Gazette Order 1546/10 Annex 2 provides that the profit split method may be applicable primarily to international transactions where these international transactions involve the transfer of unique intangibles, or applies in multiple international transactions where these international transactions are so interrelated that the taxpayer cannot evaluate each facet separately for the purpose of determining the arm's length price of any one transaction. Gazette Order 1546/10 Annex 2 provides a four-step calculation methodology as to the profit split method. The taxpayer:

1. Determines the combined net profit of the associated undertaking that arises from the international transaction in which these parties are engaged.
2. Determines the relative contribution that each of the associated parties provides. The taxpayer evaluates the relative contribution based on the functions

performed, assets employed or to be employed, and risks assumed by each enterprise. The taxpayer then evaluates the relative contribution based on reliable external market data that indicate how such a contribution would be evaluated by unrelated undertakings, performing comparable functions in similar circumstances.

3. Splits the combined net profit among the undertakings, making that split in proportion to their relative contributions, as evaluated under 2, previously.
4. Assesses the profits to arrive at an arm's length price. The Sri Lanka profit split method also permits the residual profit split method when the taxpayer can initially allocate the combined net profit amount to each undertaking. This initial allocation might provide the undertaking with a basic return that is appropriate for the type of transaction in which the taxpayer is engaged. The taxpayer needs to make this allocation by reference to market returns achieved for similar types of transactions by independent enterprises. Thereafter, the taxpayer is to apply the residual profit split remaining after the first allocation. The taxpayer can split the residual profit among the enterprise in proportion to their relative contributions. In such a case, the net profit is the summation of the profits attributable to the basic return amount plus the profits attributable to the residual amount.

Transaction Net Margin Method

The TNMM examines the net profit margin relative to an appropriate base that the taxpayer realizes from a controlled transaction. Such a base might include costs, sales, or assets. The analysis looks to the amounts that the same taxpayer would earn in a comparable uncontrolled transaction. The Sri Lanka provisions recognize that such data might not be obtainable and suggest that the taxpayer use as a guide the net margin earned by an independent enterprise on a comparable transaction.

Gazette Order 1546/10 Annex 2 provides a five-step calculation methodology as to the TNMM. The taxpayer:

1. Ascertains the net profit margin it realized by the undertaking from transactions entered into with an associated undertaking. The taxpayer is to compute these profitability amounts in relation to costs incurred, or sales affected, or assets employed or to be employed by the undertaking, or through any other relevant base.
2. Ascertains the net profit margin realized by the undertaking, or by an unrelated undertaking, from a comparable uncontrolled transaction or a number of such transactions. The taxpayer is to compute these amounts by using the same basis.
3. Adjusts the net profit margin arising in comparable uncontrolled transactions to take into account the difference, if any, between the transaction and the comparable uncontrolled transactions. Alternatively, the taxpayer is to adjust the net profit margin arising in comparable uncontrolled transactions to take into account the difference, if any, between the undertakings entering into such transactions. The taxpayer is to take into account transactions that materially affect the amount of net profit margin in the open market.

4. Calculates the net profit, which is the net profit margin realized by the undertaking.
5. Takes into account the net profit margin it establishes to arrive at the arm's length price in relation to the transaction.

ANNEX 3: APPROPRIATE PRICING METHODOLOGY—FACTORS TO CONSIDER

Gazette Order 1546/10 provides six specific factors that the taxpayer is to consider in developing its transfer pricing methodology:

1. Nature and class of the transaction. Gazette Order 1546/10 fails to define the term "class of the transaction."
2. Class or classes of the associated undertaking as entering into the transaction. The taxpayer is to consider the functions performed by the class or classes, taking into account the assets they employ or to be employed and the risks that each enterprise assumes.
3. Availability, coverage, and reliability of the data the taxpayer would need to apply the transfer pricing method.
4. Degree of comparability that exists between the transaction and the uncontrolled transaction, and between the undertaking entering into such transactions.
5. Extent to which it can make reliable and accurate adjustments to account for the differences, if any, between the transaction and the comparable uncontrolled transaction, or between the enterprises entering into such transactions.
6. Nature, extent, and reliability of the assumptions the taxpayer makes in applying the transfer pricing method.

ANNEX 4: COMPARABILITY OF AN UNCONTROLLED TRANSACTION—FACTORS TO CONSIDER

Gazette Order 1546/10 provides four specific factors that the taxpayer is to consider in comparing an uncontrolled transaction:

1. Specific characteristics of the property the taxpayer transfers or the services the taxpayer provided, in either transaction.
2. Functions performed by the respective parties to the transaction, taking into account the assets employed or to be employed by the respective parties to the transaction and the risks assumed by the respective parties to the transaction.
3. The contractual terms of the transactions that lay down explicitly or implicitly how the taxpayer and its respective parties are to divide the responsibilities, risks, and benefits. The contractual terms might or might not be formal or in writing.
4. Conditions prevailing in the markets in which the respective parties to the transactions operate. These conditions include the geographic location and size of the

markets, the laws and governmental orders in force, cost of labor, and cost of capital in the markets, overall economic development, level of competition, and whether the markets are wholesale or retail.

ANNEX 5: PRESCRIBED DOCUMENTATION

Gazette Order 1546/10 lists 13 aspects of documentation that the taxpayer is to supply:

1. Documentation concerning the ownership structure of the associated undertakings, including share ownership or other ownership interests.
2. A profile of the multinational company or group to which the company is a member. This information is required for companies for which the taxpayer has transactions. This profile is to include, for each member, the name, address, legal status, and country of tax residence. The taxpayer is to provide the ownership linkages.
3. A broad description of its business and the industry in which the taxpayer operates. The taxpayer is to provide this information for its affiliates with which it does business.
4. Details of its group or international transactions. This information is to include the nature and terms of the arrangement, including prices, details of the property being transferred or the services being provided, and the quantum and value of each such transaction or class of such transaction.
5. A description of the functions the taxpayer performs, the risks the taxpayer assumes, and the assets the taxpayer employs or will employ. The taxpayer is also to provide this information for its associated undertakings involved in the transaction.
6. Economic data that the taxpayer prepared. Such data include a record of the economic and marketing analysis, forecasts, budgets, or any other financial estimates. That data might be prepared for the business as whole and for each division or product separately. This economic data requirement applies to transactions that might be relevant to its pricing.
7. A record of uncontrolled transactions the taxpayer takes into account for analyzing their comparability with the transactions the taxpayer undertakes. Such documentation includes a record of the nature, terms, and conditions relating to any controlled transaction with third parties that might be relevant to the pricing of the transaction.
8. The analysis the taxpayer performed to evaluate the comparability of uncontrolled transactions with the taxpayer's own relevant transactions.
9. The methods it considered in determining its arm's length price. The taxpayer is to provide this arm's length analysis for each transaction or class of transaction. The taxpayer is to provide information as to the method the taxpayer selects as being the most appropriate transfer pricing method. The taxpayer should also provide explanations as to why the taxpayer selected that transfer pricing method. The taxpayer should additionally provide information to quantify the methods involved.

10. Records that demonstrate the taxpayer's working out the determination of the arm's length price. The taxpayer is to provide the details of the comparable data and financial data the taxpayer uses in applying the most appropriate transfer pricing method. The taxpayer is also to provide the adjustments the taxpayer has made to account for differences between the transaction and comparable transactions, or between the undertaking associates entering into these transactions.
11. The assumptions, policies, and price negotiations, if any, that have critically affected the taxpayer's determination of the arm's length price.
12. Details of the adjustments, if any, the taxpayer makes to its transfer prices to align them with arm's length prices under these provisions. The taxpayer is also to provide its consequent adjustments it made to the total income for tax purposes.
13. Further information, data, or document as requested by the Sri Lanka Ministry of Finance. Such information includes information or data relating to the associated undertaking that might be relevant in the determination of the arm's length price.

SUGGESTED SUPPORTING DOCUMENTS

Gazette Order 1546/10 suggests that the taxpayer provide six additional documentation facets:

1. The government of the taxpayer's country of residence of the associated enterprise, or any other country, might issue official publications, reports, studies, and databases. Gazette Order 1546/10 suggests that the taxpayer provide that information to the Sri Lanka Ministry of Finance when the Ministry requests that information.
2. Institutions of national repute might provide market study reports and technical publications. Gazette Order 1546/10 suggests that the taxpayer provide that information to the Sri Lanka Ministry of Finance when the Ministry requests that information.
3. Stock exchanges and commodity markets might provide market quotations. Gazette Order 1546/10 suggests that the taxpayer provide that information to the Sri Lanka Ministry of Finance when the Ministry requests that information.
4. Agreements and contracts entered into with associated undertakings or with unrelated enterprises as to similar transactions might be relevant to the situation. Gazette Order 1546/10 suggests that the taxpayer provide that information to the Sri Lanka Ministry of Finance when the Ministry requests that information.
5. The taxpayer and the associated enterprise might have undertaken letters or other correspondence as part of their negotiation process, documenting their terms. Gazette Order 1546/10 suggests that the taxpayer provide that information to the Sri Lanka Ministry of Finance when the Ministry requests that information.
6. The taxpayer might have issued documents in connection with transactions that reflect their accounting practices. Gazette Order 1546/10 suggests that the taxpayer provide that information to the Sri Lanka Ministry of Finance when the Ministry requests that information.

30

CHAPTER THIRTY

Taiwan Transfer Pricing

THE REPUBLIC OF CHINA (the ROC or Taiwan) enacted its transfer pricing statute in 1971, one of the first transfer pricing provisions in Asia. The ROC Ministry of Finance (MOF) later implemented transfer pricing provisions on December 28, 2004. In contrast with the transfer pricing regimes in Southeast Asia, the ROC's transfer pricing regulations require each taxpayer to prepare a transfer pricing report and to submit this transfer pricing report to the MOF far in advance of any contemplated tax audit.

ENACTMENT OF THE TRANSFER PRICING STATUTE

The ROC enacted Article 43-1 of its Income Tax Act (ITA) in 1971. The impetus for this legislation was to deal with the problem of transfer pricing and to realize "fair and legitimate" taxation impacting controlled transactions between a profit-seeking enterprise and its related parties. The ROC included provisions similar to transfer pricing in Article 50 of the Financial Holding Company of 2001 and Article 42 of the Enterprise Merger and Acquisition Act of 2002.

ITA Article 43-1 addresses the adjustment of income the government would have to undertake for non–arm's length transactions. Article 43-1A authorizes the collection by authorities in charge to adjust the calculation of the income on an enterprise in order to determine its taxable income and its tax liability. The MOF takes charge of the transfer pricing allocation process. The MOF needs to approve the collection process, and the MOF must undertake this collection process in pursuance of the arm's length principle.

The MOF can invoke Article 43-1 when a profit-seeking enterprise:

- Acts together with other enterprises or with other enterprises within or outside the Chinese territory
- Has an affiliated relationship with an enterprise, *or*
- Is directly or indirectly owned or controlled by the enterprise

The MOF can undertake this collection:

- Where these enterprises allocate revenue cost, expenses, and profits and losses among their related businesses that are incompatible with the arm's length principle, *and*
- When the taxpayer intends to avoid or reduce its income tax liabilities with the ROC

ITA Article 43-1 governs transfer pricing activities occurring within ROC domestic enterprises as well as within multinational enterprises. The tax authorities can begin the process of investigating transfer pricing adjustments even though the taxpayer meets the requirements prescribed in Article 43-1. The tax authorities in charge can undertake this investigation when they perceive that a profit-seeking enterprise has transactions with its related enterprises (e.g., through controlled transactions) that are incompatible with the arm's length principle. The authorities can start the process of investigating these adjustments so long as they have met the Article 43-1 requirements.

A similar investigation rule applies to Article 50 of the Financial Holding Company Act and to Article 42 of the Enterprise Merger and Acquisition Act. The collection authorities in charge undertake the investigation and adjustment in accordance with the arm's length principle. These collection authorities in charge are to review the transactions conducted by any company subject to these acts with related enterprises, individuals, or nonprofit organizations (i.e., controlled transactions). These collection authorities in charge should review transactions with its unrelated parties that they consider as being non–arm's length.

TRANSFER PRICING REGULATIONS

The MOF issued transfer pricing regulations (Article 43-1B) on December 28, 2004, to implement the Transfer Pricing Statute (Article 43-1A). These transfer pricing regulations govern the assessment of profit-seeking enterprise income applicable to non–arm's length transfer pricing. The MOF had promulgated the Regulations Governing the Assessment of Profit-Seeking Enterprise Income Tax on Non–Arm's Length Transfer Pricing. These transfer pricing regulations encompass seven categories of information:

1. Types of transactions covered
2. Arm's length principles
3. Transfer pricing methods
4. Requirements for disclosing information
5. Requirements for preparing transfer pricing documentation
6. Applications for advance pricing arrangements
7. Investigation, assessment, and corresponding adjustments
8. Penalties

Types of Transactions Covered

The Article 43-1B regulations encompass these transactions:

- Transfer of tangible assets
- Use of tangible assets
- Transfer of intangible assets
- Use of intangible assets
- Rendering of services
- Use of funds
- Other types of transactions, as described by the MOF

Arm's Length Principles

The ROC transfer pricing principles specify that taxpayers and tax authorities are to follow eight arm's length principles. The profit-seeking enterprises and collection authorities in charge are to evaluate whether the results of a controlled transaction are at arm's length and are to demonstrate the arm's length result. The profit center enterprise and collection authorities in charge are to undertake these eight arm's length principles in the controlled transaction context:

1. Comparability principle
2. Adoption of the "most applicable" transfer pricing method
3. Evaluation of separate transactions
4. Use of current-year data
5. Adoption of an arm's length range
6. Analysis of the reasons for losses on the part of the taxpayer
7. Separate evaluation of revenues and of expenditures
8. Any other arm's length principles, as prescribed by the MOF

Transfer Pricing Methods

At the present time, the taxpayer can use the next transfer pricing methods to evaluate whether the result of a controlled transaction is at arm's length or to evaluate the arm's length result:

- Traditional transaction methods, including:
  - Comparable uncontrolled price (CUP) method
  - Uncontrolled transaction method
  - Resale price method
  - Cost plus method
- Profit methods, including
  - Comparable profits method
  - Profit split methods

These transfer pricing methods define "applicable methods" as depending on the transaction. Profit-seeking enterprises undertaking controlled transactions are not required to check each transaction method to determine the transfer pricing method that is most appropriate. Note that some countries, including Ecuador, for example, require the taxpayer to specifically address each transfer pricing method.

Instead of the approach of testing each transaction, the profit-seeking enterprise may select one transfer pricing method or undertake a choice of transfer pricing methods to ascertain the "most appropriate" transfer pricing method. The taxpayer is to make a choice of transfer pricing methods for its circumstances based on the:

- Comparability or similarity of controlled transactions and their comparables
- Reliability of the adjustments made to eliminate these differences

Requirements for Disclosing Information

As a general matter, a profit-seeking enterprise is to disclose information regarding their related parties. This information disclosure requirement does not apply to enterprises having different tax treatments from those of their related parties. The MOF can issue these provisions with a turnover minimum and with a minimum amount as to the profit-seeking enterprise's related parties. Profit-seeking enterprises that are required to disclose information must fill out the relevant form, including an organization chart, a brief description of the related parties, a simple summary of controlled transactions, and other related information.

Requirements for Preparing Transfer Pricing Documentation

The ROC's MOF requires a profit-seeking enterprise to prepare a transfer pricing report pursuant to Article 43-1(B)(5)(a). Article 43-1(B)(5)(b) provides the specifics of the transfer pricing report.

As a general matter, a profit-seeking enterprise is to prepare a transfer pricing report when filing its income tax return. The transfer pricing report is to include its information regarding controlled transactions and other related documents, such as complete organizational structure, summaries of controlled transactions, and so forth beginning with the 2005 taxable year. However, in order to alleviate the taxpayer's burden and its compliance costs, the MOF established a safe harbor rule on December 30, 2005. Profit-seeking enterprises having controlled transactions that meet these safe harbor provisions can replace their transfer pricing report documents with other evidentiary documents that are able to sufficiently indicate that the results of these transactions are at arm's length.

Article 43-1(B)(5)(b) provides the specifics of the transfer pricing report. As a general matter, a transfer pricing report is a record of the procedures regarding the taxpayer's transfer pricing analysis. The transfer pricing report is to include these seven items at a minimum:

1. Industry analysis and economic analysis
2. Functional analysis and risk analysis of all the participants involved in the controlled transaction
3. Nature of the compliance with the arm's length principle
4. Description of the taxpayer's search for comparables
5. Description of the selection of the "most appropriate" transfer pricing method and the related comparable analysis
6. Transfer pricing methods adopted by the other related participants
7. Description applying the "most appropriate" transfer pricing method to evaluate whether the result of the controlled transaction is at arm's length, and also its conclusions concerning selected comparables, difference adjustments and assumptions, arm's length range, the conclusion and evaluation, and the transfer pricing adjustment if the transactions are not at arm's length

Applications for Advance Pricing Arrangements

Article 43-1(B)(6) provides five facets of the advance pricing arrangement (APA) procedure:

1. Application requirements
2. Application and review procedure
3. Application period
4. Tax examinations in compliance with the APA requirement
5. Advantages of using an APA

Article 43-1(B)(6)(a) provides the requirements under which a taxpayer undertaking a control transaction can apply for an APA. The profit-seeking enterprise that undertakes a controlled transaction that meets certain requirements can apply to the MOF with a view toward obtaining an APA. The three principal requirements of applying for the APA are:

1. The amount of the transactions being applied to the APA are no less than NT$ 1 billion or the annual amount of such transactions are NT$ 500 million.
2. The taxpayer did not significantly evade tax during the past three years.
3. The taxpayer will provide these documents during the time limit: documents required for an APA application, such as a business overview, relevant information from related parties and controlled transactions, and the transfer pricing report, all to be provided in its time limits.

Article 43-1(B)(6)(b), in providing the application and review process, provides that taxpayers that are deemed to qualify for an APA should file the application before the end of the first fiscal year covered by the APA. The collection authorities in charge are to review the application and make conclusions within the year. The collection authorities in charge can extend the application period for a further period of six months and, under special circumstances, can extend the time period for a further period of six months. When reaching a review of the APA application process, the collection authorities in charge are to discuss its decision with the applicants. Both the collection authorities in charge and the taxpayer should develop the APA so that both parties can follow the terms of the agreement.

Article 43-1(B)(6)(c) provides the applicable time period of the APA. Once the parties sign the APA, the APA will be effective for a period of three to five years. If there are no substantial changes to the conditions in the APA, an applicant that has fully complied with all terms of the APA may apply for an extension for another five years.

Article 43-1(B)(6)(d) provides for examinations of compliance with the APA. During the time period for which the APA is applicable, the applicant should file an annual report on the execution of the APA to the collection authorities in charge as to the taxpayer's income tax return. That annual report is akin to the U.S. concept of an annual report, and such an annual report precludes the filing of the transfer pricing report.

Article 43-1(B)(6)(e) specifies that the use of the APA has two advantages to the taxpayer:

1. The APA process provides the taxpayer with a simplified documentation requirement. The taxpayer has no need to file an annual transfer pricing report.
2. The APA provides the taxpayer with certainty for its tax liabilities. The collection authorities will reduce the probability of auditing and will determine taxable income in accordance with the APA.

Investigation, Assessment, and Corresponding Adjustments

Article 43-1(B)(7), in addressing investigation, assessment, and corresponding adjustments, addresses these issues separately:

- Investigation
- Assessment
- Corresponding adjustments

Article 43-1(B)(7)(a), in addressing transfer pricing investigations, provides that when perceived profit-seeking enterprises have non–arm's length transactions with their related parties, the collection authorities in charge may begin the process of investigation.

The authorities can conduct different procedures based on whether the enterprise being audited provides the transfer pricing documentation as required:

- In the first instance, if an enterprise provides adequate documentation, the authorities may assess its tax amount based on that documentation.
- In the second instance, if the taxpayer fails to provide that documentation, the authorities may assess the taxable amount based on the information the tax authorities gather from internal data and external data.

Article 43-1(B)(7)(b) addresses the assessment processes. For both instances described in Article 43-1(B)(7)(a), the MOF is to determine the taxpayer's taxable income in accordance with these regulations. However, in the second instance described in Article 43-1(B)(7)(a), there may be a failure of the taxpayer to determine comparables, for example, on royalty payments. In the case that the taxpayer's failure exists, the tax authorities may assess such taxable income based on standard profit margins as regulated by the MOF.

Article 43-1(B)(7)(c) provides for corresponding adjustments. The collection authority in charge might have conducted a transfer pricing investigation of profit-seeking enterprises undertaking controlled transactions pursuant to these regulations. The MOF might approve the corresponding adjustments made by the authority. The MOF should then make corresponding adjustments to the income of the counterpart of the enterprise. Both parties are liable to income tax adjustments.

The arm's length adjustment might result from an income tax assessment of the related party jurisdiction under the treaty framework. In this event, the collection authority in charge should also make a corresponding adjustment to the taxable income counterpart where that counterpart is liable to the income tax obligation, providing that the ROC views this obligation as reasonable.

Penalties

The profit-seeking enterprises might fail to comply with the Article 43-1 regulations, thereby resulting in a tax liability to the profit-seeking enterprise. The collection authority can make adjustments and assess liability to the profit-seeking enterprise as to its tax liability in accordance with ITA and Article 110. ITA is to reflect this specific tax omission or underreporting, commencing with the 2005 taxable year:

- The reported price of the controlled transaction is two times the arm's length price as assessed by the tax administration, or lower than the arm's length price. This penalty is similar in concept to one of the U.S. section 6662 transfer pricing penalties.
- The increase in taxable income of the controlled transaction adjusted and assessed by the collection authority in charge is 10% annual taxable income and 3% annual net business revenue.
- A profit-seeking enterprise that cannot provide a transfer pricing report and other documents evidencing the result that the transaction is an arm's length is subject to penalty.
- The collection authorities in charge might provide other de facto tax shortfall penalties.

CHAPTER THIRTY-ONE

Thailand Transfer Pricing

DURING THE MIDDLE of the first decade of the twenty-first century, the Revenue Department of Thailand recognized that international business transactions are continuing to increase dramatically. The Revenue Department of Thailand understood that international investment has increasingly expanded at an unprecedented rate in many countries. As a result of these developments, the Revenue Department of Thailand set up a transfer pricing regime to address these tax issues that remain in force today.

The Revenue Department of Thailand views a multinational enterprise (MNE) as being a "group of companies" having "mutual interests." The Revenue Department of Thailand views transfer pricing that takes place by the MNE as the process of trading goods or services with other MNE members. Transfer pricing, then, is the price that related contracted parties set for goods or for services where the prices may deviate from the market price. The Revenue Department of Thailand defines the market price or the arm's length price as the price on consideration, service fee, or interest that independent parties acting in good faith would charge in a commercial manner for the product or service. That product or service or loan would have the same characteristics, categories, or types of property, or service, or loan, that the first party would transfer or provide on the date provided for the date of the property transfer, the providing of services, or lending.

As part of its transfer pricing concerns, the Revenue Department of Thailand became aware of the practical problems of calculating market price. As a response to these concerns, the Revenue Department of Thailand issued a booklet titled "Determination of Market Price for Multinational Enterprises." The Revenue Department of Thailand wrote this booklet to provide businesses with guidance in determining acceptable market prices in accordance with international principles. The Revenue Department of Thailand expected that the taxpayer's preparation of adequate documentation would save time for the taxpayer and the Revenue Department of Thailand, and would reduce the burden of proof on the Revenue Department of Thailand.

TRANSFER PRICING BOOKLET

The Revenue Department of Thailand's transfer pricing booklet is composed of four separate parts:

Part 1 describes related tax laws that determine market price.
Part 2 explains methodologies the taxpayer is to use in determining market price.
Part 3 describes the process the taxpayer is to use in establishing market price.
Part 4 provides a list of documentation the taxpayer should keep.

PART 1: TAX LEGISLATION IMPACTING TRANSFER PRICING

Thailand tax authorities can price goods and services in order to prevent tax evasion caused by "manipulated transfer prices within the MNE." The Revenue Department of Thailand provides them with the following authority:

- Section 65 bis (4) (7) under the Thailand Revenue Code.
- Section 65 ter under the Thailand Revenue Code, which contains rules for computing net taxable profits for Thai companies and for Thai branches, and gives tax officers power to adjust transactions—whether domestic or international—that are not transacted at market prices. The income tax return requires taxpayers to declare that its prices for material transactions are based on market prices.
- Section 70 ter under the Thailand Revenue Code.
- Double tax agreements between Thailand and other countries.
- Standard Accounting No. 37 and No. 47.
- Paw 113/2545, a Revenue Department of Thailand departmental instruction titled "Corporate Income Tax—The Determination of Transfer Price Based on

Market Price," issued in order to provide tax officials with a standardized guide on how the taxpayer is to determine the transfer price based on market price. The Revenue Department of Thailand's departmental instruction divides Paw 113/2545 into five categories:

Clause 1: Criteria for the Calculation of Net Profits of Juristic Partnerships or Corporations for Income Tax Purposes
Clause 2: Assessment of Revenues and Expenses Based on the Market Price
Clause 3: Methodologies in Determining the Market Price
Clause 4: Documentation that the Taxpayer Should Prepare
Clause 5: Advance Pricing Arrangements (APAs)

REVENUE DEPARTMENT OF THAILAND DEPARTMENTAL INSTRUCTION PAW 113/2545

The Revenue Department of Thailand issued Departmental Instruction Paw 113/2545 to its assessment officials. The Revenue Department of Thailand intended that assessment officials would use this departmental instruction as a guideline in their examination and advice to taxpayers. The Revenue Department of Thailand intended that assessment officials would address the calculation of the juristic corporation's or partnership's net profits pursuant to Thailand's Internal Revenue Code Section 65 regarding the determination of the transfer price based on market price. In this regard, the Revenue Department of Thailand issued the assessment officials with the following instructions.

Clause 1

Clause 1 pertains to a juristic corporation or a partnership established under Thai law or under foreign law pursuant to Section 66 and Section 76 bis under the Thailand Revenue Code. Such juristic corporation or a partnership is to calculate its net profits for income tax purposes under Section 65 of the Thailand Revenue Code by undertaking these accounting activities:

- Taking into account revenues the taxpayer derives from business activities or in consequence of these business activities carried on during the accounting period
- Deducting these expenses in accordance with conditions prescribed under Section 65 bis and 65 ter under the Thailand Revenue Code

The taxpayer is to apply the revenue and expense amounts under Clause 1 by using the accrual basis. Under this accrual basis, the taxpayer is to include all revenue derived in any accounting period even if the taxpayer does not actually receive revenue during that period. The taxpayer is to reflect all expenses relevant to such revenue even if the taxpayer does not pay these amounts during that period.

Clause 2

Clause 2 pertains to a situation in which a juristic corporation or a corporation specified under Clause 1 enters a transaction with a contracting party. Paw 113/2545 gives the assessment official the power to assess the revenue and expenses based on market price when the juristic corporation or partnership:

- Receives no consideration without justifiable reason
- Receives an amount that is less than the market price without justifiable reason
- Enters into a transaction with a contracting party deriving expenditures higher than the market price without justifiable reasons

Providing that:

- The juristic corporation or partnership does not adjust revenue and expenses based on market price for income tax purposes.

The departmental instruction provides the taxpayer with two definitions:

1. Under paragraph 1, the term "market price" means the value of the consideration, service fee, or interest that is independent to the contracting parties. This market price amount is the amount that a party, acting in good faith, would charge in a commercial manner for the same characteristics, categories, or types of property, service, or loan. This market price would be transferred or would be provided on the date of the transfer of property, the date of providing services, or the date of lending.
2. The term "independent contracting parties" means contracting parties that have no direct or indirect relationship, management, control, or capital between themselves.

Clause 3

Clause 3 provides that a taxpayer can select one of four transfer price methods in computing revenue and expenses for the purposes of determining market price.

1. Comparable uncontrolled price (CUP) method
2. Resale price method
3. Cost plus method
4. Other transfer pricing methods

A taxpayer applies the CUP method by comparing the price that the taxpayer charges for consideration, the provision of services, or interest between independent contracting parties. The CUP method potentially applies where the parties transfer the same categories and types of property, or when the parties provide for loans or services under the same or similar conditions.

The taxpayer applies the resale price method by first taking into account the consideration the taxpayer receives for the transfer of property or the service fee. Under the resale price method, the purchaser of goods or services resells these goods or services to other persons who are independent parties. The purchaser of goods or services then deducts from its resale amount an appropriate gross profit amount as well as deducing the costs of the goods or services the company incurs. The taxpayer is to calculate the "appropriate gross profit" by multiplying the resale price of the property or service by the gross profit margin. The taxpayer is to determine gross profit margin from the transfer of goods or services having the same or similar properties or services to independent contracting parties.

Departmental Instruction No. Paw 113/2545 provides an example illustrating the resale cost method:

- Company G sells the goods to Company A, an associated company, at the price of 50 Baht.
- Company A then resells the same goods to Company B, an independent party, at the price of 90 Baht.
- Assume that the gross margin arising from the sale to independent contracting parties within the market selling the same goods is 20 percent of the resale price.
- Company G calculates the market price at which Company G sells goods to Company A in this way:
  - Resale price to an independent contracting party [Company A's resale of the goods to Company B] = 90 Baht
  - A's gross profit [90 Baht × 20%] = 18 Baht
  - A's market price [90 Baht – 18 Baht] = 72 Baht

The example fails to address the pricing adjustment, which would be the difference the market price of 72 Baht and the actual price of 50 Baht.

The taxpayer applies the cost method by first taking into account the cost of the property or cost of the service that the taxpayer incurs as the seller of the property or the seller of the services. Then the taxpayer takes into account the price of the property or the price of the service to the purchaser, marking up the difference with an appropriate gross profit. The taxpayer is to calculate the appropriate gross profit by multiplying the cost of the property or cost of the service with the gross profit margin derived from the transfer having the same characteristics, categories, or types of property or service to independent contracting parties.

Departmental Instruction No. Paw 113/2545 provides an example illustrating the cost plus method:

- Company G sells goods to Company A, an associated company, at a price of 75 Baht.
- The cost of goods sold is 50 Baht.
- Company K sells the same goods to Company B, an independent company, at the price of 100 Baht.

- The cost of goods sold is 60 Baht.
- The gross profit margin arising from the sale to independent parties is 40 percent of the selling price [100 Baht less 60 Baht, divided by 100 Baht] or 66.67% of the cost of goods sold [40 Baht divided by 60 Baht].
- The next mechanism determines the market price at which Company G sells goods to Company A:
  - G's cost of goods sold in its sales to Company A, an associated company, was 50 Baht.
  - G's gross profit percentage, based on K's sales to Company B, is 66.67%.
  - G's gross profit percentage is 50 Baht × 66.67%, or 33.34 Baht.
  - G's market price is 50 Baht plus 33.34 Baht, or 83.34 Baht in total.

The taxpayer might not be limited to selecting the CUP method, the resale method, or the cost plus method. The taxpayer can select other transfer pricing methods if:

- The taxpayer cannot apply the CUP method, the resale method, or the cost plus method in calculating revenue or expense in order to derive the market price.
- The consideration, service fee, or interest of other methods are "internationally accepted and commercially appropriate to the facts and circumstances as to the transfer of property, the providing of services, or lending."

Clause 4

Clause 4 establishes the level of documentation required in a transfer pricing documentation situation. These documentation rules apply in a tax investigation by an assessment official regarding the methods of calculating revenue and expense for the purpose of determining the market price under Clause 3 for a juristic corporation or partnership under Clause 1. The assessment official is to consider the next documentation providing that the:

- Documentation is actually prepared by the juristic corporation or partnership during each stage of a transaction *and*
- Corporation retains such information at its office.

Clause 4 provides the taxpayer with ten specific documentation guides:

1. Documentation that indicates the structure and relationship between business entities within the same group. Such documentation includes the structure of the business and the nature of the business that each entity carries on.
2. The business's budgets, business plans, and financial projections.
3. Documentation that indicates the taxpayer's business strategies as well as the taxpayer's reasons for adopting such strategies.
4. Documentation that indicates sales and operating results, and the nature of its transactions with business entities within the group.

5. Documentation that indicates the taxpayer's reasons for entering into international transactions with business entities within the same group.
6. Pricing policies, product profitability, relevant market information, and profit sharing for each business entity. The taxpayer is to consider the functions performed, assets utilized, and risks assumed for the related business entities.
7. Documentation that supports the selection of a particular method.
8. A taxpayer might consider applying more than one transfer pricing method. When a taxpayer does examine more than one transfer pricing method, the taxpayer should provide documentation indicating the details of the method that the taxpayer does not select and explain the reasons why the taxpayer did not select each of these transfer pricing methods. Note that Thailand's method selection documentation rules have an approach similar to the documentation selection process in Ecuador, requiring the taxpayer to pursue each transfer pricing method.
9. Documentation that the taxpayer would use as evidence, indicating the taxpayer's negotiation positions in relation to transactions with business entities within the same group, and basis for negotiation.
10. The taxpayer should include other documentation (if any) in determining the transfer price.

These ten standards are also included in Part IV within Thailand's transfer pricing rules.

The Revenue Department of Thailand employs a "direct or indirect relationship test" in ascertaining management, control, or capital. The departmental instruction defines the term "business entities within the same group" as under the first paragraph of the instruction as referring to business entities in a group of juristic corporations or partnerships having a "direct or indirect relationship" in management, control, or capital between themselves.

A juristic corporation or partnership, as specified under Clause 1, can prepare documents and evidence according to paragraph 1 in the departmental instruction. The juristic corporation or partnership might prepare documents and evidence with sufficient details to show that the taxpayer-calculated revenue and expenses in deriving the market price of a juristic corporation or partnership under Clause 3 are justified and appropriate. If the taxpayer meets this compliance requirement, the assessment officer is to adopt that method of computing revenue and expenses for purposes of determining the market price of that juristic corporation or partnership.

Clause 5

Clause 5 specifies the APA procedure that the taxpayer is to follow. A juristic corporation or partnership under Clause 1 might wish to enter into an APA with the Revenue Department for any transaction with its dependent contracting party. In the event that such a juristic corporation or partnership seeks to enter into such an APA, the juristic corporation or partnership is to submit an APA request in writing, together with relevant documentation to the Director General of Revenue Department. This document is to set forth the rules, methodologies, and conditions that the corporation or the partnership is to follow under the APA procedure.

PART 2: METHODOLOGIES IN CALCULATING MARKET PRICE

Part 2 seeks to define the term "transfer pricing methodologies which are accepted internationally." These methodologies are of two types: traditional transaction methods and transactional profit methods. There are three traditional transaction methods:

1. CUP method
2. Resale price method
3. Cost plus method

There are two types of transactional profit methods:

1. Profit split method
2. Transactional net margin method (TNMM)

PART 3: PROCESS IN ESTABLISHING THE MARKET PRICE

Clause 3 provides a four-step procedure that the taxpayer is to follow in establishing the market price:

1. Characterize the international dealings with related parties.
2. Select the "most appropriate method" in calculating the market price.
3. Apply the "most appropriate method" and determine the market price.
4. Review the first three processes to ensure that the taxpayer used the appropriate methodology.

Step 1

The taxpayer must characterize the international dealings with related parties. This characterization involves two steps:

1. The taxpayer is obligated to identify the scope, type, value, and timing of international dealings it has with related parties. The taxpayer must provide details to the Revenue Department concerning the:
   - Organizational structure and the relationship between business entities within the same business group.
   - Business's operating plans.
   - Business's minutes of the meetings of the board of directors or executives.

- External factors of the business, such as the nature of the industry, its market conditions, the structure and nature of the competition, distributors, customers, new competitors, and other economic factors affecting the business.
- Intangible assets the business uses and their ownership interest.
- Business's transactions with related parties.
- Characteristics of the business's property, service, value, and other contractual terms.

2. The taxpayer is obligated to identify the economically important activities of each business entity and to describe the operations of each business entity, that involve:
   - The functions that the business performs, including the business's economically significant functions or activities.
   - The assets the taxpayer uses, both tangible assets and intangible assets, including human resources, specifying the nature and extent of these assets the company used.
   - The risks that each of the parties assumed.

Step 2

The taxpayer is to select the "most appropriate" transfer pricing method in calculating the market price for its goods and services. The taxpayer is to:

1. Identify the data that may establish the market price between related parties. Step 2 fails to otherwise identify the data "that may establish the market price."
2. Determine the "most appropriate" transfer pricing methodology in calculating market price, making this determination based on the facts and circumstances of a particular case. Step 2 fails to specify the parameters that would make a particular transfer pricing determination as being the "most appropriate" transfer pricing method.

Step 3

The taxpayer is to apply the transfer pricing method that Step 2 determines and then calculate the market price. The market price that the taxpayer determines must be "reasonable and credible." The taxpayer must consider the data that the taxpayer obtained in Step 1 to enable comparability.

The taxpayer, in applying Step 3, should undertake these mathematical steps:

1. Adjust the data that it obtained to eliminate material differences. In examining these differences, for example, the taxpayer should account for the fact that accounting policies differ from one country to another.
2. Group data in the same manner.
3. Extend its analysis over a five-year period in order that the taxpayer can observe irregularities that it can correct where these irregularities may impact the business.

The taxpayer is to calculate the "market price" amount under Step 3. This market price amount can be either a single price amount or a range of results.

Step 4

The taxpayer is to review Steps 1 through 3 to ensure that the taxpayer applied the appropriate transfer pricing methodology. The taxpayer is to apply this review process regardless of whether the taxpayer selects one single price or selects a range of results to determine that the transfer pricing methodology is appropriate. If the taxpayer selects a transfer pricing method that is appropriate, the taxpayer is to apply the calculated price to present transactions and future transactions with related parties. Nevertheless, material changes can occur that affect the calculated price. For example, the taxpayer must again apply Steps 1 through 4 if the taxpayer determines that the information or the selected methodology is outdated, or an event occurs that directly affects the assumptions the taxpayer uses, or the taxpayer finds better information or information sources.

PROCESS OF ESTABLISHING THE MARKET PRICE

The Revenue Department of Thailand describes the process of "establishing the market price" as comprising four steps:

1. Characterize the international dealings between associated enterprises.
2. Select the most appropriate transfer pricing methodology or methodologies.
3. Apply the most appropriate transfer pricing method, and determine the market price.
4. Review the processes in Steps 1 to 3 to ensure that the taxpayer applies the appropriate transfer pricing method.

The Revenue Department provides the taxpayer with five additional notes:

1. The four steps in establishing the market price are not prescriptive and are not mandatory to taxpayers. From the vantage point of the Revenue Department, the most important objective is that the taxpayer should undertake transactions that lead to market price (i.e., a price that is appropriate and reasonable, and takes into account the facts and circumstances of the case).
2. The taxpayer is to collect and analyze information. In collecting and analyzing this information, the taxpayer should maintain sufficient, detailed information in determining market price. The information the taxpayer collects and collates depends on the size of the business and on the complexities of the transaction.
3. The taxpayer is expected to properly apply the four transfer pricing steps to the facts and circumstances of the case; and that application should normally be sufficient to establish the market price.

4. A person in the company who has the information to determine market price might be someone who is not from the finance or accounting department or section of the company.
5. Most of the information that the Revenue Department needs in ascertaining the company's transfer pricing may be already contained in business documents such as market reports and information, or business plans and budgets. Thus, the Revenue Department advises the juristic corporation or partnership to systematically gather its existing documentation. The Revenue Department states that it is not necessary for the taxpayer to produce new documentation.

GUIDELINES ON THE DETERMINATION OF MARKET PRICE

The Revenue Department of Thailand issued guidelines on May 16, 2002, on the determination of market price: Departmental Instruction No. Paw 113/2545. This instruction provides officers of the Revenue Department with guidelines of market principles and shows them how to obtain market price.

Departmental Instruction No. Paw 113/2545 empowers officers of the Revenue Department of Thailand to adjust the company's revenue and expenses when calculating the corporate income tax through an audit. The Revenue Department is to apply this audit procedure if the company:

- Receives no compensation
- Receives an amount that is less than market price without justifiable reasons
- Pays expenses at an amount more than market price without justifiable reasons

This departmental instruction provides a definition of market price that, according to the Revenue Department of Thailand, is consistent with the arm's length principle under the OECD's transfer pricing guidelines. The term "market price" under this instruction means the price that independent parties would charge to each other at the date of the transaction for the sale of assets, the providing of services, or the lending of funds, taking place under the same circumstances.

At this juncture, the Revenue Department accepts these transfer pricing methods:

- CUP method.
- Resale price method.
- Cost plus method.
- Other transfer pricing methods.
- Other methods, if the taxpayer cannot apply one of the preceding methods. Such methods include profit-based methods the OECD adopts, including the profit split method, the TNMM, and other internationally accepted methods.

Departmental Instruction No. Paw 113/2545 provides a list of documentation that taxpayers should prepare when the taxpayer undertakes these transactions. The taxpayer is to submit this list to the auditor upon request during a transfer pricing examination audit. The departmental instruction indicates that the retention of these documents and the submission of these documents to the Revenue Department of Thailand will help avoid disputes between taxpayers and government officials.

This departmental instruction provides the company with a list of ten areas in which the Revenue Department of Thailand will request detailed information.

These ten categories are the same as the preceding documentation requirements except:

- Item 8 differs in scope when a taxpayer considers the application of several alternative methods. Part IV would have the taxpayer provide documentation apart from the section of the transfer pricing method, as would the Guidelines on the Determination of Market Price. Part IV requires the taxpayer to create these documents at the same time as the taxpayer selects its transfer pricing method. The Guidelines on the Determination of Market Price fail to contain this requirement.
- Item 9 in the Guidelines on the Determination of Market Price would require the taxpayer to provide documentation evidencing the negotiating positions taken with associated enterprises. Item 9 in Part IV would require the taxpayer to provide documentation used as evidence indicating the negotiation positions taken by the taxpayer in relation to the transactions with business entities within the same group and the basis for those negotiating positions.

The reader should be forewarned that the Revenue Department of Thailand produces transfer pricing regulations only in the Thai language, which is official. The Revenue Department of Thailand provides a translation of the transfer pricing regulations into English that is not official. The bilateral APA might impact language priority, but the Revenue Department of Thailand is slow to move toward implementing bilateral APAs.

32

CHAPTER THIRTY-TWO

Vietnam Transfer Pricing

VIETNAM INTRODUCED TRANSFER pricing regulations in 2003 and then introduced formal transfer pricing regulations on December 19, 2005, through Circular 117/2005/TT-BTC. Vietnam became a World Trade Organization (WTO) member in 2006. Vietnam enacted transfer pricing regulations by statute on July 1, 2007, and the Ministry of Finance has been implementing the transfer pricing provisions. We expect the Ministry of Finance to promulgate new regulations and that these regulations will call for stricter enforcement.

The Vietnamese transfer pricing regulations provide guidance as to the definition of related party relationships, transfer pricing methodologies, benchmarking standards, mandatory transfer pricing documentation requirements, and annual filing requirements. The Vietnamese tax authorities define arm's length price as being an amount that the taxpayer objectively sets in market transactions between independent parties.

The Vietnamese transfer pricing provisions apply to inbound and to outbound related party transactions. The pricing provisions do not have a size criterion, making virtually all taxpayers subject to scrutiny. Most significantly, the Vietnamese transfer pricing provisions apply to tax-favored domestic transactions through lower rates, tax holidays, and different tax profiles. We expect the Vietnamese government to focus on international transactions, but the transfer pricing provisions cover both domestic transactions and cross-border transactions.

EXPANSIVE VIEW OF RELATED PARTY OWNERSHIP

The Vietnamese tax authorities have the most expansive view of related party ownership of any country in Asia. The Vietnamese tax authorities impose 12 specific relationship tests, including:

- Share ownership or equity ownership based on a 20% or more interest
- Control
- Management
- One party dominates the other party by controlling its output, controlling 50% or more of the party's total sales output
- One party dominates the other party by controlling its supplies, controlling 50% or more of the party's total supplies

TRANSFER PRICING METHODS

The Vietnamese transfer pricing regulations permit the taxpayer to select from any of five transfer pricing methods:

1. Comparable uncontrolled price (CUP) method
2. Resale price method
3. Cost plus method
4. Comparable profits method
5. Profit split method

Although some countries in Asia, such as Japan, establish a hierarchy of transfer pricing methods, the Vietnamese tax authorities do not impose such a hierarchy. Nevertheless, Vietnam apparently requires a "best transfer pricing method" approach. In addition, Vietnam prefers internal independent comparables to external comparables. The Vietnamese tax authorities permit the taxpayer to apply the interquartile range and to apply the median value for benchmarking and for preparing transfer pricing adjustments.

From a compliance standpoint, the Vietnamese tax authorities obligate the taxpayer to declare related party transactions on a prescribed form, GCN-01, when the taxpayer files its income tax return. The Vietnamese tax authorities obligated the company to file (or lodge) Form CGN-01 within 90 days of its financial year end.

DOCUMENTATION REQUIREMENTS

The Vietnamese tax authorities require the taxpayer to disclose the following in its annual transfer pricing filing:

- Name of the related party
- Country of residence of the related party
- Description of the transaction with the related party
- Value of the transaction
- Nature of the transaction, describing whether the transaction is tangible property, services, intangible property, or financial
- Transactions for each related party
- The transfer pricing method the taxpayer selects
- The nature of the related party relationship applicable to the transaction

The Vietnamese tax authorities require that all tax filers must "prepare and maintain contemporaneous documentation." The tax authorities, in turn, must submit the document request to the taxpayer in writing. The taxpayer must provide the transfer pricing documentation to the tax authorities within 30 working days after the tax authorities submit the written request to the taxpayer.

The Vietnamese tax authorities request specific documentation from the taxpayer:

- Organizational structure
- Related party relationships
- Business strategy
- Management
- Control
- Functions the company performs
- Related party relationships
- Transactions taking place with related parties and with independent parties
- Descriptions of products or services
- Company's transfer pricing policy
- Company's process of price setting
- Company's control structure
- Company's approval structure
- Company's contract term and contractual term process
- Analysis of the industry factors that impact the company's transfer pricing
- Method selection, and application of the "most appropriate" transfer pricing method, including comparables data and benchmarking

COMPLIANCE CONSIDERATIONS

The Vietnamese tax authorities have designed the transfer pricing regulations so as to operate under Vietnam's tax administrative law. Taxpayers must retain their transfer pricing documentation. A taxpayer's failure to meet the transfer pricing provisions may lead to deemed assessments of the tax liabilities and penalties.

The Vietnamese tax authorities impose two deadlines to submit documents to the government:

1. The first deadline—30 working days—applies to submission of standardized contemporaneous documentation to the government upon the government's written request to the taxpayer.
2. The second deadline—10 days (formerly 90 days under original transfer pricing regulations)—applies to situations in which the tax authorities consider that the taxpayer failed to apply the transfer pricing regulations or that the taxpayer intentionally applied the transfer pricing regulation incorrectly.

The Vietnamese provisions impose transfer pricing penalties for failure to retain and provide information. Such a taxpayer's failure to provide evidence may lead to the Vietnamese tax authorities' imposing arbitrary transfer pricing adjustments. The taxpayer's failure to provide evidence may lead to heavy penalties for underpayment, including lump-sum penalties.

The Vietnamese tax authorities have wide powers over taxpayers, which include:

- Heavy penalties for a wide range of tax offenses
- Failure to retain or submit documentation
- Underpayment provisions
- Evasion provisions
- Fraud provisions

The Vietnamese tax authorities impose strong penalties on taxpayers for failure to comply. The tax authorities can impose penalties in these situations:

- The tax authorities may deem an amount of tax to be payable if a taxpayer fails to provide evidence or provide transfer pricing documentation within 10 days after the government provides notice.
- The government additionally can impose heavy penalties for failure to provide information.
- The tax underpayment situation is 10% of the tax liability adjustment plus a late payment interest charge.
- The late payment interest charge is .05% per day for the period of nonpayment.
- The penalty can amount to one to three times the amount of the tax liability adjustment if the government ascertains that the taxpayer's tax practice is abusive.

The Vietnamese tax administration is contemplating making extensive changes to its transfer pricing regime. Practitioners had expected the Vietnamese tax administration to initiate the reform in 2010 or shortly thereafter, but the Vietnamese government has not issued the reform as of this writing, mid-2012. As part of the reform process, Vietnam is trying to improve its investigatory process, to develop transfer pricing databases, and to adopt information technology into its tax administration. We expect these changes might lead to more stringent enforcement.

Vietnam offered tax holidays to foreign-invested enterprises in certain manufacturing and export sectors. The tax holiday amounted to a 50% income tax reduction and lower tax rates, depending on the province in which the enterprise is located. But note that Vietnam has removed many of these tax incentives.

The Vietnamese tax officials are already engaged in transfer pricing audits. The government, in conducting a transfer pricing audit, now assesses revenue risk. The specific business sector determines the taxpayer's tax audit risk. Vietnam is expected to consistently conduct tax audits after a taxpayer's tax holiday ends. The Vietnamese government is concerned about protecting its tax base.

Some taxpayers are more susceptible than others. Persistent losses can trigger a transfer pricing audit. The Vietnamese government is concerned about persistent corporate losses. In fact, Vietnam introduced a corporate tax anti-avoidance measure effective January 1, 2009. This anti-avoidance measure addresses the shifting of losses among taxable years.

A taxpayer subject to transfer pricing audits should be concerned about corollary tax considerations. Vietnam provides strict deductions of expenses and revenue/expense matching. In addition, Vietnam caps expense deductions for interest and for marketing.

From an audit situation, the Vietnamese tax authorities postulate a normal structure and look to economic issues. The tax authorities reject intercompany service fees, in large measure because the taxpayer fails to substantiate service fees or establish the basis on which the service fee can be set.

Vietnam is seeking to set up advance pricing agreements (APAs) but has not yet set up a transfer pricing mechanism. Vietnam has an advance ruling mechanism but has not provided advance rulings in the transfer pricing context. Vietnam has apparently made private confidential APAs.

"Hot button" transfer pricing issues in Vietnam include:

- Corporate tax system
- Permanent establishment issues
- Foreign-earned income
- Tax incentives for foreign investors
- Using offshore jurisdictions to reduce taxation

Profit repatriation remains a transfer pricing issue in Vietnam in regard to the application of the double tax treaties, dividend repatriation, and foreign contractor taxation.

PART TWO

Advanced Applications

CHAPTER THIRTY-THREE

33

Services Transfer Pricing in Hong Kong and in Singapore

SERVICES ACTIVITIES ARE important for both Hong Kong and Singapore. As a consequence, the Hong Kong and the Singapore tax authorities have addressed services transfer pricing (i.e., the tax treatment for related party services that an enterprise or its associated enterprise undertake). This chapter compares and contrasts services transfer pricing in Hong Kong and Singapore. The reader should note that differences in services transfer pricing rules in Hong Kong and Singapore can impact the enterprise's choice of headquarters operations, whether for worldwide operations or for operations in the Asia-Pacific region.

SERVICES TRANSFER PRICING IN HONG KONG AND IN SINGAPORE: BASIC COMPARISON

The United States provided the primary impetus for the formation of the Organisation for Economic Co-operation and Development (OECD) following World War II as part of the Marshall Plan. The OECD now has 34 members, and is planning to increase its membership, primarily in Asia and elsewhere. The United States, then, is just one voice in formulating the OECD's transfer pricing policy. The United States, acting on its own volition, often applies transfer pricing approaches that differ from those of the OECD.

The Inland Revenue Authority of Singapore (IRAS) issued Transfer Pricing Guidelines for Related Party Loans and Related Party Services on February 23, 2009. As background, the IRAS had issued draft supplementary guidelines for related party loans and services on October 21, 2008. The draft supplementary guidelines were subject to public comment. The IRAS then took these comments into account in finalizing the Transfer Pricing Guidelines for Related Party Loans and Related Party Services.

The Hong Kong Revenue Department issued its Transfer Pricing Guidelines—Methodologies and Related Issues, doing so through the promulgation of its Departmental Interpretation and Practice Notes No. 46 in December 2009. These Hong Kong transfer pricing guidelines closely follow the OECD *Transfer Pricing Guidelines for Multinational Enterprises and Tax Administrations* (2009). It is important for the reader to note that the OECD issued *Transfer Pricing Guidelines for Multinational Enterprises and Tax Administrations* in 2010, and these 2010 regulations differ from the 2009 guidelines.

The Singapore government relies on a number of external inputs in formulating its transfer pricing policy; the three primary governmental inputs are the OECD, the United States, and Australia. Singapore transfer pricing differs from Hong Kong transfer pricing because of a myriad of factors, primarily because of developments in Australia and the United States, where the United States has failed to fully implement the 2010 OECD guidelines. Singapore, in setting up its services transfer pricing regime, tends to follow the U.S. approach regarding the treatment for services transfer pricing. In contrast, Singapore, in applying its transfer pricing documentation and its audit regime, tends to follow the Australian approach.

The Singapore services transfer pricing guidelines are more extensive than the Hong Kong transfer pricing guidelines. The Singapore services transfer pricing guidelines address three specific features the Hong Kong services transfer pricing guidelines fail to include:[1]

1. Shared services arrangements or cost pooling contracts
2. The semi-standard 5% margin
3. The list of specific enumerated services

HONG KONG SERVICES TRANSFER PRICING METHODS

The Hong Kong intragroup services arrangement provisions closely follow the OECD intragroup services provisions.[2] The term "intragroup services arrangements," as the Inland Revenue of Hong Kong use this term, encompasses a wide variety of services. Such services broadly include these categories:

- Administrative services
- Technical services

- Financial services
- Commercial services

The OECD, in its OECD *Transfer Pricing Guidelines* in Chapter VII, "Special Considerations for Intragroup Services," section 7.2, speaks of "a wide scope of services," specifically enumerating "administrative, technical, financial and commercial services" without further explanation except as to include "management, coordination and control functions for the whole group."

As a general matter, the Hong Kong Commissioner accepts the fundamental OECD *Transfer Pricing Guidelines* principles for charging for intragroup services. The Hong Kong Inland Revenue Department provides that two principal issues apply when analyzing intragroup services, according to the OECD guidelines:

1. Determining whether a member of the group rendered the service
2. Determining the arm's length charge

The OECD *Transfer Pricing Guidelines*, in Chapter VII, "Special Considerations for Intragroup Services," section 7.5, seek to apply those same performance and charging standards.

The OECD *Transfer Pricing Guidelines* set out the principal conditions under which the member is to determine whether a member of the group rendered the service. The Hong Kong transfer pricing guidelines partially quote the OECD guidelines:

> Under the arm's length principle, the question whether an intra-group service has been rendered when an activity is performed for one or more group members by another group member should depend on whether the activity provides a respective group member with economic or commercial value to enhance its commercial position.[3]

The Hong Kong transfer pricing guidelines do take into account the next material from the OECD *Transfer Pricing* guidelines, thus providing the reader with a partially obscure commentary as to this situation:

> whether an independent enterprise in comparable circumstances would have been willing to pay for the activity if performed for it by an independent enterprise or would have performed the activity in-house for itself. If the activity is not one for which the independent enterprise would have been willing to pay or perform for itself, the activity ordinarily should not be considered as an intra-group service under the arm's length principle.

SHAREHOLDER ACTIVITY AND STEWARDSHIP FUNCTIONS

The Hong Kong transfer pricing guidelines look to a delineation of shareholder activities based on the benefit that the provider of services provides. The Hong Kong guidelines specify that the OECD *Transfer Pricing Guidelines* require the intragroup service entity performing the service to determine which services:

- Relate to shareholder activities
- Benefit specific group members
- Benefit the group as a whole

The Hong Kong transfer pricing guidelines warn that the enterprise is not to re-charge the cost of shareholder activities unless the enterprise undertakes these costs of shareholder activities on behalf of the parent company by a group company. The enterprise is to re-charge the cost of the shareholder activity in such a case. The following activities normally benefit the parent company in its role of shareholder, but such activities do not benefit the subsidiaries. Nevertheless, the determination of what is shareholder activity is a matter of fact and should include:

- Meetings of the parent company's shareholders
- Issuing of shares in the parent company
- Costs of the supervisory board
- Maintaining the share register
- Activities to satisfy statutory reporting requirements of the parent company
- Audit of the parent company

As a general matter, the Hong Kong transfer pricing guidelines provide that the parent company should not receive compensation for services the company provides if these services duplicate what the subsidiary already performs or are otherwise unnecessary.[4]

FINANCIAL SERVICES AUDIT EXAMPLE

The Hong Kong transfer pricing guidelines provide a financial services audit example, Example 10.[5] Here the parent company audits the financial statements and the records of an overseas subsidiary. The parent company undertakes the audit to satisfy its own investors and to satisfy its legal requirements. The audit duplicates an audit that the overseas subsidiary performed on its own under its own domestic laws. The parent company performed this audit as a steward for its own investments rather than benefiting the overseas subsidiary company. The parent company should bear the cost of the audit it performs.

DEDUCTION OF EXPENDITURES PAID FOR INTRAGROUP SERVICES

An enterprise can incur expenditures for an intragroup arrangement under Hong Kong Inland Revenue section 16. The enterprise calculates the expenditure using a specific markup. The Hong Kong transfer pricing guidelines indicate that the enterprise can possibly deduct such an expenditure.[6] Nevertheless, the question of whether the enterprise's expenditure, having been made pursuant to the intragroup service arrangement, is deductible is a question of fact. Deductibility from a practical and business point of view depends on what the enterprise calculated the expenditure to achieve.

An enterprise can incur an expenditure for obtaining a supply of goods and services from another associated enterprise under a contract. The enterprise is to characterize such an expenditure by reference to the contractual benefits that pass to the enterprise under the contract and by the manner in which those benefits relate to the enterprise's profit-earning activities or business.

The benefits conferred by a service arrangement might provide an objective commercial explanation for the whole of the expenditure made under the service arrangement. Such a service arrangement will suffice to characterize the expenditure as an outgoing or as an expense incurred in the production of taxable profits, in the event that the service arrangement does provide such an objective commercial explanation.

There might be situations in which the benefits passing to the associated enterprise under an intragroup service arrangement do not provide an objective commercial explanation for the whole of the expenditure. The service arrangement alone, without more, will not suffice to characterize the expenditure in the event that such a lack of commercial explanation event was to occur. In such a case, the enterprise will need to undertake a broader examination of all the circumstances to determine the purposes of the expenditure.

This broader explanation of the expenditure might include an examination of the relationship between the enterprise and the services entity. Further, depending on the circumstances of the particular case, the explanation might include:

- A description of the manner in which the enterprise and the services entity have dealt with each other
- The taxpayer's purpose, motive, or intention in incurring the expenditure

"OBJECTIVE COMMERCIAL EXPLANATION" STANDARD

As a general matter, the Hong Kong transfer pricing guidelines request that the taxpayer provide an "objective commercial explanation" as to its activities. The guidelines then warn the taxpayer that a service arrangement might not be sufficient to provide an "objective commercial explanation" for the service arrangement in three situations:

1. The service fees pertaining to service arrangement are disproportionate, or are grossly excessive, measured by the benefits that the service fee arrangement provides.
2. The service fees and charges guarantee a certain profit outcome to the service entity, making that arrangement a guarantee arrangement, thus doing so without providing a "reasonable commercial arrangement."

3. The service fees and charges generate profits in the service entity. The enterprise makes these services and charges determination without the service entity showing any clear evidence that it has added value or performed any substantial functions. For example, the enterprise might make this services and charges determination without showing any clear evidence that the service entity has added value when there is no clear separation of the service entity's business activities and those of the taxpayer.

DETERMINING THE AMOUNT OF INTRAGROUP CHARGES

The enterprise must determine both the basis of charging and an appropriate margin in determining whether the amount of the charge is in accordance with the arm's length principle.[7] The OECD *Transfer Pricing Guidelines* suggest two principal methods of making the determination as to the basis of charging and the appropriate margin, based on direct charges and indirect charges.

The Hong Kong transfer pricing guidelines differentiate between direct charges and indirect charges:

- The enterprise can issue a direct charge, a charge levied by a particular affiliate for a particular service.
- The enterprise can issue an indirect charge by other means, usually through "allocation keys."

The direct charge method has the advantage of providing greater transparency.

Further, the direct charge method provides documentary evidence as to the validity of the charges. The enterprise can ascertain the amount that the enterprise is to re-charge through time sheets, charges to an account, charges to a job code, and so forth.

An indirect charge method applies where, for some reason, including the cost or burden of administrating the charge, the enterprise cannot reliably track the costs it incurs on behalf of one or more associates. The indirect charge method necessitates that the enterprise collect together all costs and share these combined costs among its beneficiaries. The indirect charge process normally requires the enterprise to make estimates of the amounts or approximate the amounts. Enterprises normally make allocations through "keys."

For example, in determining allocation keys, the enterprise can calculate the charges based on head count for human resources costs or for the number of computer terminals in use for information technology support, and so forth. The OECD *Transfer Pricing Guidelines* provide that the allocation method must be consistent with what a comparable independent enterprise would be prepared to accept.

The scope of intragroup services includes contract manufacturing activities. In such a contract manufacturing case, the group might provide the production enterprise with intensive instruction as to the items to be produced, the quality to be produced, and the quantity required. The Hong Kong transfer pricing guidelines provide that such a production enterprise bears low risks. It should be assumed that the enterprise will purchase the entire output if the contract manufacturer meets product quality requirements. The production enterprise could be considered as performing a service in that circumstance, and the cost plus method could be appropriate.

An intragroup service entity can provide services to an associated enterprise. Such a group service entity must ensure that the intragroup services entity:

- Identifies the services
- Charges for the services
- Charges for the services at arm's length
- Keeps adequate documentation

It is more satisfactory to charge an arm's length cost rather than all relevant costs when one of the following situations occur:

- The providing of the service is a principal activity of the associated enterprise.
- The profit element is significant.
- Direct charging is possible as a basis from which to determine the arm's length price.

The Hong Kong transfer pricing guidelines provide that an enterprise should include a profit element where one of the next three situations applies:

1. The service entity is engaged in the business of rendering services.
2. The service entity is providing similar services to unrelated parties.
3. The service entity provides the service as one of its principal activities.

SERVICES PROVIDED BY A PERMANENT ESTABLISHMENT

The Hong Kong transfer pricing guidelines provide that the enterprise should include a profit margin where:[8]

- The principal activity of a permanent establishment is to provide specific services to the enterprise.
- The providing of services gives a real advantage to the enterprise.
- The costs of services are a significant part of the expenses of the enterprise.

However, the Hong Kong transfer pricing guidelines indicate that there should be no markup where the providing of services is merely part of the general management activity of the enterprise taken as a whole. For example, such an enterprise might have a common system of training for all employees. In that event, the enterprise should treat the costs as being a part of general administrative expenses. The enterprise should allocate these costs on a cost basis among different parts of the enterprise, with proper share being made to the permanent establishment.

The Hong Kong transfer pricing guidelines caution that the enterprise should attribute no profits to a permanent establishment by reason of the mere purchase of the goods or merchandise for the enterprise. No notional profits should accrue to the permanent establishment if the permanent establishment merely purchases goods for the enterprise not in the course of normal business activity.

As a broad basis, the provisions of the Hong Kong Inland Revenue Ordinance and the relevant articles in the double tax agreements should allow the Commissioner to reallocate profits or adjust deductions. The Commissioner can reallocate profits and adjust deductions by substituting an arm's length profit for the consideration, if any, stipulated by the resident enterprises and the nonresident enterprises. These allocation and adjustment provisions apply where the Commissioner considers that the resident enterprises and the nonresident enterprises are not dealing at arm's length, and where the consideration is not an arm's length consideration.

SCOPE OF ACTIVITIES FOR RELATED PARTY SERVICES IN SINGAPORE

The Singapore services guidelines address the application of the arm's length principles to related party services, here termed intragroup services, when these services occur within a group of companies or businesses. The Singapore services guidelines postulate that related parties within a group would arrange for a wide array for services to one or more members of the group.[9] Such services may include, for example, these activities:

- Administrative services
- Technical services
- Financial services
- Commercial services
- Management services
- Coordination services
- Control functions

The Singapore services guidelines, then, provide an analogous scope of eligible services activities as do the OECD guidelines and the Hong Kong guidelines.

The Singapore services guidelines, similar to the OECD guidelines and the Hong Kong guidelines, do not address other services activities that the taxpayer might view as profit center activities. Such non-addressed activities and presumably non-eligible activities include:

- Sales activities
- Leasing activities
- Engineering activities
- Manufacturing activities

SINGAPORE TRANSFER PRICING SERVICES GUIDELINES

The Singapore services guidelines apply certain of the arm's length principles only on a prospective basis.[10] The first order of business, from the standpoint of the Singapore services guidelines, is to ascertain whether one party provided services to another party. However, the services guidelines fail to provide such an established set of strict criteria to determine whether one party provided services to another. The IRAS recognizes that it is not possible to establish a set of strict criteria to determine if an activity amounts to a service provided.[11] Instead, the taxpayer is to look to the surrounding facts and circumstances. Generally accepted considerations apply to determine whether one company in fact provided services to another company.

As a general matter, one party provides services to another when the provider of services receives benefits from these activities or, alternatively, when the provider of the services expects to receive benefits from such activities. Services are considered to have taken place when there is a reasonable expectation or intention of providing services conferred or received, even if the expected service does not eventually materialize.[12]

Singapore applies the "economic or commercial benefit" standard for its services. The benefit that a party receives or provides must have economic or commercial benefit such that an independent party would expect to receive or pay for that service. The benefit must be identifiable and capable of being valued. Hence, the benefit must be sufficiently direct and substantial. No service is considered to have been provided if the benefit to be derived from an activity is not what an independent party in comparable circumstances would be willing to pay for or to carry out for itself.[13]

The Singapore services guidelines recognize that it is common for a parent company, or for a designated entity within a group of companies, to undertake activities that benefit the group as a whole. Such centrally performed entities can include, for example, administrative functions, financial functions, and personnel functions. The central thrust of Singapore's service provisions are activities that an independent party would be willing to pay for or to perform for itself.[14]

As a general matter, a taxpayer views a service as having been provided when the taxpayer meets an identified need of the related party or a group of related parties by performance of these services by another related party. An independent party would have either engaged the services of a third party or performed the activities itself to fulfill the need. Consequently, although the performance of an activity confers a benefit to a related party that has no need for such activity, the enterprise is deemed to not have provided the service. When the benefit is too remote, no service is deemed provided.[15]

DIRECT CHARGING VERSUS INDIRECT CHARGING OF SERVICES

The Singapore services guidelines delineate both the direct charge method and the indirect charge method. The service provider can adopt the direct charge method or the indirect charge method, as the service provider determines:[16]

- **Direct charge method.** The service provider would identify clearly the actual work the service provider performs, the costs that the service provider expended, and the basis of making that charge. The Singapore services guideline prefers the direct charge method in charging for related party services because the direct charge method facilitates the tax authorities' review and examination. Nevertheless, the services guideline favors the direct charge method only in the context of providing specific services, such as, in an example in the services guidelines, in conducting a market survey for a particular product developed by a related party. The prerequisite for applying the direct charge method is where the beneficiary of the services and the costs incurred for the performance of the services are usually identifiable.[17]
- **Indirect charge method.** This method entails the use of an appropriate apportionment basis or allocation key to charge or to bill for services provided.[18] Such apportionment basis or allocation key includes, for example, gross sales, income, or receipts, loans and deposits, staff numbers, floor area, and asset size. The IRAS recognizes that it might not be practical for taxpayers to adopt the direct charge method for all related party services to the members belonging to the same group or to services performed specifically for individual recipients. The IRAS suggests that accounting services, for example, would be better accounted for under the indirect charge method to approximate the charges.

The central ingredient in applying the indirect charge method is the selection of the apportionment basis or the allocation key. The services guidelines imply that the service provider must select an apportionment basis or allocation key that is appropriate. This selection of the allocation key depends on the nature and use of the services.[19]

As a general matter, the most appropriate allocation key is the method that most accurately reflects the share of the benefits the beneficiary receives or expects to receive. The services guidelines acknowledge that the taxpayer selects the allocation key, and that choice is largely a question of judgment. The services guidelines expect the taxpayer to demonstrate that it has used judgment in choosing the allocation key.

The IRAS is prepared to accept the allocation key that the taxpayer adopts so long as the allocation key meets all these criteria:

- The allocation key must be reasonable.
- The allocation key must be founded on sound accounting principles.
- The taxpayer applies the allocation key consistently year to year throughout the group unless there are very good reasons for failing to do so.

ASCERTAINING THE ARM'S LENGTH FEE

After the services provider determines which charging method is appropriate, the next step is determining the arm's length fee for services the service provider provides under the Singapore services guidelines. This remuneration should be in accordance with the arm's length principle, based on a comparability analysis with an independent party.[20] The services guidelines suggest that the taxpayer undertake this analysis from the perspective of both the services provider and the recipient of the services. This charge is the amount that a service provider would charge an independent party, taking into account the service provider's costs and the amount than the recipient is willing to pay for that service. The parties are to consider what the service provider would have otherwise paid to independent parties for similar services under similar circumstances.[21]

When determining the appropriate transfer pricing method, the taxpayer is to be guided by what services guidelines term "important considerations," such as:

- Nature of the transaction
- Availability of the data
- Quality of the data

This services analysis is directly applicable to related party services.

Notwithstanding this services analysis, however, the services guidelines indicate that comparable uncontrolled price (CUP) and the cost plus methods are most often the most appropriate choices for determining the arm's length fee for related party services.[22]

ROUTINE SERVICES AND THE 5% MARKUP IN SINGAPORE

The services guidelines refer to "a common practice [in Singapore] among parent companies or group service companies to charge a 5% markup on costs incurred for providing certain routine support services." The services guidelines postulate that the services provider provides these services for the purposes of business convenience and efficiency, centralizing these routine support services within the parent company or a group service company. The services guidelines provides three such nonexclusive examples: the performance of accounting services, of payroll services, and of certain other management or administrative functions. The services guidelines then acknowledges that related companies might, in practice, based on their own business considerations, provide intragroup services to one another even when these services activities are beyond routine services.[23]

The issue as to whether a 5% cost markup conforms to the arm's length principle depends on three facets:

1. The exact nature the service provider provides
2. The actual or reasonably expected benefits the service provider provides to the recipient of the service

3. A detailed analysis of what an independent party would have been willing to pay for a similar service under similar circumstances

The IRAS is prepared to accept the current 5% markup for certain routine support services as a reasonable arm's length charge for these services on the proviso that the service provider, in providing these routine support services, does not also offer these routine support services to an unrelated party. The objective of the IRAS is to facilitate the taxpayer's compliance with the arm's length standard while maintaining a high level of adherence to the arm's length principle, based on industry norms. The services guidelines accept the practicality that performing a proper transfer pricing comparability analysis for every type of service would greatly increase the administration and compliance for the taxpayer and would increase the administrative costs of evaluating them.

The IRAS is prepared to accept the current 5% markup adopted for certain routine support services as a reasonable arm's length charge for such services. The IRAS is willing to make this determination to facilitate taxpayers' compliance with the arm's length standard while maintaining a high level of adherence to the arm's length principle. The IRAS requires, for the 5% cost markup to apply, that these routine support activities that the service provider offers to its related party are not also provided to an unrelated party.[24]

A taxpayer, in charging routine support services at a 5% markup, needs to take into account all costs for this purpose that are directly related or indirectly related to the services performed. The direct costs include, for example, materials consumed and labor expended to render these services. The indirect costs include, for example, overheads, depreciation, and telecommunication expenses that the department provides to the department providing these services.[25]

The Singapore services guidelines includes Annex A, which provides a list of routine support services that companies commonly provide on an intragroup basis across many industries. The Singapore services guidelines, in providing Annex A, use an approach analogous to the U.S. services transfer pricing rules. The IRAS can modify or expand the list of routine services in the future. These routine support services do not generate a significant arm's length markup. This list is nonexhaustive, but the taxpayer must follow the existing list of routine services:[26]

- Accounting and auditing services, including maintenance of accounting records, preparation of financial statements based on such records, ensuring authenticity and reliability of accounting records, and so forth, including the performance of operational and financial audits.
- Accounts receivable and accounts payable services, including the collation and verification of data pertaining to accounts receivable and accounts payable, undertaken for the purposes of financial reporting, aging, billing, soliciting payments from customers, payment to vendors, procurement, and so forth.
- Budgeting services, including the compilation of data for preparing budget estimates, reports, and so forth.

- Computer support services, including providing technical services and troubleshooting support services in relation to the usage of computer hardware, computer software, maintenance of intellectual property software, and so forth.
- Database administration services, including the general maintenance of computer databases, including data storage but excluding analytic services performed on stored data.
- Employee benefits services, including the administration of employee compensation and benefit plans, such as health care, life insurance, dental, employee incentive compensation, profit sharing plans, and so forth; and including the coordination with external parties, such as hospitals, insurers, and so forth to implement such benefit plans.
- General administrative services, including the performance of clerical and administrative functions such as data entry, photocopying, scanning of materials, scheduling of appointments, word processing, file maintenance, and so forth.
- Legal services, including the providing of legal services by in-house legal counsel.
- Payroll services, including the compilation and verification of employees' time worked and employee claims for reimbursable expenses to compute salaries, commissions, and reimbursements. Payroll services include the payment of paychecks and arranging credit of such payments into employees' bank accounts.
- Public relations services and corporate communications, including the handling of internal and external communications relating to corporate policies.
- Purchasing services, including the procurement of goods and services based on organization requirements or based on standards.
- Staffing and recruiting services, including the management of staffing requirements, performance issues, and staff welfare in the organization or group, and the implementation of recruitment plans, such as publicizing open positions and candidate screening, and so forth.
- Tax services, including the preparation of various tax returns, computations, refund claims, and responses to inquiries for submission to the tax authorities, the processing of tax payments, and so forth.
- Training and employee development services, including the management and implementation of employee training and development programs.

The draft of services guidelines included purchasing services, including the procurement of goods and services based on organization requirements or based on standards. The final services guidelines exclude the purchasing services category.

The IRAS is prepared to consider adding additional services on further review where taxpayers view that certain of these intragroup services are routine support services but are not included in this routine support list. The IRAS's acceptance of a 5% markup for routine services provides the taxpayer with an alternative to having the service providers undertake a detailed transfer pricing analysis. These service providers might have undertaken a detailed transfer pricing analysis that supports the charging for services at markups other than 5%. In the event that this difference occurs, the service provider should adopt that alternative markup. Once the taxpayer adopts the arm's length markup, the taxpayer should apply this markup consistently year after year throughout the group until there are material changes to the circumstances or to the services that the service provider provides. These service providers should regularly review the markup they have adopted to make sure that it continues to reflect arm's length conditions in their situations.[27]

COST POOLING CONTRACTS

The IRAS has developed a virtually new and quite useful transfer pricing technique termed "cost pooling."[28] Taxpayers can apply this cost pooling technique to certain routine services expenditures that occur among related parties with the corporate group. Cost pooling arrangements differ in numerous respects from cost contribution arrangements (or cost sharing arrangements) that taxpayers enter into primarily to develop intangible assets. Regrettably, the Singapore services guidelines fail to fully distinguish between cost pooling arrangements and cost sharing arrangements.

Taxpayers that have exceptional circumstances might find it mutually beneficial to enter into a cost pooling contract among members of the corporate group.[29] The cost pooling contract enables members of the corporate group to share in the costs of routine support services for the common use of the group to meet a common need of the members. The cost pooling arrangement allows the members of the corporate group to pool resources together in order to acquire services that meet these parameters:

- A party to the cost pooling contract must have a reasonable expectation of benefiting from or must actually benefit from the services for which costs are being shared.
- Contributions by related parties to the costs of providing the services must be made in proportion to the nature and extent of the expected benefits that each party receives.
- Each party's share of the costs in the cost pooling arrangement must be borne in the form of cash or by other monetary contributions.

The proposed services guidelines had provided that the arrangement must be necessary for the corporate group to function effectively. The final services guidelines eliminate this requirement.

The Singapore services guidelines provide additional pooling requirements:[30]

- The arrangement is to acquire services that are not the principal activities of the corporate group.
- The arrangement is not intended to be a profitable exploit of the corporate group.
- The arrangement must address mutual benefit among members of the group.

- The party to the arrangement must reasonably expect to benefit from the shared services or actually benefit from the shared services.
- The party to the arrangement must determine the contribution as to the costs of providing the service in proportion of the expected benefits that each party receives.
- Each party must bear the share of its costs in the form of cash or other contributions, and nothing else.
- To satisfy the arm's length principle, each participant's share of the costs must be consistent with the costs to which an independent party would have agreed under comparable circumstances, given the benefit the participant would have expected to derive from the services being provided.

The services guidelines provide specific parameters for the allowance of the cost pooling arrangement:[31]

- The arrangement must be termed as a proportionate share of the cost of the services.
- The arrangement can be determined on a prospective basis.
- The arrangement is to be determined with no element of markup.
- The service provider that offers its services to its related parties does not offer these same services to unrelated parties.
- The service provided to related parties is not the principal activity that the service provider is to undertake. The term "principal activity" is based on facts and circumstances, based on a 15% threshold.
- These provisions apply to Annex A services.
- The taxpayer provides sufficient documentation to show that the parties intended to pool their resources to share costs, doing so before the service provider performs the services.

The services guidelines require the taxpayer to maintain adequate documentation to support the cost allocation as being arm's length. The services guidelines required the taxpayer to maintain adequate documentation to demonstrate the sharing of expected benefits arising from providing these services. The proposed services guidelines were concerned about the taxpayer's risk of double taxation and suggested that the taxpayer retain this documentation:[32]

- Description of the type of services provided
- Rationale for selecting a specific cost method
- Nature of the related parties' contributions
- Anticipated benefits
- Calculation details

COST POOLING VERSUS PASS-THROUGH ALLOCATION ALTERNATIVES

Singapore's services guidelines address two separate procedures to aggregate and distribute services costs:

1. The cost pooling arrangement addresses the aggregation of costs by a party within the group that provides the services to the group as a whole.
2. The strict pass-through arrangement to the aggregation of costs by a third-party provider that provides the services to the group as a whole.

A group service provider occasionally might arrange and pay for services from third-party providers. The third-party provider can undertake this service on behalf of the related parties in the group, but the third party can be independent from the related party or can be related to that party. A third-party service provider or a related party service provider might have already charged the members an arm's length markup for its services. In the event that the provider has already charged the members for these costs, it may be appropriate for the group service provider to pass on these costs without incurring further markup. The parties are to pass on the costs without markup if the group service provider is merely the paying agent and the group service provider itself does not act to enhance the value of these services.

The IRAS is prepared to accept that these costs may be charged without a markup to the related party for whose benefit the services are provided. These costs must meet the listed preconditions:[33]

- The costs are the legal liabilities or the contractual liabilities of the related party.
- The group service provider is merely the paying agent, and the service provider does not itself act to enhance the value of such services.

Singapore's services guidelines provide an example of the strict cost pass-through method.[34] Assume that a group service provider incurs expenses on behalf of the related party to pay for the costs of engaging a third-party firm to provide various corporate secretarial services for its related party. The parties can identify the costs as legal or contractual liabilities of the party itself. The group service provider is the paying agent. The group service provider can pass on these costs to the related party, doing so without markup.

Singapore's services guidelines state that the group service provider is to ensure an arm's length markup for its own aggregate costs of providing the services.[35] This markup is to be reflective of the nature of the services rendered by the service provider and the extent of the value added amount that benefits the participants who receive these services. The aggregate costs that related parties incur should include its own costs incurred, if any, in facilitating the purchase of services from third-party service providers or from related party service providers. Returning to the prior example, assume that the group service provider used its own resources to arrange, select, and liaise in having the third-party firm provide corporate secretarial services. In that event, the group service provider should charge this cost to its related parties at an arm's length markup.[36]

DOCUMENTATION

The main transfer pricing circular highlights the importance of documentation. Documentation is important for loan and services transactions, and the taxpayer should refer to the main transfer pricing circular for guidance as to appropriate documentation.[37]

NOTES

1. R. Feinschreiber and M. Kent, "Singapore Issues Transfer Pricing Guidelines for Related-Party Loans and Services," *Corporate Business Taxation Monthly* (June 2009): 41; R. Feinschreiber and M. Kent, "Shared Services and Cost Pooling Arrangements," *Corporate Business Taxation Monthly* (November 2009): 25.
2. Hong Kong Transfer Pricing Guidelines, para. 90.
3. OECD, *Transfer Pricing Guidelines for Multinational Enterprises and Tax Administrations* (Paris: July 22, 2010), Chapter VII, sec. 7.6; R. Feinschreiber and M. Kent, *Transfer Pricing Handbook: Guidance on the OECD Regulations*. Chapter 20 (Hoboken, NJ: John Wiley & Sons, 2012), pp. 263–287.
4. OECD Transfer Pricing Guidelines for Multinational Enterprises and Tax Administrations, Chapter VII, sec. 7.11.
5. Hong Kong Transfer Pricing Guidelines, para. 94.
6. Hong Kong Transfer Pricing Guidelines, para. 95.
7. Hong Kong Transfer Pricing Guidelines, para. 100.
8. Hong Kong Transfer Pricing Guidelines, para. 106.
9. Singapore Transfer Pricing Guidelines for Related Party Loans and Related Party Services, 3.1.1.
10. Singapore Transfer Pricing Guidelines for Related Party Loans and Related Party Services, 3.1.2.
11. Singapore Transfer Pricing Guidelines for Related Party Loans and Related Party Services, 3.2.1.
12. Singapore Transfer Pricing Guidelines for Related Party Loans and Related Party Services, 3.2.2.
13. Singapore Transfer Pricing Guidelines for Related Party Loans and Related Party Services, 3.2.3.
14. Singapore Transfer Pricing Guidelines for Related Party Loans and Related Party Services, 3.2.4.
15. Singapore Transfer Pricing Guidelines for Related Party Loans and Related Party Services, 3.2.5.
16. Singapore Transfer Pricing Guidelines for Related Party Loans and Related Party Services, 3.3.2.

17. Singapore Transfer Pricing Guidelines for Related Party Loans and Related Party Services, 3.3.3.
18. Singapore Transfer Pricing Guidelines for Related Party Loans and Related Party Services, 3.3.4.
19. Singapore Transfer Pricing Guidelines for Related Party Loans and Related Party Services, 3.3.5.
20. Singapore Transfer Pricing Guidelines for Related Party Loans and Related Party Services, 3.3.6.
21. Singapore Transfer Pricing Guidelines for Related Party Loans and Related Party Services, 3.3.7.
22. Singapore Transfer Pricing Guidelines for Related Party Loans and Related Party Services, 3.3.8.
23. Singapore Transfer Pricing Guidelines for Related Party Loans and Related Party Services, 3.3.9.
24. Singapore Transfer Pricing Guidelines for Related Party Loans and Related Party Services, 3.3.10.
25. Singapore Transfer Pricing Guidelines for Related Party Loans and Related Party Services, 3.3.11.
26. Singapore Transfer Pricing Guidelines for Related Party Loans and Related Party Services, 3.3.12.
27. Singapore Transfer Pricing Guidelines for Related Party Loans and Related Party Services, 3.3.13.
28. Singapore Transfer Pricing Guidelines for Related Party Loans and Related Party Services, 3.3.14.
29. Singapore Transfer Pricing Guidelines for Related Party Loans and Related Party Services, 3.3.15.
30. Singapore Transfer Pricing Guidelines for Related Party Loans and Related Party Services, 3.3.16.
31. Singapore Transfer Pricing Guidelines for Related Party Loans and Related Party Services, 3.3.16.
32. Singapore Transfer Pricing Guidelines for Related Party Loans and Related Party Services, 3.3.16.
33. Singapore Transfer Pricing Guidelines for Related Party Loans and Related Party Services, 3.3.18.
34. Singapore Transfer Pricing Guidelines for Related Party Loans and Related Party Services, 3.3.18.
35. Singapore Transfer Pricing Guidelines for Related Party Loans and Related Party Services, 3.3.19.
36. Singapore Transfer Pricing Guidelines for Related Party Loans and Related Party Services, 3.3.19.
37. Singapore Transfer Pricing Guidelines for Related Party Loans and Related Party Services, 4.1.

CHAPTER THIRTY-FOUR

Permanent Establishment Parameters: Hong Kong versus India

GOVERNMENTS ACROSS ASIA are increasingly willing to assert taxation over activities of an alien business doing business in their jurisdictions. These governments are more than willing to find that the activities of the alien business create a permanent establishment in that location. This permanent establishment assertion brings with it the taxability of that enterprise in that jurisdiction together with the ensuing transfer pricing considerations. This chapter compares and contrasts permanent establishment parameters in Hong Kong and in India.

India asserts permanent establishment status based on any of the five inquiries: direct business activities, agency relationships, more-than-stewardship activities, and the power shift personnel, as well as an "entirety of the operations" approach. In contrast, Hong Kong bases its permanent establishment activities on a more amorphous standard, "the economically significant activities and responsibilities" of the nonresident enterprise.

GENERAL PERMANENT ESTABLISHMENT CONSIDERATIONS

At the outset, the reader should distinguish between Hong Kong and India by three specific permanent establishment considerations:

1. Although Hong Kong asserts that its transfer pricing regime closely follows the Organisation for Economic Co-operation and Development (OECD) *Transfer Pricing Guidelines for Multinational Enterprises and Tax Administrations*, India acknowledges that its transfer pricing rules differ more significantly from the OECD transfer pricing rules.
2. India is a party to far more double tax agreements (DTAs) than is Hong Kong.
3. As a general rule, India relies on the United Nations model treaty while Hong Kong relies on the OECD model treaty.

The term "permanent establishment" presupposes the presence of a DTA between the parties involved. A country is free to impose tax on any activities of any sort that take place within that country if the parties are not members of such a double tax treaty. As a general matter, taxpayers that extend their activities offshore rely on the presence of a DTA to limit the possibility of double taxation in the countries in which they do business. As we shall see, however, governments are increasingly bending the envelope to justify PE claims in their home jurisdictions.

One strategy of critical importance for taxpayers is the penchant of the tax authorities to investigate potential PE activities. India has an extensive audit mechanism designed to assert its PE claims. Hong Kong's approach in asserting PE claims is less developed. Both Hong Kong and India recognize the tie-in between PE and transfer pricing, a relationship that other countries are prone to ignore. The risk of double taxation is often higher in India than in Hong Kong. The difference seems to be a more aggressive stance on the part of the tax officials in India than to those in Hong Kong.

The long arm of the Indian tax authorities extends outward, often reaching beyond the geographical confines of India itself. This long arm often reaches the activities of Indian-based activities taking place abroad as well as to the activities of foreign-based enterprises undertaking activities in India. Hong Kong is less aggressive in that respect.

The DTAs of both jurisdictions provide "preparatory to" exemptions and "auxiliary from" exemptions. Thus, the treaties exempt activities that are "preparatory to" the underlying activities and activities that are "auxiliary from" these underlying activities.

PERMANENT ESTABLISHMENT CONSIDERATIONS IN INDIA

India asserts PE based on five fact-based inquiries:

1. Presence of direct business activities
2. Presence of agency relationships
3. Presence of more-than-stewardship activities

4. Presence of personnel shifts from the parent company to the subsidiary
5. Entirety of operations in India

India asserts that the presence of the parent company's direct business activities causes a PE in India. As a result, a taxpayer doing business in India is well advised to ascertain whether the direct business activities that the parent company undertakes create a PE in the subsidiary's location. The taxpayer's review of the parent company's direct business activities is a separate inquiry of the subsidiary's operations themselves. The presence of a subsidiary is not necessary for the country to find PE status. Instead, activities in India can create taxability in India regardless of the form of the enterprise in India.

The presence of an agency relationship creates causes the enterprise to constitute a PE. As a result, a taxpayer is well advised to ascertain whether the indirect relationship between the parent company and its subsidiary constitutes an agency relationship. In fact, the presence of that agency relationship might bind the parent company to the subsidiary for PE purposes. Specifically, the subsidiary can serve as the parent company's agent by negotiating, binding, entering into, or concluding contracts on behalf of the parent company. As a result, the taxpayer is well advised to examine the powers that the subsidiary exercises.

A non-Indian company engaging in activities in India that are more than stewardship might cause the Indian tax authorities to view these activities as being a PE. The taxpayer is well advised to ascertain whether the parent company's activities as to the subsidiary go beyond the stewardship level, but stewardship activities themselves are exempt for PE characterization. The parent company's more-than-stewardship activities on behalf of the subsidiary can create a PE on the part of the parent company.

The ability of the parent company to shift personnel among entities might create a PE. The taxpayer is well advised to ascertain whether the parent company's personnel being shifted to the subsidiary create a PE on the part of the parent company. The parent company might have furnished personnel, might continue to payroll the subsidiary, or might take specific responsibility for the work of its employees at the subsidiary's location.

The entirety of the operations in India, taken as a whole, may cause the Indian government to treat the enterprise in India as being a PE. Thus, the entirety of the operations in the country of operations may create PE status. The tax collector might ascertain PE as a basis of taxation apart from the four previously mentioned operational categories.

PE activities in and of themselves can cause double taxation. Thus, the country in which the subsidiary is located might be able to tax the subsidiary because of its activities in that country. This same country can impose an additional level of tax on the parent company headquartered elsewhere as well as on its subsidiary located in the jurisdiction. The country in which the subsidiary is located can look toward the activities of the parent company and then examine the relationship of the parent company toward the subsidiary. In essence, the country in which the subsidiary is located might be able to tax the parent company based on that parent company–subsidiary relationship.

PERMANENT ESTABLISHMENT CONSIDERATIONS IN HONG KONG

The Hong Kong transfer pricing guidelines provide a procedure under which Hong Kong is to enforce its attribution rules to determine the profits of a PE. This guidance governs the Hong Kong's DTAs as to the allocation of taxing rights. As a general matter, it is necessary under Treaty Article 7 to attribute profits and expenses to the Hong Kong PE if the nonresident enterprise has a PE in Hong Kong. The Hong Kong transfer pricing guidelines list eight steps in the PE process. The taxpayer is to:

1. Identify the "economically significant activities and responsibilities" of the nonresident enterprise undertaken in various places. The guidance fails to further address the scope of the "economically significant activities and responsibilities" provision.
2. Postulate the existence of the PE in Hong Kong.
3. Identify the "economically significant activities and responsibilities" of the nonresident enterprise undertaken through the PE in Hong Kong.
4. Identify the scope, type, value, and timing of the dealings of the PE.
5. Determine the character and the structure of the PE business.
6. Select the most appropriate transfer pricing methodology for attribution purposes.
7. Apply the most appropriate transfer pricing methodology to determine the arm's length outcome.
8. Implement a support process and install a review process.

The Hong Kong transfer pricing guidelines provide two main provisions as to the attribution of income and expenditures concerning PEs:

1. Inland Revenue Rules, Rule 5
2. Business Profits Article, Article 7 of the DTAs

The Hong Kong transfer pricing guidelines apply the "functionally separate approach" to determine taxability of the PE. Using the "functionally separate entity" approach, the Commissioner will treat a PE as being a separate enterprise as if this enterprise is operating at arm's length. Such an enterprise must treat PEs in Hong Kong and elsewhere as reflecting its profits and expenses. The separate entity approach operates to produce the same outcome as would transactions between two enterprises at arm's length.

The Commissioner can assess the profits of the PE of a nonresident enterprise. The Commissioner, in assessing the profits of the PE of a nonresident enterprise, can examine the separate sources of profit that the nonresident enterprise has derived from Hong Kong.

A profit is not booked in the PE in Hong Kong. Nevertheless, the PE might have to attribute the profit to the PE of the nonresident enterprise carrying on a business in Hong Kong. The PE is to reflect these PE amounts if the enterprise undertakes "economically significant activities or responsibilities" in Hong Kong.

The profit might be generated from "economically significant activities or responsibilities" outside Hong Kong. In that event, the profit will not be attributed to the PE of the nonresident enterprise in Hong Kong. The presence of "economically significant activities or responsibilities" outside Hong Kong occurs when there is another PE outside Hong Kong or when the head office undertakes the "economically significant activities or responsibilities."

The Commissioner can attribute profits to the PE in Hong Kong under Article 7(2). The Commissioner, in making such attribution of profits, is also to consider these functions:

- The significant "people functions" of the PE
- The key entrepreneurial risk-taking functions of the PE (i.e., those functions that are relevant to the assumption or acceptance or management of risks)

CHAPTER THIRTY-FIVE

35

Pacific Tax Administrators Coordinate Transfer Pricing Documentation

TRANSFER PRICING DOCUMENTATION, as a specific objective, was virtually nonexistent as recently as 1982. A few decades later, governments were requesting huge amounts of transfer pricing data from their taxpayers on an organized basis. Perhaps the high-water mark (or low-water mark, depending on your point of view) for mandatory documentation is the Pacific Association of Tax Administrators (PATA), which developed the Transfer Pricing Documentation Package. PATA members include Australia, Canada, Japan, and the United States.

BACKGROUND

The first transfer pricing documentation case was the *Toyota* case.[1] The U.S. Internal Revenue Service (IRS) audited Toyota Motor Sales USA for the 1975 to 1978 fiscal years. This was a transfer pricing audit, based on the assertion on the part of the IRS that Toyota USA shifted income to Toyota Japan. Nevertheless, Toyota USA provided the IRS with no relevant documents that the IRS could use to substantiate its assertions.[2] The IRS went to court and had the court issue a summons to Toyota Motor Sales USA to secure more data transfer pricing documentation. The IRS then had the court issue a summons to Toyota Motor Corporation, the Japanese parent corporation, to obtain transfer pricing documentation

The IRS asserted, in support of its summons, that the court had personal jurisdiction over Toyota Japan, that the IRS had the right to secure the information that it was seeking, that the litigation should take in California, and that the IRS properly "served" Toyota Japan. The court concluded that the U.S. subsidiary handled all the marketing and advertising, and there was a significant overlap of senior management and the board of directors between parent and subsidiary, which the court viewed as interlocking directorates. Toyota USA employed two dozen Japanese employees who ultimately would be returning to Japan and "derived substantial economic benefits" in the United States. In 1982, Toyota's sales exceeded $5 billion. Toyota sold 600,000 cars in the United States and paid $10 million in dividends.

The IRS alleged that Toyota Japan has all the records pertaining to Toyota USA, an argument that the court accepted. The court held that Toyota Japan purposefully exploited the U.S. market. Toyota knew that the cars were deliberately sold in the United States, so that the IRS could "serve" Toyota Japan. The IRS served the summons to Toyota USA to the person who was a senior director of Toyota Japan and president of Toyota USA. The court held that this individual had adequate notice of the suit.

The result so far was that the IRS spent a great deal of high-powered effort and money on the Toyota case. All the IRS's results were that the court treated the summons as being proper.

The IRS brought a second case against Toyota.[3] Here the court had treated the summons as being proper, and the issue then became whether the IRS could enforce the summons. Many documents that the IRS requested from Toyota were not available. Toyota destroyed backup data and supporting records, but did so in the ordinary course of business in 1982 or at a prior date. Toyota destroyed these records before Toyota received an IRS summons, and the lack of retention of records became crucial.

The court held that Toyota had to furnish one of the documents that the IRS had requested, but the IRS did not receive sufficient information to undertake a transfer pricing analysis. The IRS spent a large amount of quality time and money on the Toyota cases with nothing to show for it. The IRS sought a legislative solution to its documentation concerns when a subsidiary or parent is located outside the United States.

The U.S. tax legislation designed to obtain section 482 documentation is in response to the *Toyota* cases. The 1982 Tax Equity and Fiscal Responsibility Act included section 482 documentation rules—the first country in the world to require these documentation rules. Failure to keep or retain documents evoked a penalty of $1,000 per tax year. An audit could trigger the need for documents; the penalty then was $1,000 per month. The new provisions for the first time required basic information: name, principal place of business, country of organization, and so on. The IRS and Treasury Department issued regulations in 1985. The law included a new summons procedure.

The IRS found the 1982 provisions were substantially inadequate. The IRS suggested in 1989 that Congress should substantially increase the documentation obligations on foreign owners. Congress strengthened the documentation requirements in 1989. The IRS and Treasury Department issued proposed regulations in 1990. The IRS and Treasury Department issued final regulations in 1991.

The U.S. documentation rules required the corporation to provide related parties' data, record keeping, and reporting; provided general maintenance requirements for small and large businesses; provided specific documentation—the safe harbor concept; and required contemporaneous documentation.

The U.S. documentation rules require six categories of data under Section 1.6038A-3:[4]

1. Original entry books and transaction records—creation of records
2. Profit and loss statements
3. Pricing documents
4. Foreign country and third-party filings
5. Ownership and capital structure
6. Records of loans, services, and other nonsale transactions

PATA PROVISIONS

Tax administrators from four countries agreed in 2003 on a common set of transfer pricing documentation and procedures for achieving taxpayer agreements. These four countries—Australia, Canada, Japan, and the United States—reached this agreement under the purview of the PATA. The goal of these administrators was to set up uniform documentation with a view toward facilitating bilateral advance pricing agreements. As a result of this arrangement, one set of documentation can meet the transfer pricing documentation provisions in each country. The PATA program has had limited success because of the crushing weight of the documentation guidelines on multinational taxpayers. This section explores the facets of this onerous burden.

The PATA documentation guidelines are voluntary, so taxpayers can volunteer to use the PATA Documentation Package. The taxpayer, in volunteering to use the PATA Documentation Package, does not incur any additional requirements greater than the requirements that the PATA member would impose. All four countries are members of the OECD. Chapter V of the OECD *Transfer Pricing Guidelines* is the common thread among them. Each member, however, might act differently in implementing these provisions.

Each PATA member agreed that a multinational enterprise (MNE) will satisfy each member's documentation provisions by complying with all of the principles contained in this PATA Transfer Pricing Documentation Package (hereafter PATA

Documentation Package). As a result, an MNE that complies will avoid the imposition of PATA members' transfer pricing penalties as to documented transactions among associated enterprises resident in PATA member jurisdictions. Each PATA member reserves the right to make pricing adjustments and to assess interest due on those adjustments.

But for the PATA Documentation Package, multinational corporations would face potential difficulties in complying with the laws and administrative requirements of multiple jurisdictions. These administrative requirements are duplicative and costly. The PATA members intend to assist taxpayers to efficiently prepare and maintain useful transfer pricing documentation.

THREE OPERATIVE PRINCIPLES

A taxpayer can avoid transfer pricing penalties by complying with three operative principles under the PATA Documentation Package. The operative principles are:

1. Make reasonable efforts in establishing transfer prices in compliance with the arm's length principle.
2. Maintain contemporaneous documentation of their efforts to comply with the arm's length principle.
3. Produce the documentation that a PATA member tax administrator requests in a timely manner.

Principle One: Establishing Transfer Prices

The MNE must make reasonable efforts to establish transfer pricing in compliance with the arm's length principle. Each PATA member tax administrator can independently examine the reasonableness of the taxpayer's compliance. Such efforts on the part of the taxpayer include:

- Analysis of controlled transactions
- Searches for comparable transactions between independent enterprises dealing at arm's length
- Selection and application of transfer pricing methods that are reasonably concluded to produce arm's length results in accordance with the applicable PATA member transfer pricing rules and the relevant treaty, consistent with the OECD guidelines

Principle Two: Contemporaneous Documentation

The multinational corporation must maintain contemporaneous documentation of its efforts to comply with the arm's length principle. The PATA rules support the contemporaneous documentation requirement for these reasons:

- Contemporaneous documentation helps taxpayers and tax administrators in the examination process.
- According to the PATA rules, the contemporaneous documentation process gives taxpayers notice of the information needed to assess whether prices of controlled transactions comply with the arm's length principle. As tax practitioners, we view this objective as impractical, as it would require the taxpayer's continuous introspection over the documentation obtained.
- Contemporaneous documentation provides tax administrations with useful analysis of controlled transactions between associated enterprises.
- Contemporaneous documentation assists in minimizing controversies concerning potential transfer pricing issues.

The PATA rules define "contemporaneous documentation" in this manner: Documentation is contemporaneous if the documentation is existing or the documentation is brought into existence no later than the due date, under the rules of the PATA member, of a timely filed income tax return for the taxation year of the controlled transactions at issue. The taxpayer can take into account tax return extensions allowed by the PATA member. Contemporaneous documentation includes relevant information obtained through that date.

The PATA rules as to contemporaneous documentation represent a liberalization of the contemporaneous documentation rules under the section 482 transfer pricing rules in the United States. Taxpayers potentially facing IRS challenges to contemporaneous documentation should consider electing the PATA provisions to take advantage of the more liberal contemporaneous documentation provisions.

An analysis under the arm's length principle is generally based on:

- Information as to the associated enterprises involved in the controlled transactions
- Transactions at issue
- Relevant functions, assets, and risks
- Information derived from independent enterprises engaged in similar transactions and businesses

The PATA provisions enunciate a general contemporaneous documentation rule that impacts the taxpayer: A taxpayer must prepare and maintain the documentation for transactions or arrangements, between itself and an associated enterprise resident in another PATA jurisdiction, as necessary to demonstrate compliance with the arm's length principle.

Transfer pricing documentation that the taxpayer prepares and maintains pursuant to this PATA Documentation Package must meet this standard: The documentation needs to be adequate and of sufficient quality so as to evidence that the taxpayer reasonably concluded that it selected and applied an arm's length result. The taxpayer is to determine the arm's length result in accordance with the applicable PATA member transfer pricing rules and the relevant treaty, consistent with the OECD guidelines.

Each PATA member tax administration, in evaluating the quality of a multinational corporation's documentation, is to take into account all of the relevant facts and circumstances. Such facts and circumstances might include, for example:

- The extent to which reliable data was reasonably available and analyzed in a reasonable manner
- The significance, importance, and complexity of the taxpayer's transfer pricing issues

A PATA member tax administration may request additional information, over and above the schedule in the PATA Documentation Package, as necessary to examine the multinational corporation's conclusions as to the arm's length nature of its arrangements.

Principle Three: Timely Production of Documents

The PATA member tax administration can request documentation from the taxpayer. The taxpayer must produce this documentation to the PATA member tax administration in a timely manner to secure penalty production afforded by the PATA Documentation Package. Each PATA member has its own requirements as to timely documentation. It appears that the PATA member administration will review the documentation process early in the transfer pricing review process. PATA member administrations will treat the information the taxpayer submits as confidential.

SPECIFIC MANDATORY DOCUMENTATION

The PATA Documentation Package requires the taxpayer to maintain documents and produce these documents on request in a timely manner. This list is generally viewed as exhaustive, but the PATA members preserve an escape valve for themselves: PATA member tax administrations can request additional information from the multinational corporation as being necessary to examine its conclusions as to the arm's length nature of its arrangements. The facts and circumstances may enable the taxpayer to exclude nonapplicable documentation, such as a cost contribution arrangement (CCA) if that information is not applicable.

The PATA Documentation Package requires the taxpayer to maintain and produce these documents:

- Organization structure
- Nature of the business or industry and market conditions
- Controlled transactions
- Assumptions, strategies, policies

- CCAs
- Comparability, function, and risk analysis
- Selection of the transfer pricing method
- Application of the transfer pricing method
- Background documents
- Index to documents

Organizational Structure Requirements

The PATA Documentation Package requires the taxpayer to maintain and produce the next organizational structure documents:

- Identification of the parties in related party dealings
- Identification of associated enterprises whose transactions indirectly affect the pricing of related party dealings
- The worldwide organizational structure, including an organization chart, reflecting all associated enterprises engaged in potentially relevant transactions

Nature of the Business/Industry and Market Conditions

The PATA Documentation Package requires the taxpayer to maintain and produce the following information as to the nature of the business and industry, and the marketing conditions:

- Outline of the business.
- Relevant recent history of the taxpayer.
- Industries.
- General economic and legal issues.
- Business lines.
- Corporate business plans, to the extent that these plans provide insight into the nature and purpose of the relevant transactions between associated enterprises. The phraseology of the provision arguably suggests that the term "corporate business plans" refers only to plans within the taxable year.
- Description of the "internal procedures and controls" in place at the time of the related party dealings. The scope of the "internal procedures and controls" provision is uncertain, but this term presumably refers to internal audit issues.
- An analysis of the "economic and legal factors" that affect the pricing of the taxpayer's property and services. Nowhere does the PATA define "economic factors" or "legal factors," but it appears that economic factors should include microeconomic issues, such as the economies of scale, the age of equipment, excess capacity, and the like, and include macroeconomic factors, such as tax rates, inflation, health care costs, and the like. Legal factors should include the gamut of legal issues, such as expropriation risks, slip and fall exposure, exposure to discrimination suits, and the like, as well as contractual commitments.

- A description of the "structure, intensity and dynamics" of the relative competitive environments. It appears here that the PATA expects the taxpayer to provide a full analysis of the taxpayer's competitors, including market share.
- A description of the intangible property potentially relevant to the pricing of the taxpayer's property of services in controlled transactions. The PATA here might be referring to both technology intangibles and market intangibles.
- Annual reports and financial statements for the year to which the package relates and for the prior five years.
- Information as to the functions performed, the assets employed, and the risks assumed where these functions, assets, and risks are relevant to the transactions in question.
- Explanation of the capital structure relative to the transactions. Such capital relationships include balances and source of debt and equity funding.

Controlled Transactions

The PATA Documentation Package requires the taxpayer to maintain and produce the next information as to controlled transactions:

- Description of the controlled transactions that identify the property or services to which the transaction relates. In this regard, the taxpayer is to provide this information:
  - Any intangible rights or property attached thereto
  - Participants
  - Scope, timing, frequency of, type, and value of controlled transactions
  - All relevant related party dealings in relevant geographic markets
  - Currency of the transactions
  - Terms and conditions of the transactions
  - Relationship to the terms and conditions of each other transaction entered into between the participants
- Identification of internal data relating to the controlled transactions
- Copies of all relevant intercompany agreements

Assumptions, Strategies, and Policies

The PATA Documentation Package requires the taxpayer to maintain and produce the next information as to assumptions, strategies, and policies:

- Relevant information regarding business strategies and "special circumstances" at issue. However, the PATA views the next activities as creating special circumstances that influence the transfer pricing determination:
  - Set-off transactions
  - Market share strategies
  - Distribution channel selection
  - Management strategies

- If the taxpayer pursues a market share strategy, the taxpayer must provide documentation that:
  - Demonstrates that the taxpayer undertook the appropriate analysis before the taxpayer implemented the strategy
  - Demonstrates that the taxpayer will pursue the market share strategy only for a reasonable period
  - Reflects that the costs borne by each associated enterprise are proportionate to the projected benefits of such enterprise
- Information as to the assumptions and information regarding:
  - Factors that influence the setting prices
  - Establishment of any pricing policies for the taxpayer and the related party group as whole

Cost Contribution Arrangements

The PATA Documentation Package requires the taxpayer to maintain and produce the following information as to CCAs, assuming the taxpayer seeks to pursue a CCA. The taxpayer is to:

- Provide CCA agreements:
  - A copy of the CCA agreement that is contemporaneous with its formation.
  - A copy of the CCA revision that is contemporaneous with its revision.
  - A copy of any other agreements relating to the application of the CCA between CCA participants.
- Provide a list of:
  - Participants to the arrangement.
  - Any other associated enterprises that will benefit from the CCA.
- Explain the use of CCA property by associated enterprises that are not CCA participants.
- Provide the amounts of consideration, whether paid or payable, by these nonparticipants for the use of CCA property.
- Provide the scope of the activities to be undertaken pursuant to the CCA arrangement. These activities include any intangible or class of intangibles now in existence or intended to be developed pursuant to the CCA arrangement.
- Provide a description of each participant's interest in the results of the CCA activities. This description presumably includes contingencies, applicable currency, and timing.
- Indicate the duration of the CCA agreement.
- Describe the procedures for a participant entering into or withdrawing from the CCA agreement and describe the consequences of entering into or withdrawing from such CCA agreement.
- Explain the specifics of the buy-in and buy-out payment process within the CCA agreement.
- Explain the process for modifying the CCA agreement and the processor for withdrawing from the CCA agreement.

- Provide the total amounts of contributions incurred pursuant to the CCA agreement.
- Provide information as to the contributions that each participant provides. The taxpayer is to provide information as to the form and the value of each participant's initial contributions, including research. Then the taxpayer is to describe the manner in which the contributors are to determine their initial and ongoing contributions and how the contributors are to apply their accounting principles in this regard.
- Describe the method used to determine each participant's share of the contributions, including:
  - Projections that the taxpayer uses to estimate benefits.
  - Any rationale and assumptions the taxpayer uses that underlie the projections.
  - An explanation as to why the taxpayer selected that transfer pricing method.
- Apply a consistent accounting method to determine the contributions and benefits. This accounting method includes the taxpayer's method of translating foreign currencies. The taxpayer must explain material differences to the extent that the transfer pricing method differs materially from the accounting principles accepted in the relevant PATA member's country.
- Identify each participant's expected benefits from the CCA, including:
  - The extent of the benefits that each participant expects.
  - The formula and projections the taxpayer uses for allocating or sharing the expected benefits.
  - The rationale and assumptions the taxpayer uses underlying the expected benefits.
- Amend the future benefit assumptions and document the revised assumptions, should material differences arise between projected benefits and actual benefits realized from the CCA.
- Describe the procedure governing balancing payments. The taxpayer needs to reflect differences between projected benefits and actual benefits realized.

Comparability, Function, and Risk Analysis

The PATA Documentation Package requires the taxpayer to maintain and produce the following information as to comparability, function, and risk analysis. The taxpayer must:

- Describe the comparables, including:
  - For tangible property
    - Physical features
    - Quality
    - Availability
  - For intangible property
    - Form of the transaction
    - Type of the intangible

    - Rights to use the intangible that are assigned
    - Anticipated benefits to its use
  - For services
    - Nature and extent of the services
- Provide documentation to support material factors that could affect prices or profits in arm's length dealings.
- Provide, regarding the taxpayer and the taxpayer's comparable:
  - Factors taken into account by the taxpayer to evaluate comparability.
  - Characteristics of the property or service that the taxpayer transfers.
  - Functions that the taxpayer and its comparables perform.
  - Significance of these functions, in terms of:
    - Frequency
    - Nature and value of these functions to their respective parties
  - Assets employed, taking into consideration:
    - Age of these assets
    - Market value of these assets
    - Location of these assets
    - Other considerations
  - Risks assumed, taking into consideration:
    - Market risk
    - Financial risk
    - Credit risk
    - Other risks
  - Contract terms and conditions
  - Business strategies the taxpayer pursues
  - Economic circumstances of the business, such as:
    - Geographic location
    - Market size
    - Competitive environment
    - Availability of substitute goods and services
    - Levels of supply and demand
    - Nature and extent of government regulations
    - Cost of production
    - Other economic circumstances
- Specify the criteria that it uses, including:
    - Database screens
    - Economic considerations
  - Identify any internal comparables.
  - Specify any adjustments that it makes to the comparables and provide the reasons for making those adjustments.
  - Aggregate its analysis, providing a grouping of transactions for comparability purposes.
  - The taxpayer can use a supporting transfer pricing methodology or supporting methodologies. If the taxpayer does use the supporting methodology or

methodologies, the taxpayer is to provide this supporting methodology or methodologies.

- Such a U.S. transfer pricing methodology makes use of the interquartile range. Nevertheless, in this instance the taxpayer might ignore the interquartile range concept, in part because the United States might not be a party to the transfer pricing relationship. Nevertheless, the taxpayer might use such a range. In that event, the taxpayer must provide documentation supporting the establishment of this range.
- The taxpayer must extend its analysis over a number of years. The taxpayer must provide the reasons for selecting the years chosen, where relevant.

Selection of the Transfer Pricing Method

The PATA Documentation Package requires the taxpayer to maintain and produce the following information as to selecting the transfer pricing method. The taxpayer is to describe:

- The transfer pricing method the taxpayer selects, specifying the reasons why it selected that transfer pricing method. In this regard, for example, the taxpayer should specify the economic analysis and projections on which it relies.
- The data and methods it considered and the analysis that it performed to determine the transfer pricing method. The taxpayer is to explain why it selected other methods and did not select these methods.

Application of the Transfer Pricing Method

The PATA Documentation Package requires the taxpayer to maintain and produce the following information as to applying the transfer pricing method. The taxpayer is to:

- Document its assumptions and the judgments it made in the course of determining an arm's length outcome. The assumptions and judgments include comparability, functions, and risk analysis.
- Document all of the calculations it makes in applying the selected transfer pricing method and in making adjustment factors as to both the taxpayer and the comparable.
- Provide appropriate updates of prior-year documentation that the taxpayer relied on in the current year to reflect adjustments made for any relevant year.

Background Documents

The PATA Documentation Package requires the taxpayer to maintain and produce the following information as to background documents: The taxpayer is to retain documents that provide the foundation for transfer pricing analysis, other documents that the taxpayer used as support for its transfer pricing analysis, and documents to which the taxpayer referred in developing its transfer pricing analysis.

Index to Documents

The PATA Documentation Package requires the taxpayer to maintain and produce the following information as to the index for documents: The taxpayer is encouraged to provide an index of documents as part of its transfer pricing analysis. The taxpayer is to provide a description of the record-keeping system it uses for cataloging and assessing these documents. The United States requires the taxpayer to provide this index; other PATA members encourage the taxpayer to prepare the index. The taxpayer need not prepare the index contemporaneously.

NOTES

1. 561 F. Supp. (1983) 83-1 USTC 9302.
2. Robert Feinschreiber, one of the authors of this book, was a counsel for Toyota in this matter.
3. 569 F. Supp. 1158 (1983) 83-2 USTC 9468.
4. See Feinschreiber, R., The Safe Harbor Under Prop. Reg. 1.6038A-3(c): The Significant Industry Segment Test, *Tax Management International* 20, no. 159 (1991); Feinschreiber, *Tax Reporting for Foreign-Owned U.S. Corporations*, Chapter 6 (New York: John Wiley & Sons, 1992); Feinschreiber, *Transfer Pricing Handbook Third Edition*, Chapter 59 (New York: John Wiley & Sons, 2001).

CHAPTER THIRTY-SIX

Shared Services and Cost Pooling Arrangements in the United States and Singapore

GOVERNMENTS ARE increasing the requirements they impose on multinational taxpayers as to the allocation of services, whether these services take place inside or outside the specific governmental jurisdiction. As a result, a multinational taxpayer, on a practical basis, may need to address the treatment of a myriad number of its service costs to fulfill the compliance objectives that tax collectors impose. The taxpayer might face an uncertain future when it comes to the allocation of services costs and its need to develop complex calculations to fulfill government objectives.

Without more, such a multinational taxpayer faces the need to apply various service cost methodologies, making that determination in a plethora of circumstances. Both the Internal Revenue Service (IRS) in the United States and the Inland Revenue Authority of Singapore (IRAS) in Singapore have begun to address these transfer pricing services issues. The IRS, in recognizing these transfer pricing services concerns, permits taxpayers to set up and utilize shared services arrangements. However, as we shall see, the IRS then curtails the shared services arrangement (SSA) process, limiting the salutary benefits the SSA provides. In contrast, the Singapore provisions do not impose these cost pooling limitations.

This analysis addresses the SSA process in the United States and the cost pooling process in Singapore in regard to transfer pricing services provisions.[1]

HISTORICAL BACKGROUND

The transfer pricing services regulations have evolved over a more than 40-year period in the United States. The Treasury Department and the IRS:

- Initially issued transfer pricing services regulations on August 16, 1968.[2]
- Then issued proposed transfer pricing services regulations on September 10, 2003.[3]
- Later issued temporary transfer pricing services regulations on August 4, 2006.[4]
- Issued final transfer pricing services regulations on July 31, 2009.[5]

The shared services and cost pooling provisions in Singapore have their own history:

- The initial transfer pricing services regulations did not contain SSA provisions.
- The 2006 temporary transfer pricing services provisions provided for shared services arrangements.
- On February 23, 2009, the Government of Singapore adopted and modified the SSA provisions specified in the U.S. 2006 temporary transfer pricing provisions.
- The Treasury Department and the IRS adopted the SSA in issuing final transfer pricing services regulations on July 31, 2009.
- The Treasury Department and the IRS, in adopting the shared services arrangement, apparently did not take the Singapore provisions into account as reference.

EXPLANATION OF THE SHARED SERVICES ARRANGEMENT PROVISIONS

The final SSA provisions address three issues raised in the temporary SSA provisions:

1. Tie-in between the services cost method (SCM) and the SSA
2. Pursuit of different cost objectives
3. Applicable shared SSA

Tie-in to the Services Cost Method

The Explanation of the Provisions for T.D. 9456 categorize the SSAs as being a subset of the SCM,[6] thus making the application of the other transfer pricing services methods problematic in the SSA context. It is our view as transfer pricing practitioners that the Treasury Department and the IRS necessarily narrowed the focus of the SSA provisions by this connection to the SCM. For example, the Singapore SSA has no parallel limitation that would tie transfer pricing services to methodologies selected.

As a general matter, commentators to what became the final transfer pricing services regulations supported the SSA provisions in the temporary regulations. The commentators viewed the SSA provisions as being a useful mechanism for allocation of costs from shared services or centralized services. However, commentators did call into question the SSA restriction to "covered services" priced under the SCM.

The limitation arises as to the requirement that service not be "eligible" for the shared service arrangement. In response to that commentary concerning shared services arrangements, the IRS issued Notice 2007-5, which provides that a taxpayer can use a services cost arrangement outside the SCM context. Notice 2007-5 specifically provides that the taxpayer "may also make allocations of arm's length charges for services ineligible for the SCM that yield a benefit to multiple members of a controlled group." In such a situation in which the SCM is not eligible, the Treasury Department and the IRS provide that the flexible SCM rules for establishing the joint benefits and selecting the allocation key are inapplicable.

The Treasury Department and the IRS would employ a "more robust" analysis under the transfer pricing rules "for determining the appropriate arm's length charges, benefits, allocation keys, etc." The Treasury Department and the IRS considered providing additional SSA rules to services priced under methods other than the SCM, but the Treasury Department and the IRS concluded that such rules would be unnecessary. In any event, as stated in Notice 2007-5, the Treasury Department and the IRS are intent on denying flexibility that they afforded in the SCM context in establishing the joint benefits, and selecting the allocation key that is inapplicable in the non-SCM context.

As transfer pricing practitioners, we suggest the Treasury Department and the IRS applied a more flexible standard in determining the applicability of shared services arrangements, recognizing that the taxpayer and the IRS might not be able to ascertain whether the SCM is the best transfer pricing method until after the taxpayer compiles the necessary data and allocation key. We further suggest that the SSA process should be a separate issue from the transfer pricing services selection process. In addition, we suggest the transfer pricing services provisions recognize that SCM ineligibility is an amorphous issue, and the taxpayer might not be able to make that determination as to eligibility at the time the taxpayer formally undertakes the section 1.482-9(b)(7)(ii)(C) SSA process.

Pursuit of Different Cost Objectives

Other commentators to what became the final transfer pricing services regulations requested that the IRS respect the SSA even if a party that reasonably anticipates its benefits makes a payment to its share under the SSA to the service provider pursuant to a different arrangement. T.D. 9456 provides an example under which a controlled service provider performs services to ten taxpayers that are members of the controlled group. Nine of the service recipients agree in a written contract to allocate the arm's length charge based on a reasonable allocation basis. The tenth services recipient does not agree to these terms but instead pays for its share of the services pursuant to a separate agreement. The Treasury Department and the IRS refused to accept the validity of the SSA in such circumstances, concluding that it wants to reserve for itself the power to determine whether an agreement is an SSA based on a case-by-case determination based on facts and circumstances.

Applicable Shared Service Arrangement Standards

Other commentators to what became the final transfer pricing services regulations observed that the SSA provisions require the allocation of costs on the basis that "most reliably reflects" the participants' respective shares of "reasonably anticipated" benefits. Some of the SSA examples use the phrase "precisely known." Thus, there appears to be a disparity between the "reasonably anticipated" benefits and amounts that are "precisely known." This disparity has caused some commentators to question whether the SSA rule creates an unattainable standard or whether the SSA rule imposes a higher standard than the reasonable standard for allocation of costs in Treasury Regulation section 1.482-9(k). These commentators suggested changes to these examples.

The Treasury Department and the IRS rejected the commentators' approach to change these services cost standards. The Treasury Department and the IRS concluded that these examples do not create a standard based on "precisely known shares" of reasonably anticipated benefits. Rather, according to the Treasury Department and the IRS, the examples use hypothetical, precisely known reasonably anticipated benefits as a measuring stick to provide an easily understood comparative analysis of potential allocation keys for illustrative purposes.

SHARED SERVICES ARRANGEMENTS

Section 1.482-9(b)(7) addresses covered services that might be the subject of an SSA. In the event that covered services are subject to an SSA, sec.1.482-9(b)(7)(i) generally provides that the arm's length charge to each participant for such services will be the portion of the total costs of the services otherwise determined under the SCM of this sec. 1.482-9(b)(7) that is properly allocated to such participant pursuant to the arrangement.

Section 1.482-9(b)(7)(ii) contains the requirements for an SSA. An SSA must meet three requirements described in sec. 1.482-9(b)(7):

1. Eligibility requirements, as specified by sec. 1.482-9(b)(7)(ii)(A)
2. Allocation requirements, as specified by sec. 1.482-9(b)(7)(ii)(B)
3. Documentation requirements, as specified by sec. 1.482-9(b)(7)(ii)(C)

Section 1.482-9(b)(7)(iii) provides for definitions and special rules as to shared services arrangements.

Eligibility Requirements

Section 1.482-9(b)(7)(ii)(A) provides, as to the eligibility requirements for an SSA, that the arrangement, to be eligible for treatment under this sec. 1.482-9(b)(7), must meet these eligibility requirements:

- The arrangement must include two or more participants, as specified by sec. 1.482-9(b)(7)(ii)(A)*(1)*.
- The arrangement must include, as participants, all controlled taxpayers that "reasonably anticipate a benefit." Section 1.482-9(l)(3)(i) defines "benefit" as from one or more covered services specified in the shared services arrangement, as specified by sec. 1.482-9(b)(7)(ii)(A)*(2)*, that directly results in a "reasonably identifiable increment of economic or commercial value that enhances the recipient's commercial position or that may reasonably be anticipated to do so."
- The arrangement must be structured such that each covered service, or each reasonable aggregation of services within the meaning of sec. 1.482-9(b)(7)(iii)(B), confers a benefit on at least one participant in the SSA, as specified by sec. 1.482-9(b)(7)(ii)(A)*(3)*.

The "reasonably anticipated benefits" rule applies in ascertaining shared services. Section 1.482-9(b)(7)(ii)(B) provides, as to the allocation requirement specified in sec. 1.482-9(b)(7)(iii)(B), that the participants must allocate costs for covered services among the participants based on their respective shares of the reasonably anticipated benefits from those services. The participants are to make this determination as to benefits without regard to whether the anticipated benefits are in fact realized. "Reasonably anticipated benefits" are "benefits" as defined in sec. 1.482-9T(l)(3)(i).

Allocation of Costs

Participants must allocate the costs that are applicable to the benefits they receive. The allocation of costs that the participants select must provide the most reliable measure of the participants' respective shares of the reasonably anticipated benefits under the principles of the best method rule. See sec. 1.482-1(c) as to the definition of best method. The participant must apply the shares of the reasonably anticipated benefits allocation on a consistent basis for all participants and for all services.

The allocation to each participant in each taxable year must reasonably reflect that participant's respective share of reasonably anticipated benefits for such taxable year. The Commissioner may not adjust such allocation basis if the taxpayer reasonably concluded that the SSA, including any aggregation pursuant to sec. 1.482-9(b)(7)(iii)(B), allocated costs for covered services on a basis that most reliably reflects the participants' respective shares of the reasonably anticipated benefits attributable to such services, as provided for in sec. 1.482-9(b)(7). For allocation purposes, taxpayers need not prove to the IRS that its allocation is necessarily the best transfer pricing method, only that the taxpayer's method is reasonable and the allocation method reliably reflects respective shares of the reasonably anticipated benefits attributable to such services.

Documentation

Section 1.482-9(b)(7)(ii)(C) provides, as to the documentation requirement within the shared services provisions, that the taxpayer must maintain sufficient documentation to establish that the taxpayer satisfies the requirements of sec. 1.482-9(b)(7). The taxpayer is to include six facets to demonstrate its documentation:

1. A statement evidencing the taxpayer's intention to apply the SCM to evaluate the arm's length charge for covered services pursuant to an SSA pursuant to sec. 1.482-9(b)(7)(ii)(C)*(1)*
2. A list of the participants under the SSA pursuant to sec. 1.482-9(b)(7)(ii)(C)*(2)*
3. A list of the renderer or the renderers of covered services under the SSA pursuant to sec. 1.482-9(b)(7)(ii)(C)*(2)*
4. A description of the basis of allocation to all participants, consistent with the participants' respective shares of reasonably anticipated benefits pursuant to sec. 1.482-9(b)(7)(ii)(C)*(3)*
5. A description of any aggregation of covered services for purposes of the SSA pursuant to sec. 1.482-9(b)(7)(ii)(C)*(4)*
6. An indication whether this aggregation (if any) pursuant to sec. 1.482-9(b)(7)(ii)(C)*(4)* differs from the aggregation used to evaluate the median comparable markup for any low-margin covered services described in sec. 1.482-9(b)(3)(ii)

Section 1.482-9(b)(7)(iii) provides three definitions and special rules for SSAs:

1. Section 1.482-9(b)(7)(iii)(A) defines the term "participant" to mean a controlled taxpayer that reasonably anticipates benefits from covered services subject to an SSA that substantially complies with the requirements described in sec. 1.482-9(b)(7).
2. Section 1.482-9(b)(7)(iii)(B) provides, as to aggregation, that a taxpayer can aggregate two or more covered services that meet these criteria:
   - The aggregation takes place in a reasonable manner.
   - The aggregation takes into account all the facts and circumstances.
   - The facts and circumstances that take into account whether the relative magnitude of reasonably anticipated benefits of the participants that share the costs of such aggregated services are reasonably reflected by the allocation basis employed pursuant to sec. 1.482-9(b)(7)(ii)(B).
   - The aggregation of services under an SSA may differ from the aggregation used to evaluate the median comparable markup for any low-margin covered services described in sec. 1.482-9(b)(3)(ii).
   - However, a taxpayer seeking to aggregate services can do so provided that the taxpayer can implement such alternative aggregation on a reasonable basis, including appropriately identifying and isolating relevant costs, as necessary.
3. Section 1.482-9(b)(7)(iii)(C) provides, as to the coordination with cost sharing arrangements, that:

- A taxpayer can make an allocation to a participant in an SSA that is also a participant in a cost sharing arrangement subject to sec. 1.482-7T.
- The taxpayer can make this cost sharing arrangement allocation to the extent that such amount with respect to covered services is first allocated pursuant to the SSA under sec. 1.482-9(b)(7).
- Costs that a taxpayer allocates pursuant to an SSA may (if applicable) be further allocated between the intangible development activity under sec. 1.482-7T and other activities of the participant.

SERVICES COST METHOD EXAMPLES

The sec. 1.482-9(b)(8) regulations provide 24 examples that illustrate the SCM. The drafters do not intend an inference as to whether the presence or absence of one or more facts is determinative of the conclusion in any example. Note these factual parameters as to Examples 16 through 24: The fact patterns assume that Company P and its subsidiaries, Company X, Company Y, and Company Z, are corporations and members of the same group of controlled entities (PXYZ Group). The fact pattern assumes that Company P and its subsidiaries satisfy all of the requirements for an SSA as specified in sec. 1.482-9(b)(7)(ii) and sec. 1.482-9(b)(7)(iii).

Example 16. Shared Services Arrangement and Reliable Measure of Reasonably Anticipated Benefit (Allocation Key)

- Company P operates a centralized data processing facility that performs automated invoice processing activities and performs order generation for all of its subsidiaries.
- Company P's subsidiaries are Companies X, Y, and Z.
- Company P undertakes an SSA with Companies X, Y, and Z.
- Company P is to evaluate the shares of reasonably anticipated benefits from the centralized data processing services as part of the SSA.
- The total value of the merchandise on the invoices and orders may not provide the most reliable measure of reasonably anticipated benefits shares in determining the reasonably anticipated benefits.
- The total value of the merchandise on the invoices and orders may not provide the most reliable measure of reasonably anticipated benefits shares because value of merchandise sold does not bear a relationship to the anticipated benefits from the underlying covered services.
- The total volume of orders and invoices processed may provide a more reliable basis for evaluating the shares of reasonably anticipated benefits from the data processing services.
- Alternatively, depending on the facts and circumstances, total central processing unit time attributable to the transactions of each subsidiary may provide a more reliable basis on which to evaluate the shares of reasonably anticipated benefits.

Example 17. Shared Services Arrangement and Reliable Measure of Reasonably Anticipated Benefit (Allocation Key)

- Company P operates a centralized center that performs human resources (HR) functions.
- Such HR functions include the administration of pension, retirement, and health insurance plans that are made available to employees of its subsidiaries, Companies X, Y, and Z.
- Companies P, X, Y, and Z allocate the cost of these HR functions pursuant to a shared services arrangement.
- In evaluating the shares of reasonably anticipated benefits from these centralized services, the total revenues of each subsidiary may not provide the most reliable measure of reasonably anticipated benefit shares.
- The total revenues of each subsidiary may not provide the most reliable measure of reasonably anticipated benefit shares because total revenues do not bear a relationship to the shares of reasonably anticipated benefits from the underlying services.
- Employee headcount or total compensation paid to employees may provide a more reliable basis for evaluating the shares of reasonably anticipated benefits from the covered services.

Example 18. Shared Services Arrangement and Reliable Measure of Reasonably Anticipated Benefit (Allocation Key)

- Company P performs HR services (service A) on behalf of the PXYZ Group.
- The PXYZ Group services qualify for the SCM.
- Under the SCM, Company P determines the amount charged for these HR services pursuant to a shared services arrangement.
- Company P applies the sec. 1.482-9(b)(7) SSA.
- Service A constitutes a specified covered service described in an unspecified revenue procedure pursuant to sec. 1.482-9(b)(3)(i).
- The total services costs for service A, as otherwise determined under the SCM, is 300.
- Companies X, Y, and Z reasonably anticipate benefits from service A.
- Company P does not reasonably anticipate benefits from service A.
- Assume that if relative reasonably anticipated benefits were precisely known, the appropriate allocation of charges pursuant to sec. 1.482-9T(k) to Company X, Y, and Z for service A is:

  Service A Total cost 300, delineated as:

X	150
Y	75
Z	75

The total number of employees (employee headcount) in each company is:

Company X	600 employees
Company Y	250 employees
Company Z	250 employees

Company X, Y, Z total: 1,100 employees.

Company P allocates the 300 total services costs of service A based on employee headcount, doing so as shown:

	Service A Total Cost Company (headcount)	Allocation Key Amount
X	600	164
Y	250	68
Z	250	68
Total	1,100	300

- Based on the preceding facts, Company P may reasonably conclude that the employee headcount allocation basis most reliably reflects the participants' respective shares of the reasonably anticipated benefits attributable to service A.

Example 19. Shared Services Arrangement and Reliable Measure of Reasonably Anticipated Benefit (Allocation Key)

- Company P performs accounts payable services (service B) on behalf of the PXYZ Group.
- Company P determines the amount charged for the services under such method pursuant to an SSA based on an application of sec. 1.482-9(b)(7).
- Service B is a specified covered service described in a revenue procedure pursuant to sec. 1.482-9(b)(3)(i).
- The total services costs for service B otherwise determined under the SCM is 500.
- Companies X, Y, and Z reasonably anticipate benefits from service B.
- Company P does not reasonably anticipate benefits from service B.
- Assume that if relative reasonably anticipated benefits were precisely known, the appropriate allocation of charges pursuant to sec. 1.482-9(k) to Companies X, Y, and Z for service B is:

  Service B Company Cost

X	125
Y	205
Z	170
Total	500

The total number of employees (employee headcount) in each company is:

Company X	600
Company Y	200
Company Z	200
Total employees	1,000

The total number of transactions (transaction volume) with uncontrolled customers by each company is:

Company X	12,000
Company Y	4,000
Company Z	3,500
Total volume of transactions (transactions volume)	19,500

If Company P allocated the 500 total services costs of service B based on employee headcount, the resulting allocation would be:

	Service B Total Cost Headcount	Allocation Amount
X	600	300
Y	200	100
Z	200	100
Total	1,000	500

In contrast, if Company P used volume of transactions with uncontrolled customers as the allocation basis under the SSA, the allocation would be:

	Transaction Volume	Amount
X	2,000	105
Y	4,000	211
Z	3,500	184
Total	9,500	500

Based on these facts, Company P may reasonably conclude that the transaction volume, but not the employee headcount, allocation basis most reliably reflects the participants' respective shares of the reasonably anticipated benefits attributable to service B.

Example 20. Shared Services Arrangement and Aggregation

- Company P performs two services on behalf of PXYZ Group.
- Company P performs HR services (service A).

- Company P performs accounts payable services (service B).
- Company P applies the SCM to service A and to service B.
- Company P applies an SSA based on an application of sec. 1.482-9(b)(7), which determines the amount charged for these services.
- The example provides that service A and service B are specified covered services described in a revenue procedure.
- Rev. Proc. 2007-13 could determine the covered services pursuant to sec. 1.482-9(b)(3)(i).
- The PXYZ Group determines the total services costs under the SCM for service A is 300.
- The PXYZ Group determines the total services costs under the SCM for service B is 500.
- The PXYZ Group determines the total services costs under the SCM for service A and service B is 800.
- Company P determines that aggregation of services A and B for purposes of the arrangement is appropriate.
- Companies X, Y, and Z reasonably anticipate benefits from services A and B.
- Company P does not reasonably anticipate benefits from services A and B.
- Assume that if P precisely knew the relative reasonably anticipated benefits, the appropriate allocation of total charges pursuant to sec. 1.482-9(k) to Companies X, Y, and Z for services A and B is:

Services A and B	
X	350
Y	100
Z	350
Total Cost	800

The total volume of transactions with uncontrolled customers in each company is:

Company X	2,000
Company Y	4,000
Company Z	4,000
Total employees	10,000

The total number of employees in each company is:

Company X	600
Company Y	200
Company Z	200
Total employees	1,000

If Company P allocated the 800 total services costs of services A and B based on transaction volume or on employee headcount, the resulting allocation would be:

	Company	Aggregated Services	Allocation Key	Allocation Key:
	Headcount	Transaction Volume		Amount
X	2,000	160	600	480
Y	4,000	320	200	160
Z	4,000	320	200	160
T	10,000	800	1,000	800

In contrast, if P allocated the aggregated services AB by reference to the total U.S. dollar value of sales to uncontrolled parties (trade sales) by each company, these results would obtain:

	Aggregated Services AB	Amount
	Allocation Key: Trade Sales	
X	$400 million	314
Y	$120 million	94
Z	$500 million	392
Total	$1,020 million	800

Based on these facts, Company P may reasonably conclude that the trade sales allocation basis, but not the transaction volume or the employee headcount, most reliably reflects the participants' respective shares of the reasonably anticipated benefits attributable to services AB.

Example 21. Shared Services Arrangement and Aggregation

- Company P performs services A through P on behalf of the PXYZ Group that qualify for the SCM.
- Company P determines the amount charged for these services under such method pursuant to an SSA based on an application of sec. 1.482-9(b)(7).
- All of these services A through Z constitute either specified covered services or low-margin covered services described in sec. 1.482-9(b)(3).
- The total services costs for services A through Z otherwise determined under the SCM is 500.
- Company P determines that aggregation of services A through Z for purposes of the arrangement is appropriate.
- Companies X and Y reasonably anticipate benefits from services A through Z, and Company Z reasonably anticipates benefits from services A through X but not from services Y or Z.
- Company Z performs services similar to services Y and Z on its own behalf.
- Company P does not reasonably anticipate benefits from services A through Z.

- Assume that if relative reasonably anticipated benefits were precisely known, the appropriate allocation of total charges pursuant to sec. 1.482-9(k) to Company X, Y, and Z for services A through Z is:

	Services A–M	Services N–P	Services A–P
X	90	5	95
Y	240	5	245
Z	160		160
Total	490	10	500

The total volume of transactions with uncontrolled customers in each company is:

Company X	2,000
Company Y	4,500
Company Z	3,500
Total	10,000

Company P allocates the 500 total services costs of services A through Z based on transaction volume in this way:

Aggregated Services A–Z	Total Costs 500	Allocation Key: Transaction Volume
X	2,000	100
Y	4,500	225
Z	3,500	175
Total	10,000	500

Based on these facts, Company P may reasonably conclude that the transaction volume allocation basis most reliably reflects the participants' respective shares of the reasonably anticipated benefits attributable to services A through Z.

Example 22. Renderer Reasonably Anticipates Benefits

- Company P renders services on behalf of the PXYZ Group that qualify for the SCM.
- Company P determines the amount charged for these services under such method.
- Company P's share of reasonably anticipated benefits from services A, B, C, and D is 20% of the total reasonably anticipated benefits of all participants.
- Company P's total services cost for services A, B, C, and D charged within the group is 100.
- Based on an application of sec. 1.482-9(b)(7), Company P charges 80. P allocates this amount among Companies X, Y, and Z.

- No charge is made to Company P under the SSA for activities that it performs on its own behalf.

Example 23. Coordination with Cost Sharing Arrangement

- Company P performs HR services (service A) on behalf of the PXYZ Group.
- Such HR services qualify for the SCM.
- Company P determines the amount charged for these services under such method pursuant to an SSA based on an application of sec. 1.482-9(b)(7).
- Service A constitutes a specified covered service described in a revenue procedure pursuant to sec. 1.482-9(b)(3)(i).
- The total services costs for service A otherwise determined under the SCM is 300.
- Companies X, Y, Z, and P reasonably anticipate benefits from service A.
- Using a basis of allocation that is consistent with the controlled participants' respective shares of the reasonably anticipated benefits from the shared services, the parties allocate the total charge of 300 as shown:

X	100
Y	50
Z	25
P	125
Total	300

- In addition to performing services, P undertakes 500 of research and development (R&D) and incurs manufacturing and other costs of 1,000.
- Companies P and X enter into a cost sharing arrangement in accordance with sec. 1.482-7.
- Company P will undertake all intangible development activities under the arrangement.
- Company P devotes all its R&D activity to the intangible development activity under the cost sharing arrangement.
- Company P will manufacture, market, and otherwise exploit the product in its defined territory.
- Companies P and X will share intangible development costs in accordance with their reasonably anticipated benefits from the intangibles.
- Company X will make payments to Company P as required under sec. 1.482-7T.
- Company X will manufacture, market, and otherwise exploit the product in the rest of the world.
- A portion of the charge under the SSA is in turn allocable to the intangible development activity undertaken by Company P.
- The most reliable estimate of the proportion allocable to the intangible development activity is determined to be 500 (Company P's R&D expenses) divided by 1,500 (Company P's total noncovered services costs), or one third.

- Accordingly, one third of Company P's charge of 125, or 42, is allocated to the intangible development activity.
- Companies P and X must share the intangible development costs of the cost-shared intangibles (including the charge of 42 that is allocated under the SSA) in proportion to their respective shares of reasonably anticipated benefits under the cost sharing arrangement.
- That is, the reasonably anticipated benefit shares under the cost sharing arrangement are determined separately from reasonably anticipated benefit shares under the SSA.

Example 24. Coordination with Cost Sharing Arrangement

- The facts and analysis in Example 26 are the same as in Example 24, except that Company X also performs intangible development activities related to the cost sharing arrangement.
- Using a basis of allocation that is consistent with the controlled participants' respective shares of the reasonably anticipated benefits from the shared services, the parties allocate 300 of service costs as shown:

X	100
Y	50
Z	25
P	125
Total	300

- In addition to performing services, Company P undertakes 500 of R&D.
- Company P incurs manufacturing and other costs of 1,000.
- Company X undertakes 400 of R&D and incurs manufacturing and other costs of 600.
- Companies P and X enter into a cost sharing arrangement in accordance with sec. 1.482-7T.
- Both Companies P and X will undertake intangible development activities under the cost sharing arrangement.
- Companies P and X devote all of the R&D activity to the intangible development activity under the cost sharing arrangement.
- Both Companies P and X will manufacture, market, and otherwise exploit the product in their respective territories.
- Both Companies P and X will share intangible development costs in accordance with their reasonably anticipated benefits from the intangibles.
- Both Companies P and X will make payments as required under sec. 1.482-7T.
- A portion of the charge under the SSA is in turn allocable to the intangible development activities undertaken by Companies P and X.

- The most reliable estimate of the portion allocable to Company P's intangible development activity is determined to be 500 (Company P's R&D expenses) divided by 1,500 (P's total noncovered services costs), or one third.
- Accordingly, one third of Company P's allocated SCM charge of 125, or 42, is allocated to its intangible development activity.
- In addition, it is necessary for the taxpayer to determine the portion of the charge under the SSA to Company X that should be further allocated to Company X's intangible development activities under the cost sharing arrangement.
- The most reliable estimate of the portion allocable to Company X's intangible development activity is 400 (Company X's R&D expenses) divided by 1,000 (Company X's costs), or 40%.
- Accordingly, 40% of the 100 that was allocated to Company X, or 40, is allocated in turn to Company X's intangible development activities.
- Company X makes a payment to Company P of 100 under the shared services arrangement.
- Company X includes 40 of SCM charges in the pool of intangible development costs.

The parties' respective contributions to intangible development costs under the cost sharing arrangement are:

$$P: 500 + (0.333 \times 125) = 542$$

$$X: 400 + (0.40 \times 100) = 440$$

SINGAPORE SHARED SERVICES ARRANGEMENTS

The IRAS issued Transfer Pricing Guidelines for Related Party Loans and Related Party Services on February 23, 2009. The IRAS employs the SSA process, referring to this process as "cost pooling."[7] Singapore taxpayers can apply this cost pooling technique to certain routine services expenditures that occur among related parties with the corporate group. Cost pooling arrangements differ in numerous respects from cost contribution arrangements (or cost sharing arrangements) that taxpayers enter into primarily to develop intangible assets. Regrettably, the Singapore services guidelines fail to distinguish between cost pooling arrangements and cost sharing arrangements.

Singapore taxpayers might find it mutually beneficial to enter into a cost pooling contract among members of the corporate group.[8] The cost pooling contract enables members of the corporate group to share in the costs of routine support services for the common use of the group to meet a common need of the members. The cost pooling arrangement allows the members of the corporate group to pool resources together in order to acquire services that meet these parameters:

- A party to the cost pooling contract must have a reasonable expectation of benefiting from or actually benefit from the services for which costs are being shared.

- Contributions by related parties to the costs of providing the services must be made in proportion to the nature and extent of the expected benefits that each party receives.
- Each party's share of the costs in the cost pooling arrangement must be borne in the form of cash or by other monetary contributions.

The proposed Singapore services guidelines provided that the arrangement must be necessary for the corporate group to function effectively. The final Singapore services guidelines eliminated this requirement.

Additional pooling requirements in Singapore are:[9]

- The arrangement is to acquire services that are not the principal activities of the corporate group.
- The arrangement is not intended to be a profitable exploit of the corporate group.
- The arrangement must address mutual benefit among members of the group.
- The party to the arrangement must reasonably expect to benefit from the shared services or actually benefit from the shared services.
- The party to the arrangement must determine the contribution as to the costs of providing the service in proportion to the expected benefits that each party receives.
- Each party must bear the share of its costs in the form of cash or other contributions, and nothing else.
- To satisfy the arm's length principle, each participant's share of the costs must be consistent with the costs to which an independent party would have agreed under comparable circumstances, given the benefit the participant would have expected to derive from the services being provided.

The Singapore services guidelines provide specific parameters for the allowance of the cost pooling arrangement:[10]

- The arrangement must be termed as a proportionate share of the cost of the services.
- The arrangement can be determined on a prospective basis.
- The arrangement is to be determined with no element of markup.
- The service provider that offers its services to its related parties does not offer these same services to unrelated parties.
- The service provided to the related parties does not reflect the principal activity that the service provider is to undertake. The term "principal activity" is based on facts and circumstances, based on a 15% threshold.
- These provisions apply to Annex A specified services in Singapore.
- The taxpayer provides sufficient documentation to show that the parties intended to pool their resources to share costs, doing so before the service provider performs the services.

The Singapore services guidelines require the taxpayer to maintain adequate documentation to support the cost allocation as being arm's length. The services guidelines require the taxpayer to maintain adequate documentation to demonstrate the sharing of expected benefits arising from providing these services. The proposed services guidelines were concerned about the taxpayer's risk of double taxation and suggested that the taxpayer retain the following documentation:[11]

- Description of the type of services provided
- Rationale for selecting a specific cost method
- Nature of the related parties' contributions
- Anticipated benefits
- Calculation details

NOTES

1. R. Feinschreiber and M. Kent, "Singapore Issues Transfer Pricing Guidelines for Related-Party Loans and Services," *Corporate Business Taxation Monthly* (June 2009): 41.
2. 33 FR 5849; see R. Feinschreiber, *Paying for Intercompany Services*, Prentice-Hall U.S. Taxation of International Operations Service, January 14, 1981.
3. 68 FR 53448.
4. 71 FR 44466.
5. T.D. 9456.
6. A.1.g.
7. IRAS, Transfer Pricing Guidelines for Related Party Loans and Related Party Services, 3.3.14.
8. IRAS, Transfer Pricing Guidelines for Related Party Loans and Related Party Services, 3.3.15.
9. IRAS Transfer Pricing Guidelines for Related Party Loans and Related Party Services, 3.3.16.
10. IRAS Transfer Pricing Guidelines for Related Party Loans and Related Party Services, 3.3.16.
11. IRAS Transfer Pricing Guidelines for Related Party Loans and Related Party Services, 3.3.16.

CHAPTER THIRTY-SEVEN

37

South Korea–Japan Bilateral Investment Treaty

BILATERAL INVESTMENT treaties (BITs) are comparatively new legal structures. These treaties go back over 50 years, when Germany and Pakistan signed a bilateral investment treaty on November 25, 1959. Tax practitioners have had little opportunity to address the tax issues of these BIT agreements. The Korea–Japan BIT treaty provides an example of the tax issues relevant to the tax practitioner.

BACKGROUND

At the present time, country participants participate in more than 2,500 BITs, involving most countries in the world. Bilateral investment tax treaties are, for the most part, not tax treaties. Nevertheless, some BITs contain significant tax components. One such BIT having tax components is the Korea–Japan BIT. This treaty, perhaps uniquely, contains treaty shopping provisions.

BITS are unique among other treaties. BIT treaties give the investor significant rights vis-à-vis the treaty country, treating the host country and investor almost as equals. The investor achieves these rights through powers that its own country grants to the investor.

A BIT is distinct from an income tax convention. Countries might have income tax conventions, might have BITs, or might have both or none depending on the circumstances. BITs are akin in many respects to treaties of friendship and navigation, which also might exist with the same countries.

U.S. INVOLVEMENT IN BITS

The United States has 40 BITs in force. The United States operates its BITs through the Office of the United States Trade Representative, which is part of the Executive Office of the President. The U.S. BITs are designed to help protect U.S. foreign investment, to help market-oriented policies in partner countries, and to promote U.S. exports.

Many countries undertake BITs with large, well-developed market-driven economies. In contrast to BITs that America's treaty partners undertake, the United States has developed a BIT structure with smaller countries that only recently sought inbound investment. As a result, the U.S. BIT programs attempt to accomplish these objectives:

- Protect investment abroad, in countries where investor rights are not always protected through existing agreements. Such protections include agreements such as modern treaties of friendship, commerce, and navigation, or free trade agreements.
- Encourage the adoption of market-oriented domestic policies, where these policies treat private investment in an open, transparent, and nondiscriminatory manner.
- Support the development of international standards that are consistent with the protection objective and market-oriented policy objective.

ARBITRATION

BIT treaties typically provide an arbitration provision, enabling the investor and the host country to arbitrate disputed provisions. BIT treaties provide for arbitration under the International Centre for Settlement of Investment Disputes (ICSID) or with United Nations Commission on International Trade Law (UNCITRAL) provisions. The Korean–Japan BIT treaty contains both ICSID and UNCITRAL provisions.

ICSID ARBITRATION

Enterprises facing investment disputes with their host governments could potentially seek to resolve these disputes through the ICSID mechanism or through other dispute mechanisms. BITs might or might not specifically address these tax concerns through the ICSID dispute process.

The ICSID convention is a multilateral investment treaty that was entered into force on October 14, 1966. However, the ICSID mechanism contemplates that the parties would enter bilateral agreements as opposed to multilateral agreements.

At this writing, 155 countries have joined the ICSID Convention, of which 144 countries have ratified, accepted, or approved the ICSID Convention. Canada, Russia, and Thailand are among the countries that have joined the Convention but have not ratified, accepted, or approved it. Bolivia had been an ICSID member but denounced the Convention on May 2, 2007, effective November 3, 2007. Ecuador had been an ICSID member but denounced the convention on July 6, 2009, effective January 7, 2010. Commentators have suggested that Nicaragua and Venezuela will be leaving ICSID as well.

The ICSID Convention is an autonomous entity within the World Bank Group (i.e., the International Bank for Reconstruction and Development). Technically, the ICSID Convention is termed the Convention on the Settlement of Investment Disputes Between States and Nationals of Other States. ICSID operates through an Administrative Council, chaired by the president of the World Bank, and a Secretariat. ICSID provides facilities—legal and physical—for conciliation and arbitration of investment disputes between member countries and investors in these host countries. The Administrative Council consists of one representative of each state that has ratified the ICSID Convention. The Administrative Council meets annually in conjunction with World Bank annual meetings.

During the immediate post–World War II period, the World Bank and its presidency became involved in disputes between governments and private foreign investors. As the BITs proliferated, the World Bank and its presidency sought to institutionalize the burden of becoming involved in these investment disputes. The World Bank finances the cost of the ICSID Secretariat, but the parties to ICSID proceedings fund the cost of these proceedings through a fee system (e.g., $25,000 for an arbitration proceeding).

TREATY SHOPPING WITHIN THE BILATERAL INVESTMENT TREATY CONTEXT

Relatively few BITs include tax-oriented investment provisions. In addition, relatively few BITs having such tax provisions include a treaty shopping limitation. Consider Article 22(2) of the Agreement between the Government of the Republic of Korea and the Government of Japan for the Liberalisation, Promotion and Protection of Investment, signed at Seoul on March 22, 2002, and entered into force on January 1, 2003. The treaty applies a limited treaty shopping provisions, not limited to tax considerations.

Article 22(1) extends the scope of the BIT treaty to local governments within that jurisdiction. Article 22(1) provides, as a general matter, that, each party, in fulfilling the obligations under this agreement, is to take reasonable measures as may be necessary and as may be available to it to ensure the obligations of local governments in its territory.

Article 22(2) itself provides the treaty shopping limitations:

> Each Contracting Party to the Agreement between the Government of the Republic of Korea and the Government of Japan for the Liberalisation, Promotion and Protection of Investment reserves the right to deny the benefits of this Agreement to an investor of the other Contracting Party under specified circumstances.

Article 22(2) limits the scope of this treaty shopping to a legal person or any other entity referred to in Article 1(1)(b). Article 1(1)(b) refers to a legal person or to any other entity constituted or organized under the applicable laws and regulations of that contracting state. Such an entity includes an entity, whether for profit or not, and whether private or government owned or controlled. Such an entity includes a company, corporation, trust, partnership, sole proprietorship, joint venture, association, or organization.

The treaty, in two circumstances, would deny to the investor the benefits of the treaty if the investors of any third country own or control that investor of that other contracting party:

1. The denying contracting party does not maintain normal economic relations with the third party.
2. The investor of that contracting party has no substantial business operations in the territory of that other contracting party under whose laws it is constituted or organized.

Note that Article 22(2) fails to define "own" or "control." The treaty shopping provision, for example, would preclude alien countries such as North Korea from taking advantage of the South Korea–Japan BIT.

Article 22(2) of the agreement enforces a "most favored nation" clause regarding investment and business activities. Each contracting party in its territory is to accord investors of the contacting party and to their investments treatment no less favorable than the treatment it accords in like circumstances to investors of any third country and to their investments. Article 22(3) provides that the most favored nation provisions of Article 22(2) are not to be construed so as to extend to investors of the other contracting party and their investments any preferential treatment resulting from its membership in a free trade area, a customs union, an agreement for economic integration, or a similar international agreement.

TAX PROVISIONS WITHIN THE KOREA–JAPAN BILATERAL INVESTMENT TREATY

Article 19(1) provides that nothing in the agreement is to apply to taxation matters except as expressly provided in paragraphs 2, 3, and 4 of the article. Paragraphs 2, 3, and 4 enumerate nine articles in the agreement to which the tax matters do apply for purposes of the agreement. Note that these nine articles contain both procedural and substantive provisions.

Article 19(2) provides that Articles 1, 3, 7, 10, 22, and 23 apply to taxation matters:

- Article 1 is a definitional section, addressing the terms:
  1. "Investor"
  2. "Investment"
  3. "UNCITRAL Arbitration Rules"
  4. "ICSID Convention"
  5. "Centre" in reference to ICSID
  6. "Territory" as to contracting party
  7. "Contracting Party"

  Article 19(2), then, appears to limit the scope of the tax provisions to (1) the term "investor" and to (2) the term "investment" as to the substantive subject matter under review, including tax matters. Article 19(2) then applies to paragraphs (3) through (7) as to procedural issues under review, including tax matters.
- Article 3 provides for the procedural issues that impact national treatment. It provides investors of the other contracting party treatment that is "no less favorable" to the treatment the contracting party accords in like circumstances to its own investors, or investors of any third country, as to access to the courts of justice and to administrative tribunals. Article 19(2) extends this Article 3 national treatment provision to tax matters.
- Article 7 provides for transparency as to the publication of the contracting party's laws, regulations, and judicial decisions of general application as well as international agreements that pertain to or affect investment and business activities. Article 19(2) extends this Article 7 transparency provision to tax matters.
- Article 10 provides for fair and equitable treatment, full and constant protection and security, and limits the potential for expropriation. Article 19(2) extends this Article 10 expropriation provision to tax matters. As international tax practitioners, we take the position that the expropriation would have equal tax impact in situations in which a contracting party undertakes an expropriation of property belonging to the other contracting party.
- Article 22 provides for treaty shopping, not only in the tax context but other nontax situations as well. Article 19(2) explicitly extends this Article 22 treaty shopping provision to tax matters.
- Article 23 provides for the effective date of the Korean–Japan Agreement. Article 19(2) extends this Article 23 effective date provision to tax matters.

Article 19(3) provides that Article 14 and Article 15 apply to disputes under Article 19(2). Article 19(1) makes clear that Article 19(3) applies to tax matters under dispute.

Article 14 addresses disputes between the contracting parties themselves (i.e., situations in which the investor or the investment are not involved). Article 14 provides for the use of an arbitral tribunal to resolve such dispute, providing for application of the UNCITRAL Arbitration Rules unless the contracting parties agree otherwise. Article 19(3) provides that such a dispute includes tax matters as to Articles 1, 3, 7, 10, 20, and 23.

Article 15 addresses disputes between a contracting party and an investor of the other contracting party as to investment disputes. Article 15 provides three methods for resolving investment disputes:

1. The ICSID Convention Centre, pursuant to Article 15(3)(a)
2. The UNCITRAL Arbitration Rules, pursuant to Article 15(3)(b)
3. Any other arbitration institution or in accordance with any other arbitration rules if both parties to the dispute agree

Article 19(3) provides that such a dispute between a contracting party and an investor of the other contracting party as to investment disputes includes tax matters as to Articles 1, 3, 7, 10, 20, and 23.

Article 19(4) provides that Article 20 is to apply to taxation measures as to the matters set out in Article 19(2) (i.e., Articles 1, 3, 7, 10, 20, and 23) concerning the application of a Joint Committee representing Japan and Korea in implementing the agreement.

CHAPTER THIRTY-EIGHT

38

China–Taiwan Trade

ONCE FORBIDDEN, trade between Taiwan and mainland China (PRC) is becoming increasingly important for both countries, particularly for the smaller power, Taiwan. Multinational enterprises from either side of the Taiwan Strait face increasing risks of double taxation because both sides lack the administrative mechanisms that would otherwise preclude such anti–double taxation. More and more, transfer pricing is becoming a conflict mechanism between these two sides.

TAIWAN AND CHINA: A HISTORY LESSON

Sixty years have passed since the end of the Chinese Civil War and the promulgation of the Cross-Straits Economic Cooperation Framework Agreement (ECFA or Framework Agreement; governmental delegates signed that pact at the end of June 2010). The ECFA or framework agreement is a preferential trade agreement between the governments of the People's Republic of China (PRC) and the Republic of China (Taiwan). The ECFA curtails tariffs and commercial barriers between both sides. Multinational enterprises are increasing cross-straits trade as both sides implement the ECFA.

Many businesses that engage in cross-straits trade are related enterprises (i.e., businesses that have facilities in both the PRC and Taiwan). As such, transfer pricing is a frequent issue between parties on both sides of the strait. For historical reasons, there remains a strong well of opposition to cross-strait trade. All too often, economic nationalism affects the positions of the parties. Nevertheless, the ECFA fails to address transfer pricing issues that enterprises on both sides of the strait are facing. The ultimate objective that remains from a conflict resolution standpoint is for the two taxing jurisdictions to establish viable mechanisms that would enable the governments to allocate the combined profits of entities that are doing business in both jurisdictions.

Over the past 60 years, conflicts between the PRC and Taiwan lurked between impending war and combined economic growth. Limited military conflicts, tensions, and the instability of the cross-strait relationship was often the norm. The PRC and Taiwan, as nation-states, do not provide official recognition to each other. This lack of recognition makes agreements between these governments circuitous and convoluted.

ECONOMIC CONSIDERATIONS

Many international business executives view Taiwan as being the world's electronics powerhouse. Taiwan is known for many facets of electronics, including integrated circuits, broadband, personal computers, notebooks, motherboards, graphics cards, semiconductor foundry processes, mobile phones, cellphones, opto-electronics, LCD panels, and photovoltaic processes that convert solar energy into electricity. In addition, Taiwan manufactures biotechnology and nanotechnology products and, quite separately, manufactures bicycles and other products.

Trade with the PRC is a much greater percentage of Taiwanese sales than is the percentage of Chinese sales. As the growth continues between Taiwan and the PRC, trade with China provides a major favorable input to the Taiwanese economy. Nationalists in Taiwan view this trade with alarm, suggesting that this trade would make Taiwan more economically dependent on China. In contrast, trade with Taiwan remains relatively insignificant to China from a policy perspective. Data from the *2011 CIA World Factbook* illustrates the parameters:

	China	Taiwan
Gross domestic product	10,090 (billion USD)	822 (billion USD)
Worldwide ranking	3 (2010)	19 (2010)
GDP growth—2010	10.3%	10.8%
GDP growth—2009	9.2%	1.9%
GDP per capita	7,600 USD	35,700 USD

ONE-CHINA POLICY

Both the PRC and Taiwan have adopted a one-China policy. Either or both countries have insisted on this one-China policy from time to time. As a result of this one-China policy, both governments compete to have the world view them as being the one and only legitimate government of China. Each government objects to the use of terms such as "China–Taiwan relations" or to "PRC–ROC relations," as these terms imply the existence of a two-state solution.

Since each government does not recognize the other, the governments on both sides of the strait relate to each other only through unofficial nongovernmental, semi-official exchanges. At the present time, the PRC seeks to integrate Taiwan within its operations. It is our view that the PRC might be looking forward to there being a Taiwan Special Administrative Region (SAR) analogous to the current structure in Hong Kong and in Macao.

As part of this one-China policy, the government of the PRC has been using its influence on neighboring countries to prevent these neighbors from signing free trade agreements with Taiwan. However, to a large extent, the PRC has permitted Taiwan to piggyback its trading relationships with the PRC as East Asia moves toward economic integration. An important input to this economic integration process is the Association of South East Asian Nations (ASEAN) agreement. ASEAN members include Indonesia, Singapore, Malaysia, Brunei, the Philippines, Thailand, Burma, Vietnam, Cambodia, and Laos.

The ASEAN group plans to extend this economic integration to include China at a later date. As a result of this expansion, the ASEAN–China agreement would exclude Taiwan unless Taiwan wants to receive and accept piggyback status from China. The Taiwanese government acknowledges that the one-China policy would put Taiwan in a deleterious position with the ASEAN–China agreement but for the signing of the ECFA.

ECONOMIC COOPERATION FRAMEWORK AGREEMENT

The parties to the Cross-Straits Economic Cooperation Framework Agreement are:

- The Straits Exchange Foundation (SEF), representing the government of Taiwan.
- The Association for Relations Across the Taiwan Straits (ARATS) representing mainland China.

The détente between the PRC and Taiwan began in 2008. Since that time, SEF and ARATS have signed 15 agreements on behalf of their respective governments. The most recent of these agreements is the Cross-Strait Agreement on Intellectual Property Rights Protection and Cooperation. The PRC and Taiwan are planning more arrangements following the implementation of the ECFA. SEF and ARATS are planning to reach an arrangement for cross-strait medical cooperation, for pharmaceutical cooperation, and for health cooperation. In addition, SEF and ARATS are planning to implement an investment protection agreement.

The ECFA, after establishing its objectives and cooperation measures, addresses trade and investment issues, including trade in goods, trade in services, and investment activities. The ECFA establishes the facets of economic cooperation, including economic cooperation itself. The ECFA addresses the "early harvest" program for trade in goods and trade in services, which benefit small and medium-size providers in particular. The program enables accounting firms and financial institutions to set up operations cross-border. Both countries reduce tariffs applicable to the other country.

A number of important groups in Taiwan have opposed the ECFA. The opposition asserts that the ECFA would cause deleterious changes in Taiwan and would:

- Reduce manufacturing jobs in Taiwan
- Reduce the average salary in Taiwan
- Create a brain drain for Taiwan's management and technology expertise

Further, the ECFA opponents argue that the ECFA would lead to an influx of mainland Chinese white-collar workers and professionals in Taiwan, and that influx could adversely impact job security for the Taiwanese.

The current détente between the PRC and Taiwan has brought about extensive trade, flows of tourists, and cross-investment. Nevertheless, cross-state businesses are taking advantage of labor-rate differentials and market availability. Wage rates are substantially higher in Taiwan than in China. Taiwanese businesses are seeking a larger share of the Chinese market.

TAX CONSIDERATIONS

The Taiwanese government views cross-straits businesses as having three dynamics:

1. Historically, developmental activities, including research and development (R&D), initially took place in Taiwan. However, these developmental activities, including R&D activities, are becoming more important in the PRC.
2. Manufacturing activities increasingly taking place in the PRC.
3. Distribution activities typically take place throughout the world, not necessarily limited to Taiwan or to the PRC.

The Taiwanese government, aware of these transfer pricing issues, asked us to develop transfer pricing parameters that would allocate more profit to the multinational enterprise located in Taiwan and, by extension, would allocate more profit to the Taiwanese. In the interest of fair disclosure, Robert Feinschreiber met with Chinese officials initially in December 1992, at various cities in China at the request of China and the United Nations, to facilitate China's economic growth.

- The Taiwanese government asked us to examine both developmental activities and manufacturing activities.
- We were to focus on the transactional profit split method, which we had suggested to the Taiwanese government as a viable transfer pricing method 14 months earlier.
- The Taiwanese government asked us to ignore distribution functions of businesses. The Taiwanese government took the approach that existing applications

of transactional net margin method (TNMM) are sufficient as to these distribution activities.
- The Taiwanese government asked us to focus on transfer pricing issues facing the electronics industry.

During the current détente, which began in 2008, trade with the PRC has become an increasing share of Taiwan's international trade activities. The PRC is now Taiwan's most significant trading partner. In light of these facts, the Taiwanese government asked us to specifically address trade with the PRC and production activities when we addressed these transfer pricing concerns.

Both the PRC and Taiwan accept the Organisation of Economic Co-operation and Development (OECD) transfer pricing principles. It is our view that, while lurking transfer pricing issues will remain, the fact that each government is willing to abide by OECD transfer pricing principles will go a long way in conflict resolution.

In a larger sense, both the PRC and Taiwan want to make sure that they receive their "fair share" of the operating profits that the cross-strait company receives. The issue is, then, to determine each country's fair share of these profits. We will demonstrate that both the PRC and Taiwan can achieve many of these fair share objectives by applying the OECD's transfer pricing provisions, but we caution that the transfer pricing provisions are not always a cure-all. Nevertheless, transfer pricing mechanisms provide a range of disputes between these two governments. These transfer pricing mechanisms, even without the advance pricing arrangement (APA) process and the mutual agreement procedures (MAPs), might provide a narrower area of dispute than the countries would otherwise expect.

This conflict resolution process is not perfect—the cross-straits company might be subject to some degree of double taxation or might find itself with a tax gap. This conflict resolution approach is limited because the two governments do not recognize each other. As we shall see, intended tax-oriented remedies, such as bilateral APAs and MAPs, do not present a viable solution given the nature of the governmental institutions.

CHOICE OF TRANSFER PRICING METHOD

The OECD guidelines would have the multinational enterprise or the tax administration, when viewing transfer pricing methods, rely on one-sided transfer pricing methods or, alternatively, on two-sided transfer pricing methods. The choice between these transfer pricing methods depends on the applicable facts and circumstances.

- A one-sided transfer pricing method looks to one party as being the tested party.
- A two-sided transfer pricing method looks to testing both parties together.

Given these facts, it might be appropriate for Taiwanese multinational enterprises to consider applying a two-sided transfer pricing method, such as the transactional profit split method, to limit the exposure to double taxation.

FUNCTIONAL ANALYSIS

Taiwanese electronics manufacturers, for the most part, are highly developed, sophisticated, and highly integrated operations. These electronics manufacturers are part of a production chain that ultimately brings the electronic goods to market. Nevertheless, each such manufacturer produces items or parts that, for the most part, have no established market. In essence, such a manufacturer is producing work-in-process inventory items.

The production process for these Taiwanese manufacturers is often this:

- The Taiwanese manufacturer develops product technology that will ultimately lead to the ultimate sale of the electronic product to the ultimate consumer.
- The Taiwanese manufacturer purchases electronic parts for its manufacturing process from other unrelated electronics manufacturers in the production chain.
- The Taiwanese manufacturer adds value to the product.
- The Taiwanese manufacturer exercises quality control over the manufacturing process.
- The Taiwanese manufacturer completes its production activities before these products ultimately reach the consumer.

The production process for a Taiwanese manufacturer having PRC operations is often this:

- The Taiwanese manufacturer develops product technology that will ultimately lead to the ultimate sale of the electronic product to the ultimate consumer.
- The Taiwanese manufacturer, having this product technology, hires its related party in the PRC to produce the product en masse to the marketplace.
- The Chinese manufacturer adds value to the product.
- The Taiwanese exercise quality control over the manufacturing process in the PRC.
- The Chinese manufacturer completes the production activities before these products ultimately reach the consumer.

ANALYSIS OF THE PRODUCTION ACTIVITIES

A one-sided transfer pricing method would not be appropriate[1] to these production activities as the electronics production is part of the integrated production of highly specialized goods.[2] As such, the multinational enterprise or the tax administration would determine that a two-sided transfer pricing method (i.e., the transactional profit split method, would be the enterprise's "most appropriate" transfer pricing method).[3]

The Taiwanese manufacturer might sell its work-in-process inventories to more than one manufacturer, where one of these parties is not a related party. The presence of such an in-house comparable could provide a ready comparable. Although the ROC Tax Agency is acutely aware of such transactions taking place, our fact pattern is otherwise.

The multinational enterprise would apply a different approach to the distribution function. Once the manufacturer completed its production function, the enterprise can better address the distribution function in terms of the resale transfer pricing method, or by applying the TNMM method in lieu of the resale transfer pricing method, as analysis of the distribution now takes precedence.

Our analysis presupposes that the contract between the Taiwanese party and the PRC manufacturer does not constitute contract manufacturing or contract service activities, or otherwise create simple functions that would cause the multinational enterprise or the tax administration to apply a one-sided transfer pricing method.[4]

FACT PATTERN

The next example illustrates an operation of a long-standing Taiwanese electronics enterprise that shifts its manufacturing operations to the PRC. The Taiwanese enterprise made this shift because of the comparatively high cost of manufacturing labor in Taiwan, as it had found that it no longer was economical for the business to undertake its basic electronics manufacturing operations in Taiwan. The enterprise has retained its high-value research operations in Taiwan.

The Taiwanese operation has personnel that evaluates the company's market strategy and orders raw materials and components for further manufacturing. The Taiwanese operation directs order processing operations. In contrast, the Chinese operations develop the production flow and handle the specific manufacturing operations.

The Chinese operation sends the finished electronic products to the offshore distributors. Some of the distributors are related parties. The Chinese operation takes title to the electronic products freight on board (f.o.b.) Taipei. The distributors sell to ultimate customers located in various locations throughout the world. The Taiwanese–Chinese multinational enterprise does not advertise; the distributors handle the marketing efforts. The Chinese operation, by selling in bulk, then bills, insures, and arranges for transportation of the products. The Taiwanese operation takes on the responsibility for damaged goods and for risk of loss.

The Taiwanese operation had established initial customer relationships with the distributors, and the Taiwanese operations continue this relationship. The customers obtain their own credit lines to purchase the electronic products. The Taiwanese operation and the Chinese operation are independent of the customers' financial activities. The Chinese operation sells the electronic products f.o.b. plant.

ACCOUNTING AND TAX OPERATIONS

Both the Taiwanese operations and the Chinese operations provide extensive comparable data to each other. Taiwan and the PRC have different accounting systems, but the enterprise expects that both governments will ultimately be able to harmonize the two accounting systems.[5] The Chinese operations reflect the Chinese documentation forms,[6] and the Chinese operations provide this information to the Taiwanese operations. The Taiwanese operations provide to the Chinese operations the transfer pricing report that it had furnished to the ROC's Tax Agency.[7]

Taiwanese operations and the PRC operations have effectuated a perpetual goods-until-canceled cost plus contract. The multinational enterprise and the tax administration are in the process of evaluating the transfer pricing arrangement.

PERMANENT ESTABLISHMENT

The Taiwan operation and the Chinese operation satisfy themselves that their cross-strait activities do not constitute a permanent establishment:

- The Taiwanese operation sends different personnel on occasion to the Chinese operations.
- The Chinese operation sends engineers to Taiwan periodically to review technological updates.

TAIWANESE–CHINESE ELECTRONICS COMPANY

The next example illustrates the Taiwanese activities and the Chinese activities from a comparative standpoint.

	Taiwanese Activities	Chinese Activities	Combined Activities
Assets			
Machinery	1,600,000	2,400,000	4,000,000
Building	300,000	900,000	1,200,000
Land	100,000	200,000	300,000
Other assets—molds	0	500,000	500,000
Total assets	2,000,000	4,000,000	6,000,000
Employee Costs			
R&D	2,400,000	0	2,400,000
Engineering costs	250,000	800,000	1,050,000
Production costs	0	4,000,000	4,000,000
Other costs	350,000	200,000	550,000
Total costs	3,000,000	5,000,000	8,000,000
Personnel Count			
Number of people—R&D	80	0	80
Number of people—engineering	10	40	50
Number of people—production	0	800	800
Number of people—other facets	10	60	70
Total number of people	100	900	1,000

TRANSACTIONAL PROFIT SPLIT METHOD CRITERIA

The OECD guidelines would apply the transactional profit split method in situations in which a multinational enterprise meets one of these five criteria:

1. Creates the integrated production of highly specialized goods[8]
2. Makes unique and valuable products[9]
3. Creates unique intangibles[10]
4. Provides specialized services[11]
5. Participates in the global trading of financial instruments[12]

In the context of the trade of electronics between Taiwan and China, the first category, the creation of the integrated production of highly specialized goods, would provide the rationale for applying the transactional profit split method.

MOST APPROPRIATE TRANSFER PRICING METHOD

The guidelines would have the multinational enterprise or the tax administration apply the "most appropriate" transfer pricing method.[13] Following the concept of the "most appropriate" transfer pricing method, it appears that the multinational enterprise or the tax administration would select an allocation key that is the most appropriate allocation key. The guidelines, however, are silent in addressing the appropriateness of a selected allocation key within the transactional profit split method.

ALLOCATION KEY SYSTEM

The OECD guidelines provide that the multinational enterprise or the tax administrations can put forth four types of allocation keys:[14]

1. Allocation keys based on revenue generated
2. Allocation keys based on assets or capital—operating assets, fixed assets, intangible assets, or capital employed
3. Allocation keys based on costs—relative spending, investment in key areas, R&D, engineering, or marketing
4. Other allocation keys—incremental sales, headcounts (number of individuals involved in the "key functions that generate value" to the transaction), time spent by a certain group of employees, number of servers, data storage, or floor area of retail points

Based on the facts presented, the multinational enterprise and the tax administration should be in the process of developing allocation keys pertaining to the creation of the integrated production of highly specialized goods.

STRONG CORRELATION STANDARD

The OECD guidelines impose a "strong correlation" standard to the multinational enterprise and to the tax administration in selecting the allocation key.[15] We have covered this issue elsewhere. The guidelines fail to define the "strong correlation" standard itself.

- The guidelines apply the strong correlation standard between the tangible assets, the intangible assets, or the capital employed as to these assets or capital and the "creation of value"[16] in the asset-based allocation key context.
- The guidelines apply the strong correlation standard to relative expenses and to relative value added in the cost-based allocation key context.[17]

We anticipate that vagaries in applying the allocation key analysis will continue because the OECD guidelines fail to define the terms "strong correlation," "creation of value," and "relative value added."

SELECTING AMONG ALLOCATION KEYS

The database provides these allocation keys:

Assets	Taiwan	China
Machinery	40%	60%
Building	25%	75%
Land	33%	67%
Other assets—molds	0%	100%
Total assets	33%	67%

In this instance, it is our view that none of these allocation keys meets the strong correlation standard: the machinery allocation key, the building allocation key, the land allocation key, nor the other asset allocation key. The presence or absence of a portion of the machinery, building, land, other assets, or total assets, standing alone, appears to not affect the "creation of value" to the enterprise. As such, the asset base in China and asset base in Taiwan would then not play a role in developing the allocation key.

Now we consider the possibility of incurring employee costs as an allocation key:

Employee Costs	Taiwan	China
R&D	100%	0%
Engineering costs	24%	76%
Production costs	0%	100%
Other costs	64%	36%
Total costs	37%	63%

In this instance, the presence of employee costs correlates the relative value of these expenditures to relative added costs of these activities. The multinational enterprise would allocate these amounts based on cost-based allocation activities. Nevertheless, it appears that the multinational enterprise or the tax administration would not have a sufficient basis to exclude some employee personnel costs in favor of other employee personnel costs. We conclude that the total employee allocation key appears to be a strong correlation based on the facts at hand. That allocation would allocate 37% of the total combined income to Taiwan and would allocate 63% of the combined income to the PRC.

Now we turn our attention to applying the personnel count as an allocation key:

Personnel Count	Taiwan	China
Number of people—R&D	100%	10%
Number of people—engineering	20%	80%
Number of people—production	0%	100%
Number of people—other facets	14%	86%
Total number of people	10%	90%

In this instance, personnel counts appear to be a potentially valid "other allocation" key. The OECD guidelines specifically enumerate headcounts (i.e., the number of individuals involved in the "key functions that generate value" to the transaction as an allocation key). The key functions in this instance would be R&D, engineering, and production and possibly might include other activities as well. As a result, the total number of employees in the enterprise could well serve as an allocation key, allocating 10% of the total combined income to Taiwan and allocating 90% of the combined income to China.

The multinational enterprise in the PRC and in Taiwan, together with the tax administrations in both jurisdictions, could potentially view the allocation of the combined income as being:

Allocation Key Alternatives	Taiwan	China
Employee cost allocation key	37%	63%
Headcount allocation key	10%	90%

The Taiwanese tax authorities in this instance are likely to insist on taking 37% of the enterprise's taxable income. The enterprise in this circumstance would face extensive double taxation (37% of the combined income from Taiwan plus 90% of the combined income from China, or 127% of the combined income from both Taiwan and China) if China forces its tax position based on headcount or on applying a similar transfer pricing approach.

Most multinational enterprises, whether China based or Taiwan based, view China as being the more forceful of the two trading partners. The Taiwanese tax authorities face a dilemma: acceding to China's allocation key approach or subjecting multinational enterprises within its purview to double taxation. As this issue unfolds, we can expect pushback by the Taiwanese tax authorities, putting the onus of double taxation on the multinational enterprises themselves. As we shall see, the bilateral APA process is a much less than ideal solution.

APA PROCESS

The APA process presupposes that the contracting party has a mutual tax agreement with the contracting party's treaty partner. Thus, the OECD guidelines would apply Article 25 of the OECD Model Tax Convention for this purpose.[18] The question then becomes how Taiwanese companies and, to a lesser extent, Chinese companies cope with double taxation risks in light of the fact that China and Taiwan do not have a mutual tax agreement and, for that matter, do not recognize each other diplomatically.

The bilateral APA process requires a minimum of four stakeholders: both tax administrations and each associated multinational enterprise. The APA process might well become confrontive between a tax administration and its multinational enterprise, but the confrontive nature between two nation-states in the APA process is a different matter entirely. The multinational enterprise in such a situation is well advised to have separate tax counsel from its counterpart.

WantChinaTimes.com (Knowing China through Taiwan) reported on September 8, 2011, that Procter & Gamble (P&G) signed on September 8 a trilateral APA with Taiwan's Ministry of Finance and with Singapore's tax authority. Similar to other APAs, the purpose of this APA is for P&G to avoid paying cross-border taxes twice. The author of this piece, Wang Shin-Ren, reports that the conclusion of the APA may lead to "other international companies doing business with Taiwan and negotiating similar pacts." Whether this approach will see the end of Taiwan's diplomatic isolation remains to be seen.

SEF and ARATS are not now well positioned to represent specific multinational enterprises in the APA process. Nevertheless, as Taiwanese–China relations continue to improve, SEF and ARATS are likely to attune themselves to tax considerations.

NOTES

1. OECD, *Transfer Pricing Guidelines for Multinational Enterprises and Tax Administrations* (July 22, 2010), 2.109.
2. Guideline 1.9.
3. Guideline 2.2.
4. Guideline 2.109.
5. Guideline 2.126.
6. R. Feinschreiber and M. Kent, "Reporting Related-Party Transactions in China," *Corporate Business Taxation Monthly* (July 2009): 37.

7. R. Feinschreiber and M. Kent, "Taiwan's Transfer Pricing System," *Corporate Business Taxation Monthly* (July 2009): 33.
8. Guideline 1.9.
9. Guideline 2.109.
10. Guideline 1.9; Guideline 2.109.
11. Guideline 1.9.
12. Guideline 2.10.9
13. Guideline 2.2.
14. Guideline 2.135.
15. Guideline 2.135.
16. Guideline 2.136.
17. Guideline 2.138.
18. Guideline 4.139.

CHAPTER THIRTY-NINE

Malaysia–Singapore Allocation Keys

THE ORGANISATION of Economic Co-operation and Development (OECD), through its *Transfer Pricing Guidelines for Multinational Enterprises and Tax Administrations*, would have the multinational enterprises (MNEs) and tax administrations select the "most appropriate" transfer pricing method.[1] The multinational enterprise or the tax administration, in seeking to apply this most appropriate transfer pricing method, might apply the transactional profit split method,[2] and then would seek to apply the "most appropriate" allocation key.[3] The reader should be aware of the fact that there may be more than one viable and appropriate allocation key. The OECD does not assert that transfer pricing is an exact science.

IMPORTANCE OF ALLOCATION KEYS

The TransferPricingConsortium.com and the Inland Revenue Board of Malaysia,[4] through its Tax Academy, joint-ventured a two-day transfer pricing presentation to update tax agents with transfer pricing techniques.[5] These sessions took place on September 19 through 20, 2011, in Malaysia. A significant portion of the presentation and a question-and-answer session addressed the development of transfer pricing allocation keys, as reflected within section 2.134 through section 2.149 of the July 2010 OECD guidelines.

As part of this transfer pricing presentation, counselors Robert Feinschreiber and Margaret Kent provided an example of a small condominium residential leasing company in Malaysia and Singapore. This example illustrates how MNEs and tax administrations might apply the transactional profit split method and apply alternative allocation keys. The analysis reflects an elaboration of an example presented in the Malaysia Tax Academy with the Malaysian tax authorities. The example illustrates that the tax administration can expend less professional time and can earn a substantially greater income stream by applying allocation keys to the transactional profit split method.

SELECTION OF THE REAL ESTATE LEASING EXAMPLE

Feinschreiber and Kent selected the real estate rental leasing example for the Malaysian tax authorities for these reasons:

- The enterprise in this fact pattern has no significant tangible assets. As a result, the MNE or the tax administration, in selecting an allocation key, could well exclude tangible asset configurations.
- The enterprise in this fact pattern has no significant intangible assets. This lack of intangible assets enables the MNE or the tax administration to exclude intangible asset configurations.
- There is no viable comparable data for that real estate leasing enterprise, given its own specifics. For this reason, the MNE or the tax administration would find the transactional net margin method (TNMM) difficult to apply.
- The presence of internal accounting data would facilitate the MNE or the tax administration's application of the transactional profit split method.
- The enterprise provides extensive data for its internal operations, through its internal data, from its balance sheets and its income statements.[6]
- The enterprise earns its operating income through the presence of specialized services, the listing of residential condominium property, and the leasing of condominium property.
- These activities meet the requirements for a MNE or the tax administration to apply the transactional profit split method.[7]

WHEN THE TRANSACTIONAL PROFIT SPLIT METHOD IS THE "MOST APPLICABLE" TRANSFER PRICING METHOD

The OECD guidelines specifically direct us to the transactional profit split method in situations in which a MNE meets one of these five criteria:

1. Creates the integrated production of highly specialized goods[8]
2. Makes unique and valuable products[9]

3. Creates unique intangibles[10]
4. Provides specialized services[11]
5. Participates in the global trading of financial instruments[12]

A business can apply the transactional profit split method in situations in which the MNE:

- Creates and utilizes significant synergies
- Undertakes the integrated production of highly specialized goods
- Incurs extensive research and development (R&D) activities
- Incurs significant expenditures for its intangibles
- Participates in one or more cost contribution arrangements[13]
- Creates or provides specialized services

SPECIALIZED SERVICES

Services are "specialized" if the providers of these services require both training and expertise. That is a dictionary definition of the term "specialized services," but there is an additional specialized services facet when addressing these specialized services for tax purposes. Here the OECD guidelines mean "specialized services" as being in contradiction to the words "ordinary" and "mundane services," but the guidelines also mean that "specialized services" are the opposite of "subsidiary or incidental" services. Consider the next illustrations.

When a tax administration is examining an international real estate brokerage, the tax administration might view the listing and selling (or leasing) operations of the international real estate brokerage as a performance of a specialized service (i.e., the real estate listing agents and selling agents are the crux of the real estate business). The international real estate brokerage might need various types of service assistance, including, for example, accounting assistance. Such a tax administration might treat accounting services undertaken for the international real estate brokerage as being secondary to the international real estate brokerage activities.

Correspondingly, in a different fact pattern, the tax administration might examine an accounting firm. The tax administration might view the providing of accounting service as the performance of a specialized service in this particular instance. The accounting firm in that scenario might need secondary assistance to expand its accounting offices. Such a tax administration might treat the real estate activities that the accounting firm undertakes—such as negotiating leaseholds for the accounting firm—as being secondary to the accounting agency's prime function.

The differentiation between specialized services and subsidiary services is an important one, regardless of how the tax administration categorizes specialized services for a particular industry. The tax administration is likely to peg the taxes that the international real estate brokerage might pay based on the performance of the specialized service the real estate brokerage provides (i.e., the listing, leases, or selling the real property) based on the success of the brokers and dealers in the real estate brokerage. In contrast, the tax administration might treat services performed by other than such nonspecialized personnel as being costs or expenses that the international real estate brokerage incurs.

Tax administrations normally treat the intercompany transactions of nonspecialized personnel as being determined as part of the cost that the enterprise actually incurred. The tax administrations normally would not insist on any add-ons (such as overhead or profits) for incurring such non-specialized services costs. In contrast, tax administrations normally would insist on including add-ons for primary, specialized services costs, as being profit centers.

The next step in determining the tax allocation is for the tax administration or the international real estate brokerage to aggregate the entire income of the entire business for all of its relevant transactions.[14] The international real estate brokerage or the tax administration might aggregate these income amounts by applying harmonized tax accounting standards (i.e., by using the International Financial Reporting Standards) making this determination across all jurisdictions in which the enterprise performs these specialized services.

The final step in determining the tax allocation is for each tax administration, or the international real estate brokerage as a group, to allocate the worldwide operations in that jurisdiction.[15] The international tax brokerage or the tax administration might apply a formula or develop allocation keys. The transactional profit split method does not entirely eliminate the risk of double taxation because the tax administrations in each location might select differing—and conflicting—allocation keys.[16]

APPLYING THE TRANSACTIONAL PROFIT SPLIT METHOD

The MNE or the tax administration's application of the transactional profit split method presupposes that there are no true comparables.[17] The OECD guidelines recognize that the transactional profit split method enables the taxpayer to take into account the associated enterprise's specific and possibly unique facts and circumstances that are not present in independent enterprises.[18] Nevertheless, the OECD views the transactional profit split method as being an arm's length approach, treating the transactional profit split method as reflecting what independent enterprises would have done if faced with the same circumstances.[19]

The OECD requires the taxpayer to evaluate each party to the transaction when the taxpayer applies the transactional profit split method rather than looking at each tested party alone. The OECD views this two-sided or multisided valuation in a positive light because it will be less likely that either party to the controlled transaction will be left with an "extreme and improbable result."[20] The OECD guidelines view the dual or multisided analysis as being particularly important for a taxpayer when analyzing the contributions of the associated enterprises as to the intangible property that the associated enterprise employs in the controlled transactions.[21]

The OECD visualizes the transactional profit split method as operating in this manner:[22]

- The transactional profit split method first identifies the combined profits. The combined profits are the profits of the associated enterprises that the taxpayer is to split. The source of this combined income is the total income from the controlled transactions in which the associated enterprises are engaged.
- The transactional profit split method then splits those combined profits between the associated enterprises "on an economically valid basis." The split of the profits is to approximate the division of profits that the associated enterprises would have anticipated. The associated enterprises are to reflect the split of the profits made at arm's length.

FOUR ALLOCATION KEYS CATEGORIES

The next step in the transfer pricing process is to select potential allocation keys from the four allocation categories: allocation keys based on revenue, allocation keys based on assets or capital, allocation keys based on costs, and other allocation keys. The OECD guidelines implicitly define an allocation key as a basis on which the MNE or the tax administration can allocate operating income. The OECD guidelines provide for four types of allocation keys:[23]

1. Allocation keys based on revenue generated.
2. Allocation keys based on assets or capital. Such allocation keys could include operating assets, fixed assets, intangible assets, or capital employed.
3. Allocation keys based on costs. Such allocation keys could include relative spending, investment in key areas, R&D, engineering, or marketing.
4. Other allocation keys. Such allocation keys could include incremental sales, headcounts (number of individuals involved in the "key functions that generate value" to the transaction), time spent by a certain group of employees if there is a "strong correlation" between the time spent and the creation of combined profits, number of servers, data storage, floor area of retail points, and so forth, as appropriate, depending on the facts and circumstances of the transactions.

KEY FUNCTIONS

The OECD contemplates that the MNE or the tax administration will first determine which activities of business are "key functions" in developing the allocation key process. Functions are "key" if these functions are the essential functions of the business and generate value to this business. A functional analysis is crucial in determining which functions of the business are key.

As transfer pricing practitioners, we view "key functions that generate value" as those functions that address the integrated production of highly specialized goods, that create unique intangibles, that provide specialized services, or that participate in the global trading of financial instruments. We view the term "strong correlation" standard within the transactional profit split method as indicating causality (i.e., as effort that the enterprise expends to achieve a specified result). It might be appropriate for the MNE or the tax administration to view this "strong correlation" concept in "but for" terms. Thus, a specific activity provides a key function to the business because, without the presence of this function, the business would not generate its combined operating profits.[24]

SELECTING POTENTIAL ALLOCATION KEYS

International real estate brokerages are at the cusp of a rapidly growing multinational services industry. At the heart of this services industry, international real estate brokerages are providing "specialized services" to a myriad of clients, performing these specialized services in various locations across the world. By the term "international real estate brokerage," we mean a real estate enterprise having real estate operations in more than one country, serving as a broker or as an agent for the purpose of buying, leasing, or selling real estate for their clients in more than one country. The term "specialized services" is an important one for tax purposes, as this term determines the applicable tax category —treating this service as a profit center or as a cost.

The selection of the "most appropriate" allocation key should normally depend on the MNE and each tax administration being willing to develop harmonized tax accounting standards.[25] We assume in this example that the MNE and each tax administration have access to this harmonized accounting. One of the early steps in the audit process is for a tax administration to review financial data to make sure that the taxpayer harmonized the accounting data or, separately, harmonized the accounting results if the taxpayer fails to harmonize the data.[26]

RESIDENTIAL CONDOMINIUM LEASING EXAMPLE

The first essential step that a MNE or tax administration must undertake as part of its transfer pricing analysis is to understand the operations of the business under review. The MNE or the tax administration should rely on the functional analysis of the enterprise, together with the assets utilized, risks assumed, contractual terms, economic circumstances, and characteristics of the property being transferred.[27]

Basic Facts

The MNE or the tax administration first ascertain the following facts in our real estate condominium leasing fact pattern:

- The business under review is a small real estate leasing brokerage. The real estate brokerage has 15 real estate agents.

- Each real estate agent has the power to list property for rent from the owner of the property, and in fact lists that property for rent from owners of the properties.
- Each real estate agent has the power to lease the property to a tenant, and in fact does lease the properties to tenants.
- The real estate brokerage has offices in Malaysia and in Singapore.
- The real estate brokerage operates its leasing operations through the facilities.
- The expenses of the real estate operations in Malaysia and the operations in Singapore are essentially pro rata.
- This analytical approach would differ if the Malaysian office or the Singapore office incurred substantially more office expenses in that office than in the other office.
- The real estate agent located in Malaysia or in Singapore can lease properties in either location, in Malaysia or in Singapore.
- The list of properties to be leased operates as a shared "book of business."
- The real estate brokerage company compensates its agents through two commission structures, discussed next.
- The real estate brokerage commission to its agents is 6% in Malaysia, 5% in Singapore, before the real estate brokerage claims its "cut," based on the location in which each broker is located.
- The real estate brokerage at the physical location of the real estate agent pays half the commission to its agents and retains the other half of the commission to pay its operating expenses.
- The real estate brokerage structures its leases to residential customers only on a one-year basis.
- There are no differences among jurisdictions as to residential market availability—the condominium units are equally available in Malaysia and in Singapore.
- The real estate agency views itself as having two essential functions: the listing process and the leasing process. The real estate agency views these two functions as essentially equal in value and importance, and these two activities have an equal share of the commission they generate.
- The fact pattern would be more complex if the marketplace viewed the listing function and the leasing process as being unequal.
- There are no currency convertibility issues between Malaysia and Singapore. The rate of exchange between the Malaysian ringgit and the Singapore dollar varies through a narrow range.
- The residential preferences pertaining to leasing residential real estate property are equivalent in each jurisdiction.
- The Bumiputra discount in Malaysia is essentially equivalent to the economically based leasing preferences in Singapore.
- The real estate agency does not track cross-leases that occur (i.e., leases of Malaysian property to Singapore residents or leases of Singapore property to Malaysian residents either in Malaysia or in Singapore).

- As an audit basis, Hasil (the Malaysian tax authority) suspects that such substantial cross-border integration occurs.
- The real estate agency collaborates with other real estate brokers, sharing the listing function or the leasing function, as needed.
- The fact pattern below would have been more complex if the real estate agency sold property as well as leased property.
- The fact pattern below would have been more complex if the real estate agency rented or sold houses or the real estate agency rented or sold commercial real estate as well as leasing real estate condominium units.

RESIDENTIAL CONDOMINIUM DATABASE

The real estate enterprise provides the listed data to the Malaysian tax administration regarding the residential leases. The real estate enterprise would provide these data to the Singapore tax administration if Singapore requests this information. (Note: All amounts are in U.S. dollars.)

	Malaysia	Singapore	Total
Number of condominiums being leased	700	300	1,000
Number of rooms rented in the condominiums	3,500	1,200	4,700
Average rental per unit	10,000	20,000	13,000
Annual leased amounts	7,000,000	6,000,000	13,000,000
Number of real estate agents	10	5	15
Rentals per agent	70	60	67
Number of condominium units per property	80	200	
Value of the property being leased	140,000,000	90,000,000	230,000,000
Floor or level for flat or apartment	3	6	
Commission rate	6%	5%	
Commission generated	420,000	300,000	720,000
Agent's commission	210,000	150,000	360,000
Agent's commission per agent	21,000	30,000	
Real estate gross after commissions	210,000	150,000	360,000
Office expenses	20,000	10,000	30,000
Advertising	10,000	20,000	30,000
Net profit	180,000	120,000	300,000

SELECTING AMONG ALLOCATION KEYS

After the MNE and/or the tax administration ascertain the applicable database, they next should analyze the database to ascertain potential allocation keys. The MNE or the tax administration, in our residential leasing transfer pricing allocation example, might feasibly consider four types of allocation keys based on the real estate agency's available data:

1. **Potential revenue-based allocation keys.** The OECD guidelines, in seeking objective data, refer to "sales to independent parties"[28] as such an example. In our real estate leasing example, the amount that the enterprise earns from its commission activities appears to be such a revenue-based allocation key.
2. **Potential asset-based allocation keys.** The OECD guidelines, in describing asset-based allocation keys, refer to allocation keys based on assets or on capital. For example, the MNE or the tax administration can base such asset-based allocation key on the enterprise's operating assets, on its fixed assets, on its intangible assets, or on its capital employed.[29] Nevertheless, the facts at hand demonstrate that the residential leasing enterprise has no significant assets. Nevertheless, the MNE or the tax administration should not dismiss potential asset-based allocation keys out of hand. Rather than negating potential asset-based allocation keys, the MNE and/or the tax administration might be well advised to substitute leasing alternatives, such as leasing that would ascertain assets employed as an allocation key.
3. **Potential cost-based allocation keys.** The OECD guidelines point out that multinational taxpayers and tax administrations frequently apply relative spending and/or investment in key areas, such as in cost-based allocation keys. Such cost-based allocation keys might include R&D, engineering, or marketing.[30] In our real estate condominium example, there is no R&D and there is no engineering. The enterprise's marketing efforts are scant compared with its commission efforts. Further, the real estate leasing company is not a distributor-marketer,[31] and the enterprise fails to provide data as to other cost-based allocation keys. The issue becomes the viability of advertising expenditures as a cost-based allocation key.
4. **Potential additional allocation keys.** The OECD guidelines suggest other allocation keys, such as incremental sales, headcounts (number of individuals involved in the key functions that generate value to the transaction), or time spent by a certain group of employees.[32] The MNE or the tax administration can apply such additional allocation keys if it can ascertain a "strong correlation" between the time spent and the creation of combined profits. The MNE or the tax administration can apply an additional allocation key such as, for example, the number of servers, data storage, floor area, or retail points. In our real estate condominium example, it might be appropriate to consider the number of real estate agents as being an allocation key.

"STRONG CORRELATION" STANDARD

The OECD guidelines apply the "strong correlation" standard to the enterprise's creation of combined profits. This strong correlation standard applies to revenue-based allocation keys, to asset-based allocation keys,[33] to cost-based allocation keys,[34] and to additional allocation keys.[35] We apply two steps to implement this procedure:

1. We begin with an initial list of allocation keys that might be viable in our residential condominium database example.
2. Then we seek to apply the strong correlation standard said to exist between the functions of enterprise and the allocation key, based on the enterprise's "effort expended" for the creation of combined profits.

ALLOCATION KEYS

The MNE or the tax administration then analyzes 11 potential allocation keys in four categories:

- Potential revenue-based allocation key (1)
- Potential asset-based allocation keys (4)
- Potential cost-based allocation keys (3)
- Potential additional allocation keys (3)

Potential Revenue-Based Allocation Key

Commission-Generated Allocation Key

This commission-generated allocation key assumes that real estate agents expend effort to achieve their commissions. Here the real estate enterprise generated commissions of \$420,000 in Malaysia and \$300,000 in Singapore, \$720,000 in total. We determine that the commission-generated allocation key meets the strong correlation standard based on the agents' effort expended and the creation of combined profits. Based on these facts, Hasil could feasibly assert that, in applying the transactional profit split method to the commissions generated as an allocation key, 58.3% of the income (\$420,000/(\$420,000 + \$300,000)) was attributable to Malaysian activities.

Potential Asset-Based Allocation Keys

Properties Held for Lease Allocation Key

This leased property allocation key assumes that real estate agents expend proportionately more effort for more valuable properties than they spend for lower-value properties. Here the real estate enterprise leased residential real estate property of \$140,000,000 in Malaysia and \$90,000,000 in Singapore, \$230,000,000 in total. We determine that the leased property allocation key meets the strong correlation standard based on the agents' effort expended and the creation of combined profits. Based on these facts, Hasil could feasibly assert that, in applying the transactional profit split method to the properties held for lease as an allocation key, 60.9% of the income (\$140,000,000/(\$140,000,000 + \$90,000,000)) was attributable to Malaysian activities.

Number of Condominium Units Being Leased Allocation Key

This commission-leased allocation key assumes that real estate agents expend effort as to the property being leased to achieve their commissions. Here the real estate enterprise leased 700 condominium units in Malaysia and leased 300 condominium units in Singapore, 1,000 condominium units in total. We determine that the commission-leased, commission-generated allocation key meets the strong correlation standard based on the agents' effort expended and the creation of combined profits. Based on these facts, Hasil could feasibly assert that, in applying the transactional profit split to the number of condominium units being leased as an allocation key, 70% of the income (700/(700 + 300)) was attributable to Malaysian activities.

Number of Rooms

This number of rooms allocation key assumes that the real estate agents will devote proportionately more effort to leasing condominium structures that have more rooms than condominium structures with fewer rooms. Here the real estate enterprise determines that the number of rooms rented in the condominiums were 3,500 rooms in Malaysia and 1,200 rooms in Singapore, 4,700 rooms in total. We determine that the number of rooms allocation key does not meet the strong correlation standard based on the agents' effort expended and the creation of combined profit. We reject the number of rooms allocation key because the number of rooms does not correlate to the effort that real estate agents undertake or the creation of combined profit. But for those facts, Hasil could have asserted that, in applying the transactional profit split to the number of rooms as an allocation key, 74.5% of the income (3,500 rooms/(3,500 rooms + 1,200 rooms)) would have been attributable to Malaysian activities.

Value of the Property Being Leased

This value of property under lease allocation key postulates that the real estate agents will devote proportionately more time to leasing more valuable housing property than they would to leasing less valuable housing property. Here the real estate enterprise determines that the annual value of property being leased was $7,000,000 in Malaysia and $6,000,000 in Singapore, $13,000,000 in total. We determine that the value of property under lease allocation key meets the strong correlation standard based on the agents' effort expended and creation of combined profit. Based on these facts, Hasil could feasibly assert that, in applying the transactional profit split to the value of condominium units being leased as an allocation key, 53.8% the income ($7,000,000/($7,000,000 + $6,000,000)) was attributable to Malaysian activities.

Potential Cost-Based Allocation Keys

Agent's Commission

This agent's commission cost-based allocation key postulates that the real estate agents will devote proportionately more effort to leasing where their aggregate commissions are higher than when the commissions are less. Here the real estate enterprise determines the aggregate commission is $210,000 in Malaysia and $150,000 in Singapore, $360,000 in total. We determine that the agent's commission allocation key meets the strong correlation standard based on the agents' effort expended and the creation of combined profit. Based on these facts, Hasil could feasibly assert that, in applying the transactional profit split to the aggregate agents' commission as an allocation key, 58.3% of the income ($210,000/($210,000 + $150,000)) was attributable to Malaysian activities.

Agent's Commission per Agent

This agent's commission cost-based allocation key postulates that real estate agents earn commissions based on their activities, and the real estate agents earning higher commissions are more valuable to the real estate enterprise than those agents earning lower commissions. Here the real estate enterprise determines the agent's commission per agent is $21,000 in Malaysia and $30,000 in Singapore. We determine that the per-agent commission allocation key does not meet the strong correlation standard based on the agents' effort expended and the creation of combined profit. We reached this decision because of the lack of causality between the agent's commission structure and the revenue generated.

Real Estate Gross Revenues after Commissions

This agent's cost allocation key as to real estate gross revenues after commissions postulates that the real estate brokerage earns income based on these commission activities. Here the real estate enterprise determines its income after commissions as being $210,000 in Malaysia and $150,000 in Singapore, $360,000 in total.

We determine that the per-agent commission allocation key meets the strong correlation standard based on the agents' effort expended and the creation of combined profit. Based on these facts, Hasil could feasibly assert that, in applying the transactional profit split to the aggregate agents' commission as an allocation key, 58.3% of the income ($210,000/($210,000 + $150,000)) was attributable to Malaysian activities.

Potential Additional Allocation Keys

Number of Real Estate Agents

This number of real estate agents as an allocation key might correlate to the real estate brokerage's leasing income. The real estate enterprise has 10 real estate agents in Malaysia, 5 agents in Singapore, 15 agents in total. The number of agents the real estate enterprise adds does not indicate the agents' effort expended. Further, the number of real estate agents as an allocation key is suspect because the real estate brokerage can hire additional agents who expend little effort and fail to earn commissions. The number of real estate agents does not correlate location of real estate agent with operating commission income in the creation of combined income. We determine that the per-agent commission allocation key does not meet the strong correlation standard based on the number of real estate agents to combined profit. If the real estate enterprise were to use number of real estate agents as an allocation key, Hasil could feasibly assert that, in applying the transactional profit split based on the number of real estate agents as an allocation key, 66.7% of the income (10 agents/(10 agents + 5 agents)) would have been attributable to Malaysian activities.

Number of Condominium Units per Property Being Leased

This number of condominium units per property that customers leased might be an allocation key that conceivably might correlate to the real estate brokerage's leasing income. Nevertheless, the facts indicate that there is no causality or other connection between the number of condominium units per property the residential customers lease. We determine that the number of condominium units per property being leased as an allocation key does not meet the strong correlation standard based on the agents' effort expended and the creation of combined profit.

Floor or Level for Flat or Apartment Being Leased

The floor level or flat or apartment that the customers of the real estate agency lease might conceivably correlate to the real estate brokerage's leasing income. Nevertheless, the facts indicate that there is no causality or other connection to the number of condominium units per property the customers of the real estate agency lease. We determine that the number of condominium units per property being leased as an allocation key or the apartment being leased does not meet the strong correlation standard based on the agents' effort expended and the creation of combined profit.

Summary of Allocation Key Results

Let us combine the results we have previously ascertained:

Rejected Potential Allocation Keys

- Agent's commission
- Number of rooms
- Per-agent determination
- Number of agents in each facility
- Number of condominium units being leased
- Floor or level

	Possible Potential Allocation Keys	
Remaining Allocation Keys	Malaysia Taxable Percentage	Singapore Taxable Percentage
Commission generated	58.3	41.7
Properties held	60.9	39.1
Units leased	70.0	30.0
Value of property	53.8	46.2
Commission	58.3	41.7

Note that, in this example, as in most fact patterns, the business activities present more than one allocation key. Each of the selected allocation keys meets the strong correlation standard, and each allocation key can meet the creation of operating income criterion. The strong correlation test is a bright-line test. The determination of whether a particular allocation key meets the strong correlation test is often a matter of professional opinion. Note that professional opinions might differ.

The MNE or the tax administration might consider employing cost accountants and economists in implementing this transfer pricing analysis. In our example, consider the difference in results if the MNE or the tax administration accepted the number of agents allocation key, resulting in an allocation of 66.7% to Malaysia, or accepted advertising as being an allocation key, resulting in an allocation of 33.3% to Malaysia.

Like other facets of transfer pricing, the determination of an allocation key under the transactional profit split method provides a MNE or the tax administration with approximate transfer pricing results—a range of 53.8% to 70.0% for Malaysia and a range of 30.0% to 46.2% in Singapore. This range can cause double taxation or can cause a tax gap:

- **Double taxation exposure.** The business should realize that the transactional profit split method using allocation keys limits the risk of double taxation but does not preclude the risk of double taxation. Here, in our example, the double tax exposure can be 70% of the income in Malaysia plus 46.2% in Singapore, or 116.2% of taxable income in total.
- **Tax gap.** The business should realize that the transactional profit split method might provide situations in which the tax authorities do not tax all of the attributable income. Here, in our example, the two tax authorities might impose taxation attributable to 53.8% in Malaysia and 30% in Singapore, or 83.8% of the taxable income in total. The tax gap is 100% less 83.8%, or 16.2% net.

TRANSFER PRICING STRATEGIES

The MNE or the tax administration should consider making these six inquiries:

1. What percentage of the $300,000 profit should the Malaysian tax authorities seek to tax?

2. What percentage of the $300,000 profit should the taxpayer assert as being the correct tax in Malaysia?
3. What percentage of the $300,000 profit should the Singapore tax authorities seek to tax?
4. What percentage of the $300,000 profit should the taxpayer assert as being the correct tax in Singapore?
5. What is the extent of the taxpayer's double taxation exposure?
6. What is the extent the taxpayer can benefit from the tax gap?

CORPORATE TAX STRATEGY

The MNE corporate strategy appears to take the initiative in the first instance in setting pricing. The corporation could develop a transfer pricing strategy that meets the allocation key criteria in both Malaysia and Singapore. The taxpayer in this instance might be able to create a tax gap of 14.2% in this example by taking the first-mover advantage and by taking inconsistent positions when dealing with both Malaysia and Singapore. This tax gap should be transitory—Hasil and the Inland Revenue of Singapore may later establish discovery regimes that indicate the taxpayer's conflicting transfer pricing regimes.

MALAYSIA'S TAX STRATEGY

There might be situations in which the taxpayer, the real estate enterprise, takes the first-mover advantage and establishes an appropriate transfer pricing allocation. If the taxpayer does select such a transfer pricing result that is within the range of the allocation keys, it might be an advantage for Hasil to accept the taxpayer's transfer pricing results rather than to develop a transfer pricing result that would be in conflict. If the taxpayer fails to select such a transfer pricing result that is within the result of the allocation keys, it then would be prudent for Hasil to challenge the allocation key rather to accept this audit challenge.

Based on the next results, Hasil will find that the transactional profit split method is substantially easier to apply than is the TNMM, and will increase the yield per professional hours spent. Quite simply, it is substantially easier for Hasil to examine a company's internal records than it is to develop external data comparables. Further, it appears to be advantageous for Hasil to develop its transfer pricing specialization program, focusing on oil and gas activities, on real estate activities, and on agricultural activities and the like. We suggest that Hasil, to further implement the transactional profit split method, should consider hiring international accountants very familiar with the harmonized tax accounting process, cost accountants, and economists, together with transfer pricing experts.

NOTES

1. Promulgated July 2010; Chapter II, Part IA.
2. OECD, *Transfer Pricing Guidelines for Multinational Enterprises and Tax Administrations* (Paris: Author, July 2010), 2.108 et seq.
3. Guideline 2.134 et seq.
4. Lemaga Hasil Delam Negeri Malaysia. (Hasil) in Behasa Malay.
5. The Inland Revenue of Malaysia has more than 30 transfer pricing examiners of various levels of experience, 30 of whom attended the joint venture conference.
6. OECD, *Transfer Pricing Guidelines for Multinational Enterprises and Tax Administrations*, 2.141, 2.142.
7. Guideline 1.9.
8. Guideline 1.9.
9. Guideline 2.109.
10. Guideline 1.9; Guideline 2.109.
11. Guideline 1.9.
12. Guideline 2.109.
13. Guideline 8.19.
14. Guideline 2.124.
15. Guideline 2.131.
16. Guideline 2.133.
17. Guideline 1.9, 2.109; R. Feinschreiber and M. Kent, "What You Need to Know about the OECD's Transactional Profit Split Method," *Corporate Business Taxation Monthly* (February 2011): 29.
18. Guideline 2.112.
19. Guideline 3.39.
20. Guideline 2.113.
21. Guideline 2.109.
22. Guideline 2.108.
23. Guideline 2.135.
24. Guideline 2.131.
25. Guideline 2.136.
26. Guideline 2.126.
27. Guideline 1.36.
28. Guideline 2.132.
29. Guideline 2.135.
30. Guideline 2.135.
31. Guideline 2.138.
32. Guideline 2.136.
33. Guideline 2.136.
34. Guideline 2.138.
35. Guideline 2.135.

CHAPTER FORTY

40

Permanent Establishment Parameters

HOST COUNTRIES might be able to force multinational taxpayers to pay tax on their extended operations if the tax authorities are able to establish that these extended operations constitute a permanent establishment (PE) within their own territory. Developing and developed countries have long been asserting jurisdiction based on such PE claims. What is new to this tax regime are new methodologies—courtesy of the Organisation of Economic Co-operation and Development (OECD)—that enable tax administrations to assert a PE based on the extended operations of the multinational operations.

British-developed countries—including Australia, Canada, Hong Kong, India, Singapore, and the United States—apply long-existing common law determinations to the scope of PE activities. The host tax authority can ascertain whether its operations in a host country constitute a PE by applying common law principles. Into those established norms, the OECD formulated alternative approaches in July 2010 under which the host tax authority can ascertain whether operations in a host country constitute a PE.

We suspect that the tax authorities might view the OECD PE approach as adding to the government's present tax arsenal, not replacing the existing common law approaches to assert PE status. We suspect that the OECD's promulgation of PE principles will thus add to the tax exposure of the multinational enterprise (MNE).

OECD'S PERMANENT ESTABLISHMENT PROVISIONS

The PE issue is inherently complex in the OECD tax convention context. The model tax convention involves an interplay between Article 7 (Business Profits) and Article 5 (Permanent Establishment). The OECD made extensive changes to Article 7(2) in 2010, specifying that the profits that are attributable to the contracting state "are the profits it might expect to make, in particular in its dealings with other parts of the enterprise, as if it were a separate and independent enterprise engaged in the same or similar activities under the same or similar conditions. The contracting state would take into account the functions performed, assets used and risks assumed by the enterprise through the permanent establishment and through the other parts of the enterprise."[1] Practitioners refer to Article 7(2) as the transfer pricing rule. United Nations (UN)-based treaties have PE provisions. UN officials have specified their intent for the UN to follow the OECD in making the PE provisions.

CONSEQUENCES OF PERMANENT ESTABLISHMENT STATUS

As a general matter, if a country enters into a tax treaty with another country, such a treaty provides that the host country entering into the tax treaty can tax the income that is attributable to a PE located in that host state.[2] Such tax treaty precludes the tax authority in that country from imposing income taxation on an enterprise unless the activities of the enterprise reach the requisite threshold, that of constituting a PE. The creation of a PE provision, then, is a dual-edged sword:

- The PE provision protects the revenue in the countries in which the enterprise does business, but:
- The PE provision protects the enterprise from tax claims that the overreaching tax authority in host countries can bring.

As a general matter, a tax treaty, through its PE provision, imposes a higher threshold for tax liability than the threshold nexus standard that would otherwise apply in the nontreaty context. Consider the U.S. approach. The nontreaty nexus standard is the presence of business activities in the United States that might rise to the level of a trade or business undertaken in the United States. Such a level of business might not constitute a PE under treaty principles.[3] In contrast, the treaty PE principles would impose taxation on the enterprise's activities in the host country only if the activities reach a defined higher threshold.

The unintended creation of a PE is a continuing and growing concern for businesses having overseas operations. The operative word is "unintended." An enterprise often can obtain tax benefits from having a PE if the enterprise deliberately undertakes PE status. For example, the presence of a PE in that host country might enable the enterprise to obtain a foreign tax credit against taxes the enterprise would otherwise pay in its home location.

CONSEQUENCES OF A PERMANENT ESTABLISHMENT TO BUSINESS

The presence of a PE can be especially troublesome to the tax authority in which the PE is located and to the PE itself. Quite simply, the enterprise might not have known it is a PE in the host country and might not have registered with the tax authorities. The tax enterprise might not have met the tax authority's statute of limitations requirements because the statute of limitations period begins only from the time the enterprise first had PE status in that jurisdiction, even though the enterprise was unaware of its status.

The tax administration is likely to compel documents from the enterprise when the enterprise's activities create a PE within its jurisdiction. The tax administration might request these documents beginning from the enterprise's initial PE status in that jurisdiction. The enterprise, not being previously aware of the document requirements, might have failed to retain the requested documents prepared in prior years. The enterprise runs the risk of having to pay a myriad of penalties and taxes to that jurisdiction.

In addition, the enterprise, now being subject to documentation requirements, might also be subject to transfer pricing considerations. The tax administration might successfully seek PE status in the same manner as a subsidiary of the parent company for transfer pricing purposes. For example, the commentary 20–21 pertaining to Model Tax Convention on Income and Capital Article 7(2) discusses functional and factual analysis.

Double taxation is likely, especially when the tax authority in the host country requires the PE to pay tax retroactively for prior years. The enterprise might have paid tax to its place of incorporation and to its place of activity. The tax treaty between the enterprise's country of incorporation and its PE's physical location might provide remedies against double taxation, but these remedies would often fail to apply because of differing statute of limitations issues.

TRANSFER PRICING AND PERMANENT ESTABLISHMENT

The PE assertion brings with it the taxability of that enterprise in that host jurisdiction together with the ensuing transfer pricing considerations. The two concepts, transfer pricing and PE, are closely related, as both concepts address the determination of the income related to the entity in question. Tax authorities in a myriad of states are developing sophisticated tax collection strategies. One such collection strategy of critical importance is the penchant of the tax authorities to investigate potential PE activities.

PE became the predicate for transfer pricing. If the tax authority can ascertain the presence of these PE activities, the next focus on the part of that tax authority is to develop a transfer pricing adjustment in its favor. As a result, multinational taxpayers are increasingly facing the risk of extensive double taxation, in part because of PE claims based on an aggressive tax collector's claims.

Governments are beginning to develop transfer pricing adjustments based on the presence of PE activities. A government under the OECD approach treats the PE and the foreign enterprise as being related parties. The government's "long arm" extends outward, often reaching beyond the geographical confines of the country itself. This long arm often reaches the activities taking place abroad as well as the activities of foreign-based enterprises.

The presence of PE activities and transfer pricing adjustments between the PE and other facets of the enterprise creates double taxation. In addition, significant areas of double taxation exist between jurisdictions because of the differences in source rules. Further, significant areas of double taxation exist because of aggressive tax enforcement. Significant areas of double taxation exist when one government follows the UN tax treaty model and the counterparty applies the OECD model tax treaty.

OVERALL TAX CONSIDERATIONS

The taxpayer is well served by establishing a "worldview" of the tax liabilities it might face. The multinational taxpayer is well advised to undertake the process of aggregating its total effective tax costs on a worldwide basis. As a starting point, the multinational taxpayer then should determine the tax base and the tax rate in each jurisdiction. The multinational taxpayer should then determine the aggregate tax base and the cumulative effective tax rate.

Double taxation is becoming an increasing threat. The multinational taxpayer is likely to find that its aggregate tax base, determined on a worldwide basis, is more than 100% of the company's aggregate income. The multinational taxpayer is likely to find that its aggregate income subject to tax is substantially more than 100% of its aggregate tax base. As a result, and very importantly, the multinational taxpayer is well advised to address the conflicting tax systems simultaneously from a PE–transfer pricing prospective.

POTENTIAL FOR THE IMPOSITION OF TWO LEVELS OF TAXATION

The country in which the subsidiary is located might be able to tax the subsidiary because of the subsidiary's activities in the country. This same host country can impose an additional level of tax on the parent company headquartered elsewhere. The country in which the subsidiary is located can look toward the activities of the parent company and then examine the relationship of parent company toward the subsidiary. The host country may determine that the MNE's extended operations contribute more income to the MNE than the MNE admits. The host country sees itself as being entitled to receive more tax receipts. In essence, the country in which the subsidiary is located might be able to tax the parent company based on that parent company–subsidiary relationship. The home country can seek to tax the enterprise on its worldwide income while the host country can seek to tax its PE income.

OECD APPROACH TO DETERMINE PERMANENT ESTABLISHMENT

The OECD approach applies five specific standards to determine whether an enterprise constitutes a PE:

1. **The functionally separate entity approach.** The OECD views the PE as being a functionally separate entity. In other words, the OECD views the PE as being a separate entity from the enterprise itself. As a separate entity, there would be an expectation that the enterprise and the PE would enter cross-border transactional arrangements for sales, leases, licenses, services, and the like.
2. **Separate sources of profit.** The government can seek to ascertain the PE's separate sources of profit. In other words, if an enterprise manufactures goods in the home country and distributes the goods through a PE in the host country, the host government can seek to ascertain the income from the distribution of the goods in that country.
3. **Economically significant activities.** The government can seek to ascertain the PE's economically significant activities or responsibilities. In other words, the OECD expects the enterprise to undertake a functional analysis approach. The threshold for examining risks and functions is that the activity under consideration be "economically significant" in determining PE status.
4. **People functions.** The government can seek to ascertain the PE's significant people functions. In other words, the OECD expects the presence of people in a function as being determinative to the functions being conducted and to PE. The greater the responsibility and power the people have in the host country, the greater the probability the host country will find that those activities constitute a PE.
5. **Risk-taking functions.** The government can seek to ascertain the PE's key entrepreneurial risk-taking functions (i.e., the management of risks). In other words, the OECD would have the enterprise examine the situs of risk-taking functions when examining functional analysis for purposes of the PE.

HONG KONG APPLIES THE OECD PERMANENT ESTABLISHMENT PROVISIONS

The government of Hong Kong has established provisions that are designed to attribute profits and expenses to the Hong Kong PE if the nonresident enterprise has a

PE in Hong Kong. We have selected Hong Kong because it issued its transfer pricing provisions in December 2009, relatively contemporaneous with the OECD Article 7(2) formalization, and because the Hong Kong provisions address functional analysis and PE in the anti–tax haven context.

The Hong Kong transfer pricing guidelines provide eight steps to the PE process. The Hong Kong transfer pricing guidelines, in demonstrating this eight-step process, provide guidance as to its interpretation of the OECD PE provisions. The taxpayer is to:

1. Identify the "economically significant activities and responsibilities" of the nonresident enterprise undertaken in various places other than in Hong Kong. The guidance fails to further address the scope of the "economically significant activities and responsibilities" provision.
2. Postulate the existence of the PE in Hong Kong.
3. Identify the "economically significant activities and responsibilities" of the nonresident enterprise undertaken through the PE in Hong Kong.
4. Identify the scope, type, value, and timing of the dealings of the PE.
5. Determine the character and the structure of the PE business.
6. Select the most appropriate transfer pricing methodology for attribution purposes.
7. Apply the most appropriate transfer pricing methodology and determine the arm's length outcome.
8. Implement a support process and install a review process.

HOW HONG KONG APPLIES THE PERMANENT ESTABLISHMENT PROVISIONS

The Hong Kong transfer pricing guidelines apply the "functionally separate entity" to determine taxability of the PE. Using the "functionally separate entity" approach, the Commissioner will treat a PE as being a separate enterprise as if this enterprise is operating at arm's length. Such an enterprise must treat PEs in Hong Kong and elsewhere as reflecting its profits and expenses. The separate entity approach operates to produce the same outcome as would transactions between two enterprises at arm's length.

The Hong Kong Commissioner can assess the profits of the PE of a nonresident enterprise. The PE might earn income from more than one source. The Commissioner, in assessing the profits of the PE of a nonresident enterprise, can examine the separate sources of profit that the nonresident enterprise has derived from Hong Kong and determine what a resident (PE) enterprise's profitability should be.

The Hong Kong Special Economic Zone does not mandate that the MNE book the PE profit in the jurisdiction. Nevertheless, such a PE might have to attribute the profit to the PE of the nonresident enterprise carrying on a business on Hong Kong. The PE is to reflect these PE amounts if the enterprise undertakes "economically significant activities or responsibilities" in Hong Kong.

The profit might be generated from "economically significant activities or responsibilities" outside Hong Kong. In that event, the profit will not be attributed to the

PE of the nonresident enterprise *in* Hong Kong. The presence of "economically significant activities or responsibilities" outside Hong Kong occurs when there is another PE outside Hong Kong, or when the head office undertakes the "economically significant activities or responsibilities."

The Commissioner can attribute profits to the PE in Hong Kong under Article 7(2). The Commissioner, in making such attribution of profits, is also to consider these functions:

- The significant "people functions" of the PE
- The key entrepreneurial risk-taking functions of the PE (i.e., those functions that are relevant to the assumption or acceptance or management of risks)

COMMON LAW PERMANENT ESTABLISHMENT CRITERIA

The five OECD PE criteria are designed to integrate the PE objectives with the transfer pricing objectives. The preceding objective criteria address the presence or absence of objective facts (i.e., facts the tax authorities would know or should have known before applying the Article 7(2) transfer pricing approach). The subjective criteria might be, for example, the customers' view of the relationship between the parties, including the name of the enterprise.

However, the enterprise should undertake five fact-based common law inquiries to activities of the enterprise to ascertain the presence of a PE:

1. The presence of direct business activities
2. The presence of agency relationships
3. The presence of more-than-stewardship activities
4. The presence of personnel shifts from the parent company to the subsidiary
5. The entirety of operations

Next we examine the five facets of the PE inquiry.

DIRECT ACTIVITIES

The direct business activities by the parent company in the host country can indicate the presence of a PE in the host country. As such, a taxpayer is well advised to ascertain whether the direct business activities that the parent company undertakes create a PE in the host country. It is important to note that the taxpayer's activities as a shareholder are a separate inquiry from the subsidiary's operations in the host country and a separate inquiry from its own direct activities in the host country.

The presence of a subsidiary in the host country is not necessary for the host country to find PE status. The subsidiary's activities in the host country will be taxed in that country and the subsidiary by its very nature is a PE. The extended enterprise must run the gamut of PE assertions and the transfer pricing provisions in light of Article 7(2).

An enterprise can grow its international operations without initially focusing on its ensuing tax responsibilities. These operations can occur because of the company's overseas growth. Tax executives at a multinational business might not be aware of the PE activities that enterprise is undertaking, as non-tax people might be making its business decisions. These risks are exacerbated because of the confluence of two factors: the growth of overseas business operations and the penchant of tax preparers to prepare tax returns based on "same as last year" standard rather than reviewing the underlying facts, including the year by year changes in these facts.

Consider the next example in which Company X fails to notify the tax authorities in Country B of its business activities taking place in Country B.

- Company X began its operations in Country A, having no international operations in year 1.
- In year 2, Company X sets up a border office within Country A, trying to reach its potential customers transiting from Country B.
- In year 3, Company X sets up an occasional trading post in Country B to take advantage of seasonal and weekend traffic during the holidays.
- In year 4, Company X leases retail space and begins to sell its wares in Country B.
- In year 5, Company X advertises its goods in Country B and engages in contracts with suppliers and customers in Country B.
- In year 6, Company X manufactures its products in Country B.
- In year 7, the Country B tax authorities first assert taxability over the Company X operations and seek all Company X data from the current and prior years.

Company X is close to being considered a PE in Country B in year 3. Company X is a PE in Country B beginning in year 4.

AGENCY RELATIONSHIPS

The presence of an agency relationship can create a PE. The extended enterprise often can be an agent of the MNE in some situations, but the MNE might be an agent of an extended enterprise in other situations. A taxpayer is well advised to ascertain whether the indirect relationship between the MNE and its extended enterprise constitutes an agency relationship. That agency relationship might bind the parent company to the company for PE purposes. For example, the extended agency can serve as the company's agent by negotiating, binding, entering into, or concluding contracts on behalf of the MNE. The taxpayer is well advised to examine the powers that the agency undertakes.

The delineation in terms of agency is between a dependent agency and an independent agency. As a general matter, having a dependent agency in a jurisdiction causes that dependent agency to constitute a PE in *that* jurisdiction. In contrast, having *an* independent agency in a jurisdiction does not constitute a PE in that jurisdiction.

The law of agency, not the tax rules, takes precedence in determining the nature of the agency relationship. One such agency law, for example, is the power to conclude contracts. Thus, the power to conclude contracts determines the power and extent of an agency relationship and is often a prerequisite to creating a PE. The taxpayer can assert that a party that does not have the power to conclude contracts on behalf of the principal does not have the requisite PE for the principal. See, for example, the decision of the Supreme Court of India in *Morgan Stanley* (2007).

The presence of control within the agency context determines the nature of the relationship for tax purposes. If the agent deals with multiple parties, the tax law postulates that the agent that has more than one principal is an independent agent and that no one principal controls the agent. As a result, such an agency relationship does not constitute PE status. In contrast, the tax law presupposes that an agent having one principal is dependent on that one principal, and the principal controls that dependent agent and creates a PE. See, for example, KnoWerX Education (India) Limited, opinion by the Authority for Advance Rulings (2008).

An issue has arisen as to whether having multiple principals constitutes a PE over the agent. An agreement in concert among these principals can constitute common control over the agent. In contrast, a cross-insurance or reinvoicing arrangement does not constitute sufficient common control to create a PE.[4] Four independent property and casualty companies set up a reinsurance arrangement with Fortress Re Inc. The Tax Court held that the four insurers did not have comprehensive control over Fortress Re as a dependent agent so as to create a PE.

SHAREHOLDER ACTIVITIES IN SUBSIDIARIES' LOCATIONS

An enterprise can conduct shareholder activities in subsidiaries' locations without these activities itself constituting a PE. An enterprise that engages in activities beyond the stewardship role might find itself in a PE situation. Chapter 7.9 in the OECD guidelines delineates shareholder activities from the broader-based stewardship activities. Such stewardship nonshareholder activities include detailed planning services for particular operations, emergency management, or technical advice (troubleshooting), or, in some cases, assistance in day-to-day management.

The next activities constitute shareholder activities:

- Activities that relate to the juridical structure of the parent company itself. Such activities include the cost:
  - Of meeting the parent company's shareholders
  - Of issuing of shares in the parent company
  - Connected with the supervisory board
  - Relating to reporting requirements of the parent company, including the cost of preparing consolidated reports
  - Of raising funds for the acquisition of the participations

The taxpayer is well advised to ascertain whether the parent company's activities as to the subsidiary go beyond the shareholder relationship. Shareholder activities themselves are exempt for PE characterization. The parent company's activities can transcend the shareholder relationship as the subsidiary can create a PE on the part of the parent company.

PRESENCE OF PERSONNEL SHIFTS AMONG ENTITIES

The taxpayer is well advised to ascertain whether the parent company's personnel being shifted to the host country creates a PE on the part of the parent company. The parent company might have furnished personnel, might continue to provide payroll for subsidiary, or might take specific responsibility for the work of its employees at the foreign enterprise's location. As a result, the host country might view all activities taking place in that country as creating a PE.

ENTIRETY OF THE OPERATIONS

The entirety of the operations in the country of operations may create PE status. The tax collector might ascertain another basis of taxation apart from the four operational categories mentioned earlier.

DECLINING BUSINESSES

A multinational business might quite validly face a risk of a tax authority's overregulation of the PE claims. This overregulation is especially apparent as to a declining business. A declining business might be caught in the PE web even though the business is declining year by year.

Consider this scenario: Company X manufactures televisions in Country A, combining the TV tube with other components and a console. In addition to the company's manufacturing operations in Country A, Company X enters into a long-term contract with a manufacturer of consoles in Country B to assemble the televisions in Country B, using Company X's components and technology and locally produced consoles. Assume that the tax authority in Country B determines that Company X's activities in Country B create a PE because the technology is ongoing and requires cross-border personnel.

After decades of sustained sales, Company X's business is now supplanted by flat-screen TVs. Company X's business is declining rapidly in both Country A and Country B. Company X no longer provides technology to its Company B operations. Nevertheless, the tax authorities in Country B might continue to view Company X's operations in Country B as a PE despite the change in facts. The issue then might become whether Company X, now facing losses in Country B, can obtain net operating loss benefits in Country B or in Country A.

"PREPARATORY TO" AND "AUXILIARY FROM" EXEMPTIONS

Income tax treaties exempt activities that are preparatory to or are auxiliary from PE status. See Article 5.4f of the OECD Treaty. The issue of whether these activities are preparatory or auxiliary can be disputed. Whether activities are preparatory or auxiliary depends on the nature of the activities being conducted, the presence of revenue from the operations, and the duration of the activities being sought for the exemption.

TIME SPENT

The taxpayer should be careful that the term "permanent establishment" does not directly relate to the permanency of the enterprise. Time spent does become relevant in the construction context. Treaties differ in ascertaining time thresholds, and six months is commonplace to determine PE. An issue arises, though, whether the time period must be consecutive to reach this threshold, and whether the activities in two separate years are combined to reach the threshold amount. PE issues, especially timing, can be different for major players who have negotiation power with the host government to not be considered a PE regardless of how much presence is required to complete a task. See, for example, the Airport Authority of India's dispute before the Authority for Advance Rulings pertaining to Raytheon payments.

WILL THE OECD APPROACH PREVAIL?

The OECD approach to PE status does make sense in that the taxpayer and the tax authorities are often well positioned to assess the profits the enterprise is to make in accordance to Article 7(2) as if the enterprise were separate and independent, engaged in the same or similar activities under the same or similar conditions. This transfer pricing approach assumes that the taxpayer and the tax authorities can commit substantial expertise and effort to the transfer pricing approach and its application to the PE process.

When the taxpayer or the tax collector is unwilling or unable to apply these assumptions as to effort and expertise, perhaps because of the potentially limited tax revenues involved, we suggest that the taxpayer and tax authorities first address these more ascertainable business facets:

- The presence of direct business activities
- The presence of agency relationships

- The presence of more-than-stewardship activities
- The presence of personnel shifts from the parent company to the subsidiary
- The entirety of operations

Only time will tell whether the tax administrations will accept the OECD PE approach, reject the OECD PE approach entirely, or expand their tax arsenals.

NOTES

1. See Model Tax Convention on Income and on Capital, OECD July 22, 2010; M. Kent and R. Feinschreiber, "Permanent Establishment Parameters," Derecho Fiscal Internacional, 2011, p. 159.
2. See OECD Model Tax Convention, Articles 7 and 5.
3. See *de Amodio v. Commissioner*, U. S. Tax Court, 1960.
4. See *Taisei Fire & Marine Insurance v. Commissioner*, U.S. Tax Court 1995.

About the Authors

ROBERT FEINSCHREIBER is an experienced tax practitioner, an attorney, and a counselor based in Miami, Florida. Together with Margaret Kent, he focuses on resolving transfer pricing disputes and on developing comprehensive worldwide transfer pricing strategies for large and mid-sized businesses through TransferPricingConsortium.com. He has been quoted as an authority by the U.S. Tax Court, *Businessweek*, and *Forbes*.

Mr. Feinschreiber has been a consultant to several foreign governments in transfer pricing issues, but his primary activity is to defend international businesses. He focuses on OECD transfer pricing, transfer pricing in the United States, and transfer pricing in Asia.

MARGARET KENT is an experienced tax practitioner, an attorney, and a counselor based in Miami, Florida. Together with Robert Feinschreiber, she focuses on resolving transfer pricing disputes and on developing comprehensive worldwide transfer pricing strategies for large and mid-sized businesses through TransferPricingConsortium.com.

Ms. Kent has been a consultant to several foreign governments in transfer pricing issues, but her primary activity is to defend international businesses. She focuses on OECD transfer pricing, transfer pricing in the United States, transfer pricing in Asia, and transfer pricing in South America.

Index